Microsoft®

Access 2000

Illustrated Complete

Lisa Friedrichsen

COURSE
TECHNOLOGY

Thomson Learning™

MICROSOFT OFFICE USER SPECIALIST

APPROVED COURSEWARE

EXPERT

ONE MAIN STREET, CAMBRIDGE, MA 02142

Australia • Canada • Denmark • Japan • Mexico • New Zealand • Philippines
Puerto Rico • Singapore • South Africa • Spain • United Kingdom • United States

Microsoft Access 2000—Illustrated Complete is published by Course Technology

Senior Product Manager:	**Kathryn Schooling**
Product Manager:	**Rebecca VanEsselstine**
Associate Product Manager:	**Emily Heberlein**
Contributing Author:	**Elizabeth Eisner Reding**
Production Editor:	**Elena Montillo**
Developmental Editor:	**Rachel Biheller Bunin**
Marketing Manager:	**Karen Bartlett**
Editorial Assistant:	**Stacie Parillo**
Composition House:	**GEX, Inc.**
QA Manuscript Reviewer:	**Nicole Ashton, Jeff Schwartz, Alex White, Matt Carroll, John Freitas, John Greacen**
Text Designer:	**Joseph Lee, Joseph Lee Designs**
Cover Designer:	**Doug Goodman, Doug Goodman Designs**

For more information contact:

Course Technology
One Main Street
Cambridge, MA 02142

or find us on the World Wide Web at: www.course.com

Disclaimer

ISBN 0-7600-6072-X

Printed in the United States of America

2 3 4 5 6 7 8 9 BM 04 03 02 01 00

The Illustrated Series Offers the Entire Package for your Microsoft Office 2000 Needs

Office 2000 MOUS Certification Coverage

The Illustrated Series offers a growing number of Microsoft-approved titles that cover the objectives required to pass the Office 2000 MOUS exams. After studying with any of the approved Illustrated titles (see list on inside cover), you will have mastered the Core and Expert skills necessary to pass any Office 2000 MOUS exam with flying colors. In addition, **Access 2000 MOUS Certification Objectives** at the end of the book map to where specific MOUS skills can be found in each lesson and where students can find additional practice.

Helpful New Features

The Illustrated Series responded to Customer Feedback by adding a **Project Files list** at the back of the book for easy reference, Changing the red font in the Steps to green for easier reading, and Adding New Conceptual lessons to units to give students the extra information they need when learning Office 2000.

New Exciting Case and Innovative On-Line Companion

There is an exciting new case study used throughout our textbooks, a fictitious company called MediaLoft, designed to be "real-world" in nature by introducing the kinds of activities that students will encounter when working with Microsoft Office 2000. The **MediaLoft Web site**, available at www.course.com/illustrated/medialoft, is an innovative Student Online Companion which enhances and augments the printed page by bringing students onto the Web for a dynamic and continually updated learning experience. The MediaLoft site mirrors the case study used throughout the book, creating a real-world intranet site for this chain of bookstore cafés. This Companion is used to complete the WebWorks exercise in each unit of this book, and to allow students to become familiar with the business application of an intranet site.

Enhance Any Illustrated Text with these Exciting Products!

Course CBT

Enhance your students' Office 2000 classroom learning experience with self-paced computer-based training on CD-ROM. Course CBT engages students with interactive multimedia and hands-on simulations that reinforce and complement the concepts and skills covered in the textbook. All the content is aligned with the MOUS (Microsoft Office User Specialist) program, making it a great preparation tool for the certification exams. Course CBT also includes extensive pre- and post-assessments that test students' mastery of skills.

SAM 2000

How well do your students *really* know Microsoft Office? SAM 2000 is a performance-based testing program that measures students' proficiency in Microsoft Office 2000. SAM 2000 is available for Office 2000 in either a live or simulated environment. You can use SAM 2000 to place students into or out of courses, monitor their performance throughout a course, and help prepare them for the MOUS certification exams.

Create Your Ideal Course Package with CourseKits™

If one book doesn't offer all the coverage you need, create a course package that does. With Course Technology's CourseKits—our mix-and-match approach to selecting texts—you have the freedom to combine products from more than one series. When you choose any two or more Course Technology products for one course, we'll discount the price and package them together so your students can pick up one convenient bundle at the bookstore.

For more information about any of these offerings or other Course Technology products, contact your sales representative or visit our web site at:

www.course.com

Preface

Welcome to *Microsoft Access 2000— Illustrated Complete.* This highly visual book offers users a hands-on introduction to basic aspects of Microsoft Access 2000 and also serves as an excellent reference for future use. This book is appropriate for a full semester course, and its modular structure allows for greater flexibility—you can cover the units in any order you choose.

► Organization and Coverage

This text contains 16 units that cover basic Access skills. In these units, students learn how to create, format, and use Access databases, including tables, queries, forms, and reports.

► About this Approach

What makes the Illustrated approach so effective at teaching software skills? It's quite simple. Each skill is presented on two facing pages, with the step-by-step instructions on the left page, and large screen illustrations on the right. Students can focus on a single skill without having to turn the page. This unique design makes information extremely accessible and easy to absorb, and provides a great reference for after the course is over. This hands-on approach also makes it ideal for both self-paced or instructor-led classes.

Each lesson, or "information display," contains the following elements:

Each 2-page spread focuses on a single skill.

Clear step-by-step directions explain how to complete the specific task, with what students are to type in green. When students follow the numbered steps, they quickly learn how each procedure is performed and what the results will be.

Concise text that introduces the basic principles discussed in the lesson. Procedures are easier to learn when concepts fit into a framework.

Access 2000

Viewing the Database Window

When you start Access and open a database, the **database window** displays common Windows elements such as a title bar, menu bar, and toolbar. Clicking the Objects or Groups buttons on the Objects bar alternatively expands and collapses that section of the database window. If all the objects don't display in the expanded section, click the small arrow at the top or bottom of the section to scroll the list. The **Objects** area displays the seven types of objects that can be accessed by clicking the object type you want. The **Groups** area displays other commonly used files and folders, such as the Favorites folder. ◀━ John explores the MediaLoft-A database.

Steps

1. **Look at each of the Access window elements shown in Figure A-7**
   The Objects bar on the left side of the database window displays the seven object types. The other elements of the database window are summarized in Table A-3. Because the Tables object is selected, the buttons you need to create a new table or to work with the existing table are displayed in the MediaLoft-A Database window.

QuickTip
Your menu commands may look different depending on which window or object is in use.

2. **Click File on the menu bar**
   The File menu contains commands for opening a new or existing database, saving a database in a variety of formats, and printing. The menu commands vary depending on which window or database object is currently in use.

3. **Point to Edit on the menu bar, point to View, point to Insert, point to Tools, point to Window, point to Help, move the pointer off the menu, then press [Esc] twice**
   All menus close when you press [Esc]. Pressing [Esc] a second time deselects the menu.

4. **Point to the New button on the Database toolbar**
   Pointing to a toolbar button causes a descriptive **ScreenTip** to automatically appear, providing a short description of the button. The buttons on the toolbars represent the most commonly used Access features. Toolbar buttons change just as menu options change depending on which window and database object are currently in use.

5. **Point to the Open button on the Database toolbar, then point to the Save button on the Database toolbar**
   Sometimes toolbar buttons or menu options are dimmed which means that they are currently unavailable. For example, the Save button is dimmed because it doesn't make sense to save the MediaLoft-A database right now because you haven't made any changes to it yet.

6. **Click Queries on the Objects bar**
   The query object window provides several ways to create a new query and displays the names of previously created queries, as shown in Figure A-8. There are three previously created query objects displayed within the MediaLoft-A Database window.

7. **Click Forms on the Objects bar, then click Reports on the Objects bar**
   The MediaLoft-A database contains the Customers table, three queries, a customer entry form, and three reports.

CLUES TO USE

Viewing objects

You can change the way you view the objects in the database window by clicking the last four buttons on the toolbar. You can view the objects as Large Icons, Small Icons, in a List (this is the default view), and with Details. The Details view shows a longer description of the object, as well as the date the object was last modified and the date it was originally created.

►ACCESS A-8 **GETTING STARTED WITH ACCESS 2000**

Hints as well as trouble-shooting advice, right where you need it — next to the step itself.

Clues to Use boxes provide concise information that either expands on one component of the major lesson skill or describes an independent task that is in some way related to the major lesson skill.

Every lesson features large-size, full-color representations of what the students' screen should look like after completing the numbered steps.

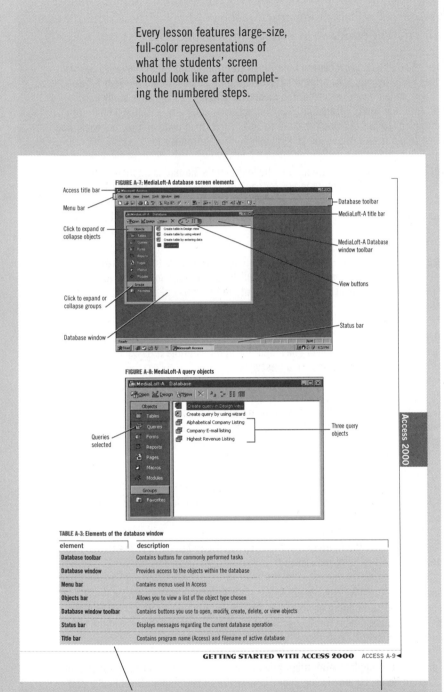

FIGURE A-7: MediaLoft-A database screen elements

Access title bar
Menu bar
Click to expand or collapse objects
Click to expand or collapse groups
Database window

Database toolbar
MediaLoft-A title bar
MediaLoft-A Database window toolbar
View buttons
Status bar

FIGURE A-8: MediaLoft-A query objects

Queries selected

Three query objects

TABLE A-3: Elements of the database window

element	description
Database toolbar	Contains buttons for commonly performed tasks
Database window	Provides access to the objects within the database
Menu bar	Contains menus used in Access
Objects bar	Allows you to view a list of the object type chosen
Database window toolbar	Contains buttons you use to open, modify, create, delete, or view objects
Status bar	Displays messages regarding the current database operation
Title bar	Contains program name (Access) and filename of active database

GETTING STARTED WITH ACCESS 2000   ACCESS A-9

Quickly accessible summaries of key terms, toolbar buttons, or keyboard alternatives connected with the lesson material. Students can refer easily to this information when working on their own projects at a later time.

The page numbers are designed like a road map. Access indicates the Access section, A indicates the first unit, and 9 indicates the page within the unit.

Other Features

The two-page lesson format featured in this book provides the new user with a powerful learning experience. Additionally, this book contains the following features:

► MOUS Certification Coverage

Each unit opener has a ⌊MOUS⌉ next to it to indicate where Microsoft Office User Specialist (MOUS) skills are covered. In addition, there is a MOUS appendix which contains a grid that maps to where specific Core and Expert Access MOUS skills can be found in each lesson and where students can find additional practice. The first eight units of this book prepare students for the Access 2000 MOUS Exam, and the complete book covers the skills needed to pass the Access 2000 Expert MOUS exam.

► Real-World Case

The case study used throughout the textbook, a fictitious company called MediaLoft, is designed to be "'real-world" in nature and introduces the kinds of activities that students will encounter when working with Microsoft Access 2000. With a real-world case, the process of solving problems will be more meaningful to students.

Students can also enhance their skills by completing the Web Works exercises in each unit by going to the innovative Student Online Companion, available at **www.course.com/illustrated/medialoft**. The MediaLoft site mirrors the case study by acting as the company's intranet site, further allowing students to become familiar with applicable business scenarios.

► End of Unit Material

Each unit concludes with a Concepts Review that tests students' understanding of what they learned in the unit. The Concepts Review is followed by a Skills Review, which provides students with additional hands-on practice of the skills. The Skills Review is followed by Independent Challenges, which pose case problems for students to solve. At least one Independent Challenge in each unit asks students to use the World Wide Web to solve the problem as indicated by a Web Work icon. The Visual Workshops that follow the Independent Challenges help students develop critical thinking skills. Students are shown completed Web pages or screens and are asked to re-create them from scratch.

Instructor's Resource Kit

The Instructor's Resource Kit is Course Technology's way of putting the resources and information needed to teach and learn effectively into your hands. With an integrated array of teaching and learning tools that offers you and your students a broad range of technology-based instructional options, we believe this kit represents the highest quality and most cutting edge resources available to instructors today. Many of these resources are available at www.course.com. The resources available with this book are:

MediaLoft Web site   Available at **www.course.com/illustrated/medialoft**, this innovative Student Online Companion enhances and augments the printed page by bringing students onto the Web for a dynamic and continually updated learning experience. The MediaLoft site mirrors the case study used throughout the book, creating a real-world intranet site for this fictitious company, a national chain of bookstore cafés. This Companion is used to complete the WebWorks exercise in each unit of this book, and to allow students to become familiar with the business application of an intranet site.

Instructor's Manual   Available as an electronic file, the Instructor's Manual is quality-assurance tested and includes unit overviews, detailed lecture topics for each unit with teaching tips, an Upgrader's Guide, solutions to all lessons and end-of-unit material, and extra Independent Challenges. The Instructor's Manual is available on the Instructor's Resource Kit CD-ROM, or you can download it from **www.course.com**.

Course Test Manager   Designed by Course Technology, this Windows-based testing software helps instructors design, administer, and print tests and pre-tests. A full-featured program, Course Test Manager also has an online testing component that allows students to take tests at the computer and have their exams automatically graded.

Course Faculty Online Companion   You can browse this textbook's password-protected site to obtain the Instructor's Manual, Solution Files, Project Files, and any updates to the text. Contact your Customer Service Representative for the site address and password.

Project Files   Project Files contain all of the data that students will use to complete the lessons and end-of-unit material. A Readme file includes instructions for using the files. Adopters of this text are granted the right to install the Project Files on any standalone computer or network. The Project Files are available on the Instructor's Resource Kit CD-ROM, the Review Pack, and can also be downloaded from www.course.com.

Solution Files   Solution Files contain every file students are asked to create or modify in the lessons and end-of-unit material. A Help file on the Instructor's Resource Kit includes information for using the Solution Files.

Figure Files   Figure files contain all the figures from the book in bitmap format. Use the figure files to create transparency masters or in a PowerPoint presentation.

WebCT   WebCT is a tool used to create Web-based educational environments and also uses WWW browsers as the interface for the course-building environment. The site is hosted on your school campus, allowing complete control over the information. WebCT has its own internal communication system, offering internal e-mail, a Bulletin Board, and a Chat room.

Course Technology offers pre-existing supplemental information to help in your WebCT class creation, such as a suggested Syllabus, Lecture Notes, Figures in the Book / Course Presenter, Student Downloads, and Test Banks in which you can schedule an exam, create reports, and more.

Access 2000

Getting Started with Access 2000

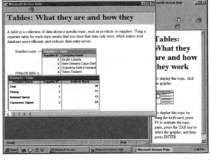

Using Tables and Queries

Contents

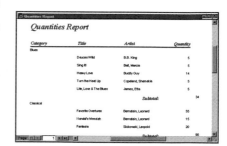

Brief Contents

Contents

Windows 98

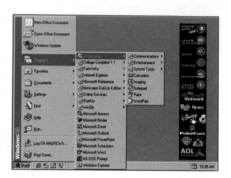

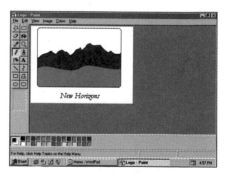

Modifying a Database Structure

Creating Multiple Table Queries

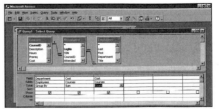

Contents

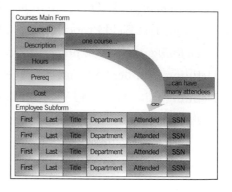

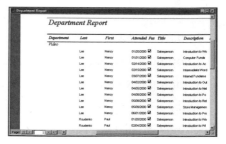

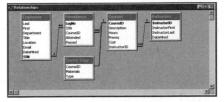

Creating Data Access Pages

Creating Advanced Queries

Contents

Creating Advanced Forms and Reports

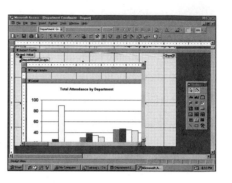

Managing Database Objects

Contents

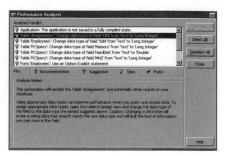

Unit
A

Getting
Started with Windows 98

Objectives

- ▶ **Start Windows and view the Active Desktop**
- ▶ **Use the mouse**
- ▶ **Start a program**
- ▶ **Move and resize windows**
- ▶ **Use menus, keyboard shortcuts, and toolbars**
- ▶ **Use dialog boxes**
- ▶ **Use scroll bars**
- ▶ **Get Help**
- ▶ **Close a program and shut down Windows**

Microsoft Windows 98 is an **operating system**, a computer program that controls how the computer carries out basic tasks such as displaying information on your computer screen and running programs. Windows 98 helps you save and organize the results of your work (such as a resume or a list of addresses) as **files**, which are electronic collections of data. Windows 98 also coordinates the flow of information among the programs, printers, storage devices, and other components of your computer system. When you work with Windows 98, you will notice many **icons**, small pictures intended to be meaningful symbols of the items they represent. You will also notice rectangular-shaped work areas known as **windows**, thus the name of the operating system. This use of icons and windows is called a **graphical user interface** (**GUI**, pronounced "gooey"), which means that you interact with the computer through the use of graphics such as windows, icons, and other meaningful words and symbols. ◢▬▬ This unit introduces you to basic skills that you can use in all Windows programs.

Starting Windows and Viewing the Active Desktop

When you turn on your computer, Windows 98 automatically starts and the Active Desktop appears. The **Active Desktop**, shown in Figure A-1, is where you organize all the information and tools you need to accomplish your computer tasks. From the desktop, you can access, store, share, and explore information seamlessly, whether it resides on your computer, a network, or the Internet. The **Internet** is a worldwide collection of over 40 million computers linked together to share information. The desktop is called "active" because, unlike in other versions of Windows, it allows you to access the Internet. When you start Windows for the first time, the desktop appears with the **default** settings, those preset by the operating system. For example, the default color of the desktop is green. If any of the default settings have been changed on your computer, your desktop will look different than in the figures, but you should be able to locate all the items you need. The bar at the bottom of your screen is called the **taskbar**, which shows what programs are currently running. Use the **Start button** at the left end of the taskbar to start programs, find and open files, access Windows Help and so on. The **Quick Launch toolbar** is next to the Start button; it contains buttons you use to quickly start Internet-related programs and show the desktop when it is not currently displayed. The bar on the right side of your screen is called the **Channel Bar**, which contains buttons you use to access the Internet. Table A-1 identifies the icons and other elements you see on your desktop. ➤ If Windows 98 is not currently running, follow the steps below to start it now.

Steps

1. Turn on your computer and monitor

Windows automatically starts and the desktop appears, as shown in Figure A-1. If you are working on a network at school or at an office, you might see a password dialog box. If so, continue to Step 2. If not, continue to the next lesson.

2. Type your password, then press [Enter]

Once the password is accepted, the Windows desktop appears on your screen.

Trouble?

If you don't know your password, see your instructor or technical support person.

CLUES TO USE

Accessing the Internet from the Active Desktop

One of the important differences between Windows 98 and previous versions of Windows is that Windows 98 allows you to access the Internet from the desktop using Internet Explorer, a program that is integrated into the Windows 98 operating system. Internet Explorer is an example of a **browser**, a program designed to access the **World Wide Web** (**WWW, the Web**). One feature of Internet Explorer is that you can use the Favorites command on the Start menu to access places on the Internet that you visit frequently. Also, you can use the Quick Launch toolbar to launch Internet-related programs and the Channel Bar to view Internet channels, which are like those on television but display Internet content. The integration of a browser into the operating system provides a seamless connection between your desktop and the Internet.

FIGURE A-1: Windows Active Desktop

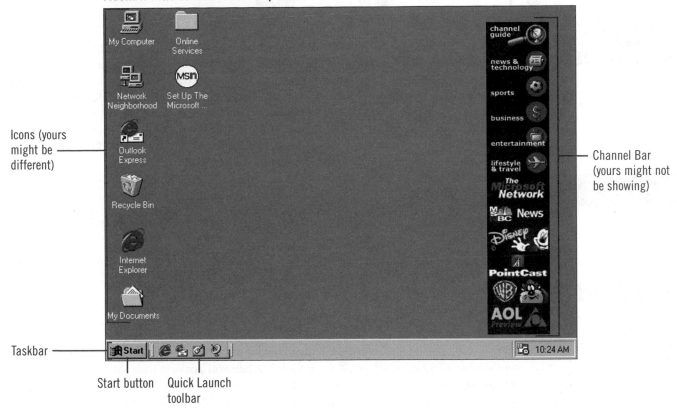

Icons (yours might be different)

Channel Bar (yours might not be showing)

Taskbar

Start button   Quick Launch toolbar

TABLE A-1: Elements of the Windows desktop

desktop element	allows you to
My Computer	Work with different disk drives and printers on your computer
Network Neighborhood	Work with different disk drives and printers on a network
Outlook Express	Start Outlook Express, an electronic mail program
Recycle Bin	Delete and restore files
Internet Explorer	Start Internet Explorer, a program you use to access the Internet
My Documents folder	Store programs, documents, graphics, or other files
Taskbar	Start programs and switch among open programs
Start button	Start programs, open documents, find a file, and more
Channel Bar	Start Internet Explorer and open channels
Quick Launch toolbar	Start Internet Explorer, start Outlook Express, show the desktop, and view channels

Using the Mouse

A **mouse** is a hand-held **input device** that you use to interact with your computer. Input devices come in many shapes and sizes; some, like a mouse, are directly attached to your computer with a cable; others function like a TV remote control and allow you to access your computer without being right next to it. Figure A-2 shows examples of common pointing devices. Because the most common pointing device is a mouse, this book uses that term. If you are using a different pointing device substitute that device whenever you see the term "mouse." When you move the mouse, the **mouse pointer** on the screen moves in the same direction. The **mouse buttons** are used to select icons and commands, which is how you communicate with the computer. Table A-2 shows some common mouse pointer shapes that indicate different activities. Table A-3 lists the five basic mouse actions. ➤ Begin by experimenting with the mouse now.

Steps

1. **Locate the mouse pointer on the desktop, then move the mouse across your desk or mousepad**
   Watch how the mouse pointer moves on the desktop in response to your movements. Practice moving the mouse pointer in circles, then back and forth in straight lines.

2. **Position the mouse pointer over the My Computer icon**
   Positioning the mouse pointer over an item is called **pointing**.

3. **With the pointer over the My Computer icon, press and release the left mouse button**
   Pressing and releasing the left mouse button is called **clicking** or single-clicking, to distinguish it from double-clicking, which you'll do in Step 7. When you position the mouse pointer over an icon or any item and click, you select that item. When an item is **selected**, it is **highlighted** (shaded differently than other items), and any action you take will be performed on that item.

4. **With the icon selected, press and hold down the left mouse button, then move the mouse down and to the right and release the mouse button**
   The icon becomes dimmed and moves with the mouse pointer; this is called **dragging**, which you use to move icons and other Windows elements. When you release the mouse button, the icon is moved to a new location.

5. **Position the mouse pointer over the My Computer icon, then press and release the right mouse button**
   Clicking the right mouse button is known as **right-clicking**. Right-clicking an item on the desktop displays a **pop-up menu**, as shown in Figure A-3. This menu lists the commands most commonly used for the item you have clicked. A **command** is a directive that provides access to a program's features.

6. **Click anywhere outside the menu to close the pop-up menu**

7. **Position the mouse pointer over the My Computer icon, then press and release the left mouse button twice quickly**
   Clicking the mouse button twice quickly is known as **double-clicking**, which, in this case, opens the My Computer window. The **My Computer** window contains additional icons that represent the drives and system components that are installed on your computer.

8. **Click the Close button** ☒ **in the upper-right corner of the My Computer window**

Trouble?

If the My Computer window opens, your mouse isn't set with the Windows 98 default mouse settings. See your instructor or technical support person for assistance. This book assumes your computer is set to all Windows 98 default settings

QuickTip

When a step tells you to "click," use the left mouse button. If it says "right-click", use the right mouse button.

TABLE A-2: Common mouse pointer shapes

shape	used to
⇖	Select items, choose commands, start programs, and work in programs
I	Position mouse pointer for editing or inserting text; called the insertion point
⧗	Indicate Windows is busy processing a command
↔	Change the size of a window; appears when mouse pointer is on the border of a window
☝	Select and open Web-based data

FIGURE A-2: Common pointing devices

Right mouse button

Left mouse button

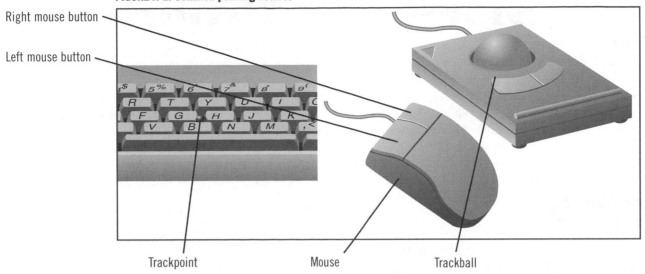

Trackpoint

Mouse

Trackball

FIGURE A-3: Displaying a pop-up menu

Selected icon

Pop-up menu

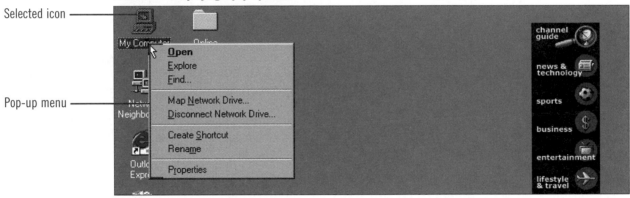

TABLE A-3: Basic mouse techniques

technique	what to do
Pointing	Move the mouse to position the mouse pointer over an item on the desktop
Clicking	Press and release the left mouse button
Double-clicking	Press and release the left mouse button twice quickly
Dragging	Point to an item, press and hold the left mouse button, move the mouse to a new location, then release the mouse button
Right-clicking	Point to an item, then press and release the right mouse button

More about the mouse: Classic style and Internet style

Because Windows 98 integrates the use of the Internet with its other functions, it allows you to choose whether you want to extend the way you click on the Internet to the rest of your computer work. With previous versions of the Windows operating system, and with the default Windows 98 settings, you click an item to select it and double-click an item to open it. When you use the Internet, however, you point to an item to select it and single-click to open it. Therefore, Windows 98 gives you two choices for using the mouse buttons: with the **Classic style**, you double-click to open items, and with the **Internet style** or **Web style**, you single-click to open items. To change from one style to another, click the Start button, point to Settings, click Folder Options, then click the Web style, Classic style, or Custom option.

Starting a Program

To start a program in Windows 98, click the Start button, which lists categories for a variety of tasks described in Table A-4. As you become familiar with Windows, you might want to customize the Start menu to include additional items that you use most often. To start a program from the Start menu, you click the Start menu, point to Programs to open the Programs submenu, then click the program you want to start. Windows 98 comes with several built-in programs, called **accessories**. Although not as feature-rich as many programs sold separately, Windows accessories are useful for completing basic tasks. In this lesson, you start a Windows accessory called **WordPad**, which is a word processing program you can use to create and edit simple documents. Table A-5 describes other popular Windows Accessories.

1. Click the **Start button** on the taskbar
The Start menu opens.

2. Point to **Programs**
The Programs submenu opens, listing the programs and categories for programs installed on your computer. WordPad is in the category called Accessories.

3. Point to **Accessories**
The Accessories menu, shown in Figure A-4, contains several programs to help you complete common tasks. You want to start WordPad, which is probably at the bottom of the list.

4. Click **WordPad**
WordPad opens and a blank document window opens, as shown in Figure A-5. Note that a **program button** appears on the taskbar, indicating that WordPad is open.

TABLE A-4: Start menu categories

category	description
Windows Update	Connects to a Microsoft Web site and updates your Windows 98 files as necessary
Programs	Opens programs included on the Start menu
Favorites	Connects to favorite Web sites or opens folders and documents that you previously selected
Documents	Opens the most recently opened and saved documents
Settings	Opens tools for selecting settings for your system, including the Control Panel, printers, taskbar and Start menu, folders, icons, and the Active Desktop
Find	Locates programs, files, folders, or computers on your computer network, or finds information and people on the Internet
Help	Provides Windows Help information by topic, alphabetical index, or search criteria
Run	Opens a program or file based on a location and filename that you type or select
Log Off	Allows you to log off the system and log on as a different user
Shut Down	Provides options to shut down the computer, restart the computer in Windows mode, or restart the computer in MS-DOS mode

FIGURE A-4: Cascading menus

Cascading menus (also called submenus)

Arrow indicates submenu

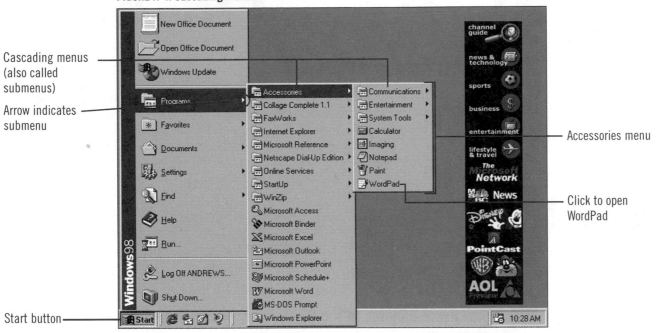

Accessories menu

Click to open WordPad

Start button

FIGURE A-5: WordPad window

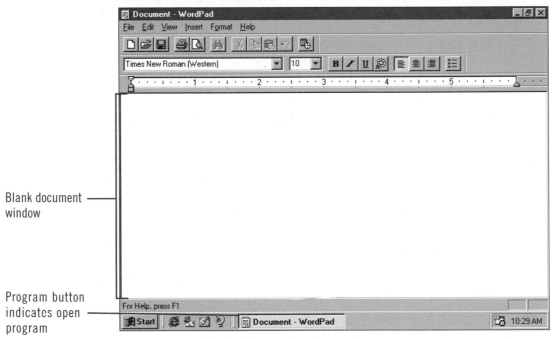

Blank document window

Program button indicates open program

TABLE A-5: Common Windows Accessories on the Accessories menu

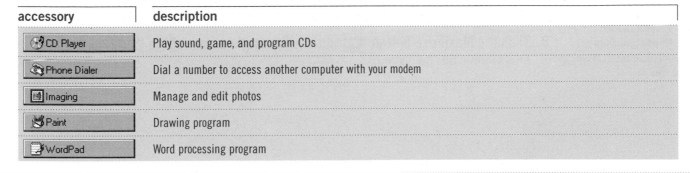

accessory	description
CD Player	Play sound, game, and program CDs
Phone Dialer	Dial a number to access another computer with your modem
Imaging	Manage and edit photos
Paint	Drawing program
WordPad	Word processing program

Windows 98

Moving and Resizing Windows

One of the powerful features of Windows is the ability to open more than one window or program at once. This means, however, that the desktop can get cluttered with the various programs and files you are using. One of the ways to keep your desktop organized is by changing the size of a window or moving it. You can do this using the standard borders and sizing buttons that are part of each window. ◄━━━ Practice sizing and moving the WordPad window now.

Steps 1 2 3 4

1. If the WordPad window does not already fill the screen, click the **Maximize button** 🔲 in the WordPad window.
   When a window is **maximized**, it takes up the whole screen.

2. Click the **Restore button** 🔳 in the WordPad window
   To **restore** a window is to return it to its previous size, as shown in Figure A-6. The Restore button only appears when a window is maximized. In addition to minimizing, maximizing, and restoring windows, you can also change the dimensions of any window.

3. Position the pointer on the right edge of the WordPad window until the pointer changes to ↔, then drag the border to the right
   The width of the window increases. You can size the height and width of a window by dragging any of the four sides individually. You can also size the height and width of the window simultaneously by dragging the corner of the window.

> **QuickTip**
>
> You can resize windows by dragging any corner, not just the lower left. You can also drag any border to make the window taller, shorter, wider, or narrower.

4. Position the pointer in the lower-right corner of the WordPad window until the pointer changes to ↘, as shown in Figure A-6, then drag down and to the right
   The height and width of the window increase at the same time. You can also position a restored window wherever you wish on the desktop by dragging its title bar.

5. Click the **title bar** on the WordPad window, as shown in Figure A-6, then drag the window up and to the left
   The window is repositioned on the desktop. The **title bar** is the area along the top of the window that displays the file name and program used to create it. At times, you might wish to close a program window, yet keep the program running and easily accessible. You can accomplish this by minimizing a window.

> **QuickTip**
>
> If you have more than one window open and you want to access something on the desktop, you can click the Show Desktop button 🔲 on the Quick Launch toolbar. All open windows are minimized so the desktop is visible.

6. In the WordPad window, click the **Minimize button** 🔲
   When you **minimize** a window, it shrinks to a program button on the taskbar, as shown in Figure A-7. WordPad is still running, but it is out of your way.

7. Click the **WordPad program button** on the taskbar to reopen the window
   The WordPad program window reopens.

8. Click the **Maximize button** 🔲 in the upper-right corner of the WordPad window
   The window fills the screen.

FIGURE A-6: Restored WordPad window

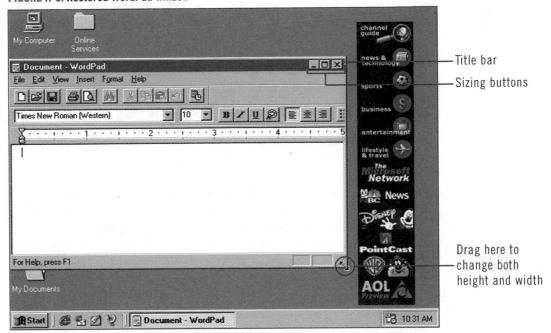

Title bar

Sizing buttons

Drag here to change both height and width

FIGURE A-7: Minimized WordPad window

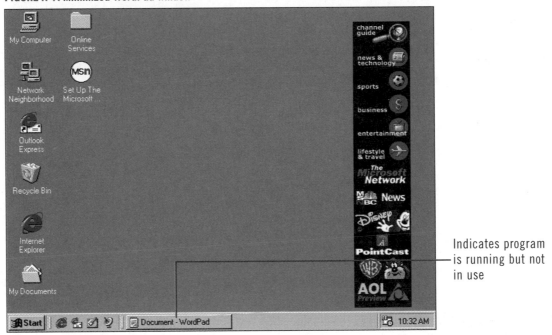

Indicates program is running but not in use

CLUES TO USE

More about sizing windows

Many programs contain two sets of sizing buttons: one that controls the program window itself and another that controls the window for the file with which you are working. The program sizing buttons are located in the title bar and the file sizing buttons are located below them. See Figure A-8. When you minimize a file window within a program, the file window is reduced to an icon in the lower-left corner of the program window, but the size of the program window remains intact.

FIGURE A-8: Program and file sizing buttons

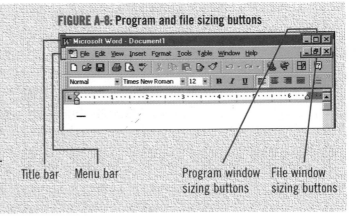

Title bar   Menu bar   Program window sizing buttons   File window sizing buttons

Windows 98

Using Menus, Keyboard Shortcuts, and Toolbars

A **menu** is a list of commands that you use to accomplish certain tasks. You've already used the Start menu to start WordPad. Each Windows program also has its own set of menus, which are located on the **menu bar** under the title bar. The menus organize commands into groups of related operations. See Table A-6 for examples of what you might see on a typical menu. A **toolbar** is a series of buttons, located under the menu bar, that you click to accomplish certain tasks. Buttons are another method for executing menu commands. ▶ You will open the Control Panel, then use a menu and toolbar button to change how the contents of the window appear.

Steps 1 2 3 4

QuickTip

You now have two windows open: WordPad and the Control Panel. The Control Panel is the **active window** (or **active program**) because it is the one with which you are currently working. WordPad is **inactive** because it is open but you are not working with it. Working with more than one window at a time is called **multitasking**.

1. Click the **Start button** on the taskbar, point to **Settings**, then click **Control Panel**

The Control Panel window opens over the WordPad window. The **Control Panel** contains icons for various programs that allow you to specify how your computer looks and performs. You use the Control Panel to practice using menus and toolbars.

2. Click **View** on the menu bar

The View menu appears, listing the View commands, as shown in Figure A-9. On a menu, a **check mark** identifies a feature that is currently enabled or "on." To disable, or turn "off" the feature, click the command again to remove the check mark. A **bullet mark** can also indicate that an option is enabled. To disable a bulleted option, you must select another option in its place.

3. Click **Small Icons**

The icons are now smaller than they were before, taking up less room in the window.

4. Press **[Alt][V]** to open the View menu

The View menu appears again; this time you opened it using the keyboard. Notice that a letter in each command on the View menu is underlined. You can select these commands by pressing the underlined letter. Executing a command using the keyboard is called a **keyboard shortcut**. You might find that you prefer keyboard shortcuts to the mouse if you find it cumbersome to reposition your hands at the keyboard each time you use the mouse.

5. Press **[T]** to select the Toolbars command

The Toolbars submenu appears with check marks next to the commands that are currently selected.

Trouble?

If the Text Labels command wasn't selected, clicking the command now will select it, and you will see the labels under the buttons. Click View, click Toolbars, then click Text Labels to deselect it.

6. Press **[T]** to deselect the Text Labels command

The buttons appear without labels below each one; now you can see the entire toolbar.

7. On the Control Panel toolbar, position the pointer over the **Views button** 🖽 but do not click yet

When you position the mouse pointer over a button (and other items), a **ScreenTip** appears, showing the name of the item, as shown in Figure A-10. ScreenTips help you learn the names of the various elements in Windows programs.

8. Click the **Views button list arrow** 🖽▾

Some toolbar buttons have an arrow, which indicates the button contains several choices. Clicking the arrow shows the choices; clicking the button itself automatically selects the command below the one that was previously selected.

9. In the list of View choices, click **Details**

The Details view includes a description of each program in the Control Panel.

FIGURE A-9: Opening a menu

Menu bar

Commands in View menu

Status bar displays description of menu

Arrow indicates submenu

Check mark

Bullet

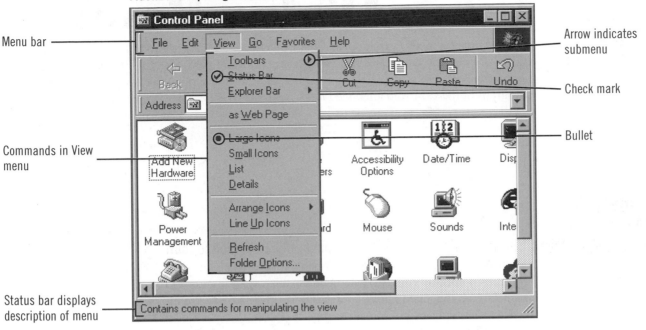

FIGURE A-10: ScreenTip in Control Panel

Toolbar

Position pointer over button to display ScreenTip

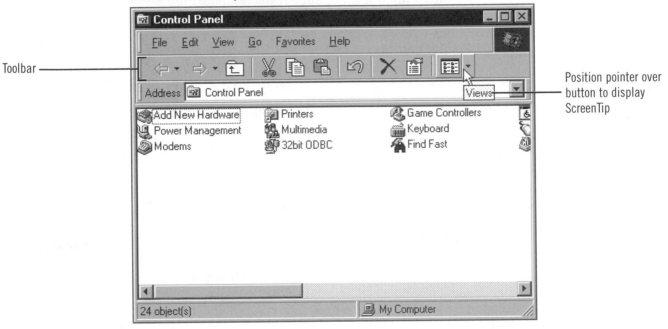

TABLE A-6: Typical items on a menu

item	description	example
Dimmed command	A menu command that is not currently available	Undo Ctrl+Z
Ellipsis	Opens a dialog box that allows you to select different or additional options	Save As...
Triangle	Opens a cascading menu containing an additional list of commands	Zoom ▶
Keyboard shortcut	A keyboard alternative to using the mouse for executing a command	Paste Ctrl+V
Underlined letter	Indicates the letter to press for the keyboard shortcut	Print Preview

Using Dialog Boxes

A **dialog box** is a window that opens when you choose a menu command that is followed by an ellipsis (...), or any command that needs more information before the program can carry out the command you selected. Dialog boxes open in other situations as well, such as when you open a program in the Control Panel. See Figure A-11 and Table A-7 for some of the typical elements of a dialog box. ◄▬▬▬ Practice using a dialog box to control your mouse settings.

Steps 1 2 3 4

1. In the Control Panel window, double-click the **Mouse icon** 👆

The Mouse Properties dialog box opens, as shown in Figure A-12. **Properties** are characteristic of a specific computer element (in this case, the mouse) that you can customize. The options in this dialog box allow you to control the way the mouse buttons are configured, select the types of pointers that appear, choose the speed of the mouse movement on the screen, and specify what type of mouse you are using. **Tabs** at the top of the dialog box separate these options into related categories.

2. Click the **Motion tab** if it is not already the frontmost tab

This tab has two boxes. The first, Pointer speed, has a slider for you to set how fast the pointer moves on the screen in relation to how you move the mouse in your hand. The second, **Pointer trail**, has a check box you can select to add a "trail" or shadow to the pointer on your screen, making it easier to see. The slider in the Pointer trail box lets you determine the degree to which the option is in effect—in this case, the length of the pointer trail.

3. In the Pointer trail box, click the **Show pointer trails check box** to select it

4. Drag the **slider** below the check box all the way to the right, then move the mouse pointer across your screen

As you move the mouse, notice the pointer trails.

5. Click the other tabs in the Mouse Properties dialog box and experiment with the options that are available in each category

After you select the options you want in a dialog box, you need to select a **command button**, which carries out the options you've selected. The two most common command buttons are OK and Cancel. Clicking OK accepts your changes and closes the dialog box; clicking Cancel leaves the original settings intact and closes the dialog box. The third command button in this dialog box is Apply. Clicking the Apply button accepts the changes you've made and keeps the dialog box open so that you can select additional options. Because you might share this computer with others, it's important to return the dialog box options back to the original settings.

6. Click **Cancel** to leave the original settings intact and close the dialog box

FIGURE A-11: Elements of a typical dialog box

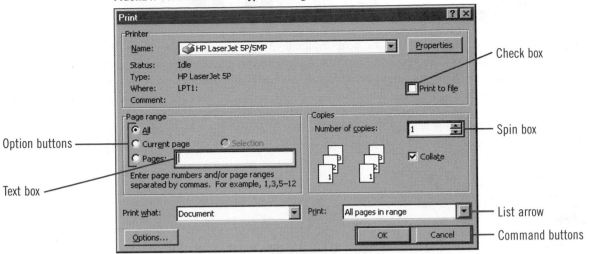

Check box

Spin box

Option buttons

Text box

List arrow

Command buttons

FIGURE A-12: Mouse Properties dialog box

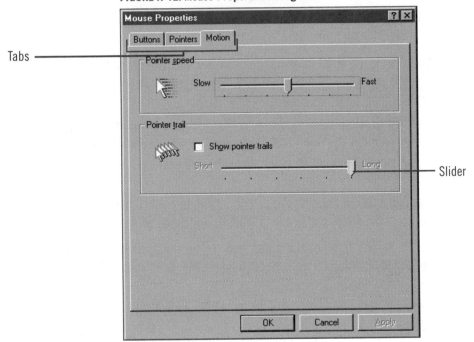

Tabs

Slider

TABLE A-7: Typical items in a dialog box

item	description	item	description
Check box	A box that turns an option on (when the box is checked) and off (when it is blank)	**List box**	A box containing a list of items; to choose an item, click the list arrow, then click the desired item
Text box	A box in which you type text	**Spin box**	A box with two arrows and a text box; allows you to scroll numerical increments or type a number
Option button	A small circle that selects a single dialog box option; you cannot check more than one option button in a list	**Slider**	A shape that you drag to set the degree to which an option is in effect
Command button	A rectangular button in a dialog box with the name of the command on it	**Tab**	A place in a dialog box where related commands and options are organized

Using Scroll Bars

When you cannot see all of the items available in a window, scroll bars appear on the right and/or bottom edges of the window. **Scroll bars** allow you to display the additional contents of the window. There are several ways you can scroll in a window. When you need to scroll only a short distance, you can use the scroll arrows. To scroll the window in larger increments, click in the scroll bar above or below the scroll box. Dragging the scroll box moves you quickly to a new part of the window. See Table A-8 for a summary of the different ways to use scroll bars. ◤ With the Control Panel window in Details view, you can use the scroll bars to view all of the items in this window.

Steps

Trouble?

If you can't see the scroll bars, resize the window until both the horizontal and vertical scroll bars appear. Scroll bars don't appear when the window is large enough to include all the information.

QuickTip

The size of the scroll box changes to reflect how many items or the amount of text that does not fit in a window. A larger scroll box indicates that a relatively small amount of the window's contents is not currently visible; you need to scroll only a short distance to see the remaining items. A smaller scroll box indicates that a relatively large amount of information is currently not visible.

1. In the Control Panel window, click the **down scroll arrow**, as shown in Figure A-13
   Clicking this arrow moves the view down one line. Clicking the up arrow moves the view up one line.

2. Click the **up scroll arrow** in the vertical scroll bar
   The screen moves up one line.

3. Click anywhere in the area below the scroll box in the vertical scroll bar
   The view moves down one window's height. Similarly, you can click in the scroll bar above the scroll box to move up one window's height.

4. Drag the **scroll box** all the way down to the bottom of the vertical scrollbar
   The view now includes the items that appear at the very bottom of the window. Similarly, you can drag the scroll box to the top of the scroll bar to view the information that appears at the top of the window.

5. Drag the **scroll box** all the way up to the top of the vertical scroll bar
   This view shows the items that appear at the top of the window.

6. Click the area to the right of the scroll box in the horizontal scroll bar
   The far right edge of the window comes into view. The horizontal scroll bar works the same as the vertical scroll bar.

7. Click the area to the left of the scroll box in the horizontal scroll bar
   You should return the Control Panel to its original settings.

8. On the Control Panel toolbar, click the **Views button list arrow** ⊞▾ , click **Large Icons**, then maximize the Control Panel window

FIGURE A-13: Scroll bars in the Control Panel

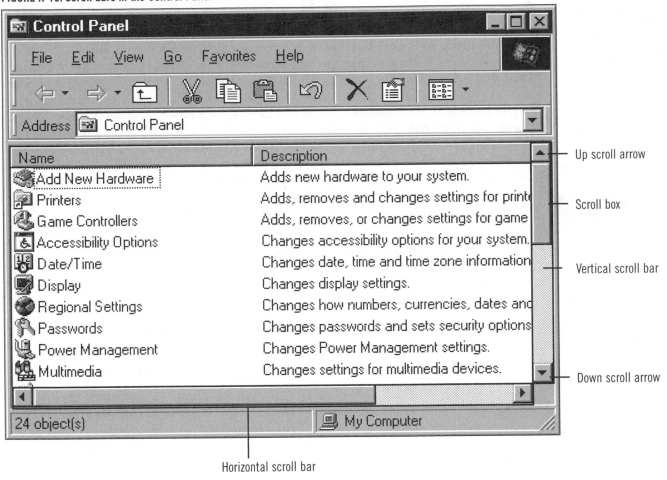

Up scroll arrow

Scroll box

Vertical scroll bar

Down scroll arrow

Horizontal scroll bar

TABLE A-8: Using scroll bars in a window

to	do this
Move down one line	Click the down arrow at the bottom of the vertical scroll bar
Move up one line	Click the up arrow at the top of the vertical scroll bar
Move down one window height	Click in the area below the scroll box in the vertical scroll bar
Move up one window height	Click in the area above the scroll box in the vertical scroll bar
Move up a large distance in the window	Drag the scroll box up in the vertical scroll bar
Move down a large distance in the window	Drag the scroll box down in the vertical scroll bar
Move a short distance side-to-side in a window	Click the left or right arrows in the horizontal scroll bar
Move to the right one window width	Click in the area to the right of the scroll box in the horizontal scroll bar
Move to the left one window width	Click in the area to the left of the scroll box in the horizontal scroll bar
Move left or right a large distance in the window	Drag the scroll box in the horizontal scroll bar

Getting Help

When you have a question about how to do something in Windows 98, you can usually find the answer with a few clicks of your mouse. **Windows Help** works like a book stored on your computer, with a table of contents and an index to make finding information easier. Help provides guidance on many Windows features, including detailed steps for completing a procedure, definitions of terms, lists of related topics, and search capabilities. To open the main Windows 98 Help system, click Help on the Start menu. From here you can browse the Help "book," or you can connect to a Microsoft Web site on the Internet for the latest technical support on Windows 98. To get help on a specific Windows program, click Help on the program's menu bar. You can also access **context-sensitive help**, help specifically related to what you are doing, using a variety of methods such as right-clicking an object or using the question mark button in a dialog box. In this lesson, you get Help on how to start a program. You also get information on the taskbar.

Steps

1. Click the **Start button** on the taskbar, then click **Help**

The Windows Help dialog box opens with the Contents tab in front, as shown in Figure A-14. The Contents tab provides you with a list of Help categories. Each "book" has several "chapters" that you can see by clicking the book or the name next to the book.

2. Click the **Contents tab** if it isn't the frontmost tab, click **Exploring Your Computer**, then click **Work with Programs** to view the Help categories

The Help window contains a selection of topics related to running programs.

3. Click **Start a Program**

The Help window appears in the right pane, as shown in Figure A-15. **Panes** divide a window into two or more sections. At the bottom of the right pane, you can click Related Topics to view a list of topics that may also be of interest. Some Help topics also allow you to view additional information about important words; these words are underlined.

4. Click the underlined word **taskbar**

A pop-up window appears with a definition of the underlined word.

5. Read the definition, then press **[Enter]** or click anywhere outside the pop-up window to close it

6. In the left pane, click the **Index tab**

The Index tab provides an alphabetical list of all the available Help topics, like an index at the end of a book. You can enter a topic in the text box at the top of the pane. As you type, the list of topics automatically scrolls to try to match the word or phrase you type. You can also scroll down to the topic. In either case, the topic appears in the right pane, as usual.

7. In the left pane, click the **Search tab**

You can use the Search tab to locate a Help topic using keywords. You enter a word or phrase in the text box and click List Topics; a list of matching topics appears below the text box. To view a topic, double-click it or select the topic, then click Display.

8. Click the **Web Help button** on the toolbar

Information on the Web page for Windows 98 Help appears in the right pane (a **Web page** is a document that contains highlighted words, phrases, and graphics that link to other pages on the Internet). You could access this Web page by clicking the "Support Online" underlined text.

9. In the Windows Help window, click the **Close button** in the upper-right corner of the window

Clicking the Close button closes the active window.

FIGURE A-14: Windows Help dialog box

Help toolbar

Help tabs

Click to view alphabetical list of Help topics

Click to search for words and phrases used in Help topics

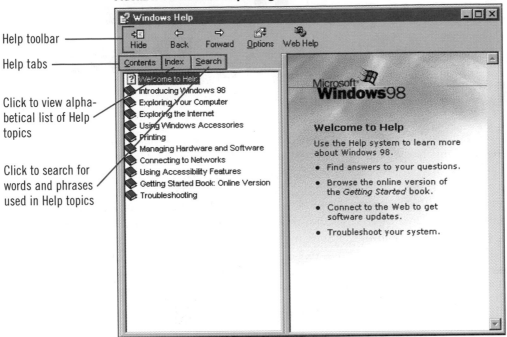

FIGURE A-15: Viewing Help on starting a program

Help topic

Hand pointer

Left pane contains Help categories and topics

Right pane contains help on the topic you select

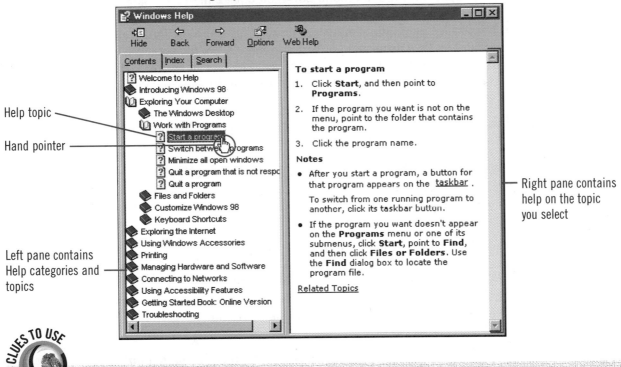

Context-sensitive help

To receive help in a dialog box, click the Help button **?** in the upper-right corner of the dialog box; the mouse pointer changes to ⬚**?**. Click the Help pointer on the item for which you need additional information. A pop-up window provides a brief explanation of the selected feature. You can also click the right mouse button on an item in a dialog box, then click the What's This? button to display the Help explanation. In addition, when you click the right mouse button in a Help topic window, you can choose commands to annotate, copy, and print the contents of the topic window. From the Help pop-up menu, you can also choose to have topic windows always appear on top of the currently active window, so you can see Help topics while you work.

Closing a Program and Shutting Down Windows

When you are finished working on your computer, you need to make sure you shut it down properly. This involves several steps: saving and closing all open files, closing all the open programs and windows, shutting down Windows, and finally, turning off the computer. If you turn off the computer while Windows is running, you could lose important data. To **close** programs, you can click the Close button in the window's upper-right corner or click File on the menu bar and choose either Close or Exit. To shut down Windows after all your files and programs are closed, click Shut Down from the Start menu, then select the desired option from the Shut Down dialog box, shown in Figure A-16. See Table A-9 for a description of shutdown options. Close all your open files, windows, and programs, then exit Windows.

Steps

1. In the Control Panel window, click the **Close button** ☒ in the upper-right corner of the window
   The Control Panel window closes.

2. Click **File** on the WordPad menu bar, then click **Exit**
   If you have made any changes to the open file, you will be prompted to save your changes before the program quits. Some programs also give you the option of choosing the Close command on the File menu in order to close the active file but leave the program open, so you can continue to work in it with a different file. Also, if there is a second set of sizing buttons in the window, the Close button on the menu bar will close the active file only, leaving the program open for continued use.

3. If you see a message asking you to save changes to the document, click **No**
   WordPad closes and you return to the desktop.

QuickTip

Complete the remaining steps to shut down Windows and your computer only if you have been told to do so by your instructor or technical support person.

4. Click the **Start button** on the taskbar, then click **Shut Down**
   The Shut Down Windows dialog box opens, as shown in Figure A-16. In this dialog box, you have the option to shut down the computer, restart the computer in Windows mode or restart the computer in MS-DOS mode.

5. Click the **Shut down option button**, if necessary

6. If you are working in a lab, click **Cancel** to leave the computer running and return to the Windows desktop
   If you are working on your own machine or if your instructor told you to shut down Windows, click **OK** to exit Windows.

7. When you see the message **It's now safe to turn off your computer**, turn off your computer and monitor

FIGURE A-16: Shut Down Windows dialog box

Click to shut down Windows

Click to restart computer in Windows mode

Click to restart computer in MS-DOS mode

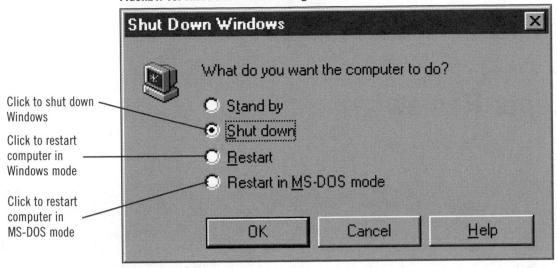

TABLE A-9: Shut down options

shut down option	function	when to use it
Shut down	Prepares the computer to be turned off	When you are finished working with Windows and you want to shut off your computer
Restart	Restarts the computer and reloads Windows	When you want to restart the computer and begin working with Windows again (your programs might have frozen or stopped working).
Restart in MS-DOS mode	Starts the computer in the MS-DOS mode	When you want to run programs under MS-DOS or use DOS commands to work with files

The Log Off command

To change users on the same computer quickly, you can choose the Log Off command from the Start menu. This command identifies the name of the current user. When you choose this command, Windows 98 shuts down and automatically restarts, stopping at the point where you need to enter a password. When the new user enters a user name and password, Windows restarts and the desktop appears as usual.

Practice

► Concepts Review

Identify each of the items labeled in Figure A-17.

FIGURE A-17

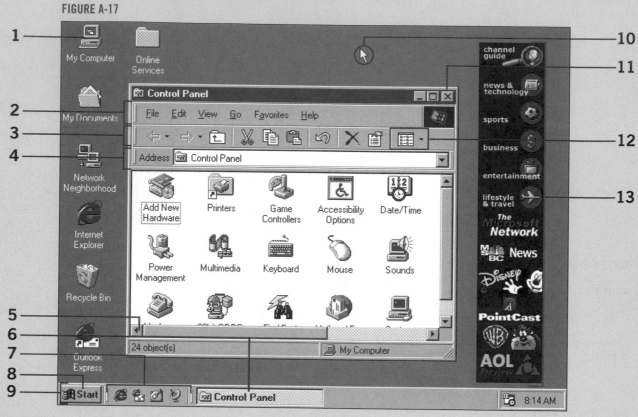

Match each of the statements with the term it describes.

14. Shrinks a window to a button on the taskbar
15. Shows the name of the window or program
16. The item you first click to start a program
17. Requests more information that you supply before carrying out command
18. Shows the Start button, Quick Launch toolbar, and any currently open programs
19. An input device that lets you point to and make selections
20. Graphic representation of program

a. Taskbar
b. Dialog box
c. Start button
d. Mouse
e. Title bar
f. Minimize button
g. Icon

Select the best answer from the list of choices.

21. The acronym GUI means
    a. Grayed user information.
    b. Group user icons.
    c. Graphical user interface.
    d. Group user interconnect.

22. **Which of the following is NOT provided by an operating system?**
    a. Programs for organizing files
    b. Instructions to coordinate the flow of information among the programs, files, printers, storage devices, and other components of your computer system
    c. Programs that allow you to specify the operation of the mouse
    d. Spell checker for your documents

23. **All of the following are examples of using a mouse, EXCEPT**
    a. Clicking the Maximize button.
    b. Pressing [Enter].
    c. Double-clicking to start a program.
    d. Dragging the My Computer icon.

24. **The term for moving an item to a new location on the desktop is**
    a. Pointing.
    b. Clicking.
    c. Dragging.
    d. Restoring.

25. **The Maximize button is used to**
    a. Return a window to its previous size.
    b. Expand a window to fill the computer screen.
    c. Scroll slowly through a window.
    d. Run programs from the Start menu.

26. **What appears if a window contains more information than can be displayed in the window?**
    a. Program icon
    b. Cascading menu
    c. Scroll bars
    d. Check box

27. **A window is active when**
    a. You see its program button on the taskbar.
    b. Its title bar is dimmed.
    c. It is open and you are currently using it.
    d. It is listed in the Programs submenu.

28. **You can exit Windows by**
    a. Double-clicking the Control Panel application.
    b. Double-clicking the Program Manager control menu box.
    c. Clicking File, then clicking Exit.
    d. Selecting the Shut Down command from the Start menu.

► Skills Review

1. **Start Windows and view the Active Desktop**
   a. Turn on the computer, if necessary.
   b. After Windows starts, identify as many items on the desktop as you can, without referring to the lesson material.
   c. Compare your results to Figure A-1.

2. **Use the mouse**
   a. Double-click the Recycle Bin icon.
   b. Drag the Recycle Bin window to the upper-right corner of the desktop.
   c. Right-click the title bar of the Recycle Bin, then click Close.

3. **Start a program.**
   a. Click the Start button on the taskbar, then point to Programs.
   b. Point to Accessories, then click Calculator.
   c. Minimize the Calculator window.

4. **Practice dragging, maximizing, restoring, sizing, and minimizing windows.**
   a. Drag the Recycle Bin icon to the bottom of the desktop.
   b. Double-click the My Computer icon to open the My Computer window.
   c. Maximize the window, if it is not already maximized.
   d. Restore the window to its previous size.
   e. Resize the window until you see both horizontal and vertical scroll bars.
   f. Resize the window until the horizontal scroll bar no longer appears.

    g. Click the Minimize button.

    h. Drag the Recycle Bin back to the top of the desktop.

5. Use menus, keyboard shortcuts, and toolbars

    a. Click the Start button on the taskbar, point to Settings, then click Control Panel.

    b. Click View on the menu bar, point to Toolbars, then click Standard Buttons to hide the toolbar.

    c. Redisplay the toolbar.

    d. Press [Alt][V] to show the View menu, then press [W] to view the Control Panel as a Web page.

    e. Note the change, then use the same keyboard shortcuts to change the view back.

    f. Click the Up One Level button to view My Computer.

    g. Click the Back button to return to the Control Panel.

    h. Double-click the Display icon.

6. Use dialog boxes.

    a. Click the Screen Saver tab.

    b. Click the Screen Saver list arrow, select a screen saver, and preview the change but do not click OK.

    c. Click the Effects tab.

    d. In the Visual effects section, click the Use large icons check box to select it, then click Apply.

    e. Note the change in the icons on the desktop and in the Control Panel window.

    f. Click the Use large icons check box to deselect it, Click the Screen Saver tab, return the scrren saver to its original setting, then click Apply.

    g. Click the Close button in the Display Properties dialog box, but leave the Control Panel open.

7. Use scroll bars

    a. Click View on the Control Panel toolbar, then click Details.

    b. Resize the Control Panel window, if necessary, so that both scroll bars are visible.

    c. Drag the vertical scroll box down all the way.

    d. Click anywhere in the area above the vertical scroll box.

    e. Click the up scroll arrow until the scroll box is back at the top of the scroll bar.

    f. Drag the horizontal scroll box so you can read the descriptions for the icons.

8. Get Help

    a. Click the Start button on the taskbar, then click Help.

    b. Click the Contents tab, then click Introducing Windows 98.

    c. Click Exploring Your Computer, click Customize Windows 98, then click How the Screen Looks.

    d. Click each of the topics and read them in the right pane.

9. Close a program and shut down Windows.

    a. Click the Close button to close the Help topic window.

    b. Click File on the menu bar, then click Close to close the Control Panel window.

    c. Click the Calculator program button on the taskbar to restore the window.

    d. Click the Close button in the Calculator window to close the Calculator program.

    e. Click the My Computer program button on the taskbar, then click the Close button to close the window.

    f. If you are instructed to do so, shut down your computer.

▶ Independent Challenges

1. Windows 98 has an extensive help system. In this independent challenge, you will use Help to learn about more Windows 98 features and explore the help that's available on the Internet.

  a. Open Windows Help and locate help topics on: adjusting the double-click speed of your mouse; using Print; and, displaying Web content on your desktop.

If you have a printer, print a Help topic for each subject. If you do not have a printer, write a summary of each topic.

  b. Follow these steps below to access help on the Internet. If you don't have Internet access, you can't do this step.

    i. Click the Web Help button on the toolbar.

    ii. Read the introduction, then click the link Support Online. A browser will open and prompt you to connect to the Internet. Once you are connected, a Web site called Support Online will appear.

    iii. Click the View Popular Topics link. Write a summary of what you find.

    iv. Click the Close button in the title bar of your browser, then disconnect from the Internet and close Windows Help.

2. You may need to change the format of the clock and date on your computer. For example, if you work with international clients it might be easier to show the time in military (24-hour) time and the date with the day before the month. You can also change the actual time and date on your computer, such as when you change time zones.

  a. Open the Control Panel window, then double-click the Regional Settings icon.

  b. Click the Time tab to change the time to show a 24-hour clock rather than a 12-hour clock.

  c. Click the Date tab to change the date to show the day before the month (e.g., 30/3/99).

  d. Change the time to one hour later using the Date/Time icon in the Control Panel window.

  e. Return the settings to the original time and format and close all open windows.

3. Calculator is a Windows program on the Accessories menu that you can use for calculations you need to perform while using the computer. Follow these guidelines to explore the Calculator and the Help that comes with it:

  a. Start the Calculator from the Accessories menu.

  b. Click Help on the menu bar, then click Help topics. The Calculator Help window opens, showing several Help topics.

  c. View the Help topic on how to perform simple calculations, then print it if you have a printer connected.

  d. Open the Tips and Tricks category, then view the Help topic on how to find out what a calculator button does.

  e. View the Help topic (under Tips and Tricks) on how to use keyboard equivalents of calculator buttons, then print the topic if you have a printer connected to your computer.

  f. Determine how many months you have to work to earn an additional week of vacation if you work for a company that provides one additional day of paid vacation for every 560 hours you work. (*Hint*: First multiply 560 times 5 days, then divide the answer by the number of hours you work in a month.)

  g. Close all open windows.

4. You can customize many Windows features to suit your needs and preferences. One way you do this is to change the appearance of the taskbar on the desktop. In this challenge, try the guidelines described to explore the different ways you can customize the appearance of the taskbar.

  a. Position the pointer over the top border of the taskbar. When the pointer changes shape, drag up an inch.

  b. Resize the taskbar back to its original size.

  c. Click the Start button on the taskbar, then point to Settings, and click Taskbar & Start Menu.

  d. In the upper-right corner of the Taskbar Properties window, click the Help button, then click each option to view the pop-up window describing the option. You need to click the Help button before clicking each option.

  e. Click each option and observe the effect in the preview area. (*Note:* Do not click OK.)

  f. Return the options to their original settings or click Cancel.

▶ Visual Workshop

Use the skills you have learned in this unit to create a desktop that looks like the one in Figure A-18. Make sure you include the following:

- Calculator program minimized
- Scroll bars in Control Panel window
- Details view in Control Panel window
- Rearranged icons on desktop; your icons may be different (*Hint*: If the icons "snap" back to where they were, they are set to be automatically arranged. Right-click a blank area of the desktop, point to Arrange Icons, then click Auto Arrange to deselect it.)
- Channel Bar closed

Use the Print Screen key to make a copy of the screen and then print it from the Paint program (see your instructor or technical support person for assistance.) Be sure to return your settings and desktop back to their original arrangement when you complete this exercise.

FIGURE A-18

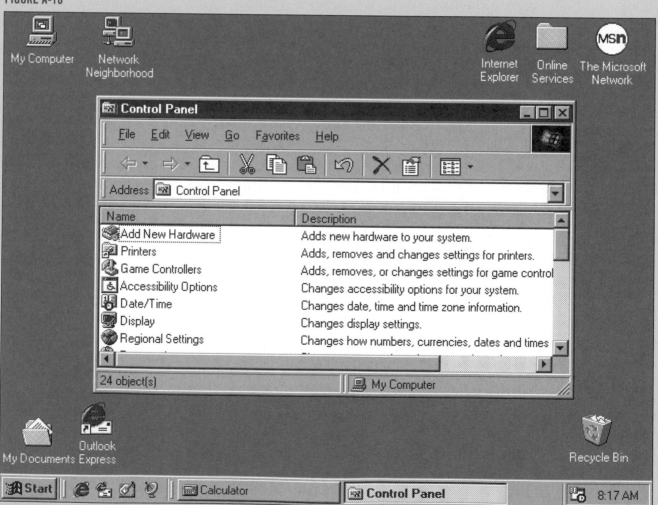

Working

with Programs, Files, and Folders

Objectives

- ► Create and save a WordPad file
- ► Open, edit, and save an existing Paint file
- ► Work with multiple programs
- ► Understand file management
- ► View files and create folders with My Computer
- ► Move and copy files using My Computer
- ► Manage files with Windows Explorer
- ► Delete and restore files
- ► Create a shortcut on the desktop

Most of your work on a computer involves creating files in programs. For example, you might use WordPad to create a resume or Microsoft Excel to create a budget. The resume and the budget are examples of **files**, electronic collections of data that you create and save on a computer. In this unit, you learn how to work with files and the programs you use to create them. You create new files, open and edit an existing file, and use the Clipboard to copy and paste data from one file to another. You also explore the file management features of Windows 98, using My Computer and Windows Explorer. Finally, you learn how to work more efficiently by managing files directly on your desktop.

Unit B

Windows 98

Creating and Saving a WordPad File

As with most programs, when you start WordPad a new, blank **document** (or file) opens. To create a new file, such as a memo, you simply begin typing. Your work is automatically stored in your computer's **random access memory (RAM)** until you turn off your computer, at which point the computer's RAM is erased. To store your work permanently, you must save your work as a file on a disk. You can save files either on an internal **hard disk**, which is built into your computer, usually drive C, or on a removable 3.5" or 5.25" **floppy disk**, which you insert into a drive on your computer, usually drive A or B. Before you can save a file on a floppy disk, the disk must be formatted. See the Appendix, "Formatting a Disk," or your instructor or technical support person for more information. When you name a file, you can use up to 255 characters including spaces and punctuation in the File Name box, using either upper or lowercase letters. ➤ In this unit, you save your files to your Project Disk. If you do not have a Project Disk, see your instructor or technical support person for assistance. First, you start WordPad and create a file that contains the text shown in Figure B-1. Then you save the file to your Project Disk.

Steps

1. **Click the Start button on the taskbar, point to Programs, point to Accessories, click WordPad, then click the Maximize button if the window does not fill your screen**
   The WordPad program window opens with a new, blank document. The blinking **insertion point** | indicates where the text you type will appear.

Trouble?

If you make a mistake, press [Back Space] to delete the character to the left of the insertion point.

2. **Type Memo, then press [Enter] to move the insertion point to the next line**

3. **Type the remaining text shown in Figure B-1, pressing [Enter] at the end of each line to move to the next line and to insert blank lines**
   Now that the text is entered, you can format it. **Formatting** changes the appearance of text to make it more readable or attractive.

QuickTip

Double-click to select a word or triple-click to select a paragraph.

4. **Click in front of the word Memo, then drag the mouse to the right to select the word**
   The text is now **selected** and any action you make will be performed on the text.

5. **Click the Center button ≣ on the Formatting toolbar, then click the Bold button B on the Formatting toolbar**
   The text is centered and bold.

6. **Click the Font Size list arrow 10 ▾, then click 16**
   A **font** is a particular shape and size of type. The text is enlarged to 16 point. One **point** is 1/72 of an inch in height. Now that your memo is complete, you are ready to save it to your Project Disk.

7. **Click File on the menu bar, then click Save As**
   The Save As dialog box opens, as shown in Figure B-2. In this dialog box, you specify where you want your file saved and also give your document a name.

Trouble?

This unit assumes that the drive that contains your Project Disk is drive A. If not, substitute the correct drive any time you are instructed to use the 3½ Floppy (A:) drive. See your instructor or technical support person for assistance.

8. **Click the Save in list arrow, then click 3½ Floppy (A:) or whichever drive contains your Project Disk**
   The drive containing your Project Disk is now active, meaning that any files currently on the disk are displayed in the list of folders and files and that the file you save now will be saved on the disk in this drive.

9. **Double-click the text in the File name text box, type Memo, then click Save**
   Your memo is now saved as a WordPad file with the name "Memo" on your Project Disk. Notice that the WordPad title bar contains the name of the file.

Opening, Editing, and Saving an Existing Paint File

Sometimes you create files from scratch, but often you may want to reopen a file you or someone else has already created. Once you open a file, you can **edit** it, or make changes to it, such as adding or deleting text. After editing a file, you can save it with the same filename, which means that you no longer will have the file in its original form, or you can save it with a different filename, so that the original file remains unchanged. ➤ In this lesson, you use **Paint**, a drawing program that comes with Windows 98, to open a file, edit it by changing a color, then save the file with a new filename to leave the original file unchanged.

Steps 123 4

1. Click the **Start button** on the taskbar, point to **Programs**, point to **Accessories**, click **Paint**, then click the **Maximize button** if the window doesn't fill the screen
   The Paint program opens with a blank work area. If you wanted to create a file from scratch, you would begin working now.

2. Click **File** on the menu bar, then click **Open**
   The Open dialog box works similarly to the Save As dialog box.

3. Click the **Look in list arrow**, then click **3½ Floppy (A:)**
   The Paint files on your Project Disk are displayed in the Open dialog box, as shown in Figure B-3.

QuickTip
You can also open a file by double-clicking it in the Open dialog box.

4. Click **Win B-1** in the list of files, then click **Open**
   The Open dialog box closes and the file named Win B-1 opens. Before you make any changes to the file, you decide to save it with a new filename, so that the original file is unchanged.

5. Click **File** on the menu bar, then click **Save As**

6. Make sure **3½ Floppy (A:)** appears in the Save in text box, select the text **Win B-1** in the File name text box if necessary, type **Logo**, then click **Save**
   The Logo file appears in the Paint window, as shown in Figure B-4. Because you saved the file with a new name, you can edit it without changing the original file.

7. Click the **Fill With Color button** 🖌 in the Toolbox, click the **Blue color box**, which is the fourth from the right in the first row
   Now when you click an area in the image, it will be filled with the color you selected. See Table B-1 for a description of the tools in the Toolbox.

8. Move the pointer into the **white area that represents the sky**, the pointer changes to 🖌, then click
   The sky is now blue.

9. Click **File** on the menu bar, then click **Save**
   The change you made is saved.

FIGURE B-1: Text to enter in WordPad

Bold button

Center button

Press [Enter]
three times
to insert
blank lines

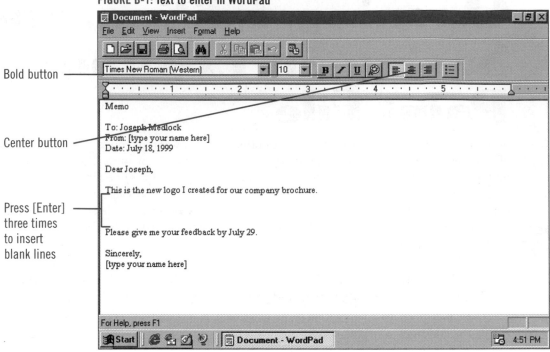

FIGURE B-2: Save As dialog box

Click to select
where to save file

Type new
filename here

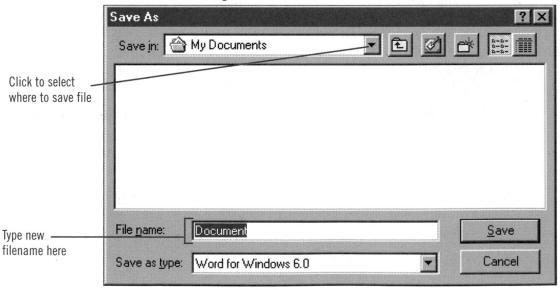

FIGURE B-3: Open dialog box

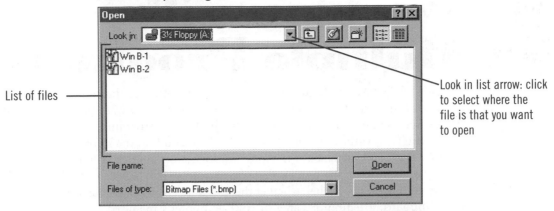

List of files ——

Look in list arrow: click to select where the file is that you want to open

FIGURE B-4: Paint file saved with new filename

Name of file displayed in title bar ——

Fill With Color button ——

Choose this blue color ——

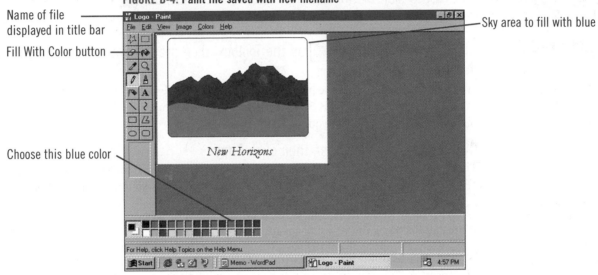

Sky area to fill with blue

TABLE B-1: Paint Toolbox buttons

tool	description	tool	description
Free-Form Select button	Selects a free-form section of the picture to move, copy, or edit	**Airbrush button**	Produces a circular spray of dots
Select button	Selects a rectangular section of the picture to move, copy, or edit	**Text button**	Inserts text into the picture
Eraser button	Erases a portion of the picture using the selected eraser size and foreground color	**Line button**	Draws a straight line with the selected width and foreground color
Fill With Color button	Fills closed shape or area with the current drawing color	**Curve button**	Draws a wavy line with the selected width and foreground color
Pick Color button	Picks up a color off the picture to use for drawing	**Rectangle button**	Draws a rectangle with the selected fill style; also used to draw squares by holding down [Shift] while drawing
Magnifier button	Changes the magnification; lists magnifications under the toolbar	**Polygon button**	Draws polygons from connected straight-line segments
Pencil button	Draws a free-form line one pixel wide	**Ellipse button**	Draws an ellipse with the selected fill style; also used to draw circles by holding down [Shift] while drawing
Brush button	Draws using a brush with the selected shape and size	**Rounded Rectangle button**	Draws rectangles with rounded corners using the selected fill style; also used to draw rounded squares by holding down [Shift] while drawing

Working with Multiple Programs

A powerful feature of Windows is that you can use more than one program at a time. For example, you might be working with a file in WordPad and want to search the Internet to find the answer to a question. You can start your **browser**, a program designed to access information on the Internet, without closing WordPad. When you find the information, you can leave your browser open and switch back to WordPad. Each program that you have open is represented by a program button on the taskbar that you click to switch between programs. You can also copy data from one file to another, whether the files were created with the same program or not, using the **Clipboard**, a temporary area in your computer's memory, and the Cut, Copy, and Paste commands. See Table B-2 for a description of these commands. In this lesson, you copy the logo graphic you worked with in the previous lesson into the memo you created in WordPad.

Steps 1 2 3 4

Trouble?

If some parts of the image or text are outside the dotted rectangle, click anywhere outside the image, then select the image again, making sure you include everything.

QuickTip

To switch between programs using the keyboard, press and hold down [Alt], press [Tab] until the program you want is selected, then release [Alt].

1. Click the **Select button** on the Toolbox, then drag a rectangle around the entire graphic, including the text
   When you release the mouse button, the dotted rectangle indicates the contents of the selection, as shown in Figure B-5. Make sure the entire image and all the text is inside the rectangle. The next action you take affects the entire selection.

2. Click **Edit** on the menu bar, then click **Copy**
   The logo is copied to the Clipboard. When you **copy** an object onto the Clipboard, the object remains in its original location and is also available to be pasted into another location.

3. Click the **WordPad program button** on the taskbar
   WordPad becomes the active program.

4. Click in the **second line** below the line that ends "for our company brochure."
   The insertion point indicates where the logo will be pasted.

5. Click the **Paste button** on the WordPad toolbar
   The contents of the Clipboard, in this case the logo, are pasted into the WordPad file, as shown in Figure B-6.

6. Click the **Save button** on the toolbar
   The Memo file is saved with the logo inserted.

7. Click the **Close buttons** in both the WordPad and Paint programs to close all open files and exit both programs
   You return to the desktop.

TABLE B-2: Overview of cutting, copying, and pasting

toolbar button	function	keyboard shortcut
Cut	Removes selected information from a file and places it on the Clipboard	[Ctrl][X]
Copy	Places a copy of selected information on the Clipboard, leaving the file intact	[Ctrl][C]
Paste	Inserts whatever is currently on the Clipboard into another location within the same file or in a different file	[Ctrl][V]

FIGURE B-5: Selecting the logo to copy and paste into the Memo file

Select button

Dotted line indicates selected area

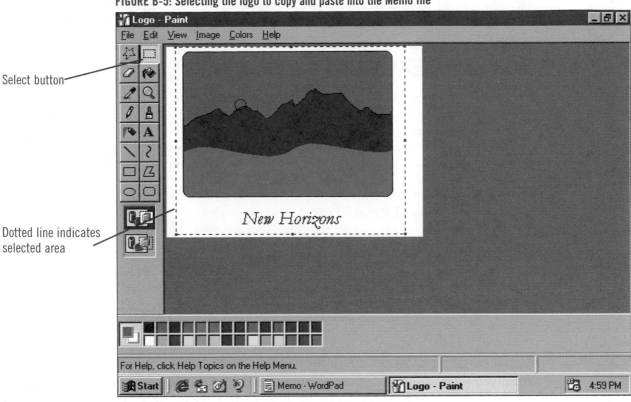

FIGURE B-6: Memo with pasted logo

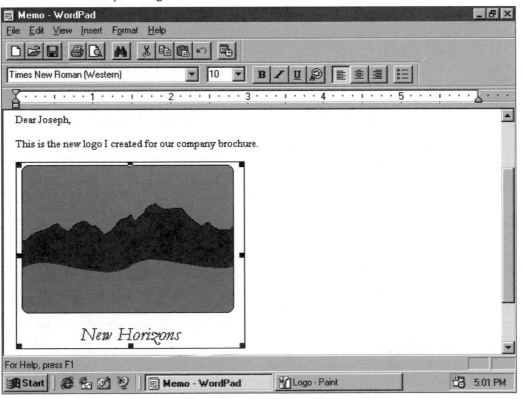

Understanding File Management

After you have created and saved numerous files using various programs, **file management**, the process of organizing and keeping track of all of your files can be a challenge. Fortunately, Windows 98 provides tools to keep everything organized so you can easily locate the files you need. There are two main tools for managing your files: My Computer and Windows Explorer. In this lesson, you preview the ways you can use My Computer and Windows Explorer to manage your files.

Details

Windows 98 gives you the ability to:

Create folders in which you can save your files

Folders are areas on a floppy disk or hard disk in which you can store files. For example, you might create a folder for your documents and another folder for your graphic files. Folders can also contain additional folders, which creates a more complex structure of folders and files, called a **file hierarchy**. See Figure B-7 for an example of how you could organize the files on your Project Disk.

QuickTip

To browse My Computer using multiple windows, click View on the menu bar, then click Folder Options. In the Folder Options dialog box, click the General tab, click Settings, then under Browse folders as follows, click the second option button. Each time you open a new folder, a new window opens, leaving the previous folder's window open so that you can view both at the same time.

Examine and organize the hierarchy of files and folders

When you want to see the overall structure of your files and folders, you can use either My Computer or Windows Explorer. By examining your file hierarchy with these tools, you can better organize the contents of your computer and adjust the hierarchy to meet your needs. Figures B-8 and B-9 illustrate how My Computer and Windows Explorer display folders and files.

Copy, move, and rename files and folders

If you decide that a file belongs in a different folder, you can move it to another folder. You can also rename a file if you decide a new name is more descriptive. If you want to keep a copy of a file in more than one folder, you can copy it to new folders.

Delete files and folders you no longer need, as well as restore files you delete accidentally

Deleting files and folders you are sure you don't need frees up disk space and keeps your file hierarchy more organized. Using the **Recycle Bin**, a space on your computer's hard disk that stores deleted files, you can restore files you deleted by accident. To free up disk space, you should occasionally empty the Recycle Bin by deleting the files permanently from your hard drive.

Locate files quickly with the Windows 98 Find feature

As you create more files and folders, you may forget where you placed a certain file or you may forget what name you used when you saved a file. With Find, you can locate files by providing only partial names or other factors, such as the file type (for example, a WordPad document, a Paint graphic, or a program) or the date the file was created or modified.

Trouble?

If the Quick View command does not appear on the pop-up menu, it means that this feature was not installed on your computer. See your instructor or technical support person for assistance.

Preview the contents of a file without opening the file in its program

After locating a particular file, use Quick View to look at the file to verify that it is the one you want. This saves time because you do not need to open the program to open the file; however, if you decide that you want to edit the file, you can open the program right from Quick View. To preview a file, right-click the selected file in My Computer or Windows Explorer, then click Quick View on the pop-up menu. A preview of the file appears in the Quick View window.

Use shortcuts

If a file or folder you use often is located several levels down in your file hierarchy, in a folder within a folder, within a folder, it might take you several steps to access it. To save time accessing the files and programs you use frequently, you can create shortcuts to them. A **shortcut** is a link that gives you quick access to a particular file, folder, or program.

FIGURE B-7: Example of file hierarchy for Project Disk files

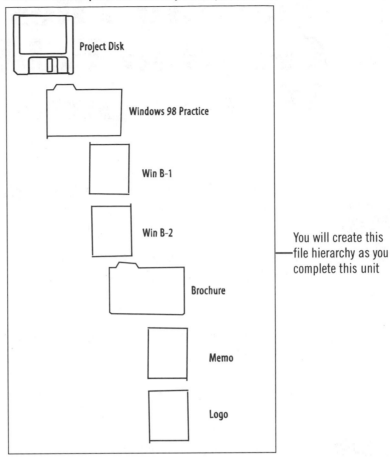

Project Disk

Windows 98 Practice

Win B-1

Win B-2

Brochure

Memo

Logo

You will create this file hierarchy as you complete this unit

FIGURE B-8: Brochure folder shown in My Computer

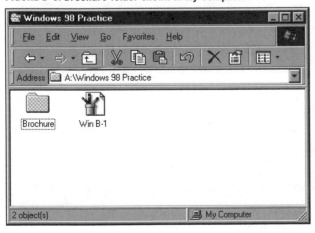

FIGURE B-9: Brochure folder shown in Windows Explorer

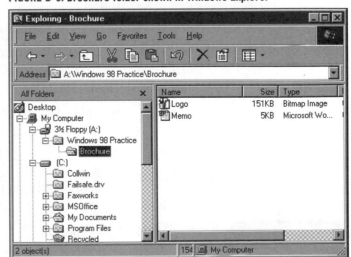

Viewing Files and Creating Folders with My Computer

My Computer shows the contents of your computer, including files, folders, programs, disk drives, and printers. You can click the icons representing these various parts of your computer to view their contents. You can manage your files using the My Computer menu bar and toolbar. See Table B-3 for a description of the toolbar buttons. ➤ In this lesson, you begin by using My Computer to move around in your computer's file hierarchy, then you create two new folders on your Project Disk that contain the files you created.

Steps

Trouble?

If you do not see the toolbar, click View on the menu bar, point to Toolbars, then click Standard Buttons. If you do not see the Address Bar, click View, point to Toolbar, then click the Address Bar.

1. Double-click the **My Computer icon** on your desktop, then click the **Maximize button** if the My Computer window does not fill the screen
My Computer opens and displays the contents of your computer, as shown in Figure B-10. Your window may contain icons for different folders, drives, printers, and so on.

2. Make sure your Project Disk is in the floppy disk drive, then double-click the **3½ Floppy (A:) icon**
The contents of your Project Disk are displayed in the window. These are the project files and the files you created using WordPad and Paint. Each file is represented by an icon, which indicates the program that was used to create the file. If Microsoft Word is installed on your computer, the Word icon appears for the WordPad files; if not, the WordPad icon appears.

Trouble?

This book assumes that your hard drive is drive C. If yours differs, substitute the appropriate drive for drive C wherever it is referenced. See your instructor or technical support person for assistance.

3. Click the **Address list arrow** on the Address Bar, as shown in Figure B-10, then click **(C:)**, or the letter for the main hard drive on your computer
The window changes to show the contents of your hard drive. The **Address Bar** allows you to open and display a drive, folder, or even a Web page. You can also type in the Address Bar to go to a different drive, folder, or Web page. For example, typing "C:\" will display drive C; typing "E:\Personal Letters" will display the Personal Letters folder on drive E, and typing "http://www.microsoft.com" opens Microsoft's Web site if your computer is connected to the Internet.

4. Click the **Back button** on the toolbar
The Back button displays the previous location, in this case, your Project Disk.

5. Click the **Views button list arrow** ▦▾ on the toolbar, then click **Details**
Details view shows not only the files and folders, but also the size of the file; the type of file, folder, or drive; and the date the file was last modified.

6. Click ▦▾, then click **Large Icons**
This view offers less information but provides a large, clear view of the contents of the disk.

7. Click **File** on the menu bar, click **New**, then click **Folder**
A new folder is created on your Project Disk, as shown in Figure B-11. The folder is called "New Folder" by default. It is selected and ready to be renamed. You can also create a new folder by right-clicking in the blank area of the My Computer window, clicking New, then clicking Folder.

Trouble?

To rename a folder, click the folder to select it, click the folder name so it is surrounded by a rectangle, type the new folder name, then press [Enter].

8. Type **Windows 98 Practice**, then press **[Enter]**
Choosing descriptive names for your folders helps you remember their contents.

9. Double-click the **Windows 98 Practice folder**, repeat Step 7 to create a new folder in the Windows 98 Practice folder, type **Brochure** for the folder name, then press **[Enter]**

10. Click the **Back button** ⇦ to return to your Project Disk

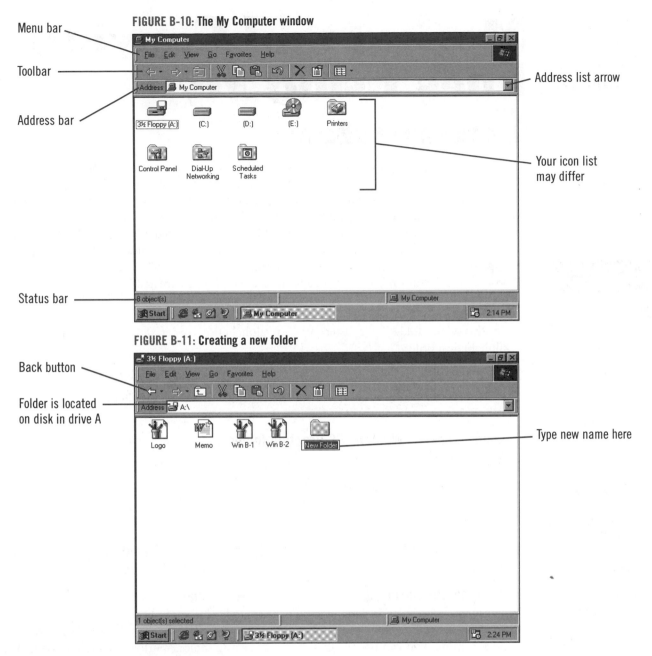

FIGURE B-10: The My Computer window

Menu bar

Toolbar

Address bar

Status bar

Address list arrow

Your icon list
may differ

FIGURE B-11: Creating a new folder

Back button

Folder is located
on disk in drive A

Type new name here

TABLE B-3: Buttons on the My Computer toolbar

button	function
⬅	Moves back to the previous location you have already visited
➡	Moves forward to the previous location you have already visited
⬆	Moves up one level in the file hierarchy
✂	Deletes a folder or file and places it on the clipboard
📋	Copies a folder or file
📋	Pastes a folder or file
↩	Undoes the most recent My Computer operation
✕	Deletes a folder or file permanently
📋	Shows the properties of a folder or file
▦	Lists the contents of My Computer using different views

Moving and Copying Files Using My Computer

You can move a file or folder from one location to another using a variety of methods in My Computer or Windows Explorer. If the file or folder and the location to which you want to move it are both visible on the desktop, you can simply drag the item from one location to the other. You can also use the cut, copy and paste commands on the Edit menu or the corresponding buttons on the toolbar. You can also right-click the file or folder and choose the Send to command to "send" it to another location—most often a floppy disk for **backing up** files. Backup copies are made in case you have computer trouble, which may cause you to lose files. ▶ In this lesson, you move your files into the folder you created in the last lesson.

Steps

QuickTip

To copy a file so that it appears in two locations, press and hold [Shift] while you drag the file to its new location.

1. Click **View**, click **Arrange Icons**, then click **By Name**
   In this view, folders are listed first in alphabetical order, followed by files, also in alphabetical order.

2. Click the **Win B-1 file**, hold down the mouse button and drag the file onto the **Windows 98 Practice folder**, as shown in Figure B-12, then release the mouse button
   Win B-1 is moved into the Windows 98 Practice folder.

3. Double-click the **Windows 98 Practice folder** and confirm that it contains the Win B-1 file as well as the Brochure folder

QuickTip

It is easy to confuse the Back button with the Up One Level button. The Back button returns you to the last location you visited, no matter where it is in your folder hierarchy. The Up One Level button displays the next level up in the folder hierarchy, no matter where you last visited.

4. Click the **Up button** 🗂 on the My Computer toolbar, as shown in Figure B–12
   You return to your Project Disk. The Up button displays the next level up in the folder hierarchy.

5. Click the **Logo file**, press and hold [Shift], then click the **Memo file**
   Both files are selected. Table B-4 describes methods for selecting multiple files and folders.

6. Click the **Cut button** ✂ on the 3½ Floppy (A:) toolbar
   The icons for the files are gray, as shown in Figure B-13. This indicates that they've been cut and placed on the Clipboard, to be pasted somewhere else. Instead of dragging items to a new location, you can use the Cut, Copy, and Paste toolbar buttons or the cut, copy, and paste commands on the Edit menu.

7. Click the **Back button** ⬅ to return to the Windows 98 Practice folder, then double-click the **Brochure folder**
   The Brochure folder is currently empty.

8. Click the **Paste button** 📋 on the toolbar
   The two files are pasted into the Brochure folder.

9. Click the **Address list arrow**, then click **3½ Floppy (A:)** and confirm that the Memo and Logo files are no longer listed there and that only the Windows 98 Practice folder and the Win B-2 file remain

10. Click the **Close button** in the 3½ Floppy (A:) window

FIGURE B-12: Dragging a file from one folder to another

Up One Level button

Drag file here

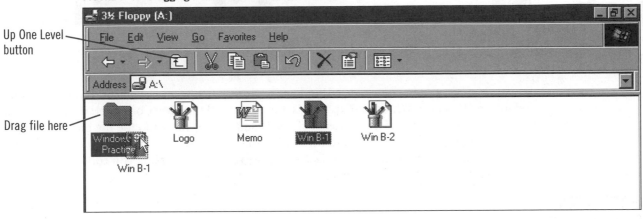

FIGURE B-13: Cutting files to move them

Gray icons indicate files have been cut

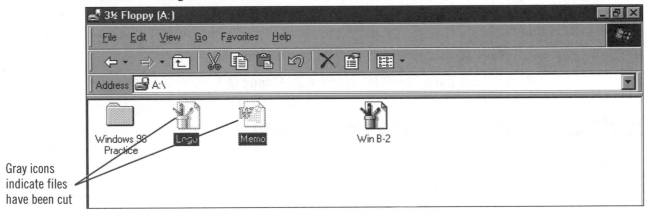

TABLE B-4: Techniques for selecting multiple files and folders

to select	use this technique
Individual objects not grouped together	Click the first object you want to select, then press [Ctrl] as you click each additional object you want to add to the selection
Objects grouped together	Click the first object you want to select, then press [Shift] as you click the last object in the list of objects you want to select; all the objects listed between the first and last objects are selected

Managing Files with Windows Explorer

As with My Computer, you can use Windows Explorer to copy, move, delete, and rename files and folders. However, **Windows Explorer** is more powerful than My Computer: it allows you to see the overall structure of the contents of your computer or network, the file hierarchy, while you work with individual files and folders within that structure. This means you can work with more than one computer, folder, or file at once. In this lesson, you copy a folder from your Project Disk onto the hard drive, then rename the folder.

Steps

Trouble?

If you do not see the toolbar, click View on the menu bar, point to Toolbars, then click Standard Buttons. If you do not see the Address Bar, click View, point to Toolbars, then click Address Bar.

1. Click the **Start button**, point to **Programs**, point to **Windows Explorer**, then click the **Maximize button** if the Windows Explorer window doesn't already fill the screen
   Windows Explorer opens, as shown in Figure B-14. The window is divided into two sides called **panes**. The left pane, also known as the **Explorer Bar**, displays the drives and folders on your computer in a hierarchy. The right pane displays the contents of whatever drive or folder is currently selected in the left pane. Each pane has its own set of scroll bars, so that changing what you can see in one pane won't affect what you can see in the other. Like My Computer, Windows Explorer has a menu bar, toolbar, and Address Bar.

2. Click **View** on the menu bar, then click **Details** if it is not already selected

3. In the left pane, scroll to and click **3½ Floppy (A:)**
   The contents of your Project Disk are displayed in the right pane.

QuickTip

When neither a + nor a – appears next to an icon, it means that the item does not have any folders in it, although it may have files, which you can display in the right pane by clicking the icon.

4. In the left pane, click the **plus sign (+)** next to 3½ Floppy (A:)
   You can use the plus signs (+) and minus signs (-) next to items in the left pane to show or hide the different levels of the file hierarchy, so that you don't always have to look at the entire structure of your computer or network. A plus sign (+) next to a computer, drive, or folder indicates there are additional folders within that object. A minus sign (-) indicates that all the folders of the next level of hierarchy are shown. Clicking the + displays (or "expands") the next level; clicking the – hides (or "collapses") them.

5. In the left pane, double-click the **Windows 98 Practice folder**
   The contents of the Windows 98 Practice folder appear in the right pane of Windows Explorer, as shown in Figure B-15. Double-clicking an item in the left pane that has a + next to it displays its contents in the right pane and also expands the next level in the hierarchy in the left pane.

Trouble?

If you are working in a lab setting, you may not be able to add items to your hard drive. Skip Steps 6, 7, and 8 if you are unable to complete them.

6. In the left pane, drag the **Windows 98 Practice folder** on top of the **C: drive icon**, then release the mouse button
   The Windows 98 Practice folder and the files in it are copied to the hard disk.

7. In the left pane, click the **C: drive icon**
   The Windows 98 Practice folder should now appear in the list of folders in the right pane. Now you should rename the folder so you can distinguish the original folder from the copy.

QuickTip

You can also rename a selected file by pressing [F2], or using the Rename command on the File menu.

8. Right-click the **Windows 98 Practice folder** in the right pane, click **Rename** in the pop-up menu, type **Practice Copy**, then press [Enter]

FIGURE B-14: The Windows Explorer window

Contents of C drive

Left pane, also known as Explorer bar

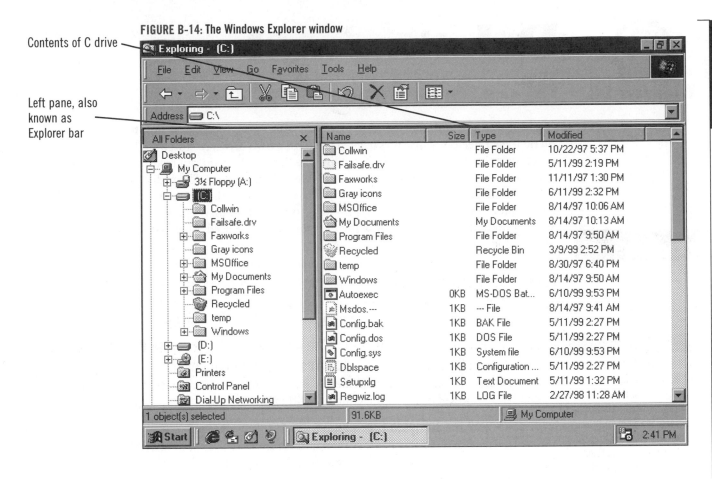

FIGURE B-15: Contents of Windows 98 Practice folder

Contents of Windows 98 Practice folder

Windows 98 Practice folder is selected in left pane

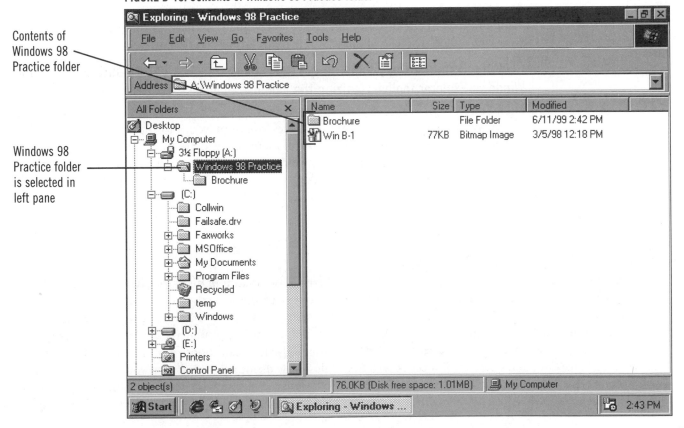

Windows 98

Deleting and Restoring Files

To save disk space and manage your files more effectively, you should **delete** (or remove) files you no longer need. Because files deleted from your hard drive are stored in the Recycle Bin until you remove them permanently by emptying the Recycle Bin, you can restore any files you might have deleted accidentally. However, if you delete a file from your floppy disk it will not be stored in the Recycle Bin—it will be permanently deleted. See Table B-5 for an overview of deleting and restoring files. ▶▶▶ There are many ways to delete files in Windows 98. In this lesson, you use two different methods for removing files you no longer need. Then, you learn how to restore a deleted file.

Steps

1. **Click the Restore button on the Windows Explorer title bar**
   You should be able to see the Recycle Bin icon on your desktop. If you can't see it, resize or move the Windows Explorer window until it is visible. See Figure B-16.

QuickTip

If you are unable to delete the file, it might be because your Recycle Bin is full, or too small, or the properties have been changed so that files are not stored in the Recycle Bin but are deleted instead. See your instructor or technical support person for assistance.

2. **Drag the Practice Copy folder from the right pane to the Recycle Bin on the desktop, as shown in Figure B-16, then click Yes to confirm the deletion**
   The folder no longer appears in Windows Explorer because you have moved it to the Recycle Bin. Next, you will examine the contents of the Recycle Bin.

3. **Double-click the Recycle Bin icon on the desktop**
   The Recycle Bin window opens, as shown in Figure B-17. Depending on the number of files already deleted on your computer, your window might look different. Use the scroll bar if you can't see the files.

4. **Click Edit on the Recycle Bin menu bar, then click Undo Delete**
   The Practice Copy folder is restored and should now appear in the Windows Explorer window. You might need to minimize your Recycle Bin window if it blocks your view of Windows Explorer, and you might need to scroll the right pane to find the restored folder. Now you should delete the Practice Copy folder from your hard drive.

5. **Click the Practice Copy folder in the right pane, click the Delete button ☒ on the Windows Explorer toolbar, resizing the window as necessary to see the button, then click Yes**
   When you are sure you no longer need files you've moved into the Recycle Bin, you can empty the Recycle Bin. You won't do this now, in case you are working on a computer that you share with other people. But, when you're working on your own machine, simply right-click the Recycle Bin icon, then click Empty Recycle Bin in the pop-up menu.

CLUES TO USE

Customizing your Recycle Bin

You can set your Recycle Bin according to how you like to delete and restore files. For example, if you do not want files to go to the Recycle Bin but rather want them to be immediately and permanently deleted, right-click the Recycle Bin, click Properties, then click the Do Not Move Files to the Recycle Bin check box. If you find that the Recycle Bin fills up too fast and you are not ready to delete the files permanently, you can increase the amount of disk space devoted to the Recycle Bin by moving the Maximum Size of Recycle Bin slider to the right. This, of course, reduces the amount of disk space you have available for other things. Also, you can choose not to have the Confirm File Delete dialog box open when you send files to the Recycle Bin. See your instructor or technical support person before changing any of the Recycle Bin settings.

FIGURE B-16: Dragging a folder to delete it

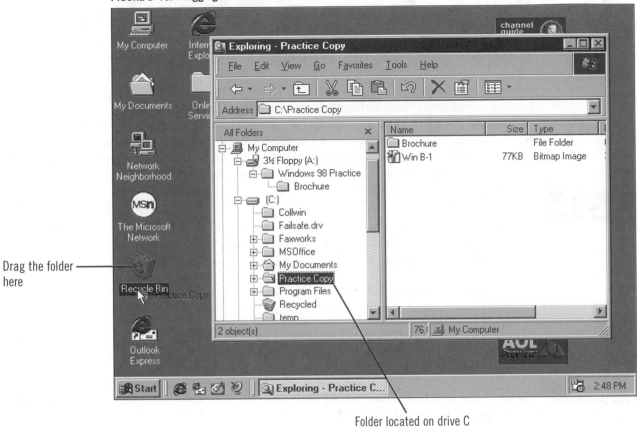

Drag the folder here

Folder located on drive C

FIGURE B-17: The Recycle Bin window

Deleted folder

TABLE B-5: Methods for deleting and restoring files

ways to delete a file	ways to restore a file from the Recycle Bin
Select the file, then click the Delete button on the toolbar	Click the Undo button on the toolbar
Select the file, then press [Delete]	Select the file, click File, then click Restore
Right-click the file, then click Delete on the pop-up menu	Right-click the file, then click Restore
Drag the file to the Recycle Bin	Drag the file from the Recycle Bin to any other location

WORKING WITH PROGRAMS, FILES, AND FOLDERS

Creating a Shortcut on the Desktop

When you use a file, folder, or program frequently, it can be cumbersome to open it if it is located several levels down in the file hierarchy. You can create a shortcut to an object and place the icon for the shortcut on the desktop or any other location you find convenient. To open the file, folder, or program using the shortcut, double-click the icon. A **shortcut** is a link between the original file, folder, or program you want to access and the icon you create. ◄━━━━ In this lesson, you create a shortcut to the Memo file on your desktop.

Steps

1. **In the left pane of the Windows Explorer window, click the Brochure folder**
   The contents of the Brochure folder appear in the right pane.

2. **In the right pane, right-click the Memo file**
   A pop-up menu appears, as shown in Figure B-18.

3. **Click Create Shortcut in the pop-up menu**
   The file named Shortcut to Memo file appears in the right pane. Now you need to move it to the desktop so that it will be accessible whenever you need it.

> **QuickTip**
>
> Make sure to use the *right* mouse button in Step 4. If you used the left mouse button by accident, right-click the Shortcut to Memo file in the right pane of Windows Explorer, then click Delete.

4. **Click the Shortcut to Memo file with the right-mouse button, then drag the shortcut to an empty area of the desktop**
   Dragging an icon using the left mouse button copies it. Dragging an icon using the right mouse button gives you the option to copy or move it. When you release the mouse button a pop-up menu appears.

5. **Click Move Here in the pop-up menu**
   A shortcut to the Memo file now appears on the desktop, as shown in Figure B-19. You might have to move or resize the Windows Explorer window to see it.

6. **Double-click the Shortcut to Memo file icon**
   WordPad starts and the Memo file opens (if you have Microsoft Word installed on your computer, it will start and open the file instead). Using a shortcut eliminates the many steps involved in starting a program and locating and opening a file.

7. **Click the Close button in the WordPad or Word title bar**
   Now you should delete the shortcut icon in case you are working in a lab and share the computer with others. Deleting a shortcut does not delete the original file or folder to which it points.

> **QuickTip**
>
> Deleting a shortcut deletes only the link; it does not delete the original file or folder to which it points.

8. **On the desktop, click the Shortcut to Memo file if necessary, press [Delete], then click Yes to confirm the deletion**
   The shortcut is removed from the desktop and is now in the Recycle Bin.

9. **Close all windows**

FIGURE B-18: Creating a shortcut

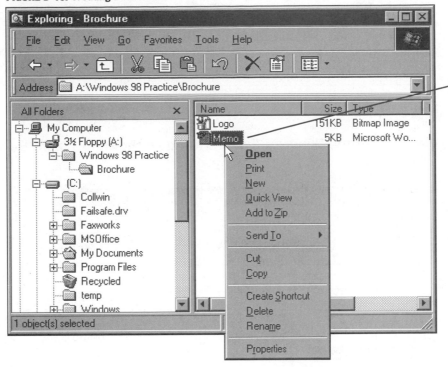

Right-click icon or filename to display pop-up menu. Your menu items may differ.

FIGURE B-19: Shortcut on desktop

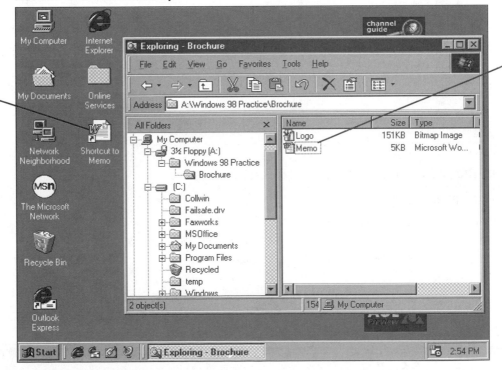

Double-click to open file

Original file located in Brochure folder

CLUES TO USE

Adding shortcuts to the Start menu

If you do not want your desktop to get cluttered with icons but you would still like easy access to certain files, programs, and folders, you can create a shortcut on the Start menu. Drag the file, program, or folder that you want to add to the Start menu from the Windows Explorer window to the Start button. The file, program, or folder will appear on the first level of the Start menu.

Practice

► Concepts Review

Label each of the elements of the Windows Explorer window shown in Figure B-20.

FIGURE B-20

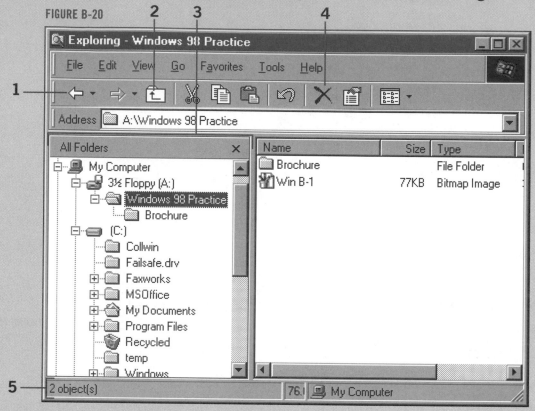

Match each of the statements with the term it describes.

6. Electronic collections of data
7. Your computer's temporary storage area
8. Temporary location of information you wish to paste into another program
9. Storage areas on your hard drive for files, folders, and programs
10. Structure of files and folders

   a. RAM
   b. Folders
   c. Files
   d. File hierarchy
   e. Clipboard

Select the best answer from the list of choices.

11. To prepare a floppy disk to save your files, you must first do which of the following?
   a. Copy work files to the disk
   b. Format the disk
   c. Erase all the files that might be on the disk
   d. Place the files on the Clipboard

12. You can use My Computer to
   a. Create a drawing of your computer.
   b. View the contents of a folder.
   c. Change the appearance of your desktop.
   d. Add text to a WordPad file.

13. Which of the following best describes WordPad?
   a. A program for organizing files
   b. A program for performing financial analysis
   c. A program for creating basic text documents
   d. A program for creating graphics

14. **Which of the following is NOT a way to move files from one folder to another?**
    a. Open the file and use the Save As command to save the file in a new location.
    b. In My Computer or the Windows Explorer, drag the selected file to the new folder.
    c. Use the Cut and Paste commands on the Edit menu while in the My Computer or the Windows Explorer windows.
    d. Use the [Ctrl][X] and [Ctrl][V] keyboard shortcuts while in the My Computer or the Windows Explorer windows.

15. **In which of the following can you view the hierarchy of drives, folders, and files in a split pane window?**
    a. Windows Explorer
    b. Programs
    c. My Computer
    d. WordPad

16. **To restore files that you have sent to the Recycle Bin:**
    a. Click File, then click Empty Recycle Bin.
    b. Click Edit, then click Undo Delete.
    c. Click File, then click Undo.
    d. You cannot retrieve files sent to the Recycle Bin.

17. **To copy instead of move a file from one folder to another, drag while pressing**
    a. [Shift].
    b. [Alt].
    c. [Tab].
    d. [Ctrl].

18. **To select files that are not grouped together, select the first file, then**
    a. Press [Shift] while selecting the second file.
    b. Press [Alt] while selecting the second file.
    c. Press [Ctrl] while selecting the second file.
    d. Click on the second file.

19. **Pressing [Backspace]**
    a. Deletes the character to the right of the cursor.
    b. Deletes the character to the left of the cursor.
    c. Moves the insertion point one character to the right.
    d. Moves the insertion point one character to the left.

20. **The size of a font is measured in**
    a. Centimeters.
    b. Points.
    c. Places.
    d. Millimeters.

21. **The Back button on the My Computer toolbar:**
    a. Starts the last program you used.
    b. Displays the next level of the file hierarchy.
    c. Backs up the currently selected file.
    d. Displays the last location you visited.

► Skills Review

If you are doing all of the exercises in this unit, you may run out of space on your Project Disk. Use a blank, formatted disk to complete the exercise if this happens.

1. **Create and save a WordPad file.**
    a. Start Windows, then start WordPad.
    b. Type a short description of your artistic abilities, pressing [Enter] several times to insert blank lines between the text and the graphic you are about to create.
    c. Save the document as "Drawing Ability" to the Windows 98 Practice folder on your Project Disk.

2. **Open and save a Paint file.**
    a. Start Paint and open the file Win B-2 from your Project Disk.
    b. Inside the picture frame, create your own unique, colorful design using several colors. Use a variety of tools. For example, create a filled circle and then place a filled square inside the circle.
    c. Save the picture as "First Unique Art" to the Windows 98 Practice folder on your Project Disk.

3. **Work with multiple programs.**
    a. Select the entire graphic and copy it to the Clipboard, then switch to WordPad.
    b. Place the insertion point in the last blank line, then paste the graphic into your document.
    c. Save the changes to your WordPad document using the same filename.
    d. Switch to Paint.
    e. Using the Fill With Color button, change the color of a filled area of your graphic.

   f. Save the revised graphic with the new name, "Second Unique Art," to the Windows 98 Practice folder.

   g. Select the entire graphic and copy it to the Clipboard.

   h. Switch to WordPad and type "This is another version of my graphic." below the first picture, then press [Enter]. (*Hint*: To move the insertion point to the line below the graphic, click below the graphic, then press [Enter].)

   i. Paste the second graphic under the text you just typed.

   j. Save the changed WordPad document as "Two Drawing Examples" to the Windows 98 Practice folder.

   k. Close Paint and WordPad.

4. View files and create folders with My Computer.

   a. Open My Computer, then insert your Project Disk in the appropriate drive if necessary.

   b. Double-click the drive that contains your Project Disk.

   c. Create a new folder on your Project Disk by clicking File, New, then Folder, and name the new folder "Review."

   d. Open the folder to display its contents (it is empty).

   e. Use the Address Bar to view your hard drive, usually (C:).

   f. Create a folder on the hard drive called "Temporary" then use the Back button to view the Review folder. (*Note:* You may not be able to add items to your hard drive.)

   g. Create two new folders in the Review folder. Name one "Documents" and the other "Artwork."

   h. Use the Forward button as many times as necessary to view the hard drive.

5. Move and copy files using My Computer.

   a. Use the Address Bar to view your Project Disk, then open the Windows 98 Practice folder.

   b. Select the two Paint files, then cut and paste them into the Artwork folder.

   c. Use the Back button as many times as necessary to view the Windows 98 Practice folder.

   d. Select the two WordPad files, then move them into the Documents folder.

   e. Close My Computer.

6. View, move and copy files.

   a. Open Windows Explorer and display the contents of the Artwork folder in the right pane.

   b. Select the two Paint files.

   c. Drag the two Paint files from the Artwork folder to the Temporary folder on the hard drive to copy them.

   d. Display the contents of the Documents folder in the right pane.

   e. Select the two WordPad files.

   f. Repeat Step c to copy the files to the Temporary folder on the hard drive.

   g. Display the contents of the Temporary folder in the right pane to verify that the four files are there.

7. Delete and restore files and folders.

   a. Resize the Windows Explorer window so you can see the Recycle Bin icon on the desktop, then scroll in Windows Explorer so you can see the Temporary folder in the left pane.

   b. Delete the Temporary folder from the hard drive by dragging it to the Recycle Bin.

   c. Select the Review folder in the left pane, then press [Delete]. Click Yes if necessary to confirm the deletion.

   d. Open the Recycle Bin, restore the Review folder and its files to your Project Disk, then close the Recycle Bin. (*Note:* If your Recycle Bin is empty, your computer is set to automatically delete items in the Recycle Bin.)

8. Create a shortcut on the desktop.

   a. Use the left pane of Windows Explorer to locate the Windows folder on your hard drive. Select the folder to display its contents in the right pane. (*Note:* If you are in a lab setting, you may not have access to the Windows folder.)

   b. In the right pane, scroll through the list of objects until you see a file called Explorer.

   c. Drag the Explorer file to the desktop to create a shortcut.

   d. Close Windows Explorer.

   e. Double-click the new shortcut to make sure it starts Windows Explorer. Then close Windows Explorer again.

   f. Delete the shortcut for Windows Explorer and exit Windows.

▶ Independent Challenges

If you are doing all of the Independent Challenges, you will need to use a new floppy disk.

1. You have decided to start a bakery business and you want to use Windows 98 to organize the files for the business.

a. Create two new folders on your Project Disk named "Advertising" and "Customers".

b. Use WordPad to create a form letter inviting new customers to the open house for the new bakery, then save it as "Open House Letter" and place it in the Customers folder.

c. Use WordPad to create a list of five tasks that need to get done before the business opens, then save it as "Business Plan" to your Project Disk, but don't place it in a folder.

d. Use Paint to create a simple logo for the bakery, save it as "Bakery Logo", then place it in the Advertising folder.

e. On a piece of paper, draw out the new organization of all the folders and files on your Project Disk, close all open programs, then exit Windows.

2. On your computer's hard drive, create a folder called "IC3". Follow the guidelines listed here to create the file hierarchy shown in Figure B-21.

a. Start WordPad, create a new file that contains a list. Save the file as "To Do List" to your Project Disk.

b. Start My Computer and copy the Memo file on your Project Disk to the IC3 folder. Rename the file "Article."

c. Copy the Memo file again to the IC3 folder on your hard drive and rename the second copy of the file "Article Two."

d. Use My Computer to copy any Paint file to the IC3 folder and rename the file "Sample Logo."

e. Copy the To Do List from your Project Disk to the IC3 folder and rename the file "Important List."

f. Move the files into the folders shown in Figure B-21.

g. Copy the IC3 folder to your Project Disk. Then delete the IC3 folder on your hard drive. Using the Recycle Bin, restore the file called IC3. To remove all your work on the hard drive, delete this folder again.

FIGURE B-21

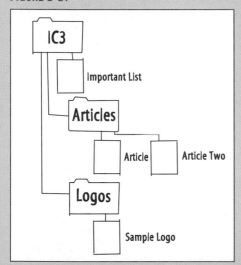

3. With Windows 98, you can access the Web from My Computer and Windows Explorer, allowing you to search for information located not only on your computer or network, but also on any computer connected to the Internet.

a. Start Windows Explorer, then click in the Address Bar so the current location (probably your hard drive) is selected, then type "www.microsoft.com"

b. Connect to the Internet if necessary. The Microsoft Web page displays in the right pane of Windows Explorer.

c. Click in the Address Bar, then type "www.course.com", then wait a moment while the Course Technology Web page opens.

d. Make sure your Project Disk is in the floppy disk drive, then click 3½ Floppy (A:) in the left pane.

e. Click the Back button list arrow, then click Welcome to Microsoft Homepage.

f. Capture a picture of your desktop by using [Print Screen]. Save the file as "Microsoft", then print it. See Independent Challenge 4 for instructions.

g. Click the Close button on the Explorer Bar.

h. Close Windows Explorer and disconnect from the Internet.

4. Create a shortcut to the drive that contains your Project Disk. Then capture a picture of your desktop showing the new shortcut by pressing [Print Screen], located on the upper-right side of your keyboard. The picture is stored temporarily on the Clipboard. Then open the Paint program and paste the contents of the Clipboard into the drawing window. Click No when asked to enlarge the Bitmap. Save the Paint file as Desktop Picture on your Project Disk and print it. Delete the shortcut when you are finished.

► Visual Workshop

Recreate the screen shown in Figure B-22, which contains the Brochure window in My Computer, two shortcuts on the desktop, and two files open. Press [Print Screen] to make a copy of the screen, then print it from Paint. See your instructor or technical support person for assistance.

FIGURE B-22

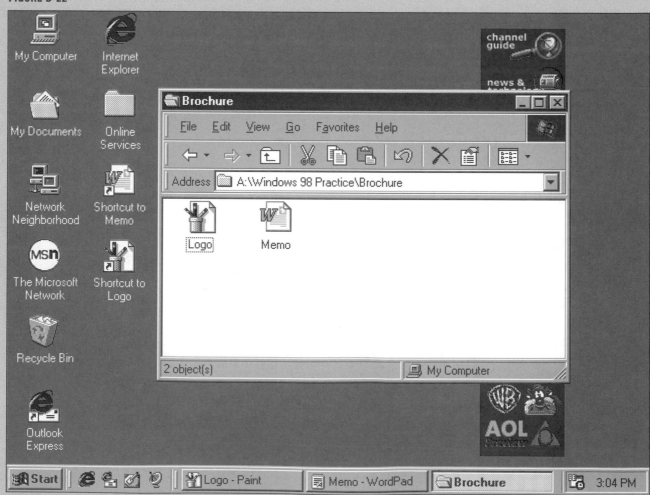

Getting
Started with Access 2000

Objectives

- MOUS ▶ **Define database software**
- MOUS ▶ **Learn database terminology**
- ▶ **Start Access and open a database**
- MOUS ▶ **View the database window**
- MOUS ▶ **Navigate records**
- MOUS ▶ **Enter records**
- MOUS ▶ **Edit records**
- MOUS ▶ **Preview and print a datasheet**
- MOUS ▶ **Get Help and exit Access**

In this unit, you will learn the purpose, advantages, and terminology of
Microsoft Access 2000, a database software. You will also learn how to
open a database and how to use the different elements of the Access
window. You'll learn how to get help. You'll learn how to navigate
through a database, enter and update data, and preview and print data.
John Kim is the director of shipping at MediaLoft, a nationwide
chain of bookstore cafés that sells books, music, and videos. Recently,
MediaLoft switched to Access from an index card system for storing and
maintaining customer information. John will use Access to enter and
maintain this critical information for MediaLoft.

Defining Database Software

Microsoft Access 2000 is a database software program that runs on Windows. **Database software** is used to manage data that can be organized into lists of related information, such as customers, products, vendors, employees, projects, or sales. Many small companies record customer, inventory, and sales information in a spreadsheet program such as Microsoft Excel. While this electronic format is more productive than writing information on index cards, Excel still lacks many of the database advantages provided by Access. Refer to Table A-1 for a comparison of the two programs. John reviews the advantages that database software has over a manual index card system.

 ### Data entry is faster and easier

Before inexpensive microcomputers, small businesses used manual paper systems, such as index cards, to record each customer, sale, and inventory item as illustrated in Figure A-1. Using an electronic database such as Access, you can create on-screen data entry forms, which make managing a database easier, more accurate, and more efficient than using index cards.

 ### Information retrieval is faster and easier

Retrieving information on an index card system is tedious because the cards have to be physically handled, sorted, and stored. Also, one error in filing can cause serious retrieval problems later. With Access you can quickly search for, display, and print information on customers, sales, or inventory.

Information can be viewed and sorted in multiple ways

A card system allows you to sort the cards in only one order, unless the cards are duplicated for a second arrangement. Customer and inventory cards were generally sorted alphabetically by name. Sales index cards were usually sorted by date. In this system, complete customer and product information was recorded on each of their individual cards as well as on the corresponding sale cards. This quickly compromises data accuracy. Access allows you to view or sort the information from one or more subjects simultaneously. For example, you might want to know all the customers who purchased a particular product or all the products purchased by a particular customer. A change made to the data in one view of Access is automatically updated in every other view or report.

 ### Information is more secure

Index cards can be torn, misplaced, and stolen. There is no password required to read them, and a disaster, such as a flood or fire, could completely destroy them. You can back up an Access database file on a regular basis and store the file at an offsite location. You can also password protect data so only those users with appropriate security clearances can view or manipulate the data.

 ### Information can be shared among several users

An index card system is limited to those users who can physically reach it. If one user keeps a card for an extended period of time, then others cannot use or update that information. Access databases are inherently multiuser. More than one person can be entering, updating, and using the data at the same time.

 ### Duplicate data entry is minimized

The index card system requires that the user duplicate the customer and product information on each sales card. With Access, you only need to enter each piece of information once. Figure A-2 shows a possible structure for an Access database to record sales.

FIGURE A-1: Using index cards to organize sales data

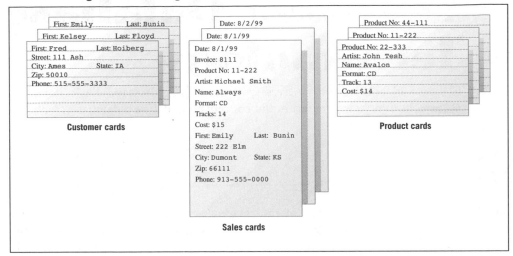

Customer cards

Sales cards

Product cards

FIGURE A-2: Using Access, an electronic relational database, to organize sales data

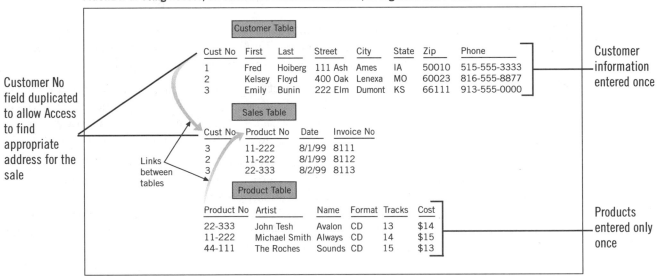

Customer No field duplicated to allow Access to find appropriate address for the sale

Links between tables

Customer information entered once

Products entered only once

TABLE A-1: Comparing Excel to Access

feature	Excel	Access
Layout	Provides a natural tabular layout for easy data entry	Provides a spreadsheet "view" as well as forms which arrange data in a variety of ways
Storage	Limited to approximately 65,000 records per sheet	Able to store any number of records up to 2 gigabytes
Linked tables	Manages single lists of information	Allows links between lists of information to reduce data entry redundancy
Reporting	Limited to a spreadsheet printout	Provides sophisticated reporting features such as multiple headers and footers and calculations on groups of records
Security	Very limited	Each user can be given access to only the records and fields they need
Multiuser capabilities	Does not allow multiple users to simultaneously enter and update data	Allows multiple users to simultaneously enter and update data
Data entry screens	Provides limited data entry screens	Provides the ability to create extensive data entry screens called forms

Learning Database Terminology

To become familiar with Access, you need to understand basic database terminology. John reviews the terms and concepts that define a database.

Details

 A **database** is a collection of information associated with a topic (for example, sales of products to customers). The smallest piece of information in a database is called a **field**, or category of information, such as the customer's name, city, state, or phone number. A **key field** is a field that contains unique information for each record. A group of related fields, such as all demographic information for one customer, is called a **record**. In Access, a collection of records for a single subject, such as all of the customer records, is called a **table**, as shown in Figure A-3.

 An Access database is a **relational database**, in which more than one table, such as the Customer, Sales, and Product tables, can share information. The term "relational database" comes from the fact that two tables are linked, or related, by a common field.

 Tables, therefore, are the most important **object** in an Access database because they contain all of the data within the database. An Access database may also contain six other objects, which serve to enhance the usability and value of the data. The objects in an Access database are tables, queries, forms, reports, pages, macros, and modules, and they are summarized in Table A-2.

 Data can be entered and edited in four of the objects: tables, queries, forms, and pages. The relationship between tables, queries, forms, and reports is shown in Figure A-4. Regardless of how the data is entered, it is physically stored in a table object. Data can be printed from a table, query, form, page, or report object. The macro and module objects are used to provide additional database productivity and automation features. All of the objects (except for the page objects, which are used to create Web pages) are stored in one database file.

TABLE A-2: Access objects and their purpose

object	purpose
Table	Contains all of the raw data within the database in a spreadsheet-like view; tables can be linked with a common field to share information and therefore minimize data redundancy
Query	Provides a spreadsheet-like view of the data similar to tables, but a query can be designed to provide the user with a subset of fields or records from one or more tables; queries are created when a user has a "question" about the data in the database
Form	Provides an easy-to-use data entry screen, which generally shows only one record at a time
Report	Provides a professional printout of data that may contain enhancements such as headers, footers, and calculations on groups of records
Page	Creates Web pages from Access objects as well as provides Web page connectivity features to an Access database, also called Data Access Page
Macro	Stores a collection of keystrokes or commands, such as printing several reports or displaying a toolbar when a form opens
Module	Stores Visual Basic programming code that extends the functions and automated processes of Access

FIGURE A-3: Tables contain fields and records

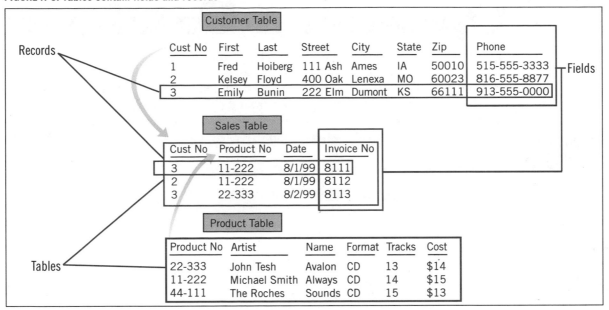

Records

Customer Table

Cust No	First	Last	Street	City	State	Zip	Phone
1	Fred	Hoiberg	111 Ash	Ames	IA	50010	515-555-3333
2	Kelsey	Floyd	400 Oak	Lenexa	MO	60023	816-555-8877
3	Emily	Bunin	222 Elm	Dumont	KS	66111	913-555-0000

Fields

Sales Table

Cust No	Product No	Date	Invoice No
3	11-222	8/1/99	8111
2	11-222	8/1/99	8112
3	22-333	8/2/99	8113

Product Table

Product No	Artist	Name	Format	Tracks	Cost
22-333	John Tesh	Avalon	CD	13	$14
11-222	Michael Smith	Always	CD	14	$15
44-111	The Roches	Sounds	CD	15	$13

Tables

FIGURE A-4: The relationship between Access objects

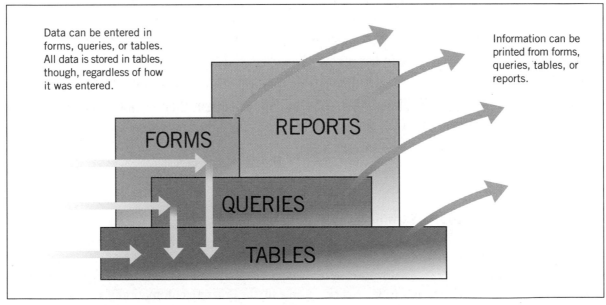

Data can be entered in forms, queries, or tables. All data is stored in tables, though, regardless of how it was entered.

Information can be printed from forms, queries, tables, or reports.

FORMS

REPORTS

QUERIES

TABLES

Unit A

Access 2000

Starting Access and Opening a Database

You can start Access by clicking the Access icon on the Windows desktop or on the Microsoft Office Shortcut Bar. Since not all computers will provide a shortcut icon on the desktop or display the Office Shortcut Bar, you can always find Access by clicking the Start button on the taskbar, pointing to Programs, and then choosing Access from the Programs menu. You can open a database from within Access or by finding the database file on the desktop, in My Computer, or in Windows Explorer, and then opening it. John starts Access and opens the MediaLoft-A database.

Steps

1. Click the **Start button** on the taskbar
   The Start button is in the lower-left corner of the taskbar. You can use the Start menu to start any program on your computer.
2. Point to **Programs**
   Access is generally located on the Programs menu. All the programs, or applications, stored on your computer can be found here.
3. Click **Microsoft Access**
   Access opens and displays the Access dialog box, from which you can start a new database or open an existing file.
4. Insert your Project Disk in the appropriate disk drive
   To complete the units in this book, you need a Project Disk. See your instructor or technical support person for assistance.
5. Click **More Files**, then click **OK**
   The Open dialog box appears, as shown in Figure A-5. Depending on the databases and folders stored on your computer, your dialog box may look slightly different.
6. Click the **Look in list arrow**, then click **3½ Floppy (A:)**
   A list of the files on your Project Disk appears in the Open dialog box.
7. Click the **MediaLoft-A** database file, click **Open**, then click the **Maximize button** on the title bar if the Access window does not fill the screen
   The MediaLoft-A database opens as shown in Figure A-6.

Trouble?

If you can't locate Microsoft Access on the Programs menu, point to the Microsoft Office group and look for Access there.

QuickTip

Make a copy of your Project Disk before you use it.

Trouble?

These lessons assume your Project Disk is in drive A. If you are using a different drive, substitute that drive for drive A in the steps.

CLUES TO USE

Personalized toolbars and menus in Office 2000

Office 2000 toolbars and menus modify themselves to your working style. The toolbars you see when you first start a program include the most frequently used buttons. To locate a button not visible on a toolbar, click the More Buttons button at the end of the toolbar to see the list of additional toolbar buttons. As you work, the program adds the buttons you use to the visible toolbars and moves the buttons you haven't used in a while to the More Buttons list. Similarly, menus adjust to your work habits. Short menus appear when you first click a menu command. To view additional menu commands, point to the double-arrow at the bottom of the menu, leave the pointer on the menu name after you've clicked the menu, or double-click the menu name. If you select a command that's not on the short menu, the program automatically adds it to the short menus. You can return personalized toolbars and menus to their original settings by clicking Tools on the menu bar, then clicking Customize. On the Options tab in the Customize dialog box, click Reset my usage data, click Yes to close the alert box, then close the Customize dialog box. Resetting usage data erases changes made automatically to your menus and toolbars. It does not affect the options you customize.

FIGURE A-5: Open dialog box

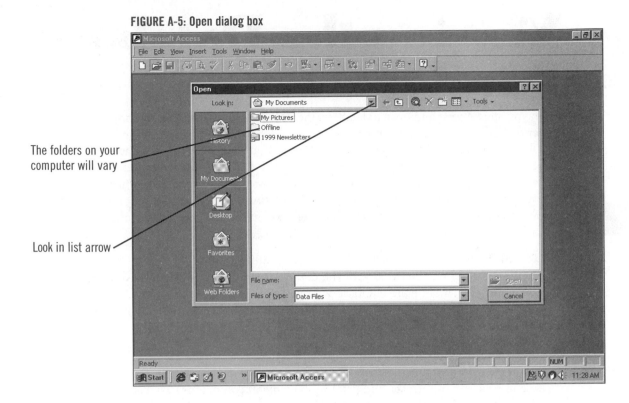

The folders on your computer will vary

Look in list arrow

FIGURE A-6: MediaLoft-A database

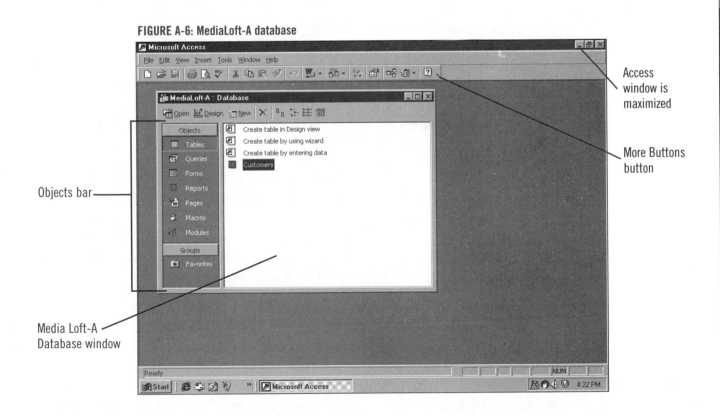

Objects bar

Media Loft-A Database window

Access window is maximized

More Buttons button

Viewing the Database Window

When you start Access and open a database, the **database window** displays common Windows elements such as a title bar, menu bar, and toolbar. Clicking the Objects or Groups buttons on the Objects bar alternatively expands and collapses that section of the database window. If all the objects don't display in the expanded section, click the small arrow at the top or bottom of the section to scroll the list. The **Objects** area displays the seven types of objects that can be accessed by clicking the object type you want. The **Groups** area displays other commonly used files and folders, such as the Favorites folder.　　　　John explores the MediaLoft-A database.

Steps

1. **Look at each of the Access window elements shown in Figure A-7**
   The Objects bar on the left side of the database window displays the seven object types. The other elements of the database window are summarized in Table A-3. Because the Tables object is selected, the buttons you need to create a new table or to work with the existing table are displayed in the MediaLoft-A Database window.

2. **Click File on the menu bar**
   The File menu contains commands for opening a new or existing database, saving a database in a variety of formats, and printing. The menu commands vary depending on which window or database object is currently in use.

3. **Point to Edit on the menu bar, point to View, point to Insert, point to Tools, point to Window, point to Help, move the pointer off the menu, then press [Esc] twice**
   All menus close when you press [Esc]. Pressing [Esc] a second time deselects the menu.

4. **Point to the New button ▢ on the Database toolbar**
   Pointing to a toolbar button causes a descriptive **ScreenTip** to automatically appear, providing a short description of the button. The buttons on the toolbars represent the most commonly used Access features. Toolbar buttons change just as menu options change depending on which window and database object are currently in use.

5. **Point to the Open button 📂 on the Database toolbar, then point to the Save button 💾 on the Database toolbar**
   Sometimes toolbar buttons or menu options are dimmed which means that they are currently unavailable. For example, the Save button is dimmed because it doesn't make sense to save the MediaLoft-A database right now because you haven't made any changes to it yet.

6. **Click Queries on the Objects bar**
   The query object window provides several ways to create a new query and displays the names of previously created queries, as shown in Figure A-8. There are three previously created query objects displayed within the MediaLoft-A Database window.

7. **Click Forms on the Objects bar, then click Reports on the Objects bar**
   The MediaLoft-A database contains the Customers table, three queries, a customer entry form, and three reports.

Viewing objects

You can change the way you view the objects in the database window by clicking the last four buttons on the toolbar. You can view the objects as Large Icons ▣, Small Icons ▸, in a List ▤ (this is the default view), and with Details ▦. The Details view shows a longer description of the object, as well as the date the object was last modified and the date it was originally created.

FIGURE A-7: MediaLoft-A database screen elements

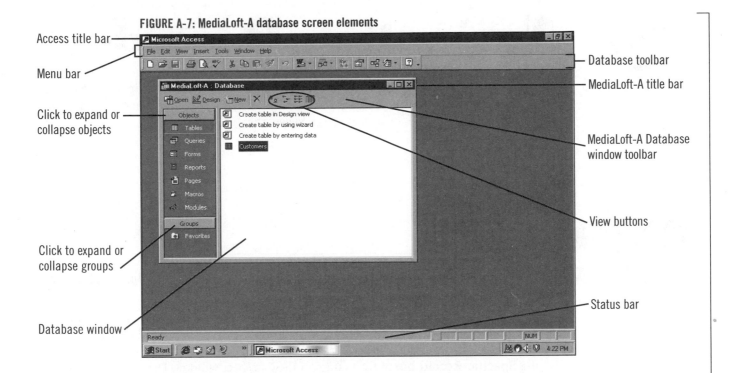

Access title bar
Menu bar
Click to expand or collapse objects
Click to expand or collapse groups
Database window

Database toolbar
MediaLoft-A title bar
MediaLoft-A Database window toolbar
View buttons
Status bar

FIGURE A-8: MediaLoft-A query objects

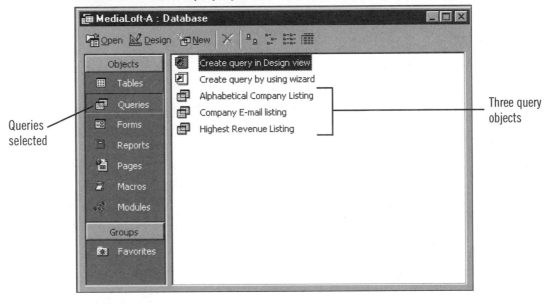

Queries selected

Three query objects

TABLE A-3: Elements of the database window

element	description
Database toolbar	Contains buttons for commonly performed tasks
Database window	Provides access to the objects within the database
Menu bar	Contains menus used in Access
Objects bar	Allows you to view a list of the object type chosen
Database window toolbar	Contains buttons you use to open, modify, create, delete, or view objects
Status bar	Displays messages regarding the current database operation
Title bar	Contains program name (Access) and filename of active database

Navigating Records

Your ability to navigate through the fields and records of a database is key to your productivity and success with the database. You navigate through the information in **Navigation mode** in the table's **datasheet**, a spreadsheet-like grid that displays fields as columns and records as rows. John opens the database and reviews the table containing information about MediaLoft's customers.

QuickTip

You can also double-click an object to open it.

1. **Click Tables on the Objects bar, click Customers, then click the Open button 📑 on the MediaLoft-A Database window toolbar**

   The datasheet for the Customers table opens, as shown in Figure A-9. The datasheet contains 27 customer records with 13 fields of information for each record. **Field names** are listed at the top of each column. The number of the selected record in the datasheet is displayed in the **Specific Record box** at the bottom of the datasheet window. Depending on the size of your monitor and the resolution of your computer system, you may see a different number of fields. If all of the fields don't display, you can scroll to the right to see the rest.

2. **Press [Tab] to move to Sprint**

   Sprint is the entry in the second field, Company, of the first record.

3. **Press [Enter]**

   The data, Aaron, is selected in the third field, First. Pressing either [Tab] or [Enter] moves the focus to the next field. **Focus** refers to which field would be edited if you started typing.

4. **Press [↓]**

   The focus moves to the Kelsey entry in the First field of the second record. The **current record symbol** in the **record selector box** also identifies which record you are navigating. The Next Record and Previous Record **navigation buttons** can also be used to navigate the datasheet.

5. **Press [Ctrl][End]**

   The focus moves to the last field of the last record. You can also use the Last Record navigation button to move to the last record.

6. **Press [Ctrl][Home]**

   The focus moves to the first field of the first record. You can also use the First Record navigation button to move to the first record. A complete listing of navigation keystrokes to move the focus between fields and records is shown in Table A-4.

Changing to Edit mode

If you click a field with the mouse pointer instead of pressing the [Tab] or [Enter] to navigate through the datasheet, you change from Navigation mode to **Edit mode**. In Edit mode, Access assumes that you are trying to edit that particular field, so keystrokes such as [Ctrl][End], [Ctrl][Home], [←], and [→] move the insertion point *within* the field. To return to Navigation mode, press [Tab] or [Enter] which moves the focus to the next field, or press [↑] or [↓] which moves the focus to a different record.

FIGURE A-9: Customers datasheet

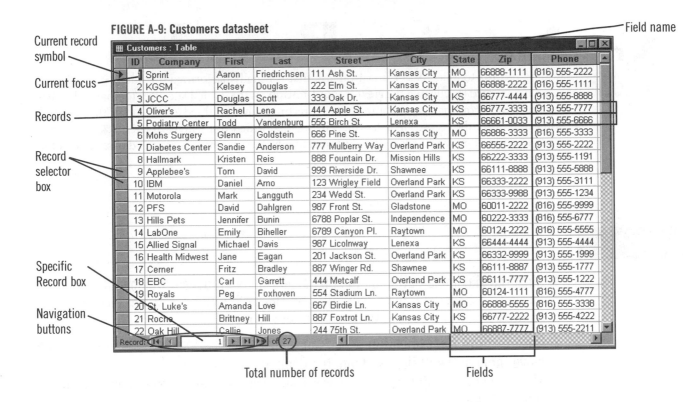

TABLE A-4: Navigation mode keyboard shortcuts

shortcut key	to move to the
[Tab], [Enter] or [→]	Next field of the current record
[Shift][Tab] or [←]	Previous field of the current record
[Home]	First field of the current record
[End]	Last field of the current record
[Ctrl][Home]	First field of the first record
[Ctrl][End]	Last field of the last record
[↑]	Current field of the previous record
[↓]	Current field of the next record
[Ctrl][↑]	Current field of the first record
[Ctrl][↓]	Current field of the last record
[F5]	Specific record

Entering Records

Adding records to a database is a critical task that is usually performed on a daily basis. You can add a new record by clicking the **New Record button** on the Table Datasheet toolbar or by clicking the New Record navigation button. A new record is always added at the end of the datasheet. You can reorder the records in a datasheet by sorting, which you will learn later. ➤ John is ready to add two new records in the Customers table. First he maximizes the datasheet window.

Steps

1. **Click the Maximize button** on the Customers Table datasheet window title bar
   Maximizing both the Access and datasheet windows displays the most information possible on the screen and allows you to see more fields and records.

2. **Click the New Record button** ▶* on the Table Datasheet toolbar, then press [Tab] to move through the ID field and into the Company field
   The ID field is an **AutoNumber** field, which automatically assigns a new number each time you add a record.

3. Type **CIO**, press [Tab], type **Lisa**, press [Tab], type **Lang**, press [Tab], type **420 Locust St.**, press [Tab], type **Lenexa**, press [Tab], type **KS**, press [Tab], type **66111-8899**, press [Tab], type **9135551189**, press [Tab], type **9135551889**, press [Tab], type **9/6/69**, press [Tab], type **lang@cio.com**, press [Tab], type **5433.22**, then press [Enter]
   The ID for the record for Lisa Lang is 28. AutoNumber fields should not be used as a counter for how many records you have in a table. Think of the AutoNumber field as an arbitrary but unique number for each record. The value in an AutoNumber field increments by one for each new record and cannot be edited or reused even if the entire record is deleted. The purpose of an AutoNumber field is to uniquely identify each new record. It logs how many records have been added to the datasheet since the creation of the datasheet, and not how many records are currently in the datasheet.

Trouble?

The ID number for the new records may be different in your database.

4. Enter the new record for Rachel Best shown in the table below

in field:	type:	in field:	type:
ID	29	Zip	65555-4444
Company	RBB Events	Phone	913-555-2289
First	Rachel	Fax	913-555-2889
Last	Best	Birthdate	8/20/68
Street	500 Sunset Blvd.	Email	Best@rbb.com
City	Manhattan	YTDSales	5998.33
State	KS		

Compare your updated datasheet with Figure A-10.

FIGURE A-10: Customers table with two new records

Table Datasheet toolbar

Two new records

New record button

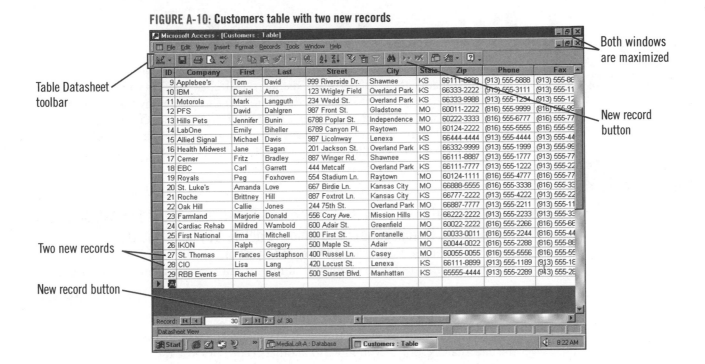

Both windows are maximized

New record button

FIGURE A-11: Moving a field

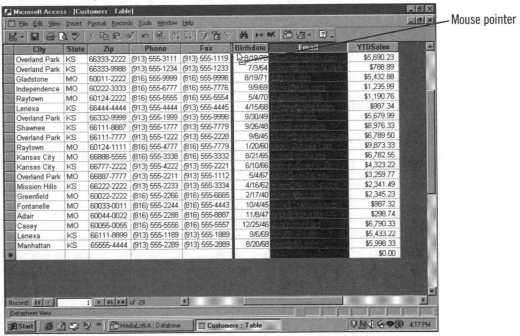

Mouse pointer

Moving datasheet columns

You can reorganize the fields in a datasheet by dragging the field name left or right. Figure A-11 shows how the mouse pointer changes to ⬚, as the Email field is moved to the left. The black vertical line represents the new location between the Fax and Birthdate fields. Release the mouse button when you have appropriately positioned the field.

Editing Records

Updating information in databases is another important daily task required to keep your database current. To change the contents of an existing record, click the field you'd like to change to switch to Edit mode, then type the new information. You can delete any unwanted data by clicking the field and using the [Backspace] and [Delete] keys to delete text to the left and right of the insertion point. Other data entry keystrokes are summarized in Table A-5. ➤ John needs to make some corrections to the datasheet of the Customers table. He starts by correcting an error in the Street field of the first record.

Steps

1. **Press [Ctrl][Home] to move to the first record, click to the right of 111 Ash St. in the Street field, press [Backspace] three times to delete St., then type Dr.**
   When you are editing a record, the **edit record symbol**, which looks like a small pencil, appears in the record selector box to the left of the current record, as shown in Figure A-12.

2. **Click to the right of Hallmark in the Company field in record 8, press [Spacebar], type Cards, then press [↓] to move to the next record**
   You do not need to explicitly save new records or changes to existing records because Access saves the new data as soon as you move to another record or close the data sheet.

3. **Click Shawnee in the City field for record 17, then press [Ctrl][']**
   The entry changes from "Shawnee" to "Overland Park." [Ctrl]['] inserts the data from the same field in the previous record.

4. **Click to the left of EBC in the Company field for record 18, press [Delete] to remove the E, press [Tab] to move to the next field, then type Doug**
   "Doug" replaces the current entry "Carl" in the First field. Notice the edit record symbol in the record selector box to the left of record 18. Since you are still editing this record, you can undo the changes.

5. **Press [Esc]**
   The Doug entry changes back to Carl. Pressing [Esc] once removes the current field's editing changes.

6. **Press [Esc] again**
   Pressing [Esc] a second time removes all changes made to the record you are currently editing. The company entry is restored to EBC. The ability to use the [Esc] key in edit mode to remove data entry changes is dependent on whether or not you are still editing the record (as evidenced by the edit record symbol to the left of the record). Once you move to another record, the changes are saved, and you return to Navigation mode. In Navigation mode you can no longer use the [Esc] key to remove editing changes, but you can click the **Undo button** ↶ on the Table Database toolbar to undo the last change you made.

7. **Press [↓] to move to Peg in the First field of record 19, type Peggy, then press [↓] to move to record 20**
   Since you are no longer editing record 19, the [Esc] key has no effect on the last change.

QuickTip
The ScreenTip for the Undo button displays the action you can undo.

8. **Click the Undo button ↶ on the Table Datasheet toolbar**
   You undo the last edit and Peggy is changed back to Peg. Access only allows you to undo your last action. You can also delete a record directly from the datasheet.

9. **Click the Allied Signal ID 15 Record Selector box, click the Delete Record button ⤫ on the Table Datasheet toolbar, then click Yes to confirm that you want to delete the record**
   You cannot undo a record deletion operation.

FIGURE A-12: Editing records

Edit record symbol

Insertion point

ID	Company	First	Last	Street	City	State	Zip	Phone	Fax
1	Sprint	Aaron	Friedrichsen	111 Ash Dr.	Kansas City	MO	66888-1111	(816) 555-2222	(816) 555-22
2	KGSM	Kelsey	Douglas	222 Elm St.	Kansas City	MO	66888-2222	(816) 555-1111	(816) 555-11
3	JCCC	Douglas	Scott	333 Oak Dr.	Kansas City	KS	66777-4444	(913) 555-8888	(913) 555-88
4	Oliver's	Rachel	Lena	444 Apple St.	Kansas City	KS	66777-3333	(913) 555-7777	(913) 555-77
5	Podiatry Center	Todd	Vandenburg	555 Birch St.	Lenexa	KS	66661-0033	(913) 555-6666	(913) 555-66
6	Mohs Surgery	Glenn	Goldstein	666 Pine St.	Kansas City	MO	66886-3333	(816) 555-3333	(816) 555-22
7	Diabetes Center	Sandie	Anderson	777 Mulberry Way	Overland Park	KS	66555-2222	(913) 555-2222	(913) 555-22
8	Hallmark	Kristen	Reis	888 Fountain Dr.	Mission Hills	KS	66222-3333	(913) 555-1191	(913) 555-11
9	Applebee's	Tom	David	999 Riverside Dr.	Shawnee	KS	66111-8888	(913) 555-5888	(913) 555-88
10	IBM	Daniel	Arno	123 Wrigley Field	Overland Park	KS	66333-2222	(913) 555-3111	(913) 555-11
11	Motorola	Mark	Langguth	234 Wedd St.	Overland Park	KS	66333-9988	(913) 555-1234	(913) 555-12
12	PFS	David	Dahlgren	987 Front St.	Gladstone	MO	60011-2222	(816) 555-9999	(816) 555-99
13	Hills Pets	Jennifer	Bunin	6788 Poplar St.	Independence	MO	60222-3333	(816) 555-6777	(816) 555-77
14	LabOne	Emily	Biheller	6789 Canyon Pl.	Raytown	MO	60124-2222	(816) 555-5555	(816) 555-55
15	Allied Signal	Michael	Davis	987 Licolnway	Lenexa	KS	66444-4444	(913) 555-4444	(913) 555-44
16	Health Midwest	Jane	Eagan	201 Jackson St.	Overland Park	KS	66332-9999	(913) 555-1999	(913) 555-99
17	Cerner	Fritz	Bradley	887 Winger Rd.	Shawnee	KS	66111-8887	(913) 555-1777	(913) 555-77
18	EBC	Carl	Garrett	444 Metcalf	Overland Park	KS	66111-7777	(913) 555-1222	(913) 555-22
19	Royals	Peg	Foxhoven	554 Stadium Ln.	Raytown	MO	60124-1111	(816) 555-4777	(816) 555-77
20	St. Luke's	Amanda	Love	667 Birdie Ln.	Kansas City	MO	66888-5555	(816) 555-3338	(816) 555-33
21	Roche	Brittney	Hill	887 Foxtrot Ln.	Kansas City	KS	66777-2222	(913) 555-4222	(913) 555-22
22	Oak Hill	Callie	Jones	244 75th St.	Overland Park	MO	66887-7777	(913) 555-2211	(913) 555-11
23	Farmland	Marjorie	Donald	556 Cory Ave.	Mission Hills	KS	66222-2222	(913) 555-2233	(913) 555-33
24	Cardiac Rehab	Mildred	Wambold	600 Adair St.	Greenfield	MO	60022-2222	(816) 555-2266	(816) 555-66
25	First National	Irma	Mitchell	800 First St.	Fontanelle	MO	60033-0011	(816) 555-2244	(816) 555-44

Record: 1 of 29

Datasheet View

TABLE A-5: Edit mode keyboard shortcuts

editing keystroke	action
[Backspace]	Deletes one character to the left of the insertion point
[Delete]	Deletes one character to the right of the insertion point
[F2]	Switches to Edit mode from Navigation mode
[Esc]	Undoes the change to the current field
[Esc][Esc]	Undoes the change to the current record
[F7]	Starts the spell check feature
[Ctrl][']	Inserts the value from the same field in the previous record into the current field
[Ctrl][;]	Inserts the current date in a date field

CLUES TO USE

Resizing datasheet columns

You can resize the width of the field in a datasheet by dragging the thin black line that separates the field names to the left or right. The mouse pointer changes to ↔ as you resize the field to make it wider or narrower. Release the mouse button when you have resized the field.

Access 2000

Previewing and Printing a Datasheet

After entering and editing the records in a table, you can print the datasheet to obtain a hard copy of it. Before printing the datasheet, you should preview it to see how it will look when printed. Often you will want to make adjustments to margins and page orientation. ⬤━━ John is ready to preview and print the datasheet.

Steps

1. Click the **Print Preview button** 🔍 on the Table Database toolbar

The datasheet appears as a miniature page in the Print Preview window, as shown in Figure A-14. The Print Preview toolbar provides options for printing, viewing more than one page, and sending the information to Word or Excel.

2. Click 🔍 on the top of the miniature datasheet

By magnifying this view of the datasheet, you can see its header, which includes the object name, Customers, in the center of the top of the page and the date on the right.

3. Scroll down to view the bottom of the page

The footer displays a page number centered on the bottom.

4. Click the **Two Pages button** 🔳 on the Print Preview toolbar

You decide to increase the top margin of the printout.

5. Click **File** on the menu bar, then click **Page Setup**

The Page Setup dialog box opens, as shown in Figure A-15. This dialog box provides options for changing margins, removing the headings (the header and footer), and changing page orientation from portrait (default) to landscape on the Page tab.

6. Double-click **1"** in the Top text box, type **2**, then click **OK**

The modified datasheet appears in the window. Satisfied with the layout for the printout, you'll print the datasheet and close the Print Preview window.

7. Click the **Print button** 🖨 on the Print Preview toolbar, then click **Close**

The datasheet appears on the screen.

CLUES TO USE

Hiding fields

Sometimes you don't need all the fields of a datasheet on a printout. To temporarily hide a field from viewing and therefore from a resulting datasheet printout, click the field name, click Format on the menu bar, and then click Hide Columns. To redisplay the column, click Format, then Unhide Columns. The Unhide Columns dialog box, shown in Figure A-13, opens. The empty columns check boxes indicate the columns that are hidden. Clicking the check boxes will bring the columns back into view on the datasheet.

FIGURE A-13: Unhide Columns dialog box

These fields are currently hidden

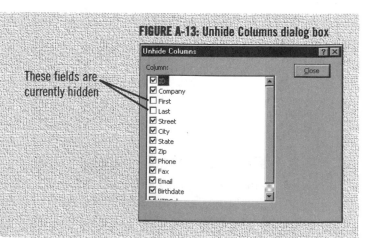

FIGURE A-14: Datasheet in print preview (portrait orientation)

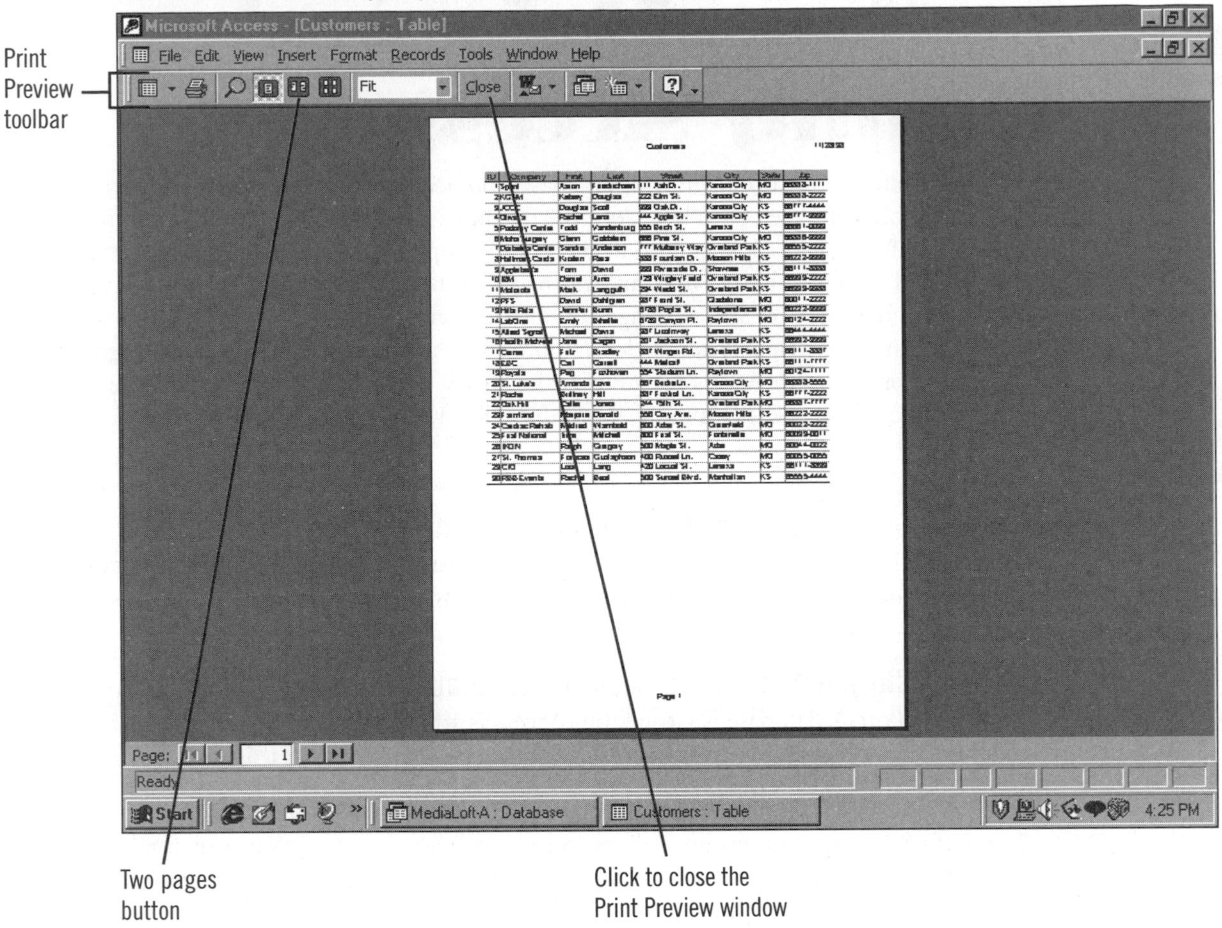

Print Preview toolbar

Two pages button

Click to close the Print Preview window

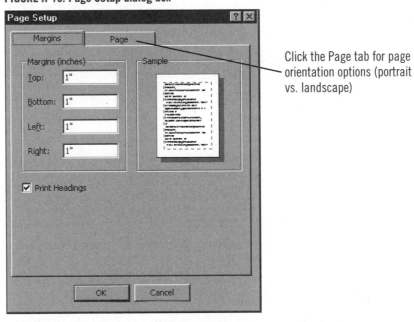

FIGURE A-15: Page Setup dialog box

Click the Page tab for page orientation options (portrait vs. landscape)

Getting Help and Exiting Access

When you have finished working in your database, you need to close the object you were working in, such as a table datasheet, and then close the database. To close a table, click Close on the File menu or click the object's Close button located in the upper-right corner of the menu bar. Once you have closed all open objects, you can exit the program. As with most programs, if you try to exit Access and have not yet saved changes to open objects, Access will prompt you to save your changes. You can use the Help system to learn more about the program and get help. ✏ John has finished working with Access for now, so he closes the Customers table and MediaLoft-A database. Before exiting, he learns more about the Help system, and then exits Access.

Steps 1 2 3 4

1. **Click the Close button for the Customers datasheet**
   The MediaLoft-A database window displays. If you make any structural changes to the datasheet such as moving, resizing, or hiding columns, you will be prompted to save those changes.

2. **Click the Close button for the MediaLoft-A Database, as shown in Figure A-16**
   The MediaLoft-A database is closed, but Access is still running so you could open another database or explore the Help system to learn more about Access at this time.

3. **Click Help on the menu bar, then click Microsoft Access Help**
   The Office Assistant opens and offers to get the help you need. You can further explore some of the concepts you have learned by finding information in the Access Help system. Table A-6 summarizes the options on the Access Help menu, which provides in-depth information on Access features.

4. **Type What is a table, click Search, click Tables: what they are and how they work, then click the graphic as shown in Figure A-17**

5. **Read the information, then click each of the five pages**

6. **Close the Access Help windows**

7. **Click File on the menu bar, then click Exit**
   You have exited Access.

Trouble?
Do not remove your Project Disk from drive A until you have exited Access.

Shutting down your computer

Never shut off a computer before the screen indicates that it is safe to do so. If you shut off a computer during the initial Windows load process (the screen displays the Windows logo and a cloud background at this time) or before the screen indicates that it is safe to do so, you can corrupt your Windows files.

FIGURE A-16: Closing a database

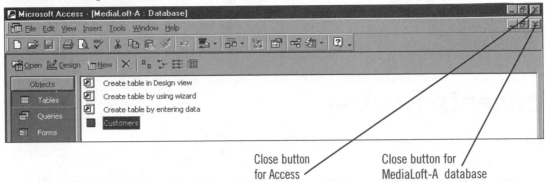

Close button
for Access

Close button for
MediaLoft-A database

FIGURE A-17: Access Help window

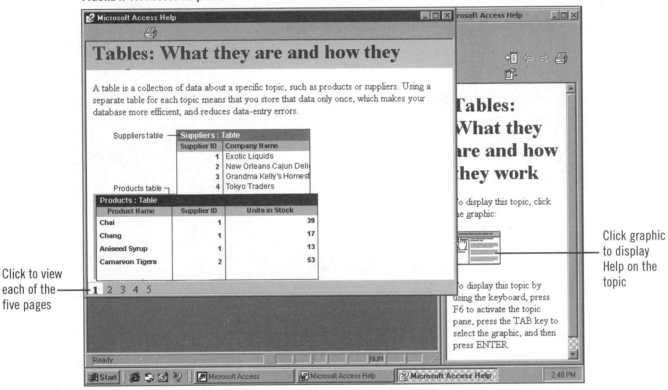

Click to view
each of the
five pages

Click graphic
to display
Help on the
topic

TABLE A-6: Help menu options

menu option	description
Microsoft Access Help	Opens the Office Assistant; type a question to open the entire Microsoft Access Help manual in a separate window in which you can search for information by the table of contents, index, or keyword
Show the Office Assistant	Presents the Office Assistant, an automated character that provides tips and interactive prompts while you are working
Hide the Office Assistant	Temporarily closes the Office Assistant for the working session
What's This	Changes the mouse pointer to ▷?; this special mouse pointer provides a short explanation of the icon or menu option that you click
Office on the Web	If you are connected to the Web, provides additional Microsoft information and support articles; this Web-based information is updated daily
Detect and Repair	Analyzes a database for possible data corruption and attempts to repair problems
About Microsoft Access	Provides the version and product ID of Access

Practice

▶ Concepts Review

Label each element of the Access window shown in Figure A-18.

FIGURE A-18

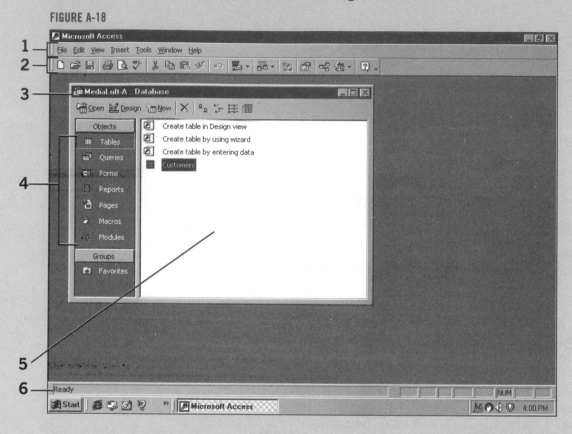

Match each term with the statement that describes it.

7. **Objects**
8. **Table**
9. **Record**
10. **Field**
11. **Datasheet**

a. A group of related fields, such as all the demographic information for one customer
b. A collection of records for a single subject, such as all the customer records
c. A category of information in a table, such as a customer's name, city, or state
d. A spreadsheet-like grid that displays fields as columns and records as rows
e. Seven types of these are contained in an Access database and are used to enter, enhance, and use the data within the database

Select the best answer from the list of choices.

12. **Which of the following is NOT a typical benefit of relational databases?**
    a. Easier data entry
    b. Faster information retrieval
    c. Minimized duplicate data entry
    d. Automatic trend analysis

13. **Which of the following is NOT an advantage of managing data with a relational database versus a spreadsheet?**
   a. Doesn't require preplanning before data is entered
   b. Allows links between lists of information
   c. Provides greater security
   d. Allows multiple users to enter data simultaneously

14. **The object that holds all of the data within an Access database**
   a. Query
   b. Table
   c. Form
   d. Report

15. **The object that provides an easy-to-use data entry screen**
   a. Table
   b. Query
   c. Form
   d. Report

16. **This displays messages regarding the current database operation**
   a. Status bar
   b. Title bar
   c. Database toolbar
   d. Object tabs

▶ Skills Review

1. **Define database software.**
   a. Identify five disadvantages of using a paper system, such as index cards, to organize database information. Write down your answers to this and the following questions using complete sentences.
   b. Identify five advantages of managing database information in Access versus using a spreadsheet product like Excel.

2. **Learn database terminology.**
   a. Explain the relationship between a field, a record, a table, and a database.
   b. Identify the seven objects of an Access database, and explain the main purpose of each.
   c. Which object of an Access database is most important? Why?

3. **Start Access and open a database.**
   a. Click the Start button, point to Programs, then click Microsoft Access.
   b. Insert your Project Disk into the appropriate disk drive, click the Open an existing file option button, click More Files, then click OK.
   c. In the Open dialog box, choose the correct drive, then open the Recycle-A database file.
   d. Identify the following items. (*Hint*: To create a printout of this screen, press [Print Screen] to capture an image of the screen to the Windows clipboard, start any word-processing program, then click the Paste button. Print the document that now contains a picture of this screen, and identify the elements on the printout.)
      - Database toolbar
      - Recycle-A database window
      - Menu bar
      - Object buttons
      - Objects bar
      - Status bar

4. **View the database window.**
   a. Maximize both the Access window and the Recycle-A Database window.
   b. Click each of the objects, then write down the object names of each type that exist in the Recycle-A database.
      - Tables
      - Queries
      - Reports
      - Pages
      - Macros
      - Modules
      - Forms

5. **Navigate records.**
   a. Open the Clubs table.
   b. Press [Tab] or [Enter] to move through the fields of the first record.
   c. Press [Ctrl][End] to move to the last field of the last record.
   d. Press [Ctrl][Home] to move to the first field of the first record.
   e. Click the Last Record navigation button to quickly move to the Oak Hill Patriots record.

6. Enter records.

a. In the Clubs table, click the New Record button, then add the following records:

Name	Street	City	State	Zip	Phone	Leader	Club Number
EBC Angels	10100 Metcalf	Overland Park	KS	66001	555-7711	Michael Garrett	8
MOT Friends	111 Holmes	Kansas City	MO	65001	555-8811	Aaron Goldstein	9

b. Move the Club Number field from the last column of the datasheet to the first column.

7. Edit records.

a. Change the Name field in the first record from "Jaycees" to "JC Club."

b. Change the Name field in the second record from "Boy Scouts #1" to "Oxford Cub Scouts."

c. Change the Leader field in the fifth record from "Melanie Perry" to "Melanie Griffiths."

d. Enter your name and personal information (make up a club name) as a new record, and enter 99 as the Club Number.

e. Delete the record for Club Number 8.

8. Preview and print a datasheet.

a. Preview the Clubs table datasheet.

b. Use the Page Setup option on the File menu to change the page orientation from portrait to landscape.

c. Print the Clubs table datasheet.

9. Get Help and exit Access.

a. Close the Clubs table object, saving the changes.

b. Close the Recycle-A database.

c. Use Office Assistant to learn more about creating a database.

d. Exit Access.

▶ Independent Challenges

1. Ten examples of databases are given below. For each example, write a brief answer for the following.

a. What field names would you expect to find in this database?

b. Provide an example of two possible records for each database.

- Telephone directory
- College course offerings
- Restaurant menu
- Cookbook
- Movie listing
- Encyclopedia
- Shopping catalog
- Corporate inventory
- Party guest list
- Members of the House of Representatives

2. You are working with several civic groups in your area to coordinate a community-wide cleanup effort. You have started a database called "Recycle-A" that tracks the clubs, their trash deposits, and the trash centers that are participating in this effort. To complete this independent challenge:

a. Start Access.

b. Open the Recycle-A database from your Project Disk, and determine the number of objects of each type that exist in the database:

- Tables
- Queries
- Reports
- Pages
- Macros
- Modules
- Forms

c. Open the Deposits table, and answer the following questions:
- How many fields does the table have?
- How many records are there in the table?

d. Close the table, then exit Access.

3. You are working with several civic groups in your area to coordinate a community-wide cleanup effort. You have started a database called "Recycle-A" that tracks the clubs, their trash deposits, and the trash centers that are participating in this effort.

To complete this independent challenge:

a. Start Access and open the Recycle-A database from your Project Disk.

b. Add the following records to the Clubs table:

Club Number	Name	Street	City	State	Zip	Phone	Leader
10	Take Pride	222 Switzer St.	Olathe	KS	66001	555-2211	David Reis
11	Cub Scouts #321	333 Ward Pkwy.	Kansas City	MO	65002	555-8811	Daniel Langguth

c. Edit the following records in the Clubs table. The Street field has changed for Club Number 6 and the Phone and Leader fields have changed for Club Number 7.

Club Number	Name	Street	City	State	Zip	Phone	Leader
6	Girl Scouts #1	55 Oak Terrace	Shawnee	KS	68777	555-4444	Jonathan Bacon
7	Oak Hill Patriots	888 Switzer	Overland Park	KS	66444	555-9988	Cynthia Ralston

d. If you haven't already, add your name and personal information (make up a club name) and enter 99 as the Club Number. Print the datasheet.

e. Close the table, close the database, then exit Access.

4. The World Wide Web can be used to collect or research information that is used in corporate databases. MediaLoft often uses their intranet for this purpose. An intranet is a group of connected networks owned by a company or organization that is used for internal purposes. Intranets use internet software to handle the data communications, such as e-mail and Web pages, within an organization. These pages often provide company-wide information. MediaLoft has developed a Web page on the intranet that provides information about their products and customers. Eventually, MediaLoft will tie these Web pages directly to their database so that the information is dynamically tied to their working database. In this exercise, you'll retrieve the new customer information recorded on the intranet Web page, and enter it directly into the MediaLoft-A database.

To complete this independent challenge:

a. Connect to the Internet, and use your browser to go to the Medialoft intranet site at http://www.course.com/illustrated/MediaLoft/

b. Click the link for Our Customers.

c. Print the page that shows the information for the two new customers.

d. Disconnect from the Internet.

e. Start Access and open the MediaLoft-A database.

f. Open the Customers table.

g. Add the new customers to the table. They will become records 30 and 31. Add your name to the table with your personal information as record 32.

h. Review your work, print the datasheet, close the MediaLoft A-database, then exit Access.

► Visual Workshop

Open the Recycle-A database on your Project Disk. Modify the existing Centers table, and enter a new record using your name as the contact and Center Number 99. The Street field for the first record has changed, the Hazardous field for the first two records has changed, and two new records have been added to the datasheet. See Figure A-19. Print the datasheet.

FIGURE A-19

	Center Number	Name	Street	City	State	Zip	Phone	Contact	Hazard
⊞	1	Trash 'R Us	989 Main	Lenexa	KS	61111	555-7777	Ben Cartwright	☐
⊞	2	You Deliver	12345 College	Overland Park	KS	63444	555-2222	Jerry Magliano	☐
⊞	3	County Landfill	12444 Pflumm	Lenexa	KS	64222	555-4422	Jerry Lewis	☐
⊞	4	Cans and Stuff	543 Holmes	Kansas City	MO	60011	555-2347	Julee Burton	☑
⊞	5	We Love Trash	589 Switzer	Kansas City	KS	60022	555-3456	Doug Morrison	☑
*									☐

Centers : Table

Record: 1 of 5

Using
Tables and Queries

Objectives

MOUS ► **Plan a database**

MOUS ► **Create a table**

MOUS ► **Use Table Design view**

MOUS ► **Format a datasheet**

MOUS ► **Understand sorting, filtering, and finding**

MOUS ► **Sort records and find data**

MOUS ► **Filter records**

MOUS ► **Create a query**

MOUS ► **Use Query Design view**

Now that you are familiar with some of the basic Access terminology and features, you are ready to plan and build your own database. Your first task is to create the tables that store the data. Once the tables are created and the data is entered, you can use several techniques for finding specific information in the database, including sorting, filtering, and building queries. ◄─── John Kim wants to build and maintain a database containing information about MediaLoft's products. The information in the database will be useful when John provides information for future sales promotions.

Planning a Database

The first and most important object in a database is the table object because it contains the **raw data**, the individual pieces of information stored in individual fields in the database. When you design a table, you identify the fields of information the table will contain and the type of data to be stored in each field. Some databases contain multiple tables linked together. John plans his database containing information about MediaLoft's products.

Details

In planning a database it is important to:

 Determine the purpose of the database and give it a meaningful name

The database will store information about MediaLoft's music products. You decide to name the database "MediaLoft," and name the first table "Music Inventory."

 Determine what reports you want the database to produce

You want to be able to print inventory reports that list the products by artist, type of product (CD or cassette), quantity in stock, and price. These pieces of information will become the fields in the Music Inventory table.

 Collect the raw data that will be stored in the database

The raw data for MediaLoft's products might be stored on index cards, in paper reports, and in other electronic formats, such as word-processed documents and spreadsheets. You can use Access to import data from many other electronic sources, which greatly increases your data entry efficiency.

 Sketch the structure of each table, including field names and data types

Using the data you collected, identify the field name and data type for each field in each table as shown in Figure B-1. The **data type** determines what type of information you can enter in a field. For example, a field with a Currency data type does accept text. Properly defining the data type for each field helps you maintain data consistency and accuracy. Table B-1 lists the data types available within Access.

Choosing between the text and number data type

When assigning data types, you should avoid choosing "number" for a telephone or zip code field. Although these fields generally contain numbers, they should still be text data types. Consider the following: You may want to enter 1-800-BUY-BOOK in a telephone number field. This would not be possible if the field were designated as a number data type. When you sort the fields, you'll want them to sort alphabetically, like text fields. Consider the following zip codes: 60011 and 50011-8888. If the zip code field were designated as a number data type, the zip codes would be interpreted incorrectly as the values 60,011 and 500,118,888; and sort in that order, too.

Field Name	Data Type
RecordingID	AutoNumber
RecordingTitle	Text
RecordingArtist	Text
MusicCategory	Text
RecordingLabel	Text
Format	Text
NumberofTracks	Number
PurchasePrice	Currency
RetailPrice	Currency
Notes	Memo

TABLE B-1: Data types

data type	description of data	size
Text	Text information or combinations of text and numbers, such as a street address, name, or phone number	Up to 255 characters
Memo	Lengthy text such as comments or notes	Up to 64,000 characters
Number	Numeric information used in calculations, such as quantities	Several sizes available to store numbers with varying degrees of precision
Date/Time	Dates and times	Size controlled by Access to accommodate dates and times across thousands of years (for example, 1/1/1850 and 1/1/2150 are valid dates)
Currency	Monetary values	Size controlled by Access; accommodates up to 15 digits to the left of the decimal point and 4 digits to the right
AutoNumber	Integers assigned by Access to sequentially order each record added to a table	Size controlled by Access
Yes/No	Only one of two values stored (Yes/No, On/Off, True/False)	Size controlled by Access
OLE Object	Pointers stored that link files created in other programs, such as pictures, sound clips, documents, or spreadsheets	Up to one gigabyte
Hyperlink	Web addresses	Size controlled by Access
Lookup Wizard	Invokes a wizard that helps link the current table to another table (the final data type of the field is determined by choices made in the wizard; a field created with the lookup data type will display data from another table)	Size controlled through the choices made in the Lookup Wizard

Creating a Table

After you plan the structure of the database, your next step is to create the database file itself, which will eventually contain all of the objects such as tables, queries, forms, and reports. When you create a database, first you name it, and then you can build the first table object and enter data. Access offers several methods for creating a table. For example, you can import a table from another data source such as a spreadsheet, or use the Access **Table Wizard**, which provides inter-active help to create the field names and data types for each field. ⬤━━ John is ready to create the MediaLoft database. He uses the Table Wizard to create the Music Inventory table.

Steps

1. Start Access, click the **Blank Access database option button** in the Microsoft Access dialog box, then click **OK**
   The File New Database dialog box opens.

2. Type **MediaLoft** in the File name text box, insert your Project Disk in the appropriate drive, click the **Save in list arrow**, click the **drive**, then click **Create**
   The MediaLoft database file is created and saved on your Project Disk. The Table Wizard offers an efficient way to plan the fields of a new table.

3. If the Office Assistant appears on your screen, click **Help** on the menu bar, click **Hide the Office Assistant**, then double-click **Create table by using wizard** in the MediaLoft Database window
   The Table Wizard dialog box opens, as shown in Figure B-2. The Table Wizard offers 25 business and 20 personal sample tables from which you can select sample fields. The Recordings sample table, which is in the Personal category of tables, most closely matches the fields you want to include in the Music Inventory table.

4. Click the **Personal option button**, scroll down and click **Recordings** in the Sample Tables list box, then click the **Select All Fields button** `>>`
   Your Table Wizard dialog box should look like Figure B-3. At this point, you can change the suggested field names to better match your database.

5. Click **RecordingArtistID** in the Fields in my new table list box, click **Rename Field**, type **RecordingArtist** in the Rename field text box, then click **OK**

6. Click **Next**
   The second Table Wizard dialog box allows you to name the table and determine if Access sets the **primary key field**, a field that contains unique information for each record.

7. Type **Music Inventory**, make sure the **Yes, set a primary key for me option button** is selected, click **Next**, click the **Modify the table design option button**, then click **Finish**
   The table opens in **Design view**, shown in Figure B-4, which allows you to add, delete, or modify the fields in the table. The primary **key field symbol** indicates that the RecordingID field has been designated as the primary key field.

Trouble?

If you don't see all the fields in the table, it is because you have different settings on your monitor. Maximize the window to see all the fields, if necessary.

FIGURE B-2: Table Wizard

Business and personal categories

Sample tables

Sample fields for the selected table

Select All Fields button

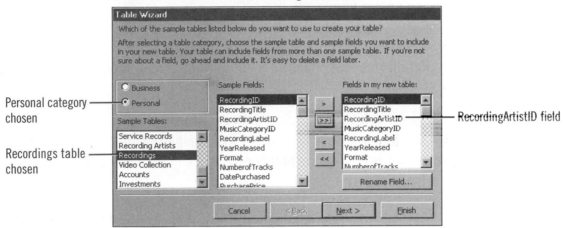

FIGURE B-3: Table Wizard with Recordings table fields

Personal category chosen

Recordings table chosen

RecordingArtistID field

FIGURE B-4: Music Inventory table in Design view

View button

Key field symbol

Field names

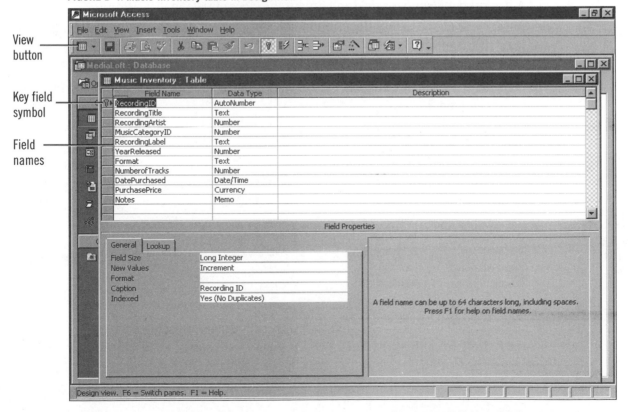

Using Table Design View

Each database object has a **Design view** in which you can modify its structure. The Design view of a table allows you to add or delete fields, add **field descriptions**, or change other field properties. **Field properties** are additional characteristics of a field such as its size or default value. Using the Table Wizard, John was able to create a Music Inventory table very quickly. Now in Design view he modifies the fields to meet his needs. MediaLoft doesn't track purchase dates or release dates, but it does need to store retail price information in the database.

Steps 1 2 3 4

QuickTip

Deleting a field from a table deletes any data stored in that field for all records in the table.

1. In the Music Inventory table's Design view, click **DatePurchased** in the Field Name column, click the **Delete Rows button** on the Table Design toolbar, click the **Year Released row selector**, click to delete the field, click the **Notes** field, then click the **Insert Rows button**

    The Year Released and Date Purchased fields are deleted from the table and a new row appears in which you can add the new field name.

2. Type **RetailPrice**, press **[Tab]**, type **C** (for Currency data type), then press **[Enter]**

    The new field is added to the Music Inventory table, as shown in Figure B-5. The data type of both the RecordingArtist and MusicCategoryID fields should be Text so that descriptive words can be entered in these fields rather than just numbers.

3. Click the **Number** data type in the RecordingArtist field, click the **Data Type list arrow**, click **Text**, click the **Number** data type in the MusicCategoryID field, click the **Data Type list arrow**, then click **Text**

    You must work in the table's Design view to make structural changes to the table.

4. Click to the right of **MusicCategoryID**, press **[Backspace]** twice, then click the **Save button** on the Table Design toolbar

    A description identifies a field and can list the types of data in that field.

5. Click the **MusicCategory Description cell**, then type **classical, country, folk, gospel, jazz, new age, rap, or rock**

    The **field size property** limits the number of characters allowed for each field.

6. Make sure the **MusicCategory** field is still selected, double-click **50** in the Field Size cell, then type **9**

    The longest entry in the MusicCategory field, "classical," is only nine characters. The finished Music Inventory table Design view should look like Figure B-6.

QuickTip

Press [Tab] to move through the RecordingID field (it's an AutoNumber field) and just type the numbers to enter the PurchasePrice and RetailPrice. The Currency format is automatically applied.

7. Click the **Datasheet View button** on the Table Design toolbar, click **Yes** to save the table, then type the following record into the new datasheet:

in field:	type:	in field:	type:
Recording ID	[Tab]	Format	CD
Recording Title	No Words	Number of Tracks	12
RecordingArtist	Brickman, Jim	Purchase Price	$10.00
Music Category ID	New Age	RetailPrice	$13.00
Recording Label	Windham Hill	Notes	

    You are finished working with the MediaLoft database for now.

8. Close the Music Inventory table, then close the MediaLoft database

    Data is saved automatically, so you were not prompted to save the record when you closed the datasheet.

FIGURE B-5: Music Inventory table with new RetailPrice field

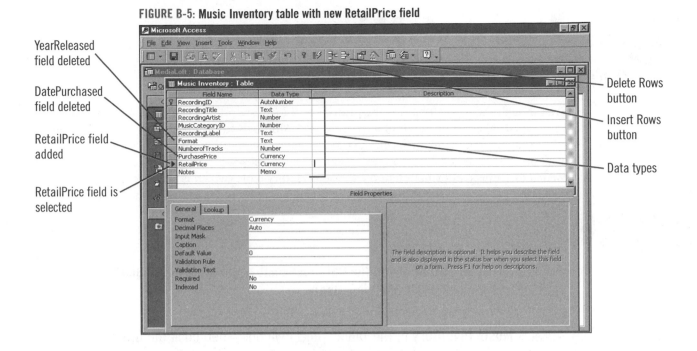

YearReleased field deleted

DatePurchased field deleted

RetailPrice field added

RetailPrice field is selected

Delete Rows button

Insert Rows button

Data types

FIGURE B-6: Description and field size properties for MusicCategory field

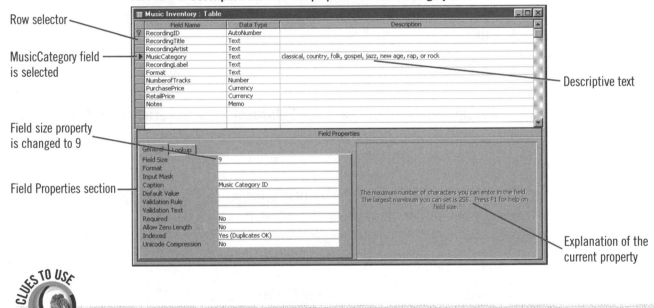

Row selector

MusicCategory field is selected

Field size property is changed to 9

Field Properties section

Descriptive text

Explanation of the current property

Learning about field properties

The properties of a field are the characteristics that define the field. Two properties are required for every field: Field Name and Data Type. Many other properties, such as Field Size, Format (the way the field is displayed on the datasheet), Caption, and Default Value, are defined in the Field Properties section of the table's Design view. As you add more property entries, you are generally restricting the amount or type of data that can be entered in the field, which also increases data entry accuracy. For example, you might change the Field Size property for a State field from the default value of 50 to 2 to eliminate an incorrect entry such as "NYY." The available field properties change depending on the data type of the selected field. For example, there is no Field Size property for a Birth Date field, because Access controls the size of fields with a Date/Time data type. Database designers often insist on field names without spaces because they are easier to reference in other Access objects. The **Caption property**, however, can be used to override the technical field name with an easy-to-read Caption entry when the field name is displayed on datasheets, forms, and reports. When you create a table using the wizard, many fields have Caption properties.

Access 2000

Formatting a Datasheet

Even though the report object is the primary tool to create professional hard copy output from an Access database, you can print a datasheet too. Although you cannot create fancy headings or insert graphic images on a datasheet, you can change the fonts and colors as well as change the gridlines to dramatically change its appearance. ➡ John has been busy entering MediaLoft's music information in the Music Inventory table (which is stored in the MediaLoft-B database). He has also simplified many of the field names. Now he will print the Music Inventory datasheet using new fonts and colors.

Steps 1 2 3 4

1. Click the **Open button** 🗁 on the Database toolbar, select the **MediaLoft-B** database from your Project Disk, then click **Open**
   The Music Inventory table has data that was entered by John Kim.

QuickTip
You can double-click a table object to open it in Datasheet view.

2. Click **Music Inventory** in the Tables Object window, then click the **Open button** 📑
   Access displays the Music Inventory table, containing 58 records, as shown in Figure B-7. You can change the font and color of the datasheet to enhance its appearance.

3. Click **Format** on the menu bar, click **Font**, click **Comic Sans MS** in the Font list, then click **OK**
   Comic Sans MS is an informal font used for personal correspondence or internal memos. It simulates handwritten text, but is still very readable. You can also change the color and format of the datasheet gridlines.

4. Click **Format** on the menu bar, click **Datasheet**, click the **Gridline Color list arrow**, then click **Red**
   The Sample box in the Datasheet Formatting dialog box displays both the vertical and horizontal gridlines as red.

5. Click the **Border list arrow**, click **Vertical Gridline**, click the **Line Styles list arrow**, click **Transparent Border**, as shown in Figure B-8, then click **OK**
   You removed the vertical gridlines separating the fields. You can also change the left and right margins, and change the page orientation from portrait to landscape to fit all the fields across the page.

6. Click **File** on the menu bar, click **Page Setup**, double-click **1"** in the Top text box, type **0.75**, press **[Tab]**, type **0.75** in the Bottom text box, press **[Tab]**, type **0.75** in the Left text box, press **[Tab]**, type **0.75** in the Right text box, click the **Page tab**, click the **Landscape option button**, then click **OK**
   Print Preview displays your formatted datasheet as it will look when printed.

7. Click the **Print Preview button** 🔍 on the Table Datasheet toolbar to preview the finished product, as shown in Figure B-9
   The red gridlines seem a bit too intense for your printout.

8. Click the **Close button** Close on the Print Preview toolbar, click **Format** on the menu bar, click **Datasheet**, click the **Gridline Color list arrow**, click **Silver**, then click **OK**
   Silver is the default gridline color.

FIGURE B-7: Music Inventory table datasheet

Music Inventory : Table

RecordingID	Title	Artist	Category	Label	Format
1	Gravity	Cook, Jesse	New Age	Columbia	CD
2	Come Walk With Me	Adams, Oleta	Gospel	CBS Records	CD
3	Greatest Hits	Winans, BeBe & C	Gospel	Benson	Vinyl
4	Tribute	Yanni	New Age	MCA	CD
5	World Café	Tree Frogs	Rap	New Stuff	CD
6	Relationships	Winans, BeBe & C	Gospel	Capitol	CD
7	No Words	Brickman, Jim	New Age	Windham Hill	CD
8	God's Property	Nu Nation	Rap	B-Rite Music	Cassette
9	Message	4 Him	Gospel	Benson	CD
10	Sacred Road	Lantz, David	New Age	Narada	Cassette
11	Mariah Carey	Carey, Mariah	Rock	Columbia	CD
12	Ironman Triathlon	Tesh, John	New Age	GTS Records	Cassette
13	Daydream	Carey, Mariah	Rock	Columbia	CD
14	Heartsounds	Lantz, David	New Age	Narada	CD
15	The Roches	Roches, The	Folk	Warner Bros. Reco	Cassette
16	Can We Go Home Now	Roches, The	Folk	Ryko	CD
17	Live at the Red Rocks	Tesh, John	New Age	GTS Records	CD
18	I'll Lead You Home	Smith, Michael	Gospel	Reunion	CD
19	Winter Song	Tesh, John	New Age	GTS Records	CD
20	December	Winston, George	New Age	Windham	CD
21	Time, Love & Tenderness	Bolton, Michael	Rock	Sony Music	CD
22	Autumn	Winston, George	New Age	Windham	Vinyl

Record: 1 of 58

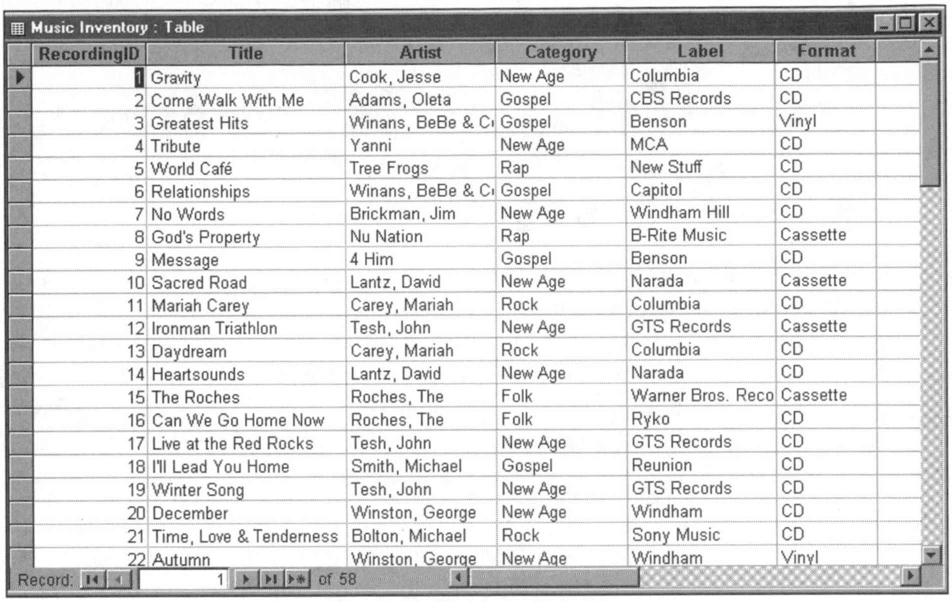

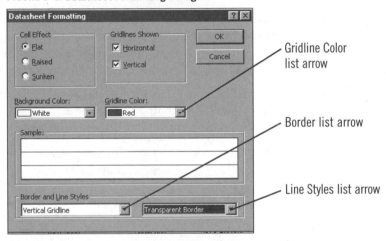

FIGURE B-8: Datasheet Formatting dialog box

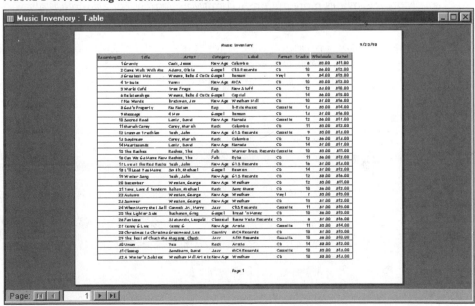

Datasheet Formatting
Cell Effect
Flat
Raised
Sunken
Gridlines Shown
Horizontal
Vertical
OK
Cancel
Background Color:
White
Gridline Color:
Red
Sample:
Border and Line Styles
Vertical Gridline
Transparent Border
Gridline Color list arrow
Border list arrow
Line Styles list arrow

FIGURE B-9: Previewing the formatted datasheet

Music Inventory : Table
Page: 1

Understanding Sorting, Filtering, and Finding

The records of a datasheet are automatically sorted according to the data in the primary key field. Often, however, you'll want to view or print records in an entirely different sort order. Or you may want to display a subset of the records, such as those within the same music category or those below a certain retail price. Access makes it easy to sort, find data, and filter a datasheet with buttons on the Table Datasheet toolbar, summarized in Table B-2. John studies the sort, find, and filter features to learn how to find and retrieve information in his database.

 Sorting refers to reorganizing the records in either ascending or descending order based on the contents of a field. Text fields sort from A to Z, number fields from the lowest to the highest value, and date/time fields from the oldest date to the date furthest into the future. In Figure B-10 the Music Inventory table has been sorted in ascending order on the Artist field. Notice that numbers sort before letters in an ascending sort order.

 Filtering means temporarily isolating a subset of records, as shown in Figure B-11. This is particularly useful because the subset can be formatted and printed just like the entire datasheet. You can produce a listing of all rock music or a listing based on any category, artist, or field in the datasheet. To remove a filter, click the Remove Filter button to view all the records in the datasheet.

 Finding refers to locating a specific piece of data, such as "Amy" or "500," within a field or an entire datasheet, similar to finding text in a word-processing document. The Find and Replace dialog box is shown in Figure B-12. The options in this dialog box are summarized below.

- **Find What:** Provides a text box for your search criteria. For example, you might want to find the text "Amy", "Beatles", or "Capitol Records" in the datasheet.

- **Look In:** Determines whether Access looks for the search criteria in the current field (in this case the Artist field) or in all fields.

- **Match:** Determines whether the search criteria must match the whole field's contents exactly, any part of the field, or the start of the field.

- **More:** Provides more options to limit your search. For example, it allows you to make your search criteria uppercase- or lowercase-sensitive.

- **Replace tab:** Provides a text box for you to specify "replacement text." In other words, you might want to search for every occurrence of "Compact Disc" and replace it with "CD" by entering "Compact Disc" as your search criteria and "CD" as your replacement text.

TABLE B-2: Sort, Filter, and Find buttons

name	button	purpose
Sort Ascending		Sorts records based on the selected field in ascending order (0 to 9, A to Z)
Sort Descending		Sorts records based on the selected field in descending order (Z to A, 9 to 0)
Filter By Selection		Filters records based on selected data and hides records that do not match
Filter By Form		Filters records based on more than one selection criteria by using the Filter By Form window
Apply Filter or Remove Filter		Applies or removes the filter
Find		Searches for a string of characters in the current field or all fields

FIGURE B-10: Records sorted in ascending order by Artist

Records sorted in
ascending order
by Artist

FIGURE B-11: Records filtered by "Rock" category

Sort Ascending
button

Sort Descending
button

Number of
records in
filtered subset

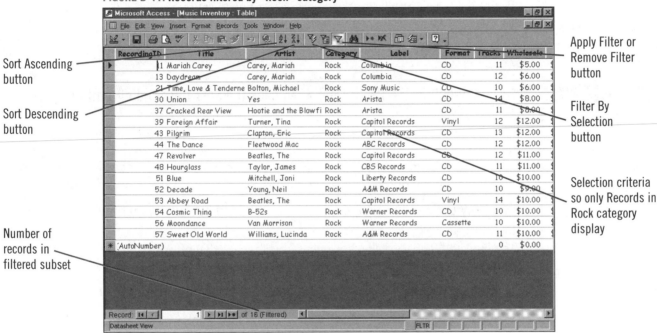

Apply Filter or
Remove Filter
button

Filter By
Selection
button

Selection criteria
so only Records in
Rock category
display

FIGURE B-12: Find and Replace dialog box

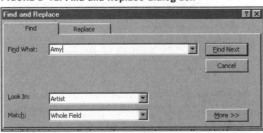

Using wildcards in Find

Wildcards are symbols you can use as substitutes for characters to find information that matches your find criteria. Access uses these wildcards: the asterisk (*) represents any group of characters, the question mark (?) stands for any single character, and the pound sign (#) stands for a single number digit. For example, to find any word beginning with "S," type "s*" in the Find What text box.

Sorting Records and Finding Data

Sorting records and quickly finding information in a database are two powerful tools that help you work more efficiently. ▟▔▔▔ John needs to create several different printouts of the Music Inventory datasheet to satisfy various departments. The Marketing department wants a printout of records sorted by title and artist. The Accounting department wants a printout of records sorted from highest retail price to lowest.

Steps 1234

1. In the Music Inventory datasheet, click **any cell** in the Title field, then click the **Sort Ascending button** 🔽 on thc Table Datasheet toolbar

    The records are listed in an A-to-Z sequence based on the data in the Title field, as shown in Figure B-13. Next you'll sort the records according to artist.

2. Click **any cell** in the Artist field, then click 🔽

    The table is sorted alphabetically in ascending order by Artist. You can preview and print a sorted datasheet at any time.

QuickTip

Scroll to the right if necessary to see this field.

3. Click **any cell** in the Retail field, then click the **Sort Descending button** 🔼 on the Table Datasheet toolbar

    The records are sorted in descending order on the value in the Retail field. The CD that sells for the highest retail price, "Skyline Firedance," is listed as the first record. To put the records back in their original order, you can click the key field, RecordingID, and click the Sort Ascending button. Access also lets you find all records based on any search word.

4. Click **any cell** in the Title field, then click the **Find button** 🔍 on the Table Datasheet toolbar

    The Find and Replace dialog box opens. You know MediaLoft will want to find the titles that are going to be hot sellers during the Christmas season.

5. Type **Christmas** in the Find What text box, click the **Match list arrow**, then click **Any Part of Field**, as shown in Figure B-14

    Access will find all occurrences of the word "Christmas" in the Title field, whether it is the first, middle, or last part of the title. "Christmas" is the search criteria.

6. Click **Find Next**, then if necessary drag the Find and Replace dialog box up and to the right to better view the datasheet

    If you started the search at the top of the datasheet, "A Family Christmas" is the first title found. You can look for more occurrences of "Christmas."

7. Click **Find Next** to find the next occurrence of the word "Christmas," then click **Find Next** as many times as it takes to move through all the records

    When no more occurrences of the search criteria "Christmas" are found, Access lets you know that no more matching records can be found.

8. Click **OK** when prompted that Access has finished searching the records, then click **Cancel** to close the Find and Replace dialog box

RecordingID	Title	Artist	Category	Label	Format	Tracks
55	A Christmas Album	Grant, Amy	Folk	Reunion Records	CD	11
46	A Family Christmas	Tesh, John	New Age	GTS Records	CD	14
32	A Winter's Solstice	Windham Hill Artists	New Age	Windham	CD	10
53	Abbey Road	Beatles, The	Rock	Capitol Records	Vinyl	14
22	Autumn	Winston, George	New Age	Windham	Vinyl	7
51	Blue	Mitchell, Joni	Rock	Liberty Records	CD	10
16	Can We Go Home Now	Roches, The	Folk	Ryko	CD	11
35	Christmas	Mannheim Steamroller	New Age	Sony Music	CD	11
28	Christmas to Christmas	Greenwood, Lee	Country	MCA Records	CD	10
31	Closeup	Sandborn, David	Jazz	MCA Records	Cassette	10
2	Come Walk With Me	Adams, Oleta	Gospel	CBS Records	CD	10
54	Cosmic Thing	B-52s	Rock	Warner Records	CD	10
37	Cracked Rear View	Hootie and the Blowfi	Rock	Arista	CD	11
13	Daydream	Carey, Mariah	Rock	Columbia	CD	12
52	Decade	Young, Neil	Rock	A&M Records	CD	10
20	December	Winston, George	New Age	Windham	CD	12
26	Fantasia	Stokowski, Leopold	Classical	Buena Vista Records	CD	6
40	Favorite Overtures	Bernstein, Leonard	Classical	CBS Records	Vinyl	5
39	Foreign Affair	Turner, Tina	Rock	Capitol Records	Vinyl	12

Record: 1 of 58

Records are sorted in
ascending order by Title

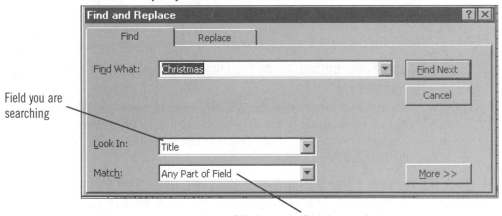

Field you are
searching

Tells Access to find the search
criteria anywhere in the selected field

Sorting on more than one field

The telephone book sorts records by last name (**primary sort field**) and when ties occur on the last name (for example, two "Smiths"), it further sorts the records by first name (**secondary sort field**). Access allows you to sort by more than one field using the query object, which you will learn more about later in this unit. Queries allow you to specify more than one sort field in Query Design view, evaluating the sort orders from left to right (the leftmost sort field is the primary sort field).

Filtering Records

Sorting allows you to reorder all the records of a datasheet. Filtering the datasheet displays only those records that match criteria. **Criteria** are rules or limiting conditions you set. For example, you may want to show only those records where the Category field is equal to "Rap," or where the PurchasePrice field is less than $10. Once you have filtered a datasheet to display a subset of records, you can still sort the records and find data just as if you were working with the entire datasheet. To make sure the Filter By Form grid is clear of any previous entries, you should click the Clear Grid button ☒. ▀▀▀ The Accounting department asked John for a printout of cassettes with a retail price of $15 or more. John uses the datasheet's filter buttons to answer this request.

Steps

1. In the Music Inventory datasheet, click the **RecordingID** field, click the **Sort Ascending button** ⬇ on the Table Datasheet toolbar, click any occurrence of **Cassette** in the Format field, then click the **Filter By Selection button** ▼ on the Table Datasheet toolbar
   Twelve records are selected, as shown in Figure B-15. Filter By Selection is a fast and easy way to filter the records for an exact match (that is, where Format field value is *equal to* Cassette). To filter for comparative data and to specify more complex criteria (for example, where PurchasePrice is *equal to* or *greater than* $15), you must use the Filter By Form feature. See Table B-3 for more information on comparison operators.

QuickTip

If you click the Field List arrow, you can pick an entry from a list of existing entries in that field.

2. Click the **Filter By Form button** 🖼 on the Table Datasheet toolbar, click the **Retail** field, then type **>=15**
   The finished Filter By Form window is shown in Figure B-16. The previous Filter By Selection criteria, "Cassette" in the Format field, is still valid in the grid. Access distinguishes between text and numeric entries by placing quotation marks around text entries. You can widen a column to display the entire criteria. Filter By Form is more powerful than Filter By Selection because it allows you to use comparison operators such as >=. Filter By Form also allows you to enter criteria for more than one field at a time where *both* criteria must be "true" in order for the record to be shown in the resulting datasheet.

3. Click the **Apply Filter button** ▼ on the Filter/Sort toolbar, then scroll to the right to display the Retail field
   Only two records are true for both criteria, as shown in Figure B-17. The Record Navigation buttons in the lower-left corner of the datasheet display how many records are in the filtered subset. You can remove the current filter to view all the records in the datasheet at any time by clicking the Remove Filter button.

4. Click the **Remove Filter button** ▼ on the Table Datasheet toolbar
   Be sure to remove existing filters before you apply a new filter or you will end up filtering the existing subset of records versus the entire datasheet. Next find all selections produced under the "A&M Records" recording label.

5. Click **any cell** in the Label field, click ⬇, **A&M Records** is selected as the Label entry, then click ▼
   Using both the sort and filter buttons, you quickly found the five records that met the "A&M Records" criteria.

6. Close the datasheet, then click **Yes** if prompted to save the changes to the Music Inventory table
   Any filters applied to a datasheet will be removed the next time you open the datasheet, but the sort order will be saved.

FIGURE B-15: **Music Inventory datasheet filtered for "Cassette" records**

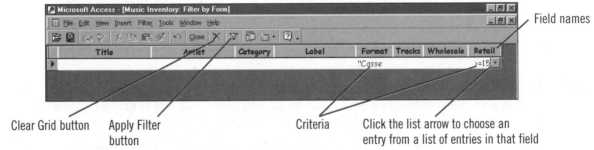

12 records are selected

All records have Cassette in Format field

FIGURE B-16: **Filter By Form grid**

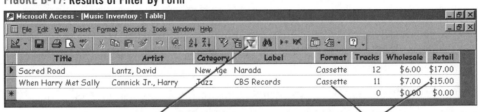

Field names

Clear Grid button   Apply Filter button

Criteria   Click the list arrow to choose an entry from a list of entries in that field

FIGURE B-17: **Results of Filter By Form**

Filter is applied and the Apply Filter button becomes the Remove Filter button

Both records have Cassette in the Format field and all records have a Retail value >=15

TABLE B-3: **Comparison operators**

operator	description	expression	meaning
>	Greater than	>500	Numbers greater than 500
>=	Greater than or equal to	>=500	Numbers greater than or equal to 500
<	Less than	<"Bunin"	Names from A through Bunim, but not Bunin
<=	Less than or equal to	<="Calloway"	Names from A through, and including, Calloway
<>	Not equal to	<>"Cyclone"	Any name except for Cyclone

Searching for blank fields

Is Null and **Is Not Null** are two other types of common criteria. Is Null criteria will find all records where no entry has been made in the field.

Is Not Null will find all records where there is any entry in the field, even if the entry is 0. Primary key fields cannot have a null entry.

Creating a Query

A **query** is a database object that creates a datasheet of specified fields and records from one or more tables. It displays the answer to a "question" about the data in your database. You can edit, navigate, sort, find, and filter a query's datasheet just like a table's datasheet. Because a query datasheet is a subset of data, however, it is similar to a filter, but much more powerful. One of the most important differences is that a query is a saved object within the database, which means that it does not need to be recreated each time you want to see that particular subset of data. A **filter** is a temporary view of the data whose criteria is discarded when you remove the filter or close the datasheet. Table B-4 compares the two. ▬▬▬▬ John uses a query to correct data in the table and then find all of the music selections in the "country" category.

Steps 1 2 3 4

1. **Click Queries on the Objects bar, then double-click Create query by using wizard**
   The Simple Query Wizard dialog box opens, allowing you to choose the table or query which contains the fields you want to display in the query. You select the fields in the order you want them to appear on the query datasheet.

> **QuickTip**
> You also can double-click a field to move it from the Available Fields list to the Selected Fields list.

2. **Click Category in the Available Fields list, click the Select Single Field button** [>], **click Title, click** [>], **click Artist, click** [>], **click Tracks, then click** [>]
   The Simple Query Wizard dialog box should look like Figure B-18.

3. **Click Next, click Next to accept the Detail option in the next dialog box, accept the title Music Inventory Query, make sure the Open the query to view information option button is selected, then click Finish**
   The query's datasheet opens, as shown in Figure B-19, with all 58 records, but with only the four fields that you requested in the query wizard. You can use a query datasheet to edit or add information.

> **QuickTip**
> The sort, filter, and find buttons work the same way whether you are working with a query or table datasheet.

4. **Double-click 10 in the Tracks cell for record 7, "No Words", then type 11**
   This record is now correct in the database.

5. **Click the Design View button** 🖾 **on the Query Datasheet toolbar**
   The **Query Design view** opens, showing you a list of fields in the Music Inventory table in the upper portion of the window, and the fields you have requested for the query in the **query design grid** in the lower portion of the window.

6. **Click the Criteria cell for the Category field, then type country, as shown in Figure B-20**
   Query Design view is the view in which you add, delete, or change the order of fields, sort the records, or add criteria to limit the number of records shown in the resulting datasheet. Any change made in Query Design view is saved with the query object.

7. **Click the Datasheet View button** 🖩 **on the Query Design toolbar**
   The resulting datasheet has four records that match the criteria "country" in the Category field. You can save a query with a name that accurately describes the resulting datasheet.

> **QuickTip**
> The only time you need to save changes in an Access database is when you make structural changes to an object in Design view.

8. **Click File on the menu bar, click Save As, type Country Music in the Save Query 'Music Inventory Query' To text box, click OK, then close the query datasheet**
   Both the Music Inventory Query and Country Music queries are saved in this database as objects that you can access in the MediaLoft-B database window.

FIGURE B-18: Simple Query Wizard dialog box

The available fields come from this object

Select Single Field button

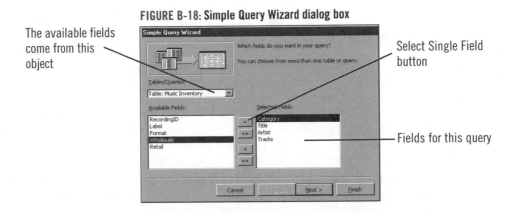

Fields for this query

FIGURE B-19: Music Inventory Query datasheet

Design View button

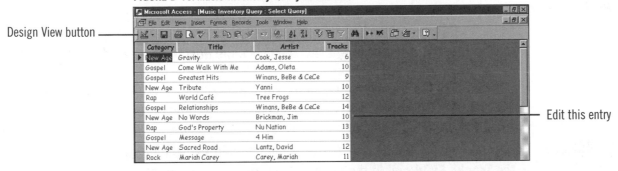

Edit this entry

FIGURE B-20: Query Design view

Datasheet View button

Music Inventory field list

Criteria cell for Category field with country criteria

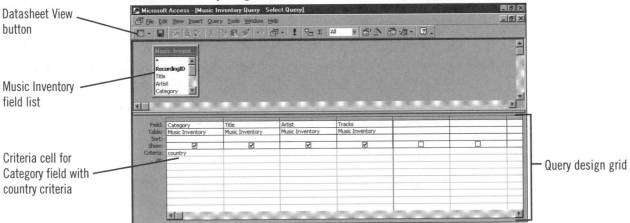

Query design grid

TABLE B-4: Queries vs. filters

characteristics	filters	queries
Are saved as an object in the database	No	Yes
Can be used to select a subset of records in a datasheet	Yes	Yes
Can be used to select a subset of fields in a datasheet	No	Yes
Its resulting datasheet can be used to enter and edit data	Yes	Yes
Its resulting datasheet can be used to sort, filter, and find records	Yes	Yes
Is commonly used as the source of data for a form or report	No	Yes
Can calculate sums, averages, counts, and other types of summary statistics across records	No	Yes
Can be used to create calculated fields	No	Yes

Access 2000

USING TABLES AND QUERIES   ACCESS B-17

Using Query Design View

Every object in the database has a Design view in which you change the structure of the object. You can build a query by using the Query Design view directly or let the Query Wizard help you. In either case, if you want to add criteria to limit the number of records that you view in the datasheet, or if you want to change the fields you are viewing, you must use the query's Design view. ⬚⬚⬚ John wants the Country Music query to also display the Retail field. In addition, he wants to add the folk music records and sort all the records according to the recording artist.

Steps

1. **Click the Country Music query** in the MediaLoft-B Database window, click the **Design button** 📐 in the database window, then click the **Restore button** 🖼 (if the window is maximized)
   Query Design view opens, displaying the current fields and criteria for the Country Music query. To add fields to the query, you can drag the fields from the upper field list and place them in any order in the grid.

   Trouble?
   You may have to scroll through the Music Inventory field list to display the Retail field.

2. **Click the Retail field** in the Music Inventory field list, then drag the **Retail field** to the **Tracks Field cell** in the query design grid
   The Query Design view now looks like Figure B-21. The Retail field is added to the query design grid between the Artist and Tracks fields. When you dropped the Retail field into the fourth column position of the query design grid, the Tracks field moved to the right to make room for the new field. You can also change the order of existing fields in the query design grid.

   QuickTip
   To remove fields from the query design grid, click the field selector, then press [Delete].

3. **In the second column, click Title**, click the **Title list arrow**, click **Artist**, click **Artist** in the third column, click the **Artist list arrow**, then click **Title**
   You have switched the order of the Title and Artist fields. You can also move fields by dragging them left and right in the query design grid by clicking the field selector, and dragging the field to the new location. The query design grid also displays criteria that limit the number of records in the resulting datasheet.

4. **Click the or: criteria cell** under the "country" criteria of the Category field, then type **folk**
   This additional criteria expression will add the folk selections to the current country selections. You also can enter Or criteria in one cell of the query design grid by entering "country" or "folk," but using two rows of the query design grid inherently joins the criteria in an Or expression.

5. **Click the Sort cell** for the Artist field, click the **Artist Sort list arrow**, then click **Ascending**
   The final Query Design view, as shown in Figure B-22, will find all records that match the Category criteria for "country" or "folk" and sort the records in ascending order by Artist. Notice that text criteria in the query design grid are surrounded by quotation marks (as were filter criteria), but that you did not need to type these characters.

6. **Click the Datasheet view button** 📄 on the Query Design toolbar
   Eight records are displayed in both the country and folk music categories, sorted in ascending order by Artist, as shown in Figure B-23.

7. **Click File** on the menu bar, click **Save As**, type **Country and Folk**, click **OK**, then click the **Print button** 🖨 on the Query Datasheet toolbar

8. **Close the query datasheet**, close the MediaLoft-B database, then exit Access

FIGURE B-21: Query Design view with new field, Retail

Scroll bar for Music Inventory field list

Field selector

Retail field in Field cell in the fourth column

Tracks field moved to the right

Field list arrow

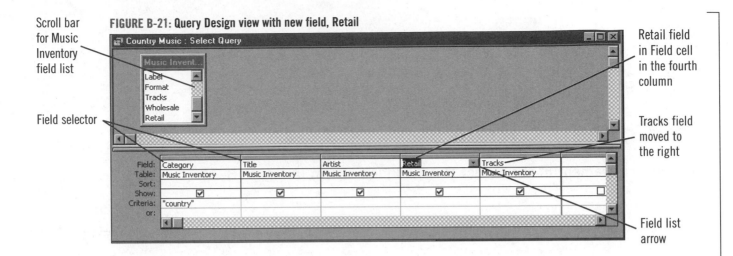

FIGURE B-22: Adding Or criteria and specifying a sort order

Field order of Artist and Title fields is changed

Or criteria for the Category field

Sort list arrow

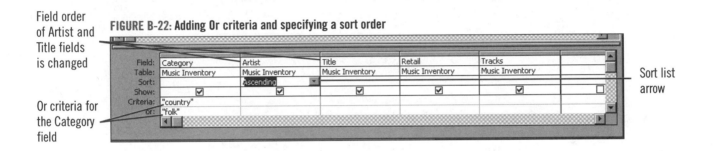

FIGURE B-23: Final query datasheet

Only Country or Folk records are displayed

Records are sorted in ascending order by Artist

Eight records are selected

Category	Artist	Title	Retail	Tracks
Country	Brooks, Garth	Garth Brooks Live	$10.00	10
Country	Brooks, Garth	The Chase	$12.00	10
Folk	Grant, Amy	A Christmas Album	$15.00	11
Folk	Grant, Amy	Heart in Motion	$13.00	11
Country	Greenwood, Lee	Christmas to Christmas	$15.00	10
Folk	Roches, The	Can We Go Home Now	$12.00	11
Folk	Roches, The	The Roches	$11.00	10
Country	Yearwood, Trisha	The Song Remembers V	$15.00	10

Record: 1 of 8

Understanding And and Or criteria

Criteria placed on different rows of the query design grid are considered Or criteria. In other words, a record may be true for *either* row of criteria in order for it to be displayed on the resulting datasheet. Placing additional criteria in the *same* row, however, is considered the And criteria. For example, if "folk" were in the Category Criteria cell and >10 in the Retail Criteria cell, *both* criteria must be true in order for the record to be displayed in the resulting datasheet.

Practice

► Concepts Review

Label each element of the Select Query window shown in Figure B-24.

FIGURE B-24

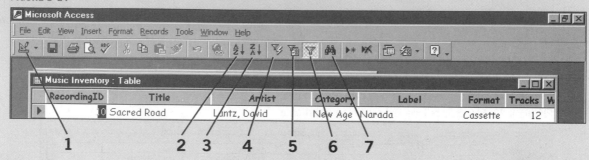

Match each term with the statement that describes it.

8. Primary key
9. Table Wizard
10. Filter
11. Data type
12. Query

a. Determines what type of data can be stored in each field
b. Provides interactive help to create the field names and data types for each field
c. A database object that creates a datasheet of specified fields and records from one or more tables
d. A field that contains unique information for each record
e. Creates a temporary subset of records

Select the best answer from the list of choices.

13. Which data type would be best for a field that was going to store birth dates?
   a. Text
   b. Number
   c. AutoNumber
   d. Date/Time

14. Which data type would be best for a field that was going to store Web addresses?
   a. Text
   b. Memo
   c. OLE
   d. Hyperlink

15. Which data type would be best for a field that was going to store telephone numbers?
   a. Text
   b. Number
   c. OLE
   d. Hyperlink

16. Each of the following is true about a filter, *except*
   a. It creates a temporary datasheet of records that match criteria.
   b. The resulting datasheet can be sorted.
   c. The resulting datasheet includes all fields in the table.
   d. A filter is automatically saved as an object in the database.

17. Sorting refers to
   a. Reorganizing the records in either ascending or descending order.
   b. Selecting a subset of fields and/or records to view as a datasheet from one or more tables.
   c. Displaying only those records that meet certain criteria.
   d. Using Or and And criteria in the query design grid.

18. **Which criteria would be used in a Category field to find all music except that in the rap category?**
    - **a.** /=/"rap"
    - **b.** <>"rap"
    - **c.** NULL "rap"
    - **d.** IS NULL "rap"

 Skills Review

1. **Plan a database.**
   - **a.** Plan a database that will contain the names and addresses of physicians. You can use the local yellow pages to gather the information.
   - **b.** On paper, sketch the Table Design view of a table that will hold this information. Write the field names in one column and the data types for each field in the second column.

2. **Create a table.**
   - **a.** Start Access and use the Blank Access database option to create a database. Save the file as "Doctors" on your Project Disk.
   - **b.** Use the Table Wizard to create a new table.
   - **c.** Make sure the Business option button is selected. In the Sample Tables list, click Contacts.
   - **d.** In the Sample Fields list box, choose each of the fields in the following order for your table: ContactID, FirstName, LastName, Address, City, StateOrProvince, PostalCode, Title.
   - **e.** Rename the StateOrProvince field as "State."
   - **f.** Name the table "Addresses," and allow Access to set the primary key field.
   - **g.** Click the Modify the table design option button in the last Table Wizard dialog box, then click Finish.

3. **Use Table Design view.**
   - **a.** In the first available blank row, add a new field called "PhoneNumber" with a Text data type.
   - **b.** Change the Field Size property of the State field from 20 to 2.
   - **c.** Insert a field named "Suite" with a Text data type between the Address and City fields.
   - **d.** Add the description "M.D." or "D.O." to the Title field.
   - **e.** Save and close the Addresses table, then close the Doctors database, but don't exit Access.

4. **Format a datasheet.**
   - **a.** Open the Doctors-B database from your Project Disk. Open the Doctor Addresses table datasheet.
   - **b.** Change the font to Arial Narrow, and the font size to 9.
   - **c.** Change the gridline color to black, and change the vertical gridline to a transparent border.
   - **d.** Change the page orientation to landscape and all of the margins to 0.5". Preview the datasheet (it should fit on one page), then print it.

5. **Understand sorting, filtering, and finding.**
   - **a.** On a sheet of paper, identify three ways that you might want to sort an address list, such as the Doctor Addresses datasheet. Be sure to specify both the field you would sort on and the sort order (ascending or descending).
   - **b.** On a sheet of paper, identify three ways that you might want to filter an address list, such as the Doctor Addresses datasheet. Be sure to specify both the field you would filter on and the criteria that you would use.

6. **Sort records and find data.**
   - **a.** Sort the Doctor Addresses records in ascending order on the Last field, then list the first two doctors on paper.
   - **b.** Sort the Doctor Addresses records in descending order on the Zip field, then list the first two doctors on paper.
   - **c.** Find the records in which the Title field contains "D.O." How many records did you find?
   - **d.** Find the records where the Zip field contains "64012." How many records did you find?

7. Filter records.

a. In the Doctor Addresses datasheet, filter the records for all physicians with the Title "D.O."

b. In the Doctor Addresses datasheet, filter the records for all physicians with the title "M.D." in the "64012" zip code, then print the datasheet.

8. Create a query.

a. Use the Query Wizard to create a new query based on the Doctor Addresses table with the following fields: First, Last, City, State, Zip.

b. Name the query "Doctors in Missouri," then view the datasheet.

c. In Query Design view, add the criteria "MO" to the State field, then view the datasheet.

d. Change Mark Garver's last name to Garvey.

9. Use Query Design view.

a. Modify the Doctors in Missouri query to include only those doctors in Kansas City, Missouri. Be sure that the criteria is in the same row so that both criteria must be true for the record to be displayed.

b. Save the query with the name "Doctors in Kansas City Missouri." Print the query results, then close the query datasheet.

c. Modify the Doctors in Kansas City Missouri query so that the records are sorted in ascending order on the last name, and add "DoctorNumber" as the first field in the datasheet.

d. Print and save the sorted query's datasheet, then close the datasheet.

e. Close the Doctors-B database and exit Access.

▶ Independent Challenges

1. You want to start a database to track your personal video collection.
To complete this independent challenge:

a. Start Access and create a new database called "Movies" on your Project Disk.

b. Using the Table Wizard, create a table based on the Video Collection sample table in the personal category with the following fields: MovieTitle, YearReleased, Rating, Length, DateAcquired, PurchasePrice.

c. Rename the YearReleased field as "Year" and the PurchasePrice field as "Price."

d. Name the table "Video Collection," and allow Access to set a primary key field.

e. Modify the Video Collection table in Design view with the following changes:
- Change the Rating field size property to 4.
- Change the Length field to a Number data type.
- Change the DateAcquired field name to DatePurchased.
- Add a field between Rating and Length called "PersonalRating" with a Number data type.
- In the description of the PersonalRating field, type: My personal rating on a scale from 1 (bad) to 10 (great).

f. Save and close the Video Collection table, and close the Movies database.

2. You work for a marketing company that sells medical supplies to doctors' offices.
To complete this independent challenge:

a. Open the Doctors-B database on your Project Disk, then open the Doctors Addresses table datasheet.

b. Filter the records to find all those physicians who live in Grandview, then print the filtered datasheet.

c. Sort the records by last name, change the font size to 12, resize the columns so all the data within each column is visible, change the page orientation to landscape, then print the datasheet.

d. Using the Query Wizard, create a query with the following fields: First, Last, Phone.

e. Name the query "Telephone Query." Sort the records in ascending order by last name, then print the datasheet.

f. Add the Title field to the third field position, then delete the First field. Save and close the query.

g. Modify the Telephone Query so that the State field is added to the fourth field position. Add criteria so that only those physicians in Missouri are shown on the resulting datasheet.

h. Print, save, and close the query. Close the Doctors-B database, then exit Access.

3. You want to create a database to keep track of your personal contacts.
To complete this independent challenge:

a. Start Access and create a new database called "People" on your Project Disk.

b. Using the Table Wizard, create a table based on the Addresses sample table in the Personal category with the following fields: FirstName, LastName, SpouseName, Address, City, StateOrProvince, PostalCode, EmailAddress, HomePhone, Birthdate.

c. Name the table Contact Info, allow Access to set the primary key field, and choose the Enter data directly into the table option in the last Table Wizard dialog box.

d. Enter at least five records into the table, making sure that two people have the same last name. Use your name for one of the records. You do not have to enter real names and addresses into the other records.

e. Press [Tab] to move through the Contact InfoID field.

f. Sort the records in ascending order by last name.

g. Adjust the column widths, change the datasheet margins, change the paper orientation, and make other adjustments, as necessary, to print the five records on one page.

h. Using the Query Wizard, create a query with the following fields from the Contact Info table in this order: LastName, FirstName, Birthdate.

i. Name the query Birthday List, and in Query Design view, sort the records in ascending order by LastName and then by FirstName.

j. Save the query as Sorted Birthday List, then view the query.

k. Change the Birthdate field to 8/20/58 for one of the records in the query datasheet.

l. Print the query's datasheet, close the query, then close the People database and exit Access.

4. MediaLoft has developed a Web site that provides information about their products and allows viewers to vote for their favorite music collections. In this exercise, you will print the Web page from the MediaLoft intranet site that records the People's choice awards. Then you will enter that information in the database, and create a query that displays only the top records.

a. Connect to the Internet, and use your browser to go to the MediaLoft intranet site at http://www.course.com/illustrated/medialoft

b. Click the link for Products to go to the Web page summarizing the most popular music selection in several categories as determined by a recent vote of customers.

c. Print the People's Choice Web page, then disconnect from the Internet.

d. Open the MediaLoft-B database, and then open the Music Inventory table in Design view.

e. Add a field called PeoplesChoice at the end of the field list with a Yes/No data type.

f. Find the six records listed on the People's Choice Web page (*Hint*: Use the Find and Sort buttons). Then place a checkmark in the PeoplesChoice field in your database for the six records to indicate that they were contest winners.

g. Using the Query Wizard, create a query that is based on the Music Inventory table with the following fields: Category, Title, Artist, Retail, PeoplesChoice.

h. Show all the Detail records, name the query "Peoples Choice Query," then modify the query so that only those records with "Yes" in the PeoplesChoice field are displayed.

i. Save and print the Peoples Choice Query datasheet.

j. Close the Peoples Choice Query, close the MediaLoft-B database, then exit Access.

Open the MediaLoft-B database and create a query based on the Music Inventory table that displays the datasheet

Access 2000

▶ Visual Workshop

Open the MediaLoft-B database and create a query based on the Music Inventory table that displays the datasheet shown in Figure B-25. Notice that only the Jazz category is displayed and that the records are sorted in a descending order on the Retail field. Save the query as "Jazz Selections" in the MediaLoft-B database.

FIGURE B-25

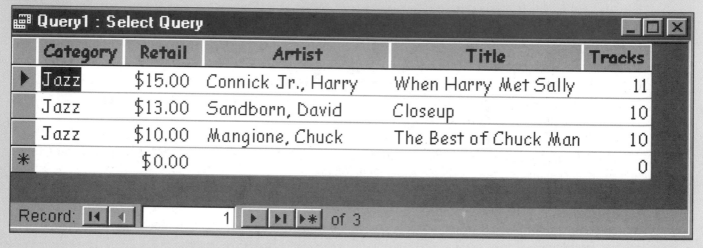

Using

Forms

Objectives

- ► **Plan a form**
- ⌐MOUS⌐ ► **Create a form**
- ⌐MOUS⌐ ► **Move and resize controls**
- ⌐MOUS⌐ ► **Modify labels**
- ⌐MOUS⌐ ► **Modify text boxes**
- ► **Modify tab order**
- ⌐MOUS⌐ ► **Enter and edit records**
- ⌐MOUS⌐ ► **Insert an image**

A **form** is an Access database object that allows you to arrange the fields of a record in any layout. Although the datasheet view of a table or query can be used to navigate, edit, and enter new information, all of the fields for one record are sometimes not visible unless you scroll left or right. A form fixes that problem by using the screen to show the fields of only one record at a time. Forms are often the primary object used to enter, edit, and find data. ⟣━━ More people are becoming excited about the MediaLoft music inventory database. They have asked John Kim to create a form to make it easier to access, enter, and update this important inventory data.

Planning a Form

Properly organized and well-designed forms make a tremendous difference in the productivity of the end user. Since forms are the primary object used to enter and edit data, time spent planning a form is time well spent. Forms are often built to match a **source document** (for example, an employment application or a medical history form) to facilitate fast and accurate data entry. Now, however, it is becoming more common to type data directly into the database rather than first recording it on paper. Form design considerations, such as clearly labeled fields and appropriate formatting, are important. Other considerations include how the user tabs from field to field, and what type of **control** is used to display the data. See Table C-1 for more information on form controls. ➤ John considers the following form design considerations when planning his Music Inventory form.

Details

 Determine the overall purpose of the form
Have a good understanding of what information you need to gather through the form. This purpose often becomes the form's title such as "Music Inventory Entry Form."

 Determine the underlying record source
The **record source** is either a table or query object, and contains the fields and records that the form will display.

 Gather the source documents used to design your form, or sketch the form by hand if a paper form does not exist
When sketching the form, be sure to list all the fields and instructions you want the form to display.

 Determine the best type of control to use for each element on the form
Figures C-1 and C-2 show examples of several controls. **Bound controls** display data from the underlying record source and are also used to edit and enter new data. **Unbound controls** do not change from record to record and exist only to clarify or enhance the appearance of the form.

TABLE C-1: Form Controls

name	used to:	bound or unbound
Label	Provide consistent descriptive text as you navigate from record to record	Unbound
Text box	Display, edit, or enter data for each record from an underlying record source	Bound
List box	Display a list of possible data entries	Bound
Combo box	Display a list of possible data entries for a field, and also provide text box for an entry from the keyboard; a "combination" of the list box and text box controls	Bound
Tab control	Create a three-dimensional aspect to a form so that controls can be organized and displayed by clicking the "tabs"	Unbound
Check box	Display "yes" or "no" answers for a field; if the box is "checked" it displays "yes" information	Bound
Toggle button	Display "yes" or "no" answers for a field; if the button is "pressed," it displays "yes" information	Bound
Option button	Display a limited list of possible choices for field	Bound
Bound image control	Display OLE data, such as a picture	Bound
Unbound image control	Display picture or clip art that doesn't change as you navigate from record to record	Unbound
Line and Rectangle controls	Draw lines and rectangles on the form	Unbound
Command button	Provide an easy way to initiate a command or run a macro	Unbound

FIGURE C-1: Sample Form Controls

Tab controls

Option group

Labels

List box

Combo box

Text boxes

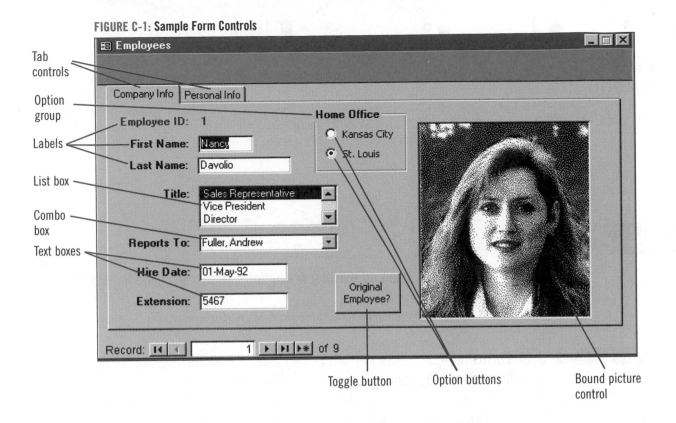

Toggle button   Option buttons   Bound picture control

FIGURE C-2: Sample Form Controls

Unbound image

Rectangle

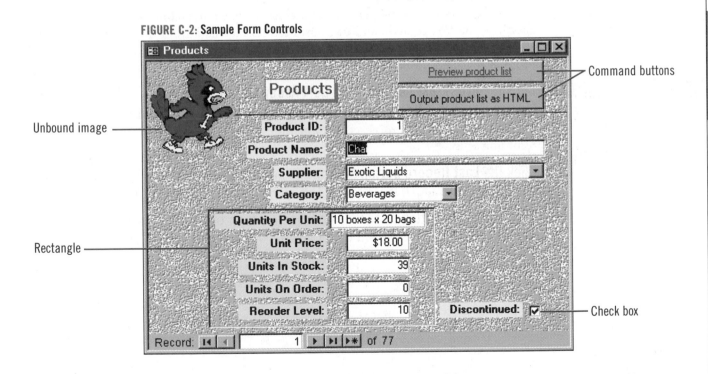

Command buttons

Check box

Creating a Form

You can create a form from scratch using **Form Design view**, or you can use the **Form Wizard** to create an initial form object that can be modified later if needed. The Form Wizard provides options for selecting fields, an overall layout, a style, and a form title. John created a sketch and made some notes on how he'd like the final Music Inventory form arranged, shown in Figure C-3. He uses the Form Wizard to get started.

Steps

1. Start Access, click the Open an existing file option button, then open the MediaLoft-C database from your Project Disk

This MediaLoft-C database contains an enhanced Music Inventory table. John added more fields and records.

QuickTip

To hide the Office Assistant, click Help on the menu bar, then click Hide Office Assistant.

2. Click Forms on the Objects bar in the MediaLoft-C Database window, then double-click Create form by using wizard

The Music Inventory table includes all of the fields required in the Music Inventory form.

3. Click the Select All Fields button [>>], click Next, click the Columnar layout option button, click Next, click the Standard style, click Next, then click Finish to accept the name Music Inventory for the form

The Music Inventory form opens in **Form view**, as shown in Figure C-4. Descriptive labels appear in the first column, and text boxes that display data from the underlying records appear in the second column. A check box control displays the yes/no data in the PeoplesChoice field. You can enter, edit, find, sort, and filter records using the form.

QuickTip

Sort, filter, and find buttons work the same way in a form as a datasheet, except that a form generally shows only one record at a time.

4. Click the Artist text box, click the Sort Ascending button [↑] on the Form View toolbar, then click the Next Record button [▶] to move to the second record

The "Adams, Oleta" record is second when the records are sorted in ascending order by recording artist.

5. Click the Last Record button [▶|] on the Music Inventory form

Neil Young's "Decade" is the last record when the records are sorted in ascending order.

6. Click the Close button on the Music Inventory form title bar to close the form

The new Music Inventory form object appears in the Forms section of the MediaLoft-C Database window.

Using AutoForm

You can quickly create a form by clicking a table or query object in the database window, and then clicking the New Object:AutoForm button [图] on the Database toolbar. AutoForm offers no prompts or dialog boxes; it instantly creates a form that displays all the fields in the previously chosen table or query using the same options as those you chose the last time you used the Form Wizard.

FIGURE C-3: Sketch of Music Inventory form

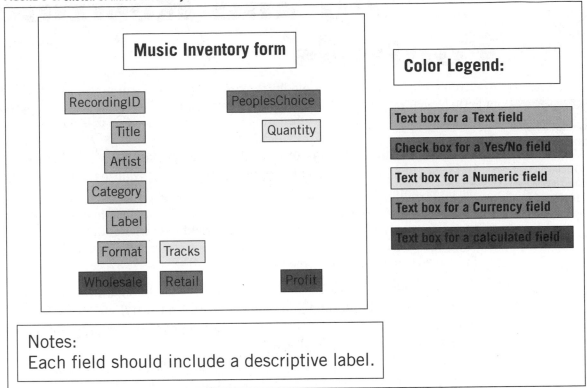

Music Inventory form

RecordingID   PeoplesChoice

Title   Quantity

Artist

Category

Label

Format   Tracks

Wholesale   Retail   Profit

Color Legend:

Text box for a Text field

Check box for a Yes/No field

Text box for a Numeric field

Text box for a Currency field

Text box for a calculated field

Notes:
Each field should include a descriptive label.

FIGURE C-4: Music Inventory form

Music Inventory form

Labels

Text boxes

Check box

Record Navigation buttons

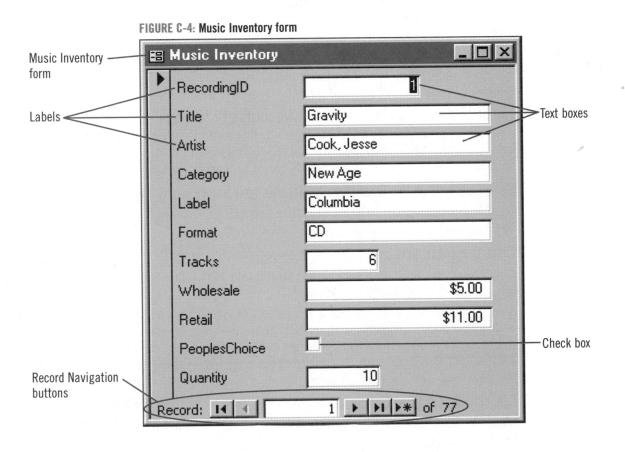

Access 2000

Moving and Resizing Controls

After you create a form, you can modify the size, location, and appearance of existing controls in Form Design view. Form Design view also allows you to add or delete controls. ➤ John moves and resizes the controls on the form to better match his original design.

Trouble?

Be sure you open the Design view of the Music Inventory form and not the Music Inventory table.

1. Click the **Music Inventory form**, click the **Design button** 🔧 in the MediaLoft-C Database window, then click the **Maximize button** to maximize the Design view of the Music Inventory form

The Design view of the Music Inventory form opens. The **Toolbox toolbar** contains buttons that allow you to add controls to the form. The **field list** contains the fields in the underlying object. You can toggle both of these screen elements on and off as needed. Widening the form gives you more room to reposition the controls.

2. Click the **Toolbox button** 🔧 on the Form Design toolbar to toggle it off (if necessary), click the **Field List button** 🔲 to toggle it off (if necessary), place the pointer on the right edge of the form, then when the pointer changes to ↔, drag the right edge to the **6"** mark on the horizontal ruler

The form is expanded so that it is 6" wide, as shown in Figure C-5. Before moving, resizing, deleting, or changing a control in any way, you must select it.

3. Click the **PeoplesChoice check box**

Squares, called **sizing handles**, appear in the corners and on the edges of the selected control. When you work with controls, the mouse pointer shape is very important. Pointer shapes are summarized in Table C-2.

Trouble?

If you make a mistake, immediately click the Undo button ↩ and try again.

4. Place the pointer on the **selected control**, when the pointer changes to ✋, drag the control so that the left edge of the label is at the **4"** mark on the horizontal ruler and the bottom edge is aligned with the **RecordingID text box**

The text boxes appear as white rectangles in this form. When you move a bound control, such as a text box or check box, the accompanying unbound label control to its left moves with it. The field name for the selected control appears in the Object list box.

QuickTip

You can move controls one pixel at a time by pressing [Ctrl] and an arrow key. You can resize controls one pixel at a time by pressing [Shift] and an arrow key.

5. Select and move the **Quantity** and **Tracks text boxes** using the ✋ pointer to match their final locations as shown in Figure C-6

Resizing controls also improves the design of the form.

6. Click the **Retail text box**, then use the ↔ pointer to drag the middle-right edge sizing handle left to the **2"** mark, click the **Wholesale text box**, then drag the middle-right edge sizing handle left to the **2"** mark

Moving and resizing controls requires great concentration and mouse control. Don't worry if your screen doesn't *precisely* match the next figure, but *do* make sure that you understand how to use the move and resize mouse pointers used in Form Design view. Precision and accuracy are naturally developed with practice, but even experienced form designers regularly rely on the Undo button.

7. Click the **Form View button** 🔳 on the Form Design toolbar, click the **Artist text box**, click the **Sort Descending button** 🔽, then click the **Sort Ascending button** 🔼 on the Form View toolbar

Your screen should look like Figure C-7.

FIGURE C-5: **Design view of the Music Inventory form**

Form View button

Horizontal ruler

Field List button

Labels

Vertical ruler

Text boxes

Toolbox button

6" mark

Right edge of form

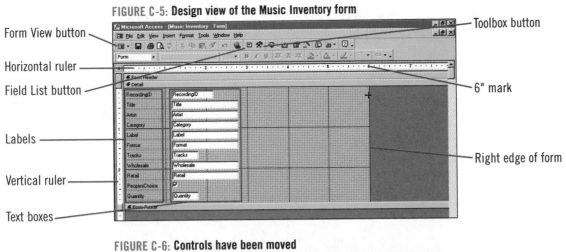

FIGURE C-6: **Controls have been moved**

Object list box

Text boxes have been moved

PeoplesChoice label and check box have been moved

"Move" mouse symbol

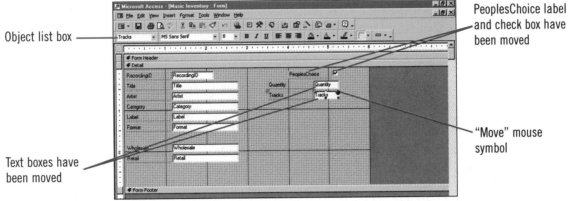

FIGURE C-7: **Reorganized Music Inventory form**

Check box

Text boxes

Labels

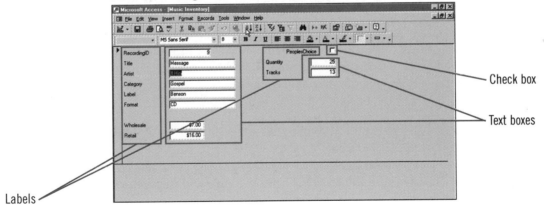

TABLE C-2: **Form Design view mouse pointer shapes**

shape	when does this shape appear?	action
⌖	When you point to any nonselected control on the form; it is the default mouse pointer	Single-clicking with this mouse pointer *selects* a control
🖐	When you point to the edge of a selected control (but not when you are pointing to a sizing handle)	Dragging this mouse pointer moves all selected controls
👆	When you point to the larger sizing handle in the upper-left corner of a selected control	Dragging this mouse pointer *moves only the single control* where pointer is currently positioned, not other controls that may also be selected
↔ ↕ ↖ ↗	When you point to any sizing handle (except the larger one in the upper-left corner)	Dragging this mouse pointer *resizes* the control

Modifying Labels

When you create a form with the Form Wizard, it places a label to the left of each text box with the field's name. Often, you'll want to modify those labels to be more descriptive or user friendly. You can modify a label control by directly editing it in Form Design view, or you can make the change in the label's property sheet. The **property sheet** is a comprehensive listing of all **properties** (characteristics) that have been specified for that control. John modifies the Music Inventory form's labels to be more descriptive.

Steps

Trouble?

If you double-click a label, you will open its property sheet. Close the property sheet by clicking its Close button, then single-click the label again.

1. **Click the Design View button** on the Form View toolbar, click the **RecordingID label** to select it, click between the **g** and **I** in the RecordingID label, then press **[Spacebar]** to insert a space

   Directly editing labels in Form Design view is tricky because you must select the label and then precisely click where you want to edit it. You can also open the label's property sheet and modify the Caption property to change the displayed text.

2. **Click the Title label**, click the **Properties button** on the Form Design toolbar, then click the **Format tab**, as shown in Figure C-8

   The Caption property controls the text displayed by the label control, and the property can be found on either the Format or the All tabs. The All tab is an exhaustive list of all the properties for a control.

Trouble?

Be sure to modify the Title label control and not the Title text box control. Text box controls must reference the *exact* field name in order to display the data within that field.

3. **Click to the left of Title** in the Caption property text box, type **Recording**, press **[Spacebar]**, then click to toggle the property sheet off

   Don't be overwhelmed by the number of properties available for each control on the form. Over time, you may want to learn about most of these properties, but in the beginning, you'll be able to make the vast majority of the property changes through menu and toolbar options rather than by accessing the property sheet itself. Labels can be aligned so that they are closer to their respective text boxes.

4. **Click the Recording ID label**, then click the **Align Right button** on the Formatting (Form/Report) toolbar

   The Recording ID label is now much closer to its associated text box. See Table C-3 for a list of techniques to quickly select several controls so that you can apply alignment and formatting changes to many controls simultaneously.

5. **Click the 0.5" mark** on the horizontal ruler to select the first column of controls, as shown in Figure C-9, then click

   All the labels in the first column are right-aligned and next to their text boxes.

6. **Click the Save button** on the Form Design toolbar, then click the **Form View button** on the Form Design toolbar

   The Music Inventory form is saved, and you can see that the labels are close to the data in the first column.

FIGURE C-8: Looking at a label's property sheet

Recording ID label has been changed

Title label is chosen

Caption property

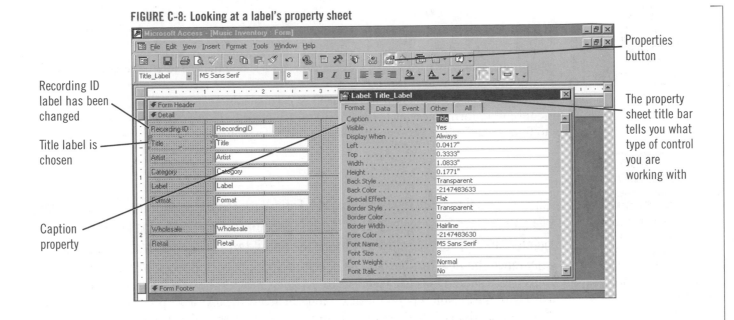

Properties button

The property sheet title bar tells you what type of control you are working with

FIGURE C-9: Selecting several labels at the same time

Clicking the 0.5" mark on the ruler

All labels in the first column are selected

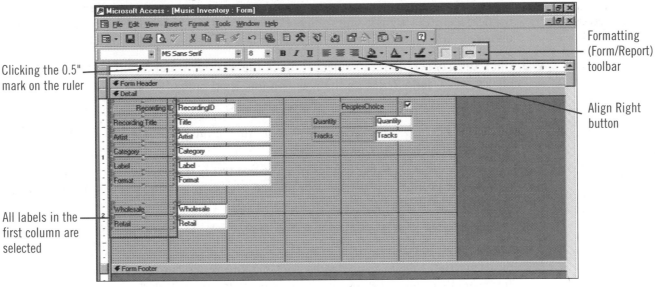

Formatting (Form/Report) toolbar

Align Right button

TABLE C-3: Selecting more than one control

technique	description
Click, [Shift]+click	Click a control, then press and hold [Shift] while clicking other controls; each one will be selected
Drag a selection box	If you drag a selection box (an imaginary box you create by dragging the pointer in Form Design view), every control that is in or touched by the edges of the box will be selected
Click in the ruler	If you click in either the horizontal or vertical ruler you will select all controls that intersect the selection line (an imaginary line you create by clicking the ruler)
Drag in the ruler	If you drag through either the horizontal or vertical ruler you will select all controls that intersect the selection line as it is dragged through the ruler

Modifying Text Boxes

Text boxes are generally used to display data from underlying fields and are therefore *bound* to that field. You can also use a text box as a **calculated control** which is not directly bound to a field but rather uses information from a field to calculate an answer. ✎ John wants the Music Inventory form to calculate the profit for each record. He uses a text box calculated control to find the difference between the Retail and Wholesale fields.

Steps 1 2 3 4

Trouble?

The Toolbox toolbar may be floating or docked on the edge of your screen. Drag the title bar of a floating toolbar or the top edge of a docked toolbar to move it to a convenient location.

1. **Click the Design View button ▣ on the Form View toolbar, click the Toolbox button ⚒ on the Form View toolbar, click the Text Box button ▣ on the Toolbox toolbar, the pointer changes to ⁺▣, click just below the Retail text box on the form, then if necessary move the new text box and label control to align with the controls above it**
Your screen should look like Figure C-10. Adding a new text box *automatically* added a new label with the default caption "Text22:". You can access the text box's property sheet to bind it to an underlying field or expression, or you can create the calculated expression directly in the text box.

Trouble?

The number in the caption "Text22" varies depending on how many controls you add to the form.

2. **Click Unbound in the new text box, type =[Retail]-[Wholesale], then press [Enter]**
When referencing field names within an expression, you *must* use square brackets and type the field name exactly as it appears in the Table Design view. You do not need to worry about uppercase and lowercase letters. The label for any expression should be descriptive.

3. **Click the Text22: label to select it, click the Text22: label again to edit it, double-click Text22, type Profit as the new caption, then press [Enter]**
The calculated text box control and associated label are modified.

Trouble?

If your calculated control did not work, return to Design view, click the calculated control, press [Delete], then repeat steps 1 through 4.

4. **Click the Form View button ▣ to view your changes, click the Ascending Sort button ▣ on the Form View toolbar**
Your screen should look like Figure C-11. The first record is $5 wholesale and sells for $11.00 retail so the profit is calculated as $6. You can use Form Design view to make a few more changes to clarify the form.

5. **Click ▣, click the Calculated text box, then click the Properties button ▣ on the Form Design toolbar**
By default, the values in text boxes that contain numeric and currency fields are right-aligned. Text boxes that contain fields with other data types or those that start as unbound controls are left-aligned. Monetary values should be right-aligned and display with a dollar sign and cents.

Trouble?

Properties are not listed in alphabetical order so you may have to scroll up or down the property sheet to find the Format and Text Align properties.

6. **Click the Format tab in the Text Box property sheet, click the Format property text box, click the Format property list arrow, scroll and click Currency, click the Text Align property text box, scroll and click the Text Align property list arrow, then click Right**

7. **Click the Properties button ▣, switch the position of the Retail and Wholesale text boxes, move and align the Profit label, resize the calculated text box (as shown in Figure C-12), then click the Form View button ▣**
The calculated profit value should display as $6.00 and be right-aligned within the text box.

FIGURE C-10: Adding a calculated text box

Toolbox button

Toolbox toolbar

Click to add a text box control

New label

New text box

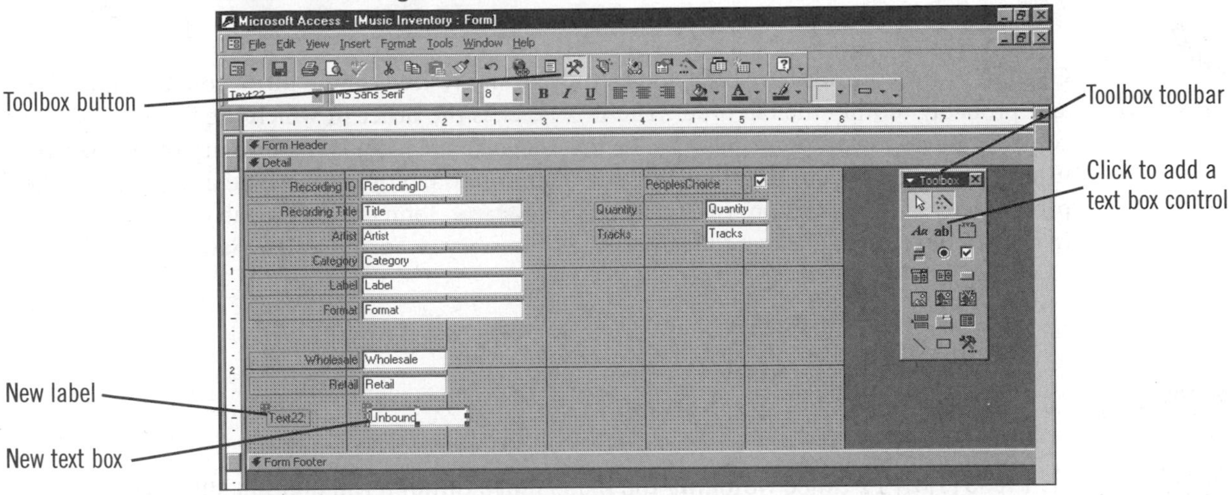

FIGURE C-11: Displaying a calculated text box

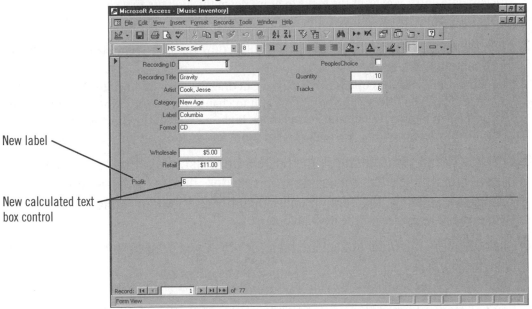

New label

New calculated text box control

FIGURE C-12: Updated Music Inventory form

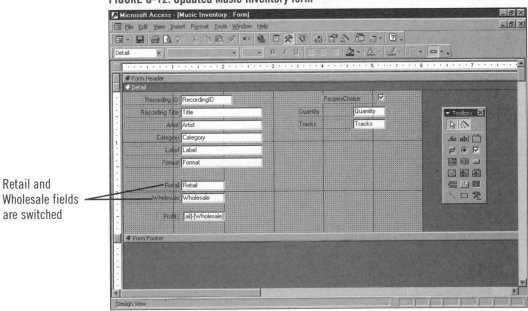

Retail and Wholesale fields are switched

Access 2000

Modifying Tab Order

Once all of the controls have been added, moved, and resized on the form, you'll want to check and probably modify the tab order. The **tab order** is the order in which the **focus** (the active control) moves as you press [Tab] in Form view. Since the form is the primary object by which users will view, edit, and enter data, careful attention to tab order is essential to maintain their productivity and satisfaction with the database. John checks the tab order of the Music Inventory form, then changes the tab order as necessary in Form Design view.

Steps

1. Press **[Tab]** 11 times watching the focus move through the bound controls of the form
Currently, focus moves back and forth between the left and right columns of controls. For efficient data entry, you want the focus to move down through the first column of text boxes before moving to the second column.

2. Click the **Design View button** 📐 on the Form View toolbar, click **View** on the menu bar, then click **Tab Order**
The Tab Order dialog box opens in which you can drag fields up or down to change their tab sequence. The Tab Order dialog box allows you to change the tab order of controls in three sections: Form Header, Detail, and Form Footer. Right now, all of the controls are positioned in the form's Detail section. See Table C-4 for more information on form sections.

3. Click the **Retail row selector** in the Custom Order list, drag it up to position it just below Format, click the **Wholesale row selector**, drag it under Retail, click the **Tracks row selector**, then drag it under Quantity as shown in Figure C-13
With the change made, test the new tab order.

4. Click **OK** in the Tab Order dialog box, then click the **Form View button** 📄 on the Form Design toolbar
Although nothing visibly changes on the form, the tab order is different.

5. Press **[Enter]** 10 times to move through the fields of the form with the new tab order
You should now be moving through all of the text boxes of the first column, with the exception of the calculated field, before you move to the second column.

6. Click the **Save button** 💾 on the Form View toolbar

FIGURE C-13: Tab Order dialog box

Tab Order
dialog box
with Detail
section
chosen

Form
Header
section

Detail
section

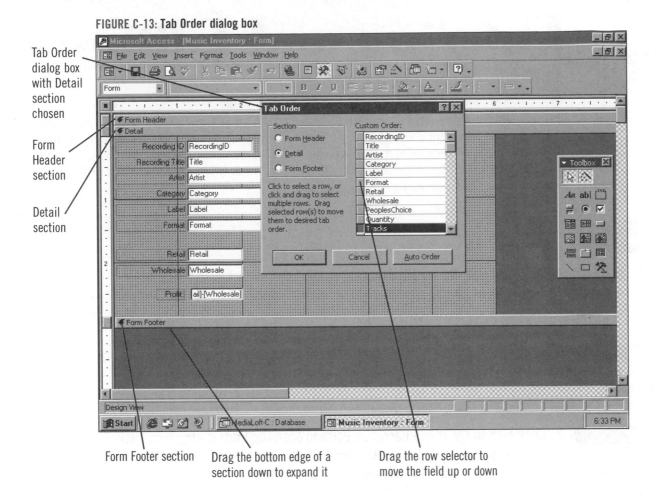

Form Footer section · Drag the bottom edge of a section down to expand it · Drag the row selector to move the field up or down

TABLE C-4: Form sections

section	description
Form Header	Controls placed in the Form Header print only once at the top of the printout; by default, this section is not "opened" in Form Design view, but can be expanded by dragging its bottom edge in Form Design view.
Detail	Controls placed in the Detail section print once for every record in the underlying table or query object; all controls created by the Form Wizard are placed in this section
Form Footer	Controls placed in the Form Footer print only once at the end of the printout; by default, this section is not "opened" in Form Design view, but it can be expanded by dragging its bottom edge down in Form Design view

Entering and Editing Records

The most important reasons for using a form are to find, enter, or edit records to the underlying object. You can also print a form, but you must be careful because printing a form often produces a very long printout because of the vertical orientation of the fields. ✍ John uses the Music Inventory form to add a new record to the underlying Music Inventory table. Then he prints the form with the data for only the new record.

Steps

1. Click the **New Record button** ⏭ on the Form View toolbar

A new, blank record is displayed. The text "(AutoNumber)" appears in the Recording ID field, which will automatically increment when you begin to enter data. The Specific Record box indicates the current record number.

2. Click the **Recording Title text box**, type **The Dance**, then enter the rest of the information shown in Figure C-14

Notice that the Profit text box shows the calculated result of $4.00. The new record is stored as record 78 in the Music Inventory table.

3. Click **File** on the menu bar, click **Print** to open the Print dialog box, click the **Selected Record(s) option button** in the Print Range section, then click **OK**

Forms are also often used to edit existing records in the database.

4. Click the **Recording Title text box**, click the **Find button** 🔍 on the Form View toolbar to open the Find and Replace dialog box, type **Mermaid Avenue** in the Find What text box, then click **Find Next**

Record 77 appears behind the Find and Replace dialog box, as shown in Figure C-15.

5. Click **Cancel** in the Find and Replace dialog box, press **[Tab]** five times to go to the Retail field, type **20**, then press **[Tab]**

Editing either the Wholesale or Retail fields automatically updates the calculated Profit field. Forms are also a great way to filter the records to a specific subset.

6. Click **Pop** in the Category text box, then click the **Filter By Selection button** 🔽 on the Form View toolbar

Twelve records were found that matched the "Pop" criteria. Previewing the records helps to determine how many pages the printout would be.

7. Click the **Print Preview button** 🔍 on the Form View toolbar

Since about three records print on a page, your printout would be four pages long.

8. Click the **Close button** on the Print Preview toolbar, then click the **Remove Filter button** 🔽 on the Form View toolbar so that all 78 records in the Music Inventory table are available

FIGURE C-14: Entering a new record into a form

Edit record symbol ——

Calculated text box
automatically
displays the answer

New Record
button

Current record number   New Record button

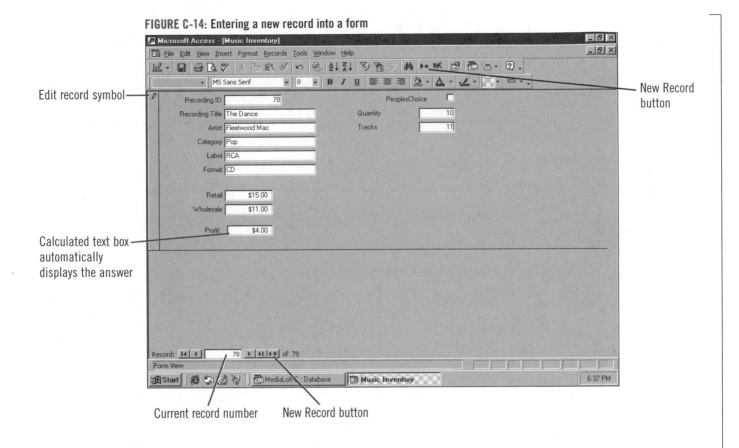

FIGURE C-15: Finding "Mermaid Avenue" using a form

Mermaid Avenue
found in Title field

Find button

Record 77

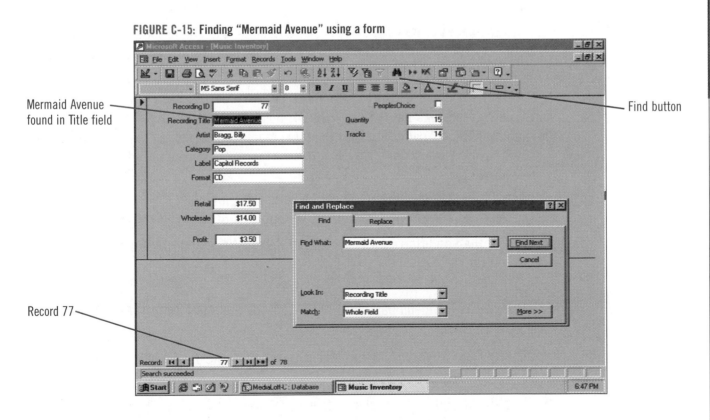

Inserting an Image

Graphic images, such as pictures, a logo, or clip art, can add style and professionalism to a form. If you add a graphic image as an unbound image to the Form Header, the image will appear at the top of the form in Form view and once at the top of the printout when printing records through a form. John adds the MediaLoft logo and a descriptive title to the Form Header section.

Steps

1. Click the **Design View button** on the Form View toolbar, place the pointer on the bottom edge of the Form Header, the pointer changes to **✛**, then drag the bottom of the Form Header section to the 1" mark on the vertical ruler
   The Form Header section is open.

2. Click the **Image button** on the Toolbox toolbar, the pointer changes to **⁺🖾**, then click in the **Form Header section** at the 1" mark on the horizontal ruler
   The Insert Picture dialog box opens. The MediaLoft image file you want to insert in the Form Header is on the Project Disk.

3. Click the **Look in list arrow**, click the drive containing your Project Disk, click **smallmedia**, then click **OK**
   The MediaLoft logo appears in the Form Header, surrounded by handles, as shown in Figure C-16. Form header titles add a finishing touch to a form.

QuickTip

If you need your name on the printed solution, enter your name as a label below the MediaLoft Music label.

4. Click the **Label button** on the Toolbox toolbar, the pointer changes to **⁺A**, click to the right of the **MediaLoft logo** in the Form Header section, type **MediaLoft Music**, then press **[Enter]**
   Labels can be formatted to enhance the appearance on the form.

5. Click the **Font Size list arrow**, click **24**, point to the **upper-right resizing handle**, then drag the **⤢** pointer so that the label **MediaLoft Music** is completely displayed
   If you double-click a label's sizing handle, the label will automatically adjust to display the entire caption.

6. Click the **Form View button** on the Form Design toolbar
   You can go directly to a specific record by typing the record number in the specific record box.

7. Click in the **specific record box** on the Record Navigation buttons, type **11**, then press **[Enter]**
   Compare your form with Figure C-17.

8. Click **File** on the menu bar, click **Print**, click the **Selected Record(s) option button**, then click **OK**

9. Click the **Close button** on the Music Inventory form, then click **Yes** to save any changes if necessary

10. Close the MediaLoft-C database, then exit Access

FIGURE C-16: Adding an image to the Form Header section

1" mark on the ruler

MediaLoft logo

Label button

Image button

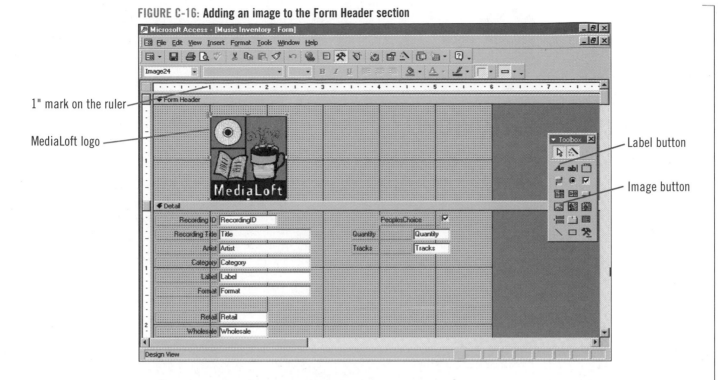

FIGURE C-17: The final Music Inventory form

MediaLoft logo

New label serves as form title

Form Header section

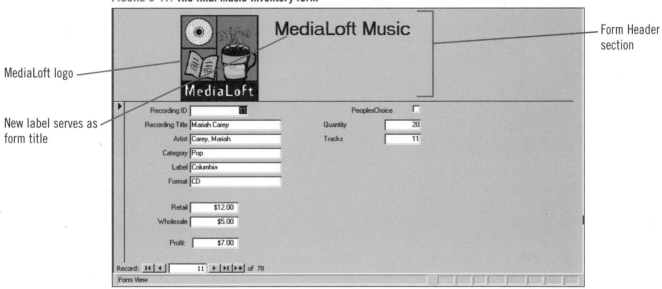

Creating a hyperlink from an image

Once an image is added to a form, you can convert it to a hyperlink by using its property sheet to modify the control's **Hyperlink Address** property in Form Design view. Depending on what you enter for the Hyperlink Address property, clicking the hyperlinked image in Form view opens another file, Access object, Web address, or e-mail address. For example, C:\Colleges\JCCCDescriptions.doc is the Hyperlink Address property entry to link a Word document at the specified drive and folder location; http://www.jccc.net creates a link between the image and the specified Web address.

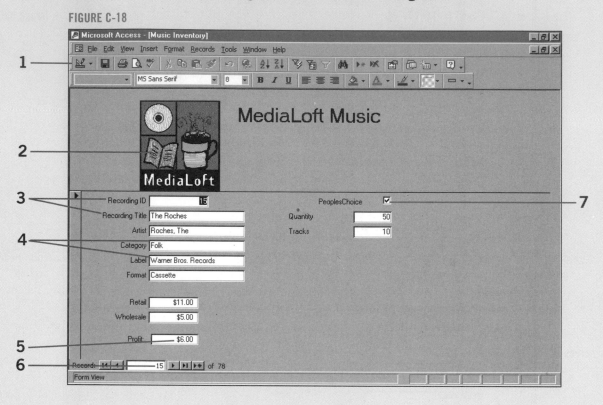

Practice

► Concepts Review

Label each element of the Form Design window shown in Figure C-18.

FIGURE C-18

Match each term with the statement that describes it.

- **8. Sizing handles**
- **9. Detail section**
- **10. Bound control**
- **11. Tab order**
- **12. Form**
- **13. Calculated control**

a. An Access database object that allows you to arrange the fields of a record in any layout; you use it to enter, edit, and delete records

b. Displays data from a field in the underlying record source

c. Black squares that appear in the corners and edges of the selected control

d. The way in which the focus moves from one bound control to the next

e. Uses a text box and an expression to display an answer

f. Controls placed here print once for every record in the underlying table or query object

Select the best answer from the list of choices.

14. Every element on a form is called a
- **a.** Property.
- **b.** Control.
- **c.** Piece.
- **d.** Handle.

15. The pointer used to resize a control is
- **a.** ⟷⟷
- **b.** ↔
- **c.** ✋
- **d.** 👆

16. The most common bound control is the
- **a.** Label.
- **b.** Text box.
- **c.** Combo box.
- **d.** Check box.

17. The most common unbound control is the
- **a.** Label.
- **b.** Text box.
- **c.** Combo box.
- **d.** Image.

18. The _____ view is used to modify form controls.
- **a.** Form
- **b.** Datasheet
- **c.** Print Preview
- **d.** Design

Skills Review

---

1. Plan a form.
a. Plan a form to use for the data entry of business contacts by looking at several business cards.
b. Write down the organization of the fields on the form. Determine what type of control you will use for each bound field.
c. Identify the labels you would like to display on the form.

2. Create a form.
a. Start Access and open the Membership-C database from your Project Disk.
b. Click the Forms button in the Membership-C Database window, then double-click the Create form by using wizard option.
c. Base the form on the Contacts table, and include all of the fields.
d. Use a Columnar layout, a Standard style, and title the form "Contact Entry Form."
e. Display the form with data.

3. Move and resize controls.
a. Open and maximize the Design View window for the Contact Entry Form.
b. Widen the form so that the right edge is at the 6" mark on the horizontal ruler.
c. Move the LNAME text box and corresponding label to the right of the FNAME text box.
d. Move the DUESOWED and DUESPAID text boxes and corresponding labels to the right of the address controls.
e. Resize the PHONE and ZIP text boxes to be the same size as the CITY text box.
f. Move the PHONE text box and corresponding label between the FNAME and COMPANY controls.

4. Modify labels.
a. Right align all of the labels.
b. Modify the FNAME label to FIRST NAME, the LNAME label to LAST NAME, the DUESOWED label to DUES OWED, and the DUESPAID label to DUES PAID.

5. Modify text boxes.
a. Add a new text box below the DUESPAID text box.
b. Type the expression =[DUESOWED]-[DUESPAID] in the new unbound text box. (*Hint*: Remember that you must use the *exact field names* in a calculated expression.)
c. In the property sheet for the new calculated control, change the Format property to Currency.
d. Right align the new calculated text boxes.
e. Change the calculated text box label from Text20: to BALANCE.
f. Move and resize the new calculated control and label so that it is aligned beneath the DUESOWED and DUES-PAID controls.

6. Modify tab order.
a. Change the Tab order so that pressing [Tab] moves the focus through the text boxes in the following order: FNAME, LNAME, PHONE, COMPANY, STREET, CITY, STATE, ZIP, DUESOWED, DUESPAID, BALANCE text box

7. Enter and edit records.

a. Use the Contact Entry Form to enter the following new records:

	FIRST NAME	LAST NAME	PHONE	COMPANY	STREET
Record 1	Jane	Eagan	555-1166	Cummins Construction	1515 Maple St.
Record 2	Mark	Daniels	555-2277	Motorola	1010 Green St.

	CITY	STATE	ZIP	DUES OWED	DUES PAID
1 con't.	Fontanelle	KS	50033-	$50.00	$25.00
2 con't.	Bridgewater	KS	50022-	$50.00	$50.00

b. Print the Mark Daniels record.

c. Find the Lois Goode record, enter IBM in the Company text box, then print that record.

d. Filter for all records with a Zip entry of 64145. How many records did you find?

e. Sort the filtered 64145 zip code records in ascending order by Last Name, then print the first one.

8. Insert an image.

a. In Form Design view, expand the Form Header section to the 1" mark on the vertical ruler.

b. Use the Image control to insert the handin1.bmp file found on your Project Disk in the Form Header.

c. Centered and below the graphic file, add the label MEMBERSHIP INFORMATION in a 24-point font. Be sure to resize the label so that all of the text is visible.

d. Add your name as a label in the Form Header section.

e. View the form using the Form view.

f. Print the selected record.

g. Close the form, close the database, then exit Access.

▶ Independent Challenges

1. As the office manager of a cardiology clinic, you need to create a new patient data entry form. To complete this independent challenge:

a. Open the Clinic-C database from your Project Disk.

b. Using the Form Wizard, create a form that includes all the fields in the Demographics table, using the Columnar layout and Standard style. Title the form "Patient Entry Form."

c. In Form Design view, widen the form to the 6" mark, then move the DOB, Gender, Ins Code, and Entry Date controls to a second column to the right of the existing column. DOB should be next to Last Name.

d. Switch the positions of the State and Zip controls.

e. Modify the Medical Record Number label to MR Number, the Address 1 label to Address, the DOB label to Birthday, and the Ins Code label to Insurance.

f. Change the tab order so State is above Zip.

g. Use the newly created form to add a record using your own personal information. Enter 2000 for the MR Number, BCBS for the Insurance, and 2/1/00 for the Entry Date.

h. Print the form with the new record you just added about yourself.

i. Close the Patient Entry Form, close the Clinic-C database, then exit Access.

2. As office manager of a cardiology clinic you want to build a form that quickly calculates a height to weight ratio value based on information in the Outcomes Data table.

    To complete this independent challenge:

a. Open the Clinic-C database from your Project Disk.

b. Using the Form Wizard, create a form based on the Outcomes Data table with only the following fields: MR#, Height, and Weight.

c. Use the Columnar layout and Standard style, and name the form "Height to Weight Ratio Form."

d. In Design view, widen the form to the 4" mark on the horizontal ruler, then add a text box to the right half of the form.

e. Close the Field list if necessary.

f. Enter the expression =[Height]/[Weight] in the unbound text box.

g. Modify the calculated expression's label from Text6: (the number may vary) to Ratio.

h. Resize the Ratio label so that it is closer to the calculated expression control, then right-align the Ratio label.

i. Change the format property of the calculated control to Fixed.

j. Open the form header and enter your name as a label.

k. View the form.

l. Print the form for the record for MR# 006494.

m. Sort the records in descending order by Height, then print the record with the tallest height entry.

n. Close the Height to Weight Ratio Form, close the Clinic-C database, then exit Access.

3. As office manager of a cardiology clinic you want to build a form to enter new insurance information.
    To complete this independent challenge:

a. Open the Clinic-C database from your Project Disk.

b. Using the Form Wizard, create a form based on the Insurance Company Information table, and include all of the fields.

c. Use the Columnar layout, Standard style, and accept the default title for the form "Insurance Company Information."

d. Change the label Insurance Company Name to just "Insurance Company."

e. Resize the State text box so that it is the same size as the City text box.

f. Expand the Form Header section, and add the graphic image Medical.bmp found on your Project Disk to the left side of the Form Header section.

g. Add a label "Insurance Entry Form" and another for your name to the right of the medical clip art in the Form Header section.

h. Increase the size of the Insurance Entry Form label to 18 points. Resize the label to display the entire caption.

i. Switch to Form view, then find and print the Cigna record.

j. Filter for all records with a State entry of KS. Print those records.

k. Close the Insurance Company Information Form, close the Clinic-C database, then exit Access.

4. As a new employee in the Market Research department for MediaLoft, you use the World Wide Web to find information on competitors' Web sites, specifically as it relates to Web-based forms.

To complete this independent challenge:

a. Connect to the Internet, use your browser to go to the MediaLoft intranet site at http://www.course.com/illustrated/ MediaLoft, then click the link for the Research Center.

b. Click the link for www.amazon.com, and explore its Web site until you find a Web-based form that requests information about you as a customer or an order that you'd like to place. Print that online form.

c. Use the MediaLoft Research Center to find the home pages of at least three other Internet-based book and/or music stores.

d. Find and print one Web-based data entry form from each of the three sites that you found.
(*Note*: You may have to pretend that you are actually making an online purchase in order to view and print these forms, so be sure to cancel the transaction if you do not intend to purchase any products. Never enter credit card or payment information if you are not serious about finalizing the sale.)

e. Disconnect from the Internet.

f. Draw a sketch to design a form that MediaLoft can use to take orders online. You can use the Music Inventory table in the MediaLoft database as your guide for product information.

g. List all the fields, the data types, and any labels and images for your order form.

► Visual Workshop

Using the Clinic-C database, create the form based on the Demographics table, as shown in Figure C-19. Notice that the label "Patient Form" is 24 points and has been placed in the Form Header section. The clip art, medstaff.bmp, can be found on the Project Disk. The image has been placed on the right side of the Detail section, and many controls had to be resized in order for it to fit. Also notice that the labels are right-aligned. You also need to correct the gender entry for this record.

FIGURE C-19

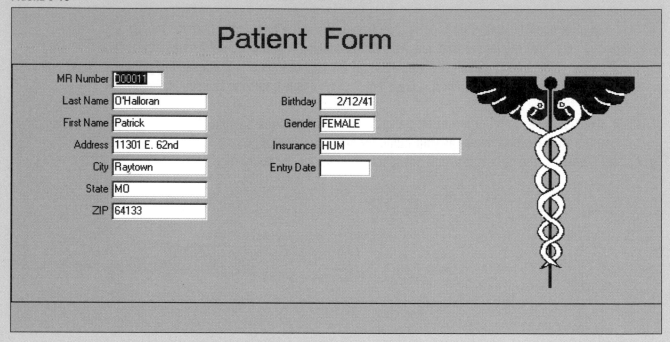

Using

Reports

Objectives

MOUS ► **Plan a report**

MOUS ► **Create a report**

MOUS ► **Group records**

MOUS ► **Change the sort order**

MOUS ► **Modify an expression**

MOUS ► **Align controls**

MOUS ► **Format controls**

► **Create mailing labels**

A **report** is an Access object used to create printouts. You cannot enter or edit data through a report. Although data displayed in a report can be viewed on the screen, it is usually sent to a printer. Access reports can be based on the fields and records of either a table or a query object, can include extensive formatting embellishments such as clip art and lines, and can include professional headers and footers. Reports can also include meaningful calculations such as subtotals on groups of records. ◢━━ John Kim wants to produce reports that he can distribute to MediaLoft employees who do not yet have access to the MediaLoft database.

Planning a Report

Without clear communication, the accuracy and integrity of information being discussed can be questioned, misinterpreted, or obscured. Hard copy reports are often the primary tool used to communicate database information at meetings, with outsiders, and with top executives. Although the **Report Wizard** can help you create an initial report object that you can later modify, the time spent planning your report not only increases your productivity but also ensures that the overall report meets its intended objectives. John has been asked to provide several reports on a regular basis to the MediaLoft executives. He plans his first report that summarizes inventory quantities within each music category.

Steps

John uses the following guidelines to plan his report:

Identify a meaningful title for the report

The title should clearly identify the purpose of the report and be meaningful to those who will be reading the report. The title is created with a label control placed in the **Report Header** section. **Sections** are the parts of the report that determine where a control will display on the report. See Table D-1 for more information on report sections. Just like forms, every element on a report is a control.

Determine the information (the fields and records) that the report will show

You can base a report on a table, but usually you create a query to gather the specific fields from the one or more tables upon which to base the report. Of course, using a query also allows you to set criteria to limit the number of records displayed by the report.

Determine how the fields should be laid out on the report

Most reports display fields in a horizontal layout across the page, but you can arrange them in any way you want. Just as in forms, bound text box controls are used on a report to display the data stored in the underlying records. These text boxes are generally placed in the report **Detail** section.

Determine how the records should be sorted and/or grouped within the report

In an Access report, the term **grouping** refers to sorting records *plus* providing a section before the group of records called the **Group Header** section and a section after the group of records called the **Group Footer** section. These sections include additional controls that often contain calculated expressions such as a subtotal for a group of records. The ability to group records is extremely powerful and only available through the report object.

Identify any other descriptive information that should be placed at the end of the report or at the top or bottom of each page

You will use the **Report Footer**, **Page Header**, and **Page Footer** sections for these descriptive controls. John has sketched his first report in Figure D-1.

FIGURE D-1: Sketch of the Quantities Report

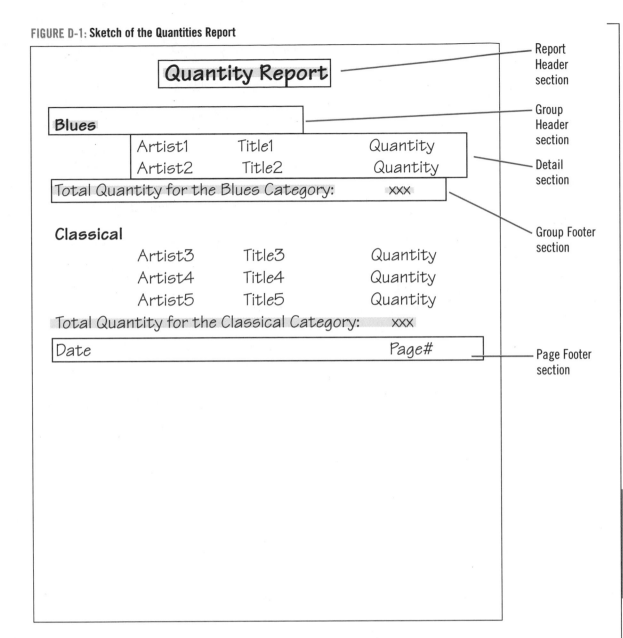

TABLE D-1: Report sections

section	where does this section print?	which controls are most commonly placed there?
Report Header	At the top of the first page of the report	Label controls containing the report title; can also include clip art, a logo image, or a line separating the title from the rest of the report
Page Header	At the top of every page (but below the report header on page one)	Descriptive label controls often acting as column headings for text box controls in the Detail section
Group Header	Before every group of records	Text box control for the field by which the records are grouped
Detail	Once for every record	Text box controls for the rest of the fields
Group Footer	After every group of records	Text box controls containing calculated expressions, such as subtotals or counts, for the records in that group
Page Footer	At the bottom of every page	Text box controls containing page number or date expression
Report Footer	At the end of the entire report	Text box controls containing expressions such as grand totals or counts that calculate an answer for all of the records in the report

Creating a Report

You can create reports in Access in **Report Design view**, or you can use the **Report Wizard** to help you get started. The Report Wizard asks questions that guide you through the initial development of the report, similar to the Form Wizard. In addition to questions about which object the report is based, which fields you want to view in the report, and the style and layout of the report, the Report Wizard also asks how you want report records to be grouped and sorted. John uses the Report Wizard to create the Quantities Report he planned on paper.

1. Start Access, click the **Open an existing file option button**, then open the **MediaLoft-D** database from your Project Disk
   This database contains an enhanced Music Inventory table and several queries from which you will base your reports.

2. Click **Reports** on the Objects bar in the MediaLoft-D Database window, then double-click **Create report by using wizard**
   The Report Wizard dialog box opens. You'll use the Selection Quantities query for this report. Another way to quickly create a report is by selecting a table or query, clicking the New Object list arrow on the Database toolbar and then selecting AutoReport. AutoReport, however, does not give you a chance to review the options provided by the Report Wizard.

3. Click the **Tables/Queries list arrow**, click **Query: Selection Quantities**, click **Category** in the Available Fields list, click the **Select Single Field button** [>], click **Title**, click [>], click **Artist**, click [>], click **Quantity**, then click [>]
   The first dialog box of the Report Wizard should look like Figure D-2. The Report Wizard also asks grouping and sorting questions that determine the order and amount of detail provided on the report.

Trouble?
You can always click Back to review previous dialog boxes within a wizard.

4. Click **Next**, click **Next** to move past the grouping levels question, click the **first sort order list arrow** in the sort order dialog box, then click **Category**
   At this point you have not specified any grouping fields, but specified that you want the fields sorted by Category. You can use the Report Wizard to specify up to four sort fields in either an ascending or descending sort order for each field.

5. Click **Next**, click **Next** to accept the **Tabular** layout and **Portrait** orientation, click **Corporate** for the style, click **Next**, type **Quantities Report** for the report title, verify that the **Preview the report option button** is selected, then click **Finish**
   The Quantities Report opens in Print Preview, as shown in Figure D-3. It is very similar to the sketch created earlier. Notice that the records are sorted by the Category field.

Why reports should be based on queries

Although you can use the first dialog box of the Report Wizard to select fields from different tables without first creating a query to collect those fields into one object, it is not recommended. If you later decide that you want to add more fields to the report or limit the number of records in the table, you will find it very easy to add fields or criteria to an underlying query object to meet these new needs. To accomplish this same task without using an intermediary query object requires that you change the properties of the report itself, which most users find more difficult.

FIGURE D-2: **First Report Wizard dialog box**

Base the report on
the Selection
Quantities query

Select Single Field
button

Fields selected for
the report

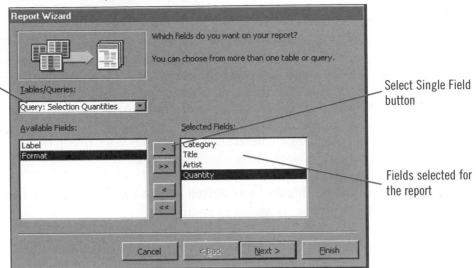

FIGURE D-3: **Quantities Report in Print Preview**

Report Header

Page Header

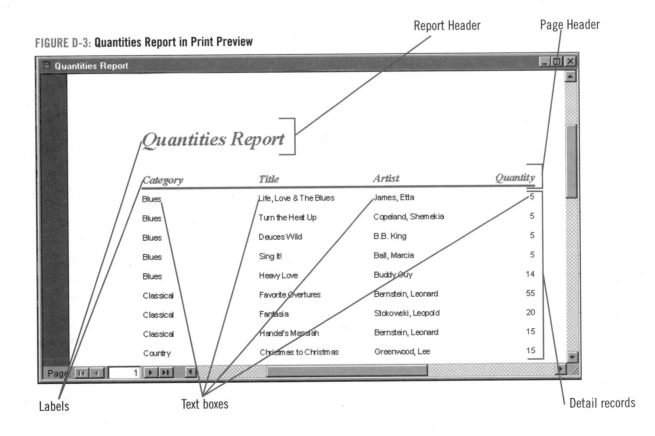

Labels

Text boxes

Detail records

Grouping Records

Grouping refers to sorting records on a report *plus* providing an area above and below the group of records in which additional controls can be placed. These two sections of the report are called the Group Header and Group Footer. You can create groups on a report through the Report Wizard, or you can change an existing report's grouping and sorting fields in Report Design view. Just as with forms, you make all structural changes to a report in the object's Design view. John wants to group the Quantities Report by Category instead of simply sorting it by Category. In addition, he wants to add controls to the Group Header and Group Footer to clarify and summarize information within the report.

Steps 1 2 3 4

Trouble?
If a property has a predetermined set of options, a list arrow will display when you click that property's text box in the property sheet.

1. **Click the Design View button** 📐 **on the Print Preview toolbar to switch to Report Design view, as shown in Figure D-4**
Report Design view shows you the sections of the report as well as the controls within each section. Labels and text boxes are formatted similarly in Report Design view. You can click a control and then click the Properties button to view the title bar of the property sheet to determine the nature of a control. Report Design view is where you change grouping and sort fields.

2. **Click the Sorting and Grouping button** 📑 **on the Report Design toolbar, click the Group Header text box, click the Group Header list arrow, click Yes, click the Group Footer text box, click the Group Footer list arrow, then click Yes**
Specifying "Yes" for the Group Header and Group Footer properties opens those sections of the report in Report Design view.

3. **Click** 📑 **to close the dialog box, click the Category text box in the Detail section, then drag the textbox with the** 🖐 **pointer directly up into the Category Header section**
By placing the Category text box in the Category Header, it will print once for each new group rather than once for each record. You can add calculated subtotal controls for each category of records by placing a text box in the Category Footer section.

QuickTip
The Field list, Toolbox toolbar, and property sheet may or may not be visible, but you can turn them on and off by clicking their respective toggle buttons. You can move them by dragging their title bars.

4. **If the Toolbox toolbar is not visible, click the Toolbox button** 🔧 **on the Report Design toolbar, click the Text Box button** abl **on the Toolbox toolbar, then click in the Category Footer section directly below the Quantity text box**
Your screen should look like Figure D-5. You can use the label and text box controls in the Category Footer section to describe and subtotal the Quantity field respectively.

5. **Click the Text13: label in the Category Footer section to select it, double-click Text13, type Subtotal, then press [Enter]**

Trouble?
If you double-click the edge of a control, you open the control's property sheet.

6. **Click the unbound text box control in the Category Footer section to select it, click the unbound text box control again to edit it, then type =sum([Quantity])**
The expression that calculates the sum of the Quantity field is now in the unbound text box control. Calculated expressions start with an equal sign. When entering an expression, the field name must be referenced exactly and surrounded by square brackets.

7. **Click the Print Preview button** 🔍 **on the Report Design toolbar, then scroll through the report as necessary**
The new report that groups and summarizes records by Category appears, as shown in Figure D-6. Since the Category text box was moved to the Category Header section, it prints only once per group of records. Each group of records is trailed by a Group Footer that includes the Subtotal label as well as a calculated field that subtotals the Quantity field.

8. **Click Close on the Print Preview toolbar, click the Save button** 💾, **then click the Quantities Report Close button to close the report**
The Quantities Report is now an object in the MediaLoft-D Database window.

FIGURE D-4: Quantities Report Design view

Field List button

Toolbox button

Sorting and Grouping button

Properties button

Sections

Labels

Toolbox toolbar

Text boxes

Field list

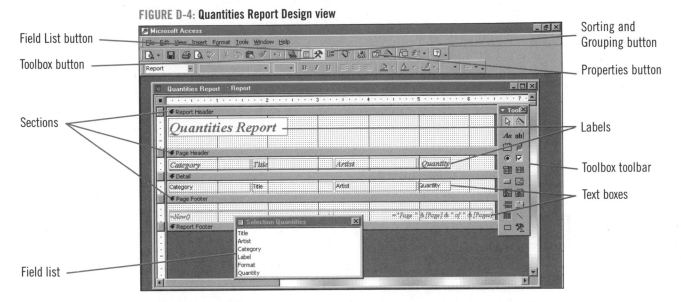

FIGURE D-5: Adding controls to the group footer section

Category Header

Category text box moved up from Detail section into Category Header section

Category Footer

Text Box button

New text box

New label

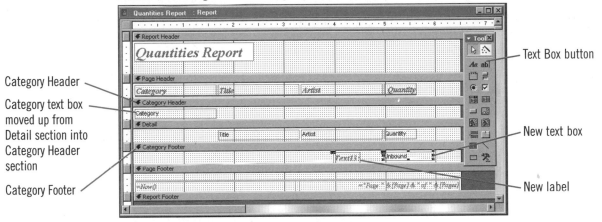

FIGURE D-6: The Quantities Report grouped by Category

Group Header (Category is the grouping field)

Report Header

Page Header

Detail

Group Footer (Category is the grouping field)

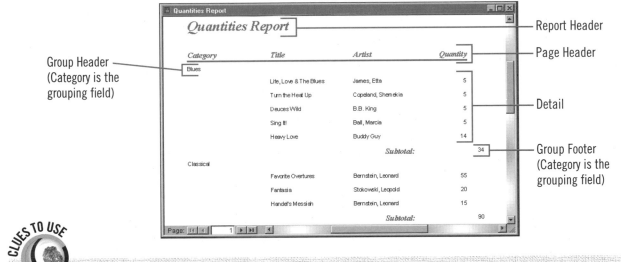

Access 2000

Clues to Use

Adding a field to a report

Clicking the Field List button 🔲 on the Report Design toolbar toggles the field list of the underlying table or query object. To add a field from this list to the report, simply drag it from the Field list to the appropriate position on the report. This action creates both a label control that displays the field name and a text box control that displays the value of the field from the underlying records.

Changing the Sort Order

Grouping records is really just sorting them with the additional ability to create a Group Header or Group Footer section on the report. The grouping field acts as a primary sort field. You can define further sort fields too. When you further sort records within a group, you order the Detail records according to a particular field. The Report Wizard prompts you for group and sort information at the time you create the report, but you can also group and sort an existing report by using the Sorting and Grouping dialog box in Report Design view. ▶━━━ John wants to modify the Quantities Report so that the Detail records are sorted by the Artist field within the Category group.

Steps 1 2 3 4

1. Click the **Quantities Report** in the MediaLoft-D Database window, then click the **Design button** 🖉

   The Quantities Report opens in Report Design view.

2. Click the **Sorting and Grouping button** 📇 on the Report Design toolbar, click the **second row Field/Expression text box**, click the **Field/Expression list arrow**, then click **Artist**

   The Sorting and Grouping dialog box looks like Figure D-7. There is no Sorting and Grouping indicator in the Artist row selector. Both the Group Header and Group Footer Group properties are "No" which indicates that the Artist field is providing a sort order only.

3. Click 📇 to toggle the Sorting and Grouping dialog box off, then click the **Print Preview button** 🔍 on the Report Design toolbar

   Part of the report is shown in Print Preview, as shown in Figure D-8. You can use the buttons on the Print Preview toolbar to view more of the report.

4. Click the **One Page button** 🔳 on the Print Preview toolbar to view one miniature page, click the **Two Pages button** 🔳 to view two miniature pages, click the **Multiple Pages button** 🔳, then drag to **1x4 Pages** in the grid as shown in Figure D-9

   The Print Preview window displays the four pages of the report in miniature. Regardless of the zoom magnification of the pages, however, you can click the **Zoom pointer** 🔍 to quickly toggle between two zoom magnifications.

5. Point to the **last subtotal** on the last page of the report with the 🔍 pointer, click to read the number **92**, then click again to return the report to its former four-page magnification level

6. Click the **Close** button on the Print Preview toolbar, then click the **Save button** 🖫 on the Report Design toolbar

FIGURE D-7: Specifying a sort order

Sorting and Grouping indicator

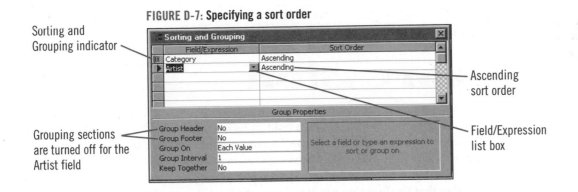

Ascending sort order

Grouping sections are turned off for the Artist field

Field/Expression list box

FIGURE D-8: The Quantities Report sorted by Artist

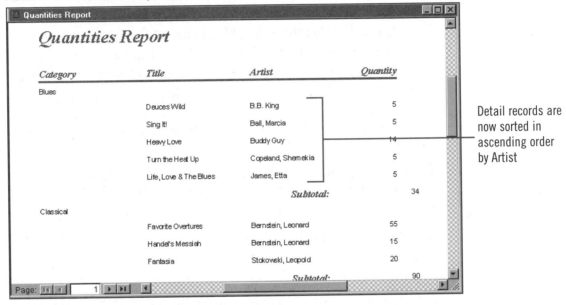

Detail records are now sorted in ascending order by Artist

FIGURE D-9: Print Preview

One Page button

Two Pages button

Multiple Pages button

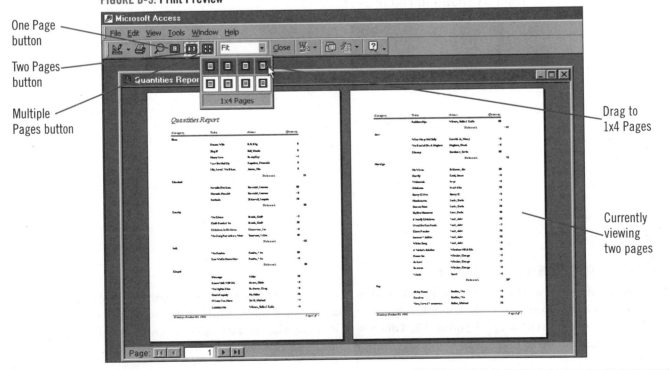

Drag to 1x4 Pages

Currently viewing two pages

Modifying an Expression

An **expression** is a combination of fields, operators (such as +, -, / and *) and functions that result in a single value. A **function** is a built-in formula provided by Access that helps you quickly create a calculated expression. See Table D-2 for examples of common expressions that use Access functions. Notice that every calculated expression starts with an equal sign, and when it uses a function, the arguments for the function are placed in parentheses. **Arguments** are the pieces of information that the function needs to create the final answer. Calculated expressions are entered in text box controls. John adds a calculated expression to the Quantities Report that uses the Count function to count the number of records within each music category.

Steps 1234

1. Make sure the Quantities Report is in Report Design view, click the **=Sum([Quantity])
   text box** in the Category Footer section, click the **Copy button** 📄 on the Report
   Design toolbar, click in a **blank area** in the left part of the Category Footer section,
   then click the **Paste button** 📋 on the Report Design toolbar
   The text box and accompanying label are copied and pasted, as shown in Figure D-10.
   Modifying a copy of the existing calculated expression control helps reduce errors and saves
   on keystrokes.

2. Click the copied **Subtotal label** in the Category Footer section to select it, double-
   click **Subtotal** to select the text, type **Count**, then press **[Enter]**
   The label is only descriptive text. The text box is the control that actually calculates the count.

3. Click the copy of the **=Sum([Quantity]) text box** to select it, double-click **Sum** to
   select it, type **count**, then press **[Enter]**
   The expression now counts the number of records in each group.

4. Click the **Print Preview button** 🔍 on the Report Design toolbar to view the updated
   report, click the **One Page button** 🔲 on the Print Preview toolbar, then scroll and
   zoom as shown in Figure D-11

Using the Office Clipboard

The Office Clipboard works together with the Windows Clipboard to let you copy and paste multiple items within or between the Office applications. The Office Clipboard can hold up to 12 items copied or cut from any Office program. The Clipboard toolbar displays the items stored on the Office Clipboard. The collected items remain on the Clipboard and are available to you until you close all open Office applications.

FIGURE D-10: Copying and pasting a calculated control

Copy button

Paste button

New label control

New text box control

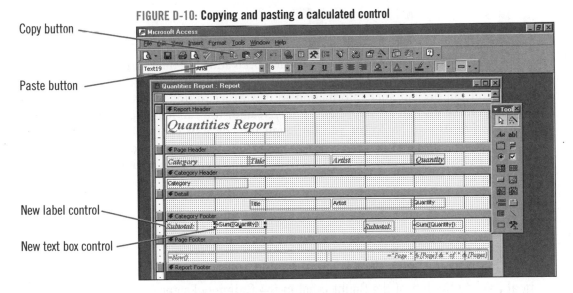

FIGURE D-11: Previewing the Count calculated control

New label control

New text box control

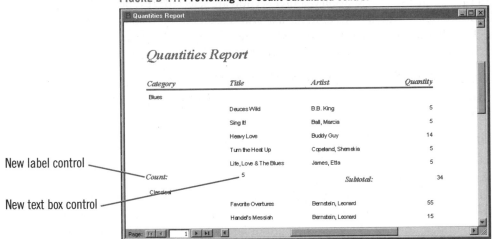

TABLE D-2: Common Access expressions

category	sample expression	description
Arithmetic	=[Price]*1.05	Multiplies the Price field by 1.05 (adds 5% to the Price field)
Arithmetic	=[Subtotal]+[Shipping]	Adds the value of the Subtotal field to the value of the Shipping field
Page Number	=[Page]	Displays the current page number, such as 5, 6, or 10
Page Number	="Page "&[Page]	Displays the word "Page," a space, and the current page number, such as Page 5, Page 6, or Page 10
Text	=[FirstName]&" "&[LastName]	Displays the value of the FirstName and LastName fields in one control separated by a space
Text	=Left([ProductNumber],2)	Uses the **Left** function to display the first two characters in the ProductNumber field
Aggregate	=Avg([Freight])	Uses the **Avg** function to display an average of the values in the Freight field
Aggregate	=Count([FirstName])	Uses the **Count** function to display the number of records that contain an entry in the FirstName field
Aggregate	=Sum([Tracks])	Uses the **Sum** function to display the total value from the Tracks field
Date	=Date()	Uses the **Date** function to display the current date in the form of mm-dd-yy, such as 10-23-00 or 11-14-01

Aligning Controls

Once the information that you want to present has been added to the appropriate section of a report, you may also want to rearrange the data on the report. By aligning controls in columns and rows, you can present your information so it is easier to understand. There are several **alignment** commands that are important to understand. You can left-, right-, or center-align a control *within its own border*, or you can align the edges of controls *with respect to one another.* John aligns several controls on the Quantities Report to improve the readability and professionalism of the report. His first task is to right-align all of the controls in the Category Footer.

Steps

1. **Click the Design View button** ⊞ **on the Print Preview toolbar, then click in the vertical ruler to the left of the Count label in the Category Footer section**
   All four controls in the Category Footer section are selected. Text boxes that display numeric fields are right-aligned by default; the labels and text boxes you added in the Category Footer section that display calculated expressions are left-aligned by default. You can use the same techniques for selecting controls in Report Design view as you did in Form Design view.

2. **Click the Align Right button** ▤ **on the Formatting (Form/Report) toolbar**
   Your screen should look like Figure D-12. Now the information displayed by the control is right-aligned within the control.

3. **With the four controls still selected, click Format on the menu bar, point to Align, then click Bottom**
   The bottom edges of the four controls are now aligned with respect to one another. The Align command on the Format menu refers to aligning controls with respect to one another. The Alignment buttons on the Formatting toolbar refer to aligning controls within their own borders. You can also align the right or left edges of controls in different sections.

4. **Click the Quantity label in the Page Header section, press and hold [Shift], click the Quantity text box in the Detail section, click the =Sum([Quantity]) text box in the Category Footer section, release [Shift], click Format on the menu bar, point to Align, then click Right**
   The right edges of the Quantity label, Quantity text box, and Quantity calculated controls are aligned. With the edges at the same position and the information right-aligned within the controls, the controls form a perfect column on the final report. You can extend the line in the Page Header section to better define the sections on the page.

Trouble?
Don't drag beyond the 6" mark or the printout will be wider than one sheet of paper.

5. **Click the blue line in the Page Header section, press and hold [Shift], point to the right sizing handle, when the pointer changes to** ↘ **, drag the handle to the 6" mark, then release [Shift]**
   By pressing [Shift] when you draw or resize a line, the line remains perfectly horizontal as you drag it left or right.

6. **Click the Print Preview button** ▣ **on the Report Design toolbar, then scroll and zoom**
   Your screen should look like Figure D-13.

FIGURE D-12: **Working with the alignment buttons**

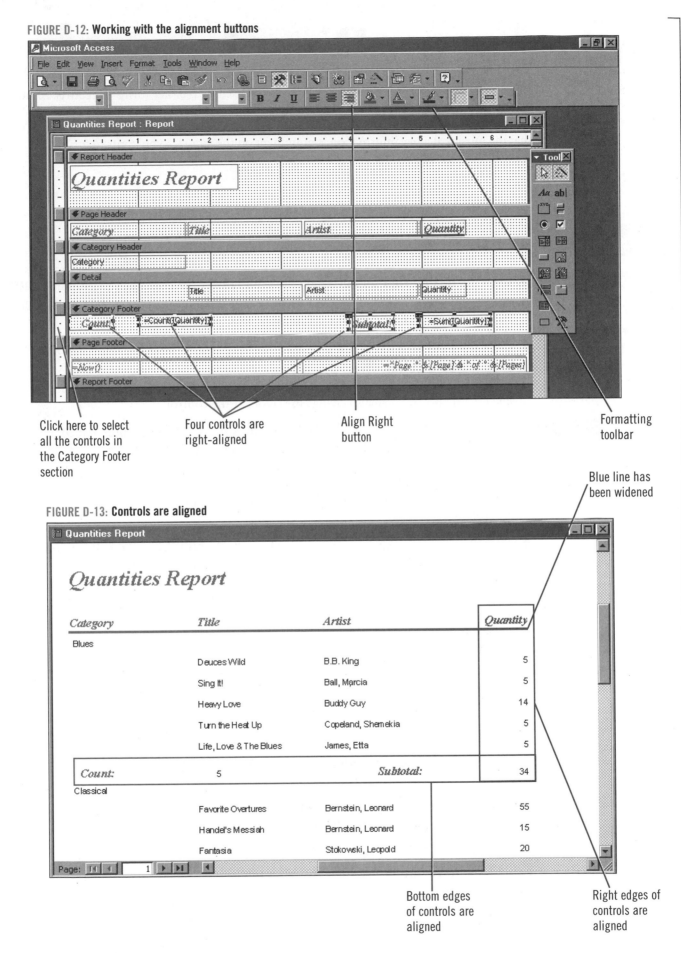

Click here to select
all the controls in
the Category Footer
section

Four controls are
right-aligned

Align Right
button

Formatting
toolbar

Blue line has
been widened

FIGURE D-13: **Controls are aligned**

Bottom edges
of controls are
aligned

Right edges of
controls are
aligned

Formatting Controls

Formatting refers to enhancing the appearance of the information. Table D-3 lists several of the most popular formatting commands which can be used with either forms or reports. Although the Report Wizard provides many formatting embellishments on a report, you often want to improve upon the report's appearance to fit your particular needs. John doesn't feel that the music category information is prominent on the report, so he wants to format that control to change its appearance.

Steps

QuickTip

If you need your name on the printed solution, add a label to the Report Header that displays your name.

1. Click the **Design View button** on the Print Preview toolbar, click the **Toolbox button** to toggle it off, then click the **Category text box** in the Category Header section
   Before you can format any control, it must be selected.

2. Click the **Font size list arrow** on the Formatting (Form/Report) toolbar, click **11**, then click the **Bold button**
   Increasing the font size and applying bold are common ways to make information more visible on a report. You can also change the colors of the control.

Trouble?

If the default color on the Font/Fore Color button is red, click the button.

3. With the Category text box still selected, click the **Font/Fore Color list arrow**, then click the **Red box** (third row, first column on the left), as shown in Figure D-14
   Many buttons on the Formatting (Form/Report) toolbar include a list arrow that you can click to reveal a list of choices. When you click the color list arrow, a palette of available colors is displayed. You can change the background color of the Category text box using the palette.

4. With the Category text box still selected, click the **Fill/Back Color list arrow**, then click the **light gray box** (fourth row, first column on the right)
   When you print colors on a black and white printer, they become various shades of gray. So unless you always print to a color printer, be careful about relying too heavily on color formatting, especially background shades that often become solid black boxes when printed on a black and white printer or fax machine. Fortunately, Access allows you to undo your last command if you don't like the change you've made. You must pay close attention, however, because you can only undo your very last command.

5. With the Category text box still selected, click the **Undo button** on the Report Design toolbar to remove the background color, click the **Line/Border Color list arrow**, then click the **blue box** (second row, third column from right)

6. Click the **Print Preview button** on the Report Design toolbar
   The screen should look like Figure D-15.

7. Click **File** on the menu bar, click **Print**, type **1** in the From text box, type **1** in the To text box, click **OK**, then click **Close** on the Print Preview toolbar
   The first page of the report is printed.

8. Click the **Save button**, then close the Quantities Report

FIGURE D-14: Working with color formats

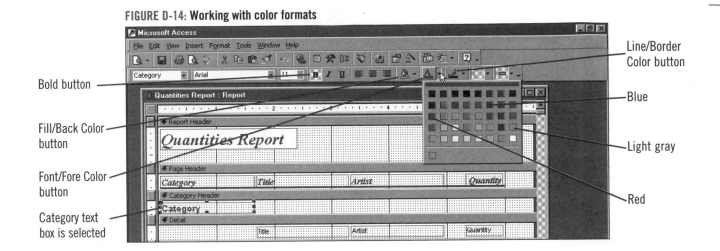

Bold button

Fill/Back Color button

Font/Fore Color button

Category text box is selected

Line/Border Color button

Blue

Light gray

Red

FIGURE D-15: Formatted Quantities Report

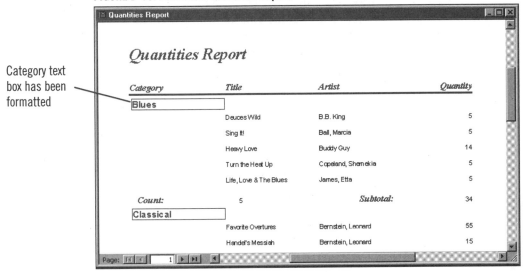

Category text box has been formatted

TABLE D-3: Popular formatting commands

button	button name	description
B	Bold	Toggles bold on or off for the selected control(s)
I	Italic	Toggles italics, on or off for the selected control(s)
U	Underline	Toggles underline on or off for the selected control(s)
≡	Align Left	Left-aligns the selected control(s) within its own border
≡	Center	Center-aligns the selected control(s) within its own border
≡	Align Right	Right-aligns the selected control(s) within its own border
◇ ▾	Fill/Back Color	Changes the background color of the selected control(s)
▲ ▾	Font/Fore Color	Changes the text color of the selected control(s)
✎ ▾	Line/Border Color	Changes the border color of the selected control(s)
▭ ▾	Line/Border Width	Changes the style of the border of the selected control(s)
▱ ▾	Special Effect	Changes the special visual effect of the selected control(s)

Creating Mailing Labels

Mailing Labels are used for many business purposes such as identifying paper folders and providing addresses for mass mailings. Once you enter raw data into your Access database, you can easily create mailing labels from this data using the **Label Wizard**. John has been asked to create labels for the display cases in the MediaLoft stores with the Artist and Title fields only. The labels are to be printed in alphabetical order by Artist and then by Title. John uses the Label Wizard to get started.

Steps

Trouble?

If you don't see Avery, click English units of measure, click the Filter by manufacturer list arrow, then click Avery.

1. Click **Reports** on the Objects bar in the MediaLoft-D Database window, click the **New button**, click **Label Wizard** in the New Report dialog box, click the **Choose the table or query where the object's data comes from list arrow**, click **Music Inventory**, then click **OK**

   The Label Wizard dialog box opens requesting that you specify information about the characteristics of the label, as shown in Figure D-16. Avery 5160 labels are one of the most popular sizes. Avery 5160 label sheets have three columns and ten rows of labels for a total of 30 labels per page.

2. Click **5160**, then click **Next**

   The next wizard dialog box allows you to change the font, font size, and other text attributes. Larger fonts will be easier to read and will fit on this label since there are only two fields of information.

Trouble?

If your system doesn't have the Comic Sans MS font, choose another font appropriate for music labels.

3. Click the **Font size list arrow**, click **11**, click the **Font name list arrow**, scroll and click **Comic Sans MS** (a sample appears in the Sample box), then click **Next**

   The next wizard dialog box, which shows you the prototype label, allows you choose which fields you want to include in each label as well as their placement. Any spaces or punctuation that you want on the label must be entered from the keyboard. Also, if you want to put a field on a new line, you must press [Enter] to move to a new row of the prototype label.

QuickTip

You can double-click the field name in the Available Fields list to move it to the Prototype label list.

4. Click **Artist**, click the **Select Single Field button**, press [Enter], click **Title**, then click ▶

   Your screen should look like Figure D-17.

5. Click **Next**

   The next wizard dialog box asks about sorting.

6. Double-click **Artist** for your primary sort field, double-click **Title** for your secondary sort field, then click **Next**

   You should give your labels a descriptive name.

7. Type **Artist-Title Labels** to name the report, click **Finish**, then click the **Zoom pointer** to see a full page of labels

   The labels should look like Figure D-18.

8. Click **Close** on the Print Preview toolbar to see the Artist-Title Labels report in Design view, click the **Save button**, then click the **Print button**

9. Click **File** on the menu bar, then click **Exit** to exit Access

FIGURE D-16: Label Wizard

Avery 5160 label type

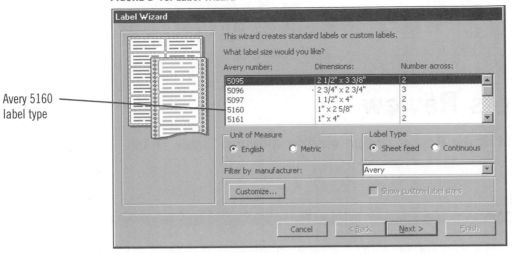

FIGURE D-17: The prototype label

Select Single Field button

Artist field

Title field

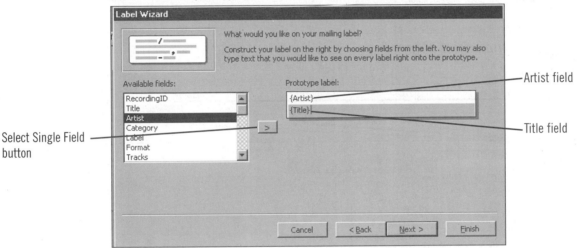

FIGURE D-18: The Artist-Title Labels report

Labels are 3 columns by 10 rows on each page

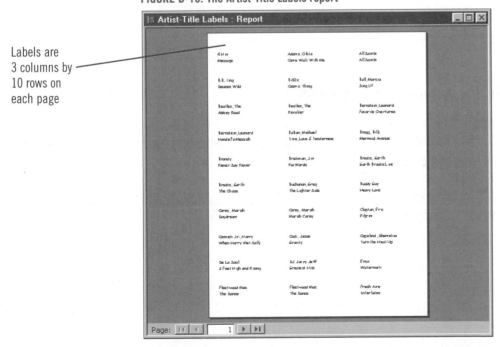

Practice

▶ Concepts Review

Label each element of the Report Design window shown in Figure D-19.

FIGURE D-19

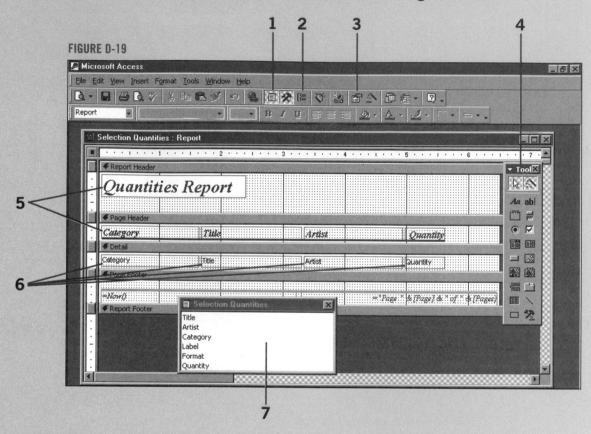

Match each term with the statement that describes it.

8. Function	**a.** Part of the report that determines where a control will display on the report
9. Section	**b.** Sorting records *plus* providing a section before and after the group of records
10. Detail section	**c.** An Access object used to create paper printouts
11. Report	**d.** Enhancing the appearance of the information
12. Formatting	**e.** A built-in formula provided by Access that helps you quickly create a calculated expression
13. Grouping	**f.** Prints once for every record

Select the best answer from the list of choices.

14. Press and hold which key to select more than one control in Report Design view?
   a. [Ctrl]
   b. [Alt]
   c. [Shift]
   d. [Tab]

15. Which type of control is most likely found in the Detail section?
   a. Label
   b. Text box
   c. Combo box
   d. List box

16. Which type of control is most likely found in the Page Header section?
   a. Label
   b. Combo box
   c. Command button
   d. Bound image

17. A calculated expression is most often found in which report section?
   a. Report Header
   b. Detail
   c. Formulas
   d. Group Footer

18. Which of the following would be the appropriate expression to count the number of records using the FirstName field?
   a. =Count(FirstName)
   b. =Count[FirstName)
   c. =Count{FirstName}
   d. =Count([FirstName])

19. To align the edges of several controls with respect to one another, you use the alignment commands on the
   a. Formatting toolbar.
   b. Standard toolbar.
   c. Print Preview toolbar.
   d. Format menu.

▶ Skills Review

1. **Plan a report.**
   a. Pretend that you are looking for a job. Plan a report to use for tracking job opportunities. To gather the raw data for your report, find a newspaper with job listings in your area of interest.
   b. Identify the Report Header, Group Header, and Detail sections of the report by using sample data based on the following information:
      • The title of the report should be "Job Opportunity Report."
      • The records should be grouped by job title. For example, if you are interested in working with computers, job titles might be "Computer Operator" or "Computer Analyst." Include at least two job title groupings in your sample report.
      • The Detail section should include information on the company, contact, and telephone number for each job opportunity.

2. **Create a report.**
   a. Start Access and open the Club-D database on your Project Disk.
   b. Use the Report Wizard to create a report based on the Contacts table.
   c. Include the following fields for the report:
      STATUS, FNAME, LNAME, DUESOWED, DUESPAID
   d. Do not add any grouping or sorting fields.
   e. Use the Tabular layout and Portrait orientation.
   f. Use a bold style and title the report "Contact Status Report."
   g. Preview the first page of the new report.

3. **Group records.**
   a. In Report Design view, open the Sorting and Grouping dialog box, and group the report by the STATUS field in ascending order. Open both the Group Header and Group Footer sections, then close the dialog box.
   b. Move the STATUS text box in the Detail section up to the left edge of the STATUS Header section.
   c. Preview the first page of the new report.

4. **Change the sort order.**
   a. In Report Design view, open the Sorting and Grouping dialog box, then add LNAME as a sort field in ascending order immediately below the STATUS field.
   b. Preview the first page of the new report.

5. **Modify an expression.**
   a. In Report Design view, add a text box control in the STATUS Footer section directly below the DUESOWED text box in the Detail section.
   b. Delete the accompanying label to the left of the unbound text box.
   c. Add a text box control in the STATUS Footer section directly below the DUESPAID text box in the Detail section.
   d. Delete the accompanying label to the left of the unbound text box by clicking the label, then pressing [Delete].
   e. Add an unbound label to the report header, and type your name as the label.
   f. Modify the text boxes so that they subtotal the DUESOWED and DUESPAID fields respectively. The calculated expressions will be =Sum([DUESOWED]) and =Sum([DUESPAID]).
   g. Preview both pages of the report, then print both pages of the report.

6. **Align controls.**
   a. In Report Design view, right-align the new calculated controls in the STATUS Footer section.
   b. Select the DUESOWED text box in the Detail section, and the =Sum([DUESOWED]) calculated expression in the STATUS Footer, then right-align the controls with respect to one another.
   c. Select the DUESPAID text box in the Detail section, and the =Sum([DUESPAID]) calculated expression in the STATUS Footer, then right-align the controls with respect to one another.

7. **Format controls.**
   a. Select the two calculated controls in the STATUS Footer, click the Properties button, then change the Format property on the Format tab to Currency. Close the property sheet.
   b. Select the STATUS text box in the STATUS Header section, change the font size to 12 points, bold and italicize the control, then change the background color to bright yellow.
   c. Preview the report, check the new totals, save the report, print it, then close the report.

8. **Create mailing labels.**
   a. Use the Label Wizard and the Contacts table to create mailing labels using Avery 5160 labels.
   b. The text should be formatted as Arial, 10 points, Light font weight, black, with no italic or underline attributes.
   c. The prototype label should be organized as follows:
   FNAME LNAME
   COMPANY
   STREET
   CITY, STATE ZIP
   d. Sort the labels by the ZIP field.
   e. Name the report "Mailing Labels."
   f. Print the first page of the labels, save the report, then close it.
   g. Exit Access.

► Independent Challenges

1. You have been hired to create several reports for a physical therapy clinic.
To complete this independent challenge:

a. Start Access and open the Therapy-D database from your Project Disk.

b. Using the Report Wizard, create a report using all of the fields from the Location Financial Query.

c. View your data by Survey, group by Street, sort in ascending order by PatientLast, and sum both the AmountSent and AmountRecorded fields.

d. Use the Stepped layout, Portrait orientation, and Soft Gray style.

e. Name the report "Location Financial Report."

f. Modify the AmountSent and AmountRecorded labels in the Page Header section to "Sent" and "Recorded" respectively.

g. Change the font/fore color of the labels in the Page Header section to bright blue.

h. Widen the Street text box label in the Street Header section to twice its current size, and change the border color to bright blue.

i. Save and print the report.

j. Exit Access.

2. You have been hired to create several reports for a physical therapy clinic.
To complete this independent challenge:

a. Start Access and open the Therapy-D database from your Project Disk.

b. Using the Report Wizard, create a report using all of the fields from the Therapist Satisfaction Query except for the Initials and First fields.

c. View the data by Survey. Do not add any grouping levels and do not add any sorting levels.

d. Use the Tabular layout, Portrait orientation, and Casual style.

e. Title the report "Therapist Satisfaction Report," then print the report.

f. In Report Design view, group the report by Last, and open both the Group Header and Group Footer sections.

g. Further sort the records by PatientLast.

h. Move the Last text box from the Detail section up into the Last Header section.

i. Remove bold from all of the labels in the Page Header section.

j. Add text boxes in the Last Footer section directly below the Courtesy and Knowledge text boxes in the Detail section. Enter the calculated controls =Avg([Courtesy]) and =Avg([Knowledge]) respectively. Delete their accompanying labels, and resize the new calculated controls so that they are a little narrower than the Courtesy and Knowledge text boxes in the Detail section.

k. Open the property sheet for the two new calculated controls, and change the Format property on the Format tab to "Fixed."

l. Right-align the two new calculated controls within their own borders. Also, align the right edge of the =Avg([Courtesy]) control with respect to the Courtesy text box in the Detail section. Right-align the edges of the =Avg([Knowledge]) and Knowledge text boxes with respect to each other.

m. Align the top edges of the new calculated controls.

n. Drag the right edge of the report to the left so the report is 6½" wide (if necessary).

o. Save, preview, and print the report.

p. Exit Access.

3. Use the knowledge and skills that you have acquired about Access to create an attractive report that includes information about colleges and universities that offer programs in computer science. Create a database containing this information, and then design a report that displays the data. Gather information from libraries, friends, and the Web to enter into the database.

To complete this independent challenge:

a. Start Access and create a new database called "Colleges" on your Project Disk. Include any fields you feel are important, but make sure you include the institution's name, state, and whether it is a 4- or 2-year school.

b. Find information on schools that offer programs in computer science. If you are using the Web, use any available search engines.

c. Compile a list of at least 15 institutions, and enter the 15 records into a table named "Computer Science Schools."

d. Create a report that includes all the fields in the table Computer Science Schools, and group by the field that contains the information on whether it is a 4- or 2-year school.

e. Sort the records in ascending order by the state, then by the institution's name.

f. Use an appropriate style and title for your report. Insert your initials at the end of the report title so you can identify it.

g. Save, preview, and print the report.

h. Exit Access.

4. As an assistant in the marketing department at MediaLoft, you are often asked to create mailing labels for the MediaLoft store locations. You have decided to create a small database that stores information about the stores so that you can quickly create the labels using the Label Wizard.

To complete this independent challenge:

a. Start Access and create a new database on your Project Disk called "MediaLoft Locations."

b. Connect to the Internet, use your browser to go to the MediaLoft intranet site at http://www.course.com/illustrated/MediaLoft, then click the About link for the page with the MediaLoft store locations.

c. Print the Web page that displays the store locations.

d. Disconnect from the Internet, and switch to the Access window.

e. Create a table called "Stores" with the following fields (each field's data type should be Text): StoreName, Street, City, State, Zip, Phone

f. Using the Stores datasheet, type each store location into the database. Pay close attention to capitalization and spelling.

g. Using the Label Wizard, create mailing labels with the store address information on Avery 5160 labels.

h. Format the label with any decorative font, a 12-point font size, and bright red text.

i. Use the following label prototype:
StoreName
Street
City, State Zip

j. Name the label report "Store Address Labels," and print the report.

k. Save and close the report, then exit Access.

Visual Workshop

Use the Club-D database on your Project Disk to create the report based on the CONTACTS table shown in Figure D-20. The Report Wizard and the Corporate style were used to create this report. Note that the records are grouped by the CITY field and sorted within each group by the LNAME field. A calculated control that counts the number of records is displayed in the Group Footer.

FIGURE D-20

Membership by City

CITY	LNAME	FNAME	PHONE
Bridgewater			
	Daniels	Mark	555-2277
Count: 1			
Fontanelle			
	Eagan	Jane	555-1166
Count: 1			
Industrial Airport			
	Braven	Mary	555-7002
Count: 1			
Kansas City			
	Alman	Jill	555-6931
	Bouchart	Bob	555-3081
	Collins	Christine	555-3602
	Diverman	Barbara	555-0401
	Duman	Mary Jane	555-8844
	Eahle	Andrea	555-0401
	Eckert	Jay	555-7414
	Hammer	Mike	555-0365
	Hubert	Holly	555-6004
	Mackintosh	Helen	555-9414
	Mayberry	Mitch	555-0401
	Olson	Marcie	555-1388
	Parton	Jeanette	555-8773
	Walker	Shirley	555-0403
Count: 14			

Modifying

a Database Structure

Objectives

- MOUS ▶ **Examine relational databases**
- MOUS ▶ **Plan related tables**
- MOUS ▶ **Create related tables**
- MOUS ▶ **Define Text field properties**
- MOUS ▶ **Define Number and Currency fields**
- MOUS ▶ **Define Date/Time and Yes/No fields**
- MOUS ▶ **Define field validation properties**
- MOUS ▶ **Create one-to-many relationships**

In this unit, you will add new tables to an existing database and link them in one-to-many relationships to create a relational database. You will also modify several field properties such as field formatting and field validation to increase data entry accuracy. ◀━━ David Dumont, director of training at MediaLoft, has created an Access database to track the courses attended by MediaLoft employees. Courses include hands-on computer classes, business seminars, and self-improvement workshops. Because a single-table database will not meet all of his needs, he will use multiple tables of data and link them together to create a relational database.

Examining Relational Databases

A **relational database** is a collection of related tables that share information. The goals of a relational database are to satisfy dynamic information management needs and to eliminate duplicate data entry wherever possible.  MediaLoft employees have tried to track course attendance using a Training database in a single Access table called "Attendance Log," as shown in Figure E-1. Although only four records are shown in this sample, David sees a data redundancy problem because there are multiple occurrences of the same employee and same course information. He knows that data redundancy in one table is a major clue that the database needs to be redesigned. Therefore, David studies the principles of relational database design.

 ### A relational database is based on multiple tables of data. Each table should be based on only one subject

Right now the Attendance Log table in the Training database contains three subjects: Courses, Attendance, and Employees. Therefore, you have to duplicate several fields of information in this table every time an employee takes a course. Redundant data in one table creates a need for a relational database.

 ### Each record in a table should be uniquely identified with a key field or key field combination

A **key field** is a field that contains unique information for each record. Typically, an employee table contains an Employee Identification (EmployeeID) field to uniquely identify each employee. Often, the Social Security Number (SSN) field serves this purpose. Although using the employee's last name as the key field might accommodate a small database, it is a poor choice because the user cannot enter two employees with the same last name.

 ### Tables in the same database should be related, or linked, through a common field in a one-to-many relationship

To tie the information from one table to another, a single field of data must be common to each table. This common field will be the key field in one of the tables, creating the "one" side of the relationship; the field data will be listed "many" times in the other table, creating a **one-to-many relationship**. Table E-1 shows common examples of one-to-many relationships between two database tables.

Attendance Log

Course Description	Prerequisite	Date	Employee
Internet Fundamentals	Computer Fundamentals	2/7/2000	Maria Abbott
Internet Fundamentals	Computer Fundamentals	2/7/2000	Lauren Alber
Introduction to Access	Computer Fundamentals	3/6/2000	Maria Abbott
Introduction to Access	Computer Fundamentals	3/6/2000	Lauren Alber

Redundant data is shaded the same color

Redundant data is shaded the same color

TABLE E-1: **One-to-many relationships**

table on "one" side of relationship	table on "many" side of relationship	linking field	description
Products	Sales	ProductID	A ProductID field must have a unique entry in a Products table, but will be listed many times in a Sales table as multiple copies of that item are sold
Customers	Sales	CustomerID	A CustomerID field must have a unique entry in a Customers table, but will be listed many times in a Sales table as multiple sales are recorded for the same customer
Employees	Promotions	EmployeeID	An EmployeeID field must have a unique entry in an Employees table, but will be listed many times in a Promotions table as the employee is promoted over time
Vendors	Products	VendorID	A VendorID field must have a unique entry in a Vendors table, but will be listed many times in the Products table if multiple products are purchased from the same vendor

Planning Related Tables

Careful planning is crucial to successful relational database design and creation. Duplicated data is not only error-prone and inefficient to enter, but it also limits the query and reporting capabilities of the overall database. After studying the concepts of solid relational database design, David is ready to apply those concepts and redesign MediaLoft's Training database. He uses the following steps to move from a single table of data to the powerful relational database capabilities provided by Access.

Details

List all of the fields of data that need to be tracked

Typically, these fields are already present in existing tables or paper reports. Still, it is a good idea to document each field in order to examine all fields at the same time. This is the appropriate time to determine if there are additional fields of information that do not currently exist on any report that should be tracked. David lists the fields he wishes to track, including fields about employee information, course information, and attendance information.

Group fields together in subject matter tables

The new MediaLoft training database will track courses attended by employees. It will contain three tables: Courses, Employees, and Attendance. David organizes the fields he listed under their appropriate table name.

Identify key fields that exist in tables

Each table should include a key field or key field combination in order to uniquely identify each record. David will use the SSN field in the Employees table, the CourseID field in the Courses table, and an automatically incrementing (AutoNumber data type) LogID field in the Attendance table to handle this requirement.

Link the tables with a one-to-many relationship via a common field

By adding an SSN field to the Attendance table, David creates a common field in both the Employees and Attendance tables that can serve as the link between them. Similarly, by adding a CourseID field to the Attendance table, David creates a common field in both the Attendance and Courses tables that can serve as the link. For a valid one-to-many relationship, the linking field must be designated as the key field in the "one" side of the one-to-many relationship. The final sketch of David's redesigned relational database is shown in Figure E-2.

FIGURE E-2: One-to-many relationships

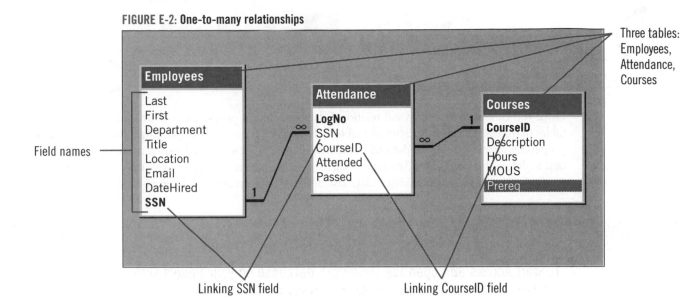

Field names

Linking SSN field

Linking CourseID field

Three tables:
Employees,
Attendance,
Courses

Identifying key field combinations

Identifying a single key field may be difficult in some tables. Examine, for instance, a table that records employee promotions over time that includes three fields: employee number, date, and pay rate. None of the fields individually could serve as a valid key field because none are restricted to unique data. The employee number and date together, however, could serve as a valid **key field combination** because an employee would get promoted only once on any given date; uniquely identifying the record.

Creating Related Tables

Once you have developed a valid relational database design on paper, you are ready to define the tables in Access. All characteristics of a table including field names, data types, field descriptions, field properties, and key fields are defined in the table's **Design view**. In a relational database, it is important to define the length and data type of the linking field the same way in both tables to create a successful link. ✐ Using his new database design, David creates the Attendance table.

Steps 1 2 3 4

1. **Start Access and open the Training-E database on your Project Disk**
   The Courses and Employees tables already exist in the database.

2. **Click Tables on the Objects Bar if it is not already selected, then click the New Table button ⊞ in the Training-E database window**
   You will enter the fields for the Attendance table directly into the table's Design view.

3. **Click Design View in the New Table dialog box, then click OK**
   Field names should be as short as possible, but long enough to be descriptive. The field name entered in a table's Design view is used as the default name for the field in all later queries, forms, and reports.

QuickTip

Press [Enter] or [Tab] to move to the next column in a table's Design view window.

4. **Maximize the Table1: Table window, type LogNo, press [Enter], type a to select the AutoNumber Data Type, then press [Enter] twice to bypass the Description column and move to the second row**
   The LogNo is a unique number used to identify each record in the Attendance table (each occurrence of an employee taking a course). The AutoNumber data type, which automatically sequences each new record with the next available integer, works well for this field. When entering data types, you can type the first letter of the data type; for example, type "T" for Text, "D" for Date/Time, or "C" for Currency. You can also click the Data Type list arrow, then select the data type from the list.

5. **Type the other fields, entering the data types as shown in Table E-2**
   Field descriptions entered in a table's Design view are optional. In Datasheet view, the description of a field appears in the status bar, and therefore provides further clarification about what type of data should be entered in the field. The SSN field will serve as the linking field between the Attendance and Employee tables. The CourseID field will serve as the linking field between the Attendance and Courses tables. You are not required to use the same field name in both tables, but doing so makes it easier to understand the link between the related tables later.

6. **Click LogNo in the Field Name column, then click the Primary Key button 🔑 on the Table Design toolbar**
   The LogNo field serves as the primary key field in this table.

7. **Click the Save button 🖫 on the Table Design toolbar, type Attendance in the Table Name text box in the Save As dialog box, then click OK**
   The completed Table Design view for the Attendance table is shown in Figure E-3.

8. **Click the Attendance: Table Design Close Window button**
   The Attendance table is now displayed as a table object in the Training-E database window.

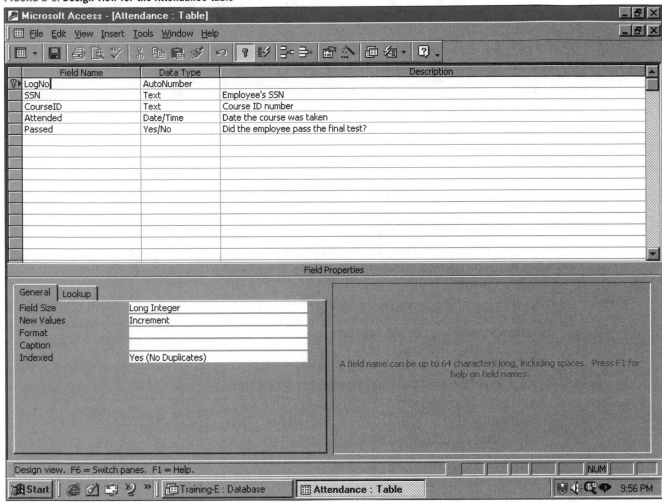

field name	data type	description
SSN	Text	Employee's SSN
CourseID	Text	Course ID number
Attended	Date/Time	Date the course was taken
Passed	Yes/No	Did the employee pass the final test?

Comparing linked tables to imported tables

A **linked table** is a table created in another database product, or another program such as Excel, that is stored in a file outside the open database. You can add, delete, and edit records in a linked table from within Access, but you can't change its structure. An **imported table** creates a copy of the information from the external file and places it in a new Access table in your database.

Defining Text Field Properties

Field properties are the characteristics that apply to each field in a table, such as field size, default value, or field formats. Modifying these properties helps ensure database accuracy and clarity because they restrict the way data is entered and displayed. You modify field properties in Table Design view. ~~~~~~ David decides to make field property changes to several text fields in the Employees table. He modifies the size and format properties.

Steps 1 2 3 4

1. Click the **Tables button** on the Objects bar in the database window if it is not already selected, click the **Employees table**, then click the **Design button** 🔲 in the Training-E database window

   The Employees table opens in Design view. The Field Properties panel (the lower half of the Table Design view window) changes to display the properties of the selected field, which depend on the field's data type. For example, when a field with a Text data type is selected, the Field Size property is visible. However, when a field with a Date/Time data type is selected, Access controls the Field Size property, so the property is not displayed. Most field properties are optional, but if they require an entry, Access provides a default value.

2. Click the **SSN field name**, look at the Field properties, then click each of the **field names** while viewing the Field Properties panel

   ### QuickTip
   Fifty is the default field size for a text field.

3. Click the **Last field name**, double-click **255** in the **Field Size text box** in the Field Properties, then type **30**

   Changing this property to 30 should accommodate even the longest entry for Last Name.

   ### QuickTip
   Press [F6] to quickly move between the upper and lower panels of Table Design view.

4. Change the **Field Size property** to **30** for the following Field Names: **First, Department**, **Title**, **Location**, and **Email**

   Changing the Field Size property to **30** for each of these text fields in this table should accommodate all the entries. The **Input Mask property** controls both the values that users can enter into a text box control and provides a visual guide for users as they enter data.

   ### Trouble?
   Insert the Office 2000 CD to install the Input Mask Wizard if necessary.

5. Click the **SSN field name**, click the **Input Mask text box** in the Field Properties panel, click the **Build button** 🔳 to start the Input Mask Wizard, click **Yes** to save the table, then click **Yes** when warned about losing data

   ### QuickTip
   You can enter the Input Mask directly in the field properties.

6. Click **Social Security Number** in the Input Mask list, click **Next**, click **Next** to accept **000-00-0000** as the default input mask, click **Next** to accept the option to store the data **without the symbols in the mask**, then click **Finish**

   The Design view of the Employees table should now look like Figure E-4. Notice that the SSN field is chosen, and the Field Properties panel displays the Input Mask property.

7. Click the **Save button** 🔳 on the Table Design toolbar, then click the **Datasheet View button** 🔳 on the Table Design toolbar

8. Maximize the datasheet, press [**Tab**] seven times to move to the SSN field for the first record, then type **115774444**

   The SSN Input Mask property creates an easy-to-use visual pathway to facilitate accurate data entry. See Table E-3 for more information on Text field properties.

9. Close the Employees table

FIGURE E-4: Changing Text field properties

Employees Table

SSN field is selected

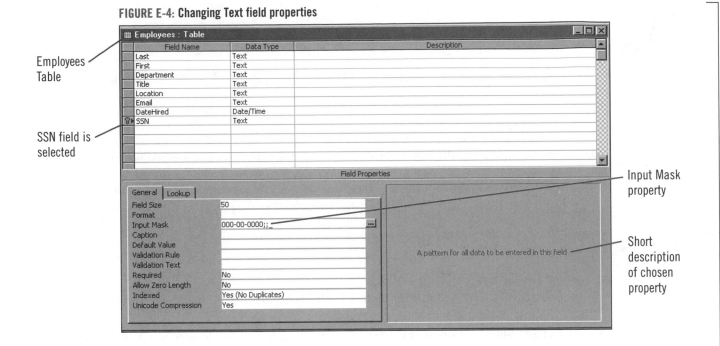

Input Mask property

A pattern for all data to be entered in this field

Short description of chosen property

TABLE E-3: Common Text field properties

property	description	sample field name	sample property entry
Field Size	Controls how many characters can be entered into the field	State	2
Format	Controls how information will be displayed and printed < forces all characters to *display* lowercase even though the data is stored in the same way it was entered > forces all characters to *display* uppercase even though the data is stored in the same way it was entered @ requires that an entry be made & does not require that an entry be made	State	>
Input Mask	Provides a pattern for data to be entered; contains three parts separated by semicolons	Phone	(999)000-0000;1;_
Caption	A label used to describe the field. When a Caption property isn't entered, the field name is used to describe the field	Emp#	Employee Number
Default Value	Value that is automatically entered in the given field for new records	City	Kansas City
Required	Determines if an entry is required for this field	LastName	Yes

CLUES TO USE

Defining input mask property parts

Input mask properties contain three parts. The first part controls what type of data can be entered and how it will be displayed: 9 represents an optional number; 0 represents a required number, ? represents an optional letter; L represented a required letter. The second part determines whether all displayed characters (such as dashes in the SSN field) are stored in the field, or just the entry. The 0 (zero) entry stores all characters. The 1 (one) entry stores only the entered characters. The third part determines which character Access will display for the space where a character is typed in the input mask. Common entries are the asterisk (*), underscore (_), or pound sign (#).

Defining Number and Currency Fields

Even though some of the properties for Number and Currency fields are the same as for Text fields, each field type has its own specific list of valid properties. Numeric and Currency fields have very similar properties because they both contain numbers. One important difference, however, is that a Currency field limits the user's control over the field size. Therefore, you would use a Currency field to prevent rounding off during calculations. A Currency field is accurate to fifteen digits to the left of the decimal point and four digits to the right. ➤ The Courses table contains both a Number field (Hours), and a Currency field (Cost). David modifies the properties of these two fields.

Steps 1234

1. Click the **Courses table**, click the **Design button** 🔲 in the Training-E database window, then click the **Hours field**

   The Field Size property for a Number field defaults to Long Integer. See Table E-4 for more information on common Number field properties.

2. Click the **Field Size text box** in the Field Properties, click the **Field Size list arrow**, then click **Byte**

3. Click the **Cost field**, click the **Decimal Places text box** in the Field Properties, click the **Decimal Places list arrow**, then click **0**

   Your screen should look like Figure E-5. Because all of MediaLoft's courses are priced at a round dollar value, there is no need to display zero cents in each field entry.

4. Click the **Save button** 🔲 on the Table Design toolbar, then click the **Datasheet View button** 🔲 on the Table Design toolbar

   Since none of the entries in any of the fields were longer than the new field size entries, you won't lose any data.

5. Press **[Tab]** twice to move to the **Hours** field for the first record, type **1000**, then press **[Tab]**

   Because 1,000 is larger than the Byte field size for the Hours field will allow, you are cautioned with an Access error message indicating that the value isn't valid for this field.

6. Click **OK**, press **[Esc]** to remove the inappropriate entry in the Hours field, then press **[Tab]** three times to move to the **Cost** field

   The Cost field currently displays all data rounded to the nearest dollar.

7. Type **199.75** in the **Cost** field, then press **[↓]**

   Because this field has been formatted to display no cents, remainders are rounded to the nearest dollar and $200 is displayed in the datasheet. Even though remainders of cents are rounded when displayed on the datasheet, 199.75 is the actual value stored in the field. Formatting does not change the actual data, but only the way it is displayed.

8. Close the Courses table

FIGURE E-5: Changing Currency and Number field properties

Courses table

Cost field is chosen

Decimal Places property

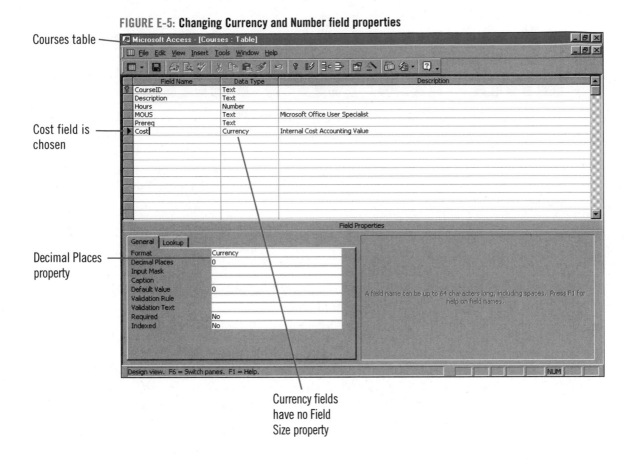

Currency fields have no Field Size property

TABLE E-4: Common numeric and currency field properties

property	description	sample field name	sample property entry
Field size (Number field only)	Determines the largest number that can be entered in the field, as well as the type of data (e.g. integer or fraction) • Byte stores numbers from 0 to 255 (no fractions) Integer stores numbers from −32,768 to 32,767 (no fractions) • Long Integer stores numbers from −2,147,483,648 to 2,147,483,647 (no fractions) • Single stores numbers (including fractions with six digits to the right of the decimal point) times 10 to the −38th to +38th power • Double stores numbers (including fractions with over 10 digits to the right of the decimal point) in the range of 10 to the −324th to +324th power	Quantity	Integer
Decimal Places	The number of digits to the right of the decimal separator	Dues	0

Defining Date/Time and Yes/No Fields

A Date field's Format property is designed specifically to show dates in just about any format such as January 5, 2003; 05-Jan-03; or 1/5/2003. Many of a Date field's other properties such as Input Mask, Caption, and Default Value are very similar to Text and Number field types. David wants the database to display all Date fields with four digits for the year, so there is no confusion regarding the century. He will also ensure that the Yes/No field is displayed as a check box versus a text entry of "Yes" or "No."

Steps

1. Click the **Attendance table**, click the **Design button** in the Training-E database window, then click the **Attended field name**

You want the dates of attendance to display as 01/17/2000 instead of as 1/17/00. You must work with the Attended field's Format property.

2. Click the **Format text box** in the Field Properties, then click the **Format list arrow**

Although several predefined Date/Time formats are available, none matches the format you want. To define a custom format, enter symbols that represent how you want the date to appear in the Format property text box.

3. Type **mm/dd/yyyy**, then press **[Enter]**

The updated Format property for the Attended field shown in Figure E-6 forces the date to appear with two digits for the month, two digits for the day, and four digits for the year. The parts of the date will be separated by forward slashes. You want the Passed field to display a check box for this control. The Display Control property is on the Lookup tab.

QuickTip

Click a property, then press [F1] to open the Microsoft Access Help window to the specific page that describes that property.

4. Click the **Passed field name**, click the **Lookup tab** in the Field Properties, click the **Display Control textbox**, then click the **Display Control property's list arrow**

A Yes/No field may appear as a check box in which "checked" equals "yes" and "unchecked" equals "no," as a text box that displays "yes" or "no," or as a combo box that displays "yes" and "no" in the drop-down list.

5. Click **Check Box** in the Display Control list

The linking SSN field in the Attendance table must be the same data type and size as it is in the Employees table.

6. Click the **SSN field**, click the **General tab** in the Field Properties, click the **Input Mask text box**, click the **Build button** , click **Yes** to save the table, click **Social Security Number** in the Input Mask Wizard dialog box, click **Next,** click **Next**, click **Finish**, click the **Datasheet View button** on the Table Design, then click **Yes** when prompted

Entering records tests the property changes.

QuickTip

You can click a checkbox control or press the spacebar. Click or press the spacebar a second time to clear the checkmark.

7. Press **[Tab]** to move to the SSN field, type **115774444**, press **[Tab]**, type **Comp1**, press **[Tab]**, type **1/31/00**, press **[Tab]**, then press **[Spacebar]**

Your screen should look like Figure E-7. Double-check that the SSN and Attended fields are formatting correctly too.

8. Press **[Enter]**, press **[Tab]** to move through the LogNo field, type **222334444**, press **[Tab]**, type **Comp1**, press **[Tab]**, type **1/31/00**, press **[Tab]**, then press **[Spacebar]**

FIGURE E-6: Changing Date/Time field properties

Attendance table

Attended field is chosen

Custom Format property change is made

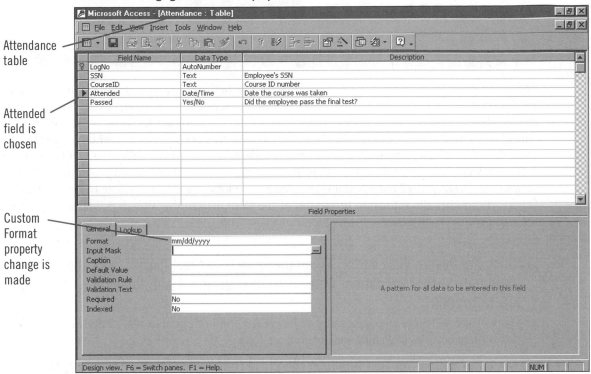

FIGURE E-7: Testing field property changes

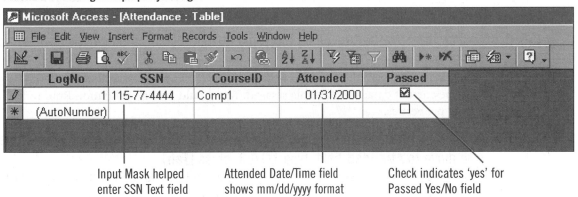

Input Mask helped enter SSN Text field

Attended Date/Time field shows mm/dd/yyyy format

Check indicates 'yes' for Passed Yes/No field

Planning for the 21st century

The default Format property (General) for a Date/Time field assumes that dates entered as 1/1/30 to 12/31/99 are twentieth-century dates (1930–1999), and those entered as 1/1/00 to 12/31/29 are twenty- first century dates (2000–2029). If you wish to enter dates outside these ranges, you must enter all four digits of the date.

Defining Field Validation Properties

The **Validation Rule** and **Validation Text** field properties can help you eliminate unreasonable entries by establishing criteria for the entry before it is accepted into the database. For example, the Validation Rule property of a Gender field might be modified to allow only two entries: "male" or "female." The Validation Text property is used to display a message when a user tries to enter data that doesn't pass the Validation Rule property for that field. Without a Validation Rule entry, the Validation Text property is meaningless. ━━━ MediaLoft started providing in-house courses on January 17, 2000. Therefore, it wouldn't make sense to enter a date before that time. David will modify the validation properties of the Date field in the Attendance table to prevent the entry of incorrect dates.

Steps 1 2 3 4

1. Click the **Design View button** on the Table Datasheet toolbar, click the **Attended field**, click the **Validation Rule text box** in the Field Properties, then type **>=1/17/2000**
   This property forces all course dates to be greater than or equal to 1/17/2000. See Table E-5 for more examples of Validation Rule expressions.

2. Click the **Validation Text text box**, then type **Date must be on or after 1/17/2000**
   The Validation Text property will appear in a dialog box to explain to the user why a field entry that doesn't pass the Validation Rule criteria cannot be accepted. The Design view of the Attendance table should now look like Figure E-8. Access changed the entry in the Validation Rule property to appear as >=#1/17/00#. Pound signs (#) are used to surround date criteria. Access assumes that years entered with two digits in the range 30 and 99 refer to the years 1930 through 1999, whereas digits in the range 00 and 29 refer to the years 2000 through 2029. If you wish to indicate a year outside these ranges, you must enter all four digits of the year.

3. Click the **Save button** on the Table Design toolbar, then click **Yes** when asked to test the existing data
   Because all dates in the Attended field are more recent than 1/17/00, there are no date errors in the current data, and the table is saved. You should test the Validation Rule and Validation Text properties.

4. Click the **Datasheet View button** on the Table Design toolbar, press **[Tab]** three times to move to **Attended field**, type **1/1/99**, press **[Tab]**
   Because you tried to enter a 1999 date in the Attended field of the Attendance datasheet, the Validation rule that you entered appears in a dialog box. See Figure E-9.

5. Click **OK** to close the Validation Rule dialog box
   You know that the Validation Rule and Validation Text properties work properly.

6. Press **[Esc]** to reject the invalid date entry

7. Close the Attendance table

FIGURE E-8: Using the Validation properties

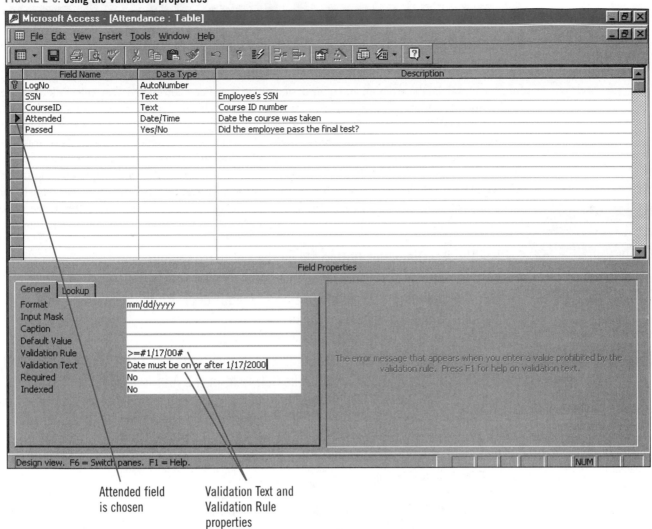

Attended field
is chosen

Validation Text and
Validation Rule
properties

FIGURE E-9: Validation Rule dialog box

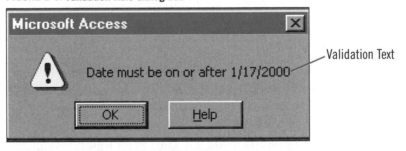

Validation Text

TABLE E-5: Validation Rule expressions

data type	validation rule expression	description
Number or Currency	>0	The number must be positive
Number or Currency	>10 And <100	The number must be between 10 and 100
Number or Currency	10 Or 20 Or 30	The number must be 10, 20, or 30
Text	"IA" Or "NE" Or "MO"	The entry must be IA, NE, or MO
Date/Time	>=#1/1/93#	The date must be on or after 1/1/1993
Date/Time	>#1/1/80# And <#1/1/90#	The date must be between 1/1/1980 and 1/1/1990

Creating One-to-Many Relationships

Once the initial database design and table design phase have been completed, you must link the tables together in appropriate one-to-many relationships. Some field properties that do not affect how the data is stored (such as the Format property), can be changed after the tables are linked, but other properties (such as the Field Size property), cannot be changed once tables are linked. Therefore, it is best to complete all of the table and field design activities before linking the tables. Once the tables are linked, however, you can design queries, reports, and forms with fields from multiple tables. David's initial database sketch revealed that the SSN field will link the Employee table to the Attendance table and that the CourseID field will link the Courses table to the Attendance table. David will now define the one-to-many relationships between the tables of the Training-E database.

1. Click the **Relationships button** on the Database toolbar

   The Show Table dialog box opens and lists all three tables in the Training-E database.

2. Click **Employees** on the **Tables tab**, click **Add**, click **Attendance**, click **Add**, click **Courses**, click **Add**, then click **Close**

   All three tables have been added to the Relationships window.

3. Maximize the window, click **SSN** in the **Employees table Field List**, then drag the **SSN field** from the Employees table to the SSN field in the Attendance table

   Dragging a field from one table to another in the Relationships window links the two tables with the chosen field and opens the Edit Relationships dialog box as shown in Figure E-10. **Referential integrity** helps ensure data accuracy.

4. Click the **Enforce Referential Integrity check box** in the Edit Relationships dialog box, then click **Create**

   The **one-to-many line** shows the linkage between the SSN field of the Employees table and the Attendance table. The "one" side of the relationship is the unique SSN for each record in the Employees table. The "many" side of the relationship is identified by an infinity symbol pointing to the SSN field in the Attendance table. The CourseID field will link the Courses table to the Attendance table.

5. Click the **CourseID field** in the Courses table, then drag it from the Courses table to the **CourseID field** in the Attendance table

6. Click the **Enforce Referential Integrity check box**, then click **Create**

   The finished Relationships window should look like Figure E-11. Print the Relationships window to show structural information including table names, field names, key fields, and relationships between tables.

7. Click **File** on the menu bar, click **Print Relationships**, click the **Print button** on the Print Preview toolbar, click the **Close Window button**, click **Yes** to save the report, click **OK** to accep the default report name, click the **Relationships Window Close button**, then click **Yes** to save changes

   When tables are related with one-to-many relationships, their datasheets will show an **expand button**, to the left of the record that can be clicked to show related records in a **subdatasheet**. When the related records appear, the expand button becomes a **collapse button**, which can be clicked to close the related records window.

8. Double-click the **Courses table**, then click the **Comp1 Expand button**

   Your screen should look like Figure E-12.

9. Close the Training-E database, then exit Access

FIGURE E-10: Edit Relationships dialog box

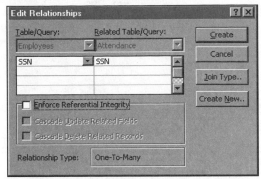

FIGURE E-11: Final Relationships window

"Many" side of one-to-many relationship

"One" side of one-to-many relationship

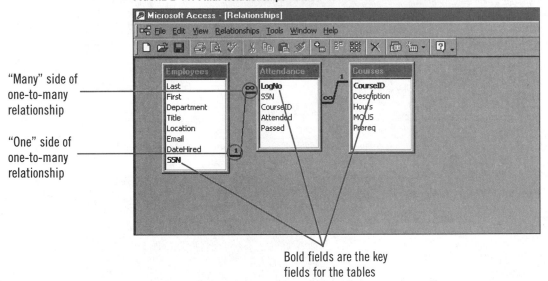

Bold fields are the key fields for the tables

FIGURE E-12: A subdatasheet allows you to view related records

Expand button

Collapse button

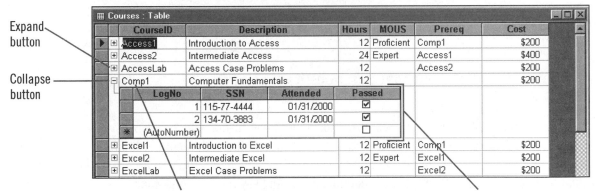

One record in the Courses table is related to two records in the Attendance table through the common CourseID field

Subdatasheet

Enforcing referential integrity

Referential integrity ensures that no orphaned records are entered or created in the database. An **orphan record** happens when information in the linking field of the "many" table doesn't have a matching entry in the linking field of the "one" table. For MediaLoft, referential integrity ensures that SSN entries added to the Attendance table are first recorded in the Employees table. Also, referential integrity prevents the user from deleting a record from the Employees table if a matching SSN entry is present in the Attendance table.

Practice

► Concepts Review

Identify each element of the table Design view shown in Figure E-13.

FIGURE E-13

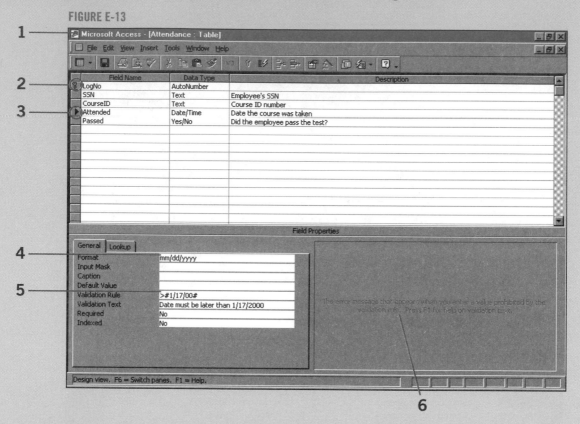

Match each term with the statement that describes its function.

7. Primary Key	**a.** Several tables linked together in one-to-many relationships
8. Field Properties	**b.** A field that holds unique information for each record in the table
9. Design view	**c.** Where all characteristics of a table, including field names, data types, field
10. Validation Rule and	descriptions, field properties, and key fields, are defined
Validation Text	**d.** Characteristics that apply to each field of a table, such as field size, default
11. Relational database	values, or field formats
	e. Helps you eliminate unreasonable entries by establishing criteria for the entry

Select the best answer from the list of choices.

12. Which of the following steps would probably help eliminate fields of duplicate data in a table?
  a. Redesign the database and add more tables.
  b. Redesign the database and add more fields.
  c. Change the formatting properties of the field in which the duplicate data existed.
  d. Change the validation properties of the field in which the duplicate data existed.

13. Which of the following is **NOT** defined in the table's Design view?
   a. Key fields
   b. Duplicate data
   c. Field lengths
   d. Data types

14. Which of the following is **NOT** a common data type?
   a. Text
   b. Alpha
   c. Number
   d. Date/Time

15. Which feature helps the database designer make sure that one-to-many relationships are preserved?
   a. Validation Text property
   b. Validation Rule property
   c. Field formatting
   d. Referential integrity

16. Which character is used to identify dates in a validation expression?
   a. " (double quote)
   b. ' (single quote)
   c. # (pound sign)
   d. & (ampersand)

17. Which Format Property Option displays all characters in the field as uppercase?
   a. <
   b. >
   c. !
   d. @

▶ Skills Review

1. **Examine relational database requirements.**
   a. Examine your address book.
   b. Write down the fields you will need.
   c. Examine which fields contain duplicate entries.

2. **Plan related tables.**
   a. Start Access.
   b. Use the Blank Access Database option button to create a new database file.
   c. Type "Membership-E" as the File name then create the database on your Project Disk.
   d. Click Tables on the Objects bar, then click the New Table button.

3. **Create related tables.**
   a. Use Design view to create the new table using the following field names with the given data types: First, Text; Last, Text; Street, Text; Zip, Text; Birthday, Date/Time; Dues, Currency; MemberNo, Text; CharterMember, Yes/No.
   b. Identify MemberNo as the primary key field.

c. Save the table as "Names," then close it.

d. Use Design view to create a new table using the following fields with the given data types: Zip, Text; City, Text; State, Text.

e. Identify Zip as the primary key field.

f. Save the table as "Zips," then close it.

g. Use Design view to create a new table using the following fields with the given data types: MemberNo, Text Activity Date, Date/Time; Hours, Number.

j. Save the table without a primary key field, name it "Activities," then close it.

4. Define text field properties.

a. Open the Zips table in Design view.

b. Change the Field Size property of the State field to 2.

c. Change the Field Size property of the Zip field to 5.

d. Save the changes and close the Zips table.

e. Open the Names table in Design view.

f. Use the Input Mask Wizard to create the Input Mask property for the Zip field in both the Zips and Names tables. Choose the Zip Code input mask, and use the other default options provided by the Input Mask Wizard.

g. Change the Field Size property of the First, Last, and Street fields to 30.

h. Change the Field Size property of the MemberNo field to 5.

i. Save the changes and close the Names and Zips tables.

j. Open the Activities table in Design view.

k. Change the Field Size property of the MemberNo field to 5.

l. Save the change and close the Activities table.

5. Define number and currency field properties.

a. Open the Names table in Design view.

b. Change the Decimal Places property of the Dues field to 0.

c. Save the change and close the Names table.

d. Open the Activities table in Design view.

e. Change the Field Size property of the Hours field to Byte.

f. Save the change and close the Activities table.

6. Define the Date/Time and Yes/No field properties.

a. Open the Names table in Design view.

b. Change the Format property of the Birthday field to m/d/yyyy.

c. Check to ensure that the Display Control property of the CharterMember field is set to check box.

d. Save the changes and close the Names table.

e. Open the Activities table in Design view.

f. Change the Format property of the ActivityDate field to m/d/yyyy.

g. Save the change and close the Activities table.

7. Define field validation properties.

a. Open the Zips table in Design view.

b. Click the State field name, click the Validation Rule text box, then type ="IA" OR "KS" OR "MO"

c. Click the Validation Text text box, then type "State must be IA, KS, or MO"

d. Save the change and close the Zips table.

8. Create one-to-many relationships.

a. Open the Relationships window.

b. Add all three tables to the Relationships window in this order: Activities, Names, Zips.

c. Close the Show Table dialog box.

d. Drag the Zip field from the Zips table to the Zip field in the Names table, creating a one-to-many relationship from the Zips table to the Names table.

e. Enforce Referential Integrity for the relationship.

f. Drag the MemberNo field from the Names table to the MemberNo field in the Activities table, creating a one-to-many relationship from the Names table to the Activities table.

g. Enforce Referential Integrity for the relationship.

h. Save the changes to the Relationships layout.

i. Print the Relationships window.

j. Close the Relationships report, and save it with the given name.

k. Close the Relationships window.

l. Close the Memberships-E database.

 # Independent Challenges

1. As the manager of a music store's instrument rental program, you have decided to create a database to track instrument rentals to school children. The fields you need to track can be organized with four tables: Instruments, Rentals, Customers, and Schools, as shown below.

To complete this independent challenge:

a. Sketch how the fields could be organized into four tables: Instruments, Rentals, Customers, and Schools. The sketch should show the fields listed in a vertical field list similarly to how they appear in the Relationships window.

b. Determine if there are key fields in the tables. Place a "K" beside those fields in your sketch.

c. Determine how the tables should be linked using one-to-many relationships. This may involve adding a linking field to a table to establish the connection. Draw a linking line between these fields using the one-to-many symbols at the appropriate ends of the linking line.

d. Create and save a database called "Music Store-E".

e. Create the four tables in the Music Store-E database using the following information. Note that the Primary Key fields are bold in the table.

table	field name	data type	table	field name	data type
Customers	FirstName	Text	Instruments	Description	Text
	LastName	Text		**SerialNo**	Text
	Street	Text		MonthlyFee	Currency
	City	Text			
	State	Text			
	Zip	Text			
	CustNo	AutoNumber			
	SchoolNo	Number			
Schools	SchoolName	Text	Rentals	**RentalNo**	AutoNumber
	SchoolNo	AutoNumber		CustNo	Number
				SerialNo	Text
				Date	Date/Time

f. Change the Field Size property of the following fields:

table	fields	change the Field Size property to:
Customers	FirstName, LastName, Street, City	30
Customers	State	2
Customers	Zip	9
Instruments	SerialNo	10
Rentals	SerialNo	10

g. Add a Validation Rule property to the Date field of the Rentals table that only allows dates of 1/1/00 or later to be entered into the database. The property entry is >=#1/1/00#.

h. Add a Validation Text property to the Date field that states "Dates must be on or later than 1/1/2000".

i. Create one-to-many relationships to link the tables as follows. Be sure to enforce referential integrity as appropriate.

"one" table	"many" table	linking field
Customers	Rentals	CustNo
Instruments	Rentals	SerialNo
Schools	Customers	SchoolNo

j. Print the Relationships window of the database, making sure that all fields of each table are visible.

k. Compare the printout to your original sketch. How do the database designs differ?

2. You want to document the books you've read in a relational database. You will design the database on paper including the tables, field names, data types, and relationships.

To complete this independent challenge:

a. On paper, create three balanced columns by drawing two vertical lines from the top to the bottom of the paper. At the top of the first column write the label "Table." At the top of the second column write the label "Field Name," and at the top of the third column write the label "Data Type."

b. In the middle column, list all of the fields that need to be tracked to record information about the books you've read. You'll want to track such information as the book title, category (such as Biography, Mystery, or Science Fiction), rating (a numeric value from 1–10 that indicates how satisfied you were with the book), date you read the book, author's first name, and author's last name.

c. In the first column, identify the table where this field would be found. (*Hint:* You should identify two tables of information for this listing of fields.)

d. Identify the key fields found in the tables by circling the field name. If you do not find any fields that are good candidates for key fields, you may have to create additional fields. (*Hint:* Each book has an ISBN— International Standard Book Number—which is a unique number assigned to every book. To uniquely identify each author, you will have to create a new field called AuthorNo.)

e. In a third column, identify the appropriate data type for each field.

f. On a new piece of paper, sketch the fields as they would appear in the Relationships window of Access. Be sure to include these elements:
- Two tables with their respective field lists
- Circled key fields in each table

- A linking line drawn between the field common to each table. (*Hint:* To complete the linking line, you may have to add a field to one of the tables to create the common link. Remember that the "one" side of the relationship must be a key field.) Be sure that your linking line shows the "one" and "many" symbols at the appropriate ends of the linking line, just as it does in the Access Relationships window.

3. You have been asked by your employer to create a database that documents blood donations by employees over the year. You first design the database on paper and include the tables, field names, data types, and relationships, and then you create the database in Access.

To complete this independent challenge:

a. On paper, create three balanced columns by drawing two vertical lines from the top to the bottom of the paper. At the top of the first column write the label "Table." At the top of the second column write the label "Field Name," and at the top of the third column write the label "Data Type."

b. In the middle column, list all of the fields that need to be tracked to record information about the blood donations. You'll want to track information such as employee name, employee Social Security number, employee department, employee blood type, date of donation, and hospital the donation was given to. Also, you'll want to track basic hospital information, such as the hospital name and address.

c. In the first column, identify the table where this field would be found. (*Hint:* You should identify three tables of information for this listing of fields. Each employee can donate many times in one year, and each hospital can receive many donations.)

d. Identify the key fields found in the tables by circling the field name. If you do not find any fields that are good candidates for key fields, you may have to create additional fields. (*Hint:* Employees are uniquely identified by their SSN, and hospitals by a unique HospitalNo. An AutoNumber field called "DonationNo" uniquely identifies each donation.)

e. In a third column, identify the appropriate data type for each field.

f. On a new piece of paper, sketch the fields as they would appear in the Relationships window of Access. Be sure to include these elements:
- Three tables with their respective field lists.
- Circle the key fields in each table.
- Draw the linking line between the field common to each table. (*Hint:* To complete the linking line, you may have to add a field to one of the tables to create the common link. Remember that the "one" side of the relationship must be a key field.) Be sure that your linking line shows the "one" and "many" symbols at the appropriate ends of the linking line, just as it does in the Access Relationships window.

g. Start Access and open a new, blank database, then create the database you just designed.

h. Name the database "Donations", save and close Donations, then exit Access.

4. MediaLoft has developed a company intranet site that gives employees access to company-wide information. In this independent challenge, you'll check the intranet site to find new courses requested by MediaLoft employees.

a. Connect to the Internet and use your browser to go to the MediaLoft intranet site at http://www.course.com/illustrated/MediaLoft/.

b. Click the link for Training.

c. Click the link for New Courses, and print the Web page.

d. Start Access, then open the Training-E database.

e. Enter the three new courses found on the Web page into the Courses table.

f. Print the Courses table, then close the Courses table.

g. Close the Training-E database.

h. Exit Access.

► Visual Workshop

Open the Training-E database, create a new table called "Vendors" using the Table Design view shown in Figure E-14 to determine field names and data types. Additional property changes include changing the Field Size property of the VState field to 2, the VendorID and VPhone fields to 10, and all other text fields to 30. Be sure to specify that the VendorID field is the Primary Key field.

FIGURE E-14

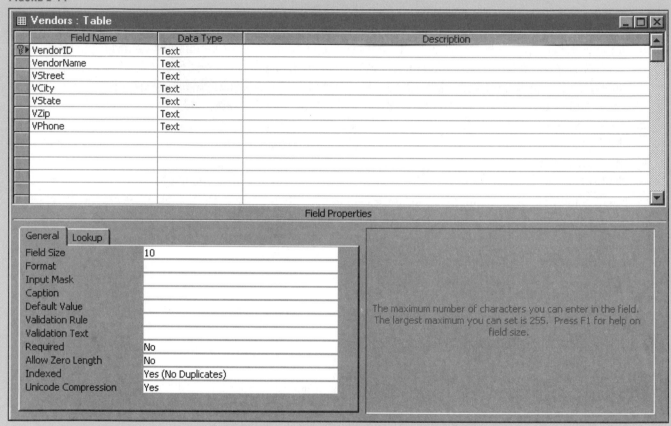

Creating
Multiple Table Queries

Objectives

- ► **Create select queries**
- ► **Sort a query on multiple fields**
- ► **Develop AND queries**
- ► **Develop OR queries**
- ► **Create calculated fields**
- ► **Build summary queries**
- ► **Create crosstab queries**
- ► **Modify crosstab queries**

In this unit, you will create **queries**, which are database objects that answer questions about the data by pulling fields and records that match specific criteria into a single datasheet. A **select query** retrieves data from one or more linked tables and displays the results in a datasheet. Queries can also be used to sort records, develop new calculated fields from existing fields, or develop summary calculations such as the sum or average of the values in a field. **Crosstab queries** present information in a cross-tabular report, similar to pivot tables in other database and spreadsheet products. David Dumont has spent several days entering information into the Attendance table to record which employees are taking which classes. Now, he can create select queries and crosstab queries to analyze the data in the database.

Access 2000

Creating Select Queries

You develop queries by using the Query Wizard or by directly specifying requested fields and query criteria in **Query Design view**. The resulting query datasheet is not a duplication of the data that resides in the original table's datasheet, but rather a logical view of the data. If you change or enter data in a query's datasheet, the data in the underlying table (and any other logical view) is updated automatically. Queries often are used to present and sort a subset of fields from multiple tables for data entry or update purposes. ✎ David creates a query to answer the question, "Who is taking what course?" He pulls fields from several tables into a single query object to display a single datasheet that answers this question.

Steps

1. Start Access and open the **Training-F** database on your Project Disk

2. Click the **Queries button** 📑 on the Objects bar in the Training-F Database window, then double-click **Create query in Design View**

   The Query1 Select Query Design view window opens and the Show Table dialog box opens listing all the tables in the database. You use the Show Table dialog box to add the tables that contain the fields you need to the Query Design view.

Trouble?

If you add a table to Query Design view twice by mistake, click the title bar of the extra field list, then press [Delete].

3. Click **Employees**, click **Add**, click **Attendance**, click **Add**, click **Courses**, click **Add**, then click **Close**

   The upper pane of Query Design view displays **field lists** for the three tables. Each table's name is in its field list title bar. You can drag the title bar of the field lists to move them or drag the edge of a field list to resize it. Key fields are bold, and serve as the "one" side of the one-to-many relationship between two tables. Relationships are displayed with **one-to-many join lines** between the linking fields, as shown in Figure F-1. The fields you want displayed in the datasheet must be added to the columns in the lower pane of the Query Design view.

QuickTip

Double-click a field name to place it in the next available column of the query grid.

4. Click the **First field** in the Employees table field list, then drag the **First field** to the Field cell in the first column of the query design grid

   The order in which the fields are placed in the query design grid is their order in the datasheet.

QuickTip

If you need to add a field to the query that isn't currently displayed, click the Show Table button 📑 to add the new table.

5. Drag the **Last field** from the Employees table to the Field cell in the second column, drag the **Attended field** from the Attendance table to the third column, drag the **Description field** from the Courses table to the fourth column, then drag the **Hours field** from the Courses table to the fifth column

   Your Query Design view should look like Figure F-2. You may delete a field from the lower pane by clicking the field selector above the field name and pressing [Delete]. Deleting a field from the query design grid removes it from the logical view of this query's datasheet, but does not delete the field from the database. A field is physically defined and the field's contents are physically stored in a table object only.

6. Click the **Hours field selector**, press [Delete] to remove the field from the query design grid, then click the **Datasheet View button** 📰 on the query Design toolbar

   The datasheet looks like Figure F-3. The resulting datasheet shows the four fields selected in Query Design view and displays 153 records. The records represent the 153 different times a MediaLoft employee has attended a MediaLoft class. Shayla Colletti appears in eleven records because she has attended eleven classes.

FIGURE F-1: Query Design view with multiple tables

Table names

Fields in the
Employees table

One-to-many
link lines

Query design grid

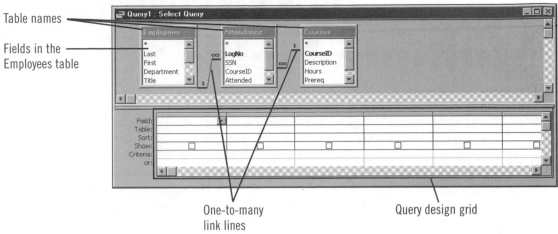

FIGURE F-2: Query Design view with five fields in the query grid

Field selector

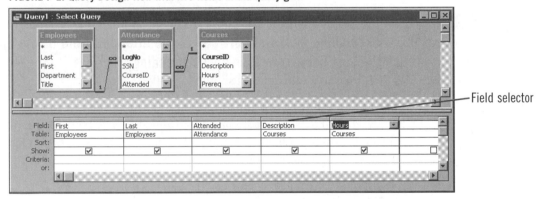

FIGURE F-3: Query datasheet showing related information from three tables

153 courses have
been taken

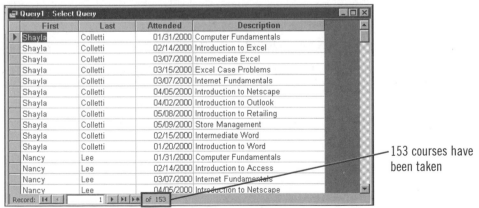

Resizing Query Design view

Drag the resize bar up or down to provide more room for the upper (field lists) or lower (query design grid) parts of Query Design view. By dragging the resize bar down, you may have enough room to enlarge each field list so that you can see all of the field names in each table, but still have enough room to show all of the information in the query design grid.

Sorting a Query on Multiple Fields

Sorting refers to reorganizing the records in either ascending or descending order based on the contents of a field. Queries allow you to specify more than one sort field in Query Design view, evaluating the sort orders from left to right. The leftmost sort field is the primary sort field. Sort orders defined in Query Design view are saved with the query object. If no sort orders are specified in the query design grid, the records are sorted by the primary key field of the first table that has a field in the query. David wishes to put the records in alphabetical order based on the employee's last name. If more than one record exists for an employee (if the employee has attended more than one class), David wants to further sort the records by the date the course was attended.

Steps

1. Click the **Design View button** on the Query Datasheet toolbar
   To sort the records according to David's plan, the Last field must be the primary sort, and the Attended field the secondary sort field.

2. Click the **Sort cell** of the **Last field** in the query design grid, click the **Sort list arrow**, click **Ascending**, click the **Sort cell** of the **Attended field** in the query design grid, click the **Sort list arrow**, then click **Ascending**
   The resulting query design grid should look like Figure F-4.

3. Click the **Datasheet View button** on the Query Design toolbar
   The records of the datasheet are now listed alphabetically by the entry in the Last field, then in chronological order by the entry in the Attended field, as shown in Figure F-5. You notice that Maria Abbott has attended six classes, but that her name has been incorrectly entered in the database as "Marie." Fix this error in the query datasheet.

4. Type **Maria**, then press [↓]
   This update shows that you are using a properly designed relational database because changing any occurrence of an employee's name should cause all other occurrences of that name to be automatically updated. The employee name is physically stored only once in the Employees table, although it is displayed in this datasheet once for every time the employee has attended a course.

5. Click the **Close Window button** to close the Select Query, click **Yes** when prompted to save the changes, type **Employee Progress Query** in the Query Name text box, then click **OK**
   The query is now saved and listed as an object in the Queries window in the Training-F database window.

QuickTip

You can resize the columns of a datasheet by pointing to the right column border that separates the field names, then dragging ╂ left or right to resize as needed. You can double-click ╂ to automatically adjust the column width to fit the widest entry.

QuickTip

If you need to identify your printout, include your name or initials in the query name and it will print in the header of the datasheet.

FIGURE F-4: Specifying multiple sort orders in Query Design view

Records will be sorted by Last, then by Attended

Resize bar

Show check box

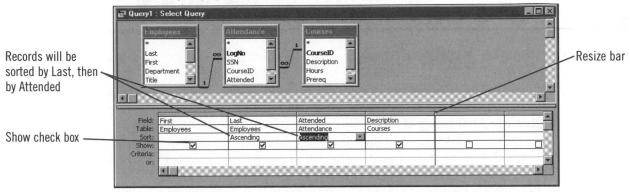

FIGURE F-5: Records sorted by Last, then Attended

Primary sort field

Secondary sort field

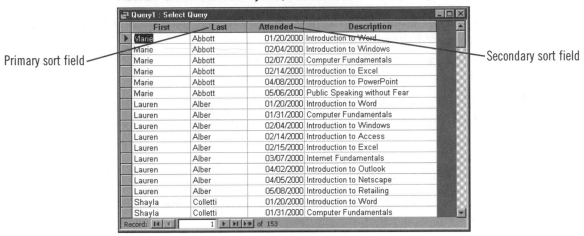

FIGURE F-6: Query grid for sorting out of order

Sort order is defined using fields that do not appear on the datasheet

Show check boxes are unchecked

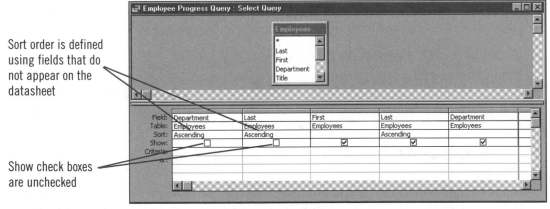

Specifying a sort order different from the field order in the datasheet

You cannot modify the left-to-right sort order hierarchy in Query Design view. However, if you wish to have the fields in the datasheet appear in a different order than that by which they are sorted, there is a simple solution, as shown in Figure F-6. Suppose you want the fields First, Last, and Department to appear in a datasheet in that order, but want to sort the records by Department, then by Last. The Department and Last fields are the first two fields in the design grid with the appropriate sort order specified, but their Show Check Boxes are unchecked, so these columns do not display in the datasheet. The resulting datasheet would sort the records by Department, then Last, and display the First, Last, and Department fields.

Developing AND Queries

Using Access you can query for specific records that match two or more criteria. **Criteria** are tests, or limiting conditions, for which the record must be true to be selected for a datasheet. To create an **AND query** in which two or more criteria are present, enter the criteria for the fields on the same Criteria row of the query design grid. If two AND criteria are entered for the same field, the AND operator separates the criteria in the Criteria cell for that field. ◄━━ David is looking for a person to assist the Access teacher in the classroom. In order to compile a list of potential candidates, he creates an AND query to find all employees who have taken MediaLoft's Access courses and passed the exams.

Steps

1. Click the **Employee Progress query**, then click the **Design View button** 📐 on the Query Datasheet toolbar

Instead of creating a query from scratch, you can modify the Employee Progress query. The only additional field you have to add to the query is the Passed field.

QuickTip

If you wanted the Attendance field to be in one of the first four, just drag and drop it there. The existing field in that column, as well as any fields to the right, will move over one column to the right to accommodate the addition.

2. Scroll the **Attendance table field list**, then double-click the **Passed field** to move it to the fifth column in the query design grid

MediaLoft offers several Access courses, so the criteria must specify all the records that contain the word "Access" anywhere in the Description field. You'll use the asterisk (*), a **wildcard character** that represents any combination of characters, to create this criteria.

3. Click the **Description field Criteria cell**, type ***access***, then click the **Datasheet View button** 🔲 on the Query Design toolbar

The resulting datasheet as shown in Figure F-7, shows thirteen records that match the criteria. The resulting records all contain the word "access" in some part of the Description field, but because of the placement of the asterisks, it didn't matter *where* (beginning, middle, or end) the word was found in the Description field entry. Additional criteria are needed to display a datasheet with only those records where the student passed the final exam.

4. Click the **Design View button** 📐 on the Query Datasheet toolbar, click the **Passed field Criteria cell**, then type **yes**

The resulting query design grid is shown in Figure F-8. Notice that Access entered double quotation marks around the text criterion in the Description field and added the **Like operator**. See Table F-1 for more information on Access operators.

5. Click **Datasheet View button** 🔲 on the Query Design toolbar to view the resulting records

Multiple criteria added to the same line of the query design grid (AND criteria) must *each* be true for the record to appear in the resulting datasheet, thereby causing the resulting datasheet to display *fewer* records. Only nine records contain "access" in the Description field and "yes" in the Passed field.

6. Click **File** on the menu bar, click **Save As** to save this query with a new name, type **Potential Access Assistants** in the Save Query 'Employee Progress Query' To: text box, then click **OK**

The query is saved with the new name, Potential Access Assistants, as a new object in the MediaLoft-F database.

7. Close the Potential Access Assistants datasheet

FIGURE F-7: Datasheet for Access records

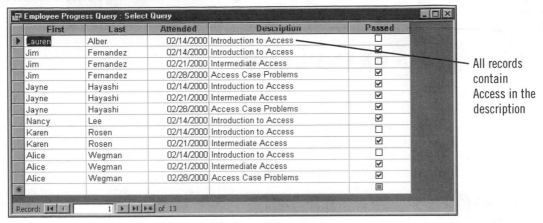

All records contain Access in the description

FIGURE F-8: AND criteria

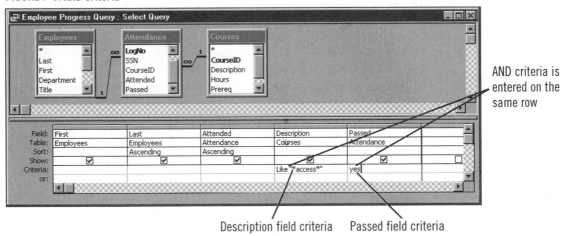

AND criteria is entered on the same row

Description field criteria   Passed field criteria

TABLE F-1: Comparison operators

operator	description	example	result
>	greater than	>50	Value exceeds 50
>=	greater than or equal to	>=50	Value is 50 or greater
<	less than	<50	Value is less than 50
<=	less than or equal to	<=50	Value is 50 or less
<>	not equal to	<>50	Value is any number other than 50
Between...And	finds values between two numbers or dates	Between #2/2/95# And #2/2/98#	Dates between 2/2/95 and 2/2/98, inclusive
In	finds a value that is one of a list	In("IA","KS","NE")	Value equals IA or KS or NE
Null	finds records that are blank	Null	No value has been entered
Is Not Null	finds records that are not blank	Is Not Null	Any value has been entered
Like	finds records that match the criteria	Like "A"	Value equals A
Not	finds records that do not match the criteria	Not 2	Numbers other than 2

Developing OR Queries

AND queries *narrow* the number of records in the resulting datasheet by requiring that a record be true for multiple criteria in one criteria row. **OR queries** *expand* the number of records that will appear in the datasheet because a record needs to be true *for only one* of the criteria rows. OR criteria are entered in the query design grid on different lines (criteria rows). Each criteria row of the query design grid is evaluated separately, adding the records that are true for that row to the resulting datasheet. ▬▬▬ David is looking for an assistant for the Excel courses. He modifies the Potential Access Assistants query to expand the number of records to include those who have passed Excel courses.

Steps

1. Click the **Potential Access Assistants** query, then click the **Design button** 📝 in the Training-F database window

To add OR criteria, you have to enter criteria in the "or" row of the query design grid.

2. Click the **or Description criteria cell** below Like "*access*", then type ***excel***

As soon as you click elsewhere in the query grid, Access will assist you with criteria **syntax** (rules by which criteria need to be entered) by automatically entering the Like operator when necessary. It also automatically adds double quotes to surround text criteria in Text fields, and pound signs (#) to surround date criteria in Date/Time fields. The criteria in Number, Currency, and Yes/No fields are not surrounded by any characters.

3. Click the **or Passed criteria cell** below Yes, then type **yes**

If a record matches *either* row of the criteria grid, it is included in the query's datasheet. Each row is evaluated separately, which is why it was necessary to put the Yes criteria for the Passed field in both rows of the grid. Otherwise, the second row would pull all records where "excel" is in the description regardless of whether the test was passed or not. Figure F-9 shows the OR criteria in the query design grid.

4. Click the **Datasheet View button** 🔳 on the Query Design toolbar

The resulting datasheet displays 28 records, as shown in Figure F-10. All of the records contain course Descriptions that contain the word Access or Excel as well as "Yes" in the Passed field. Also, notice that the sort order (Last, then Attended) is still in effect.

5. Click **File** on the menu bar, click **Save As**, click between **"Access"** and **"Assistants"**, type **or Excel**, press **[Spacebar]**, then click **OK**

This query is saved as a separate database object.

6. Close the Potential Access or Excel Assistants query

The Training-F database displays the three queries you created.

FIGURE F-9: OR criteria

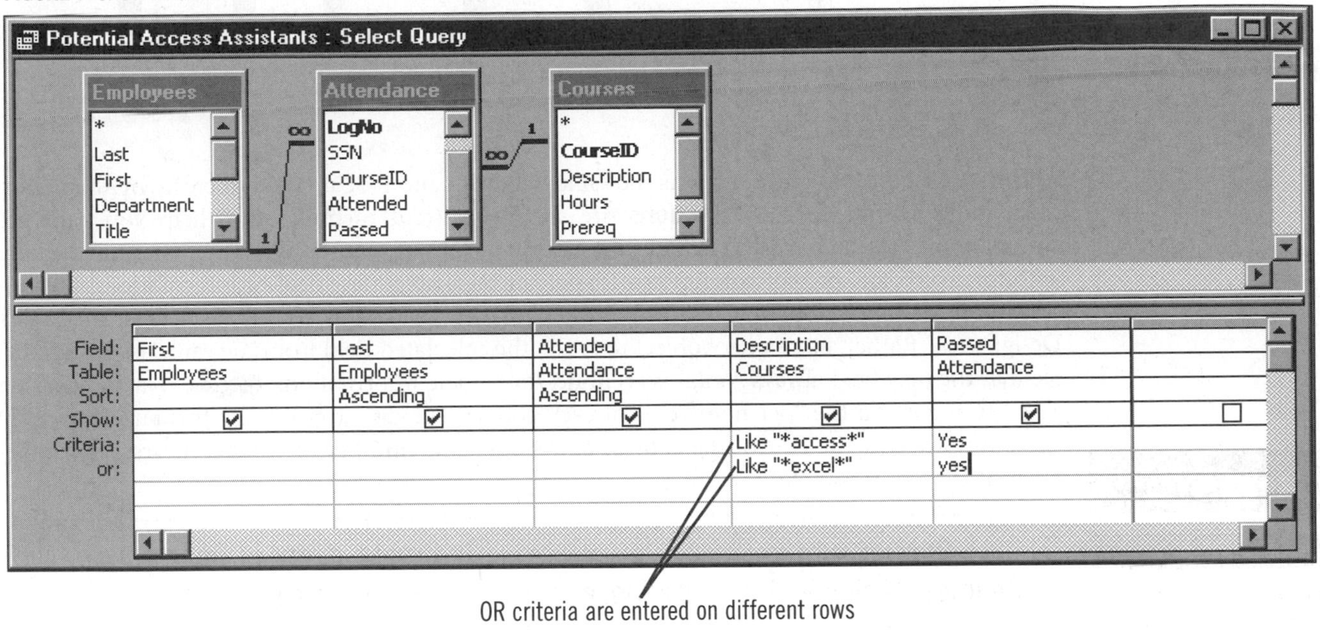
Potential Access Assistants : Select Query
Employees
*
Last
First
Department
Title
Attendance
LogNo
SSN
CourseID
Attended
Passed
Courses
*
CourseID
Description
Hours
Prereq
Field: First | Last | Attended | Description | Passed
Table: Employees | Employees | Attendance | Courses | Attendance
Sort: Ascending | Ascending
Show:
Criteria: Like "*access*" | Yes
or: Like "*excel*" | yes
OR criteria are entered on different rows

FIGURE F-10: OR criteria adds more records to the datasheet

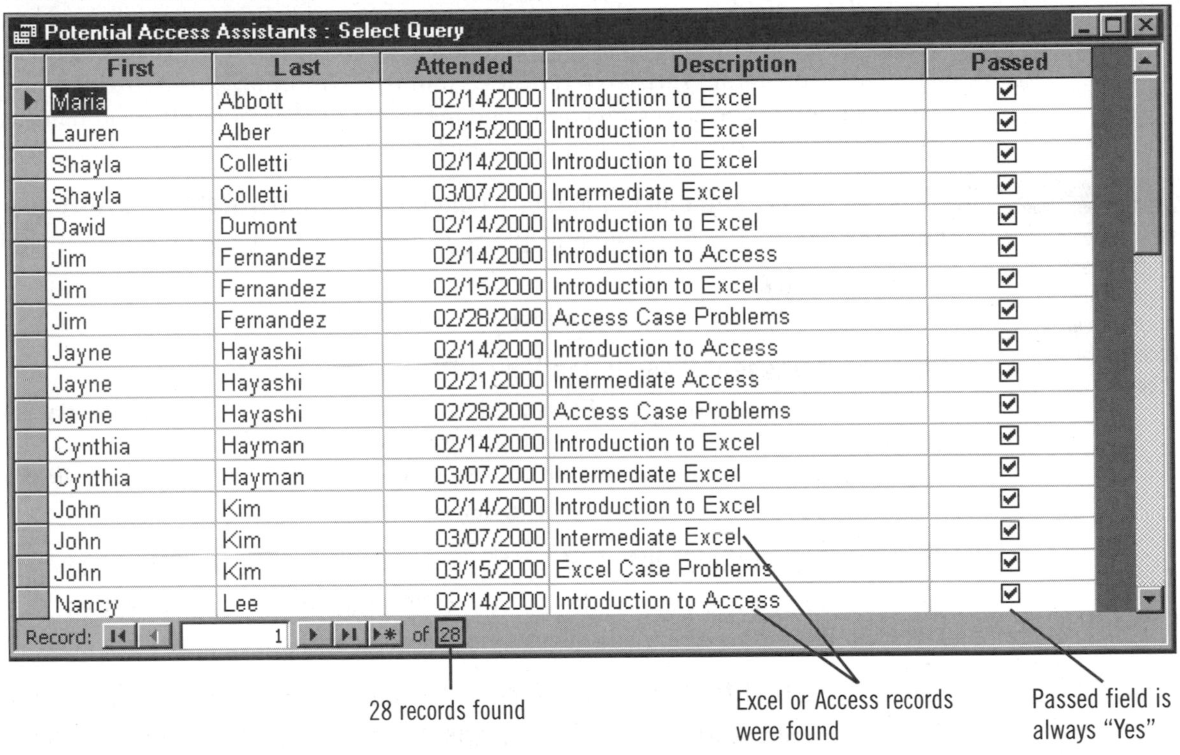
Potential Access Assistants : Select Query
First | Last | Attended | Description | Passed
Maria | Abbott | 02/14/2000 | Introduction to Excel
Lauren | Alber | 02/15/2000 | Introduction to Excel
Shayla | Colletti | 02/14/2000 | Introduction to Excel
Shayla | Colletti | 03/07/2000 | Intermediate Excel
David | Dumont | 02/14/2000 | Introduction to Excel
Jim | Fernandez | 02/14/2000 | Introduction to Access
Jim | Fernandez | 02/15/2000 | Introduction to Excel
Jim | Fernandez | 02/28/2000 | Access Case Problems
Jayne | Hayashi | 02/14/2000 | Introduction to Access
Jayne | Hayashi | 02/21/2000 | Intermediate Access
Jayne | Hayashi | 02/28/2000 | Access Case Problems
Cynthia | Hayman | 02/14/2000 | Introduction to Excel
Cynthia | Hayman | 03/07/2000 | Intermediate Excel
John | Kim | 02/14/2000 | Introduction to Excel
John | Kim | 03/07/2000 | Intermediate Excel
John | Kim | 03/15/2000 | Excel Case Problems
Nancy | Lee | 02/14/2000 | Introduction to Access
Record: 1 of 28
28 records found
Excel or Access records were found
Passed field is always "Yes"

CLUES TO USE

Using wildcard characters in query criteria

To search for a pattern, use a ? (question mark) to search for any single character and an * (asterisk) to search for any number of characters. Wildcard characters are often used with the Like operator. For example, the criterion Like "10/*/97" would find all dates in October of 1997, and the criterion Like "F*" would find all entries that start with the letter F.

Creating Calculated Fields

Arithmetic operators and functions shown in Table F-2 and F-3, are used to create mathematical calculations within Access. **Functions** are special shortcut formulas that help you calculate common answers such as counts and subtotals on groups of records, a loan payment if working with financial data, or the current date. If you can calculate a new field of information based on existing fields in a database, never define the new piece of data as a separate field in the table's Design view. Rather, use a query object to create the calculated field from the raw data to guarantee that the new field always contains accurate, up-to-date information. David has been asked to report on the "per hour" cost of each course. The data to calculate this answer already exists in the Cost (the cost of the course) and Hours (the number of contact hours per course) fields of the Courses table.

Steps

1. Click **Queries** on the Objects bar, double-click **Create query in Design view**, click **Courses**, click **Add**, then click **Close** in the Show Table dialog box
   The Courses field list is in the upper pane of the query window.

2. Double-click the **Description field**, double-click the **Hours field**, then double-click the **Cost field**
   A **calculated field** is created by entering a new descriptive field name followed by a colon in the Field cell of the query design grid followed by an expression. An **expression** is a combination of operators such as + (plus), − (minus), * (multiply), or / (divide); raw values (such as numbers or dates), functions; and fields that produce a result. Field names used in an expression are surrounded by square brackets.

3. Click the blank **Field cell** of the fourth column, type **Hourly Rate:[Cost]/[Hours]**, then drag the ↔ on the right edge of the fourth column selector to the right to display the entire entry
   The query design grid should now look like Figure F-11.

4. Click the **Datasheet View button** 📖 on the Query Design toolbar
   It is not necessary to show the fields used in the calculated expression in the datasheet (in this case, Hours and Cost), but viewing these fields beside the new calculated field helps confirm that your new calculated field is working properly. The Hourly Rate field appears to be accurate, but the data is not formatted well.

5. Click the **Design View button** 📐 on the Query Datasheet toolbar, right-click the calculated **Hourly Rate field** in the query design grid, then click **Properties**
   The Field Properties dialog box opens. This new field represents dollars per hour.

6. Click the **Format text box**, click **Format property list arrow**, click **Currency**, close the property sheet, then click the **Datasheet View button** to display the records
   The data shown in the Hourly Rate field is now rounded to the nearest cent.

7. Press **[Tab]** twice, type **300** in the Introduction to Access Cost field, then press **[Enter]**
   The resulting datasheet is shown in Figure F-12. The Hourly Rate field was updated to the correct value as soon as the Cost field was updated.

8. Press **[Esc]** to reverse the Introduction to Access Cost field change, click the **Save button** 💾, type **Hourly Rate** in the Save As dialog box, click **OK**, then close the datasheet

FIGURE F-11: Entering a calculated field in Query Design view

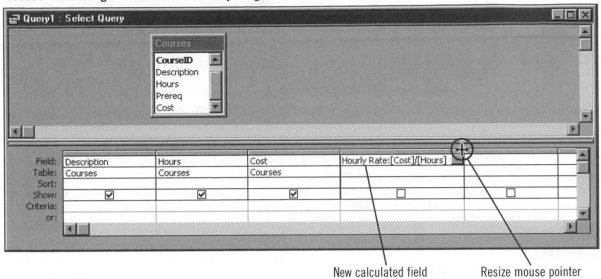

New calculated field   Resize mouse pointer

FIGURE F-12: Formatting and testing the calculated field

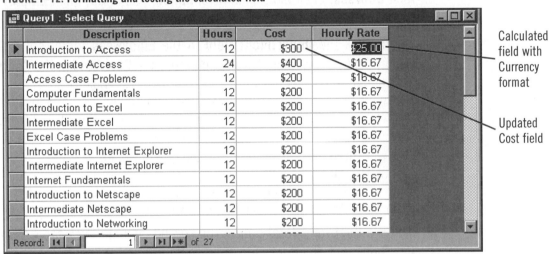

Calculated field with Currency format

Updated Cost field

TABLE F-2: Arithmetic operators

operator	description
+	Addition
–	Subtraction
*	Multiplication
/	Division
^	Exponentiation

TABLE F-3: Common functions

function	sample expression and description
DATE	DATE()-[BirthDate] Calculates the number of days between today and the date in the BirthDate field
PMT	PMT([Rate],[Term],[Loan]) Calculates the monthly payment on a loan where the Rate field contains the monthly interest rate, the Term field contains the number of monthly payments, and the Loan field contains the total amount financed
LEFT	LEFT([Lastname],2) Returns the first two characters of the entry in the Lastname field
RIGHT	RIGHT([Partno],3) Returns the last three characters of the entry in the Partno field
LEN	LEN([Description]) Returns the number of characters in the Description field

Building Summary Queries

As your database grows, you will probably be less interested in individual records and more interested in information about groups of records. A **summary query** can be used to calculate information about a group of records by adding appropriate **aggregate functions** to the Total row of the query design grid. Aggregate functions also create calculations, but are special functions in that they calculate information about a *group of records* rather than a new field of information for *each record*. Aggregate functions are summarized in Table F-4. Some aggregate functions such as Sum can be used only on fields with Number or Currency data types, but others such as Min, Max, or Count can be used on Text fields, too. ➤ The Accounting Department has asked David for a "cost by department" report that shows how many classes employees of each department have attended as well as the summarized costs for these courses. He builds a summary query to provide this information.

Steps

1. Click **Queries** on the Objects bar (if necessary), then double-click **Create query in Design view**

   You need all three tables to develop this query.

2. Click **Courses**, click **Add**, click **Attendance**, click **Add**, click **Employees**, click **Add**, then click **Close** in the Show Table dialog box

3. Double-click the **Department field** in the Employees table, double-click the **Cost field** in the Courses table, then double-click the **Cost field** in the Courses table again

   Even though you don't explicitly use fields from the Attendance table, you need this table in your query to tie the fields from the Courses and Employees tables together. You added the Cost field to the query grid twice because you wish to compute two different summary statistics on the information in this field (a subtotal and a count).

4. Click the **Totals button** Σ on the Query Design toolbar

   The Total row is added to the query grid below the Table row. This is the row that you use to specify how you want the resulting datasheet summarized. You want to group the resulting datasheet by the Department field, but summarize the data in the Cost fields.

5. Click the **Cost field Total cell** in the second column, click the **Group By list arrow**, click **Sum**, click the **Cost field Total cell** in the third column, click the **Group By list arrow**, then click **Count**

   Your Query Design view should look like Figure F-13.

6. Click the **Datasheet View button** ▦ on the Query Design toolbar

   As you can see from the resulting datasheet, the Accounting Department had $3,500 of internal charges for the 16 classes its employees attended. By counting the Cost field in addition to summing it, you know how many records were combined to reach the total $3,500 figure. You can sort summary queries, too.

7. Click any entry in the **SumOfCost** field, then click the **Sort Descending button** ↓ on the Query Datasheet toolbar

   The resulting datasheet is shown in Figure F-14, listing the in-house training costs in a highest to lowest order for all of the 11 departments at MediaLoft. If you wanted to permanently store this sort order, you would specify it in Query Design view, where it would be stored as part of the query object.

8. Click the **Save button** 🖫, type **Internal Costs**, click **OK**, click the **Print button** 🖨 on the Query Datasheet toolbar, then close the datasheet

FIGURE F-13: Summary Query Design view

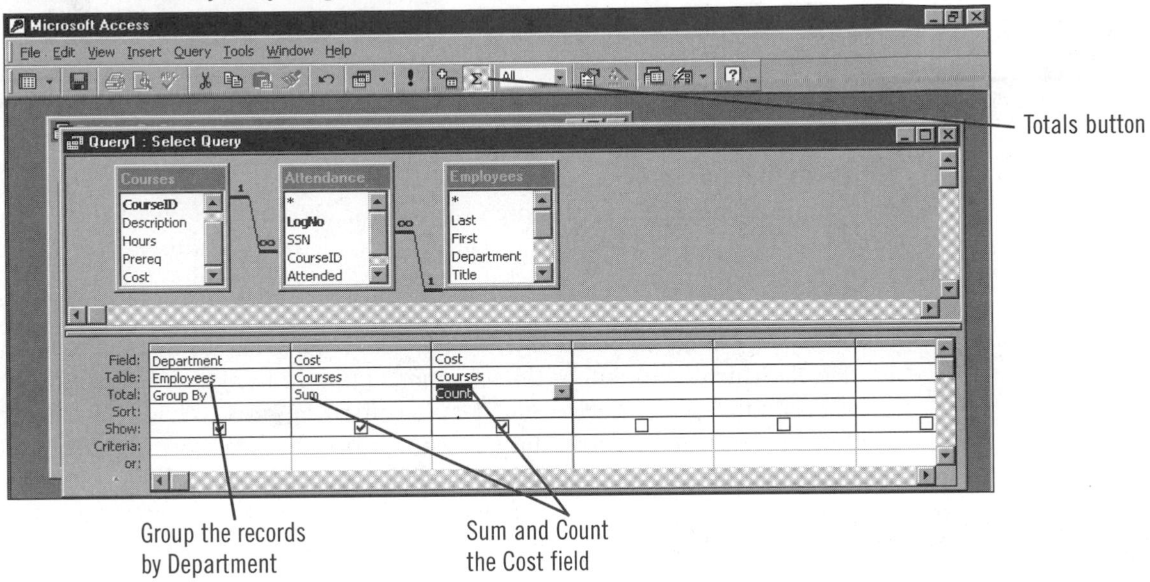

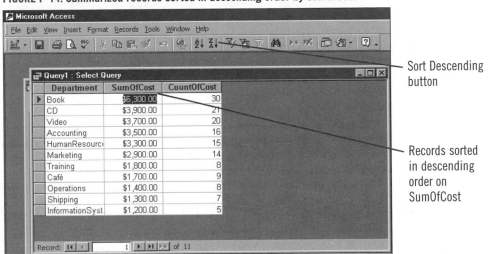

Totals button

Group the records by Department

Sum and Count the Cost field

FIGURE F-14: Summarized records sorted in descending order by SumOfCost

Sort Descending button

Records sorted in descending order on SumOfCost

TABLE F-4: Aggregate Functions

aggregate function	used to find the
Sum	Total of values in a field
Avg	Average of values in a field
Min	Minimum value in the field
Max	Maximum value in the field
Count	Number of values in a field (not counting null values)
StDev	Standard deviation of values in a field
Var	Variance of values in a field
First	Field value from the first record in a table or query
Last	Field value from the last record in a table or query

Creating Crosstab Queries

Crosstab queries provide another method of summarizing data by creating a datasheet in which one or more fields are chosen for the row headings, another field is chosen for the column headings, and a third field, usually a numeric field, is summarized within the datasheet itself. If you wish to base the crosstab query on fields from multiple tables, the first step to creating a crosstab query is to assemble the fields in a single select query. Then you create the final crosstab query based upon the intermediary query object by using the **Crosstab Query Wizard** to identify which fields will be the row and column headings, and which field will be summarized within the grid of the crosstab datasheet itself. David wishes to expand the information in the Internal Costs query to summarize the total cost for each course within each department. This is a good candidate for a crosstab query because he is summarizing information by two fields, one that will serve as the row heading (Description) and one that will serve as the column heading (Department) for the final crosstab datasheet.

Steps

1. Click **Queries** on the objects bar (if necessary), click **Internal Costs**, then click the **Design View button** in the Training-F database window
   Instead of creating the intermediate select query from scratch, a couple of modifications to the Internal Costs query will quickly provide the fields you need.

2. Click the **Totals button** Σ on the Query Design toolbar, click the **Cost Field cell** for the third column, click the **Cost list arrow**, then click **Description**
   The intermediary select query should look like Figure F-15. You removed the summary functions (the Total row on the query design grid), then changed the second Cost field to the Description field. It is important to save the query with an appropriate name.

3. Click **File** on the menu bar, click **Save As**, type **Crosstab Fields** in the **Save Query 'Internal Costs' To:** text box, click **OK**, then close the query
   You can build the Crosstab query using the Crosstab Query Wizard.

Trouble?

The Create query by using wizard option from the database window is used only to create a select query, so you must click the New button to use the other query wizards.

4. Click the **New button** in the database window, click **Crosstab Query Wizard** in the New Query dialog box, then click **OK**
   The Crosstab Query Wizard dialog box opens. The first question asks you which object contains the fields for the crosstab query.

5. Click the **Queries option button** in the View section, click **Crosstab Fields** in the list of available queries, then click **Next**
   The next questions from the Crosstab Query Wizard will organize how the fields are displayed in the datasheet.

QuickTip

You can click the Back button within any wizard to review previous choices.

6. Click **Description** for the row heading, click the **Select Single Field button** >, click **Next**, click **Department** to specify the column heading, then click **Next**
   The next wizard dialog box asks you to identify the field that is summarized within the body of the crosstab report. Since the Cost field is the only field left, it is automatically chosen, but you still need to specify a function that will determine the way the Cost field is calculated.

7. Click **Sum** in the Functions list
   Your Query Wizard dialog box should look like Figure F-16.

8. Click **Next**, type **Crosstab Query** in the query name text box, then click **Finish**
   The final crosstab query is shown in Figure F-17.

9. Print the resulting datasheet

FIGURE F-15: Select query upon which the crosstab query will be based

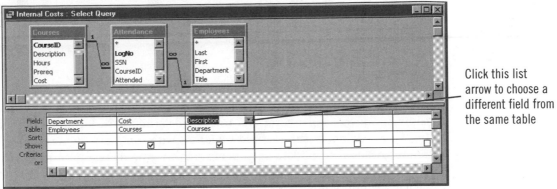

Click this list arrow to choose a different field from the same table

FIGURE F-16: Crosstab Query Wizard

Department field is the column heading

Description field is the row heading

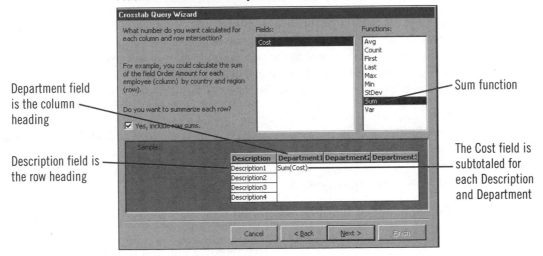

Sum function

The Cost field is subtotaled for each Description and Department

FIGURE F-17: Crosstab Query datasheet

Descriptions are row headings

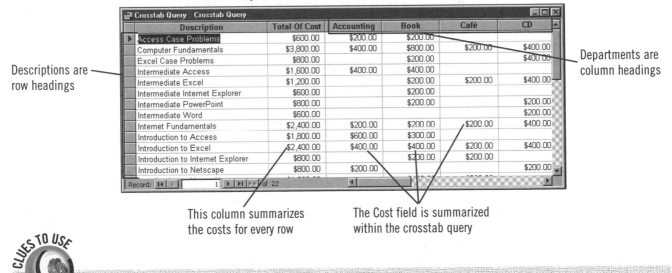

Departments are column headings

This column summarizes the costs for every row

The Cost field is summarized within the crosstab query

CLUES TO USE

Defining types of Query Wizards

The **Simple Query Wizard** is an alternative way to create a select query, rather than going directly into Query Design view. The **Find Duplicates Query Wizard** is used to determine whether a table contains duplicate values in one or more fields. The **Find Unmatched Query Wizard** is used to find records in one table that don't have related records in another table. To invoke the Find Duplicates, Find Unmatched, or Crosstab Query Wizards, you must click the New button when viewing the query objects within the opening database window.

Modifying Crosstab Queries

Once a crosstab query is created, it can be modified in Query Design view, just like a select query can. Crosstab queries use two additional rows in the query grid: the "Totals" row (similar to a summary query) and a "Crosstab" row that determines the location of the field (column heading, row heading, or summarized value). As with summary queries, crosstab query datasheets cannot be used to update data, because every row represents a summarization of multiple records of data. ⬛ David will use Query Design view to modify the crosstab query so that he has a count of how many people within each department took each class.

Steps

1. **Click the Design View button 📝 on the Query Datasheet toolbar**
   Query Design view for the Crosstab Query opens, as shown in Figure F-18. The Totals and Crosstab rows are displayed in the query grid. If you had not used the Query Wizard to create this query, you could still display these rows and, therefore, make any existing select query into a crosstab query by selecting the Query Type button and choosing the Crosstab Query from the list.

2. **Click Sum in the Total row for Cost field, click the list arrow, then click Count**
   This field determines the calculation performed on the field within the body of the crosstab report. Now it will count the number of people within each department that took each class rather than sum the Cost data.

3. **Click Sum in the Total row for the Total of Cost: Cost field, click the list arrow, then click Count**
   This field determines the second **row heading** and will now count how many courses of each description were taken for all departments.

4. **Click the Datasheet View button 🞑 on the Query Design toolbar, then click the Save button 💾 on the Query Datasheet toolbar**
   The modified crosstab query that counts the number of times each course was taken for employees within each department is shown in Figure F-19.

5. Print the resulting datasheet

6. Close the datasheet, then close the Training-F database

7. Exit Access

FIGURE F-18: Query Design view of a crosstab query

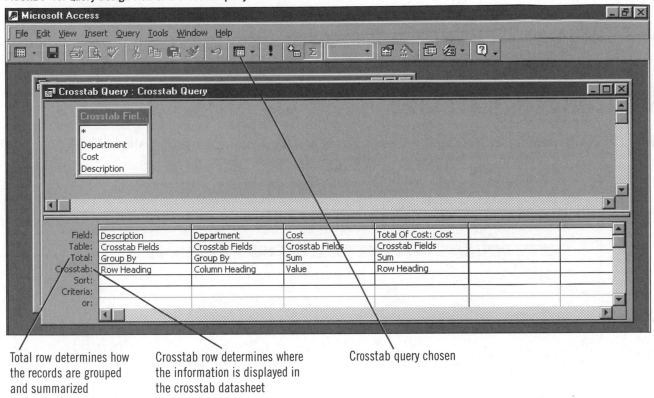

Total row determines how
the records are grouped
and summarized

Crosstab row determines where
the information is displayed in
the crosstab datasheet

Crosstab query chosen

FIGURE F-19: Modified crosstab query that counts courses taken

Description	Total Of Cost	Accounting	Book	Café	CD
Access Case Problems	3	1	1		
Computer Fundamentals	19	2	4	1	
Excel Case Problems	4		1		
Intermediate Access	4	1	1		
Intermediate Excel	6		1	1	
Intermediate Internet Explorer	3		1		
Intermediate PowerPoint	4		1		
Intermediate Word	3				
Internet Fundamentals	12	1	1	1	
Introduction to Access	6	2	1		
Introduction to Excel	12	2	2	1	
Introduction to Internet Explorer	4		1	1	
Introduction to Netscape	4	1			

Record: 1 of 22

A total of 19 Computer
Fundamentals courses
were taken

Accounting Department
employees took 2 Introduction
to Excel courses

Practice

► Concepts Review

Identify each element of the Design view window and Select query window shown in Figure F-20.

FIGURE F-20

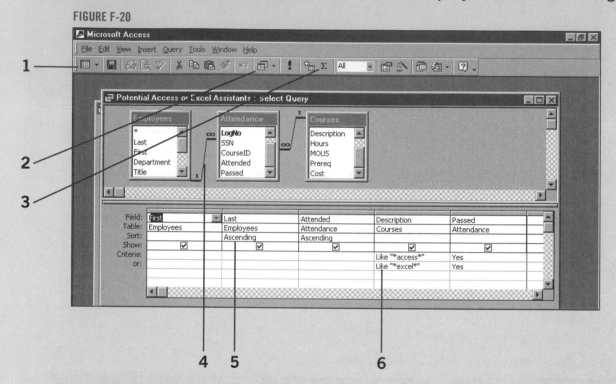

Match each term with the statement that describes its function.

7. Query
8. Arithmetic operators
9. And
10. Sorting
11. Criteria

a. Placing the records of a datasheet in a certain order
b. Used to create mathematical calculations in a query
c. A database object that answers questions about the data
d. Conditions that select only certain records
e. Operator used to combine two expressions

Select the best answer from the list of choices.

12. The query datasheet can best be described as a
   a. Duplication of the data in the underlying table's datasheet.
   b. Logical view of the selected data from an underlying table's datasheet.
   c. Separate file of data.
   d. Second copy of the data in the underlying tables.

13. **Queries are often used to:**
    a. Create copies of database files.
    b. Eliminate the need to build multiple tables.
    c. Create option boxes and list boxes from which to choose field values.
    d. Present a subset of fields from multiple tables.

14. **When you update data in a table that is displayed in a query:**
    a. You must also update the query.
    b. You must relink the query to the table.
    c. The data is automatically updated in the query.
    d. You have the choice whether or not you want to update the data in the query.

15. **To assemble several fields from different tables, use a(n):**
    a. Select Query.
    b. Update Query.
    c. Delete Query.
    d. Append Query.

16. **The order in which records are sorted is determined by:**
    a. The order in which the fields are defined in the underlying table.
    b. The alphabetic order of the field names.
    c. The left-to-right position of the fields in the query design grid.
    d. The ascending fields are sorted first in the query design grid, then the descending fields are sorted second.

17. **Crosstab queries are used to:**
    a. Summarize information based on fields in the column and row headings of the report.
    b. Update several records at the same time.
    c. Select fields for a datasheet from multiple tables.
    d. Calculate price increases on numeric fields.

▶ # Skills Review

1. **Create select queries.**
   a. Start Access and open the database Membership-F.
   b. Create a new select query in Design View using both the Names and Zips tables.
   c. Add the following fields to the query design grid in this order:
      First, Last, and Street from the Names table
      City, State, and Zip from the Zips table
   d. Enter your own last name in the Last field of the first record.
   e. Save the query as "Basic Address List", view the datasheet, print the datasheet, then close the query.

2. **Sort a query on multiple fields.**
   a. Open the Design view for the Basic Address List query. You wish to modify the query so that it is sorted in ascending order by Last, then by First, but you do not want to change the order of the fields in the resulting datasheet.
   b. Drag another First field to the right of the Last field in the query design grid to make the first three fields in the query design grid First, Last, and First.

c. Add the ascending sort criteria to the second column and third column fields, and uncheck the Show check box in the third column.

d. Use Save As to save the query as "Sorted Address List", view the datasheet, print the datasheet, then close the query.

3. Develop AND queries.

a. Return to the Design view for the Basic Address List. You wish to modify the "Basic Address List" query so that only those people from Kansas with a last name that starts with "M" are chosen.

b. Enter M* (the asterisk is a wildcard) in the criteria row for the Last field to choose all people whose last name starts with M. Access assists you with the syntax for this type of criterion and enters "Like M*" in the cell when you click elsewhere in the grid.

c. Enter "KS" as the criterion for the State field. Be sure to enter the criteria on the same line in the query design grid to make the query an AND query. You should have six records in this datasheet.

d. Enter your own hometown in the City field of the first record.

e. Save the query as "Kansas M Names", view, print, then close the datasheet.

4. Develop OR queries.

a. Modify the "Kansas M Names" query so that only those people from KS with a last name that starts with either "M" or "C" are chosen. Do this by entering the OR criterion C* on the or row for the Last field in the query design grid.

b. Be sure to also type the KS criterion on the or row for the State field in the query design grid to make sure that your query doesn't display all names that start with C, but only those who also live in Kansas.

c. Save the query as "Kansas C or M Names", view the datasheet (there should be nine records), print the datasheet, then close the query.

5. Create calculated fields.

a. Create a new select query using Design view using only the Names table. You want to determine the number of days old each person is based on the information in the Birthday field.

b. Add the following fields from the Names table to the query design grid in this order: First, Last, Birthday.

c. Create a calculated field called "Days Old" in the fourth column of the query design grid by entering the expression: Days Old:Date()-[Birthday].

d. Sort the query in descending order on the calculated Days Old field.

e. Select the calculated Days Old field using the column Field selector, open the Property sheet, format the Days Old field with a Standard format, and enter "0" in the Decimal Places property text box.

f. Save the query as "Days Old", view the datasheet, print the datasheet, then close the query.

6. Build summary queries.

a. Create a new select query using Design view, then add the Names and Activities tables.

b. Add the following fields: First and Last from the Names table, Hours from the Activities table.

c. Add the Total row to the query design grid and change the function for the Hours field from Group By to Sum.

d. Sort in descending order by Hours.

e. Save the query as "Total Hours", view the datasheet, print the datasheet, then close the query.

7. Create crosstab queries.

a. First create a select query with the fields City and State from the Zips table, and Dues from the Names table. Save it as "Crosstab Fields".

b. Click the New button when viewing query objects, then start the Crosstab Query Wizard, and base the crosstab query on the Crosstab Fields query you just created.

c. Select City as the row heading and State as the column heading, and sum the Dues field within the crosstab datasheet.

d. Save and name the query "Crosstab of Dues by City and State".

e. View, print, then close the datasheet.

8. Modify crosstab queries.

a. Open the Crosstab of Dues by City and State query in Design view.

b. Change the Sum function to Count for both the Dues and the Total of Dues: Dues fields.

c. View, print, then close the datasheet without saving it.

d. Close the database, then exit Access.

▶ Independent Challenges

1. As the manager of a music store's instrument rental program, you have created a database to track instrument rentals to schoolchildren. Now that several rentals have been made, you wish to query the database for several different datasheet printouts to analyze school information.

To complete this independent challenge:

a. Start Access and open the database Music Store-F.

b. Create a query that pulls the following fields in the following order into a datasheet, then print the datasheet: SchoolName from Schools table, Date from Rentals table, Description from Instruments table. (*Hint:* You will need to add the Customers table to this query to make the connection between the Schools table and the Rentals table even though you don't need any Customers fields in this query's datasheet.)

c. Sort ascending by SchoolName, then ascending by Date.

d. Save the query as "School Rentals", enter your high school name in the first record, then print the datasheet.

e. Modify the School Rentals query by deleting the Description field. Then, use the Totals button to group the records by SchoolName and to count the Date field. Print the datasheet and save the query as "School Count". (*Note:* Include your name or initials as part of the query name if you need to identify your prinout.)

f. Use the Crosstab Query Wizard to create a crosstab query based on the School Rentals query. Use Description as the row heading and SchoolName as the column heading. Count the Date field.

g. Save the query as "School Crosstab", then view, print, and close it.

h. Modify the "School Rentals" query so that only those schools with the word "Elementary" in the SchoolName field are displayed. (*Hint:* You will have to use wildcard characters in the criteria.) Twelve elementary schools should be displayed.

i. Save the query as "Elementary Rentals", then view, print, and close the datasheet.

j. Close the Music Store-F database and exit Access.

Access 2000

2. As the manager of a music store's instrument rental program, you have created a database to track instrument rentals to schoolchildren. Now that several rentals have been made, you wish to query the database to analyze customer and rental information.

To complete this independent challenge:

a. Start Access and open the database Music Store-F.

b. Create a query that pulls the following fields in the following order into a datasheet, and print the datasheet:
FirstName and LastName from the Customers Table
Description and MonthlyFee from the Instruments Table
(*Hint:* You will need to add the Rentals table to this query to make the connection between the Customers table and the Instruments table even though you don't need any Rentals fields in this query's datasheet.)

c. Sort ascending by LastName.

d. Save the query as "Customer Rentals", enter your own last name in the first record's LastName field, and print the datasheet.

e. Modify the Customer Rentals query by deleting the FirstName and LastName fields. Then, use the Totals button to group the records by Description and to sum the MonthlyFee field.

f. Add another MonthlyFee field as a third column to the query grid, and use the Count function to find the total number of rentals within that group.

g. Sort ascending by the Description field.

h. Save the query as "Monthly Instrument Income".

i. View, print, and close the datasheet.

j. Close the Music Store-F database and exit Access.

3. As the manager of a music store's instrument rental program, you have created a database to track instrument rentals to schoolchildren. The database has already been used to answer several basic questions, and now that you've shown how easy it is to get the answers using queries, more and more questions are being asked. You will use queries to analyze customer and rental information.

To complete this independent challenge:

a. Start Access and open the database Music Store-F.

b. Create a query that pulls the following fields in the following order into a datasheet:
Description and MonthlyFee from the Instruments Table
Zip and City from the Customers Table
(*Hint:* You will need to add the Rentals table to this query to make the connection between the Customers table and the Instruments table even though you don't need any Rentals fields in this query's datasheet.)

c. Sort ascending by Zip, and within Zip by Description. (*Hint:* You will have to add the Zip field to the query grid twice to accomplish this task. Uncheck the Show check box on the Zip field column that you do not wish to display in the datasheet.)

d. Save the query as "Zip Analysis". (*Note:* Include your name or initials as part of the query name if you need to identify your printout.)

e. View, print, and close the datasheet.

f. Modify the Zip Analysis query by adding criteria to find the records where the Description is "viola".

g. Save this query as "Violas". The datasheet should have three records. Print the datasheet.

h. Modify the Violas query with AND criteria that further specifies that the City must be "Des Moines".

i. Save this query as "Violas in Des Moines". The datasheet should have only one record. Print the datasheet.

j. Modify the "Violas" query with OR criteria that finds all violas OR violins, regardless of where they are located.

k. Save this query as "Violas and Violins". The datasheet should have five records. Print and close the datasheet.

l. Using the Crosstab Query Wizard, create a crosstab query based on the School Analysis query that uses the Description field for the row headings and the SchoolName field for the column headings, and that counts the RentalNo field.

m. Save the crosstab query as "Crosstab School and Instrument", preview the datasheet, then print the datasheet in landscape orientation so that it fits on one page.

n. Close the Music Store-F database and exit Access.

4. Check the MediaLoft Intranet site to find cost information about public training courses that the Accounting Department has gathered. Then create a query to determine if your in-house courses are similar in length and cost.

To complete this independent challenge:

a. Connect to the Internet and use your browser to go to the MediaLoft Intranet site at http://www.course.com/illustrated/MediaLoft/

b. Click the link for Training.

c. Click the link for Public Courses, and print the Web page.

d. Start Access and open the Training-F database.

e. Create a query that lists the following fields from the Courses table in the following order: Description, Hours, Cost.

f. Sort the records in ascending order by Description.

g. Save the query as "Competitor Analysis". (*Note:* If you need to identify your printout, include your name or initials in the query name.)

h. View and print the resulting datasheet.

i. Compare the Competitor Analysis query to the results you found on the Web site. Who offers less expensive training, MediaLoft or the competition?

j. Print the datasheet, exit Access.

▶ **Visual Workshop**

Open the Training-F database and create a new query to display the datasheet as shown in Figure F-21. Notice that the records are sorted alphabetically by the date the course was attended, then by last name. Save the query as "History of Attendance". (*Note:* If you need to identify your work on the printout, add your initials as part of the query name). Print the query.

FIGURE F-21

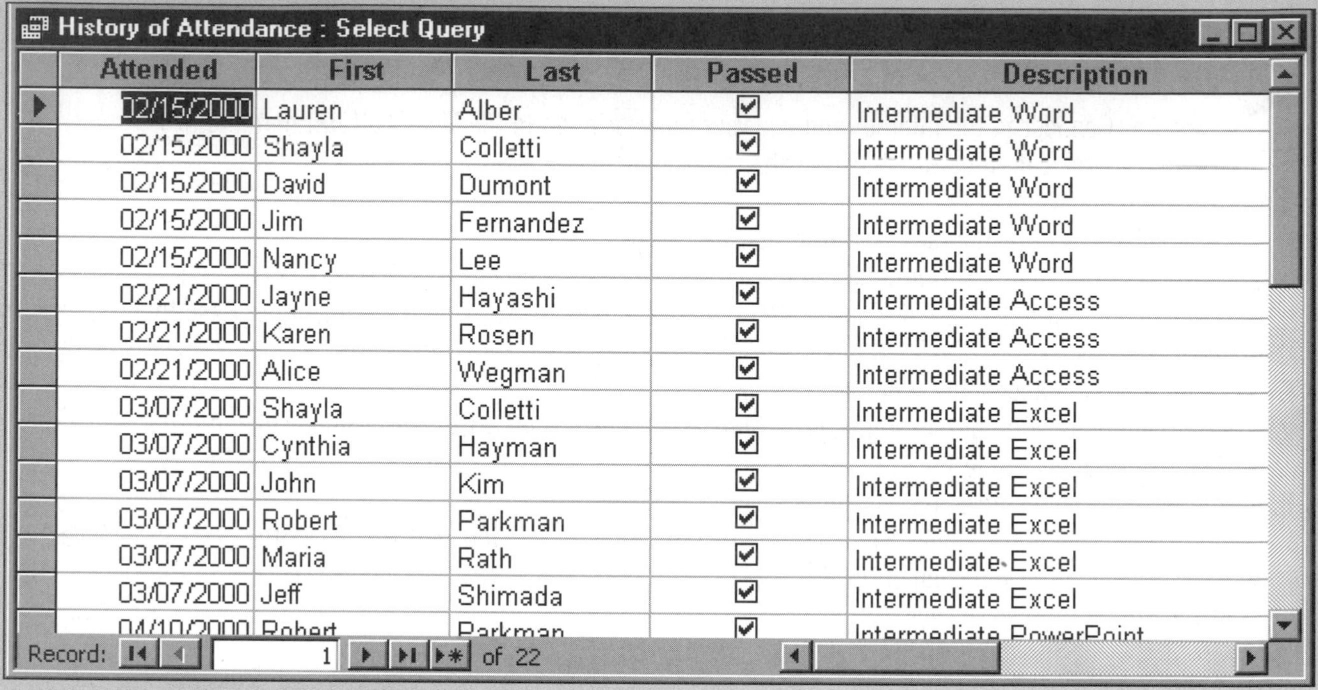

Attended	First	Last	Passed	Description
02/15/2000	Lauren	Alber	☑	Intermediate Word
02/15/2000	Shayla	Colletti	☑	Intermediate Word
02/15/2000	David	Dumont	☑	Intermediate Word
02/15/2000	Jim	Fernandez	☑	Intermediate Word
02/15/2000	Nancy	Lee	☑	Intermediate Word
02/21/2000	Jayne	Hayashi	☑	Intermediate Access
02/21/2000	Karen	Rosen	☑	Intermediate Access
02/21/2000	Alice	Wegman	☑	Intermediate Access
03/07/2000	Shayla	Colletti	☑	Intermediate Excel
03/07/2000	Cynthia	Hayman	☑	Intermediate Excel
03/07/2000	John	Kim	☑	Intermediate Excel
03/07/2000	Robert	Parkman	☑	Intermediate Excel
03/07/2000	Maria	Rath	☑	Intermediate Excel
03/07/2000	Jeff	Shimada	☑	Intermediate Excel
04/10/2000	Robert	Parkman	☑	Intermediate PowerPoint

History of Attendance : Select Query

Record: ◄ ◄ 1 ► ►► ►* of 22

Developing
Forms and Subforms

Objectives

- ► **Understand the form/subform relationship**
- ► **Create subforms using the Form Wizard**
- MOUS ► **Create subforms using queries**
- MOUS ► **Modify subforms**
- MOUS ► **Add combo boxes**
- MOUS ► **Add option groups**
- MOUS ► **Add command buttons**
- MOUS ► **Add records with a form/subform**

Viewing, finding, entering, and editing data in a database must be easy and straightforward for all database users. A **form** can be designed to present data in any logical screen arrangement and serve as the primary interface for most database users. Forms contain **controls** such as labels, text boxes, combo boxes, and command buttons to help identify and enter data. Forms with **subform** controls allow you to show a record and its related records from another object (table or query) at the same time. For example, on one screen you may wish to see customer information as well as all of the orders placed by the customer. Well-designed form/subforms will encourage fast, accurate data entry, and will shield the data entry person from the complexity of underlying tables, queries, and datasheets. David develops a single form that shows employee information at the top of the form and all of the classes that an employee has attended at the bottom. This requires a subform control. He also upgrades the usability of the forms by adding various controls such as combo boxes, option groups, and command buttons.

Understanding the Form/Subform Relationship

A **subform** control is actually a form within a form. The primary form is called the **main form**, and it contains the subform control. The subform shows related records that are linked to the single record currently displayed in the main form. The relationship between the main form and subform is often called a **parent/child relationship**, because the "parent" record in the main form is linked to many "children" records displayed in the subform. The link between the main form and subform is established through a linking field common to both, the same field that is used to establish the one-to-many relationship between underlying tables in the database. Creating forms with subforms requires careful planning, so David studies form/subform planning guidelines before he attempts to create the forms in Access.

Sketch the layout of the form/subform on paper, identifying which fields belong in the main form and which belong in the subform

David has sketched two forms with subforms that he wants to create. Figure G-1 displays employee information in the main form and attendance information in the subform. Figure G-2 displays course information in the main form and employee information in the subform.

Determine whether you are going to create separate queries upon which to base the main form and subform, or if you are going to use the Form Wizard to collect fields from multiple tables upon which to create the form and subform objects

This decision may have important consequences later because it determines the form's recordset. The **recordset** is the fields and records that will appear on the form. To modify the recordset of forms created solely through the Form Wizard, you have to modify the form's **Record Source property**, where the recordset is defined. When the form is based on an intermediate query, changing the query object automatically updates the Record Source property for the form, because the query object name *is* the Record Source property entry for that form.

If you use the Form Wizard to create a form with fields from multiple tables without an intermediary query object, the Record Source property of the form often displays an **SQL (Structured Query Language) statement**. This SQL statement can be modified to change the recordset, but obviously requires some knowledge of SQL.

Create the form and subform objects based on the appropriate intermediary queries. If intermediary queries were not created, use the Form Wizard to gather the fields for both the form and subform

David uses the Form Wizard technique as well as the intermediary query technique so that he can compare the two.

FIGURE G-1: Employees Main Form with Attendance Subform

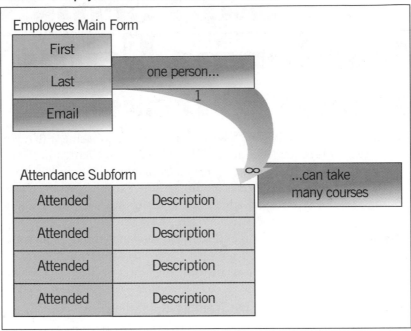

FIGURE G-2: Courses Main Form with Employee Subform

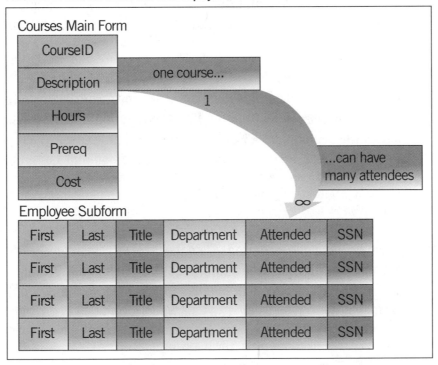

Access 2000

Creating Forms with Subforms Using the Form Wizard

A form displays the fields of a table or query in an arrangement that you design, based on one of five general **layouts**: Columnar, Tabular, Datasheet, Chart, and PivotTable. **Columnar** is the most popular layout for a main form, and **Datasheet** is the most popular layout for a subform. See Table G-1 for more information on the different form layouts. Once the main form is created, the subform control is added in the main form's Form Design view. If you create the form/subform through the Form Wizard, however, both objects are created in one process. David creates a form and subform showing employee information in the main form and course information in the subform. He creates the form/subform objects without first creating intermediary query objects by using the power of the Form Wizard.

1. Start Access and open the **Training-G** database

2. Click **Forms** on the Objects bar, then double-click **Create form by using wizard** in the Training-G Database window
   The **Form Wizard** appears and prompts you to select the fields of the form. You need five fields that are stored in three different tables for the final form/subform.

QuickTip

Double-click the field name to move it from the Available to Selected Fields list.

---

3. Click the **Attended field**, click the **Select Single Field button** >, click the **Tables/Queries list arrow**, click **Table: Courses**, click the **Description field**, click >, click the **Tables/Queries list arrow**, click **Table: Employees**, click the **First field**, click >, click the **Last field**, click >, click the **Email field**, then click >
   The Form Wizard dialog box should look like Figure G-3. Next, you must decide how to view the data. Arranging the form by Employees places the fields from the Employees table in the main form, and the Attended and Description fields in a subform.

QuickTip

Use the Standard style when saving a database to a Project Disk with limited space. The other styles contain graphics that increase the storage requirements of the form.

---

4. Click **Next**, click **by Employees**, click the **Form with subform(s) option button** (if necessary), click **Next**, click the **Datasheet option button** (if necessary) as the layout for the subform, click **Next**, click **Standard** (if necessary) as the style for the main form, click **Next**, then click **Finish** to accept the default form and subform names
   The final Employees main form and Attendance Subform is shown in Figure G-4. Two sets of navigation buttons appear, one for the main form and one for the subform. The navigation buttons show that 19 employees are in the recordset and that the first employee has attended 11 courses. You can resize the form and subform control to display more information.

Trouble?

To select the subform control, click its edge.

---

5. Click the **Design View button** on the Form View toolbar, click the **Employees Form Maximize button**, click the **subform control** so that sizing handles appear, then drag the subform control bottom middle sizing handle to the horizontal scroll bar at the bottom of the screen using ↕, as shown in Figure G-5
   The controls on the Attendance Subform appear within the subform control, and can be modified, just like controls in the main form.

6. Click the **Form View button** on the Form Design toolbar to view the resized subform, click the **Save button**, then close the **Employees** form
   The Employees form and the Attendance Subform appear with other form objects in the Training-G database window.

FIGURE G-3: Form Wizard

Choose Table or Query

Select Single Field button

Fields within the Selected table or query

From Attendance table

From Courses table

From Employees table

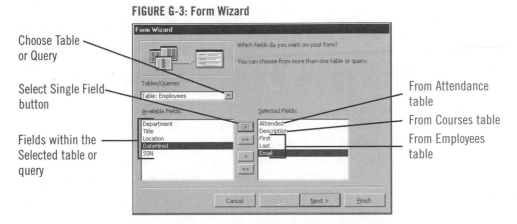

FIGURE G-4: Employees Main Form/Attendance Subform

Employees main form

Attendance Subform

Main form navigation buttons

Subform navigation buttons

Shayla attended 11 classes

19 employees

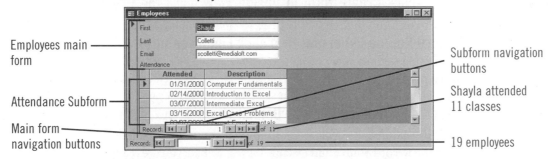

FIGURE G-5: Resizing the Attendance Subform

Attendance Subform is selected object

Subform control

Drag sizing handle down to scroll bar to enlarge the subform

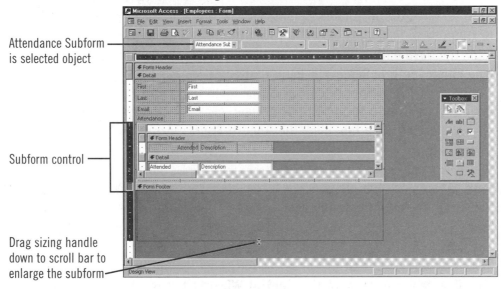

TABLE G-1: Form layouts

layout	description
Columnar	Each field appears on a separate line with a label to its left, one record for each screen
Tabular	Each field appears as a column heading and each record as a row. Multiple records appear just like they do in a datasheet, but you have more design control and flexibility. For example, you can change elements such as colors, fonts, headers, or footers
Datasheet	Each field appears as a column heading and each record as a row. The datasheet layout shows multiple records, but formatting options, except for resizing columns, are limited
Chart	Numeric fields appear in a chart (graph) format
PivotTable	Fields are chosen for column and row headings, and a field is summarized in the intersection of the appropriate column and row in a cross-tabular format

Creating Subforms Using Queries

Another way to create a form with a subform is to create both forms separately, basing them on either table or query objects, then linking the two forms together in a form/subform relationship. Although creating the forms by building them on separate query objects takes more work than building the form/subform using the Form Wizard, the benefit is your ability to quickly change the form's recordset by modifying the underlying query. ➤ David creates a form and subform showing course information in the main form and employee information in the subform using query objects that he has already created.

Steps

Trouble?

If the property sheet doesn't show the word "Form" in the title bar, click the Form Selector button.

1. Double-click **Create form in Design View**, click the **Properties button** 🖹 on the Form Design toolbar to display the form's property sheet, click the **Data tab**, click the **Record Source list arrow**, then click **Employee Info**
   The Employee Info query's field list (which supplies the recordset for the form) opens. Another initial property to consider is the **Default View** property, which determines the form's appearance. Datasheet layout is a popular style for subforms because it arranges the fields horizontally.

2. Click the **Format tab**, click the **Default View text box**, click the **Default View list arrow**, click **Datasheet**, then click 🖹 to toggle the property sheet off
   With the Record Source and Default View specified, you are ready to add the fields to the form.

QuickTip

Point to the Field list title bar to display the object name as a ScreenTip.

3. Double-click the **Employee Info field list title bar**, drag the **selected fields** using 🖾 to the top of the Detail section at the **1" mark** on the horizontal ruler, as shown in Figure G-6, then click the **Field list button** 🖹 to toggle the field list off

4. Click the **Save button** 🖫 on the Form Design toolbar, the Save As dialog box opens, type **Employee Info Sub** in the Form Name text box, click **OK**, then close the form
   The subform will display the Employees who took each course.

5. Double-click **Create form in Design View**, click 🖹 to display the form's property sheet, click the **Data tab**, click the **Record Source property list arrow**, then click **Courses Info**
   The main form requires all of the fields from the Courses Info query.

Trouble?

If you drag and position the fields incorrectly on the form, click Undo 🔄 and try again.

6. Click 🖹 to close the property sheet, double-click the **Courses Info Field list title bar**, drag the **selected fields** using 🖾 to the top of the Detail section at the **1" mark** on the horizontal ruler, click 🖹 to close the Field list, then maximize the form
   The main form is created. Now add the subform to it.

Trouble?

If you get a message box to install the Subform Wizard, insert your Office 2000 CD, then follow the instructions to install the feature.

7. Click the **Toolbox button** 🔨 on the Form Design toolbar to display the Toolbox toolbar (if necessary), be sure the **Control Wizards button** 🖹 is selected, click the **Subform/Subreport button** 🖼 on the Toolbox toolbar, then use ⁺🖽 to drag a 6" wide and 2" high rectangle to place the subform just below the Cost controls as shown in Figure G-7
   If you drag a control beyond the edges of an existing form, the form will automatically enlarge to accept the control. The SubForm Wizard appears.

8. Click **Employee Info Sub** as the existing data for the subform, click **Next**, verify that **Show Employee Info for each record in Courses Info using CourseID** is selected, click **Next**, verify the name **Employee Info Sub**, click **Finish**, then click the **Form View button** 🖹
   The final form/subform is shown in Figure G-8. The first of 27 courses, Access1, is displayed in the main form. The six employees who completed that course are displayed in the subform.

FIGURE G-6: Creating the Employee Info Sub

Field list button

Properties button

1" mark on horizontal ruler

Form Selector button

Employee Info Field list

Drag from the highlighted Field list to the 1" mark

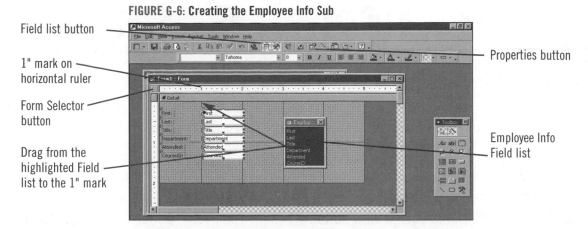

FIGURE G-7: Adding a subform control

Control Wizards button

Subform/Subreport button

Drag a box from the upper-left corner to the lower-right corner of the subform

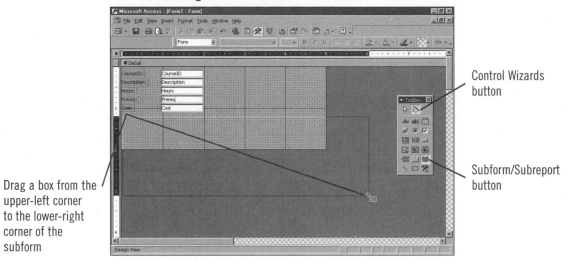

FIGURE G-8: Courses Main Form / Employee Info Subform

Employee Info Sub Subform in Datasheet view

6 employees took this course

27 courses

Subform's horizontal scroll bar

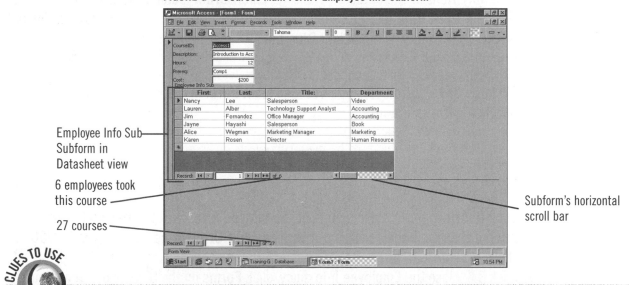

CLUES TO USE

Linking the form and subform

If the form and subform do not appear to be correctly linked, examine the subform's property sheet, paying special attention to the **Link Child Fields** and **Link Master Fields** properties on the Data tab. These properties tell you which field serves as the link between the main form and subform. The field specified for this property should be present in the queries that underlie the main and subforms, and is the same field that creates the one-to-many relationship.

Modifying Subforms

Because the form/subform arrangement packs so much information on one screen, it is important to modify and format the form/subform to present the data clearly. If the subform is displayed in Datasheet view, you can use resize, hide, or move the columns. You can also change the subform's font, grid color, or background color directly in Form view. When viewing the subform control in Design view, you can directly modify the subform's controls just as you can directly modify the main form's controls. David likes the form/subform arrangement that displays each course in the main form and each employee who has taken that course in the subform, but he will improve upon the subform's design to display the employee subform information a little more clearly.

Steps

1. **Click the Design View button** 📝 **on the Form View toolbar, click the subform control, drag the middle right sizing handle to the 7" mark on the horizontal ruler, as shown in Figure G-9, then release the mouse button**
   Widening the subform control will allow you to display more fields at the same time. Even though the fields of the subform appear to be in a vertical arrangement in the subform control, the "Datasheet" Default View property forces them to display horizontally, like a datasheet. Other options for a form's Default View property are shown in Table G-2.

2. **Click the Form View button** 📄 **on the Form Design toolbar to view the widened subform**
   The appearance of a horizontal scroll bar on the subform tells you that not all of the fields are visible on the subform's datasheet, but you can resize the columns of the datasheet directly in Form view.

3. **Point to the First and Last field name column separator, double-click with ✛ to automatically adjust the column to accommodate the widest entry, then double-click each field name column separator in the subform**
   Your screen should look like Figure G-10. Notice that the horizontal scroll bar disappears when all fields within the subform are visible. Formatting the datasheet makes it more appealing to the user.

4. **Click any field in the subform, click the Line/Border color button list arrow** 🖊️, **click the Dark Blue box** (first row, second from right), **click the Fill/Back color list arrow** 🎨, **then click the Light Blue box** (last row, fourth from the right)
   You can format the datasheet to best represent the data using line colors, special effects, and fill colors as well as changing the fonts and character formatting.

5. **Click the Save button** 💾, **type Courses Main Form in the Form Name text box, click OK, then close the form**
   You can always sort, filter, and find records directly on a form or subform, but filters are not saved with the form object. By basing form objects on associated queries, however, you can easily modify the form's recordset by modifying the underlying query. MediaLoft's Accounting Department wants to use this form to display only those employees who attended class in January 2000.

6. **Click Queries on the Objects bar, click Employee Info, click the Design button** 📝 **in the database window, click the Attended field Criteria cell, then type 1/*/00, as shown in Figure G-11**

7. **Click** 💾, **close the Employee Info query, click Forms on the Objects bar, then double-click Courses Main Form to open it**
   The Employee InfoSub Subform is based on the Employee Info query and does not display any records for the first course, Access1, because no employees attended this course in January of 2000.

8. **Press [Page Down] three times to move to CourseID Comp1, which is record 4**
   The Comp1 course displays 10 records in the subform, indicating that 10 employees took this course in January 2000.

FIGURE G-9: Widening a subform

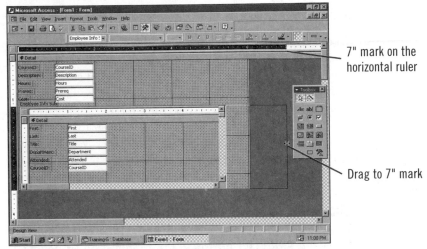

7" mark on the horizontal ruler

Drag to 7" mark

FIGURE G-10: Resizing columns of a subform

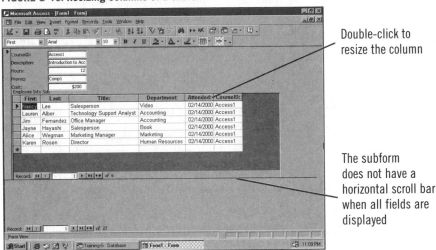

Double-click to resize the column

The subform does not have a horizontal scroll bar when all fields are displayed

FIGURE G-11: Changing the criteria of an underlying query

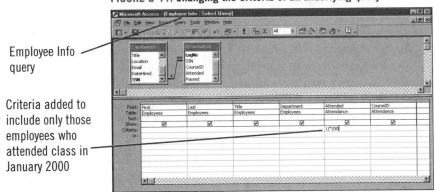

Employee Info query

Criteria added to include only those employees who attended class in January 2000

TABLE G-2: Default View property options for forms

default view property	description
Single Form	Displays one record at a time. Gives the user full ability to format the controls placed on the form in Design view and is the most common Default View property entry.
Continuous Form	Displays multiple records at a time, and is often used as the Default View property for subforms. Gives the user the ability to format the controls in Design view.
Datasheet	Displays multiple records at the same time in a datasheet arrangement regardless of how they are formatted in Design view. This is the most common Default View property choice for subforms.

Adding Combo Boxes

By default, fields are added to a form as text boxes, but sometimes other controls such as list boxes, combo boxes, or options buttons would handle the data entry process more easily or quickly for a particular field. Both the **list box** and **combo box** controls provide a list of values from which the user can choose an entry. A combo box also allows the user to make an entry from the keyboard; therefore, it is a "combination" of the list box and text box controls. You can create a combo box by using the Combo Box Wizard to guide your actions, or you can change an existing text box into a combo box control. David changes the Prereq text box (which specifies if a prerequisite course is required in the main form) from a text box into a combo box to allow users to choose from the existing courses offered at MediaLoft.

Steps 1 2 3 4

1. Click the **Design View button**, click the **Prereq text box**, then press **[Delete]**
   You can add the Prereq field back to the form as a combo box.

2. Click the **Field List button** to toggle it on (if necessary), click the **Toolbox button** to toggle it on (if necessary), click the **Control Wizards button** to toggle it on (if necessary), click the **Combo Box button** on the Toolbox toolbar, click the **Prereq field** in the field list, then drag the **Prereq field** with ⁺≣ to the space where the Prereq text box was positioned
   The Combo Box Wizard appears. You want the Prereq combo box to display the CourseID and Description information from the Courses table.

3. Click **I want the combo box to look up the values in a table or query** (if necessary), click **Next**, click **Courses**, click **Next**, double-click the **CourseID field**, double-click the **Description field**, click **Next**, double-click ◄╫► on the right edge of the Description column selector to widen it, click **Next**, click **Next** to accept that the value will be stored in the Prereq field, then click **Finish** to accept the Prereq label
   Your screen will look similar to Figure G-12.

QuickTip

Press and hold **[Ctrl]**, then press the →, ←, ↑, or ↓ keys to move the control precisely.

4. Position the **Prereq combo box** between the Hours and Cost fields, click the **Prereq combo box right resizing handle**, drag ↔ to the **3" mark** on the horizontal ruler, click the **Description text box**, then drag the **Description text box right sizing handle** with ↔ to the **3" mark** on the horizontal ruler
   Your screen will look similar to Figure G-13. Your final step will be to change the Cost text box into a combo box as well. MediaLoft has only three internal charges for its classes, $100, $200, and $400, which you want to display in the combo box.

5. Right-click the **Cost text box**, point to **Change To**, then click **Combo Box**
   This action changed the control from a text box to a combo box without the aid of the Combo Box Wizard. Therefore, you need to specify where the combo box will get its values directly in the control's property sheet.

6. Click the **Properties button**, click the **Data tab** (if necessary), click the **Row Source Type text box**, click the **Row Source Type list arrow**, then click **Value List**
   The combo box will get its values from the list entered in the Row Source property.

Trouble?

Be sure to enter semicolons between the values in the Row Source property.

7. Click the **Row Source property text box**, type **$100; $200; $400**, click the **Limit to List property list arrow**, click **Yes**, then click to close the property sheet
   The entries in the Row Source property list become the values for the combo box's list. By changing the Limit to List property to "Yes," the user cannot enter a new entry from the keyboard.

8. Click the **Save button**, click the **Form View button**, click the **Cost combo box list arrow**, then click **$400**
   The updated form with two combo boxes should look like Figure G-14.

FIGURE G-12: Adding the Prereq combo box

Prereq field added
as a combo box

Combo Box button

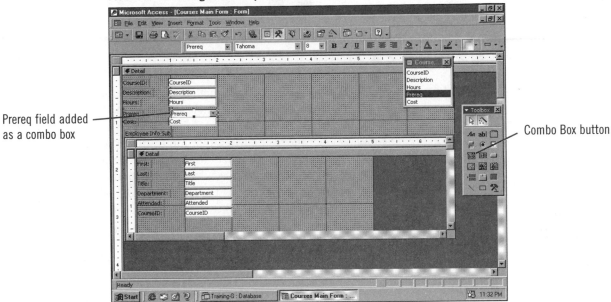

FIGURE G-13: Moving and resizing controls

Controls are resized
to 3" mark on the
horizontal ruler

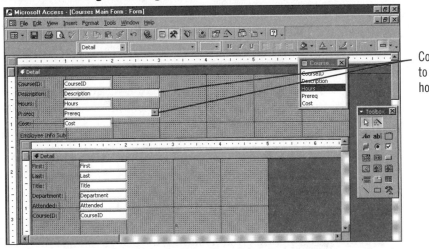

FIGURE G-14: Adding the Cost combo box

New Combo boxes

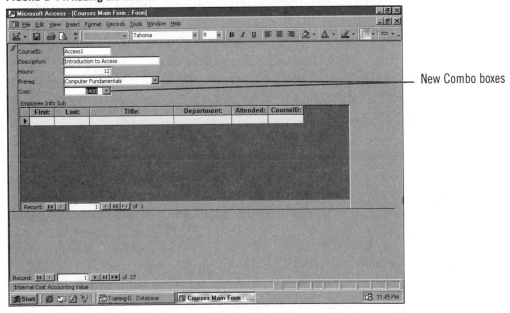

Access 2000

Adding Option Groups

An **option group** is a special type of bound control that is often used when a limited number of values are available for a field. The option group control uses **option button** controls (sometimes called radio buttons) to determine the value that is placed in the field. One option button exists for each possible entry. When the user clicks an option button, the numeric value associated with that option button is entered into the field bound to the option group. Option buttons within an option group are mutually exclusive, which means that only one can be chosen at a time. MediaLoft's classes are offered in 6-, 8-, 12-, and 16-hour formats. Because this represents a limited number of options, David uses an option group control for the Hours field to further simplify the Courses Main Form.

Steps

1. Click the **Design View button** ![icon], click the **Hours text box**, then press **[Delete]**
   You can add the Hours field back to the form as an option group.

2. Click the **Option Group button** ![icon] on the Toolbox, click the **Hours field** in the field list, then, using ![icon], drag the **Hours field** to the upper-right corner of the form at about the 5" mark on the horizontal ruler
   The Option Group Wizard appears to help guide the process of developing an option group. The first question asks about label names for the option buttons.

3. Type **6 hrs**, press **[Tab]**, type **8 hrs**, press **[Tab]**, type **12 hrs**, press **[Tab]**, type **16 hrs**, click **Next**, choose **No, I don't want a default**, then click **Next**
   The next question prompts you for the actual values associated with each option button.

4. Type **6**, press **[Tab]**, type **8**, press **[Tab]**, type **12**, press **[Tab]**, type **16**, click **Next**, click **Next** to accept **Hours** as the field that the value is stored in, click **Next** to accept **Option button controls** in an **Etched style**, type **Classroom Hours** as the caption, then click **Finish**
   An option group can contain option buttons, check boxes, or toggle button controls. The most common choice, however, are option buttons in an etched style. The **Control Source property** of the option group identifies the field it will update. The **Option Value property** of each option button identifies what value will be placed in the field when that option button is clicked. The new option group and option button controls are shown in Figure G-15.

5. Click the **Form View button** ![icon] to view the form with the new control, then click the **16 hrs option button**
   Your screen should look like Figure G-16. You changed the Access1 course from 12 to 16 hrs. You just found out that MediaLoft is offering 24-hour classes, so you have to add another button to the group.

QuickTip

The option group control will darken when you are adding an option button to it.

6. Click ![icon], click the **Option Button button** ![icon] on the Toolbox toolbar, then click below the **16 hrs option button** in the new option group
   Your screen should look like Figure G-17. This option button in the group will represent 24-hour classes. Change the new option button's label and option value.

Trouble?

The option number may vary.

7. Click the **Option18 label** once to select it, double-click the **Option18 text**, then type **24 hrs**

8. Double-click the new **option button** to open the property sheet, click the **Data tab** (if necessary), double-click **5** in the **Option Value property text box** to select it, type **24**, click the **Properties button** ![icon] to close the property sheet, move the **24 hrs option button control** as necessary to align it with the other option buttons, click the **Save button** ![icon], then click ![icon] to observe the new option button

FIGURE G-15: Adding an Option Group with option buttons

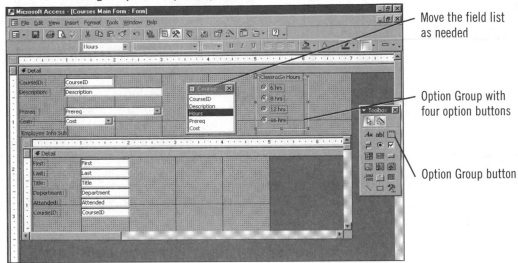

Move the field list as needed

Option Group with four option buttons

Option Group button

FIGURE G-16: Using an Option Group

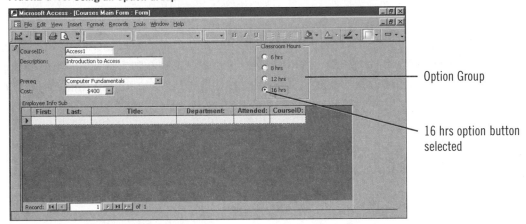

Option Group

16 hrs option button selected

FIGURE G-17: Adding another option button

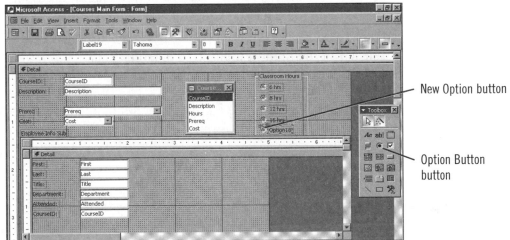

New Option button

Option Button button

CLUES TO USE

Protecting data

You may not want all the data that appears on a form to be able to be changed by all users who view that form. You can design forms to limit access to certain fields by changing the enabled and locked properties of a control. The Enabled property specifies whether a control can have the focus in Form view. The Locked property specifies whether you can edit data in a control in Form view.

Adding Command Buttons

A **command button** is a powerful unbound control used to initiate a common action such as printing the current record, opening another form, or closing the current form. In Form view, the user clicks a command button to run the specified action. Command buttons are often added to the **form header** or **form footer** sections. **Sections** determine where controls appear and print. See Table G-3 for more information on form sections. ➤ David adds a command button to the Courses Main Form form header section to help the users print the current record.

Steps 1 2 3 4

1. Click the **Design View button** 🖳, click **View** on the menu bar, wait a second or two for the menu to expand (if necessary), then click **Form Header/Footer**
   The form header opens.

2. Click the **Command Button button** ▭ on the Toolbox toolbar, then click in the **Form Header at the 5" mark** on the horizontal ruler
   The Command Button Wizard opens, listing over 30 of the most popular actions for the command button, organized within six categories.

QuickTip

Resize the Form Header section to make more room for the button, if necessary.

3. Click **Record Operations** in the Categories list, click **Print Record** in the Actions list, click **Next**, click **Next** to accept the choice to display a **Picture of a Printer** on the button, type **Print Current Record** as the button name, then click **Finish**
   Your screen should look like Figure G-18. By default, the Print button 🖨 on the Standard toolbar prints the entire recordset displayed by the form creating a very long printout. Therefore, adding a command button to print only the current record is very useful.

QuickTip

To help identify your printouts, you can add your name as a label to the Detail section of the Courses Main Form.

4. Click the **Form View button** 🖼 to view the new command button, press [Page Down] three times to navigate to the fourth record, click the new **Print Record command button**, then save and close the form
   The fourth record for the Computer Fundamentals class contains ten records in the subform that still displays only the January attendees as defined by the Employee Info query. You can adjust the left and right margins so that the printout fits neatly on one page.

5. Click **File** on the menu bar, click **Page Setup**, click the **Margins tab** (if necessary), press [Tab] three times to select 1 in the Left text box, type **0.5**, press [Tab] once to select 1 in the Right text box, type **0.5**, then click **OK**
   The **Display When** property of the Form Header controls when the controls in that section display and print.

6. Click 🖳, double-click the **Form Header section** to open its property sheet, click the **Format tab** (if necessary), click the **Display When property text box**, click the **Display When list arrow**, click **Screen Only**, then click the **Properties button** 🖺 to close the property sheet
   You don't want the command button on the printouts.

Trouble?

If your printout is still too wide for one sheet of paper, pull the right edge of the form to the left in Form Design view to narrow it.

7. Click the **Save button** 🖫, click 🖼, click the **Next Record button** ▶ several times on the Courses Main Form to navigate to the fourth record (Comp1), then click the **Print Record command button** to print the Comp1 record using the new command button
   Your final Courses Main Form should look like Figure G-19, and your printout should fit on one page, without displaying the form header.

8. Close the **Courses Main Form**

FIGURE G-18: Adding a command button

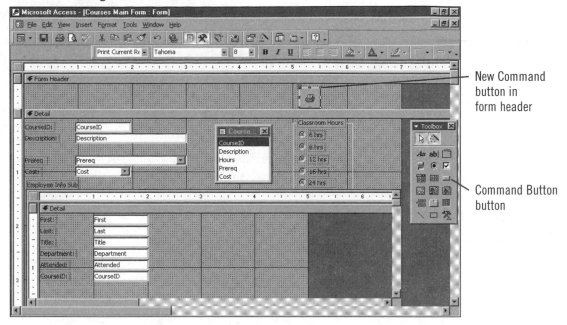

New Command button in form header

Command Button button

FIGURE G-19: The final Courses Main Form

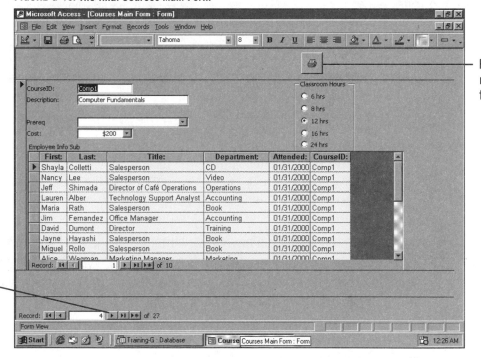

Print Record command button in form header

Next Record navigation button for Courses Main Form

TABLE G-3: Form Sections

section	description
Detail	Appears once for every individual record
Form Header	Appears at the top of the form and often contains command buttons or a label with the form's title
Form Footer	Appears at the bottom of the form and often contains command buttons or a label with instructions on how to use the form
Page Header	Appears at the top of a printed form with information such as page numbers or dates. The Page Header and Page Footer sections can be added to the form by clicking View on the menu bar, then clicking Page Header/Footer
Page Footer	Appears at the bottom of a printed form with information such as page numbers or dates

Adding Records with a Form/Subform

If you want to use the form/subform objects for data entry in addition to finding and viewing data, you must carefully plan the forms to make sure that all of the necessary fields are present that are required to add a record. For example, you cannot add a new employee to a main form unless the SSN field is present in the main form because the SSN is the key field. ◄━━ David built a form/subform for data entry purposes that displays all fields for each employee in the main form. The subform displays fields that reflect which classes that employee has attended. He uses this form/subform to add new employees as well as record new classes that employees have attended.

Steps

1. Double-click the **Employee Details Main Form** in the database window, maximize the form, then press **[Page Down]** once to view the second record for Nancy Lee
   Your screen should look like Figure G-20. Since the SSN field is listed in the main form, this form could be used to add new employees. You can also use the subform to add another class to the list that Nancy has attended.

2. Click the **New Record button** ►✱ on the subform navigation buttons, press **[Tab]** twice to move through the LogNo and SSN fields, then type **Project1** in the CourseID field
   The LogNo field is an AutoNumber data type, so it will automatically increase to the next available number as determined by the records in the Attendance table. The SSN field is automatically filled in with Nancy Lee's SSN because it serves as the linking field between the main and subforms.

3. Press **[Enter]** to move the focus to the Description field, press **[Enter]**, type **6/1/00** in the Attended field, press **[Enter]**, press **[Spacebar]** to enter a check in the Passed field, then press **[Enter]** to complete the record
   The CourseID entry (when added to the CourseID field of the Attendance table) automatically pulls the associated Description field entry from the Courses table, as shown in Figure G-21. Now enter a new employee into the main form.

   QuickTip
   A pencil icon in the margin of the form indicates the record is being edited.

4. Click ►✱ on the main form navigation buttons, click in the **First Name text box**, type **Kelsey**, press **[Tab]**, type **Wambold**, press **[Tab]**, type **Video**, press **[Tab]**, type **Salesperson**, press **[Tab]**, type **San Francisco**, press **[Tab]**, type the address **kwambold@medialoft.com**, press **[Tab]**, type **9/1/00**, press **[Tab]**, type **999881111**, then press **[Tab]**
   Kelsey has been added as a new employee in the database. When she starts taking courses, this form will be useful to track her attendance.

5. Close the **Employee Details Main Form**, close the **Training-G** database, then exit **Access**

FIGURE G-20: The Employee Details Main Form and Attendance Update Subform

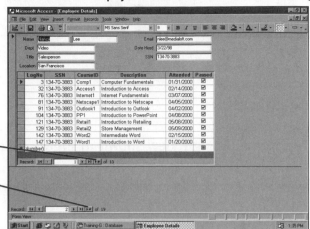

Subform New Record button

Main form New Record button

FIGURE G-21: Adding a record to the subform

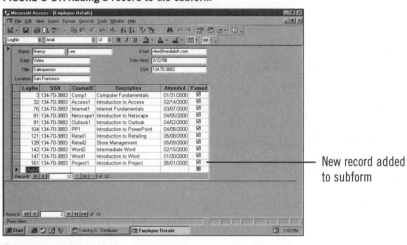

New record added to subform

FIGURE G-22: The Employee Details Main Form as a Web page

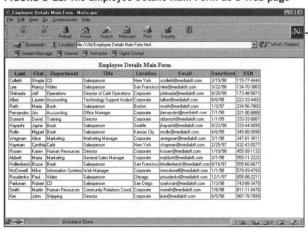

Netscape browser is displaying this Web page

CLUES TO USE

Saving a form as a Web page

You can save any form as a Web page in an **HTML** (Hypertext Markup Language, the language used to develop World Wide Web pages) file format. However, unless you create a **Data Access Page**, a database object used to create Web pages that interact with a live Access database, you will not be able to use the Web page to enter or edit data. Use the Export option on the File menu to save a form as an HTML document. You have the option of applying an HTML template that contains formatting instructions. Figure G-22 shows how the fields from the Employee main form would appear when they are exported from Access into an HTML file and are opened in browser software such as Microsoft Internet Explorer or Netscape Navigator.

Practice

▶ Concepts Review

Identify each element of the form's Design View shown in Figure G-23.

FIGURE G-23

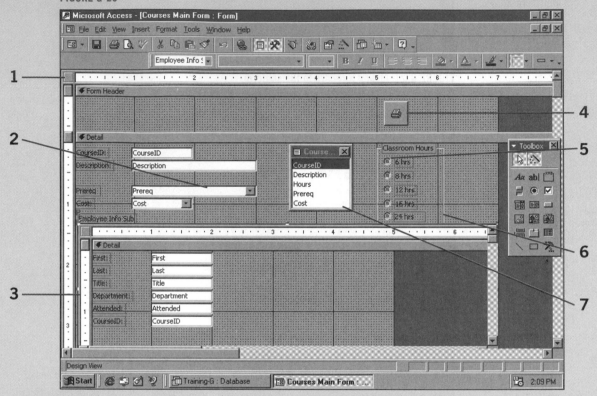

Match each term with the statement that describes its function.

8. **Option group**	**a.** Elements you add to a form such as labels, text boxes, and list boxes
9. **Controls**	**b.** A control that shows records that are related to one record shown in the main form
10. **Command button**	**c.** An unbound control that, when clicked, executes an action
11. **Subform**	**d.** A bound control that is really both a list box and a text box
12. **Combo box**	**e.** A bound control that displays a few mutually exclusive entries for a field

Select the best answer from the list of choices.

13. **Which control would work best to display two choices for a field?**
    a. Text box
    b. Label
    c. Option group
    d. Command button

14. **Which control would you use to print a form?**
    a. Option group
    b. List box
    c. Text box
    d. Command button

15. **Which control would you use to display a drop-down list of 50 states?**
    a. Check box
    b. Field label
    c. List box
    d. Combo box

16. **To view linked records within a form use a:**
    a. Subform.
    b. List box.
    c. Design template.
    d. Link control.

▶ Skills Review

1. **Understand the form/subform relationship.**
    a. Start Access and open the Membership-G database.
    b. Click the Relationships button on the Database toolbar.
    c. Click File on the menu bar, wait a second or two for the expanded menu to appear, then click Print Relationships.
    d. The Relationships for Membership-G will appear as a previewed report. Click the Print button on the Print Preview toolbar to print the report, close the preview window without saving the report, and then close the Relationships window. If you need to include your name on the printout, go to Design view and add your name as a label on the report.
    e. Based on the one-to-many relationships defined in the Membership-G database, sketch two form/subform combinations that you might want to create.

2. **Create subforms using the Wizard.**
    a. Click Forms on the Objects bar in the Membership-G database window.
    b. Double-click Create form by using wizard.
    c. Select all of the fields from both the Activities and the Names tables.
    d. View the data by Names.
    e. Accept a datasheet layout for the subform.
    f. Accept a standard style.
    g. Accept the default titles for the forms.
    h. Find the record for Lois Goode (record number 3) and enter your own first and last names in the appropriate text boxes.

i. Resize the columns of the datasheet in the subform so that all of the data is clearly visible.

j. Click File on the menu bar, then click Print. Click the Selected records option button in the Print dialog box to print only the data for your name.

k. Close the Names form.

3. **Create subforms using queries.**

a. Open the "Zips in IA or MO" query in Design view, and add the criteria to find only those records from IA or MO in the State field.

b. Using either the Form Wizard or Form Design view, build a form based on the "Zips in IA or MO" query using all three fields in the query.

c. Open the Zips in IA or MO form in Design view, and add a subform control about 5" wide by about 3" tall below the three text boxes.

d. Use the Subform Wizard to specify that the subform will use an existing query, then select all of the fields in the Dues query to be part of the subform.

e. Allow the wizard to link the form and subform so that they "Show Dues for each record in Zips in IA or MO using Zip".

f. Accept Dues subform as the subform's name.

g. Maximize the form, expand the size of the subform, move the subform as necessary, and resize the datasheet column widths so that all of the information in the subform is clearly visible. You will know you are done when the horizontal scroll bar does not display in Form view and text from the subform doesn't overlap the main form.

h. Format the datasheet so the First field entry always appears as red text and the Zip field entry always appears as blue text.

i. Find the record for Zip 64105 (the sixth record), enter your last name in the Last field of the first record, and print only that record.

j. Save and close the Zips in IA or MO form.

4. **Modify subforms.**

a. Click the Queries tab and open the Zips in IA or MO query in Design view.

b. Delete the criteria that specifies that only the records with State values of IA or MO appear in the recordset.

c. Save the modified query as "All Zips".

d. Close the all Zips query.

e. Click the Forms tab and open the Zips in IA or MO form in Design view.

f. Open the property sheet for the form, and change the Record Source property from "Zips in IA or MO" to "All Zips".

g. Save the form and navigate to record number 13, which displays Zip 64145 for Shawnee, Kansas.

h. Change the city to the name of your hometown, then print this record.

i. Close the form, then right-click it and choose Rename.

j. Save the updated form with the name "Zips".

5. **Add combo boxes.**

a. Open the Names form in Design view and delete the Zip text box.

b. Add the Zip field back to the same location as a combo box, using the Combo Box Wizard.

c. The Combo Box Wizard should look up values from a table or query.

d. Choose the Zips table and the Zip field within the Combo Box Wizard.

e. Store the value in the Zip field, label the Combo Box Zip.

f. Reposition the new Zip label and combo box as necessary, save the form, and display it in Form view.

g. Navigate to the second record, change the address to your own, and change the Zip to 50266 using the new combo box. Print the second record.

6. Add option groups.

  a. Open the Names form in Design view, then delete the Dues text box.

  b. Add the Dues field back to the form below the CharterMember check box control using an Option Group control with the Option Group Wizard.

  c. Enter "$25" and "$50" as the label names, and accept $25 as the default choice.

  d. Change the values to "25" and "50" to correspond with the labels.

  e. Store the value in the Dues field, choose option buttons with an etched style, and enter the caption "Annual Dues".

  f. Save the form, display it in Form view, find the record for Jerry Martin (you can use the Find command from the Edit menu), change the first name to your own, and change the Annual Dues to "$50".

  g. Print the updated Martin record.

7. Add command buttons.

  a. Open the Names form in Design view.

  b. Open the Form Header to display about 0.5" of space, then add a command button to the upper-right corner using the Command Button Wizard.

  c. Choose the Print Record action from the Record Operations category.

  d. Display the text "Print Current Record" on the button, then name the button "Print".

  e. Save the form and display it in Form view.

  f. Navigate to the record with your own name, change the birth date to your own, and print the record using the new Print Current Record command button.

8. Add records with a subform.

  a. Navigate to the first record for Mark Daniels, then click in the subform.

  b. Add two records with the following information:

ActivityDate:	Hours:
3/1/00	4
3/2/00	8

  c. Print the updated record using the Print Current Record command button.

  d. Why is it unnecessary to enter the MemberNo data in the subform? Write a brief answer on your printout.

  e. Use the Export option from the File menu to save the Names form as an HTML document. Do not use an HTML template.

  f. Open the HTML document you created from the Names form in either Netscape or Internet Explorer, whichever browser is available on your system, then print the document.

  g. Close the browser window, return to the Access window, close the Names form, close the Membership-G database, and exit Access.

► **Independent Challenges**

1. As the manager of a music store's instrument rental program, you have created a database to track instrument rentals to schoolchildren. Now that several rentals have been made, you wish to create a form/subform to facilitate the user's ability to enter a new rental record.

To complete this independent challenge:

  a. Start Access and open the database Music Store-G.

  b. Using the Form Wizard, create a new form based on all of the fields in the Customers and Rentals tables.

  c. View the data by Customers, choose both a Datasheet layout for the subform and a Standard style, and accept the default form titles of "Customers" and "Rentals Subform."

  d. Add another record to the rental subform by pressing [Tab] through both the RentalNo and CustNo fields, which will be filled in automatically, and typing "888335" as the SerialNo entry and "5/1/00" as the Date entry.

e. Close the new Customers form.

f. Add the description of the instrument to the subform information. To do this, create a new query in Design view.

g. Add the Rentals and Instruments tables, then close the Show Table dialog box.

h. Add all of the fields from the Rentals table and the Description field from the Instruments table to the query, save the query with the name "Rental Description", and close it.

i. Open the Rentals Subform in Design view, then change the Record Source property of the form from "Rentals" to "Rental Description".

j. Open the form's field list and drag the Description field to the right of the Date text box in the Detail section. Don't worry if the field doesn't perfectly line up with the others or if the Description label seems to be "on top" of other controls. Because the Default view of this form is set to Datasheet, this form will appear as a datasheet regardless of the organization of the controls in Design view.

k. Close the property sheet and the Rentals Subform, saving it when prompted.

l. Open the Customers form and note the new field in the subform that describes the type of instrument rented. Enter your last name in the LastName text box that currently displays "Bacon" and print the first record.

m. Close the Music Store-G database, save the changes, and exit Access.

2. As the manager of a music store's instrument rental program, you have created a database to track instrument rentals to schoolchildren. You add command buttons to a form to make it easier to use.

To complete this independent challenge:

a. Start Access and open the database Music Store-G.

b. Using the Form Wizard, create a form/subform using all the fields of both the Customers and Schools tables.

c. View the data by Schools, use a Datasheet layout for the subform, and a Standard style.

d. Accept the default names of "Schools" and "Customers Subform" for the titles.

e. Maximize the form and resize the columns of the subform so that as many fields as possible can be displayed. Save the form.

f. In Design view, widen the subform to the 6.5" mark on the horizontal ruler.

g. In Design view, add two command buttons in the Form Header using the Command Button Wizard. The first button should print the current record and display the text "Print School Record." The second button should add a new record and display the text "Add New School." Name the buttons appropriately.

h. Modify the Form Header "Display When" property so that this section appears only on the screen and not when printed.

i. Display the form in Form view, resize the columns of the datasheet (if necessary) to display all fields, add your own name and address as a new record in the datasheet of the first record, then use the Print School Record button to print that record.

j. Click the Add New School button, then add the name of your elementary school to the SchoolName field, allow the SchoolNo to increment automatically, and add the name of an elementary school teacher as the first record within the subform.

k. Use the Print School Record button to print this new school record.

l. Close the Schools form, saving it if prompted, then close the Music Store-G database and exit Access.

3. As the manager of a music store's instrument rental program, you have created a database to track instrument rentals to schoolchildren. Now that the users are becoming accustomed to forms, you add a combo box and option group to make the forms easier to use.

To complete this independent challenge:

a. Start Access and open the database Music Store-G.

b. Using the Form Wizard, create a form/subform using all the fields of both the Instruments and Rentals tables.

c. View the data by Instruments, use a datasheet layout for the subform, and a Standard style.

d. Enter the names "Instruments Main Form" and "Rental Information" as the form and subform titles, respectively.

e. Maximize the form, open it in Design view, and delete the Condition text box and label.

f. Using the Field List and the Toolbox toolbar, add the Condition field to the same location using the Combo Box Wizard. Choose "I will type in the values that I want", then enter "Poor", "Fair", "Good", and "Excellent" as the values for the first and only column.

g. Store the value in the Condition field, and label the new combo box as "Condition".

h. Move and resize the new combo box as necessary.

i. Delete the MonthlyFee textbox and associated label.

j. Using the Field List and the Toolbox toolbar, add the MonthlyFee field to the upper-right corner of the form using the Option Group Wizard.

k. Enter the Label Names as "$35", "$40", "$45", and "$50"; there should be no default option, and the values entered should be "35", "40", "45", and "50", respectively.

l. Store the value in the Monthly Fee field, and use option buttons with an etched style.

m. Caption the option group "Monthly Fee", then save the form and view it in Form view.

n. Navigate to the record for the cello, Serial Number 1234568, change the Monthly Fee to "$45", choose "Excellent" for the Condition, and add a new rental record in the subform. The RentalNo is an AutoNumber field and will record "20" automatically, enter "10" for the CustNo, tab through the SerialNo field that is already linked to the main form, and enter the date of your next birthday as the Date entry.

o. Use the Selected Record option in the Print dialog box, invoked by clicking Print from the File menu, to print only that record.

p. Save and close the Instruments Main Form, exit Music Store-G, and exit Access.

4. MediaLoft developed an intranet site that provides internal information to their employees. The Accounting Department created an example of a form that they would like to develop and add as a Web page on the MediaLoft intranet for easy access by others. In this independent challenge, you will find the prototype form on the intranet site. Print it, then create the form in the Training-G database.

a. Connect to the Internet and use your browser to go to the MediaLoft intranet site at http://www.course.com/illustrated/MediaLoft/

b. Click the link for Training.

c. Click the link for User Requests, and print the Web page.

d. Disconnect from the Internet, start Access, then open the Training-G database.

e. Create a query with the following fields: Department from the Employees table, LogNo and Attended from the Attendance table, and Description, Hours, and Cost from the Courses table.

f. Sort the query by Department, and then by Attended. Add criteria so that only the records in the Accounting Department are shown. (You should have 16 records.) Save and name the query "Accounting Query".

g. Create a new form in Form Design view, and set the form's Record Source property to the Accounting Query and the Default View property to Datasheet. Add all fields from the field list to the form. Save the form as "Accounting Form".

h. View the Accounting Form in form view, change the date on the first record by entering "1/21/00" in the Attended field, then save and close the Accounting Form.

i. Use the Export option from the File menu to export the Accounting Form to your floppy disk (A:\) as an HTML document. (*Hint*: Change the Save as type: option in the Export Form 'Accounting Form' As dialog box to HTML Documents). When prompted, click OK without specifying a special HTML template.

j. Start your browser (Internet Explorer or Netscape), use the Open option from the File menu to open the Accounting Form HTML file from your Project Disk, print it, and compare it to the earlier printout from the intranet site. The printouts should look exactly the same, except for the updated date in the first record.

k. Close your browser window, close the Training-G database, and exit Access.

▶ Visual Workshop

Start Access, then open the Training-G database. Create a new form, as shown in Figure G-24, using the Form Wizard. The First, Last, and Department fields are pulled from the Employees table, the Description field comes from the Courses table, and the Attended and Passed fields come from the Attendance table. Name the form "Employee Basics" and the subform "Test Results." The Department combo box contains the following entries: Accounting, Book, Café, CD, Human Resources, Marketing, Operations, Shipping, Training, and Video. The command buttons in the Form Header print the current record and close the form.

FIGURE G-24

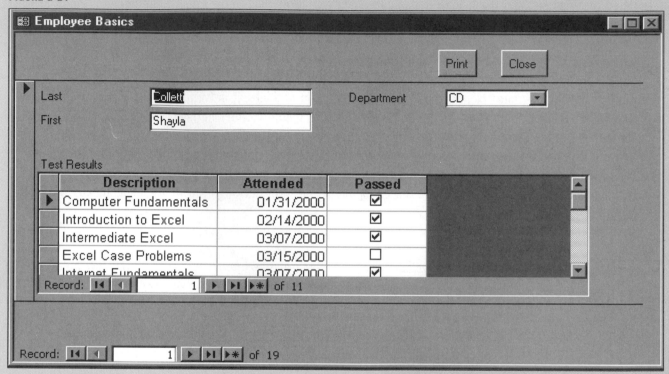

Building
Complex Reports

Objectives

- MOUS ► **Use the Database Wizard**
- MOUS ► **Import data**
- MOUS ► **Create a report from a parameter query**
- MOUS ► **Enhance reports**
- MOUS ► **Add lines and rectangles**
- MOUS ► **Use the Format Painter and AutoFormats**
- MOUS ► **Insert an image**
- MOUS ► **Secure the database**

Although you can print data in forms and datasheets, **reports** give you more control over how data is printed and greater flexibility in presenting summary information such as subtotals on groups of records. Because a report definition (the report object itself) can be saved, it can be created once and then used many times. Printed reports always reflect the most up-to-date data in a consistent format each time they are printed. As with form designs, report designs allow you to add bound controls such as text boxes and calculated controls, and unbound controls such as lines, graphics, or labels. ◄──── Other departments have noted the initial success of David's Training database, and now he is being asked to report the information in new ways. David uses the database to report information electronically, by using the Access import and export features. David also uses database management features such as database compacting to make the database easier to manage. Advanced reporting and formatting features such as parameter prompts, group footer calculations, conditional formatting, images, colors, and lines help David enhance his reports.

Using the Database Wizard

The **Database Wizard** is a powerful Access tool that creates a sample database file for a general purpose such as inventory control, event tracking, or expenses. It also creates objects that you can use or modify. The Accounting Department tracks a training budget to determine how various departments are using MediaLoft's in-house classes. Although David could create a quarterly paper report with this information, he decides to report this information electronically by creating a separate Access database for the Accounting Department into which he can send historical information on course attendance and costs from the Training database.

1. Start Access, click the **Access database wizards, pages, and projects option button** in the Microsoft Access dialog box, click **OK**, then click the **Databases tab**
   The Databases tab of the New Dialog box is shown in Figure H-1.

2. Click **Expenses** in the New dialog box, then click **OK**
   When you create a new database, you must first name the database file regardless of whether it is created by a wizard or from scratch.

3. Click the **Save In: list arrow**, click the **3½ Floppy (A:)** option to save the file on your Project Disk, double-click **expenses1** in the File name text box, type **Accounting**, click **Create**, then click **Next**
   The dialog box shown in Figure H-2 opens. The sample database will include four tables and their associated fields.

4. Click **Expense report information** in the Tables list, then click **Next**

5. Click **Standard**, click **Next**, click **Corporate**, click **Next**, type **Accounting** as the database title, click **Next**, make sure the **Yes, start the database check box** is checked, then click **Finish**
   It takes several seconds for Access to build all of the objects for the Accounting database and then open the Main Switchboard form, as shown in Figure H-3. When you use the Database Wizard, Access creates a **switchboard**, a special Access form that displays command buttons that help make the database easier to use.

6. Click the **Main Switchboard Close button**, maximize the **Accounting database window**, review the available forms, click **Reports** on the Objects bar, then click the **Tables** on the Objects bar
   These objects can be used, modified, or deleted like any user-created object.

7. Click the **Employees table**, click the **Design button** 📐, click the **Insert Rows button** 🔁 on the Table Design toolbar, type **Department**, press **[Tab]**, click the **Data Type list arrow**, then click **Lookup Wizard**
   The Lookup Wizard opens. Use the Lookup Wizard to provide department choices.

8. Click **I will type in the values that I want option button**, click **Next**, press **[Tab]**, then type **Accounting**, press **[Tab]**, type **Book**, press **[Tab]**, type **Cafe**, press **[Tab]**, type **CD**, press **[Tab]**, type **Human Resources**, press **[Tab]**, type **Information Systems**, press **[Tab]**, type **Marketing**, press **[Tab]**, type **Operations**, press **[Tab]**, type **Shipping**, press **[Tab]**, then type **Video**

9. Click **Next**, click **Finish** to accept the Department label, click the **Datasheet View button** 🔳, click **Yes** to save the table, then click the **Department field list arrow**
   The Lookup Wizard provides the values in the Department list, but you could also type a new value into the Department field if desired.

FIGURE H-1: Database wizards

New dialog box

Database wizards are available on the Databases tab

View buttons

Picture relates to selected Database wizard

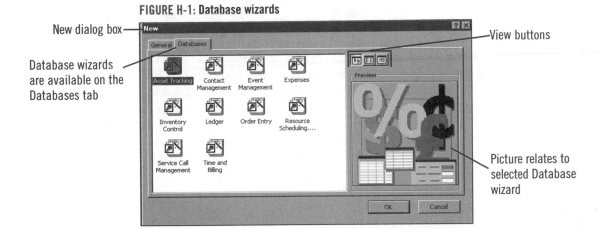

FIGURE H-2: Tables and fields within the Expenses Database Wizard

This database will have four tables

Check or uncheck fields to add them to the selected table

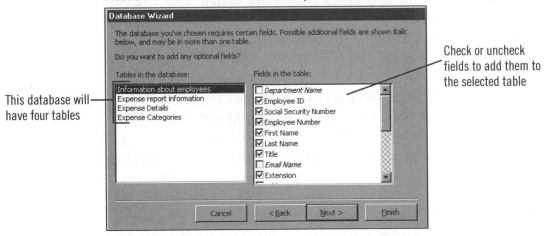

FIGURE H-3: Main Switchboard form for the Accounting database

Main Switchboard Close button

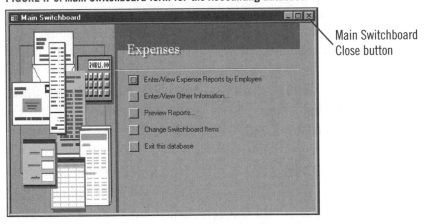

CLUES TO USE

Using the Lookup Wizard

The **Lookup Wizard** is a powerful Access feature that allows a field to "look up" values from a list you type (called a **value list**) or from another table or query. It is not a data type such as Text, Number, or Yes/No. However, the Lookup Wizard helps you determine the final data type for the field based on the values you enter in the list. A lookup field often improves data entry speed, accuracy, and comprehension. A field that has lookup properties will automatically appear as a combo box control when added to a form or viewed on a datasheet. Lookup properties for a specific field can be examined on the Lookup Tab of the field's properties in Table Design view.

Importing Data

Importing is a process to quickly convert data from an external source, such as Excel or another database program, into an Access database. The Access import process copies the data from the original source and pastes the data in the Access database. Therefore, if you update data in either the original source or in the imported copy in Access, the other copy is not updated. See Table H-1 for more information on the types of data that Access can import. ✎ Now that the Accounting database has been created, David imports the historical cost and attendance information into it. The integrity of the information will remain intact because the Accounting Department will not be updating or changing the data, but only creating reports.

Steps

Trouble?

You can't import from the Training database if it is opened in another Access window.

1. Click the **Employees table Close button**, click **File** on the menu bar, point to **Get External Data**, click **Import**, click the **Look in list arrow**, locate your **Project Disk**, click **Training**, then click **Import**
The Import Objects dialog box opens, as shown in Figure H-4. Any object in the Training-H database can be imported into the Accounting database.

2. Click **1QTR-2000**, click **Courses**, click the **Queries tab**, click **Accounting Query**, click the **Reports tab**, click **Accounting Report**, then click **OK**
The four selected objects are imported into the Accounting database.

3. Click **Tables** on the Objects bar, then click the **Details button** 🔳 in the database window
The Created and Modified dates of both the 1QTR-2000 and the Courses tables should be today's date. If you update these tables in the future, the Modified date will change, but not the Created date.

QuickTip

By default, objects in the database window are sorted by name.

4. Click the **Modified column heading** to sort the Table objects in ascending order on the date they were modified, then click the **Name column heading**

5. Click **Queries** on the Objects bar to make sure that the Accounting Query has been imported, click **Reports** (Your screen should look like Figure H-5.), point to the **Name column heading divider** to display the ↔ pointer, then double-click ↔
The column expands to accommodate the widest entry in the Name column. This database will also track department codes that are stored in an Excel spreadsheet.

6. Click **File** on the menu bar, point to **Get External Data**, click **Import**, click the **Look in: list arrow**, locate your **Project Disk**, click the **Files of type list arrow**, click **Microsoft Excel**, click **Deptcodes**, then click **Import**
The Import Spreadsheet Wizard guides you through the rest of the import process.

7. Click **Next**, make sure the **First Row Contains Column Headings** check box is checked, click **Next**, make sure the **In a New Table option button** is selected, click **Next**, click **Next** to accept the default field information, click the **Choose my own primary key option button**, make sure **Code** is displayed in the primary key list box, click **Next**, type **Codes** in the Import to Table text box, click **Finish**, then click **OK**
The Deptcodes spreadsheet is now a table in the Accounting database.

8. Double-click **Codes** to open it, then review the codes as a datasheet
The Accounting Department has more work to do before they can use their new database. They must determine if they are going to use the other tables created by the Database Wizard; if they are going to add, modify, or delete any of the existing fields; and most importantly, how they are going to link the tables in one-to-many relationships.

9. Close the codes datasheet, then close the Accounting database

FIGURE H-4: Import Objects dialog box

Tables tab is chosen —

Table objects in the — Training-H database

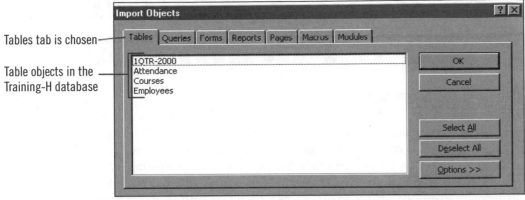

FIGURE H-5: Database window with Details

Resize column pointer

Details button

Column heading for Name of object

Column heading for Created date

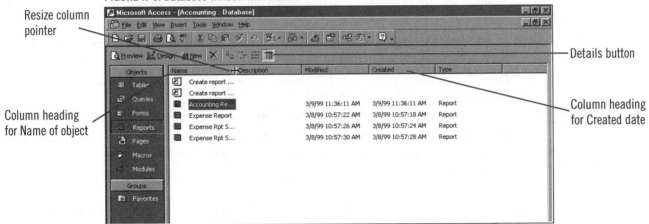

TABLE H-1: Data sources Microsoft Access can import

data source	version or format supported
Microsoft Access database	2.0, 7.0/95, 8.0/97, 9.0/2000 (Note: Access version 7.0 is also known as Access version 95. Access version 8.0 is also known as Access 97, and so forth.)
Microsoft Access project	9.0/2000
dBASE	III, III+, IV, and 5
Paradox, Paradox for Windows	3.x, 4.x, and 5.0
Microsoft Excel	3.0, 4.0, 5.0, 7.0/95, 8.0/97, and 9.0/2000
Lotus 1-2-3	.wks, .wk1, .wk3, .wk4
Microsoft Exchange	All versions
Delimited text files	All character sets
Fixed-width text files	All character sets
HTML	1.0 (if a list) 2.0, 3.x (if a table or list)
SQL tables, Microsoft Visual Foxpro, and other data sources that support ODBC protocol	ODBC (Open Database Connectivity) is a protocol for accessing data in SQL (Structured Query Language) database servers.

Creating a Report from a Parameter Query

If you create a report or form by basing it on a **parameter query**, it will display a dialog box prompting you for criteria to customize the **recordset** of the object each time you use it. For example, you might base a report on a parameter query that prompts for date, department, or state criteria so that only those records that are true for that are used for the report. David has been asked by many departments to provide a paper report of which employees have attended which classes. Rather than create a query and corresponding report object for each department, he builds one parameter query that prompts for the Department field criteria and one report object based on this parameter query.

Steps 1 2 3 4

Trouble?

If you are using floppy disks, the Training-H database is on the second Project Disk.

Trouble?

The parameter criteria must be surrounded by [square brackets], not by (parentheses), <angle brackets>, or {curly brackets}.

QuickTip

If you want to customize your printouts, place a label control in the Report Header section that contains your name.

1. Open the **Training-H** database from your Project Disk, click **Queries** 🗐 on the Objects bar, click **Department Query**, then click the **Design button** 📐
   Department Query opens in Design view. It uses fields from all three of the original tables: Courses, Attendance, and Employees.

2. Click the **Department field Criteria cell**, type **[Enter department name:]**, press **[Enter]**, place the pointer on the **right edge of the Department field column selector**, then drag the ✛ pointer to the right to display the entry
   You can see the entire parameter criteria entry, as shown in Figure H-6. Query criteria, including parameter criteria, are not case sensitive.

3. Click the **Datasheet view button** 🔳, type **cd** in the Enter department name text box in the Enter Parameter Value dialog box, then click **OK**
   The resulting datasheet shows that the CD department employees attended 21 classes. The parameter criteria entry works.

4. Click the **Save button** 🖫, then close the Department Query datasheet
   Use the Report Wizard to quickly create a report based on the Department Query.

5. Click **Reports** 🗐 on the Objects bar, double-click **Create report by using wizard**, click the **Tables/Queries list arrow**, click **Query: Department Query**, click the **Select All Fields button** >> , click **Next**, then click **by Attendance**
   View choices are actually ways to group the records with multiple fields in the group header.

6. Click **Next**, click **Department**, click the **Select Single Field button** > , click **Next**, click the **first sort order list arrow**, click **Last**, click the **second sort order list arrow**, click **First**, click the **third sort order list arrow**, then click **Attended**
   Your Report Wizard sorting and summary dialog box should look like Figure H-7. The rest of the wizard options determine group calculations (summary options), layout, and style information. The Summary Options dialog box allows you to calculate the subtotal, average, or minimum or maximum value for several fields.

7. Click the **Summary Options button**, click the **Hours Sum check box**, click **OK**, click **Next**, click the **Stepped option button**, click the **Portrait option button**, click **Next**, click **Corporate** for the style, click **Next**, type **Department Report** in the title text box, then click **Finish**
   Because the report is based on the Department Query (a parameter query), the entry in the dialog box will determine which department's records will appear on the report.

8. Type **video**, then click **OK**
   The final report should look similar to Figure H-8.

9. Click the **Print button** 🖶 on the Print Preview toolbar

FIGURE H-6: Creating a parameter query

Resize column pointer

Parameter criteria entry

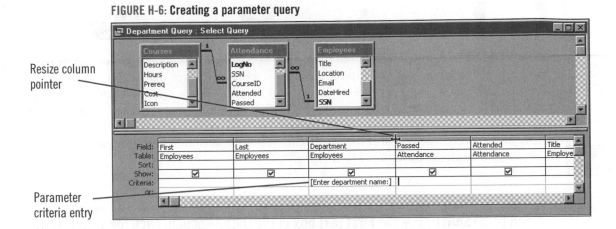

FIGURE H-7: Report Wizard sorting order and Summary Options dialog box

First sort order

Second sort order

Third sort order

Summary Options button

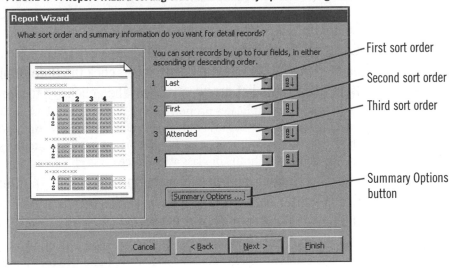

FIGURE H-8: Final Department Report

Records are grouped by Department

Only the Video department is displayed

Records are sorted by Last name

Because there are not two employees with the same last and first name, the records are further sorted by the date in the Attended field

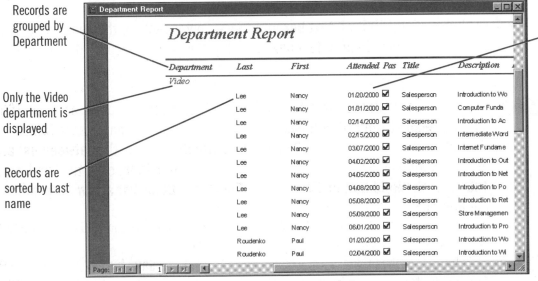

Enhancing Reports

Conditional formatting allows you to change the appearance of a control on a form or report based on criteria you specify. **Grouping controls** is a handy feature that allows you to identify several controls in a group in order to quickly and easily apply the same formatting properties to them. Other report embellishments such as hiding duplicate values and group footer calculations improve the clarity of the report. ✎ David wants to improve the appearance and clarity of the Department Report by using techniques such as hiding duplicate values, grouping controls, and applying conditional formatting.

Steps 123 4

1. Click the **Design View button** 🖉, click the **Last text box** in the Detail section, press and hold **[Shift]**, click the **First text box** in the Detail section, click the **Title text box**, release **[Shift]**, click **Format** on the menu bar, then click **Group**
   The three text boxes have been grouped and can now be formatted or modified simultaneously. Group selection handles surround the group, so when you click on *any* control in a group, you select *every* control in the group.

2. Click the **Properties button** 🖹 on the Report Design toolbar, click the **Format tab** on the Multiple selection property sheet, click the **Hide Duplicates text box**, click the **Hide Duplicates list arrow**, click **Yes**, then click 🖹 to close the property sheet
   With the Hide Duplicates property set to Yes, the First, Last, and Title values will print only once per employee. Because only one department shows on this report, there is no need for the Department Footer because the Report Footer presents the same calculation. To subtotal the number of hours of class attendance for each person, you need a Last Footer section.

3. Click the **Sorting and Grouping button** 📳, select the **Department field**, click the **Group Footer list arrow**, click **No**, click **Yes** to delete the group section, click the **Last field**, click the **Group Footer list arrow**, click **Yes** to display a footer every time the Last field changes, then click 📳 to close the Sorting and Grouping dialog box
   The Department Footer section was removed and the Last Footer section was added.

4. Click the **=Sum([Hours]) text box** in the Report Footer, click the **Copy button** 🖹 on the Report Design toolbar, click the **Last Footer section**, then click the **Paste button** 🖺
   Your screen should look like Figure H-9. This calculated control in the Last group footer summarizes the number of hours for each person.

5. Click the **=Sum([Hours]) text box** in the Last Footer section, then use the ✋ pointer to drag the **=Sum([Hours]) text box** to the right edge of the report, directly under the Hours text box in the Detail section
   Both calculated controls will be selected for conditional formatting.

6. Click the **=Sum([Hours]) text box** in the Last Footer section, press and hold **[Shift]**, click the **=Sum([Hours]) text box** in the Report Footer section, release **[Shift]**, click **Format** on the menu bar, click **Conditional Formatting**, click the **between list arrow** in the Conditional Formatting dialog box, click **greater than**, click the text box, type **100**, click the **Bold button** 🅱, click the **Font/Fore Color list arrow** 🄰, then click the **Red box** on the palette
   Your screen should look like Figure H-10. The conditional formatting will display the subtotaled hours in bold and red if the calculation exceeds 100.

7. Click **OK** in the Conditional Formatting dialog box, click the **Save button** 🖫, click the **Print Preview button** 🔍, type **book** in the Enter Parameter Value dialog box, then click **OK**
   The Department Report for the Book department should look like Figure H-11.

8. Close the Print Preview window, save the report, then close it

FIGURE H-9: Department Report in Design view

Last Footer section

Pasted
=Sum([Hours]) text
box

Report Footer section

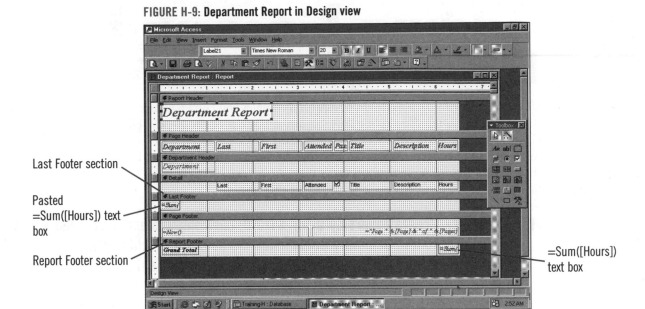

=Sum([Hours])
text box

FIGURE H-10: Conditional Formatting dialog box

Select "greater than"

Bold button

Font/Fore Color
button

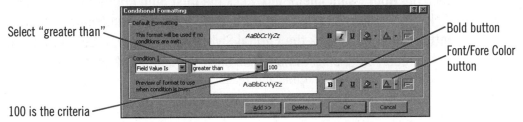

100 is the criteria

FIGURE H-11: Final Department Report for the Book department

Duplicate values
are hidden

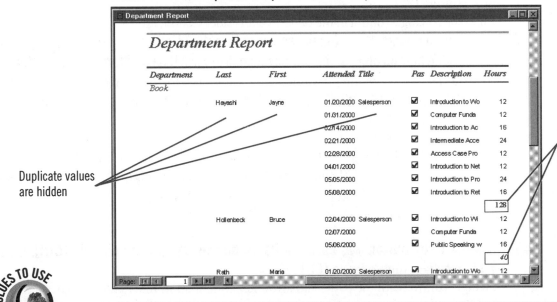

Hours are subtotaled
for each person, and
conditional formatting
is applied for values
greater than 100

Applying Conditional Formatting

Conditional Formatting is an excellent tool to highlight important data in a report. For example, you could change the color, background, or style of a text box control, such as a Sales field, if its value exceeds $1,000. Later, if the value of the Sales field becomes less than $1,000, Access would reapply the default formatting for the control.

Adding Lines and Rectangles

Unbound controls such as labels, lines, and rectangles can enhance the clarity of the report. The Report Wizard often creates line controls at the bottom of the Report Header, Page Header, or Group Header sections that visually separate the parts of the report. Lines and boxes can be formatted in many ways. ➤ The Personnel Department has asked David to create a report that lists all of the courses and subtotals the courses by hours and costs. David uses line and rectangle controls to enhance the appearance of this report.

Steps 1 2 3 4

1. Double-click **Create report by using wizard**, click the **Tables/Queries list arrow**, click **Query: Course Summary Query**, click the **Select All Fields button** ⏩, click **Next**, click **by Attendance**, click **Next**, double-click **Department** to add it as a grouping field, then click **Next**

   After determining the grouping field(s), the wizard prompts for the sort fields.

2. Click the **first sort field list arrow**, click **Attended** to sort the detail records by the date the classes were attended, then click the **Summary Options button**

QuickTip

Printing the first and last pages of a report will help you see where controls are placed in Design view.

3. Click the **Hours Sum check box**, click the **Cost Sum check box**, click **OK**, click **Next**, click the **Outline 2 Layout option button**, click the **Landscape Orientation option button**, click **Next**, click the **Formal** Style, click **Next**, type **Course Summary Report** as the report title, click **Finish**, then click the **Zoom Out pointer** 🔍 on the report

   Figure H-12 shows several line and rectangle controls. These controls are sometimes very difficult to locate in Design view because they are placed against the edge of the section or the border of other controls. The easiest place to click the line control in the Detail section is between the Passed check box and Description text box controls.

Trouble?

Maximize the report if necessary.

QuickTip

To be sure you select the right control, verify that line 34 displays in the Object list box on the Formatting Form/Report toolbar.

4. Click the **Design View button** 📐, click the **line control** in the Detail section, then press **[Delete]**

   To find the rectangle control in the Department Header section, expand the size of that section.

5. Point to the **top edge of the Detail section** so that the pointer changes to ✛, drag down 0.5", click the **bottom edge of the rectangle control**, click the **Line/Border Color button list arrow** 🖌 on the Formatting (Form/Report) toolbar, click the **bright blue box** in the second row, click the **Line/Border Width list arrow** ▭, then click **2** (a measurement of line width)

   Your screen should look like Figure H-13. Short double lines under the calculations in the Report Footer section indicate grand totals.

QuickTip

When working in Design view, and especially when using the line control—which requires precise mouse movements—click the **Undo button** ↺ to reverse your last action as needed.

6. Click the **Line button** ╲ on the Toolbox toolbar, press and hold **[Shift]**, drag a line from the **left edge =Sum([Hours]) text box** to the **right edge of the =Sum([Cost]) text box** in the Report Footer section, then release **[Shift]**

   Copying and pasting lines create an exact duplicate of the line that can be moved to a new location.

7. Click the **Copy button** 📋, click the **Paste button** 📋, press and hold **[Ctrl]**, press **[↑]** five times, then release **[Ctrl]**

   Moving a control with the **[Ctrl]** and arrow key combination moves it one picture element (**pixel**) at a time.

8. Click the **line control** below the Course Summary Report label in the Report Header section, point to the **line** so the pointer changes to 🖐, drag the **line** straight down until it rests just above the Page Footer section, click the **Print Preview button** 🔍, then click the **Last Page Navigation button** ⏭

   Your screen should look like Figure H-14.

FIGURE H-12: First page of Course Summary Report

Rectangle control

Line controls

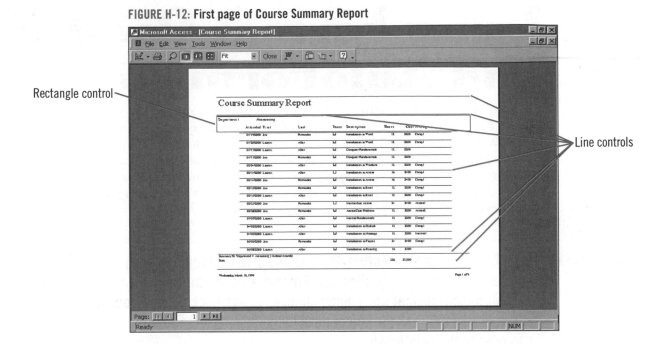

FIGURE H-13: Course Summary Report in Design view

Line/Border Width button

Line/Border Color button

Line control deleted

Drag top edge of Detail section down to expand the Department Header section

Rectangle control is selected

Line button

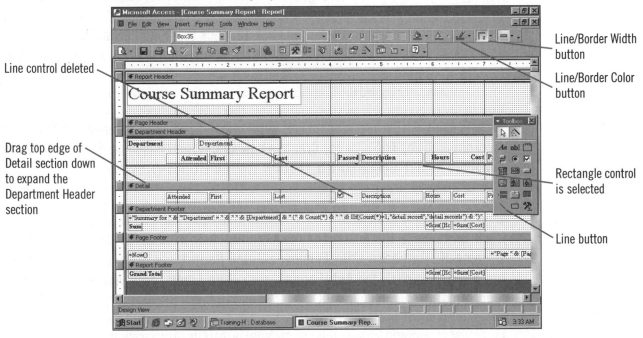

Line was moved from the bottom of the Report Header section to the bottom of the Department Footer section

Lines added to indicate a grand total

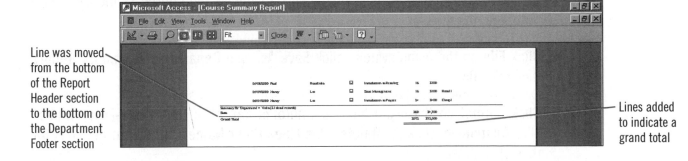

Using Format Painter and AutoFormats

The **Format Painter** is a handy tool used to copy formatting properties from one control to another. **AutoFormats** are predefined formats that you can apply to a form or report and include such items as background pictures, font, color, and alignment choices. Once you have developed a form or report format that you wish to save and apply to other objects, you can add it to the list of AutoFormats provided by Access. ✐ David uses the Format Painter to change the characteristics of other lines on the report, then saves the report's formatting scheme as a new AutoFormat so that he can apply it to other reports he creates.

Steps 1 2 3 4

QuickTip

Double-clicking the Format Painter button will allow you to "paint" more than one control.

1. Click the **Design View button** 🖾, click the **blue rectangle control** in the Department Header section, double-click the **Format Painter button** 🖌 on the Formatting (Form/Report) toolbar (the pointer changes to ▷🖌), click the **line control** in the Report Header section, click the **line control** in the Department Footer section, then click 🖌 to release the paintbrush
   Both lines are now bright blue and the same width as the rectangle control.

QuickTip

Press [Esc] to release the Format Painter.

2. Click the **Attended label** in the Department Header section, click the **Font list arrow**
   `Times New Roman ▾` on the Formatting (Form/Report) toolbar, click **Arial**, click the **Font size list arrow** `10 ▾` click **11**, click the **Align Left button** 📄, double-click 🖌, click the **First**, **Last**, **Passed**, **Description**, **Hours**, **Cost**, and **Prereq labels** in the Department Header section, then click 🖌
   The Format Painter copied the font face, font size, and alignment properties from the Attended label in the Department Header section to the other labels, as shown in Figure H-15.

3. Click **Format** on the menu bar, click **AutoFormat**, click the **Customize button** in the AutoFormat dialog box, click the **Create a new AutoFormat based on the Report 'Course Summary Report' option button**, click **OK**, type **Blue Lines-*(Your Name)***, then click **OK**
   The AutoFormat dialog box should look similar to Figure H-16 (many other AutoFormats may appear). Saving the formatting characteristics of the report as a new AutoFormat will allow you to apply them later to other reports in the Training-H database.

4. Click **OK** to close the AutoFormat dialog box, click **Window** on the menu bar, click **Training-H : Database**, click **Employee Detail Report**, click the 🖾, click **Format** on the menu bar, click the **AutoFormat**, click **Blue Lines-[*Your Name*]** in the Report AutoFormats list, then click **OK**
   Your screen should look like Figure H-17. The AutoFormat you applied changed the formatting properties of lines and labels in this report. AutoFormats that you create are available every time you use the Report Wizard (report AutoFormats) and Form Wizard (form AutoFormats).

5. Click the **Save button** 💾, close the report, then click the **Course Summary Report button** on the taskbar
   The Design view of the Course Summary Report appears on your screen.

6. Click **File** on the menu system, click **Save As**, type **Department Summary Report**, then click **OK**
   Delete the Blue Lines-[Your Name] AutoFormat.

7. Click **Format** on the menu bar, click **AutoFormat**, click **Blue Lines-[Your Name]**, click **Customize**, click the **Delete 'Blue Lines-[Your Name]' option button**, click **OK**, then click **Close**

8. Save and close the Department Summary Report

Font list arrow

Format Painter button

Attended label

Align Left button

Font size list arrow

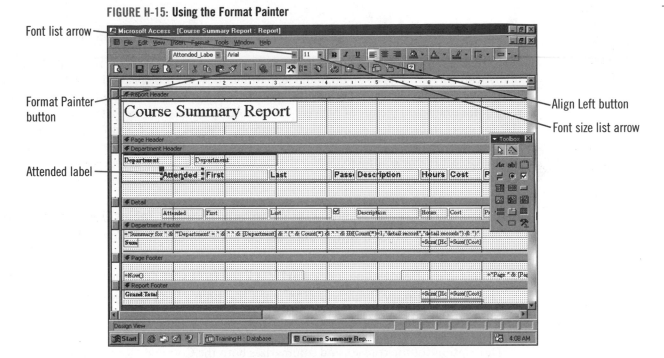

New Report AutoFormat

Customize button

Sample shows the new AutoFormat characteristics

Label formatting changed

Line formatting changed

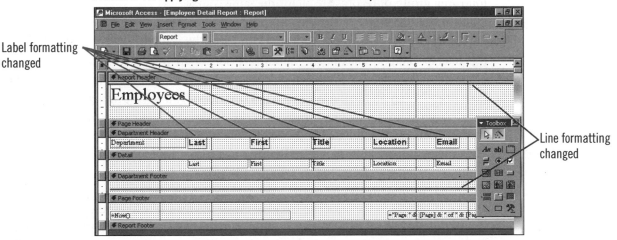

Access 2000

Displaying only summary reports

Sometimes you may not want show all the details of a report, but only a portion of it, such as the group summary information that is calculated in the Group Footer section. You can accomplish this by deleting all controls in the Detail section. Calculated controls in a Group Footer section will still calculate properly even if the individual records used within the calculation are not displayed on the report.

Inserting an Image

Multimedia controls, those that display picture, sound, motion, or other nontextual information. A control that displays an unbound logo would most likely be placed in the Report Header section, and a control that is bound to a field that contains multimedia information for each record (for example a picture of each employee) would be placed in the Detail section. See Table H-2 for more information on multimedia controls. David added an Icon field to the Courses table that contains a descriptive picture that represents the course's content. He uses the Bound Object Frame control to display this picture for each course in a new report.

1. Double-click **Create report by using wizard**, click the **Tables/Queries list arrow**, click **Query: Microsoft Office Classes**, click the **Select All Fields button** >> , click **Next**, click **by Attendance**, then click **Next**

2. Double-click **Description**, click **Next**, click the **first sort order list arrow**, click **Last**, click the **Summary Options button**, click the **Hours Sum check box**, click the **Cost Sum check box**, click **OK**, then click **Next**
   This report groups the records by Description, sorts them by Last (name) within Description (of the course), and summarizes both the Cost and Hours fields.

3. Click the **Outline 1 Layout option button**, click the **Landscape Orientation option button**, click **Next**, click the **Casual** style, click **Next**, type **Microsoft Office Classes** as the report title, click **Finish**, then click the 🔍 on the Print Preview screen
   The first page of the report appears in miniature, as shown in Figure H-18. The wizard created a large control for the picture for each course.

Trouble?

Close the Field list if necessary.

4. Click the **Design View button** 🔲, click the large **icon bound image control** in the Detail section, press and hold **[Shift]**, click the **Icon label** in the Description Header section, click the **Description label** in the Description Header section, release **[Shift]**, then press **[Delete]**
   The Icon field can be added to the Description Header section to help announce that the following group of records are all for the same course.

Trouble?

Be sure to delete the Description label control on the left and not the Description text box control on the right.

5. Point to the **top edge of the Description Footer section**, drag the ✛ pointer up to the bottom of the controls in the Detail section, click the **Bound Object Frame button** 🖼 on the Toolbox toolbar, click in the **upper-left corner of the Description Header section**, place the pointer on the **Bound Object Frame control lower-right corner sizing handle**, then drag ↖ up and to the left to the **0.5" mark** on both the horizontal and vertical rulers
   Your screen should look like Figure H-19. Every time you add a control from the Toolbox toolbar, you get an accompanying label. In this case, you do not need the label.

Trouble?

The label control is partially behind the new frame.

6. Click the new **label control**, press **[Delete]**, place the pointer on the **top edge of the Detail section**, then drag ✛ up to the bottom of the controls in the Description Header section
   You need to **bind** the frame to the Icon field, which means you change a bound control's **source property** to the associated field name of the field it will represent.

7. Double-click the **Bound Object Frame control** to open its property sheet, click the **Data tab**, click the **Control Source property list arrow**, click **Icon**, click the **Format tab**, click the **Border Style property list arrow**, click **Transparent**, click the **Properties button** 🗒 to close the property sheet, click the **Save button** 🖫, click the **Print Preview button** 🔖, click 🔍 on the screen, then maximize the report window
   Your screen should look like Figure H-20. The icons for both Access and Excel appear in their respective course Description Header sections.

8. Print the report, close the Print Preview window, then close the Microsoft Office Classes report

FIGURE H-18: Microsoft Office Classes report

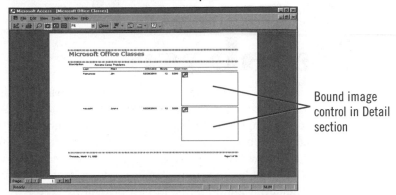

Bound image
control in Detail
section

FIGURE H-19: Microsoft Office Classes report in Design view

New label

Bound Object Frame

Resized Detail
section

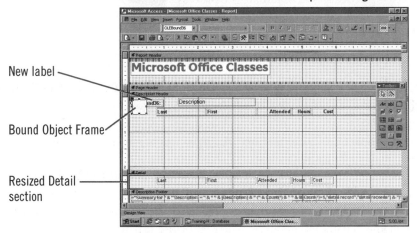

FIGURE H-20: Final Microsoft Office Classes report

Bound Object
Control displays
the Icon picture
in the Description
Header section

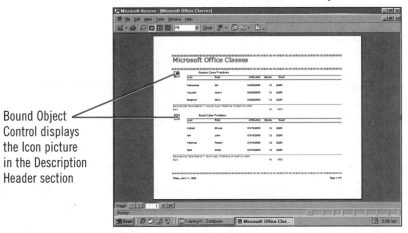

TABLE H-2 Multimedia controls

control name	toolbox icon	bound or unbound	used to display	form/report section where this control is most likely placed	
Image		Unbound	an unbound picture, piece of clip art, or logo	Form Header	Report Header or Page Header
Unbound Object Frame		Unbound	a sound or motion clip a document or spreadsheet	Form Header not often used on a form	Report Footer
Bound Object Frame		Bound	information contained in a field with an OLE data type	Detail	Detail or Group Header

Securing the Database

When you delete data and objects in an Access database, the database can become fragmented and use disk space inefficiently. **Compacting** the database rearranges the data and objects to improve performance by reusing the space formerly occupied by the deleted objects. The compact process also checks to see if the database is damaged and, if so, attempts to repair it. A good time to back up a database is right after it has been compacted. If hardware is stolen or destroyed, a recent backup (most database administrators recommend that databases be backed up each night) can minimize the impact of that loss to the business. Use Windows Explorer to copy individual database files and floppy disks, or use back-up software like Microsoft Backup to create back-up schedules to automate the process. ➤ David needs to secure the Training database. He starts by compacting the database, then backing it up by using Windows Explorer to make a copy.

Steps

1. Click **Tools** on the menu bar, point to **Database Utilities**, click **Compact and Repair Database**
   Access 2000 allows you to compact and repair an open database, but it's a good practice to use the "Compact on Close" feature, which compacts the database every time it is closed.

2. Click **Tools** on the menu bar, click **Options**, click the **General tab** of the Options dialog box, then click the **Compact on Close** check box (if it is not already created)
   The Options dialog box is shown in Figure H-21. **Compact on Close** automatically compacts and repairs the database when you close it if the size can be reduced by at least 256 KB. It is not checked (turned on) by default.

3. Click **OK**, close the **Training-H** database, exit **Access**, right-click the **Start button**, then click **Explore**
   You'll use Windows Explorer, as shown in Figure H-22, to make a copy of your Project Disk.

4. Right-click **3½ Floppy (A:)** in the Folders list, then click **Copy Disk**
   The Copy Disk dialog box opens, as shown in Figure H-23. This command allows you to copy an entire floppy disk from one disk to another without first copying the contents to the computer's C: hard drive.

5. Click **Start**
   Windows Explorer will start copying your original Project Disk, the **source disk**, and will prompt you to insert the blank disk, the **destination disk**, where the files will be pasted.

6. When you are prompted to insert the destination disk, do so and click **OK**
   Explorer was able to copy all of the files from the Project Disk to the blank disk with one process. Sometimes you are prompted to reinsert the source disk and then the destination disk because all of the files cannot be copied in one process.

7. Click **Close** in the Copy Disk dialog box, then close **Windows Explorer**

8. Label the disk and place it in a safe place

FIGURE H-21: Options dialog box

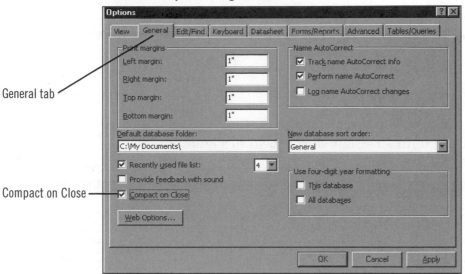

General tab

Compact on Close

FIGURE H-22: Windows Explorer

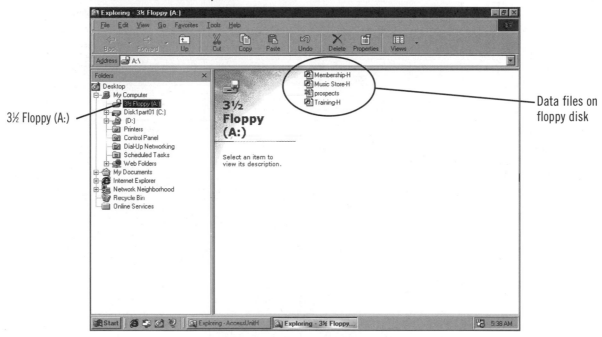

3½ Floppy (A:)

Data files on floppy disk

FIGURE H-23: Copy Disk dialog box

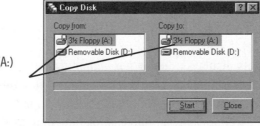

Make sure 3½ Floppy (A:) is chosen in both the Copy from: and Copy to: locations

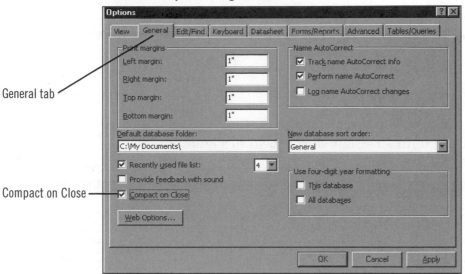

Compacting a database automatically

Microsoft Access can automatically compact a database file every time you close it. Choose the Options from the Tools menu, then click the General tab. Click the Compact on Close check box, then click OK.

Compacting does not occur when you close the database unless the file size would be reduced by more than 256 KB. It also does not occur if you close the database while another person is using it.

Practice

► Concepts Review

Identify each element of the form's Design view shown in Figure H-24.

FIGURE-H-24

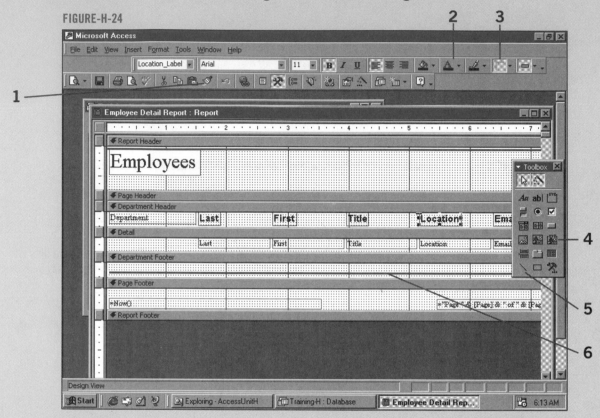

Match each term with the statement that describes its function.

7. Image control
8. Parameter Query
9. Bound Object Frame
10. Format Painter
11. Importing

a. A process to quickly convert data from an external source into an Access database
b. This displays a dialog box prompting you for criteria each time you open it
c. Used to display information contained in a field with an OLE data type
d. Used to copy formatting properties from one control to another
e. Used to display an unbound picture, clip art item, or logo

Select the best answer from the list of choices.

12. **Which control would work best to present sound clips of each employee's voice stored in a Voice field with an OLE data type?**
    a. Text box
    b. Label
    c. Bound Object Frame
    d. Unbound Object Frame

13. **Which control would you use to separate groups of records on a report?**
    a. Option group
    b. Image
    c. Bound Object Frame
    d. Line

14. **Which wizard would you use to create a database from scratch?**
    a. Database Wizard
    b. Table Wizard
    c. Records Wizard
    d. Lookup Wizard

15. **Which wizard would you use to provide a value list for a field?**
    a. Database Wizard
    b. Lookup Wizard
    c. Value List Wizard
    d. Field Wizard

16. **Which of the following programs or file types cannot serve as a source for data imported into Access?**
    a. Excel
    b. Lotus 1-2-3
    c. Lotus Notes
    d. HTML

► Skills Review

1. **Use the Database Wizard.**
   a. Start Access, click the Access database wizards, pages, and projects option button in the Microsoft Access dialog box, then click OK.
   b. Double-click the Contact Management Wizard, and create the new database with the name "Contacts" on a new, blank Project Disk. _DRIVE C Access class UNIT H DISK 3_
   c. Follow the prompts of the Database Wizard and accept all of the default field suggestions. Use the Standard style for screen displays and the Soft Gray style for printed reports.
   d. Accept the name Contact Management as the title of the database.
   e. After all of the objects are created, close the Main Switchboard form, then close the Contacts database.

2. **Import Data.**
   a. Use Windows Explorer to copy the Excel file prospects from Project Disk 2 to the new Project Disk that contains the Contacts database.
   b. Open the Contacts database.
   c. Click File on the menu bar, point to Get External Data, then click Import.
   d. In the Import dialog box, click the Files of type list arrow, click Microsoft Excel, click prospects on your Project Disk, then click the Import button in the Import dialog box.

e. In the Import Spreadsheet Wizard, make sure that the Show Worksheets option button is selected, click Next, check the First Row Contains Column Headings check box, click Next, click the In an Existing Table list arrow, click Contacts, click Next, then click Finish.

f. Click OK when prompted that the import was successful, then open the Contacts table in Design view.

g. Modify the Region field using the Lookup Wizard Data Type by typing the following values. Press [Tab] as you type each value in the column: East, Midwest, North, South, West. Use "Region" for the label.

h. Save the table, then open it in Datasheet view.

i. Add your personal information as a new record using "East" as the entry for the Region, regardless of where you live.

j. Print the datasheet in landscape orientation, then close the datasheet.

3. **Create a Report from a Parameter Query.**

a. Start a new query in Design view, then add the Contacts table.

b. Add the following fields to the Query Design grid in this order: FirstName, LastName, City, StateOrProvince, Region.

c. Enter the following parameter criteria to the Region field: [Enter Region:].

d. Save the query, naming it "Customer Regions", then close the query.

e. Using the Report Wizard, create a new report basing it on the Customer Regions query.

f. Select all the fields, group the report by Region, sort ascending by LastName, and choose a Block layout, a Portrait orientation, and a bold style.

g. Accept the name Customer Regions for your report title.

h. When prompted for the region, enter "East".

i. Open the report in Design view and add a label to the Report Footer with the text "Created by [Your Name]".

j. Save, print, and close the report.

k. Close the Contacts database.

4. **Enhance Reports.**

a. Open the Membership-H database.

b. Using the Report Wizard, create a report on the Query: Member Activity Log using all of the fields in that query.

c. Group the fields by Last, sort ascending by ActivityDate, and Sum the Hours field.

d. Use the Outline 2 layout, Portrait orientation, Compact style, and accept the name Member Activity Log as the report title.

e. Open the report in Design view and select the =Sum([Hours]) calculated field in the Last Footer section.

f. Use the Conditional Formatting from the Format menu to change Font/Fore color to bold and bright blue if the value is greater than or equal to 10.

g. Add a label to the Report Footer section, with the text "Created by [Your Name]", then save the report and print the last page.

h. Open the property sheet for the First text box in the Detail section and set the Hide Duplicates property to Yes.

i. Group the controls in the Report Footer section, then format the group with a bright blue Font/Fore color.

j. Save and print the report.

5. **Add Lines and Rectangles.**

a. Open the Member Activity Log report in Design view, then delete the following controls:
Last, First, and Dues labels in the Last Header section
First and Dues text boxes in the Detail section
Line in the Detail section (*Hint*: It is between the ActivityDate and Hours text boxes.)
Line in the Last Header section (*Hint*: It is a short line just above the Last text box.)
Rectangle in the Last Header section (*Hint*: You will probably have to expand the section to find it.)

b. Move the ActivityDate label in the Last Header section and the ActivityDate text box in the Detail section to the right, so that they are right beside the Hours controls.

c. Move the line control at the top of the Last Footer section to the bottom of the Last Footer section.

d. Draw two short lines under the =Sum([Hours]) control in the Report Footer to indicate a grand total.

e. Use the Save As option from the File menu to save the report as the "Simplified Member Activity Log" and print the first page.

6. Use the Format Painter and AutoFormats.

a. Open the Simplified Member Activity Log in Design view.

b. Format the ActivityDate label in the Last Header section with a bold Tahoma font.

c. Use the Format Painter to copy that format to the Last text box and the Hours label in the Last Header section.

d. Change the color of the lines in the Report Header section to bright red.

e. Create a new AutoFormat named "Red Lines-[Your Name]" based on the Simplified Member Activity Log report.

f. Print the first page of the Simplified Member Activity Log report, then save and close it.

g. Open the Member Activity Log report in Design view, and use the AutoFormat option from the Format menu to apply the Corporate format.

h. Use the Customize button in the AutoFormat dialog box to delete the "Red Lines-[Your Name]" style.

i. Preview, then print the first page of the Member Activity Log report. Save and close the report.

7. Insert an Image.

a. Use the Report Wizard to create a report using all the fields from the Team Members query except for the Team field.

b. Do not group the records, but sort them in ascending order on the Last, then on the First fields.

c. Use a Columnar layout and a Portrait orientation.

d. Apply a Bold style, and accept the name Team Members as the title.

e. In Design view, use the Bound Object Frame control to add a frame to the right of the Last text box in the Detail section. Delete the frame's accompanying label. Be sure to move and resize the frame and right edge of the report so that they do not go beyond the 6.5" mark.

f. On the Data tab of the property sheet for the frame, change the Control Source property to Team.

g. On the Format tab of the property sheet for the frame, change the Size Mode property to Zoom and change the Border Style to Transparent.

h. Put a label control in the Report Header that displays your name, then save, preview, and print the report.

i. Close the Membership-H database and exit Access.

8. Secure the Database.

a. Start Access.

b. Use the Database Utilities option on the Tools menu to Compact and Repair the database.

c. Close the Membership-H database and exit Access.

d. Start Explorer, right-click on the 3½ Floppy (A:) option, then click Copy Disk.

e. Follow the prompts to make a back-up copy of your Project Disk to a new, blank disk.

f. Exit Windows Explorer.

▶ Independent Challenges

1. As the manager of a music store's instrument rental program, you have created a database to track instrument rentals to schoolchildren. Now that several instruments have been purchased, you often need to print a report listing the particular instruments in inventory. You will create a single instrument inventory report based on a parameter query that prompts the user for the type of instrument to be displayed on the report.

To complete this independent challenge:

a. Start Access and open the database Music Store-H.

b. Create a query with the following fields from the Instruments table:
Description, SerialNo, MonthlyFee, Condition

c. Add the following parameter criteria entry in the Description field:
[Enter the type of instrument:]

d. Save the query with the name "Instruments by Type".

e. Using the Report Wizard, create a report on the Instruments by Type query, and select all of the fields.

f. Group by the Description field, sort in ascending order by the SerialNo field, use a Stepped layout, use a Portrait orientation, apply a Corporate style, and title the report "Instruments in Inventory".

g. Enter "Cello" when prompted for the type of instrument.

h. Open the report in Design view and add a rectangle control to the left side of the Report Footer about 1" tall and 2" wide.

i. Add a label control to the Report Footer inside the rectangle control that displays your name.

j. Display the report with the Cello criteria, and print it.

k. Save and close the Instruments in Inventory report.

l. Close the Music Store-H database and exit Access.

2. As the manager of a music store's instrument rental program, you have created a database to track instrument rentals to schoolchildren. Now that several instruments have been rented, you need to create a conditionally formatted report that lists which school has the highest number of rentals from the store.

To complete this independent challenge:

a. Start Access and open the database Music Store-H.

b. Open the Schools table in Datasheet view and click the expand button to the left of Oak Hill Elementary to show the related records in the students table.

c. Click the collapse button, then close the datasheet.

d. Using the Report Wizard, create a report with the following fields from the following tables:
Schools: SchoolName
Instrument: Description, MonthlyFee
Rentals: Date

e. View and group the data by SchoolName, sort in ascending order by Date, and Sum the MonthlyFee field.

f. Use an Outline 1 layout, Portrait orientation, and Casual style.

g. Title the report "School Summary Report".

h. Open the report in Design view and click the =Sum([MonthlyFee]) control in the SchoolNo Footer section.

i. Use the Conditional Formatting option on the Format menu to specify that the field be Bold and have a bright yellow Fill/Back Color if it is greater than or equal to 200.

j. Add a label to the right side of the report that displays your name, and save the report.

k. Print the first page of the report.

l. Close the School Summary Report, then close the Music Store-H database and exit Access.

3. As the manager of a music store's instrument rental program, you have created a database to track instrument rentals to schoolchildren. Build a report that shows pictures of instruments.

To complete this independent challenge:

a. Start Access and open the database Music Store-H.

b. Double-click the Create a report in Design View option.

c. Click the Properties button, then choose "Instrument Sampler" as the Record Source property on the Data tab.

d. Open the Field list, then drag the three fields (Description, MonthlyFee, and Picture) to the left side of the Detail section, and arrange them in a vertical column.

e. Open the Properties sheet for the Picture Bound Object Frame. Make sure that the Size Mode property is set to Zoom (which resizes the picture to the size of the control and is especially necessary when the picture itself is larger than the actual control) and the Border Style property is set to Transparent.

f. Use the Page Header/Footer option on the View menu to close the Page Header and Page Footer sections.

g. Use the Report Header/Footer option on the View menu to open the Report Header and Report Footer sections.

h. Add a label to the Report Header section that displays your name.

i. Apply the Bold Autoformat.

j. Add a horizontal line to the bottom of the Detail section to separate the individual records.

k. Save the report with the name "Instrument Sampler Report".

l. Preview and print the first page of the report.

m. Close the Instrument Sampler Report, exit Music Store-H, and exit Access.

4. MediaLoft has developed a Web site that provides internal information to their employees. The Information Systems Department has created a sample report (just a mock up) that they would like to have developed, and have placed it as a Web page on the MediaLoft intranet for easy access by others. In this independent challenge, you'll find the prototype form on the Web site, print it, then create the real thing in the Training-H database.

a. Connect to the Internet and use your browser to go to the MediaLoft intranet at http://www.course.com/illustrated/MediaLoft/

b. Click the link for Training.

c. Click the link for User Report Requests, and print the Web page.

d. Close your browser window and disconnect from the Internet, start Access, then open the Training-H database.

e. Using the Report Wizard, create a report using the Description field from the Courses table, and Attended and Passed fields from the Attendance table.

f. View the data by Courses, group by Passed, and sort in ascending order by Attended.

g. Use a Stepped layout, a Portrait orientation, and a Formal style.

h. Title the report "Achievement Report".

i. In Design view, click the Sorting and Grouping button, change the CourseID Group Footer and the Passed Group Footer property to Yes, and close the Sorting and Grouping dialog box.

j. Add a text box control to the Passed Footer section just below the Attended text box with the expression =Count([Attended]), then delete the extra label that was created in the Passed Footer section.

k. Add a horizontal line to the CourseID Footer, then compare your report with the one you printed in step c. In Design view, make any changes to the report necessary to more closely match the request from the Information Systems Department.

l. Add a label to the Report Header section with your name, save the report, then print the first page.

m. Close the Achievement Report and the Training-H database.

n. Exit Access.

Access 2000

Visual Workshop

Open the Training-H database and create a new report as shown in Figure H-25 using the Report Wizard. Gather the First, Last, and Department fields from the Employees table and the Description and Hours fields from the Courses table. Sum the Hours, sort in ascending order by the Description, and use the Outline 1, Portrait, and Corporate Wizard options. Enter your name as a label in the Report Header if you need to identify your printout.

FIGURE H-25

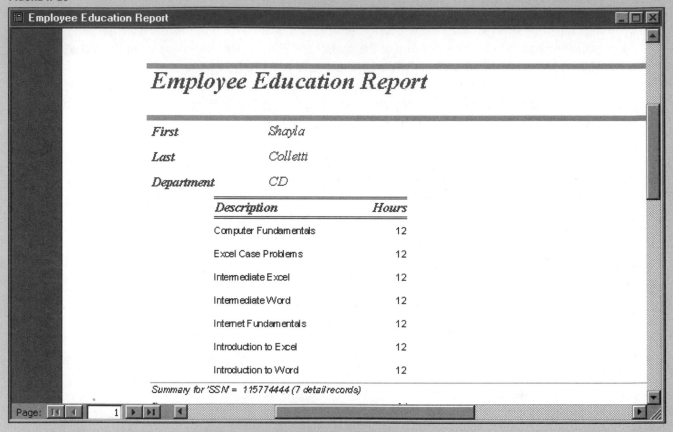

Sharing

Access Information with Other Office Programs

Objectives

- ► **Examine Access Objects**
- [MOUS] ► **Examine Relationships Between Tables**
- ► **Importing Data from Excel**
- [MOUS] ► **Link Data to an Excel worksheet**
- [MOUS] ► **Create Hyperlinks**
- [MOUS] ► **Analyze Data with Excel**
- ► **Copy Records to Word**
- [MOUS] ► **Export Data to Excel**

Access is a powerful relational database program that can share data with many other application Microsoft Office 2000 software products. Choosing the right tool for each task is important because you often need to use features from one program and data stored in another type of file. For example, you might want to use financial data in an Excel spreadsheet as part of an Access database. Or, you might want to copy records from an Access query into a Word document that will be published to the Internet. Before you copy or link Access data to another program, however, you should determine if the capability exists within Access. David Dumont, director of training at MediaLoft, has developed an Access database that tracks courses, employees, and course attendance for the internal education provided by MediaLoft. David will share Access data with other software applications to provide each MediaLoft department the data they have requested in a format they can use.

Examining Access Objects

In order to become proficient with Access, it is important for you to understand the capabilities of the seven Access objects. ▰▰▰▰ David reviews key Access terminology and the seven Access objects.

Details

A **database** is a collection of data associated with a topic (for example, the training each employee at MediaLoft has received). The smallest piece of information in a database is called a **field,** or category of information such as the employee's name, e-mail address, or department. A **key field** is a field that contains unique information for each record such as an employee's Social Security number. A group of related fields, such as all descriptive information for one employee, is called a **record**. A collection of records for a single subject, such as all of the employee records, is called a **table.** When a table object is opened, the fields and records are displayed as a **datasheet**, as shown in Figure I-1.

Tables are the most important **objects** within an Access database because they contain all of the data within the database. An Access database also may contain six other object types that serve to enhance the usability and value of the data. The objects in an Access database are **tables, queries, forms, reports, pages, macros,** and **modules,** and are summarized in Table I-1.

Query objects are based on tables; and form, page, and report objects can be based on either tables or queries. Data can be entered and edited in four of the objects—tables, queries, pages, and forms—but is always stored in tables. These relationships are shown in Figure I-2. The macro and module objects are used to provide additional database productivity and automation features such as **GUI (graphical user interface)** screens and buttons, which surround and mask the complexity of the underlying objects. All of the objects are stored in one database file.

TABLE I-1 **Access objects**

object	purpose
Table	Contains all of the raw data within the database in a spreadsheet-like view; can be linked with a common field to share information and therefore minimize data redundancy
Query	Provides a spreadsheet-like view of the data that is similar to tables, but can display a subset of fields and/or records from one or more tables; created when a user has a "question" about the data in the database
Form	Provides an easy-to-use data entry screen that generally shows only one record at a time
Report	Provides a professional printout of data that may contain enhancements such as headers, footers, and calculations on groups of records; mailing labels can also be created from report objects
Page	Creates Web pages from Access objects as well as Web page connectivity features to an Access database
Macro	Stores a collection of keystrokes or commands such as printing several reports in a row or displaying a toolbar when a form opens
Module	Stores Visual Basic programming code that extends the functions and automated processes of Access

FIGURE I-1: Table datasheet

Employees table opened as a datasheet

3 records

Title field entries

Key field

Field names

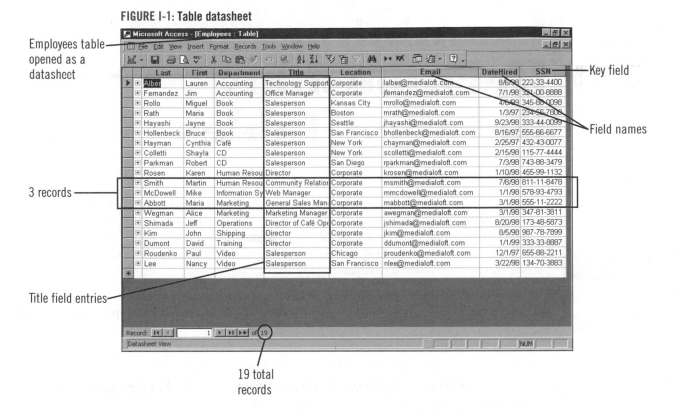

19 total records

FIGURE I-2: Objects of an Access database

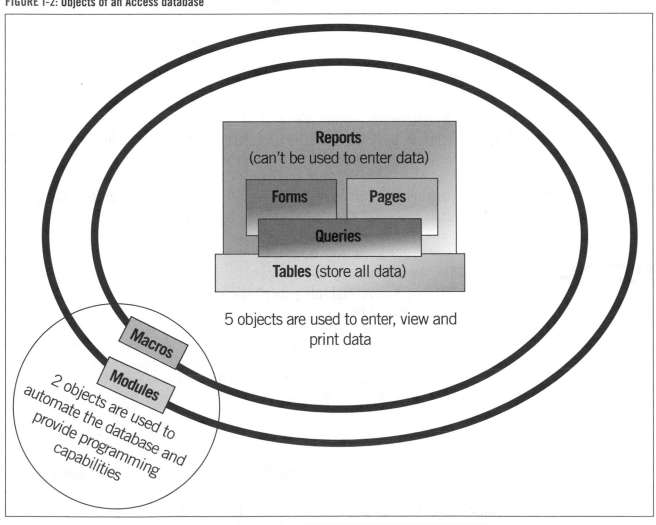

Access 2000

Examining Relationships Between Tables

An Access database is a **relational database** in that more than one table can share information, or "relate." The key benefit of organizing your data into a relational database is minimized redundant data. The ability to link separate tables of data improves the accuracy, speed, and flexibility of a relational database. The process of designing a relational database is called **normalization**, and involves determining the appropriate fields, tables, and table relationships. Relationship types are summarized in Table I-2. ➤ David develops an Instructors table to store one record for each teacher. He relates the Instructors table to the Courses table so that it participates in the relational database.

Steps 1 2 3 4

1. Start Access, open the **Training-I** database on your Project Disk, click **Tables** on the Objects bar, maximize the database window, then double-click the **Instructors table**
   The InstructorID field serves as the **primary key field** so it contains unique data for each record in the Instructors table. The Instructors table should be related to the Courses table with a one-to-many relationship because each instructor teaches many courses.

2. Click the **Instructors Table Close Window button**, click the **Courses table**, then click the **Design button** 📝 in the database window
   A matching field, often called the **foreign key field**, must be added to the table on the "many" side of a one-to-many relationship to link with the primary key field of the "one" table.

3. Click the **Field Name cell** in the first blank row, type **InstructorID**, press **[Tab]**, press **N** to select a Number data type, press **[Tab]**, type **Foreign Key** as shown in Figure I-3, click the **Save button** 💾, then close the Courses table Design view window
   The linking field for both tables is created.

4. Click the **Relationships button** 🔗 on the Database toolbar, click the **Show Table button** 🔲 on the Relationships toolbar, click **Instructors**, click **Add**, then click **Close**
   The Instructors table appears in the Relationships window without any relationships to other tables. Primary key fields appear in bold.

5. Drag the **InstructorID field** from the Instructors table to the **InstructorID field** in the Courses table, then click **Create** in the Edit Relationships dialog box
   The link between the Courses and Instructors tables has been established, but the linking line doesn't display the "one" and "many" sides of the relationship.

6. Double-click the **relationship line** between the Instructors and Courses tables, then click the **Enforce Referential Integrity check box**, see Figure I-4
   The **Enforce Referential Integrity** option does not allow values to be entered in the foreign key field that are not first entered in the primary key field. It also does not allow records to be deleted in the "one" table if related records exist in the "many" table. **Cascade Update Related Fields** automatically updates the data in the foreign key field when the matching primary key field is changed. **Cascade Delete Related Records** automatically deletes all records in the "many" table if the record with the matching key field in the "one" table is deleted.

7. Click **OK** in the Edit Relationships dialog box
   Printing the Relationships window shown in Figure I-5 creates a valuable report that helps you remember what fields are in which tables.

8. Click **File** on the menu bar, click **Print Relationships**, click the **Print button** 🖨 on the Print Preview toolbar, click **Close**, click 💾, accept the default report name **Relationships for Training-I**, then close the Relationships window

FIGURE I-3: Adding the foreign key field to the Courses table in Design view

Courses table

New InstructorID field to serve as the foreign key

Description

Number data type

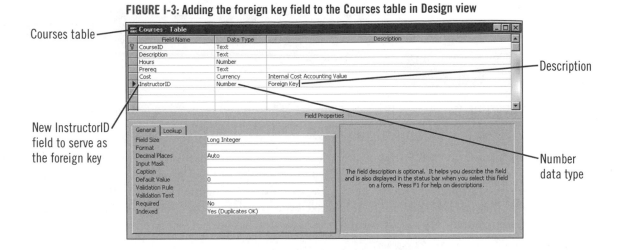

FIGURE I-4: Edit Relationships dialog box

"one" table

"many" table

Enforce Referential Integrity check box

Linking field between the tables

These options change data in the "many" table

Relationship type

FIGURE I-5: Relationships window

The primary key field in the "one" table

The foreign key field in the "many" table

One-to-many link with enforce referential integrity

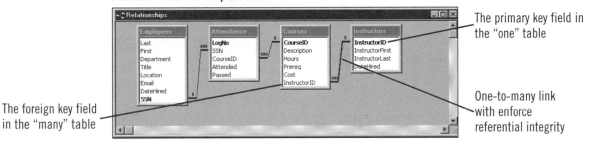

TABLE I-2: Relationship types

relationship	description	example	notes
One-to-One	A record in Table X has no more than one matching record in Table Y.	A student table would have no more than one matching record in a graduation table that tracks the student's graduation date and major.	Not common, because all fields related this way could be stored in one table; sometimes used to separate rarely used fields from a table to improve the overall performance of the database
One-to-Many	A single record in Table X has many records in Table Y.	One product can be sold many times, one customer can make many purchases, one teacher can teach many courses, and one student can take many courses.	Most common type of relationship
Many-to-Many	A record in Table X has many records in Table Y, and a record in Table Y has many records in Table X.	One employee can take several courses, and the same course can be taken by several employees. (In the MediaLoft database, the Attendance table serves as the junction table between the Courses and Employees tables.)	It is impossible to directly create many-to-many relationships in Access. Instead, a third table, called a junction table, must be established between the original tables. The junction table contains foreign key fields that link to the primary key fields of each of the original tables and establishes separate one-to-many relationships with them. The junction table serves as the "many" side of each relationship.

Importing Data from Excel

Importing is a process to quickly convert data from an external source into an Access database. You can import data from one Access database to another, or from many other data sources such as Excel, dBase, Paradox, FoxPro, HTML, or delimited text files. A **delimited text file** contains one record on each line, with the fields separated by a common character such as a comma, tab, or dash. Often, external numerical data is stored in an Excel spreadsheet, because many people are comfortable with the easy-to-use spreadsheet structure of Excel. ◄──── Karen Rosen, Director of Human Resources, has asked the Training Department to add three new courses to the current offerings. Information about the courses has been entered into an Excel spreadsheet called New Courses.

Steps 1234

1. Click **File** on the menu bar, point to **Get External Data**, click **Import**, click the **Look in: list arrow**, locate your Project Disk, click the **Files of Type list arrow**, click **Microsoft Excel**, then double-click **New Courses**

The Import Spreadsheet Wizard dialog box opens, as shown in Figure I-6.

2. Click **Next**, then verify that the **First Row Contains Column Headings check box** is checked

The second dialog box of the Import Spreadsheet Wizard, shown in Figure I-7, is extremely important. In order to successfully import data from an Excel spreadsheet to an existing table, the spreadsheet fields (columns) must be consistent with the fields of the Access table.

3. Click **Next**, click the **In an Existing Table list arrow**, click **Courses**, click **Next**, click **Finish**, then click **OK**

The three records from the New Courses spreadsheet were successfully imported into the Courses table of the Training-I database.

4. Double-click the **Courses** table to open its datasheet

The Courses datasheet, with the three new records, is displayed in Figure I-8. By default, the records in the Courses table sort by the primary key field, CourseID. Note that the new records do not have any values in the Prereq field, but they do have entries in the InstructorID field. Even if the field is **null** (contains nothing), the number and type of fields in the Excel spreadsheet must be consistent with the Access table to successfully import the Excel data. If you import an Excel spreadsheet into a new table, Access will choose an appropriate data type and field name for each field in the new table.

5. Close the **Courses** datasheet

Now that the Excel data has been imported into the Access Training-I database, it can link to many other tables of data to create valuable queries, forms, and reports, and therefore it can serve the varied needs of simultaneous users.

FIGURE I-6: Import Spreadsheet Wizard's first dialog box

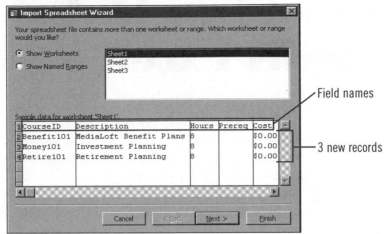
Field names

3 new records

FIGURE I-7: Import Spreadsheet Wizard's second dialog box

First row contains
field names

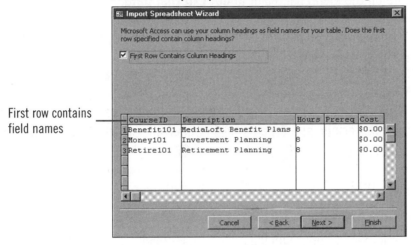

FIGURE I-8: Courses table with three new imported records

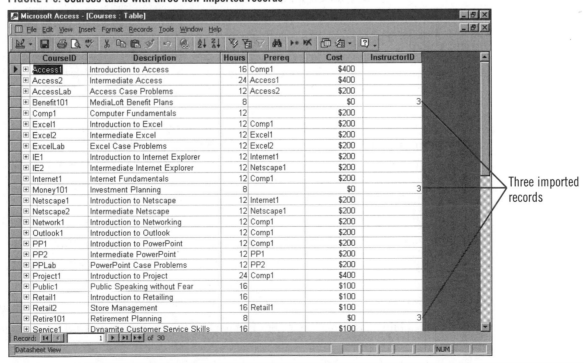
Three imported records

Linking Data with Excel

Linking connects an Access database to data in an external file such as another Access, dBase, or Paradox database; an Excel or Lotus 1-2-3 spreadsheet; a text file; an HTML file; and other data sources that support **ODBC** (**Open Database Connectivity**) standards. If you link, data can be entered or edited in either the original file or the Access database even though the data is only stored in the original file. Changes to data in either location are automatically made in the other. **Importing**, in contrast, makes a duplicate copy of the data in the Access database, so changes to either the original data source or the imported Access copy have no affect on the other. David asked the new instructors to make a list of all of their class materials. They created this list in an Excel spreadsheet, and wish to maintain it there. David creates a link to this data from within the Training database.

1. Click **File** on the menu bar, point to **Get External Data**, then click **Link Tables**

The Link dialog box opens, listing Access files in the current folder.

Trouble?

If your Project Disk files do not display in the Link dialog box, click the Look in: list arrow to locate your Project Disk.

2. Click the **Files of Type list arrow**, click **Microsoft Excel**, click **Course Materials** in the files list, then click **Link**

The Link Spreadsheet Wizard appears, as shown in Figure I-9. Data can be linked from different parts of the Excel spreadsheet. The data you want is on Sheet 1.

3. Click **Next**, click the **First Row Contains Column Headings check box** to specify **CourseID**, **Materials**, and **Type** as field names, click **Next**, type **Course Supplies** as the Linked Table Name, click **Finish**, then click **OK**

The Course Supplies table appears in the database window with a linking Excel icon, as shown in Figure I-10. A linked table can and must participate in a one-to-many relationship with another table if it is to share data with the rest of the tables of the database.

4. Click the **Relationships button** ⬚ on the Database toolbar, click the **Show Table button** ⬚, double-click **Course Supplies**, then click **Close**

Rearranging the tables in the Relationships window can improve the clarity of the relationships.

QuickTip

If you update data in a linked table, it will update the original source.

5. Drag the **Course Supplies table title bar** to a position under the Attendance table, drag the **CourseID field** in the Courses table to the **CourseID field** in the Course Supplies table, then click **Create** in the Edit Relationships dialog box

A one-to-many relationship is established between the Courses and Course Supplies tables. You cannot establish referential integrity when one of the tables is a linked table, but the table can now participate in queries, forms, pages, and reports that use fields from multiple tables. Your screen should look like Figure I-11.

6. Click the **Save button** ⬚, close the **Relationships window**, double-click the **Course Supplies table** to open it, click the **New Record button** ⬚ on the Table Datasheet toolbar, type **Access1**, press **[Tab]**, type **MediaLoft.mdb**, press **[Tab]**, then type **File**

You added a new record. When first creating a linked table, you should check the original data source, the Course Materials Excel file, to make sure that the data was automatically updated there.

7. Close the **Course Supplies table**, right-click the **Start button** in the taskbar, click **Explore**, locate your Project Disk, double-click the **Course Materials Excel file** to open it in Excel, then press **[Page Down]**

The new Access1 record should be visible in row 40 of the Excel spreadsheet.

8. Click **File** on the menu bar, click **Exit** to close the worksheet and exit Excel, then close Explorer

FIGURE I-9: Link Spreadsheet Wizard dialog box

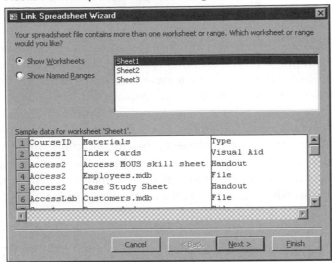

FIGURE I-10: Course Supplies table is linked from Excel

Excel linking icon

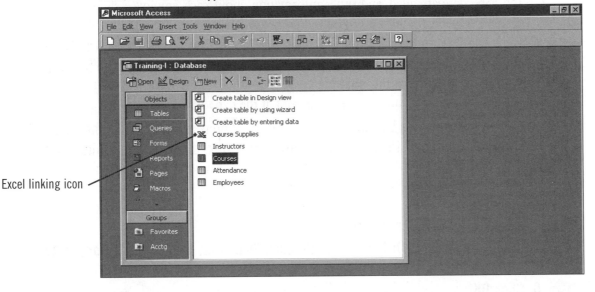

FIGURE I-11: Relationships window with Course Supplies table

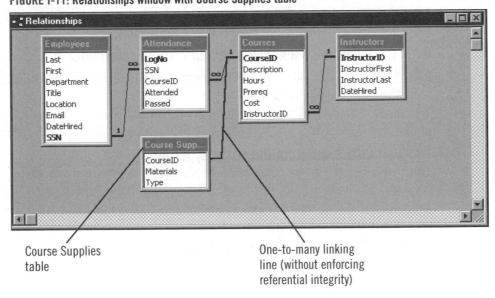

Course Supplies table

One-to-many linking line (without enforcing referential integrity)

Creating Hyperlinks

A **hyperlink** is a label, button, or image that when clicked automatically opens another object, document or graphic file, e-mail message, or World Wide Web page. Hyperlinks can be added as labels, pictures, or buttons on a form. A field with a **hyperlink data type** can be defined in a table's Design view so that the datasheet displays and stores different hyperlink information for each record. David created a Word document called "Directions to MediaLoft Corporate" that gives detailed directions to the San Francisco training facility. Within the Word document he created two **bookmarks**, specific locations within the document marked by a bookmark code, called "fromTheNorth" and "fromTheSouth" that identify the beginning of the paragraph that describes each route. Because employees often ask for detailed directions to the training facility when they sign up for a course, David will create hyperlinks to these instructions from the Courses form.

Steps

1. Click **Forms** on the Objects bar, then double-click the **Courses form** to open it in Form view

   The Courses form displays course information in the main form, whereas the subform logs the SSN, date attended, and other information about each employee signed up for each course. Create hyperlinks from the Courses form to the Directions document.

2. Click the **Design View button** 📐, click the **Toolbox button** 🗲, click the **Label button** 🗛 on the Toolbox, click ⁺A in the **Detail section** of the form at the 5" mark, then type **Directions from the north**

   Any label on a form can become a hyperlink if the hyperlink properties are entered.

3. Click the **Properties button** 🗐 to open the label property sheet, click the **Format tab** (if necessary), click the **Hyperlink Address text box**, then click the **Build button** 🔳

   The Insert Hyperlink dialog box appears, as shown in Figure I-12. This dialog box helps you link to a file, Web page, database object, or e-mail address.

4. Click **File**

   The Link to File dialog box opens.

5. Locate your Project Disk, then double-click **Directions to MediaLoft Corporate**

   The filename appears in the Type the file or Web page name text box.

6. Click **OK**

   The entry for the Hyperlink Address property appears in the label's property sheet. Use the Hyperlink SubAddress property to specify the bookmark name within the Directions document to link to a specific paragraph within the document.

7. Click the **Hyperlink SubAddress text box**, type **FromTheNorth**, click 🗐 to close the property sheet, then click the **Form View button** 🗐 on the Form Design toolbar to view the updated Courses form

   Your screen should look like Figure I-13. By default, a hyperlink label appears in blue and is underlined. This style is similar to the way hyperlinks usually appear on Web pages.

8. Click the **Directions from the north hyperlink**

   The Directions document appears in Word, as shown in Figure I-14. A hyperlink that has been clicked changes from blue to purple, similar to Web hyperlinks. You can copy, paste, and modify the hyperlink to create a link to the directions from the south bookmark within the Directions document.

9. Close the Word window, then save and close the Courses form

> **QuickTip**
>
> The mouse pointer changes to 🖑 when pointing to a hyperlink.

> **QuickTip**
>
> Bookmarks cannot have any spaces in them. The name of the bookmark in the document must exactly match the Hyperlink SubAddress.

FIGURE I-12: Insert Hyperlink dialog box

Hyperlinks can link
to these items

File button

Existing file and
Web page
subcategories (your
list will be different)

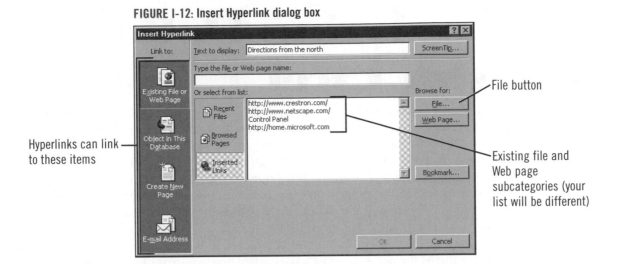

FIGURE I-13: Hyperlink label displayed in Form view

Hyperlink label

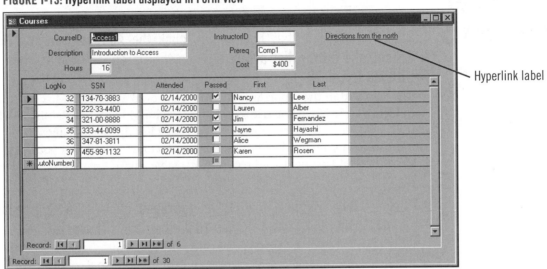

FIGURE I-14: Directions to the Media Loft Corporate Word document with bookmark highlighted

Directions to
MediaLoft Corporate
Word document

Back button

FromTheNorth
bookmark

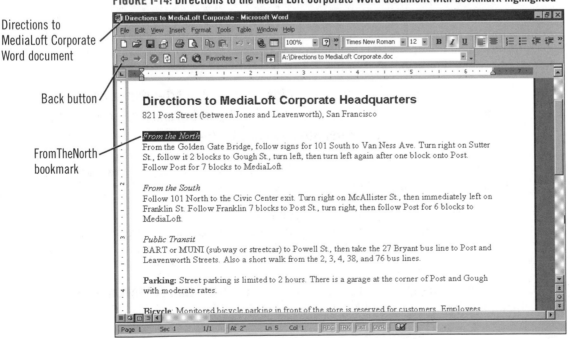

Analyzing Data with Excel

Excel, the spreadsheet software program within the Microsoft Office Suite, is an excellent tool for projecting numeric trends into the future. For example, you may wish to analyze the impact of a price increase on budget or income projections by applying several different numbers. This reiterative analysis is sometimes called "what-if" analysis. **What-if analysis** allows a user to apply assumptions interactively to a set of numbers and watch the resulting calculated formulas update instantly. This is a very popular use for Excel. You can use the **Analyze It with MS Excel** feature to quickly copy Access data to Excel. ➤ David has been asked by the Accounting Department to provide some Access data in an Excel spreadsheet so they can analyze how various percentage increases in the cost of the Access classes would affect each of the departments. He has gathered the raw data into a report, called Access Courses Report, and will use the power of Excel to analyze the impact of increased costs.

Steps 1 2 3 4

Trouble?

It takes several seconds for Access to export and create the .xls file. If a dialog box opens indicating that the file already exists, click Yes to replace the existing file.

1. Click **Reports** on the Objects bar, click the **Access Courses Report**, click the **OfficeLinks button list arrow** 📄▾ on the Database toolbar, then click **Analyze It with MS Excel** 📊

   The data within the report was automatically exported into an Excel spreadsheet, as shown in Figure I-15. When you use the Analyze It with MS Excel or Publish It with MS Word buttons, the spreadsheet or document you create has the same name as the Access object, and it is usually automatically saved in the My Documents folder of your C: drive. You can send the **recordset** (the fields and records) of a table, query, form, or report object to Excel using the Analyze It with MS Excel button.

2. Click cell **G1** (column G, row 1), type **Increase**, click cell **A16**, type **Increase %**, click cell **A17** (column A, row 17), type **10%**, then press **[Enter]**

   Cell G2 will contain a formula that calculates the additional increase in cost (in column E) for the Access classes. Cell A17 stores an "assumption" that will be used in the formula, the 10% growth factor.

3. Click cell **G2**, type **=E2*A17**, then press **[Enter]**

   Your screen should look like Figure I-16. All formulas in Excel begin with an equal sign. This formula multiplies the cost value in cell E3 by 10% to calculate the $20.00 increase for the Introduction to Access class. The Accounting Department completed this Excel spreadsheet analysis in another spreadsheet file.

4. Click **File** on the Excel menu bar, click **Close** to close the **Attendance Log Report file**, click **No** if prompted to save changes, click the **Open button** 📂, locate your Project Disk, then double-click the **Final Attendance Log Report**

   The Final Attendance Log Report has subtotaled and graphed the increased cost for Access classes for each department, as shown in Figure I-17. The 10% cost increase assumption in cell A22 is shaded bright yellow.

5. Click cell **A22**, type **12%**, then press **[Enter]**

   By changing assumption values, Excel automatically updates all dependent formulas and graphs. You can enter any number in cell A22 to see "what if" the percentage increased by different amounts.

6. Click **File** on the Excel menu bar, click Exit to close **Final Attendance Log Report**, then click **Yes** if prompted to save the changes

FIGURE I-15: Attendance Log Report spreadsheet

Access Courses Report data in an Excel spreadsheet

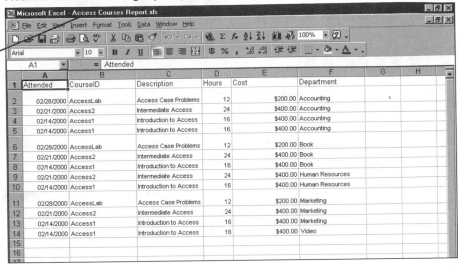

FIGURE I-16: Entering assumptions and formulas in an Excel spreadsheet

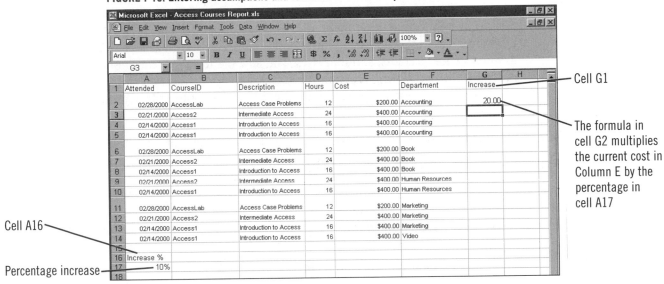

Cell G1

The formula in cell G2 multiplies the current cost in Column E by the percentage in cell A17

Cell A16

Percentage increase

FIGURE I-17: Performing "what-if" analysis

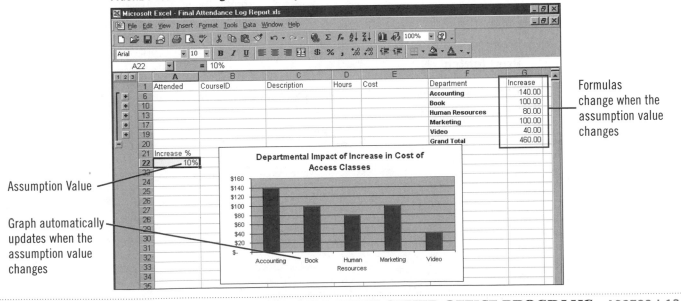

Formulas change when the assumption value changes

Assumption Value

Graph automatically updates when the assumption value changes

Copying Data to Word

Word, the word processing program within the Microsoft Office Suite, is a premier tool for entering, editing, and formatting large paragraphs of text. You may wish to copy the recordset from an Access table, query, form, or report into a Word document in order to integrate the Access data with a larger word-processed document. You can use the **Publish it with MS Word** feature to quickly copy Access data to Word. You can send the **recordset** (the fields and records) of a table, query, form, or report object to Word using the Publish It with MS Word button. Table I-3 lists a variety of other techniques for copying Access data to Word. ✐ David has been asked to comment on the Access courses his department has provided. He will use the Office Links buttons to send the Access Courses Report to Word, then summarize his thoughts about the classes in a paragraph of text in the Word document.

Trouble?

If a dialog box appears indicating that the file already exists, click Yes to replace the existing file.

1. Click **Access Courses Report**, click the **OfficeLinks button list arrow** 📄▾ on the Database toolbar, then click **Publish It with MS Word** 📄

   The records from the Access Courses Report object appear in a Word document with an **RTF** (**rich text format**) file format, as shown in Figure I-18. The RTF format does not support all advanced Word features, but it does support basic formatting embellishments such as multiple fonts, colors, and font sizes. The RTF file format is commonly used when two different word processing programs need to use the same file. You can send the **recordset** (the fields and records) of a table, query, form, or report object to Word using the Publish It with MS Word button.

2. Press **[Enter]** three times to increase the space between the top of the document and the Access information, press **[Ctrl][Home]** to position the insertion point at the top of the document, then type the following:

   To: Management Committee
   From: [*type your name*]
   Re: Analysis of Access Courses
   Date: [*type the current date*]

   The following information shows the recent demand for Access training. The information is sorted by department, and shows that the Accounting Department has had the greatest demand for Access courses. Since Access databases are currently being developed in many MediaLoft areas, I predict that the demand for Access training will increase in the near future.

3. Proofread your document, which should now look like Figure I-19, then click the **Print button** 🖨

4. Click **File** on the menu bar, click **Exit**, then click **No** to close the Access Courses Report document without saving it

FIGURE I-18: Publishing an Access report to Word

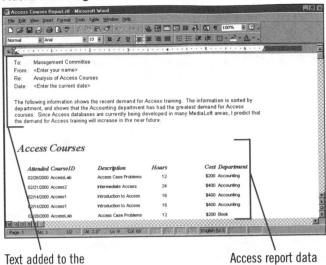

FIGURE I-19: Using Word to enter text

Text added to the Word document

Access report data

TABLE I-3: Techniques to copy Access data to other applications

technique	button or menu option	description
OfficeLinks buttons		Sends selected data to Excel or Word
	Analyze It with MS Excel	Sends a selected table, query, form, or report object's records to Excel
	Publish It with MS Word	Sends a selected table, query, form, or report object's records to Word
	Merge It with MS Word	Helps merge the selected table or query recordset with a Word document
Office Clipboard	Copy and Paste	Copies selected fields and records in a datasheet or a record in a form to the Clipboard. Open a Word document or Excel spreadsheet, click where you want to paste the data, then click the Paste button. The copied data remains on the Office Clipboard until you close all open Office applications in case you want to paste it again.
Exporting	File on the menu bar, then Export	Copies information from an Access object into a different file format
Drag and drop	Right-click an empty space on the taskbar, then choose the Tile Windows Horizontally or Tile Windows Vertically option	With the windows tiled, drag the Access table, query, form, or report object icon from the Access window to the target (Excel or Word) window. You cannot drag an object icon from one window to the next if the windows are maximized.

Creating form letters with Merge It to MS Word

You can merge the information in a table or query with a Word document to create form letters by clicking the object, then clicking the Merge It to MS Word button. Word will start and load a blank document that will serve as the form letter. Type the standard text into the document, then use the Insert Merge Field button on the Mail Merge toolbar to position the table or query fields in the appropriate positions in the letter. Merge the Access data into the form letter by clicking the Merge to New Document button also on the Mail Merge toolbar within Word.

Access 2000

Exporting Data

Exporting is a way to send Access information to another database, spreadsheet, or file format. Exporting is the opposite of importing. Importing is a process to copy and paste information *into* an Access database, whereas exporting is a process used to copy and paste data *out of* the database. Unlike linking, importing and exporting retain no connection between the original source of data. Therefore, when exporting data, changes in either the original Access database or the exported copy do not affect the other. Table I-4 shows the data formats that Microsoft Access can export data to. ▄◢◣ Jim Fernandez, Office Manager of the MediaLoft Accounting Department, has requested that David export the first six months of training activity into an Excel spreadsheet. Jim wants to use his Excel skills to further analyze the historical training activity data using Excel formulas and graphing tools. David gathered the fields that Jim requested into a query called Accounting Data. David also will provide Jim with a list of the courses offered by the MediaLoft Training Department. David never misses an opportunity to take advantage of the power of Access.

Steps

QuickTip

You can also right-click an object in the database window and click Export from the shortcut menu.

1. **Click Queries on the Objects bar, click Accounting Data, click File on the menu bar, then click Export**
   The Export Query 'Accounting Data' To… dialog box opens, requesting information on the location and format for the exported information.

2. **Locate your Project Disk, click the Save as type list arrow, click Microsoft Excel 97-2000, then click Save**
   The fields and records in the Accounting Data query have been exported to an Excel file.

3. **Right-click the Start button in the taskbar, click Explore, locate your Project Disk, then double-click the Accounting Data Excel file to open it, right-click the Exploring button on the task bar, then click Close**
   Your screen should look like Figure I-20. Each field became a column and each record a row of data within Excel. A common reason to export Access information to Excel is to use Excel's extensive graphing (charting) capabilities. Yet another way to export Access information to Excel is the **drag-and-drop** method.

4. **Click File on the menu bar, click Close to close the Accounting Data file (but leave Excel open), click the New button ▢ on the Excel Standard toolbar to open a new workbook, right-click an empty space on the taskbar, then click Tile Windows Vertically**
   Depending upon how many programs you have open, you may have several windows tiled on the screen. If they are too small to work with, close or minimize the windows you do not need and retile the windows. Your screens should look like figure I-21.

5. **Click Tables on the Objects bar in the Access window, click Courses in the Training-I Database window, then drag the Courses table icon to cell A1 in the Excel window**
   Your screen should look like Figure I-22. You can drag any table or query object from an Access database window to an Excel window. This action copies the recordset from the Access object to the Excel spreadsheet just as export or copy and paste does.

6. **Close the Excel window without saving the changes, then close the Training-I database**

7. **Exit Access**

FIGURE I-20: Excel Accounting Data file

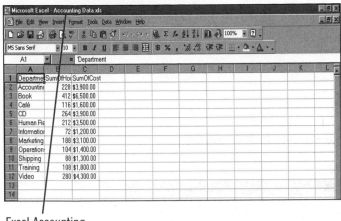

Excel Accounting
Data file

FIGURE I-21: Tiling Windows

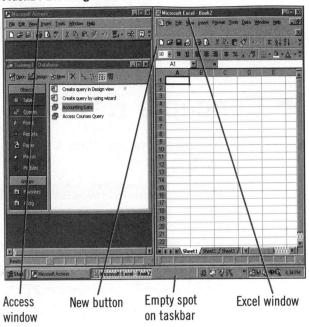

Access   New button   Empty spot   Excel window
window   on taskbar

FIGURE I-22: Drag-and-Drop to Excel

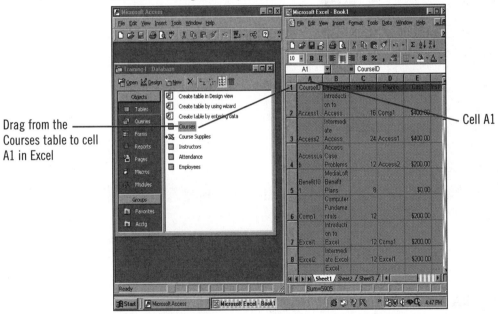

Drag from the
Courses table to cell
A1 in Excel

Cell A1

TABLE I-4: Data formats Microsoft Access can export

application	version or format supported	application	version or format supported
Microsoft Access database	2.0, 7.0/95, 8.0/97, 9.0/2000	Lotus 1-2-3	.wk1 and .wk3
Microsoft Access project	9.0/2000	Delimited text files	All character sets
dBASE	III, III+, IV, and 5	Fixed-width text files	All character sets
Paradox, Paradox for Windows	3.x, 4.x, and 5.0	HTML	1.0 (if a list) 2.0, 3.x (if a table or list)
Microsoft Excel	3.0, 4.0, 5.0, 7.0/95, 8.0/97, 9.0/2000	SQL tables, Microsoft Visual Foxpro, and other data sources that support ODBC protocol	Visual FoxPro 3.0, 5.0, and 6.x

Practice

► Concepts Review

Identify each element of the form's Design view shown in Figure I-23.

FIGURE I-23

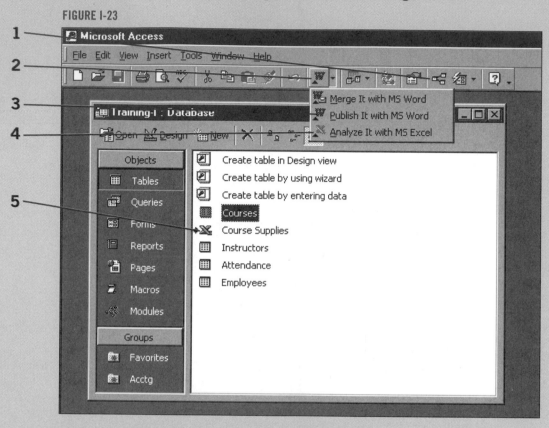

Match each term with the statement that describes its function.

6. hyperlink
7. junction table
8. linking
9. what-if analysis
10. key field
11. normalization

a. A field that contains unique information for each record
b. Testing different assumptions in a spreadsheet
c. Contains foreign key fields that link to the primary key fields of each of two other tables
d. The process of determining the appropriate fields, records, and tables when designing a relational database
e. A way to connect to data in an external source without copying it
f. A label, button, or image placed on a form that when clicked automatically opens another object, file, e-mail message, or Web address

Select the best answer from the list of choices.

12. Which of the following is NOT an Access object?
   a. Spreadsheet
   b. Report
   c. Table
   d. Query

13. Which of the following is NOT part of the normalization process?
   a. Determining the appropriate fields for the database
   b. Identifying the correct number of tables within the database
   c. Establishing table relationships
   d. Creating database hyperlinks

14. Which of the following is NOT true about linking?
   a. Linking does not duplicate data
   b. Changes to linked data will be updated in the original data source
   c. Changes to the original data source will be displayed in the linked data
   d. Linking is the same thing as copying and pasting

15. Which of the following software products would most likely be used to analyze and graph the effect of several potential price increases?
   a. Word
   b. Excel
   c. Access
   d. PowerPoint

16. Which of the following is NOT an OfficeLinks button?
   a. Analyze it with MS Excel
   b. Publish it with MS Word
   c. Present it with MS PowerPoint
   d. Merge it with MS Word

▶ Skills Review

1. Examine Access Objects.
   a. Start Access, then open the Machinery-I database from your Project Disk.
   b. On a separate piece of paper, list the seven Access objects and the number of each type that exist in the Machinery-I database.
   c. List each Access table name, then use the table's Datasheet and Design views to write down the number of records and fields within each table.

2. Examine Relationships.
   a. Click the Relationships button on the Database toolbar.
   b. Drag the ProductID field from the Products table to the ProductID field of the Inventory Transactions table to create a one-to-many relationship between those tables.
   c. Click Enforce Referential Integrity in the Edit Relationships dialog box, then click Create.

 d. Drag the PurchaseOrderID field from the Purchase Orders table to the PurchaseOrderID field of the Inventory Transactions table to create a one-to-many relationship between those tables.

 e. Click Enforce Referential Integrity in the Edit Relationships dialog box, then click Create.

 f. Print the Relationships, then save and close the Relationships window.

3. **Importing Data from Excel.**

 a. Click File on the menu bar, point to the Get External Data option, then click Import.

 b. In the Import dialog box, change the Files of type list to Microsoft Excel, then import the Machinery Employees Excel file on your Project Disk.

 c. In the Import Spreadsheet Wizard, be sure to specify that the first row contains column headings and that five data records are imported in a new table.

 d. Do not make any changes to fields you are importing, and be sure to select the EmpNo field as the table's primary key.

 e. Name the new table "Employees".

 f. Click the Relationships button on the Database toolbar.

 g. Drag the EmpNo field from the Employees table to the EmployeeID field of the Purchase Orders table.

 h. Click Enforce Referential Integrity in the Edit Relationships dialog box, then click Create.

 i. Save and close the Relationships window.

4. **Link Data to Excel.**

 a. Click File on the menu bar, point to the Get External Data option, then click Link Tables.

 b. In the Link dialog box, change the Files of type list to Microsoft Excel, then link to the Machinery Vendors Excel file on your Project Disk.

 c. In the Link Spreadsheet Wizard, be sure to specify that the first row contains column headings and that five data records are linked.

 d. Name the new table "Vendors".

 e. Open the Relationships window.

 f. Click the Show Table button on the Relationship toolbar.

 g. Double-click the Vendors table in the Show Table dialog box to add it to the Relationships window, then close the Show Table dialog box.

 h. Drag the VendorNo field from the Vendors table to the SupplierID field of the Purchase Orders table.

 i. Drag the title bars of the field lists in the Relationships window to more clearly present the relationships between the tables.

 j. Save and close the Relationships window.

5. **Create Hyperlinks.**

 a. Open the Product Entry Form in Design view.

 b. Add a label with the caption "Product Contacts" to the right side of the form.

 c. In the Hyperlink Address property of the Product Contacts label, click the Build button, then browse for the Product Contacts file (it is a Word document) on your Project Disk.

 d. Close the new label's property sheet, and display the Product Entry Form in Form view.

 e. Click the Product Contacts hyperlink, which will open the Product Contacts Word document, then print and close the Product Contacts Word document.

 f. Save and then close the Product Entry Form.

6. Analyze Data with Excel.

a. Click the Reports button on the Object bar, click the Every Product We Lease report, click the Office Links List arrow, then click the Analyze It with MS Excel button to send the information to Excel.

b. Press [Tab] seven times to move to column H, type "Tax" in cell H1, then press [Enter] to move to cell H2.

c. In cell H2, type =6%*D2, the formula to calculate tax that is 6% of the Unit Price, then press [Enter].

d. Print the Excel spreadsheet, then close the Every Product We Lease spreadsheet without saving the changes. Don't exit Excel.

7. Copy Data to Word.

a. Click the Machinery-I Database button on the taskbar to open the window on your screen.

b. Click the Reports button on the Objects bar, click the Every Product We Lease report, click the Office Links list arrow, then click the Publish It with MS Word button to send the information to Word.

c. Click to the right of the "We" in the title and type "Lease".

d. Press [Ctrl][Home] to go to the top of the document, press the [Enter] key twice, then press [Ctrl][Home] to return to the top of the document.

e. Type the following at the top of the document:
INTERNAL MEMO
From: [*Your Name*]
To: Sales Staff
Date: [*Today's Date*]
When quoting prices to customers over the phone, do not forget to mention the long lead times on the Back Hoe and Thatcher products. We usually do not keep these expensive items in stock.

f. Proofread the document, then print it.

g. Close the document without saving changes, then exit Word.

8. Export Data.

a. Right-click an empty space on the taskbar, then choose Tile Windows Vertically.

b. Click Tables on the Objects bar in the Access window, click the New button on the Excel standard toolbar, then drag the Products table icon to cell A1 in the Excel window.

c. Maximize the Excel window, click cell A9, and type your name.

d. Print the Excel spreadsheet, then close the Excel window without saving the Excel spreadsheet.

e. Maximize the Access window, then click the Employees table.

f. Choose File from the menu bar, then Export.

g. Locate your Project Disk, choose Microsoft Excel 97-2000 as the option in the Save as type list, and save the spreadsheet with the name "Employees".

h. Close the Machinery-I database and exit Access.

▶ Independent Challenges

1. As the manager of a college women's basketball team, you have created a database called Basketball-I that tracks the players, games, and player statistics. You need to complete the table relationships as well as import some of the statistics that were created in an Excel file.

To complete this independent challenge:

a. Start Access and open the database Basketball-I.

b. Click the Relationships button and create a one-to-many relationship using the GameNo field between the Games table and the Stats table. Enforce referential integrity.

c. Similarly, create a one-to-many relationship using the PlayerNo field between the Players and Stats table. Note that the Stats table should be the "many" side of both relationships.

d. Close the Relationships window.

e. Click the File menu, point to Get External Data, click Import, locate your Project Disk and display Excel files in the Import dialog box, then Import the BB Stats spreadsheet.

f. Make sure that the first row contains column headings, and store the data in the existing Stats table.

g. Open the Stats table and press [Page Down] several times to make sure that the records for PlayerNo 30 and 35 were successfully imported, then close the Stats table.

h. Enter one new record in the Players table with your own information, using a PlayerNo of 99, then close the Players table.

i. Open the Players Query in Design view, double-click the link line between the Players and Stats tables to open the Join Properties dialog box, click option 2 to include all records from 'Players' and only those records from 'Stats' where the joined fields are equal, then click OK.

j. Open the Players Query in datasheet view, then print it. Jamie Johnson and your name should be the last two records. Because neither you nor Jamie has played in a game yet, you do not have any corresponding statistics.

k. Close the Basketball-I database and exit Access.

2. As the manager of a women's college basketball team, you have created a database called Basketball-I that tracks the players, games, and player statistics. You wish to link to an Excel file that contains information on the player's course load and create a hyperlink on a form to a Word document that gives more detailed information about each player.
   To complete this independent challenge:

a. Start Access and open the database Basketball-I.

b. Click the File menu, point to Get External Data, click Link Tables, locate your Project Disk and display Microsoft Excel files in the Import dialog box, then Link the Course Load spreadsheet.

c. Make sure that the first row contains column headings, and link the data to a new table called "Course Load".

d. If you have not already done so, enter one new record in the Players table with your own information, using a PlayerNo of 99, then close the Players table.

e. Open the Course Load table from within Access, enter two more new records for PlayerNo 99 (you) with your own ClassNo (try to think of unique ClassNos that will differentiate your printout from that of the other students) and Grade information, print the datasheet, then close the table.

f. Click the Relationships button, click the Show Table button, then double-click the Course Load table to add it to the Relationships window.

g. Close the Show Table dialog box, then drag the PlayerNo field from the Players table to the PlayerNo field of the Course Load table and create a one-to-many relationship between the tables.

h. Save and close the Relationships window.

i. Open the Player Information Form in Design view, then add a label to the right side of the form with the caption "Player Profiles".

j. In the Hyperlink Address property of the new label, browse for the file BB Player Information Word document.

k. Close the property sheet of the new label, save the form, view it in Form view, display the last record for PlayerNo 99 (your record), then use the Selected Record option from the Print dialog box (choose File, then Print from the menu system) to print only that record.

l. Click the Player Profiles hyperlink to display the BB Player Information document, create a blank line at the top of the document and enter your name there, print the document, then close the document.

m. Close the Basketball-I database and exit Access.

3. As the manager of a women's college basketball team, you have created a database called Basketball-I that tracks the players, games, and player statistics. You wish to copy and export some of the information in the Basketball-I database to other applications such as Excel and Word.

To complete this independent challenge:

a. Start Access and open the database Basketball-I.

b. Click the Games table, then choose the Analyze It with MS Excel option from the OfficeLinks button on the Database toolbar. (If a dialog box indicating that the file already exists appears, click Yes to replace the existing file.)

c. Click cell H1, type "Margin", then click cell H2 and type the following Excel formula: =E2-F2

d. Scroll and click cell A25 and type your name, change the print settings (use the Page Setup option on the File menu) to a landscape orientation, then print the spreadsheet.

e. Close the spreadsheet without saving the changes.

f. Return to the Basketball-I database, click Reports on the Objects bar, click the Player Statistics report, then click the Publish It with MS Word option from the OfficeLinks button on the Database toolbar. (If a dialog box opens indicating that the file already exists, click Yes to replace the existing file.)

g. Enter two blank lines at the top of the document, then add the following text there:
Name: [*Your Name*]
Date: [*Today's Date*]
Subject: Offensive Statistics
The following statistics show the number of field goals, three-point completions, and field goals completed for selected players and games.

h. Print the first page of the document. (Use the Print option from the File menu and choose the Current Page option.)

i. Close the document without saving changes.

j. Close the Basketball-I database and exit Access.

4. MediaLoft has developed a Web site that provides internal information to its employees. In this independent challenge, you'll add a hyperlink to a form in the Training-I database that allows the user to link to this Web page.

To complete this independent challenge:

a. Start Access, open the Training-I database, click the Forms on the Objects bar, then open the Employees form in Design view.

b. Add a label to the right side of the form with the caption "MediaLoft Home Page".

c. In the Hyperlink Address property of the new label, enter the following WorldWide Web address: http://www.course.com/illustrated/MediaLoft/ (*Hint*: You do not need to use the Builder button to enter this address.)

d. Close the properties sheet, save the Employees form, and open it in Form view.

e. Connect on to the Internet (if necessary).

f. Return to the Employees form and click the MediaLoft Home Page hyperlink label.

g. Print the MediaLoft Web page.

h. Return to the Employees form, view the form in Design view, and add a label with your name to the lower-right corner of the form.

i. Save the Employees form, display it in Form view, then print the first record.

j. Close the Employees form, then exit the Training-I database.

▶ Visual Workshop

Use any technique you wish (drag-and-drop, export, Analyze It with MS Excel, or copy and paste) to copy the Field Goal Stats query to an Excel spreadsheet shown in Figure I-24. Enter the formula =B2/C2 in cell D2 to determine the field goal percentage. Enter your name in cell F2, then print the first page of the spreadsheet.

FIGURE I-24

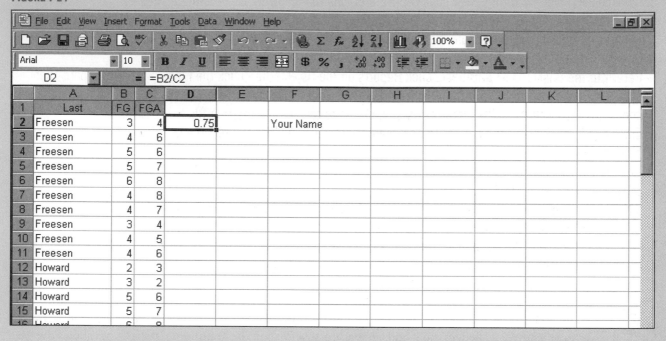

Creating
Data Access Pages

Objectives

▶ **Understand the World Wide Web**
⌐MOUS⌐ ▶ **Use hyperlink fields**
⌐MOUS⌐ ▶ **Create pages for interactive reporting**
▶ **Create pages for data entry**
▶ **Create pages for data analysis**
▶ **Work in Page Design view**
▶ **Insert hyperlinks to other pages**
▶ **Publish Web pages to Web servers**

The Internet has an enormous wealth of information, unlimited potential for business opportunity, and ability for instant global communication. A tremendous amount of energy is being focused on how to connect **World Wide Web pages**, which are hyperlinked documents that make the Internet easy to navigate, directly to underlying databases. Linked pages enable employees, customers, or vendors to view, find, enter, edit, analyze, and order products via an Internet connection rather than having direct access to the database file. Access 2000 provides a connection between Web pages and an Access database through the **page** object. ◢━━ MediaLoft employees are located throughout the United States, and David Dumont would like to give them the ability to access the Training-J database via the Internet.

Understanding the World Wide Web

Creating Web pages that dynamically interact with an Access database is an exciting process that involves many underlying technologies. Understanding how the Internet, the World Wide Web, and Web pages interact is extremely important in order to successfully connect a Web page to an underlying Access database. David reviews some of the history and key terminology of the Internet and World Wide Web to better prepare himself for the task of connecting a Web page to an Access database.

Details

The **Internet** is a worldwide network of computer networks that sends and receives information through a common **protocol** (set of rules) called **TCP/IP** (Transmission Control Protocol/Internet Protocol).

The Internet supports many services including:

- **E-Mail:** electronic mail
- **File Transfer:** uploading and downloading files
- **Newsgroups:** similar to e-mail, but messages are posted in a "public mailbox" that is available to any subscriber rather than sent to one individual
- **World Wide Web (WWW):** a vast number of linked documents stored on thousands of different Web servers

The Internet has experienced tremendous growth in the past decade partly because of the following three major factors:

- In the early 1990s, the U.S. government lifted restrictions on commercial Internet traffic, causing explosive growth in electronic commerce activities.
- Technological innovations resulted in breakthroughs in hardware such as faster computer processors and storage devices, and in networking media such as fiber-optics and satellite transmission.
- Less expensive and easier-to-use Internet systems and program software were developed for both **clients** (your computer) and **servers** (the computer that "serves" the information to you from the Internet).

Behind all of these innovations are many amazing people. Of special note is the scientist who saw the need to easily share real-time information with colleagues. This scientific initiative grew into today's World Wide Web. Table J-1 introduces more Internet and World Wide Web terminology. Figure J-1 shows how hyperlinks work on a Web page.

FIGURE J-1: Hyperlinks on a Web page

URL

Hyperlinks can be pictures, clip art, or text.

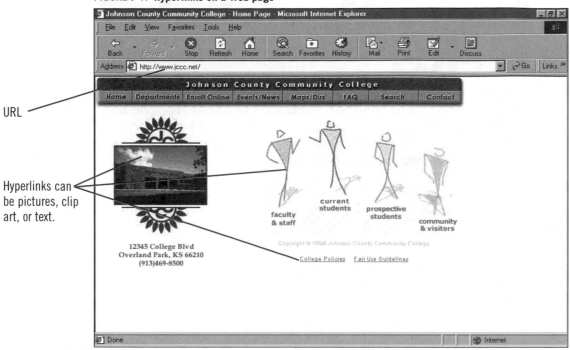

TABLE J-1: Internet and World Wide Web terminology

term	definition
Web page	A special type of file created with HTML code that contains hyperlinks to other files
Web server	A computer that stores Web pages
Hyperlink	Text (usually underlined), an image, or an icon on a Web page that when clicked, presents another Web page. Hyperlinks can jump to another part of the same Web page, a different page on the same Web server, or to a different Web server in another part of the world.
HTML	Hypertext Markup Language. HTML is a special programming language used to create Web pages. An HTML programmer writes HTML code to create a Web page. Nonprogrammers create HTML Web pages using FrontPage or by converting files such as Word, Excel, and PowerPoint files into HTML Web pages using menu options within those programs.
Browser	Software such as Microsoft's Internet Explorer (IE) or Netscape Navigator used to find and display Web pages. HTML files created through the Access Page object are best displayed with IE version 5 or later.
ISP	Internet Service Provider. To access the Internet from a home computer, your computer first must dial an ISP that connects your computer with the Internet. National ISPs include America Online, The Microsoft Network, and Sprint's Earthlink Internet. Hundreds of regional and local ISPs exist as well.
Modem	Short for *mod*ulate-*dem*odulate. A modem is hardware (usually located inside the computer) that converts digital computer signals to analog telephone signals to allow a computer to send and receive information across ordinary telephone lines.
URL	Uniform Resource Locator. Each resource on the Internet (including Web pages) has an address so that other computers can accurately and consistently locate and view it. http://www.course.com/products/ is the URL for the Web page that displays information about Course Technology, Inc. (the publisher of this textbook.) There is never a space in a URL.
Domain name	The middle part of a URL, such as www.course.com. The middle part of the domain name is often either the company's name or words that describe the information you will find at that site. The last part of the domain name indicates the type of site, such as commercial (com), educational (edu), military (mil), organizational (org), or governmental (gov).
Home page	The first page displayed on a Web server.

Using Hyperlink Fields

A **Hyperlink field** is a field defined with the Hyperlink data type in Table Design view. The entry in a hyperlink field can be a **Universal Naming Convention (UNC) path** or a **Uniform Resource Locator (URL) address.** Table J-2 gives more information about networks. URLs may also specify an Internet e-mail address, a newsgroup address, an intranet Web page address, or a file on a local area network. ✎ Many MediaLoft employees have requested more information about the internal classes. To accommodate these requests, David creates a Hyperlink field called Online Resources to store the URL for a World Wide Web page that contains up-to-date information on the subject of the class.

Steps

1. Start **Access**, open the **Training-J** database from your Project Disk, click **Tables** on the Objects bar, click the **Courses table**, click the **Design button** 🔲 in the Database window, then maximize both the database and the table windows (if not already maximized)
   The Courses table opens in Design view, where you can add fields and specify their properties.

2. Click the first empty **Field Name cell** below InstructorID, type **Online Resources**, press **[Tab]**, press **h**, click the **Save button** 🔲, then click the **Datasheet View button** 🔲
   The Courses table with the new Online Resources field opens in datasheet view.

> **QuickTip**
> The first part of an Internet Web address (http://) can be omitted when entering a URL into a hyperlink field.

3. Press **[Tab]** six times to move to the new Online Resources field, type **www.microsoft.com/access**, press **[↓]** point to the right edge of the **Online Resources field name**, double-click ↔, then click 🔲
   Your screen should look like Figure J-2. The column is widened to display all of the data in the Online Resources field. Note that hyperlinks appear underlined in bright blue just like text hyperlinks on Web pages.

> **QuickTip**
> [Ctrl]['] copies the entry in the field of the previous record to the same field of the current record.

4. Press **[Ctrl][']**, then press **[↓]**

5. Point to **www.microsoft.com/access** in either record so that the pointer changes to 🖑, then click **www.microsoft.com/access**
   If you are currently connected to the Internet and have Microsoft Internet Explorer browser software loaded on your computer, your screen should look similar to Figure J-3. Netscape Communicator is another popular browser program that will also open and display HTML files. Web pages are continually updated as new information is announced, so the content of the Web page itself may vary. If you are not already connected to the Internet, your **dialer** (software that helps you dial and connect to your ISP) may appear. Once connected to your ISP, the Microsoft Access Web page should appear.

> **QuickTip**
> Visited links will change to the color purple.

6. Click the **Courses: Table button** in the taskbar, click the **Online Resources field** for record 5 (Introduction to Excel), type **www.microsoft.com/excel**, click the **Online Resources field** for record 11 (Introduction to Netscape), type **www.netscape.com**, then press **[Enter]**
   Hyperlink entries can point to a different Web page on the same Web server or to an entirely different Web server.

7. Click **www.netscape.com**
   The Netscape Netcenter Web page appears on your screen.

8. Right-click the **Courses: Table button** on the taskbar, click **Close**, click **Yes** to save the changes to the layout of the table, then close any open browser windows

FIGURE J-2: A hyperlink entry

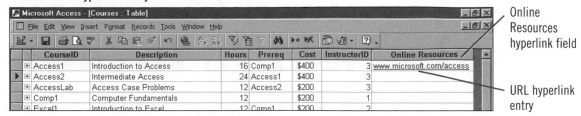

Online Resources hyperlink field

URL hyperlink entry

FIGURE J-3: www.microsoft.com/access Web page

Microsoft Internet Explorer (browser software)

URL

Web page

TABLE J-2: Types of networks

type of network	description
LAN (local area network)	Connects local resources such as file servers, user computers, and printers by a direct cable. LANs do not cross a public thoroughfare such as a street because of distance and legal restrictions on how far and where cables can be pulled.
WAN (wide area network)	Created when a LAN is connected to an existing telecommunications network, such as the phone system, to reach resources across public thoroughfares such as streets and rivers
Internet	Largest WAN in the world, spanning the entire globe and connecting many diverse computer architectures
Intranet	WANs that support the same services as the Internet (i.e., e-mail, Web pages, and file transfer) and are built with the same technologies (e.g., TCP/IP communications protocol, HTML Web pages, and browser software), but are designed and secured for the internal purposes of a business. To secure intranet information and resources from outsiders, passwords and data encryption techniques are used.

CLUES TO USE

Understanding the Universal Naming Convention (UNC)

Universal Naming Convention (UNC) is another naming convention (in addition to URL) to locate a file on a network. The structure of a UNC is \\server\sharedfoldername\filename. UNCs are used for local resources, such as a file stored on a local area network. URL addresses are used for Web pages on the Internet or a company intranet.

Creating Pages for Interactive Reporting

The **page** object, also called the **data access page (DAP)**, is a special Access object used to create Web pages designed for viewing, editing, and entering data stored in a Microsoft Access database. Data access pages may also include data from other sources such as Microsoft Excel or a Microsoft SQL Server database. You create data access page objects in Access, but the Web pages they create are separate HTML files stored outside the Access database file. DAPs appear when you click Pages on the Objects bar. Table J-3 describes three major purposes for a DAP. David uses the page object to publish interactive reports from the Training-J database that can be viewed using Internet Explorer.

1. Click **Pages** on the Objects bar, then double-click **Create data access page by using wizard**

   You can create a page object using a wizard or develop it from scratch in Design view.

2. Click the **Tables/Queries list arrow**, click **Query: Attendance Details**, click the **Select All Fields button** , click **Next**, click **Department** as the grouping level, click the **Select Field button** , then click **Next**

   The Page Wizard prompts for sorting fields as well as a page title.

Trouble?

Click the Page View button if you are viewing Page Design view instead of Page view.

3. Click the **first sort list arrow**, click **Last**, click **Next**, type **Department Training Information**, click the **Open the page option button**, then click **Finish**

   Your screen should look like Figure J-4. The **Expand button** indicates that detail records grouped within the Accounting Department can be viewed by clicking that button. The **navigation buttons** are similar to those for a datasheet or form. The **filter** and **sort buttons** appear on the right side of the navigation buttons of a page object and provide filtering and sorting capabilities to the person who is viewing this information as a Web page when the data access page is posted to an Internet or intranet Web server.

Trouble?

If your page doesn't display correctly, click the Page Design View button, then click the Page View button.

4. Click the **Expand button** , click **1/31/00** in the Attended text box, then click the **Sort Ascending button** on the Attendance Details 1 of 16 navigation bar

   Your screen should look like Figure J-5. The Expand button has become the **Collapse button**. When clicked, the Collapse button collapses the detail records within that group.

Trouble?

When you click a text box on a data access page used for interactive reporting, you may not see the blinking insertion point inside the text box.

5. Click the **Last Record button** on the Attendance Details Department 1 of 11 navigation buttons to display the Video group, click , click **Lee** in the Last field, then click the **Filter by Selection button** on the Attendance Detail 1 of 21 navigation buttons

   Your screen should look like Figure J-6.

6. Click the **Remove Filter button** on the Attendance Details 1 of 11 toolbar to view all 21 detail records within the Video department, click the **Save button** on the Page View toolbar, locate your Project disk, type **Department Training** in the File name text box, then click **Save**

   You do not need to save the HTML file with the same name as the corresponding DAP, but it helps keep them organized if they have similar names. An HTML file named Department Training has been saved to your Project Disk. Internet Explorer opens HTML files as Web pages.

7. Close the Department Training Information page object window

FIGURE J-4: Department Training Information data access page

Page Design View button

Expand button

Department Navigation buttons

Filter and Sort buttons

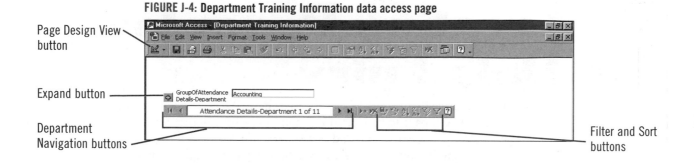

FIGURE J-5: Expanded and sorted data access page

Last field is listed at the top because that's how the detail records are sorted

Attended field

Accounting employees took 16 classes

Detail record for the Accounting Department

Sort Ascending button

11 different departments

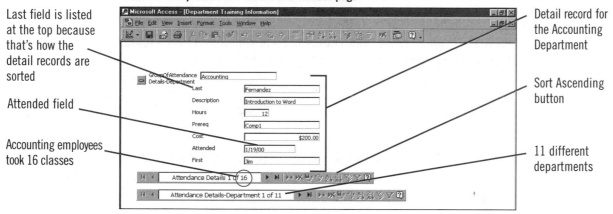

FIGURE J-6: Filtered data access page

Within the video department, Nancy Lee attended 11 classes

"Lee" entry in Last text box

Filter by Selection button

Department Last Record button

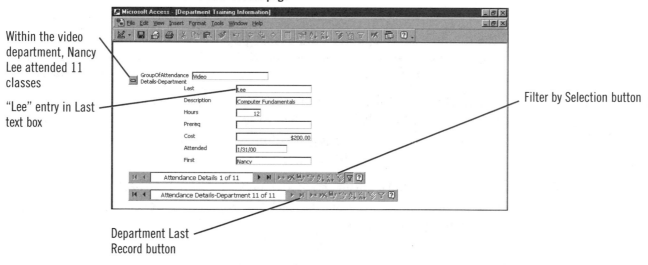

TABLE J-3: Purposes for data access pages

purpose	description
Interactive reporting	To publish summaries of information using sorting, grouping, and filtering techniques.
Data entry	To view, add, and edit records
Data analysis	To analyze the data using pivot tables and charts

Creating Pages for Data Entry

Using a data access page for data entry is similar to using an Access form except that the data access page also creates a Web page to be viewed through Microsoft Internet Explorer. Within the data access page you can view, enter, edit, and delete data, just like in a form. ◄━━━ The Human Resources department has offered to help David find, enter, and update information on instructors. David creates a data access page based on the Instructors table within the Training-J database to give the HR department the ability to also view and update this data using Internet Explorer.

Steps

1. **Double-click the Create data access page by using wizard, click the Tables/Queries list arrow, click Table: Instructors, click the Select All Fields button >> , click Next, then click Finish to accept the rest of the defaults**
   The data access page opens in **Page Design view**, as shown in Figure J-7. The Toolbox and the Alignment and Sizing toolbars may be open. The Field list, which organizes fields and objects much like Internet Explorer organizes files and folders, is open. Page objects contain controls just as reports and forms do.

2. **Click the Page View button 🔲 on the Page Design toolbar to view the data access page, click the Save button 💾 on the Page View toolbar, locate your Project Disk, type Instructor Updates in the File name text box, then click Save**
   The Instructors data access page shows the three records that are currently in the Instructors table. You *could* use this page object within Access to enter or edit data, but the purpose of a data access page isn't for data entry (forms are much more powerful data entry tools if you have direct access to the database file). The real power of the data access page object is its ability to create dynamic HTML files (Web pages) that can be used to enter and update data by people who *do not* have direct access to the database, but who *do* have Internet Explorer browser software.

3. **Close the Instructor Updates data access page**
   Use Microsoft Internet Explorer to open the Instructor Updates HTML file to make changes to the Training-J database *even though you are not directly using the Training-J database file.*

4. **Click Start on the taskbar, point to Programs, click Internet Explorer (IE), click File on the IE menu bar, click Open, click Browse in the Open dialog box, locate your Project Disk, click Instructor Updates.htm, click Open, then click OK**
   The Instructor Updates.htm file opens in Internet Explorer, as shown in Figure J-8.

5. **Click the New Record button ▸✱ on the navigation bar, type Sarah, press [Tab], type Chalupa, press [Tab], type 9/1/00, click the Previous Record button ◂ , then click the Next Record button ▸**
   You verify that the record for Sarah Chalupa was entered successfully.

6. **Close Internet Explorer, click the Training-J database button on the taskbar, click Tables on the Objects bar, then double-click the Instructors table to open it in Datasheet view**
   Your screen should look like Figure J-9. The new record appears in the table. You used an HTML Web page opened in Internet Explorer to dynamically update an underlying Access database. If you had been using the Internet or a company intranet, the Instructor Updates.htm file would have to have been stored on a Web server rather than your Project Disk. To open the Instructor Updates.htm file on a Web server, you have to enter the URL or UNC address for the file.

7. **Close the Instructors datasheet**

> **Trouble?**
> You do not need to be connected to the Internet to load Web pages stored in your Project Disk.

> **Trouble?**
> You cannot press [Page Up] and [Page Down] to move from record to record when viewing records through an HTML file.

FIGURE J-7: Page Design view

Page View button

Field List button

Alignment and Sizing toolbar

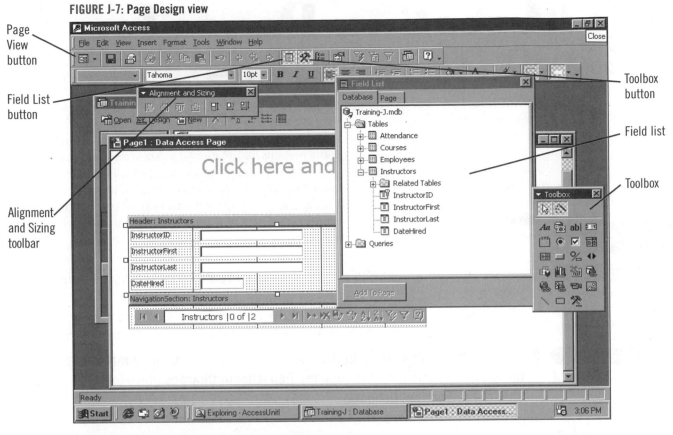

Toolbox button

Field list

Toolbox

FIGURE J-8: Instructor Updates.htm Web page opened in Internet Explorer

Internet Explorer is the active program

Instructor Updates. htm file from Project Disk in drive A

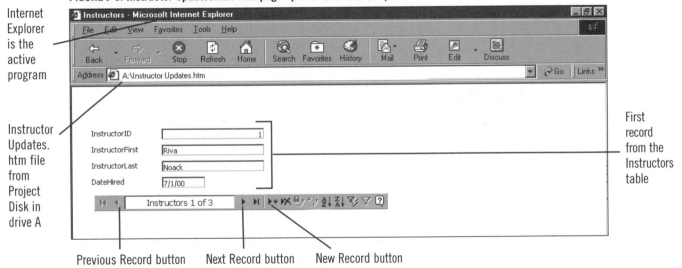

First record from the Instructors table

Previous Record button   Next Record button   New Record button

FIGURE J-9: Updated Instructors table

Instructors table

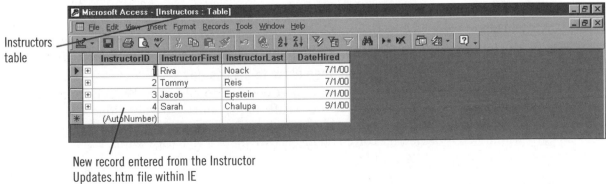

New record entered from the Instructor Updates.htm file within IE

Creating Pages for Data Analysis

A **PivotTable list** is a bound control created in Design view of a data access page. It helps you analyze data by allowing you to organize data in many different ways. In a pivot table, one field is used for the column heading, one field is used for the row heading, and one field is summarized for each column and row. The PivotTable list control presents information in a data access page in a way that is similar to how a Crosstab query presents data in a query. You cannot use the PivotTable List control to edit, delete, or add new data. In this respect, DAPs created for data analysis using the PivotTable List control are similar to those created for interactive reporting. Neither can be used to update data. David creates a data access page using the PivotTable list control so that information about course attendance can be viewed in many different ways.

1. Click **Pages** on the Objects bar, double-click **Create data access page in Design view**, then maximize the Design View window
   The Design view of a page, as shown in Figure J-10, is very similar to that of a form or report. Table J-4 summarizes some of the key terminology used in Design view.

2. Click the **Office PivotTable button** 🖾 on the Toolbox, click the **Queries Expand button** 🟦 in the Field list, then drag the **Department Charges** query into the upper-left area of the **Section: Unbound**
   The Layout Wizard helps guide you through the rest of the process.

3. Click the **PivotTable List option button**, click **OK**, then click 🗐 to toggle the Field list off
   Your screen should look like Figure J-11. The four fields within the Department Charges query are the column headings in the PivotTable List control.

4. Point to the **middle sizing handle** on the right edge of the PivotTable List control, drag ↔ to the right edge of the section to view the Cost field, then click the **Page View button** 🖾 on the Page Design toolbar
   The data access page appears within Access, and the fields display interactive list arrows.

5. Click the **Department list arrow**, click the **(Show All) check box** to clear all of the check marks, scroll and click the **Video checkbox**, then click **OK**
   Only the records with "Video" in the Department field appear. Choices made within these lists are temporary and are not saved with the page object, so every time you open the page, all of the records are visible.

6. Click the **Design View button** 🖾, **click the PivotTable List control**, right-click the **Description field name**, click **Move to Row Area**, then click 🖾
   Your screen should look like Figure J-12. The Description field entries are now organized as row headings, and the other fields from the Department Charges query still appear as column headings. The PivotTable List control's major benefit is its ability to quickly rearrange data in many different ways.

7. Click the **Save button** 🖫 on the Page View toolbar, locate your Project Disk, type **Department Pivot**, click **Save**, then close to access page
   The new Department Pivot data access page object is stored within the Training-J database window and the Department Pivot HTML file is stored on your Project Disk. The PivotTable List control looks and behaves the same way whether you access it as a DAP within Access or view the corresponding HTML file as a Web page within IE.

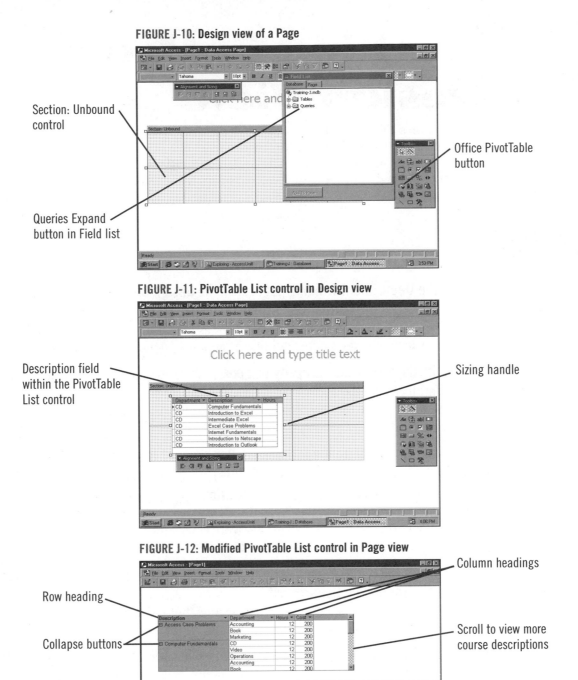

FIGURE J-10: Design view of a Page

Section: Unbound control

Queries Expand button in Field list

Office PivotTable button

FIGURE J-11: PivotTable List control in Design view

Click here and type title text

Description field within the PivotTable List control

Sizing handle

FIGURE J-12: Modified PivotTable List control in Page view

Column headings

Row heading

Collapse buttons

Scroll to view more course descriptions

TABLE J-4: Design view terminology

term	definition
Field list	List that contains all of the field names that can be added to an object in Design view
Toolbox toolbar	Toolbar that contains all of the bound and unbound controls that can be added to the object in Design view
Control	Each individual element that can be added, deleted, or modified in an object's Design view
Bound controls	Controls that display data from an underlying recordset. Common bound controls are text boxes, list boxes, and pivot table lists
Unbound controls	Controls that do not display data from an underlying recordset. Common unbound controls for a page are labels, lines, and toolbars
Sections	Areas of the object that contain controls. Sections determine where and how often a control will appear or print
Properties	Characteristics that further describe the selected object, section, or control

Access 2000

Working in Page Design View

Like every other object within Access, page objects have a Design view that you use to modify the object's structure. Page Design view closely resembles that of Form and Report Design view, but there are some key differences, as identified in Table J-5. David works in Page Design view to add a caption and some formatting enhancements to the Department Training Page object.

Steps

1. **Click the Department Training page, click the Design button** in the Database window, **then click the Sorting and Grouping button** on the Page Design toolbar
   The Sorting and Grouping dialog box opens, as shown in Figure J-13. Several options are available, including the ability to display a caption section and record navigation section.

2. **Click the Caption Section property text box, click the Caption section property list arrow, click Yes, then click**
   The Sorting and Grouping dialog box closes. The Caption section is often used for descriptive labels.

3. **Click the GroupOfAttendance Details-Department label** in the Header: Attendance Details-Department section, **press [Delete], click the Label button** on the Toolbox, **click on the left side of the Caption section, then type DEPARTMENTS**
   Your screen should look similar to Figure J-14. Many of the moving and resizing skills you learned in Form and Report Design view work exactly the same way in Page Design view, so you can move and resize controls if necessary.

4. **Click Click here and type title text** at the top of the page, **then type Attendance Records Grouped by Department**
   The body of the page is not a part of any section, but rather is the title text for the HTML Web page that this DAP creates.

5. **Click the Save button** on the Page Design toolbar, **then click the Page View button**
   The changes you made to the Department Training page are displayed in the Page view.

6. **Close the Department Training page object**
   The Department Training page looks and behaves the same whether you are viewing it in Page view through Access or as a Web page opened in Internet Explorer.

7. **Start Internet Explorer, click File** on the menu bar, **click Open, click Browse, locate** your Project Disk, **double-click Department Training, then click OK**
   After a few moments, the Department Training HTML file opens within Internet Explorer, as shown in Figure J-15.

8. **Close Internet Explorer**

FIGURE J-13: Sorting and Grouping dialog box for the Data Access page

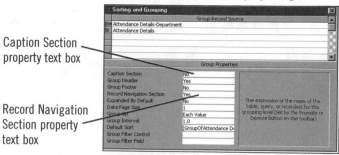

Caption Section
property text box

Record Navigation
Section property
text box

FIGURE J-14: Adding label controls

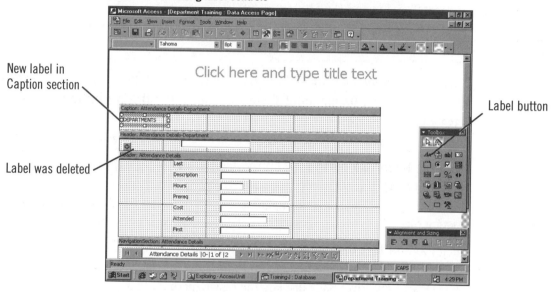

New label in
Caption section

Label was deleted

Label button

FIGURE J-15: Viewing the updated Web page in Internet Explorer

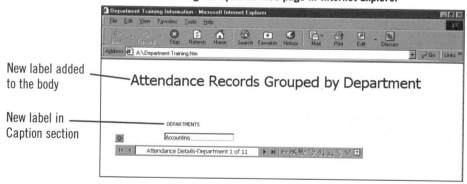

New label added
to the body

New label in
Caption section

TABLE J-5: New Features within Page Design view

item	description
Body	Basic design surface of the data access page that displays text, controls, and sections. When viewed in Page view or in Internet Explorer, the content in the body automatically adjusts itself to fit the size of the browser
Sections	New sections within a page object include the record navigation section used to display the navigation toolbar and the caption section used to display text. Neither of these two new sections can contain bound controls
Positioning	By default, the position of text, sections, and other elements in the body of a page are relative to one another (determined by the preceding content on the page)
Toolbox	Several new controls are displayed in the Toolbox toolbar that are specific to page objects, including the Office PivotTable, Expand, and Record Navigation controls
Field list	The Field List window displays *all* Tables, Queries, and associated fields within them. The Page tab of the Field list displays the bound controls and grouping choices within the Details section

Inserting Hyperlinks to Other Pages

Once the Access page objects are finished, you may wish to connect them using hyperlinks. Hyperlinks allow the user to access one Web page from another with a single click, just like World Wide Web pages reference other Web pages throughout the Internet. You add hyperlinks to pages in Page Design view. Then, when you browse through the pages, you can jump between them by clicking the hyperlinks. David wants to create a hyperlink between the Department Training and Department Pivot data access pages so that one page can be accessed from the other. He uses Page Design view to add the hyperlinks to both pages.

Steps

1. Click the **Training-J** database button in the taskbar (if necessary), click **Pages** on the Objects bar, click **Department Pivot**, then click the **Design button** in the database window
   Hyperlink controls are added to page objects by using the Hyperlink control.

2. Click the **Hyperlink button** on the Toolbox, then click the hyperlink pointer in the page body above the left edge of the Section: Unbound control
   The Insert Hyperlink dialog box opens, as shown in Figure J-16. You may choose links from existing files, Web pages, pages in this database, new pages, or e-mail addresses.

3. Click **Page in This Database**, click **Department Training** from the Select a page in this database list, click **OK**, then click the **Page View button** on the Page Design toolbar
   The Department Pivot page displays the new hyperlink. Pointing to a hyperlink on a page displays information about the hyperlink.

Trouble?
If Netscape opens the Web page, you may want to change file type associations within Explorer so that IE is used to open HTML files.

4. Place the pointer over **Department Training** so that the pointer changes to 🖑, observe the ScreenTip, then click the **Department Training hyperlink** to test the link
   The Department Training Web page with records grouped by department should be displayed within an IE window. Now add a hyperlink to go from the Department Training Web page back to the Department Pivot Web page.

5. Click the **Department Pivot button** in the taskbar to return to Access, save and close the **Department Pivot** page, click **Department Training** page object in the Training-J database window, then click

6. Click on the Toolbox, then click on the **page body** above the left edge of the Caption: Attendance Details-Department section

7. Click **Page in This Database** in the Insert Hyperlink dialog box, click the **Department Pivot** page, click **OK**, then click

Trouble?
To make sure that IE is displaying the latest version of a Web page, click the Refresh button on the IE Standard Buttons toolbar.

8. Click the **Department Pivot hyperlink**, then click the **Print button** on the IE Standard Buttons toolbar
   The Department Pivot Web page should open in IE, as shown in Figure J-17. Now you can move between the two pages by clicking their hyperlinks.

9. Close IE, then close the Training-J database, saving any changes.

FIGURE J-16: Insert Hyperlink dialog box

Existing file or Web Page button is currently chosen

Click to view Page in This Database

Inserted Links is chosen

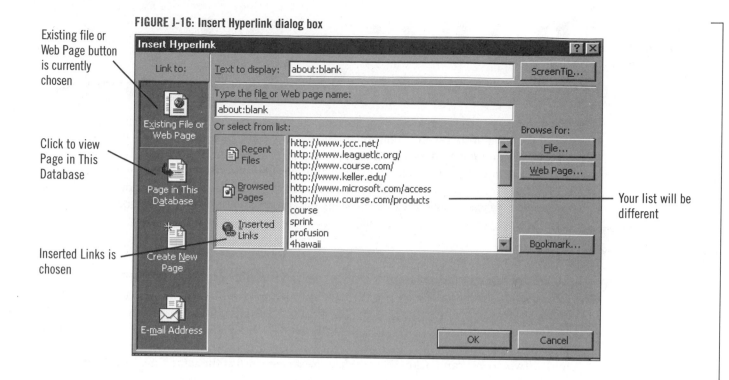

Your list will be different

FIGURE J-17: Department Pivot Web page viewed through IE

Refresh button

Print button

Hyperlink

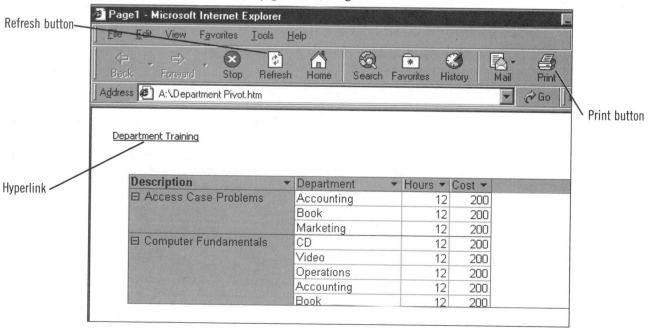

CREATING DATA ACCESS PAGES ACCESS J-15

Publishing Web Pages to Web Servers

Making Web pages available over the Internet or a company intranet requires publishing your Web pages to a **Web server**, a computer devoted to storing and downloading Web pages. Web servers contain **Web folders**, which are special folders dedicated to storing and organizing Web pages. Once your Web page files are stored appropriately, **clients**, computers with appropriate browser and communication software that have access to the Web folder, may download and use those files. ➤ David reviews the steps necessary to publish the Instructor Updates Web page for use over MediaLoft's intranet.

Details

Store the Access database in a shared network folder on the Web server

On a network, most folders are not available to everyone, so you must be sure to put the Access database in a folder that the appropriate people have permission to use (**shared network folder**). Access databases are inherently **multi-user**, so that many people can enter and update information at the same time, provided they are given permission to use the files inside that folder. Two people cannot, however, update the same record at the same time (**record locking**). Also, it doesn't matter whether the individuals are accessing the Access database through the database file itself (for example, two people updating the same database using forms or datasheets) or whether they are using Web pages created by DAPs.

Use the Access database to create DAPs, which in turn create dynamic HTML Web pages

Save the HTML Web page files in the same shared network folder as the Access database

It is not required that the database and HTML files be in the same folder, but this helps keep them organized.

Give the users the URL or UNC address to access the Web pages using IE

URLs are used to access Internet Web pages. UNCs can be used when the file is located on the same local area network as the client computer. As users access the Web pages, the underlying Access database will be updated automatically.

Use professional networking resources as necessary

Publishing a Web page to a Web Folder on a Web Server is very similar to saving an existing file with a new name in a new location, but the existing networking infrastructure (including connectivity between the Web server and your computer), along with appropriate security clearances, needs to be in place before you can save Web pages to any location on a company intranet or on the Internet. This requires the knowledge and skills of professionals dedicated to the field of computer networking. People who build networking infrastructures are often called **network administrators**. Those who work with Web Servers, Web Folders, and supporting Internet technologies are often called **Webmasters**. Table J-6 provides more tips and information about working with Web pages and Access. Figure J-18 illustrates the infrastructure involved with publishing a Web page to a Web server.

FIGURE J-18: Publishing to a Web server

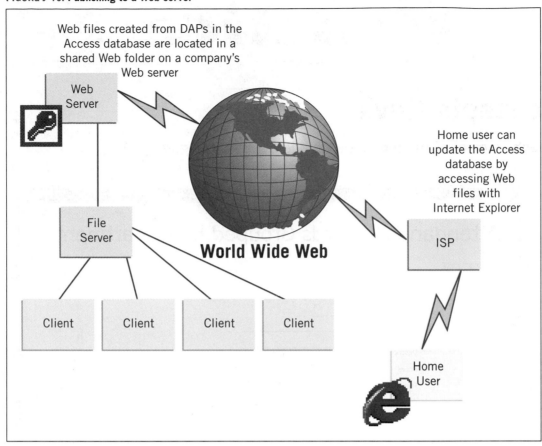

Web files created from DAPs in the Access database are located in a shared Web folder on a company's Web server

Home user can update the Access database by accessing Web files with Internet Explorer

World Wide Web

Web Server

File Server

ISP

Client Client Client Client

Home User

TABLE J-6: Tips for Working with Web pages and Access

to:	do this:
Open dynamic HTML files created by Access in a browser other than IE—dynamic files display live data from the underlying Access database	Use the Export option on the File menu to create server-generated HTML files from tables, queries, and forms (Save as file type ASP for Microsoft Active Server Pages or IDC/HTX Microsoft IIS 1-2 file types.) Server-generated HTML files pages are dynamic, and therefore show current data, but are read-only.
Open static HTML files created by Access in a browser other than IE—static files display data that is current only as of the moment that the Web page was created	Use the Export option on the File menu to create static HTML files from tables, queries, forms, and reports. The files display a snapshot of the data at the time the static HTML file was created.
Open an HTML file created by another program in Access	Right-click the file in the Open dialog box, then click Open in Microsoft Access on the pop-up menu.

Practice

► Concepts Review

Identify each element of the form's Design View shown in Figure J-19.

FIGURE J-19

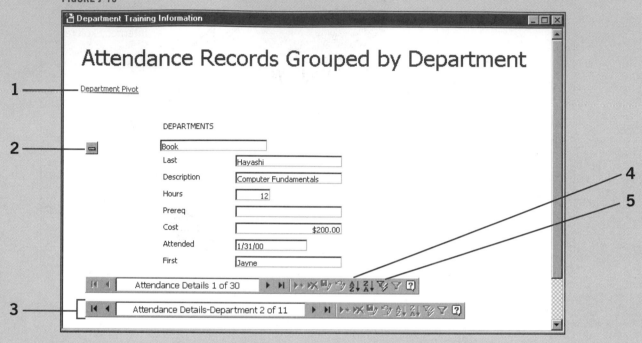

Match each term with the statement that describes its function.

6. data access page
7. URL
8. HTML
9. World Wide Web pages
10. browser
11. World Wide network of computer networks

a. Programming language used to create Web pages
b. Software loaded on a microcomputer and used to find and display Web pages
c. Access 2000 object that provides a connection between Web pages and an Access database
d. Internet
e. Web page address
f. Hyperlinked documents that make the Internet easy to navigate

12. **The communications protocol for the Internet is**
    a. TCP/IP.
    b. HTML.
    c. URL.
    d. ISP.

13. **To connect to the Internet through your home computer, you must first call a(n):**
    a. URL
    b. ISP
    c. Home page
    d. Webmaster

14. **Which of the following is NOT a service provided by the Internet?**
    a. E-mail
    b. File transfer
    c. World Wide Web
    d. Cable TV

15. **Which of the following is browser software?**
    a. Windows NT
    b. Internet Explorer
    c. Microsoft Access
    d. Microsoft Excel

16. **Which of the following is a special type of Web page designed for viewing, editing, and entering data stored in a Microsoft Access database?**
    a. Browser
    b. Home page
    c. Data access page
    d. Pivot table

17. **Making Web pages created through Access available to other users is called**
    a. Publishing.
    b. Uploading.
    c. Transferring.
    d. Rendering.

▶ Skills Review

1. **Understanding the World Wide Web.**
   a. Interview five people and ask them if they have recently used the World Wide Web for the following purposes. If the answer is "Yes," ask them to also identify the URL for the Web page.

   - To sell or purchase a product or service
   - For entertainment
   - To index or reference other Internet resources (search engines)
   - To gather information
   - To take a class

   b. Ask five people who access the Internet from home who they use as their ISP, then write down the names.

2. **Using Hyperlink Fields.**

   a. Open the Machinery-J database, then open the Products table in Design view.

   b. Add a new field named "HomePage" with a Hyperlink Data Type.

   c. Save the Products table, open it in Datasheet view, then enter the following home page URLs into the new field for the first six records:

   > 1) www.toro.com
   > 2) www.caseih.com
   > 3) www.snapper.com
   > 4) www.deere.com
   > 5) www.troybilt.com
   > 6) www.stihl.com

   d. Click the link for www.deere.com and print the first page. If you are not already connected to the Internet, your dialer may appear, prompting you to connect with your chosen ISP. Once connected to your ISP, the John Deere home page should appear.

3. **Creating Pages for Interactive Reporting.**

   a. Click Pages on the Objects bar and double-click Create data access page by using wizard.

   b. Select the ProductName and the ReorderLevel fields from the Products table, then select the TransactionDate and UnitPrice fields from the Inventory Transactions table.

   c. Group the fields by ProductName, and sort in ascending order by TransactionDate.

   d. Type "Product Activity" for the page title, then open the new page in Page view.

   e. Open the Design view, maximize the Design view window, click in the title text area of the body of the Page and type the title "*Your Name's* Garden Shop Orders".

   f. Click the Page View button, click the Product Name text box, sort the ProductName in descending order, expand the ProductName group, then navigate to the 7/1/99 TransactionDate record within the Weed Wacker ProductName and print the page.

   g. Save the HTML file as "Garden Orders" on your Project Disk, then close the page.

4. **Creating Pages for Data Entry.**

   a. Click Pages on the Objects bar, then double-click Create data access page by using the wizard.

   b. Select all of the fields in the Products table.

   c. Do not add any grouping levels, but sort the records in ascending order on ProductName.

   d. Title the page "Product Update Page".

   e. In Design view, click in the title text area of the body of the page and type the title "Your Name's Products".

   f. Save the HTML file as "Products" on your Project Disk, then open Products.htm within Internet Explorer.

   g. Find and change the price of the "Mulcher" from $69.50 to $79.50 by changing the 6 to a 7, then print the Web page within Internet Explorer in which you made this change.

   h. Navigate to the next record within IE, then back to the Mulcher record to make sure that the price change was saved. Close IE.

   i. Open the Products table in the Machinery-J database, and make sure the Mulcher record now displays $79.50 as the Unit Price.

   j. Close the Products table within the Machinery-J database and the Products Web page within IE.

5. **Creating Pages for Data Analysis.**

   a. Click Pages on the Objects bar, then double-click Create data access page in Design view.

   b. Open the Field list window if necessary, then click the Expand button to the left of the Queries folder.

   c. Drag the Products Query to the upper-left corner of the Section: Unbound control, click the PivotTable List option button, then click OK.

   d. Click the PivotTable control to select it, right-click the ProductName field in the PivotTable control, then choose Move to Row Area.

e. Resize the control so that all three columns are clearly visible.

f. Click in the title text area of the body of the page and type the title "*Your Name's* Units Ordered Page", then display the page in Page view.

g. Use the TransactionDate list arrow to select only the 7/1/99 dates, then print the page.

h. Save the HTML file as Units Ordered to your Project Disk.

6. **Working in Page Design view.**

a. Open the Products page in Design view, then modify all of the labels in the first column so that a space exists between the descriptive words (e.g., change "ProductName" to "Product Name"). (*Hint*: Change these labels by clicking them once to select them, then clicking them again to edit them, just as you would the label control of any form or report.)

b. Click and drag across "*Your Name's* Products" in the body. Format the text to a bright blue, Britannic Bold font. (*Hint*: Use the Formatting (Page) toolbar just as you would when you format a control for any form or report.)

c. Save the changes.

7. **Inserting Hyperlinks to other Pages.**

a. Open the Products page in Design view, use the Hyperlink button on the toolbox to add a hyperlink control named "Units ordered" above the upper-left corner of the Header: Products section. Create the hyperlink so that it opens the Units Ordered page.

b. Save the Products page and close it.

c. Open the Units Ordered page in Design view, then add a hyperlink control named "Products" that opens the Products page above the upper-left corner of the Section: Unbound control.

d. Save the Units Ordered page and close it.

e. Open the Units Ordered Web page in IE, then click the Products hyperlink to make sure it works.

f. From the opened Products Web page, click the Units Ordered hyperlink to make sure it works.

g. Print the Units Ordered Web page within IE, close IE, and close the Machinery-J database.

8. **Publishing Web Pages to Web Servers.**

a. Call your ISP and ask for information about the requirements to publish Web pages to their Web server. (If you are not currently connected to the Internet from home, research any ISP of your choice.)

b. If your ISP does not allow members to publish Web pages, continue researching ISPs until you find one that allows members to publish Web pages.

c. Print the documentation on how to publish Web pages to the ISP's Web server.

d. Open IE and type "www.geocities.com" in the Address list box. Follow the links on the Web page to determine how to create your own Web page at the geocities Web site, then print the documentation.

▶ Independent Challenges

1. As the manager of a college women's basketball team, you wish to enhance the Basketball-J database to include hyperlink field entries for opponents. You also wish to develop several Web pages to report information on player statistics. To complete this independent challenge:

a. Start Access and open the database Basketball-J from your Project Disk.

b. Open the Games table in Design view, then add a field named "Web Site" with a Hyperlink Data Type.

c. Save the Games table, then open it in Datasheet view.

d. For the second record, enter www.creighton.edu in the Web Site field.

e. For the fifth record, enter www.drake.edu in the Web Site field.

f. Click the www.drake.edu link to display the Web page for Drake University, then print the first page.

g. Close the Drake Web page, save and close the Games table, click Pages on the Objects bar, then double-click Create data access page by using wizard.

h. Add all of the fields in the Players Query, group by Last, do not specify any sort fields, and title the page "Player Stats".

i. In Design view, change the label "GroupofPlayersQuery-Last" to "Last".

j. In Design view, click in the title text area of the body of the page and type the title "Iowa State Women's Basketball". Include your initials in the title if you have to identify your name on the printed solution.

k. Save the HTML file as "Player Stats" on your Project Disk, then close the Player Stats DAP in Access.

l. Open the Player Stats HTML file in Internet Explorer, navigate to the player whose last name is Freesen.

m. Click the Expand button to display all of sort the records within the last name of Freesen, sort in descending order on the date, then print that record.

n. Close the Basketball-J database and exit Access.

o. Exit Internet Explorer.

2. As the manager of a college women's basketball team, you wish to enhance the Basketball-J database by developing a Web page to enter new game information.

To complete this independent challenge:

a. Start Access and open the database Basketball-J from your Project Disk.

b. Click Pages on the Objects bar, then double-click Create data access page by using the wizard.

c. Add all of the fields from the Games table, do not add any grouping levels, sort the records in ascending order by Date, and accept Games as the title for the page.

d. In Design view, click in the title text area of the body of the Page and type the title "ISU Games". Include Your Initials in the title if you have to identify your name on the printed solution.

e. Save the HTML file as "Games" to your Project Disk, then open the Games HTML file in IE.

f. Enter the following new record as record 23:

Date:	3/1/01
GameNo:	(No entry required, this is an AutoNumber field. You will not see the AutoNumber entry until you move to a new record, then return to this one.)
Opponent:	State Univ NY-Binghamton
Mascot:	Colonials
Home-Away:	H
Home Score:	100
Opponent Score:	52
Web Site:	www.binghamton.edu

g. Navigate to the first record, then back to the last. (*Note*: The AutoNumber entry for the new record, 23, is automatically entered.)

h. Print this new record, then close IE.

i. Check the Games table to verify the entry in the Basketball-J database.

j. Close the Basketball-J database and exit Access.

3. As the manager of a college women's basketball team, you wish to enhance the Basketball-J database by developing a Web page to display player statistical information as a pivot table.

To complete this independent challenge:

a. Start Access and open the database Basketball-J from your Project Disk.

b. Click Pages on the Objects toolbar, then double-click Create data access page in Design view.

c. Expand the Queries folder in the Field List, then drag the Players Query to the upper-left corner of the Section: Unbound control.

d. Choose the PivotTable List option, then close the Field list.

e. Widen the pivot table control so that all of the seven fields are clearly displayed.

f. Click in the title text area of the body of the Page and type the title "Game Stats". Include your initials in the title if you have to identify your name on the printed solution.

g. Select the pivot table control, right-click the Opponent field, then choose Move to Row Area.

h. Save the HTML file as "Game Stats" to your Project Disk, then close the Game Stats page within Access.

i. Open the Game Stats HTML file within Internet Explorer, click the Last list arrow in the pivot table, click the Show all check box (to clear it), then click the Freesen check box to display only Sydney Freesen's statistics.

j. Print this Web page showing Sydney Freesen's statistics, then close Internet Explorer.

k. Close the Basketball-J database and exit Access.

4. MediaLoft has developed a Web site that provides internal information to their employees. In this independent challenge, you'll find information posted to the Web site from potential new instructors (independent contractors), then enter those records into the Training-J database.

a. Open the Training-J database, click Pages on the Objects bar, then use the Page Wizard to create a new data access page based on all of the fields in the Instructors table.

b. Do not use any grouping levels or sort fields, and title the page "HR Instructors".

c. Save the HTML file as "HR Instructors" to your Project Disk, then open it in Internet Explorer.

d. In a separate IE window, connect to the Internet, then go to the MediaLoft intranet site at http://www.course.com/illustrated/MediaLoft

e. Click the link for Training, then click the link for New HR Instructors.

f. Print this Web page, then close this IE window.

g. Open the IE window that displays the HR Instructors HTML file you created, then enter the four new instructors in the Web page. (*Hint*: The InstructorID field is an AutoNumber field, so you will not type in it.)

h. Add yourself as the ninth new instructor, with a hire date of 11/1/00.

i. Close all IE windows, then return to the Training-J Access database and open the Instructors table.

j. Print the Instructors datasheet, then close the Training-J database and exit Access.

Access 2000

▶ Visual Workshop

As the manager of a college women's basketball team, you wish to enhance the Basketball-J database by developing a Web page to display player scoring information as a pivot table. Figure J-20 shows the data access page, called ISU Scoring, that you need to create. Develop the page in Design view, use the Scoring query as a pivot table control. You will have to move the Home-Away field and the Last field to the Row Area. Include your initials in the title text area. Save the HTML file with the name "Scoring" to your Project Disk. View and print the page in IE. Close all open applications.

FIGURE J-20

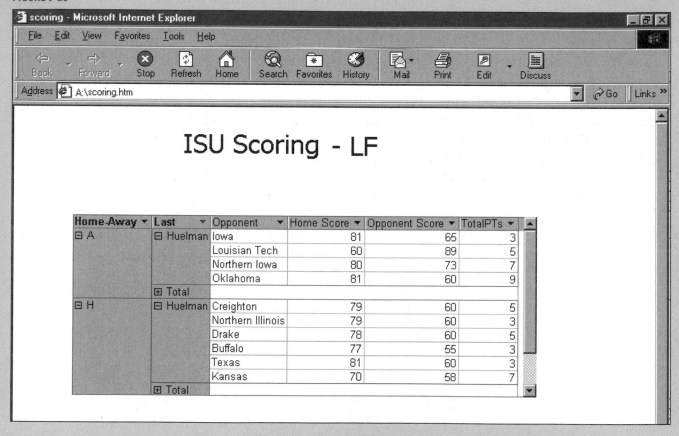

Creating
Advanced Queries

Objectives

- MOUS ▶ **Query for Top Values**
- MOUS ▶ **Create an Advanced Parameter Query**
- MOUS ▶ **Modify Query Properties**
- MOUS ▶ **Create an Update Query**
- MOUS ▶ **Create a Make-Table Query**
- MOUS ▶ **Create an Append Query**
- MOUS ▶ **Create a Delete Query**
- MOUS ▶ **Specify Join Properties**

Queries are database objects that answer questions about the data. The most common query is the **select query**, which displays fields and records that match specific criteria into a single datasheet. Other types of queries, such as top value, parameter, and action queries, are powerful tools for displaying, analyzing, and updating data. An **action query** is one that makes changes to the data. There are four types of action queries: delete, update, append, and make-table. ✎ David Dumont, director of training at MediaLoft, has become very familiar with the capabilities of Access. Users come to David with extensive data-analysis and data-update requests, confident that he can provide the information they need. David uses powerful query features and new query types to handle these requirements.

Querying for Top Values

Once a large number of records are entered into a table of a database, it is less common to query for all of the records, and more common to list only the most significant records by choosing a subset of the highest or lowest values from a sorted query. The **Top Values** feature within the Query Design view allows you to respond to these types of requests. ➤ Employee attendance at MediaLoft classes has grown. To help plan future classes, David wants to print a datasheet listing the names of the top five classes, sorted by number of students per class. David creates a summarized select query to find the total number of attendees for each class, then uses the Top Values feature to find the five most attended classes.

Steps

1. Start Access, open the **Training-K** database, click **Queries** on the Objects bar, click the **New button** in the database window, click **Design View**, then click **OK**
   You need fields from both the Attendance and Courses tables.

2. Double-click **Attendance**, double-click **Courses**, then click **Close** in the Show Table dialog box
   Query Design view now displays two related tables in the upper portion of the screen.

3. Double-click **LogNo** in the Attendance table, then double-click **Description** in the Courses table
   You want to count the LogNo entries for each course Description.

QuickTip

Click the Datasheet View button at any time during the query design development process to view the resulting datasheet.

4. Click the **Totals button** Σ on the Query Design toolbar, click **Group By** for the LogNo field, click the **Group By list arrow**, then click **Count**
   You identified the fields and summarized the records by counting the LogNo entries for each Description. Your screen should look like Figure K-1. Sorting determines which records will be on "top."

5. Click the **LogNo field Sort cell**, click the **LogNo field Sort list arrow**, then click **Descending**
   A descending order will put the courses most attended by MediaLoft employees, those with the highest count, at the top.

6. Click the **Top Values list arrow** [All ▼] on the Query Design toolbar
   The Top Values feature is used to display a subset of the records. You can select a number or percentage from the list or enter a specific value or percentage. See Table K-1 for more information on how to use the Top Values feature.

7. Click **5**, then click the **Datasheet View button** on the Query Design toolbar
   Your screen should look like Figure K-2. The Introduction to Access course and the Computer Fundamentals course both had 19 attendees. If more than one course had 14 attendees (a summarized value of 14 in the CountOfLogNo field), then all courses that "tied" for fifth place would have been displayed too.

8. Click the **Save button** on the Query Datasheet toolbar, type **Top 5 Courses**, click **OK**, then close the datasheet
   The Top 5 Courses query appears as a query object in the database window.

FIGURE K-1: Designing a summary query for top values

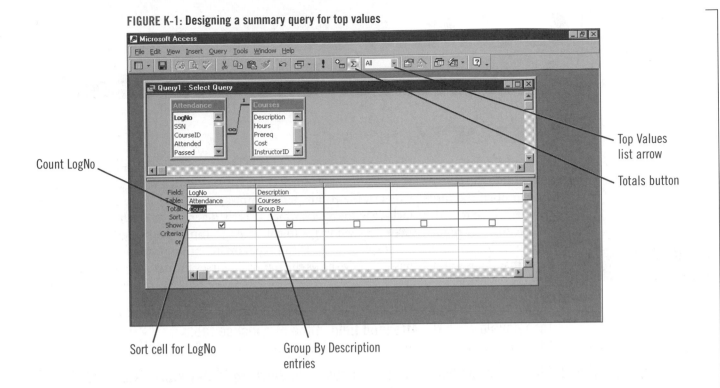

Count LogNo

Top Values list arrow

Totals button

Sort cell for LogNo

Group By Description entries

FIGURE K-2: Top Values datasheet

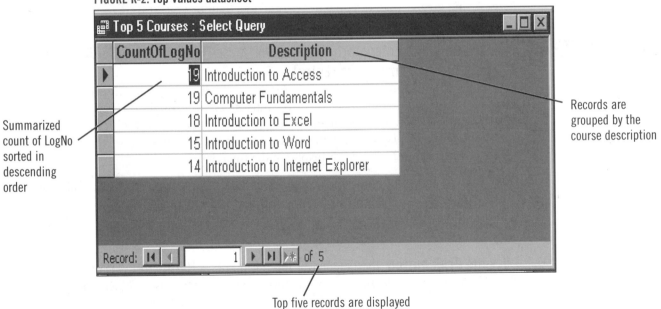

Summarized count of LogNo sorted in descending order

Records are grouped by the course description

Top five records are displayed

TABLE K-1: Top Values options

action	to display
Click 5, or 25, or 100 from the Top Values list	Top 5, 25, or 100 records
Enter a number such as 10 in the Top Values text box	Top 10 (in this case) records
Click 5% or 25% from the Top Values list	Top 5 or 25 percent of records
Enter a percentage, such as 10%, in the Top Values text box	Top 10 percent (in this case) of records

Creating an Advanced Parameter Query

A **parameter query** displays a dialog box prompting you for information to enter as limiting criteria each time the query runs. You can build a form or report based on a parameter query, too. When you open the form or report, the parameter prompt appears. The entry in the prompt determines which records to include in the query, which in turn, determines which records to display in the form or report. ➤ David wants to enhance the Top 5 Courses query to display the top five courses within a specific date range. He adds parameter prompts to the Top 5 Courses query so that the resulting datasheet only shows the top five courses for the dates he specifies.

Steps 1 2 3 4

1. Click the **Top 5 Courses query**, click the **Design button** 🗎 in the database window, then double-click the **Attended field** in the Attendance table
   The Attended field contains the date that the course was taken.

2. Click the **Attended field Criteria cell**, type **Between [Enter start date:] And [Enter end date:]**, then click the **Datasheet View button** 🖩
   Your screen should look like Figure K-3. Parameter criteria must be entered within [square brackets]. The **Between ... And** operator will help you find all records on or between two dates. Using greater than or equal to, >=, and less than or equal to, <=, operators works in the same way.

3. Type **1/1/00** in the Enter start date text box, press **[Enter]**, type **6/30/00** in the Enter end date text box, then press **[Enter]**
   Your screen should look like Figure K-4. The datasheet displays the top five courses attended between 1/1/00 and 6/30/00. Because three courses tied for fifth place, seven records are displayed instead of five. You can enter as many parameter criteria entries in as many fields as you wish. Access displays the parameter prompts one at a time, and uses the entries you've made to determine which records belong in the final datasheet.

4. Click **File** on the menu bar, click **Save As**, click to the left of the word **"Courses"** in the text box, type **– Parameter – Your Initials**, then click **OK**
   Because the object name always appears in the header of a datasheet printout, descriptive query names can help identify the information or creator of the information.

5. Click the **Print button**, then close the Top 5 Courses – Parameter – Your Initials query
   The Top 5 Courses – Parameter – Your Initials query appears as an object in the database window.

FIGURE K-3: A parameter prompt

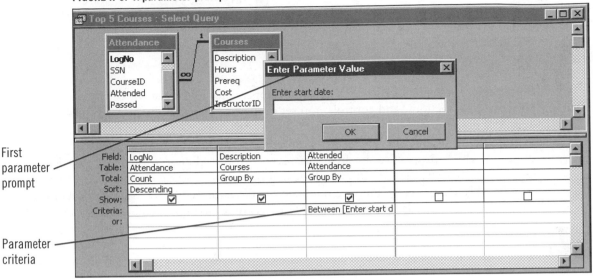

First parameter prompt

Parameter criteria

FIGURE K-4: Top 5 Courses – Parameter query

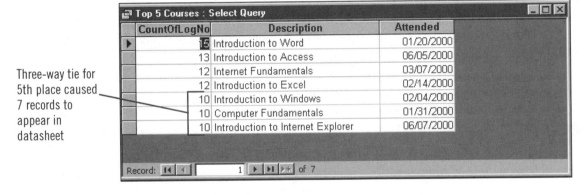

Three-way tie for 5th place caused 7 records to appear in datasheet

CLUES TO USE

Concatenating a parameter prompt to a wildcard character

You can concatenate parameter prompts with a wildcard character such as the asterisk (*) to create more flexible queries. For example, the entry: LIKE [Enter the first character of the company name:] & "*" placed in the Criteria cell of the Company field searches for companies that begin with a specified letter. The entry: LIKE "*" & [Enter any character(s) to search by:] & "*" placed in the Criteria cell of the Company field searches for words that contain the specified characters anywhere in the field. The ampersand (&) is used to concatenate items in an expression and double quotation marks (" ") are used to surround text criteria.

Modifying Query Properties

Properties are characteristics that define the appearance and behavior of the database itself; objects, fields, sections, and controls. You set properties by using the **property sheet** for that item. The property sheet can be displayed in many ways, such as right-clicking the item you wish to examine or modify, and then clicking Properties. The title bar of the property sheet always indicates which properties are being displayed. If you change a field's properties within Query Design view, they are modified for that query only. If you change a field's properties within Table Design view, they are modified for the entire database. ◄▬▬▬ David uses the query and field properties of the Department Charges query to improve the datasheet's appearance.

Steps 1234

1. Right-click the **Department Charges** query, then click **Properties**

   The Department Charges Properties dialog box opens, providing information about the query and also allowing you to enter a description for the query.

   QuickTip

   Click the column headings to sort the objects in ascending or descending order.

2. Type **Lists the department, description, hours, and cost**, click **OK**, click the **Details button** ▦ in the Training-K database window, then maximize the database window

   Five columns of information about each query object appear, as shown in Figure K-5. The Description property entry appears in the Description column.

3. Click the **Design button** ◩ on the database toolbar, right-click to the right of the Employees table, click **Properties**, click the **Recordset Type text box**, click the **Recordset Type list arrow**, then click **Snapshot**

   Your screen should look like Figure K-6. Viewing the query property sheet from within Query Design view gives a complete list of the query's properties. The Snapshot property makes the Recordset not updateable.

   Trouble?

   Separate the new field name from the calculated expression with a colon (:) and be sure to surround field names in [square brackets].

4. Close the **Query Properties dialog box**, click the **blank Field cell** in the **fifth** column, type **PerHour:[Cost]/[Hours]**, then click the **Datasheet View button** ▦

   The datasheet appears with the cost per hour calculated in the fifth column, but the calculated values are hard to read because they are unformatted.

   Trouble?

   The title bar of the property sheet should say "Field Properties." If it doesn't, close the dialog box and try again.

5. Click the **Design View button** ◩, right-click the **PerHour field**, then click **Properties**

   The Field Properties dialog box allows you to change field properties within this query. When you start making an entry in a property, a short description of the property appears in the status bar.

6. Click **Format text box**, click the **Format list arrow**, click **Currency**, click the **Decimal Places text box**, click the **Decimal Places list arrow**, click **2**, click the **Caption property text box**, then type **Cost Per Hour**

   Your screen should look like Figure K-7.

7. Close the property sheet, click the ▦ on the Query Design toolbar, type **Video** in the Department field for the first record to view the message in the status bar

   The message "This recordset is not updateable" appears because the query Recordset Type property was set to "Snapshot," which allows you to view the records but not update them. The caption and formatting properties of the calculated field clarify the information.

8. Save and close the Department Charges query

FIGURE K-5: Details

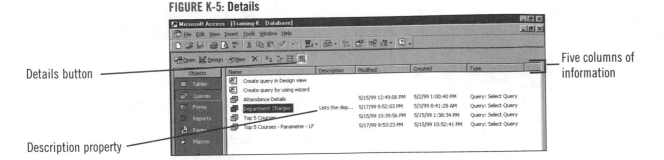

Details button

Description property

Five columns of information

FIGURE K-6: Query property sheet

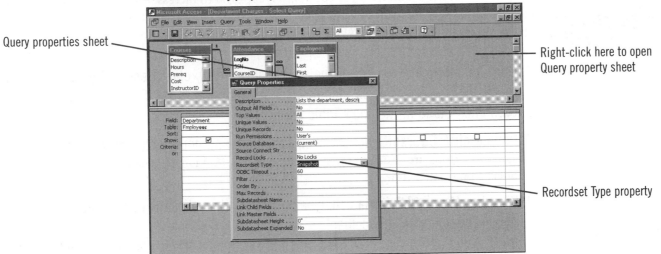

Query properties sheet

Right-click here to open Query property sheet

Recordset Type property

FIGURE K-7: Field property sheet

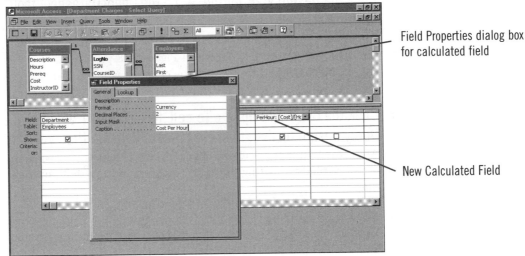

Field Properties dialog box for calculated field

New Calculated Field

CLUES TO USE

Optimizing queries using indexes and SQL

Indexes are used to speed up queries that are often sorted or grouped. For example, if you commonly sort by a LastName field, setting the **Indexed property** to Yes would improve the performance of any query that also sorted or grouped by the LastName field. You can only set the Indexed property of a field in Table Design view, but if you know **SQL** (Structured Query Language) you can create an index on a field within a query. SQL is a national standard database language for querying a wide range of relational database products. If you want to query an Access database in a manner that is beyond the capabilities of the Query Design view, knowledge of SQL is required. To access the SQL statements for any query, click the Datasheet View list arrow ▦▾ and choose SQL View. To add an index, use the SQL CREATE INDEX statement.

Creating an Update Query

An **action query** makes changes to the data of many records. There are four types of action queries: delete, update, append, and make-table. See Table K-2 for more information on action queries. An **update query** is a type of action query that makes a change to the data of the tables. For example, you may wish to increase the price of a product in a particular category by 5% or change an area code with one operation. ➡ The Training Department upgraded their equipment on June 1, and David has been given approval to increase by 5% the internal cost of all courses provided after that date to cover the upgrade expense. He creates an update query to change the data in the tables to reflect the cost increase.

Steps

1. Click the **New button** 📇 on the database window, click **Design View** in the New Query dialog box, click **OK**, double-click **Attendance** in the Show Table dialog box, then click **Close** in the Show Table dialog box

2. Double-click **CourseID**, double-click **Attended**, and double-click **Cost**
   The three fields are added to the query design grid. You have to change only those courses offered on or after June 1.

3. Click the **Attended Criteria cell**, type **>=6/1/00**, then click the **Datasheet View button** 📇 on the Query Design toolbar
   Every action query starts as a select query. Always look at the datasheet of the select query before initiating any action that will change data to make sure which records will be affected.

4. Click the **Design View button** 📐 on the Query Datasheet toolbar, click the **Query Type button list arrow** 📇▾ on the Query Design toolbar, then click **Update Query** 📇
   The Query Type button displays the Update Query icon and the Update To: row appears in the query design grid, as shown in Figure K-8. All action query icons include an exclamation point that indicates data will be changed when you click the Run button on the Query Design toolbar.

5. Click the **Cost field Update To cell**, type **[Cost]*1.05**, click the **Run button** 📇 on the Query Design toolbar, then click **Yes** to indicate that you want to update 41 rows
   Any time you run an action query, Access prompts you with an "Are you sure?" message before actually updating the data. The Undo button will not undo changes made by action queries.

6. Click 📇 on the Query Design toolbar
   Your screen should look like Figure K-9. The datasheet of an update query shows only the updated field.

7. Close the update query without saving the changes
   You rarely need to save an update query, because once the data has been updated, you don't need the query object anymore. Also, if you double-click an action query of any type from the database window, you run the query. Therefore, don't save any queries that you won't need again, especially action queries.

FIGURE K-8: Creating an update query

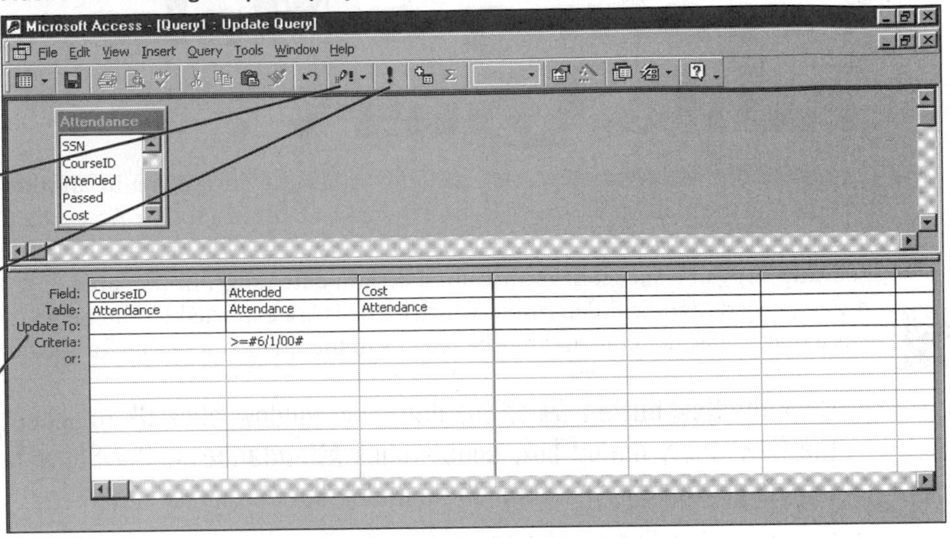

Update Query chosen

Run button

Update To: row

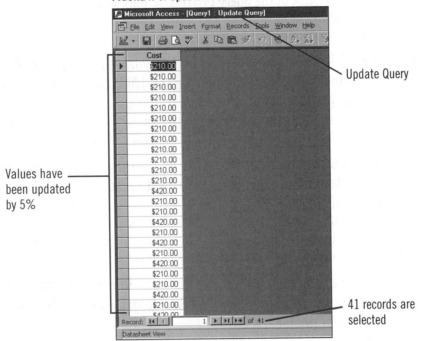

FIGURE K-9: Updated cost fields

Update Query

Values have been updated by 5%

41 records are selected

TABLE K-2: Action queries

type of action query	query icon	description	example
Delete		Deletes a group of records from one or more tables	Remove products that are discontinued or for which there are no orders
Update		Makes global changes to a group of records in one or more tables	Raise prices by 10 percent for all products
Append		Adds a group of records from one or more tables to the end of a table	Merge the product table from a business you just acquired to the existing product table for the company
Make-Table		Creates a new table from all or part of the data in one or more tables	Export records to another Access database, make a backup copy of a table, or create reports that display data from a specified point in time

Creating a Make-Table Query

A **make-table query** creates a new table in either the current or in another Access database. When using the make-table query feature to make a table in another Access database, it works like an export feature. Sometimes the make-table query is used to create a backup copy of a table or a backup copy of a subset of records for a certain date range. In the latter case, date criteria used in the query design grid determine which records are exported to the new table. ➤ David uses a make-table query to archive the records in the Attendance table for the first quarter of 2000.

Steps

1. Click the **New button** 📠 on the database window, click **OK** to accept Design View in the New Query dialog box, double-click **Attendance** in the Show Table dialog box, then click **Close** in the Show Table dialog box

2. Double-click the *** (asterisk)** at the top of the Attendance table's field list
   Putting the asterisk in the query design grid puts all of the fields in that table in the grid. Later, if fields are added to this table, they also will be automatically added to this query because of the asterisk.

3. Double-click the **Attended field** to add it to the second column of the query grid, click the **Attended field Criteria cell**, type **<4/1/00**, then click the **Attended field Show check box** to uncheck it
   Your screen should look like Figure K-10. Before changing this select query into a make-table query, it is always a good idea to view the datasheet.

4. Click the **Datasheet View button** 📰 on the Query Design toolbar, click any entry in the **Attended field**, then click the **Sort Descending button** 📉 on the Query Datasheet toolbar
   The descending sort on the Attended field allows you to check that no records on or after 4/1/00 are present in the datasheet. (*Note*: None of the cost values for these records were updated because the previous update query affected courses on or after 6/1/00.)

5. Click the **Design View button** 📐, click the **Query Type list arrow** 🔽, click the **Make-Table Query button** 🔳, type **First Quarter 2000 Attendance Log** in the Table Name text box, then click **OK**
   Your screen should look like Figure K-11. The Query Type button displays the Make Table icon. The make-table query is ready to be run, but the new table has not yet been created. Action queries do not delete, update, append, or make data until you click the Run button.

6. Click the **Run button** ❗ on the Query Design toolbar, click **Yes** when prompted that you are about to paste 102 records, then close but do not save the query
   Make-table queries are rarely saved unless you intend to use them again.

7. Click **Tables** on the Objects bar, then double-click **First Quarter 2000 Attendance Log** to view the new table's datasheet
   All 102 records were pasted into the new table, as shown in Figure K-12. Field properties such as the input mask for the SSN field and the check box display for the Passed field were not duplicated, but you could modify the Design view of this table to change the appearance of the fields just like you could for any other table. (*Note*: -1 is sometimes used to designate "yes" and 0 is used to designate "no" in a Yes/No field).

8. Close the First Quarter 2000 Attendance Log table

FIGURE K-10: Using the asterisk in a query grid

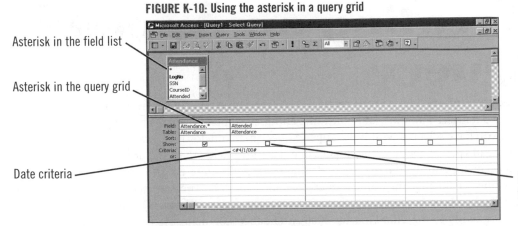

Asterisk in the field list

Asterisk in the query grid

Date criteria

Field will not display in the resulting datasheet

FIGURE K-11: Creating a make-table query

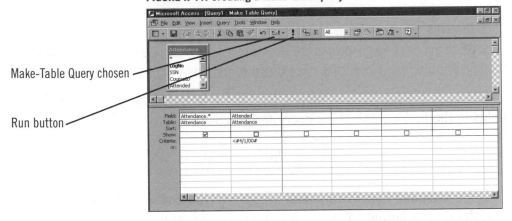

Make-Table Query chosen

Run button

FIGURE K-12: First Half 2000 Attendance Log datasheet

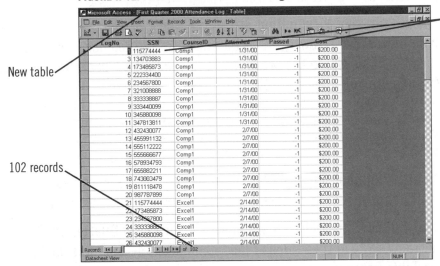

Field properties were not duplicated

New table

102 records

Resolving Year 2000 Issues

If you type only two digits of a date, Access assumes that the digits 00 through 29 are for the years 2000 through 2029. If you type 30 through 99, Access assumes the years refer to 1930 through 1999. If you want years outside these ranges, you must type all four digits of the year or customize the way two-digit date entries are interpreted by using the Microsoft Office 2000 Resource Kit. If you want Access to display all dates with four digits, regardless of how they are entered, click the "Use four-digit year formatting" check box found on the General tab of the Options dialog box. Click the Tools menu item, then click Options to open the Options dialog box.

Creating an Append Query

An **append query** adds a group of records to an existing table in either the current or in another Access database. The most difficult thing about an append query is making sure that all of the fields you have selected within the append query match fields in the target table where you wish to append (paste) them. If the target table has more fields than the append query, the append query will append the data in the matching fields and ignore the other fields. If the target table is lacking a field that the append query contains, an error message will appear indicating that there is an unknown field name that will cancel the action. ✦ David would like to append April's records to the First Quarter 2000 Attendance Log table. He uses an append query to do this, then he renames the table to accurately reflect its contents.

Steps 1 2 3 4

1. Click **Queries** 🔳 on the Objects bar, click the **New button** 🔳 on the database window, click **OK** to accept Design view in the New Query dialog box, double-click **Attendance** in the Show Table dialog box, then click **Close** in the Show Table dialog box

2. Double-click the **Attendance table's field list title bar**, then drag the **highlighted fields** to the first column of the query design grid
   Double-clicking the title bar of the field list highlights all of the fields, so you were able to add all the fields to the query grid quickly. An append query does not allow the same field to be referenced twice, even if the show check box is cleared for one occurrence of the field.

3. Click the **Attended field Criteria cell**, type **>=4/1/00 and <=4/30/00**, then click the **Datasheet View button** 🔳 on the Query Design toolbar
   There should be 29 records with an April date in the Attended field.

4. Click the **Design View button** 🔳 on the Query Datasheet toolbar, click the **Query Type button list arrow** 🔳▾ on the Query Design toolbar, click **Append Query** 🔳, click the **Table Name list arrow** in the Append dialog box, click **First Quarter 2000 Attendance Log**, then click **OK**
   Your screen should look like Figure K-13. The Query Type button displays the Append Query icon, and the Append To row was added to the query design grid. You would use the Append To row to choose fields in the target table if they were different than the query fields. The append action is ready to be initiated by clicking the Run button.

5. Click the **Run button** 🔳 on the Query Design toolbar, click **Yes** to indicate that you want to append 29 rows, then close the query without saving the changes

6. Click **Tables** on the Objects bar, double-click the **First Quarter 2000 Attendance Log**, click any entry in the Attended field, then click the **Sort Descending button** 🔳 on the Table Datasheet toolbar
   The April records were appended to the table for a total of 131 records, as shown in Figure K-14.

7. Close the First Quarter 2000 Attendance Log without saving changes, right-click **First Quarter 2000 Attendance Log** in the database window, click **Rename**, type **Jan-April 2000 Log**, then press **[Enter]**
   The backup table with attendance records from January through April 2000 has been renamed.

FIGURE K-13: Creating an append query

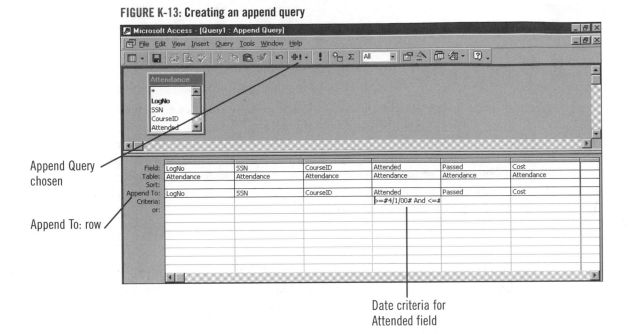

Append Query chosen

Append To: row

Date criteria for Attended field

FIGURE K-14: Updated table with appended records

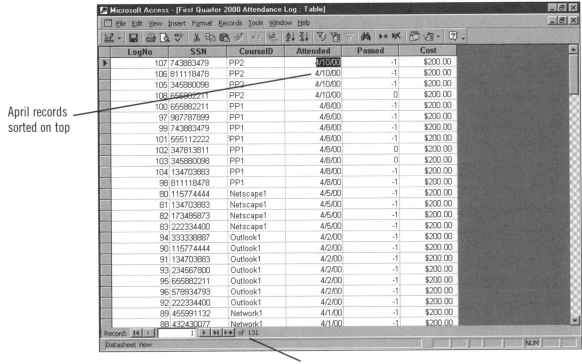

April records sorted on top

131 records

Creating a Delete Query

A **delete query** deletes a group of records from one or more tables as defined by a query. Delete queries always delete entire records, and not just selected fields within records, so they should be used carefully. Since the delete query destroys records without the ability to undo the action, it is wise to always have a current backup of the database before running any action query, especially the delete query. ◄━━━ Now that David has the first four months of attendance records archived in the Jan-April 2000 Log table, he wishes to delete them from the Attendance table. He uses a delete query to accomplish this task.

Steps 1 2 3 4

1. Click **Queries** on the Objects bar, click the **New button** 📖 on the database window, click **OK** to accept Design view in the New Query dialog box, double-click **Attendance** in the Show Table dialog box, then click **Close** in the Show Table dialog box

2. Double-click the *** (asterisk)** at the top of the Attendance table's field list, then double-click the **Attended** field
   All the fields from the Attendance table are added to the first column of the query design grid, and the Attended field is added to the second column of the query design grid.

3. Click the **Attended field Criteria cell**, type **<=4/30/00**, then press **[Enter]**
   It is important to check the datasheet to make sure that you have selected the same 131 records that are in the Jan-April 2000 Log table.

4. Click the **Datasheet View button** 📖 on the Query Design toolbar to confirm that there are 131 records in the datasheet, click the **Design View button** 📖 on the Query Datasheet toolbar, click the **Query Type button list arrow** 📖▾, then click **Delete Query** ✕!
   Your screen should look like Figure K-15. The Query Type button displays the Delete Query icon, and the Delete row was added to the query design grid. The delete action is ready to be initiated by clicking the Run button.

5. Click the **Run button** ❗ on the Query Design toolbar, click **Yes** to confirm that you want to delete 131 rows, then close the query without saving the changes.

6. Click **Tables** on the Objects bar, double-click **Attendance**, click **any entry in the Attended field**, then click the **Sort Ascending button** 📖 on the Table Datasheet toolbar
   The oldest records should start in the month of May, as shown in Figure K-16. All prior records were deleted by the delete query.

7. Save and close the Attendance table datasheet

FIGURE K-15: Creating a delete query

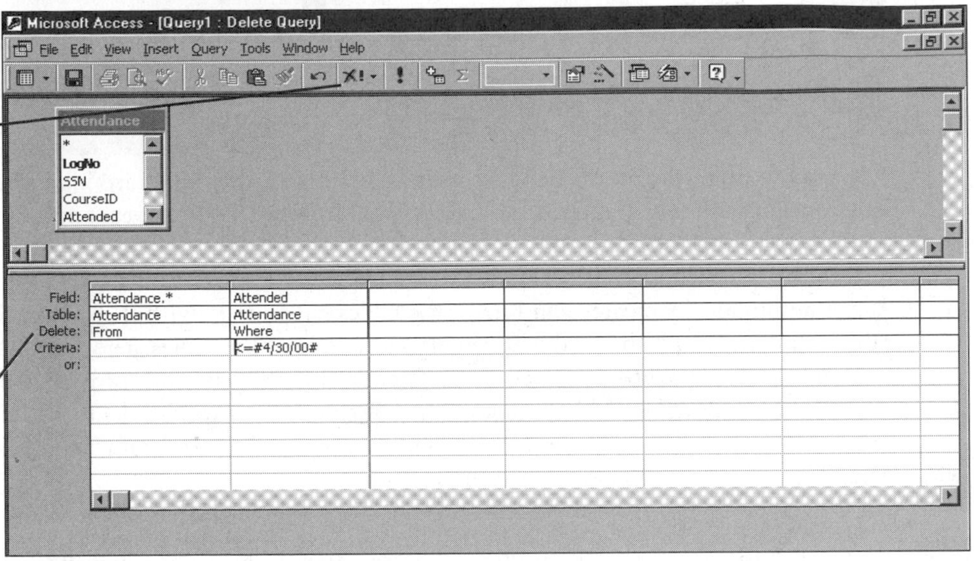

Delete Query chosen

Delete: row

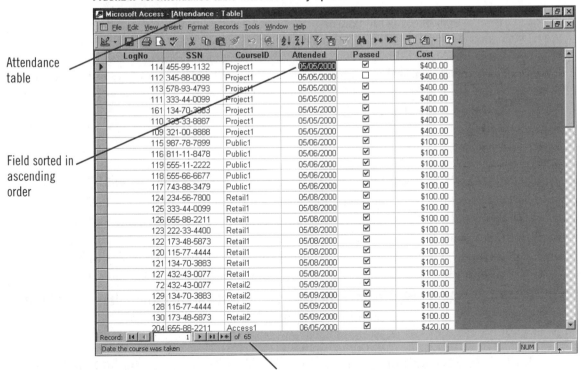

FIGURE K-16: Attendance table without January-April records

Attendance table

Field sorted in ascending order

65 records remain

Specifying Join Properties

When more than one table's field list is used in a query, the tables are joined as defined in the Relationships window. If referential integrity was enforced, a "1" appears next to the table whose field serves as the "one" side of the one-to-many relationship, and an infinity sign (∞) appears next to the table whose field serves as the "many" side. If no relationships have been established, Access automatically creates join lines if the tables have a field with the same name and comparable data type, and if the field is a primary key in one of the tables. The "one" and "many" symbols do not appear, however, because referential integrity is not enforced. You can edit this relationship by double-clicking the join line. ✈ David would like to create a query to find out which courses have never been attended. He modifies the join properties between the Attendance and Courses table to get this answer.

Steps

QuickTip

Right-click a blank spot in the upper portion of the query design grid, then click Relationships to quickly open the Relationships window.

Trouble?

Double-click the middle portion of the join line, not the "one" or "many" symbols.

1. Click **Queries** on the Object bar, click the **New button** 🔲, click **OK** to accept Design view, double-click **Courses**, double-click **Attendance**, then click **Close**

   Because the Courses and Attendance tables already have a one-to-many relationship with referential integrity enforced in the Relationships window, the join line appears, linking the two tables using the CourseID field common to both.

2. Double-click the **one-to-many join line** between the field lists

   The Join Properties dialog box opens, as shown in Figure K-17, showing which tables and fields participate in the join. The lower half of the dialog box shows that, by default, option 1 is chosen, which specifies that the query will display only records where joined fields from *both* tables are equal. That means that if any courses exist in which there was no matching attendance record, those courses would not appear in the resulting datasheet.

3. Click the option **2 option button**

   By choosing option 2, you are specifying that you wish to see all of the records in the Courses table, regardless of whether there are any matching records in the Attendance table. Because referential integrity is enforced, option 3 would be the same as option 1, because referential integrity makes it impossible to enter records in the Attendance table that do not have a corresponding record in the Courses table.

4. Click **OK**

   The join line's appearance changes as shown in Figure K-18.

5. Double-click **CourseID** from the Courses field list, double-click **Description** from the Courses field list, double-click **Attended** from the Attendance field list, double-click **Cost** from the Attendance field list, then click the **Datasheet View button** 🔲

   All courses are listed in the datasheet. The ones with corresponding attendance records have an entry in the Attended and Cost fields. By using a filter, you can quickly display those with no entry in the Attended field to determine exactly which courses have not been attended.

6. Click the **Access2 Attended field** (it is null), then click the **Filter by Selection button** 🔽 on the Query Datasheet toolbar

   The 18 filtered records represent those courses as shown in Figure K-19.

7. Click the **Save button** 🔲 on the Query Datasheet toolbar, type **No Attendance Since 5/1/00 – Your Initials** in the Query Name text box, click **OK**, click the **Access2 Attended field**, click 🔽 (to refilter for null values), then click the **Print button** 🖨

8. Close the datasheet, then exit Access

FIGURE K-17: Join Properties dialog box

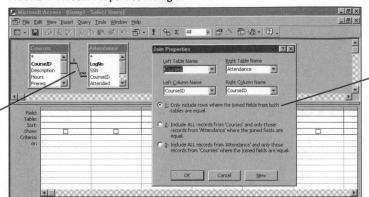

Double-click join line to open the Join Properties dialog box

Default join property

FIGURE K-18: The join line's appearance changes when its properties are changed

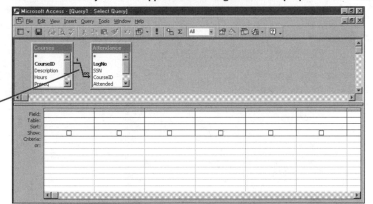

Join line's appearance shows that *all* records from the Courses table will be included in the datasheet

FIGURE K-19: Filtering for courses with no attendance records

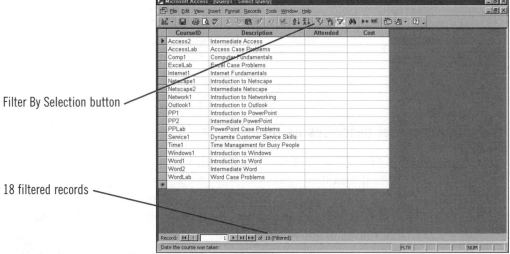

Filter By Selection button

18 filtered records

Reviewing referential integrity

Referential integrity between two tables may be established when tables are joined in the Relationships window, and it ensures that no orphaned records are entered or created in the database. An **orphan record** happens when information in the linking field of the "many" table doesn't have a matching entry in the linking field of the "one" table. For the Training-K database, for example, referential integrity ensures that CourseNo entries added to the Attendance table are first recorded in the Courses table. Also, referential integrity prevents the user from deleting a record from the Courses table if matching CourseNo entries are present in the Attendance table.

Practice

► Concepts Review

Identify each element of the form's Design view shown in Figure K-20.

FIGURE K-20

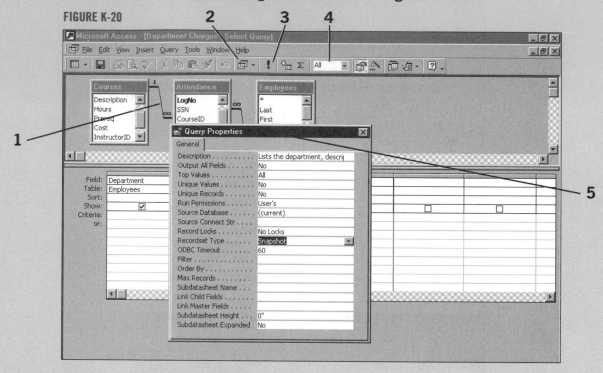

Match each term with the statement that describes its function.

6. Top values query
7. Select query
8. Action query
9. Properties
10. Snapshot
11. Parameter query

a. Displays a dialog box prompting you for information to enter as criteria
b. Makes changes to the data
c. Displays only the highest or lowest values from a sorted query
d. Displays fields and records that match specific criteria into a single datasheet
e. Makes the Recordset not updateable
f. Characteristics that define the appearance and behavior of almost everything within the database

Select the best answer from the list of choices.

12. **The entry for the Recordset Type query property that does not allow you to modify any of the data is**
    a. No Updates.
    b. Snapshot.
    c. Referential Integrity.
    d. Dynaset (No Nulls).

13. **Which of the following shows the proper way to enter parameter criteria in the query design grid?**
    a. >=(Type minimum value here:)
    b. >=Type minimum value here: }
    c. >=[Type minimum value here:]
    d. >=Type minimum value here:

14. **You cannot use the Top Values feature to:**
    a. Display a subset of records.
    b. Show the top 30 records.
    c. Update the top 10 records.
    d. Show the bottom 10 percent of records.

15. **Which of the following is not an action query?**
    a. Union query
    b. Delete query
    c. Make-table query
    d. Append query

16. **Which of the following precautions should you take before running a delete query?**
    a. Check the resulting datasheet to make sure the query selects the right records.
    b. Have a current backup of the database.
    c. Understand the relationships between the records you are about to delete in the database.
    d. All of the above

17. **When querying tables in a one-to-many relationship with referential integrity enforced, which records will appear (by default) on the resulting datasheet?**
    a. Only those with matching values in both tables
    b. All records from the "one" table, and only those with matching values from the "many" side
    c. All records from the "many" table, and only those with nonmatching values from the "one" side
    d. All records from both tables will appear at all times

▶ Skills Review

1. **Query for Top Values.**
    a. Start Access then open the Seminar-K database.
    b. Create a select query with the EventName field from the Events table and the RegistrationFee field from the Registration table.
    c. Add the RegistrationFee field a second time, then click the Totals button. In the Total row of the query grid, Group By the EventName field, Sum the first RegistrationFee field, and count the second Registration Fee field.
    d. Sort in descending order by the Summed RegistrationFee field.
    e. Enter 2 in the Top Values list box to display the top two seminars in the datasheet.
    f. Save the query as "Top 2 Seminars – Your Initials", view the resulting datasheet, print the datasheet, then close the datasheet.

2. Create an Advanced Parameter Query.

    a. Create a select query with the AttendeeLastName field from the Attendees table, and the EventName and Date fields from the Events table. (*Hint*: You'll need to add the Registration table to this query as well as join the Attendees and Events tables.)

    b. Add the parameter criteria "Between [Enter Start Date:] And [Enter End Date:]" in the Date field.

    c. Specify an ascending sort order on the Date field.

    d. Click the Datasheet View button, then enter "5/1/00" as the start date and "6/30/00" as the end date in order to find everyone who has attended a seminar in May or June of the year 2000. You should view 22 records.

    e. Save the query as "May and June Seminar Attendance – Your Initials", then print the datasheet.

3. Modify Query Properties.

    a. Open the "May and June Seminar Attendance – Your Initials" query in Design view, open the property sheet for the query, change the Recordset Type property to Snapshot, then close the query property sheet.

    b. Right-click the Date field, and click Properties from the shortcut menu to open the Field Properties dialog box. Enter "Date of Seminar" as the Caption property, change the Format property to Medium Date, then close the property sheet.

    c. Display the records for the months of May and June of 2000, and print the datasheet.

    d. Save and close the query.

4. Create an Update Query.

    a. Create a select query and select all the fields from the Registration table.

    b. Add criteria to find those records in which the RegistrationDate is on or after 5/1/00. View the datasheet, and observe and note the values in the RegistrationFee field. There should be six records. Expand the columns to view all of the data.

    c. In Design view, change the query to an update query, then enter "[RegistrationFee]+5" in the RegistrationFee field Update To cell in order to increase each value in that field by $5.

    d. Run the query to update the six records.

    e. Change the query back to a select query, then view the datasheet to make sure that the RegistrationFee fields were updated properly.

    f. Close the query without saving the changes.

5. Create a Make-Table Query.

    a. Create a select query and select all the fields from the Registration table.

    b. Add criteria to find those records in which the RegistrationDate is on or before 3/31/00.

    c. View the datasheet. There should be 15 records.

    d. In Design view, change the query into a make-table query that creates a new table in the current database with the Table Name "1Qtr2000 – Your Initials".

    e. Run the query to paste 15 rows into the 1Qtr2000 – Your Initials table.

    f. Close the query without saving it, click Tables on the Objects bar, open the 1Qtr2000 – Your Initials table, view the 15 records, print the datasheet, then close it.

6. Create an Append Query.

    a. Create a select query and select all the fields from the Registration table.

    b. Add criteria to find those records in which the RegistrationDate occurred on any day during April 2000. (*Hint*: Use the criteria >=4/1/00 and <=4/30/00.)

    c. View the datasheet. There should be one record.

    d. Change the query to an append query that appends to the 1Qtr2000 – Your Initials table.

    e. Run the query to append the row into the 1Qtr2000 – Your Initials table.

    f. Close the query without saving it.

    g. Rename the 1Qtr2000 – Your Initials table to "Jan-Apr2000 – Your Initials", open the datasheet (there should be 16 records), print it, then close it.

7. Create a Delete Query.

   a. Create a select query and select all the fields from the Registration table.

   b. Add criteria to find those records in which the RegistrationDate occurred before May 1, 2000.

   c. View the datasheet. There should be 16 records.

   d. Change the query into a delete query.

   e. Run the query that deletes 16 records from the Registration table.

   f. Close the query without saving it.

   g. Open the Registration table in datasheet view to confirm that there are only six records, then close it.

8. Specify Join Properties.

   a. Create a select query with the following fields: AttendeeFirstName and AttendeeLastName from the Attendees table, and RegistrationFee from the Registration table.

   b. Double-click the link between the Attendees and Registration tables to open the Join Properties dialog box. Click the option button to include *all* records from Attendees and only those records from Registration where the joined fields are equal. Click OK to close the dialog box.

   c. View the datasheet, and add your own first and last name as the last record, but do not enter anything in the RegistrationFee field for your record.

   d. Print the datasheet, save the query with the name "Current Attendees", then close the datasheet.

   e. Close the Seminar-K database and exit Access.

► Independent Challenges

1. As the manager of a college women's basketball team, you wish to create several queries using the Basketball-K database.

   To complete this independent challenge:

   a. Start Access and open the database Basketball-K.

   b. Open the Players Query in Design view and add parameter criteria to prompt the user to enter a start and end date in the Date field like the following: Between [Enter start date:] and [Enter end date:]

   c. Display the datasheet for all of the records in the year 2000. There should be 42 records.

   d. Use the Save As option on the File menu to save the query with the name "2000 – Your Initials", then print the datasheet.

   e. In Design view of the 2000 - Your Initials query, sort in descending order on the TotalPts field, then choose 5% for Top Values.

   f. Display the datasheet for all of the records in the year 2001. There should be two records.

   g. Use the Save As option on the File menu to save the query with the name "2001 – Top 5% - Your Initials", then print the datasheet.

   h. Close the 2001 – Top 5% - Your Initials query.

   i. Open the Scoring query in Design view, then add a new calculated field between the Opponent Score and Last fields with the following expression: Win%:[Home Score]/[Opponent Score]

   j. View the datasheet to make sure that the Win% field calculates properly. Because the home score is generally greater than the opponent score, most values will be greater than 1.

   k. In Design view, open the property sheet of the Win% field to change the Format property of the Win% field to "Percent" and the Decimal Places property to "0".

   l. View the datasheet, use the Save As feature to save the query as "Scoring – Your Initials", then print it.

   m. Close the Scoring – Your Initials query and the Basketball-K database, and exit Access.

2. As the manager of a college women's basketball team, you wish to enhance the Basketball-K database and need to create several action queries using the Basketball-K database.

To complete this independent challenge:

a. Start Access and open the database Basketball-K.

b. Create a new select query that includes all of the fields from the Stats table.

c. Add criteria to find all of the statistics for those records with the GameNo field equal to 1, 2, or 3. There should be 18 records.

d. Change the query to a Make-Table query to paste the records into a table in the current database called "Games 1, 2, and 3 – Your Initials".

e. Run the query to paste the 18 rows, then close the query without saving it.

f. Open the Games 1, 2, and 3 – Your Initials table's datasheet and print it.

g. Create another new select query that includes all of the fields from the Stats table.

h. Add criteria to find all of the statistics for those records with the GameNo field equal to 4 or 5. There should be 12 records.

i. Change the query to an append query to append the records to the Games 1, 2, and 3 – Your Initials table.

j. Run the query to append the 12 rows, then close the query without saving it.

k. Rename the Games 1, 2, and 3 – Your Initials table to the "Games 1-5 – Your Initials" table.

l. Open the Games 1-5 – Your Initials table's datasheet, then print it. There should be 30 records.

m. Close the Games 1-5 – Your Initials table, close the Basketball-K database, then exit Access.

3. As the manager of a college women's basketball team, you wish to query the Basketball-K database to find specific information about each player.

To complete this independent challenge:

a. Start Access and open the database Basketball-K.

b. Create a query in Design view with the Players and Stats tables.

c. Double-click the linking line to open the Join Properties dialog box, and change the join properties to include ALL records from "Players" and only those from "Stats" where the joined fields are equal.

d. Add the First and Last fields from the Players table, and the Reb-O, Reb-D, and Assists fields from the Stats table.

e. View the datasheet, then scroll to see if there are any players who do not have rebounding or assist statistics.

f. Click an empty Reb-O field, then click the Filter By Selection button to filter for only those players with null Reb-O statistics.

g. Add your name as the last record, but do not enter anything in the three statistics fields.

h. Print the datasheet, save the query as Redshirts, then close the datasheet.

i. Close Basketball-K and exit Access.

4. MediaLoft has developed a Web site that provides internal information to their employees. In this independent challenge, you'll find query requests posted to the Web site that you will complete using the Training-K database.

a. Connect to the Internet, go to the MediaLoft intranet site at
http://www.course.com/illustrated/MediaLoft

b. Click the link for Training, click the link for Query Requests, then Print the page.

c. Open the Training-K database, click the Queries on the Objects bar, then create the query requested on the printed Web page by including the InstructorFirst and InstructorLast fields from the Instructors table, and the Description field from the Courses table.

d. Double-click the join line to open the Join Properties dialog box, and modify the join properties to include all records from "Instructors" and only those from "Courses" where the joined fields are equal.

e. View the datasheet, add your name in a new record if it doesn't already exist in the datasheet (do not enter a Description in that record), then print the datasheet.

f. Save the query as Instructor Assignments – Your Initials, then close the query and the Training-K database, and exit Access.

► Visual Workshop

As the manager of a college women's basketball team, you wish to create a query from the Basketball-K database with the fields shown. The query is a parameter query that prompts the user for a start and end date. Figure K-21 shows the datasheet where the start date of 12/1/00 and end date of 12/31/00 are used. Save and name the query "Offense – Your Initials", then print the datasheet.

FIGURE K-21

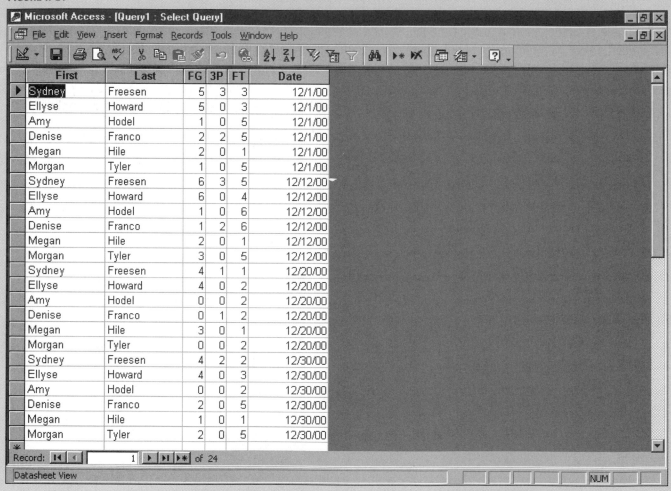

First	Last	FG	3P	FT	Date
Sydney	Freesen	5	3	3	12/1/00
Ellyse	Howard	5	0	3	12/1/00
Amy	Hodel	1	0	5	12/1/00
Denise	Franco	2	2	5	12/1/00
Megan	Hile	2	0	1	12/1/00
Morgan	Tyler	1	0	5	12/1/00
Sydney	Freesen	6	3	5	12/12/00
Ellyse	Howard	6	0	4	12/12/00
Amy	Hodel	1	0	6	12/12/00
Denise	Franco	1	2	6	12/12/00
Megan	Hile	2	0	1	12/12/00
Morgan	Tyler	3	0	5	12/12/00
Sydney	Freesen	4	1	1	12/20/00
Ellyse	Howard	4	0	2	12/20/00
Amy	Hodel	0	0	2	12/20/00
Denise	Franco	0	1	2	12/20/00
Megan	Hile	3	0	1	12/20/00
Morgan	Tyler	0	0	2	12/20/00
Sydney	Freesen	4	2	2	12/30/00
Ellyse	Howard	4	0	3	12/30/00
Amy	Hodel	0	0	2	12/30/00
Denise	Franco	2	0	5	12/30/00
Megan	Hile	1	0	1	12/30/00
Morgan	Tyler	2	0	5	12/30/00

Record: 1 of 24

Creating
Advanced Forms and Reports

Objectives

- **▶ Add Check Boxes and Toggle Buttons**
- **▶ Use Conditional Formatting**
- **▶ Create Custom Help**
- **▶ Add Tab Controls**
- **▶ Add Charts**
- **▶ Modify Charts**
- **▶ Add Subreport Controls**
- **▶ Modify Section Properties**

Advanced controls such as tab controls, charts, and subreports are powerful communication tools. Conditional formatting allows you to highlight exceptional information within a form or report to more clearly present key information. Knowing how to use these advanced features to enhance forms and reports will improve the value of your database to every user. David Dumont wants to enhance existing forms and reports to more professionally and clearly present the information. David will use powerful form and report controls and features such as check boxes, conditional formatting, tab controls, charts, and subreports to improve the training database's forms and reports.

Adding Check Boxes and Toggle Buttons

A **check box** is a control that is often used to display Yes/No fields on a form because it can appear in only one of two ways: checked or unchecked. The checked state intuitively means on, yes, or true, and the unchecked state means off, no, or false. It is much easier for a user to answer questions on a form by using the mouse to click a check box control than to type the word "True" or "Yes" in a text box control. By default, Access represents any field with a Yes/No data type as a check box control on a form, regardless of whether the field was added to the form through the Form Wizard, AutoForm options, or in Form Design view. ➤ David would like to improve the visual appeal of the Employee Course Attendance form and Attendance Subform. He changes the properties of the Attendance Subform and a Yes/No field.

Steps

1. Open the **Training-L** database, click **Forms** on the Objects bar, then double-click the **Employee Course Attendance form**

   The form opens in Form view and the Attendance Subform appears as a datasheet within it.

   Trouble?
   If the subform appears as a white rectangle, click the Form View button, then click the Design View button to refresh the screen.

2. Click the **Design View button** 📝 on the Form View toolbar, then maximize the **Employee Course Attendance form** window

   Your screen should look like Figure L-1. In order to change the appearance of the controls on the subform, the Default View property for the form has to be changed from Datasheet (which allows no special formatting) to Continuous Forms.

3. Double-click the **subform's Select form button**, click the **Format tab** (if necessary) on the property sheet, click the **Default View text box**, click the **Default View list arrow**, click **Continuous Forms**, then click the **Form View button** 📧

   Your screen should look like Figure L-2. The property sheet for the currently selected control, the Last text box, appears because Access allows you to change the properties of some bound controls in Form view. Some modifications can be made only in Design view, however, such as adding, deleting, moving, or resizing a control, or modifying an unbound control such as a label.

4. Close the **property sheet**

   Because of the change to the subform's Default View property, the subform now displays the records in exactly the same way that they appear formatted in Design view, and not as a datasheet.

5. Click 📝 on the Form View toolbar, click the **Passed check box** to select it, right-click the **Passed check box**, point to **Change To**, then click **Toggle Button**

   Changing a control into a different control can be accomplished only in Design view. See Table L-1 for more information on which controls are interchangeable by using the "Change To" shortcut menu option.

6. Point to the **middle-right resize handle** on the toggle button, drag ↔ to the right edge of the form, click the **toggle button**, type **Click if Yes**, then click 📧

   Your screen should look similar to Figure L-3. Notice that when the value is "yes," the toggle button appears indented or "pushed in." The text displayed on the button can be changed using the Caption property on the Format tab in the toggle button's property sheet.

7. Click the **Save button** 💾 on the Form View toolbar

   The changes are saved to the Employee Course Attendance form and the Attendance Subform.

8. Close the Employee Course Attendance form

FIGURE L-1: Form and subform in Design view

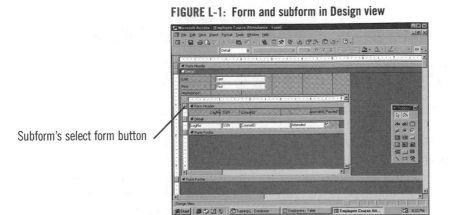

Subform's select form button

FIGURE L-2: Form view displaying the property sheet

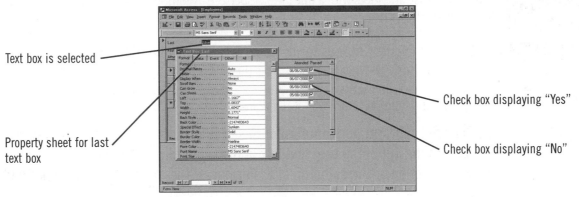

Text box is selected

Property sheet for last text box

Check box displaying "Yes"

Check box displaying "No"

FIGURE L-3: Command buttons displaying "yes" and "no" values

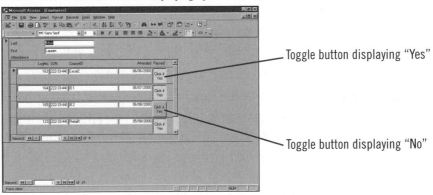

Toggle button displaying "Yes"

Toggle button displaying "No"

TABLE L-1: Interchangeable bound controls

control	can be interchanged with	used most commonly when the field has:
Text box	List box, combo box	An unlimited number of choices such as a Price, LastName, or Street field
List box	Text box, combo box	A limited number of predefined values such as Manager, Department, or State fields
Combo box	Text box, list box	A limited number of common values, yet you still need the ability to enter a new value from the keyboard, such as the City field
Check box	Toggle button, option button	Only two values, "yes" or "no," such as a Veteran field
Option button	Check box, toggle button	A limited number of values, such as "female" or "male" for a Gender field. The option button is most commonly used in conjunction with an option group that can contain several option buttons, each representing a possible value for the field
Toggle button	Check box, option button	Only two values, "yes" or "no," and you want the appearance of the field to look like a button rather than a check box

Using Conditional Formatting

Conditional Formatting can be used to determine the appearance of a field on a form or report based on its value, a value in another field, or when the field has the focus. **Focus** is the ability to receive user input through the keyboard or mouse. Conditional formatting provides a way to alert the user to exceptional situations as data is being entered or reported. Format changes include changing the text color, background color, or style of the control. If you conditionally format a control based on a value in another field, you must use an **expression**, a combination of field names, operators, and values that calculate an answer. ▰▰▰ The users of the Courses form (which includes the Course-Employee Subform) would like David to modify the form so that they can quickly identify those course attendees with a title of "Salesperson." Additionally, David uses conditional formatting to more clearly show which text box has the focus.

Steps 123 4

Trouble?

If the subform appears as a white rectangle, click the Form View button, then click the Design View button to refresh the screen.

1. Double-click the **Courses form**, view the overall layout of the form and subform, then click the **Design View button** 📐 on the Form View toolbar
   The subform represents each person who attended the course, and the main form provides four fields of information about the course.

2. Click the **subform horizontal ruler** to select the subform, click the **subform vertical ruler** to the left of the **Last text box** in the subform to select all four text boxes in the Detail section of the subform, click **Format** on the menu bar, then click **Conditional Formatting**
   The Conditional Formatting dialog box opens. The first condition will highlight the field with the focus.

3. Click the **Condition 1 list arrow**, click **Field Has Focus**, click the **Condition 1 Fill/Back Color list arrow** 🎨▾, then click **bright yellow** (fourth row, third box from the left)
   The second condition will highlight which attendees have the title of "Salesperson."

QuickTip

You can include up to three conditions in the Conditional Formatting dialog box.

4. Click **Add** in the Conditional Formatting dialog box, click the **Condition 2 list arrow**, click **Expression is**, press [Tab], type [Title]="Salesperson", click the **Condition 2 Bold button** 🅱, click the **Condition 2 Font/Fore Color list arrow** 🅰▾, then click **bright red** (third row, first box from the left)
   Your screen should look like Figure L-4. When an expression is used in the Conditional Formatting dialog box, the expression must evaluate to be either "true," which turns the formatting on, or "false," which turns the formatting off.

5. Click **OK**, click the **Form View button** 📧 on the Form Design toolbar, then click **Colletti** (the first field value in the first record) in the subform
   Your screen should look like Figure L-5.

6. Press [Tab] three times to move the focus to the Salesperson entry for the first record, press [Delete], then press [Tab]
   Your screen should look like Figure L-6, in which the first record in the subform is no longer red and boldface. Conditional formatting reverts to default formatting if the condition is no longer true.

QuickTip

You can also click the Undo button 🔙 on the Form View toolbar to undo the last action.

7. Click **Edit** on the menu bar, then click the **Undo Saved Record button** 🔙
   The Title Salesperson is restored for the first record and it is in red boldface text.

8. Save then close the Courses form

FIGURE L-4: Conditional Formatting dialog box

Field Has Focus

Expression

Expression Is

Back/Fill Color button

Bold button

Font/Fore Color button

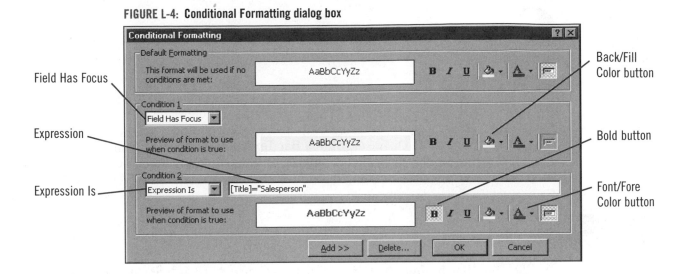

FIGURE L-5: The control with the focus is bright yellow

This control has the focus

Conditional formatting for [Title]= "Salesperson"

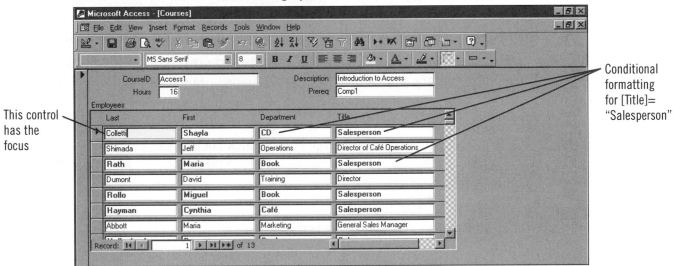

FIGURE L-6: Conditional formats change as data is edited

Title value is no longer "Salesperson"

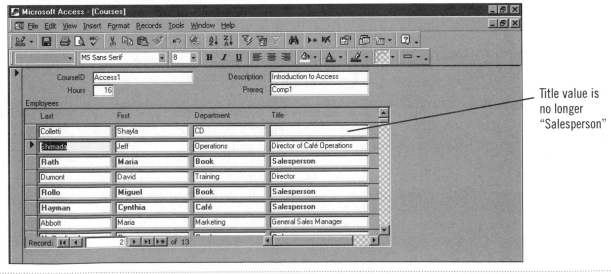

Creating Custom Help

You can create several types of custom Help for a form or a control on a form. If you want to display a textual tip that pops up over a control when you point to it, use the **ControlTip Text** property for that control. Or, use the **Status Bar Text** property to display helpful information about a form or control in the status bar. ⟶ David wants to allow other users to enter new course records as those courses become available. He quickly creates a new form based on the Courses table, then adds custom help to guide the new users as they enter the data.

1. Click the **New button** 📇 in the database window, click **AutoForm: Columnar**, click the **Choose the table or query where the object's data comes from list arrow**, click **Courses**, then click **OK**

   A Courses form is created. You can modify the ControlTip Text and Status Bar Text properties for text boxes and other bound controls from Form view.

2. Click **View** on the menu, click **Properties**, click the **Other tab** in the CourseID text box property sheet, click the **ControlTip Text property text box**, type **Use a 1 suffix for an introductory course**, press [Enter], then point to the **CourseID text box**

   A control tip pops up, as shown in Figure L-7. You can view and enter a long entry using the Zoom dialog box.

> **QuickTip**
>
> Click a property, then press [Shift][F2] to open the Zoom dialog box for that property.

3. Right-click the **ControlTip Text property**, click **Zoom**, click to the right of the word "**course**" in the Zoom dialog box, press [Spacebar], then type **and a 2 suffix for an intermediate course**

   The Zoom dialog box should look like Figure L-8.

4. Click **OK**, then click the **Prereq text box**

   The property sheet now shows the properties for the Prereq text box.

> **QuickTip**
>
> Click a property, then press [F1] to open the Microsoft Access Help window for the specific explanation of that property.

5. Click the **Status Bar Text text box** in the Text Box Prereq property sheet

   When the property sheet is open, a short description of the selected property appears in the status bar.

6. Right-click the **Status Bar Text text box**, click **Zoom**, type **Comp1 can be waived by achieving an 80% score on the Computers 101 test**, click **OK**, then close the property sheet

7. Click **File** on the menu bar, click **Save As**, type **Courses Entry Form** in the Save From Form 1 To text box, click **OK**, then close the property sheet and the form

8. Double-click **Courses Entry Form** in the database window, then click the **Prereq text box**

   Your screen should look like Figure L-9. The status bar displays the entry in the Status Bar Text property for this control. Unbound properties such as labels do not have a Status Bar Text property because they cannot have the focus. A label can have a ControlTip Text property that displays text when you point to the label. A label's ControlTip Text property can be modified only in Form Design view, because that's the only place you can select an unbound control in order to access its property sheet.

9. Close the Courses Entry form

FIGURE L-7: Using the ControlTip Text property

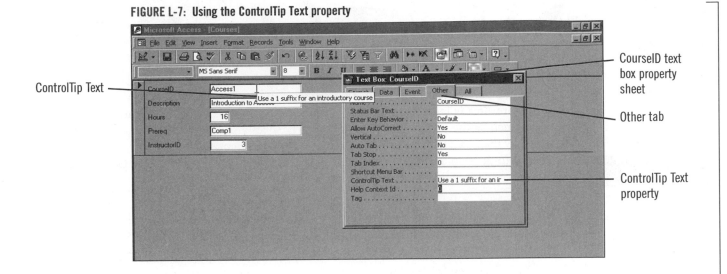

ControlTip Text

CourseID text box property sheet

Other tab

ControlTip Text property

FIGURE L-8: Zoom dialog box

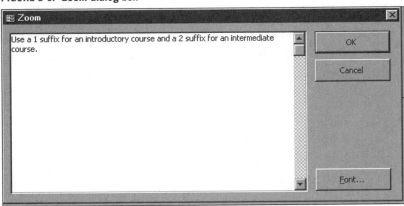

FIGURE L-9: Using the Status Bar Text property

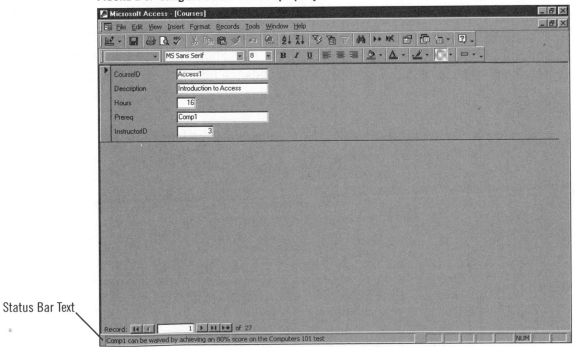

Status Bar Text

Access 2000

Adding Tab Controls

The **tab control** is a powerful unbound control used to organize a form and give it a three-dimensional look by presenting several "pages" on a single form. When you want to show a lot of information on a form at one time, the tab control is an excellent tool to logically organize many fields. You are already familiar with using tab controls because they are used in many Access dialog boxes such as the property sheet. The property sheet also uses tabs to organize properties identified by their category name in the tab (Format, Data, Event, Other, and All). ◄━━ David has started to develop an Employee Update Form, but wants to use the tab control to organize and present employee information in an easy-to-use way.

Steps

1. Click the **Employee Update Form**, click the **Design View button** ▨ in the database window, click the **Toolbox button** ✖ to toggle the Toolbox on (if necessary), click the **Tab Control button** ▣ on the Toolbox toolbar, then click just below the **First label** in the Detail section of the form
   Your screen should look like Figure L-10. The tab control appears with two "pages," with the default names of Page17 and Page18, on the respective tabs.

2. Double-click **Page17** to open its property sheet, click the **Other tab**, verify Page17 is selected in the Name text box, type **Personnel Info**, click the **Page18 tab** on the form, double-click **Page18** in the Name text box of the property sheet, type **Course Attendance**, then close the property sheet
   The tabs now describe the information they will contain.

3. Click the **Personnel Info tab**, click the **Field List button** ▣ on the Form Design toolbar to toggle it on (if necessary), click **Department** in the field list, press and hold [Shift], click **SSN** in the field list (you may have to scroll) to select all fields between the Department and SSN, release [Shift], then drag the **highlighted fields** to the middle of the Personnel Info page
   Your screen should look like Figure L-11. The six fields are added to the Personnel Info page on the tab control. You can add any control, even a subform control, to a page.

4. Click the **Course Attendance tab**, click the **Subform/Subreport button** ▣ on the Toolbox, click the **upper-left corner of the Course Attendance page**, click the **Use existing Tables and Queries** option button in the SubForm Wizard dialog box, click **Next**, click the **Select All Fields button** ⏩, click **Next**, click **Show Attendance for each record in Employees using SSN**, click **Next**, type **Attendance Info**, then click **Finish**
   The tab control as well as the entire form has been automatically widened to better accommodate the wide subform control.

5. Click the **Form View button** ▣, click the **Course Attendance tab**, then maximize the Employee Update Form window
   Your screen should look similar to Figure L-12.

6. Click ▨, right-click the **Course Attendance tab**, click **Insert Page**, double-click **Page27** to open the property sheet, click the **Other tab** (if necessary), double-click **Page27**, type **Course Feedback**, close the property sheet, click ▣, then click all three tabs
   You probably want to move and resize several of the controls on this form before using it, but for now the Course Feedback tab is prepared and ready for you to add controls to it in Design view to hold information for a future time.

7. Save and close the Employee Update Form

FIGURE L-10: Adding a tab control

New tab control

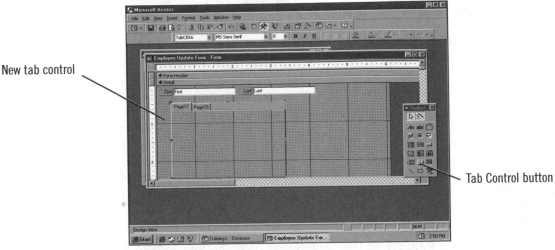

Tab Control button

FIGURE L-11: Adding fields to a tab control

Field List button

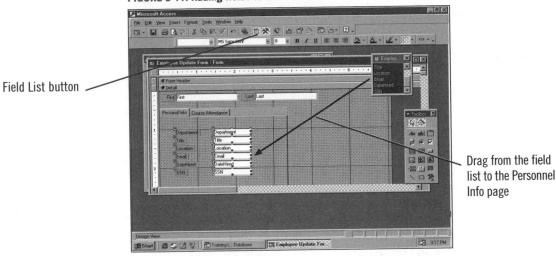

Drag from the field list to the Personnel Info page

FIGURE L-12: The tab control in Form View

Course Attendance tab

Attendance Info subform

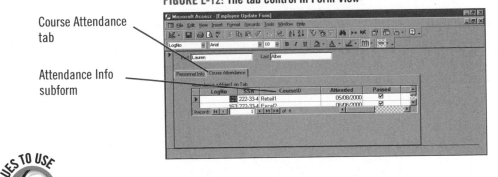

Access 2000

CLUES TO USE

Referencing controls with Text## and Page##

Access sequentially numbers each control on a form and uses that number in the Name property for the control. The label and tab control that display the name property as part of the control, you see the sequential number in the name of the control. For example, when adding a tab control to the form, the word "Page" plus the sequential number of that control are used as the default entry for the Name property

and appear on the tab itself. If you add a control and then delete it, that sequential number is not used over. Since users build their forms in different ways, adding and deleting controls as necessary, it is common to reference the new label or tab controls as "Text##" or "Page##" because the exact number represented by ## will be different from user to user.

Access 2000

Adding Charts

Charts, sometimes called graphs, are visual representations of numeric data that help users see comparisons, patterns, and trends in data. Charts can be inserted on a form, report, or data access page object. Access provides a **Chart Wizard** that steps you through the process of creating charts within forms and reports. Before using the Chart Wizard, however, you must determine what data you want the graph to show. Often you'll use an intermediate query to gather the specific fields that you wish to graph into one object before using the Chart Wizard to create the graph, especially if the data comes from multiple tables or if you wish to graph a subset of records. ▟ David created a Department Summary query with two fields: Attended from the Attendance table and Department from the Employees table. Instead of reporting this information as a datasheet of summarized numbers, he uses the report object's Chart Wizard to visually display a total count of attendance by department.

Steps

1. Click **Reports** on the Objects bar, click the **New button** ▣ in the database window, click **Chart Wizard**, click the **Choose the table or query where the object's data comes from** list arrow, click **Department Summary**, then click **OK**
   The Chart Wizard starts and presents the fields in the Department Summary query.

> **QuickTip**
> Click any chart button to read a description of that chart in the lower-right corner of the Chart Wizard dialog box.

2. Click **the Select All Fields button** ▣▣, then click **Next**
   The next Chart Wizard dialog box, shown in Figure L-13, determines the type of chart that will be created. See Table L-2 for more information on common chart types. Column Chart, the button in the first row, first column on the left, is the default chart type.

3. Click **Next**
   The next dialog box determines which fields will be used for the x-axis, bar, and series (legend) areas of the chart. For this chart, you want the bars to represent a count of the Attended field. The Department field should be used as x-axis labels.

> **QuickTip**
> If you drag a numeric field into the Data area, you can double-click the button to change the way it is summarized to Sum, Avg, Min, or Max value of the field.

4. Drag the **Attended field button** from the field buttons on the right to the **Data** area, then drag the **Attended by month button** from the Series area out of the chart area, as shown in Figure L-14
   Since the Attended field holds date data, bars should count the number of entries.

5. Click **Next**, type **Total Attendance by Department** in the title for your chart text box, then click **Finish**
   Your chart should look similar to Figure L-15. The chart is difficult to read as it currently appears, but Access provides charting tools to improve the appearance of charts.

FIGURE L-13: Chart types

Column Chart

Line Chart

Area Chart

Pie Chart

Chart type description

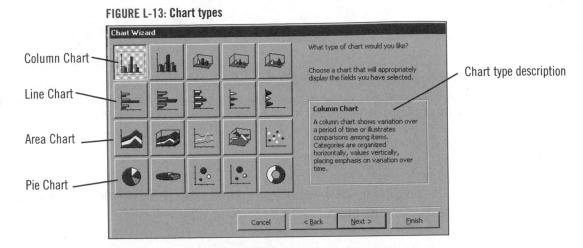

FIGURE L-14: Determining chart layout

Preview Chart button

Data fields

Series (legend) fields

X-axis fields

Field button

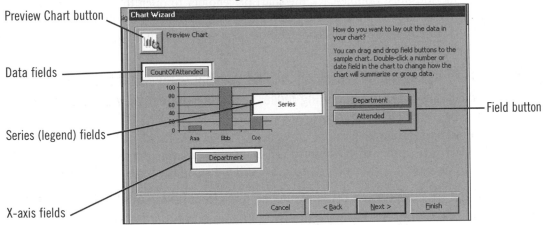

FIGURE L-15: Total Attendance by Department chart

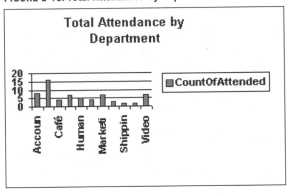

TABLE L-2: Common chart types

chart type	chart icon	most commonly used to show	example
Column		Comparisons of values	Each bar represents the annual sales for a different product for the year 2000
Line		Trends over time	Each point on the line represents monthly sales for one product for the year 2000
Pie		Parts of a whole	Each slice represents total quarterly sales for a company for the year 2000
Area		Cumulative totals	Each section represents monthly sales by representative, stacked to show the cumulative total sales effort for the year 2000

Modifying Charts

All charts are modified in Design View of the form or report where the chart exists. Modifying a chart is challenging because Design View doesn't show you the actual chart values and elements, but rather shows you a chart placeholder that represents the embedded chart object. ➤ David sees that the chart would be clearer if he removes the legend and resizes the chart to better display the values on the axes. He makes all modifications to the existing chart in Report Design view.

Steps

QuickTip

The hashed border of the chart placeholder control indicates that the Chart is in edit mode.

1. Click the Design View button 📷**, maximize the Report Design View window, then double-click the chart to edit it**

The chart is now ready to be edited, as shown in Figure L-16. You can delete, move, or resize the chart object without double-clicking it, but if you want to modify any of the chart elements, you must double-click the chart placeholder to open the chart menu bar and toolbar. If you double-click the edge of the chart placeholder, you will open its property sheet. All chart editing and formatting is done in Report Design view, but the actual chart data displays only in Print Preview.

Trouble?

You may have to click the More Buttons button 📷 on the Chart toolbar to locate the Legend button.

2. Click the Legend button 📷 **on the Chart toolbar to toggle off the legend, click outside the chart to exit chart editing mode, click the Print Preview button** 📷 **on the Chart toolbar, then click the chart**

Your chart should look similar to Figure L-17. Because the chart has only one series of bars, a clear title (rather than a legend) can be used to describe the series. Most of the elements, including the y-axis labels and bars, are still too small to clearly display the information.

Trouble?

Be sure you work within the vertical ruler in the Detail section.

3. Click 📷 **on the Print Preview toolbar, click the chart placeholder to select the control, then drag the lower-right sizing handle down and to the right to the 5" mark on the horizontal ruler and the 3.5" mark on the vertical ruler**

With the chart placeholder resized, you can expand the size of the chart within it.

Trouble?

Click the View Datasheet button 📷 on the Standard toolbar to close the chart's datasheet if it opens.

4. Double-click the chart placeholder, then drag the lower-right corner sizing handle of the fuzzy border of the chart to just within the border of the chart placeholder, as shown in Figure L-18

You can modify any element such as the labels on the x-axis or y-axis, but you must select them before you change or format them.

QuickTip

The Category Axis is the x-axis, and the Value Axis is the y-axis.

5. Click the East label to select the Category Axis, click the Font Size list arrow 📷**, click 8, click the Total Attendance by Department Chart Title, click** 📷**, click 10, click outside the chart to exit chart edit mode, click** 📷 **on the Report Design toolbar, then click the chart**

The final chart is shown in Figure L-19. It clearly shows that the Book Department has far more attendees at MediaLoft's internal training courses than any other department.

6. Click File on the menu bar, click Save As, type Department Graph-Your Initials, then click OK

7. Click the Print button 📷**, then close the Department Graph-Your Initials report**

FIGURE L-16: Editing a chart in Design view

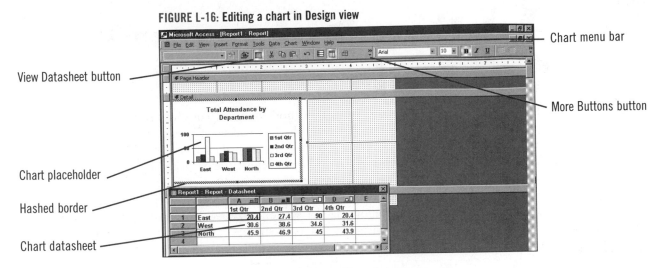

Chart menu bar

View Datasheet button

More Buttons button

Chart placeholder

Hashed border

Chart datasheet

FIGURE L-17: Chart still needs improvement

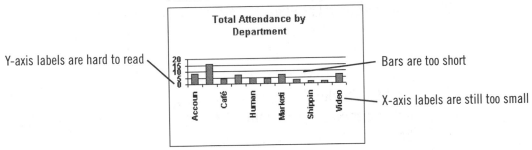

Y-axis labels are hard to read

Bars are too short

X-axis labels are still too small

FIGURE L-18: Increasing the chart size

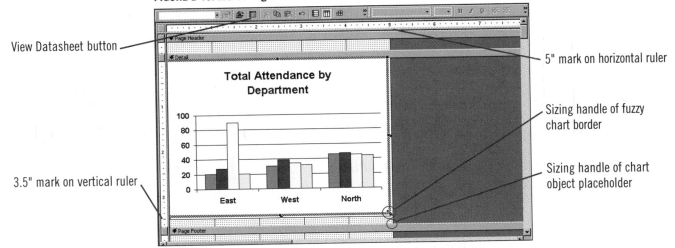

View Datasheet button

5" mark on horizontal ruler

Sizing handle of fuzzy chart border

Sizing handle of chart object placeholder

3.5" mark on vertical ruler

FIGURE L-19: Final chart

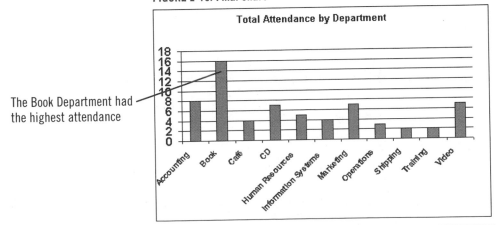

The Book Department had the highest attendance

Adding Subreport Controls

Steps 1 2 3 4

A **subreport control** displays a report within another report. The **main report** contains the subreport control. You use the subreport control when you want to link two reports together to automate printing. You also can use a subreport control when you want to change the order in which information normally prints. If you want report totals (generally found in the Report Footer section, which prints on the last page) to print on the first page, you could use a subreport control that calculates report grand totals in the subreport's Report Footer section and place it in the main report's Report Header section. Now that David has created the Department Graph report, he wishes to add it as a subreport to the bottom of the Report Footer section of the Department Enrollment report so that it is viewed and printed at the same time.

1. Click the **Department Enrollment** report, click the **Design button** in the database window, scroll to the bottom of the report, then use the ✛ pointer to drag the bottom edge of the report down **1"**
   You've expanded the size of the Report Footer section to make room for the subreport control.

2. Click the **Toolbox button** on the Report Design toolbar to toggle it on (if necessary), click the **Subform/Subreport button** on the Toolbox, then click below the **Grand Total label** in the Report Footer section
   The SubReport Wizard opens, as shown in Figure L-20.

3. Click the **Use an existing report or form option button**, click **Department Graph Report-Your Initials**, click **Next**, click **Finish** to accept the name **Department Graph-Your Initials** for the subreport, maximize the Report Design view window (if necessary), then scroll down to view the Report Footer section
   The subreport control appears in Report Design view, as shown in Figure L-21, and expands the size of the report to accommodate the large control. You can modify a subreport's controls directly within the main report just as you can modify a subform's controls within a main form.

4. Click the **Print Preview button** on the Report Design toolbar, then click the **Last page button** on the navigation buttons
   Your screen should look like Figure L-22. The Report Footer section contains the subreport and, therefore, displays the graph on the last page.

5. Close the Department Enrollment report, then save the changes when prompted

FIGURE L-20: SubReport Wizard

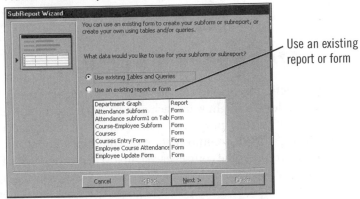

Use an existing report or form

FIGURE L-21: Subreport in Report Design view

Report Footer section

Grand Total label

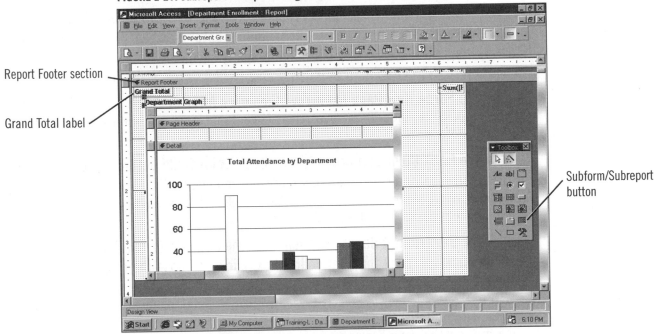

Subform/Subreport button

FIGURE L-22: Department graph displayed as a subreport

Page Header controls

Report Footer controls

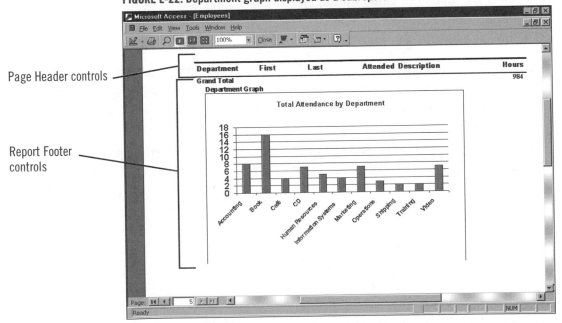

Modifying Section Properties

Report **section properties** can be modified to help determine how the sections of the report print. For example, you might want each group's header section to always print at the top of a new page. Other report section properties control formatting issues such as the section's back color property. See Table L-3 for more information on common section properties. ◄ David doesn't want the Detail records (the courses each employee has attended) of the Department Enrollment report to span two pages. In addition, he'd like the records for each new department to start at the top of a new page. He makes these section property changes in Report Design view.

Steps

1. **Click the Department Enrollment report, click the Design button in the database window, double-click the Department Footer section to open its property sheet, then click the Format tab in the property sheet**
   The property sheet for the Department Header section opens, as shown in Figure L-23.

2. **Click the Force New Page list arrow, then click After Section**
   This property change will force the report to continue at the top of the next page after the Group Footer prints.

3. **Click the Back Color text box, click the Back Color Build button , click the light yellow box (second column on the top row), then click OK**
   Now the entire section will appear with a light yellow background color in print preview, and on the printout if a color printer is used.

4. **Click the Department Header section, click the Back Color text box in the property sheet, click , click the light yellow box, click OK, close the property sheet, click the Print Preview button , then Zoom Out**
   Your screen should look like Figure L-24. By modifying section properties, you have clarified where the group starts and stops by shading those sections, and have forced a page break at the end of each Group Footer.

5. **Click , click the Label button on the Toolbox toolbar, click to the right of the Department Enrollment label in the Report Header section, type Your Name, click the Save button , then click **

6. **Click File on the menu bar, click Print, click the Pages option button in the Print Range section, type 1 in the From text box, click the To text box, type 1, then click OK**
   The first page of the Department Enrollment report showing the section shading is sent to the printer.

7. **Close the Department Enrollment report, close MediaLoft-L database, then exit Access**

FIGURE L-23: Using Section Properties

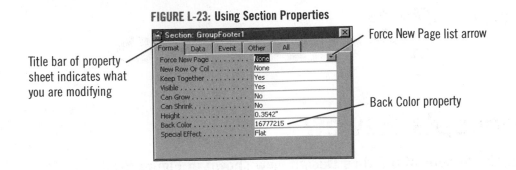

Title bar of property sheet indicates what you are modifying

Force New Page list arrow

Back Color property

FIGURE L-24: Using Section Colors

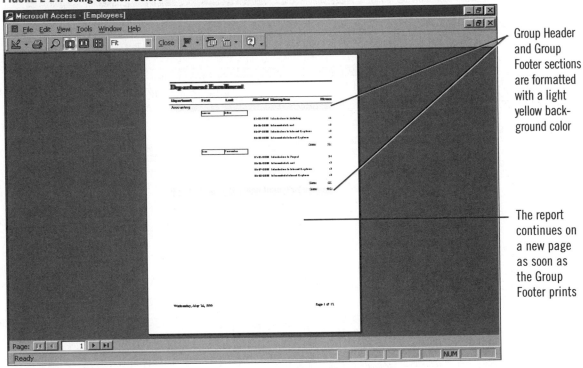

Group Header and Group Footer sections are formatted with a light yellow background color

The report continues on a new page as soon as the Group Footer prints

TABLE L-3: Common report section properties

property	options	description
Force New Page	None (default) Before Section After Section Before and After	Determines whether a section starts on the current page or a new page, or whether a new page starts after the section
New Row or Col	None (default) Before Section After Section Before and After	Often used to specify that a Group Header prints at the top of a new column in a multiple-column report
Visible	Yes (default) No	Determines whether the section is visible in Print Preview
Keep Together	Yes (default) No	Determines whether the records in that section must print on the same page or whether they can span multiple pages
Back Color	Number that corresponds to a color	Controls the color of the background of that section

Access 2000

Practice

▶ Concepts Review

Identify each element of a form's Design view shown in Figure L-25.

FIGURE L-25

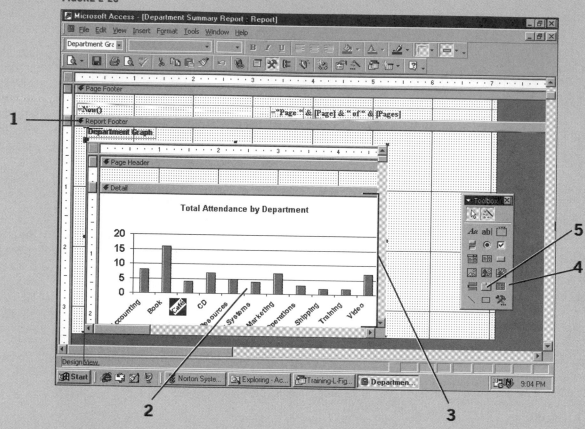

Match each term with the statement that describes its function.

6. Focus
7. Tab control
8. Sections
9. Conditional formatting
10. Charts
11. Check box

a. Allows you to change the appearance of a control on a form or report based on criteria you specify
b. Visual representations of numeric data
c. The ability to receive user input through the keyboard or mouse
d. Determine where and how controls print on a report
e. A control that is often used to display Yes/No fields on a form
f. An unbound control used to organize a form and give it a three-dimensional look

Select the best answer from the list of choices.

12. **Which controls are NOT interchangeable?**
    a. Text box and combo box
    b. Combo box and list box
    c. Check box and toggle button
    d. Check box and option group

13. **When would you most likely use a toggle button control?**
    a. For a field with a limited set of choices
    b. For a field with only two choices: Yes or No
    c. In place of a command button
    d. In place of an unbound label

14. **You would most likely use which control for a City field?**
    a. List box
    b. Combo box
    c. Check box
    d. Command button

15. **To display text that pops up over a control when you point to it, you would modify which control property?**
    a. ControlTip Text
    b. Status Bar Text
    c. Popup Text
    d. Help Text

16. **Which type of chart would you most likely use to show an upward sales trend over several months?**
    a. Pie
    b. Column
    c. Scatter
    d. Line

17. **Which type of control would you use to display report totals as the first page of a report?**
    a. Report Footer
    b. Subreport
    c. Calculated Properties
    d. Main Report

 ## Skills Review

1. **Adding Check Boxes and Toggle Buttons.**
    a. Start Access and open the Seminar-L database from your Project Disk.
    b. Open the Attendees form in Form view, and check the EarlyBirdDiscount check box for the first record in the subform of the first person, Phuong Pham.
    c. Open Design view of the Attendees form. If the subform doesn't display the controls (but rather a white box), click the Form View button, then click Design view a second time in order to see the controls in the subform.

d. Change the Default View property of the subform to Continuous Forms. (*Hint*: Open the property sheet for the form in the subform control.)

e. Change the EarlyBirdDiscount check box into a toggle button.

f. Expand the subform's height about one inch, then expand the size of the EarlyBirdDiscount toggle button to the width of the subform.

g. Add the text "Click for Early Bird Discount" to the toggle button (either by typing directly on the button or by modifying the toggle button's Caption property).

h. Close the property sheet, then view the form in Form view. Expand the size of the subform control using Design View to clearly display three records in the subform when viewed in Form view.

i. Open the form in Form view, and click the toggle button to enter "Yes" in the EarlyBirdDiscount field for the second record in the subform for Phuong Pham.

j. Enter your own last name in place of "Pham" and print only this record.

k. Save and close the form.

2. Using Conditional Formatting.

a. Open the Attendees form in Design view.

b. Click the RegistrationDate text box, then press and hold [Shift] while clicking the RegistrationFee text box to select both controls in the Detail section of the subform. If you see a white box for the subform control, click the Form View button, then the Design View button to refresh the screen.

c. Click Format on the menu bar, click Conditional Formatting, set Condition 1 to Expression Is, then set the criteria to [RegistrationFee]>10

d. Format the Condition 1 for this expression so any values meeting the criteria display as bold, with a bright blue Font/Fore Color. Close the Conditional Formatting dialog box.

e. Save the changes.

f. Still in Design view, select both the AttendeeFirstName and AttendeeLastName text box controls in the Detail section of the main form.

g. Click Format on the menu bar, click Conditional Formatting, then set Condition 1 to Field Has Focus.

h. The Condition 1 format should be black text against a light blue Fill/Back color.

i. Display the form in Form view, then enter your own first name in place of "Phuong."

j. Change the Registration Fee to $11 for the first record in the subform, then tab through the record to make sure that both the RegistrationDate and RegistrationFee text boxes are conditionally formatted.

k. Save the form, print the first record, then close the form.

3. Creating Custom Help.

a. Open the Attendees form in Design view.

b. Open the property sheet for the EarlyBirdDiscount toggle button, then select the Other tab.

c. Enter the following as the ControlTip Text property: "To qualify, registration must be one month before the event." Use the Zoom dialog box if you wish.

d. Use the Zoom dialog box to enter the following as the Status Bar Text property: "Discounts can also be given for group registrations."

e. Close the property sheet, save the form, then open the form in Form view.

f. Point to the button for the third record in the subform to make sure that the ControlTip Text property works.

g. Point to, then click the command button for the third record in the subform to make sure that the Status Bar Text property works.

h. Close the Attendees form.

4. Adding Tab Controls.
a. Open the Events form in Design view.

b. Add a tab control under the Event Name label.

c. Modify the Page5 Name property of the first tab to be "Event Info".

d. Modify the Page6 Name property of the second tab to be "Participants".

e. Open the Field List, then add the Location, Date, and AvailableSpaces fields from the Field List to the middle of the Event Info page.

f. Add a subform to the Participants page, using the Subform Wizard to guide your actions. Click the Existing tables or queries option button. Select the RegistrationDate field from the Registration table, and the AttendeeFirstName and AttendeeLastName fields from the Attendees table.

g. Link the main form to the subform by using the "Show Registration for each record in Events using EventID" option.

h. Name the subform "Registration".

i. Expand the height of the subform control to fill the page, then view the form in Form view.

j. Click the Participants tab to make sure both tabs work correctly, then print the first record twice, once with the Event Info tab displayed and once with the Participants tab displayed.

k. Save and close the Events form.

5. Adding Charts.
a. Click Reports on the Objects bar, then click the New button in the database window.

b. Click the Chart Wizard, choose Registration as the table or query where the object's data comes from, then click OK.

c. Choose the EventID and RegistrationFee as the fields for the Chart.

d. Choose a Column Chart type.

e. Sum the RegistrationFee field in the Data area, and use the EventID field as the x-axis. (*Hint*: These should be the defaults, but click the Preview Chart button to make sure.)

f. Title the chart "Registration Fee Totals-Your Initials".

g. Print the chart, then save the report as "Registration Fee Totals".

6. Modifying Charts.
a. Open Registration Fee Totals in Design view.

b. Double-click the chart to edit it.

c. Remove the legend, and increase the size of both the control and the chart within it to as large as will comfortably fit on your screen.

d. Click any value in the y-axis to select it, choose Format on the menu bar, then click the Number option.

e. Click the Number tab in the Format Axis dialog box, click the Currency category, change the Decimal places text box to 0, then click OK in the Format Axis dialog box.

f. Click outside the chart object to return to Report Design view, preview the report with the chart, print it, save the changes, then close the Registration Fee Totals report.

7. Adding Subreport Controls.
a. Use the Report Wizard to create a report on all of the fields in the Events table.

b. Do not add any grouping levels, but sort the records in ascending order by EventID.

c. Use a Tabular layout, a Portrait orientation, and a Casual style.

d. Title the report "Event Information".

e. Open Event Information in Design view.

f. Increase the size of the Report Footer section by about one inch.

g. Add a subreport control to the upper-left part of the Report Footer section.

h. Use the SubReport Wizard to guide your actions in creating the subreport. Click the Registration Fee Totals report in the first dialog box, and accept the name "Registration Fee Totals" as the subreport's name in the second.

i. Preview the report, print it, then save and close the Event Information Report.

8. Modifying Section Properties.

a. Use the Report Wizard to create a report on all of the fields in the Registration table, and the EventName field in the Events table.

b. View the data by Events, but do not add any grouping levels or sorting fields.

c. Use an Outline 2 layout, a Landscape orientation, and a Compact style.

d. Title the report "Event Details".

e. Open Event Details in Design view, then open the property sheet for the Events_EventID Header section.

f. Change the Force New Page property on the Format tab to Before Section. Change the Back Color property to light blue. (*Hint*: Use the Build button to locate the color on the palette.)

g. Close the property sheet, add your name as a label in the Report Header section, preview the report, then print the first two pages.

h. Save and close the Event Details report.

i. Close Seminar-L and exit Access.

▶ Independent Challenges

1. As the manager of a college women's basketball team, you wish to enhance the forms within the Basketball-L database. To complete this independent challenge:

a. Start Access and open the database Basketball-L from your Project Disk.

b. Click the Forms button on the Object bar, then double-click the Create form by using wizard option.

c. Choose all of the fields in the Players table.

d. Use a Columnar layout, a Standard style, and title the form "Player Information."

e. Maximize the Player Information form, open it in Design view, then change the Lettered? check box into a toggle button with the text "Click if earned a varsity letter".

f. Resize the toggle button so that it is as wide as the form and clearly displays the text.

g. Open the toggle button's property sheet and add the following ControlTip Text property: "Must have 200 minutes of playing time to letter".

h. In the toggle button's property sheet, add the following Status Bar Text property: "For the year 2000".

i. Close the property sheet, display the form in Form view, enter your own last name in the first record, then click the toggle button to indicate you've earned a varsity letter.

j. Print the first record, save the form, then close the Player Information form and the Basketball-L database.

k. Exit Access.

2. As the manager of a college women's basketball team, you wish to enhance the forms within the Basketball-L database. To complete this independent challenge:

a. Start Access and open the database Basketball-L from your Project Disk.

b. Open the Player Statistics form in Design view.

c. Add a tab control just below the Last label.

d. Modify the Page5 Name property of the first tab to be "Player Background".

e. Modify the Page6 Name property of the second tab to be "Statistics".

f. Add the Height, PlayerNo, Year, Position, HomeTown, and HomeState fields from the Field List to the middle of the Player Background page.

g. Add a subform to the Statistics page based on all the fields from the Stats table.

h. Link the main form to the subform by using the "Show Stats for each record in Players using PlayerNo" option.

i. Name the subform "Stats subform".

j. Expand the height of the subform control to fill the page, then view the form in Form view.

k. Click the Participants tab to make sure both tabs work correctly, then print the first record.

l. Save and close the Player Statistics form.

m. Close the Basketball-L database, then exit Access.

3. As the manager of a college women's basketball team, you wish to create a chart from the Basketball-L database to summarize three-point goals.

To complete this independent challenge:

a. Start Access and open the Basketball-L database from your Project Disk.

b. Click the Reports button on the Objects bar, click the New button in the database window, click Chart Wizard, then choose the Stats table.

c. Choose the PlayerNo, 3P (three pointers), and 3PA (three pointers attempted) fields for the chart.

d. Choose a Column Chart.

e. Drag the 3PA field to the Data area of the chart so that both the SumOf3P and SumOf3PA fields are in the Data area, and the PlayerNo field is in the Axis area of the chart.

f. Title the chart "3 Pointers – Your Initials".

g. Print the chart, then close and save the report as "3 Pointers".

h. Close the Basketball-L database, then exit Access.

4. MediaLoft has developed a Web site that provides internal information to its employees. In this independent challenge, you'll surf the Internet to find Web pages that present information organized similarly to how tab controls are used on Access forms.

a. Connect to the Internet, go to the MediaLoft intranet site at http://www.course.com/illustrated/MediaLoft

b. Click the link for Research, click the link for Competition: Other Bookstores, and browse for a Web page that organizes information on "pages" accessed by clicking "tabs" in a manner similar to how tab controls are used within Access forms.

c. If you are not familiar with Web browsing techniques, click the Back button until you return to the MediaLoft Research page, where you can start a new search.

d. When you find a Web page that contains "tab-like" controls to organize information, print the Web page and circle the tab controls.

e. Close your browser window, then disconnect from the Internet.

► Visual Workshop

As the manager of a college women's basketball team, you wish to create a form that highlights outstanding statistics if either their scoring or their rebounding totals are equal to or greater than 10 for an individual game effort. Start Access and open the Basketball-L database. Open the Players form in Design view, and use the conditional formatting feature to format the FG (field goals), 3P (three-point shots), and FT (free throws) text boxes in the Stats Subform1 to have a bright yellow background if the following expression that totals their scoring for that game is true: 2*[FG]+3*[3P]+[FT]>=10. Conditionally format the Reb-O (offensive rebounds) and Reb-D (defensive rebounds) text boxes to be have a light blue background if the following expression that totals rebounds is true: [Reb-O]+[Reb-D]>=10. Display the second record for Ellyse Howard, which should look like Figure L-26. Print the form.

FIGURE L-26

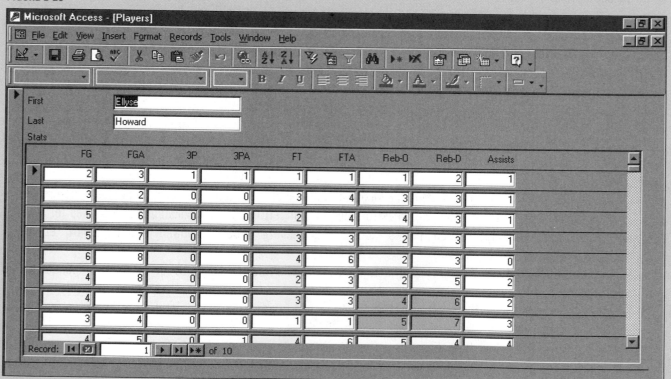

Managing

Database Objects

Objectives

- ► **Work with Objects**
- MOUS ► **Use the Documenter**
- ► **Group Objects**
- ► **Modify Groups**
- ► **Create a Dialog Box**
- ► **Create a Pop-up Form**
- MOUS ► **Create a Switchboard**
- ► **Modify a Switchboard**

As your database grows in size and functionality, the number of objects (especially queries and reports) will grow as well. Your ability to find, rename, delete, and document objects as well as your proficiency to present objects in an organized way to other database users through groups and switchboards will become important skills. ➤ Kristen Fontanelle is the network administrator at MediaLoft headquarters. She has developed a working database to document MediaLoft computer equipment in use throughout the company. The large quantity of objects within the database makes it increasingly difficult to find and organize information. Kristen will use powerful Access documentation, object grouping, and switchboard features to manage the growing database.

Working with Objects

Working with Access objects is very similar to working with files in Windows Explorer. For example, the **View buttons** (Large Icons, Small Icons, List, and Details) on the database window toolbar can be used to arrange the objects in four different ways just as files can be arranged within Explorer. Similarly, you right-click an object within Access to open, copy, delete, or rename it just as you would right-click a file within Explorer. ◀▬▬ Kristen wants to work with several objects to improve the database window interface. She deletes, renames, sorts, and adds descriptions to several objects.

Steps 1 2 3 4

1. Start Access, open the **Technology-M database** on your Project Disk, maximize the database window, click **Queries** on the Objects bar, then click the **Details button** 🔲 on the database window toolbar

   Your screen should look like Figure M-1, with five columns of information for each object: Name, Description, Modified (date the object was last changed), Created (date the object was originally created), and Type. By default, objects are sorted in ascending order by name, and the Description column is blank.

QuickTip
Point to the line between column headings, then drag ✛ left or right to resize that column.

2. Click the **Modified column heading** to sort the objects in ascending order on the date they were last modified, click **Modified column heading** again to sort the objects in descending order on the date they were last modified, then click the **Name column heading**

   The query objects are now sorted in ascending order by name. The Description column is a special object property that is used to further describe the object.

3. Right-click the **Equipment Specs query**, then click **Properties**

   The Equipment Specs Properties dialog box opens, as shown in Figure M-2.

4. Type **Includes RAM, hard drive, and processor information for PCs**, then click **OK**

   Part of the description appears in the database window and helps describe the object. If an object is no longer needed, you should delete it to free up disk space and keep the database window organized.

5. Right-click the **Employees Query**, click **Delete**, then click **Yes** when prompted

   Even though object names can be 64 characters long and can include any combination of letters, numbers, spaces, and special characters except a period (.), exclamation point (!), accent (`), or brackets ([]), they should be kept short yet descriptive. Short names make them easier to reference in other places in the database such as in the Record Source property for a report.

6. Right-click the **Human Resources query**, click **Rename**, type **HR**, press [Enter], right-click the **Information Systems query**, click **Rename**, type **IS**, then press [Enter]

   Your final screen should look like Figure M-3. With shorter query names, all of the object names are visible in the database window without resizing the columns.

FIGURE M-1: Viewing object details

Details button

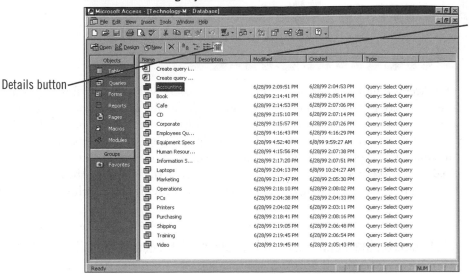

Modified column heading

FIGURE M-2: Equipment Specs Properties dialog box

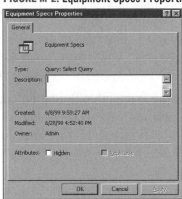

FIGURE M-3: Final Query object window

Description

Queries were renamed

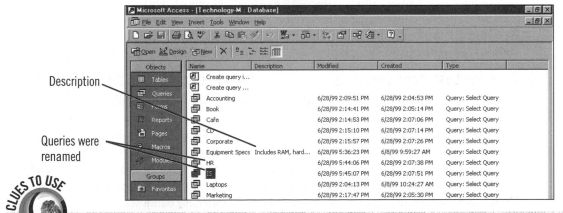

Access 2000

CLUES TO USE

Updating names with Name AutoCorrect

Name AutoCorrect fixes discrepancies between references to field names, controls, and objects when you rename them. For example, if a report is based on a query named "Department Income," and the query name is changed to "Dept Inc," the Name AutoCorrect feature will automatically update the Record Source property for the report to "Dept Inc." Similarly, if a query includes a field name of "LastName" that changes to "LName" in the Design view of the original table, the Name AutoCorrect feature will update the field name reference within the query as well. Name AutoCorrect will not repair references in Visual Basic code, replicated databases, linked tables, or a number of other database situations. Click Tools on the menu bar in the database window, click Options, and then click the General tab to view the Name AutoCorrect options. By default, the first two of the three Name AutoCorrect options should be checked.

Using the Documenter

As your Access database becomes more successful, users will naturally find new ways to use the data. Your ability to modify an existing database will revolve largely around your understanding of existing database objects. Access provides an analysis feature called the **Documenter** that creates reports on the properties and relationships between the objects in your database. This documentation is especially helpful to those who need to use the database but did not design the original tables. Kristen uses the Documenter to start creating the paper documentation that will support the Technology-M database for other MediaLoft employees.

Steps 1234

1. Click **Tools** on the menu bar, point to **Analyze**, click **Documenter**, then click the **Tables tab**
The Documenter dialog box opens, displaying tabs for the object types.

2. Click **Options** in the Documenter dialog box
The Print Table Definition dialog box, shown in Figure M-4, opens. This dialog box gives you some control over what type of documentation you wish to print for the table. The documentation for each object type varies slightly. For example, the documentation on forms and reports would include information on controls and sections.

3. Click **Cancel** in the Print Table Definition dialog box
You work through the Documenter dialog box, deciding which objects and options you want to document. Clicking the Select All button is a fast way to select all of the objects on that tab. You can also select or deselect individual objects by clicking the check box beside their name.

QuickTip

Information about the progress of Documenter will appear in the status bar.

4. Click **Select All**, click the **Forms tab**, click **Select All**, then click **OK**
Documenter is now creating a report about all of the table and form objects in the Technology-M database, and will display it as an Access report. This can be a lengthy process (several minutes) depending on the speed of your computer and the number of objects that Documenter is examining. When completed, your screen will look like Figure M-5, which shows a report that displays information about the first table, Assignments, on the first page.

5. Click the **Last Page button** in the navigation buttons, click the **Previous Page button**, then scroll down so that your screen looks like Figure M-6
The report contains about three pages of documentation for each table, and about six pages per form. The properties for each control on the form are listed in two columns. Because most form controls have approximately 50 properties, you can quickly see why the documentation that lists each control and section property can become so large. You can print or send the report to a Word document using the OfficeLinks buttons, but you cannot work in the report's Design view or save the report as an object within the database window.

6. Click the **Close button** on the Print Preview toolbar

FIGURE M-4: Print Table Definition dialog box

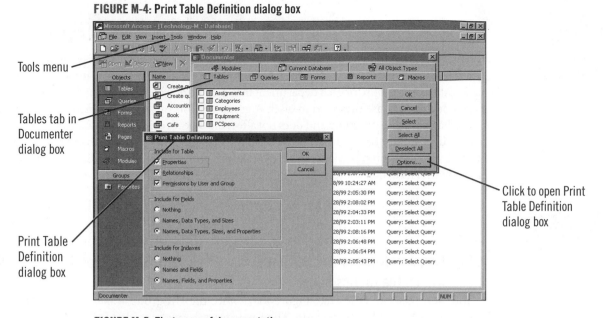

Tools menu

Tables tab in Documenter dialog box

Print Table Definition dialog box

Click to open Print Table Definition dialog box

FIGURE M-5: First page of documentation

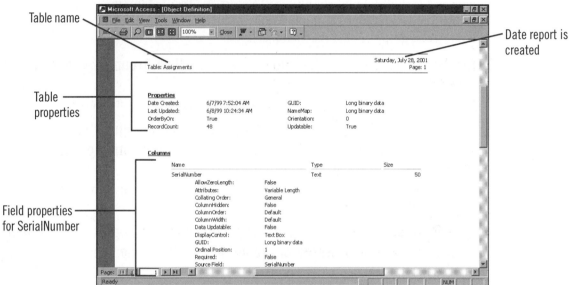

Table name

Date report is created

Table properties

Field properties for SerialNumber

FIGURE M-6: Second to last page of documentation

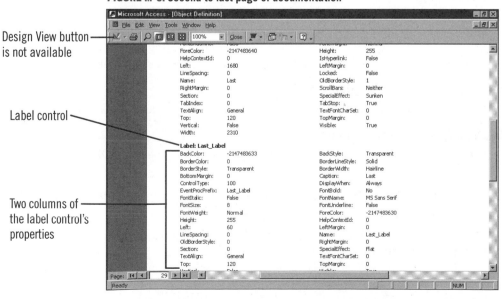

Design View button is not available

Label control

Two columns of the label control's properties

Grouping Objects

Viewing every object in the database window can be cumbersome when your database contains many objects. Objects can be placed in **groups** to help you easily organize or classify objects. For example, you might create a group for each department that uses the database so that the forms and reports used by each department are presented as a set. A group consists of **shortcuts** (pointers) to the database objects that belong to the group and does not affect the object's original location. To work with groups, click the **Groups bar** below the Objects bar in the Database window. Kristen organizes the objects in the Technology-M database by creating groups for the objects used by two different departments: Human Resources (HR) and Accounting.

Steps

1. **Right-click Favorites on the Groups bar, click New Group, type HR, click OK, then click HR on the Groups bar**
   Your screen should look like Figure M-7. Since the HR group was just created, there are no objects referenced in that group. The Favorites group is provided for every new Access database and is similar in function to the Favorites folder used in other Microsoft applications. Within an Access database, the Favorites group organizes *objects* rather than files because it is an Access group (rather than a folder).

2. **Right-click Favorites on the Groups bar, click New Group, type Accounting, then click OK**
   With the two new groups in place, you are ready to organize objects according to these groups.

3. **Click Queries on the Objects bar, drag the Accounting query into the Accounting group, drag the Equipment Specs query into the Accounting group, then drag the HR query into the HR group**
   Shortcuts to these three queries have been placed in their respective groups; the original objects do not move.

4. **Click Reports on the Objects bar, drag the Accounting report into the Accounting group, drag the Human Resources report into the HR group, then click Accounting on the Groups bar**
   Your screen should look like Figure M-8, with three shortcut icons representing two queries and one report in the Accounting group. Because both an original query and a report object were named "Accounting," Access added a "1" to the second "Accounting" shortcut icon. These shortcuts are just pointers to the original objects and, therefore, do not change the name of the original object. You can open or design an object by clicking its shortcut icon. You also can drag an object to more than one group, thereby creating more than one shortcut to it.

5. **Click Groups on the Groups bar**
   Clicking Groups expands the Groups bar and collapses the Objects bar, as shown in Figure M-9.

6. **Click Groups on the Groups bar**
   Clicking Groups when it is expanded collapses the Groups bar. The Objects bar works in the same way.

7. **Place the pointer on the top edge of Groups, and drag up with the ⬍ mouse pointer to just below Modules on the Objects bar**
   Displaying all of the Objects and all of the Groups is a good way to arrange the Objects and Groups bars when you start a new Access database.

FIGURE M-7: Creating groups

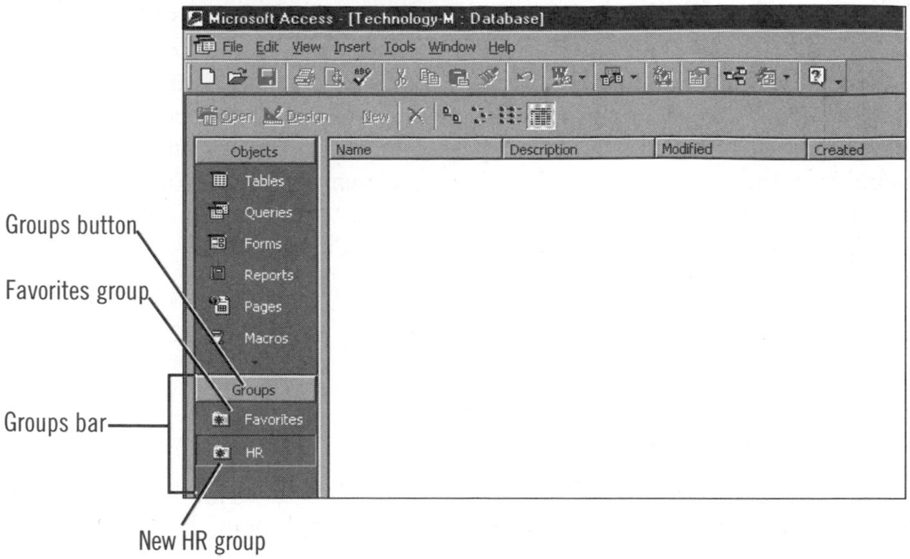

Groups button

Favorites group

Groups bar

New HR group

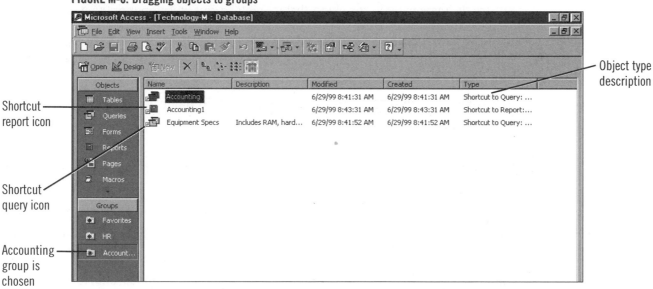

FIGURE M-8: Dragging objects to groups

Shortcut report icon

Shortcut query icon

Accounting group is chosen

Object type description

FIGURE M-9: Expanding groups

Groups are expanded

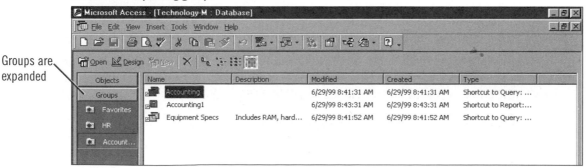

Access 2000

Modifying Groups

Once groups are created and object shortcuts are added to them, you modify the shortcuts in each group similarly to how you work with the actual objects themselves. For example, you can delete, rename, copy, or print a shortcut by right-clicking it and choosing the appropriate command from the short-cut menu. The biggest difference between working with shortcuts and actual objects is that if you delete a shortcut, you do not permanently delete the object. Groups also can be renamed and deleted. Kristen modifies both the groups and the shortcuts within them to clarify the Technology-M database.

Steps 1234

1. Right-click the **Accounting1 shortcut** in the Accounting group, click **Rename**, type **Accounting Report Sorted by Name**, press **[Enter]**, point to the **right edge of the Name column** so that the pointer changes to ↔, then double-click the column separator

   The Name column resizes to display the full shortcut name. A shortcut name does not have to have the same name as the object that it points to, but, it is important that the shortcuts be clearly named. The shortcut icon to the left of the shortcut indicates the type of object it represents. See Tables M-1 and M-2 for information about a popular object and field type naming convention developed by the Kwery Corporation, called the Leszynski Naming Convention.

2. Right-click **Accounting** on the Groups bar, click **Rename Group**, type **Acctg**, then press **[Enter]**

   The Groups bar should look like Figure M-10.

3. Right-click **Acctg**, click **New Group**, type **IS** in the New Group dialog box, then press **[Enter]**

4. Drag the **Equipment Specs shortcut** from the Acctg group to the IS group

   Shortcuts to the same object can be found in multiple groups. They can have the same or different names within each group.

5. Click **IS** on the Groups bar, double-click the **Equipment Specs shortcut** in the IS group to open the query's datasheet, double-click **32** in the Memory field for the second record (SerialNo RT55XLQ5), type **64**, then close the datasheet

   Edits and entries made to data in this query's datasheet (whether you opened the datasheet from the original query object or from a shortcut) are stored in the original table object.

6. Click **Tables** on the Objects bar, double-click the **PCSpecs table** to open its datasheet, then click the **Sort Descending button** ⧗ on the Table Datasheet toolbar

   The records are sorted in descending order on SerialNo, as shown in Figure M-11. Note that the entry for the Memory field for SerialNo RT55XLQ5 is 64.

7. Close the PCSpecs datasheet without saving changes

FIGURE M-10: Modifying groups

Renamed shortcut

Right edge of the Name column

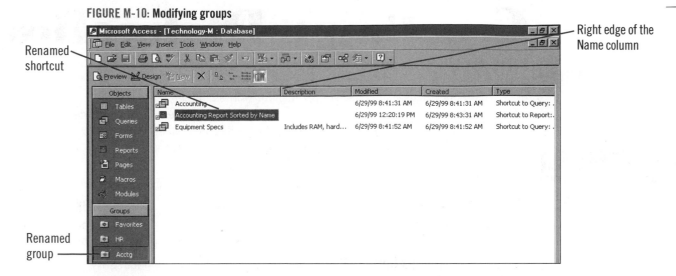

Renamed group

FIGURE M-11: A change made through a shortcut

Edit made through shortcut

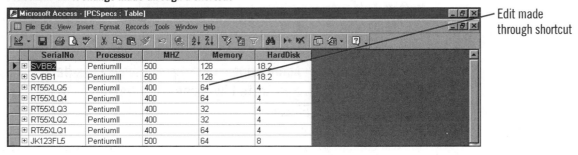

TABLE M-1: Leszynski Naming Convention for objects

object	tag	example
Table	tbl	TblEmployees
Form	frm	FrmEmployeeEntry
Query	qry	qryIncome2000
Report	rpt	rptAccount1Qtr
Macro	mcr	McrHRToolbar

TABLE M-2: Leszynski Naming Convention for data types

field data type	tag	example
Currency	cur	CurRetail
Date/Time	dtm	DtmSaleDate
Number (Integer)	int	IntDistrictNo
Number (Double)	dbl	DblMicrons
Number (Single)	sng	SngMillimeters
Memo	mem	MemComments
OLE Object	ole	OlePicture
Text	str	StrFName
Yes/No	ysn	YsnGoldClub

Creating a Dialog Box

A **dialog box** is a special form that is used to display information or to prompt a user for a choice. For example, you might create a dialog box to prompt the user to select a report to print. Dialog boxes are used to simplify the Access interface rather than forms used in their traditional role (to support easy, accurate data entry). Special form properties such as **Border Style** and **Auto Center** make a form appear like a dialog box. Kristen would like to create a dialog box that gives access to the three reports that the Accounting Department regularly prints. Then she'll add a shortcut to the dialog box in the Accounting group to simplify the printing process.

Steps

1. Click **Forms** on the Objects bar, click the **New button**, then click **OK**
   A dialog box is not bound to an underlying table or query and doesn't use the form's Record Source property. A dialog box often contains command buttons to automate tasks.

2. Click the **Toolbox button** on the Form Design toolbar (if necessary), verify that the **Control Wizards button** is selected on the Toolbox, click the **Command Button button** on the Toolbox, then click ⁺☐ in the upper-left corner of the form
   The **Command Button Wizard** dialog box opens.

3. Click **Report Operations** in the Categories list, click **Preview Report** in the Actions list, click **Next**, click **Accounting** as the report choice, click **Next**, click the **Text option button**, press **[Tab]**, type **Sorted by Name**, click **Next**, type **Name** in the button name text box, then click **Finish**
   The command button appears in Form Design view, as shown in Figure M-12. The dialog box will contain two more buttons to preview the other two Accounting reports.

4. Click ▭, click ⁺☐ below the first command button, click **Report Operations** in the Categories list, click **Preview Report** in the Actions list, click **Next**, click **Accounting Manufacturer**, click **Next**, click the **Text option button**, press **[Tab]**, type **Sorted by Manufacturer**, click **Next**, type **Mfg**, then click **Finish**

5. Click ▭, click ⁺☐ below the second command button, click **Report Operations** in the Categories list, click **Preview Report** in the Actions list, click **Next**, click **Accounting MHz**, click **Next**, click the **Text option button**, press **[Tab]**, type **Sorted by Speed**, click **Next**, type **Speed**, then click **Finish**
   The Design view of the form should look like Figure M-13.

Trouble?

Every command button must be given a unique name that is referenced in underlying Visual Basic code. Deleting a command button from Design view does not delete the underlying code, so each new button name must be different, even if the button has been deleted.

6. Double-click the **Form Selector button** to open the form's property sheet, click the **Format tab**, click the **Border Style text box**, click the **Border Style list arrow**, then click **Dialog**
   The **Dialog** option for the Border Style property indicates that the form will have a thick border and can include only a title bar, a close button, and a control menu button. The form cannot be maximized, minimized, or resized.

7. Click the **Navigation Buttons text box**, click the **Navigation Buttons list arrow**, click **No**, click the **Record Selectors text box**, click the **Record Selectors list arrow**, then click **No**

8. Close the property sheet, restore the form, resize the form to 3" wide by 3" tall, save the form as **Accounting Reports**, then click the **Form View button**
   Restoring and resizing the form best displays the property changes you made to the Border Style, Navigation Buttons, and Record Selectors properties as shown in Figure M-14.

9. Click the **Sorted by Speed command button**
   The report sorts the PCs in the Accounting Department in descending order by MHz (megahertz).

10. Close the **Accounting MHz report**, then close the **Accounting Reports form**

FIGURE M-12: Adding a command button

Command button's
name

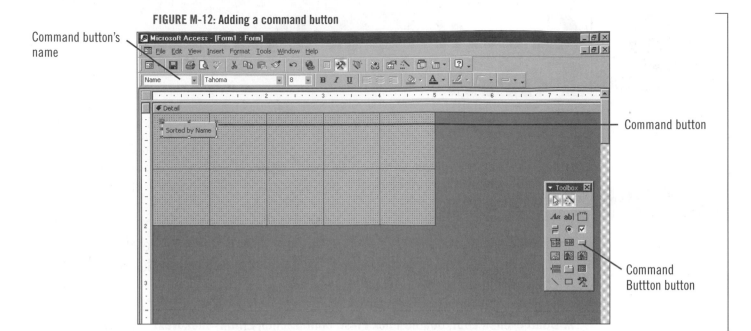

Command button

Command
Buttton button

FIGURE M-13: The final dialog box in Form Design view

Form Selector
button

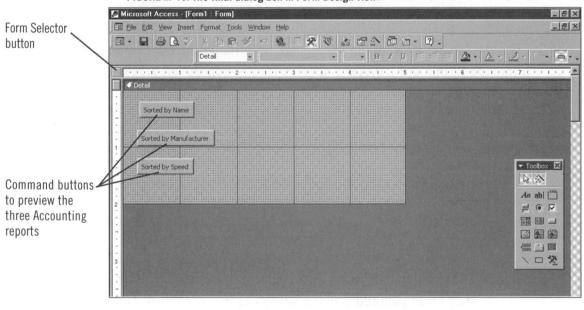

Command buttons
to preview the
three Accounting
reports

FIGURE M-14: The final dialog box in Form view

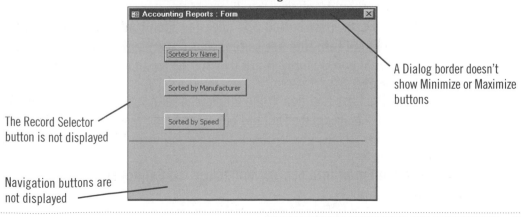

A Dialog border doesn't
show Minimize or Maximize
buttons

The Record Selector
button is not displayed

Navigation buttons are
not displayed

Creating a Pop-up Form

A **pop-up form** is another special type of form that stays on top of other open forms, even when another form is active. For example, you might want to create a pop-up form to give the user detailed information about an employee that isn't always visible on the main form. A command button is usually used to open the pop-up form. ➤ Kristen creates a pop-up form to access employee e-mail information, and adds a command button on the Employees form to open the pop-up form.

Steps

1. Click **Forms** on the Objects bar, click the **New button** 📄 in the database window, click **Form Wizard**, click the **Choose the table or query where the object's data comes from list arrow**, click **Employees**, then click **OK**
   You need only three fields of information in the pop-up form.

2. Double-click **Last**, double-click **First**, double-click **Email**, click **Next**, click **Tabular** for the layout, click **Next**, click **Standard** for the style, click **Next**, type **Email Info** for the title of the form, then click **Finish**
   The Email Info form opens in Form view, as shown in Figure M-15. You can modify the form so that it behaves as a pop-up form in Form Design view.

3. Click the **Design View button** 📐, double-click the **Form Selector button**, click the **Other tab** in the form's property sheet, click the **Pop Up list arrow**, click **Yes**, close the property sheet, save the form, then close the form
   With the Email Info pop-up form created, you are ready to connect it via a command button to the Employees form.

4. Double-click the **Employees form** to open it in Form view, then maximize the Employees form
   The Employees form contains four bound fields: Last, First, Department, and Title, as well as a subform that displays the equipment assigned to that employee.

5. Click 📐 on the Form view toolbar, place the pointer on the **right edge of the form**, then drag ↔ to the **6.5"** mark on the horizontal ruler
   The command button will be placed in the upper-right corner of the form.

6. Click the **Command Button button** ▭ on the Toolbox, click ⁺▭ to the right of the Title text box, click **Form Operations** in the Categories list, click **Open Form** in the Actions list, click **Next**, click the **Email Info** form, click **Next**, click the **Open the form and show all the records option button**, click **Next**, click the **Text option button**, press **[Tab]**, type **Email Addresses**, click **Next**, type **Email** as the name of the button, then click **Finish**
   Your screen should look similar to Figure M-16.

7. Click the **Form View button** 📄, click the **Email Addresses command button**, then drag the **Email Info title bar** so that your screen looks like Figure M-17
   The power of pop-up forms is that they stay on top of all other forms and can be turned on and off as needed by the user.

8. Click in the **Last text box** in the Employees form, click the **Sort Ascending button** ⬆, double-click **Maria** in the First text box of the Employees form, type **Mary**, then press **[Tab]**
   "Maria" also changed to "Mary" in the pop-up form because both forms are tied to the underlying Employee table.

9. Close the **Email Info** pop-up form, close the **Employees** form and save the changes when prompted

FIGURE M-15: Creating the Email Info pop-up form

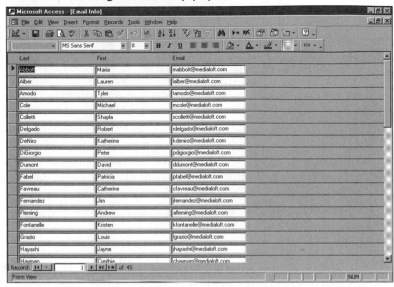

FIGURE M-16: Adding a command button to the Employees form

Command button's name

New command button

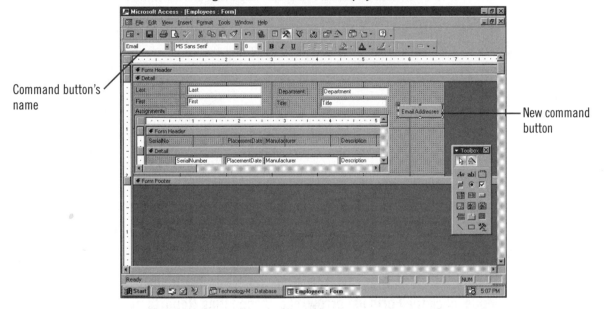

FIGURE M-17: The final form and pop-up form

Employees form

Command button

Title bar

Pop-up form

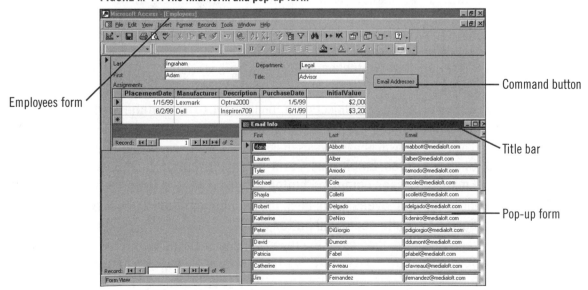

Creating a Switchboard

A **switchboard** is a special type of Access form that uses command buttons to simplify and secure the database. Switchboards are created and modified by using the **Switchboard Manager**. Using the Switchboard Manager requires very little knowledge of form design techniques, control types, or property settings. The Switchboard Manager is an Access **Add-In**, an extra feature that is not a part of the core Access program. A typical Access installation will include the Switchboard Manager as well as a few other Microsoft-supplied Add-Ins. More Add-Ins that extend the capabilities of Access are available through third-party vendors, and many can be downloaded from the Microsoft Web site. ◆ Kristen creates a switchboard form to make the database extremely easy to navigate.

Steps 1 2 3 4

1. Click **Tools** on the menu, point to **Database Utilities**, click **Switchboard Manager**, then click **Yes** when prompted to create a switchboard
   The Switchboard Manager dialog box opens, displaying one switchboard with the name of "Main Switchboard (Default)." One switchboard is always identified as the default switchboard, a designation that can be used to automatically open the switchboard form when the database opens.

2. Click **Edit** in the Switchboard Manager dialog box
   The Edit Switchboard Page dialog box opens. There are no items currently on the switchboard form.

3. Click **New**
   The Edit Switchboard Item dialog box opens, asking for three important items: Text (a label on the switchboard form that identifies the corresponding command button), Command (which corresponds to a database action that will be chosen), and Switchboard (which further defines the command button action). The Switchboard option changes depending on the action chosen in the Command list.

4. Type **Open Employees Form** in the Text text box, click the **Command list arrow**, click **Open Form in Edit Mode**, click the **Form list arrow**, then click **Employees**
   The Edit Switchboard Item dialog box should look like Figure M-18.

5. Click **OK** to add the first command button to the switchboard, click **New**, type **Accounting Reports** in the Text text box, click the **Command list arrow**, click **Open Form in Edit Mode**, click the **Form list arrow**, click **Accounting Reports**, then click **OK**
   The Edit Switchboard Page dialog box should look like Figure M-19. Each entry in this dialog box represents a command button that will appear on the final switchboard. Recall that the object "Accounting Reports" is a form with three command buttons that allow the user to preview three different reports.

6. Close the Edit Switchboard Page dialog box, then close the Switchboard Manager dialog box

7. Click **Forms** on the Objects bar, double-click the **Switchboard form**, then click the **Switchboard Restore Window button** (if it is maximized)
   The finished switchboard opens in Form view, as shown in Figure M-20.

8. Click the **Open Employees Form command button** on the Switchboard, click the **Email Addresses command button** on the Employees form, close the **Email info form**, close the **Employees form**, click the **Accounting Reports command button**, click the **Sorted by Name command button** in the Accounting Reports dialog box, maximize the report window, then close the report window and the Accounting Reports dialog box
   You have successfully tested the Switchboard, which should be on the screen. Most users consider Switchboard forms to be the easiest way to navigate through the objects of a large database.

FIGURE M-18: Edit Switchboard Item dialog box

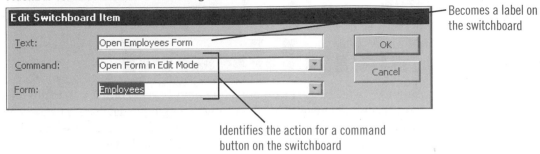

Becomes a label on the switchboard

Identifies the action for a command button on the switchboard

FIGURE M-19: Edit Switchboard Page dialog box

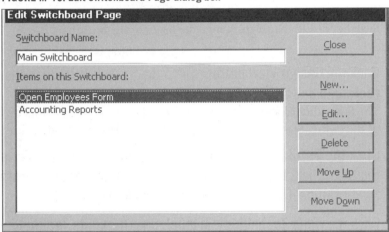

FIGURE M-20: Finished Switchboard

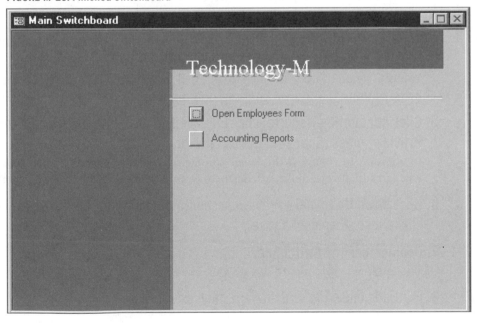

Modifying a Switchboard

Although switchboard forms don't *appear* to be very complex, in reality they are probably much more technically involved than any other form in the database. The Switchboard Manager hides that complexity by providing a series of dialog boxes you can use to add, delete, move, and edit the command buttons displayed on the switchboard. Cosmetic changes to a switchboard form, such as changing the label that serves as the title of the form, or changing form colors, can be accomplished in the form's Design view, but *always* use the Switchboard Manager to make changes to the command buttons and associated labels. ✐ Kristen is happy with the initial switchboard form she created, but she would like to improve it by changing the title, colors, and order of the command buttons. She uses Form Design view to make the formatting changes and the Switchboard Manager to change the order of the buttons.

Steps

1. Click the **Design View button** 🖾 on the Form View toolbar, then click the **dark green rectangle** on the left of the Detail section

The Switchboard form is in Design view. The dark green colors on the left and top portion of the switchboard are actually just clip art, added to provide color to the form.

QuickTip

If you need to uniquely identify your switchboard, add a label to the upper-right corner with your name.

2. Click the **Fill/Back Color button list arrow** 🎨▾ on the Formatting (Form/Report) toolbar, click **bright yellow**, click the **dark green rectangle** on the top of the Detail section, click 🎨▾, then click **bright red**

Trouble?

The Switchboard Manager creates a table called Switchboard Items that stores a record of information for each item in each switchboard. Deleting this table deletes all switchboards created within the database.

3. Click the **white Technology-M label**, drag the **white Technology-M label** using ✋ up into the red rectangle, click the **gray Technology-M** label, then press **[Delete]**

Your screen should look like Figure M-21. Other than changing colors, the title label, and adding or deleting clip art, there isn't much more you should modify in Form Design view when you are working with a switchboard. The Switchboard Manager gives you all the power you need to make changes to the command buttons.

4. Save and close the switchboard, click **Tools** on the menu, point to **Database Utilities**, click **Switchboard Manager**, then click **Edit**

You can create more than one switchboard form, and chain them together through command buttons. In this case, you have only one switchboard.

5. Click **Accounting Reports**, click **Edit**, click to the left of the **A** in the Text text box, type **Preview**, press **[Spacebar]**, then click **OK**

In addition to changing the labels connected to each command button on a switchboard, you can add, delete, move, or edit them from the Edit Switchboard Page dialog box.

6. Click **Move Up** to make Preview Accounting Reports the first item in the switchboard, click **Close**, then click **Close**

7. Double-click the **Switchboard** form to open it in Form view

The modified switchboard should look like Figure M-22.

8. Print and close the switchboard, then exit Access

FIGURE M-21: Switchboard in Design view

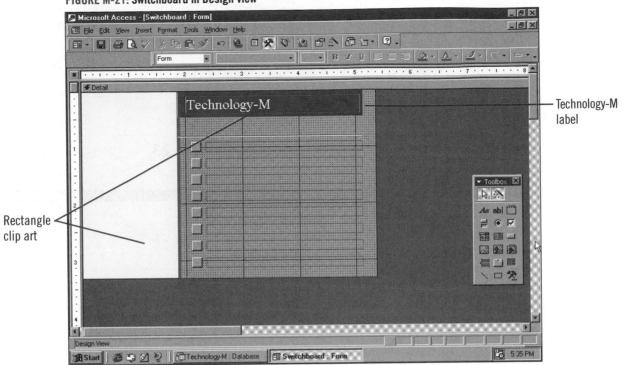

Rectangle
clip art

Technology-M
label

FIGURE M-22: Modified Switchboard

Command button
label was modified
using the Switchboard
Manager

Order has been
changed using
the Switchboard
Manager

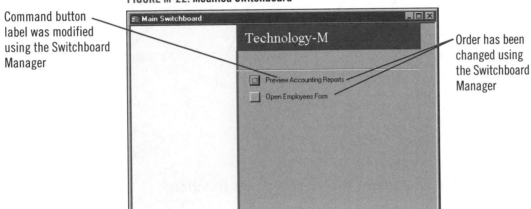

Illustrating Access features with Sample Databases

Microsoft provides four sample databases with
Access 2000 that illustrate many different ways to use
Access objects and features. All four databases are
installed on first use in a default installation (or can
be installed to your hard drive directly from the

Microsoft Office 2000 CD from the Microsoft
Access for Windows; Sample Databases installation
category). The Northwind database, in particular,
provides several examples of exciting switchboards
and dialog boxes.

Practice

► Concepts Review

Identify each element of the database window shown in Figure M-23.

FIGURE M-23

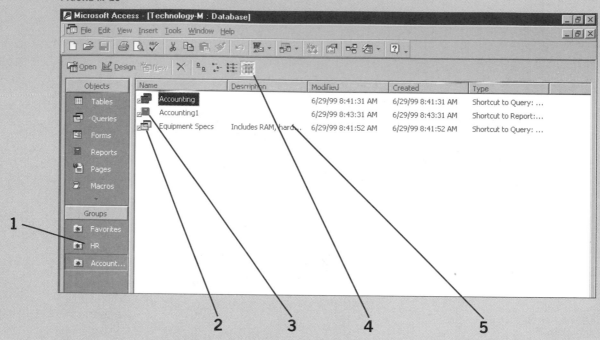

Match each term with the statement that describes its function.

6. Group
7. Pop-up form
8. Shortcut
9. Add-In
10. Documenter
11. Switchboard

a. Creates reports on the properties and relationships between the objects in your database
b. Pointer to database objects
c. Special type of form that stays on top of other open forms, even when another form is active
d. Special type of Access form that uses command buttons to simplify and secure access to database objects
e. Extra feature that is not a part of the core Access program
f. Helps you easily organize and classify objects

Select the best answer from the list of choices.

12. Which View button do you use to see the date that the object was created?
- **a.** List
- **b.** Small Icons
- **c.** Date
- **d.** Details

13. Which feature fixes discrepancies between references to field names, controls, and objects when you rename them?
- **a.** Documenter
- **b.** Renamer
- **c.** Name AutoCorrect
- **d.** Switchboard Manager

14. If you wanted to add another command button to a switchboard, which technique would you use?
- **a.** Modify the switchboard in Form Design view.
- **b.** Modify the switchboard in Report Design view.
- **c.** Use the Switchboard Manager.
- **d.** Use the Switchboard Analyzer.

15. Which technique would NOT provide much help to organize the Access objects that the Human Resources (HR) Department most often uses?
- **a.** Create a report that lists all HR employees.
- **b.** Create a switchboard that provides command buttons to the appropriate HR objects.
- **c.** Create a dialog box with command buttons that reference the most commonly used HR reports.
- **d.** Create an HR group and add shortcuts to the objects the HR Department most commonly uses.

16. Northwind is the name of a sample
- **a.** Switchboard form.
- **b.** Database.
- **c.** Pop-up form.
- **d.** Dialog box.

17. A dialog box is really a _____ with special property settings.
- **a.** Table
- **b.** Form
- **c.** Macro
- **d.** Report

▶ Skills Review

1. Working with Objects.
- **a.** Open the Basketball-M database.
- **b.** Click the Details button to view the details, click Reports on the Objects bar, then resize the Name column so that the entire report name is visible in the database window.

    c. Right-click the Player Field Goal Stats report, click Properties, type "Forwards and Guards" as the Description, then click OK.

    d. Click Queries on the Objects bar, right-click the Games query, click Rename, then type "Score Delta" as the new query name.

    e. Open the Games Summary Report in Design view, open the report property sheet, then check the Record Source property on the Data tab. Because the Games Summary Report was based on the former Games Query object, the new query name should appear in the Record Source property. (*Hint*: If the query name, Score Delta, doesn't appear in the Record Source property, click the Record Source property list arrow, then click Score Delta. Check the AutoCorrect options. From the database window, click Tools on the menu bar, click Options, click the General tab, then check the Name AutoCorrect options. By default, the first two of the three Name AutoCorrect options should be checked. Close the Options dialog box by clicking OK.)

    f. Close the property sheet, then save and close the report.

2. Using the Documenter.

    a. Click Tools on the menu bar, point to Analyze, then click Documenter.

    b. Click the Tables tab, click Select All, click the Reports tab, click the Games Summary Report check box, then click OK

    c. Watch the status bar to track the Documenter's progress.

    d. The final report is 20 pages long. Click File on the menu bar, click Print, click the Pages option button, type "1" in the From text box, type "1" in the To text box, then click OK to print the first page.

    e. Click File on the menu bar, click Print, click the Pages option button, type "20" in the From and To text boxes, then click OK to print page 20.

    f. Close the report created by Documenter.

3. Grouping Objects.

    a. Right-click Favorites on the Groups bar, click New Group, then type Forwards to create a new group named "Forwards".

    b. Drag the Forward Field Goals query to the Forwards group, then drag the Forward Field Goal Stats report to the Forwards group. Verify that the shortcuts are on the Forwards group.

    c. Create a new group named "Guards", then add shortcuts for the Guard Field Goals query and Guard Field Goal Stats report objects to it. Verify that the shortcuts are on the Guards group.

4. Modifying Groups.

    a. Click Forwards on the Groups bar, right-click the Forward Field Goals query shortcut, then rename the shortcut as "Forward FG Query".

    b. Rename the Forward Field Goal Stats report as "Forward FG Report".

    c. Click Guards on the Groups bar. Rename the Guard Field Goals query shortcut as "Guard FG Query".

    d. Rename the Guard Field Goal Stats report shortcut to "Guard FG Report".

    e. Click Forwards on the Groups bar, double-click the Forward FG Query shortcut, then enter your own name to replace Amy Hodel on any record her name currently occupies. As soon as you move off the record you are editing, the change will be made to the underlying Players table, which will update every record in this datasheet.

    f. Print the datasheet, then close it.

5. Creating a Dialog Box.

    a. Start a new form in Design view. Do not select any underlying tables or queries.

    b. Using the Toolbox, add a command button to the upper-left corner of the form using the Command Button Wizard. Select Report operations from the Categories list, then select Preview Report from the actions list since this is a form to preview the Games Summary Report.

    c. The Text for the button should be "Preview Games Summary Report" and the name of the button should be "Games".

    d. Using the Toolbox and the Command Button Wizard, create a second command button below the first to preview the Player Field Goal Stats report.

e. The Text for the button should be "Preview Player FG Stats" and the name of the button should be "Players".

f. Below the two buttons, add a label to the form with your name in it.

g. Open the Form's property sheet, click the Format tab, change the form's Border Style property to Dialog, change the form's Record Selectors property to No, then change the form's Navigation Buttons property to No.

h. Close the property sheet, restore the form (if it is maximized), resize it to approximately 3" wide by 3" tall, save the form as "Team Reports", click the Form View button, test the buttons, then print the form.

6. **Creating a Pop-up Form.**

   a. Using the Form Wizard, create a form with the following fields from the Players table: First, Last, and PlayerNo.

   b. Use a Tabular layout, a Standard style, and title the form "Player Pop-up".

   c. In Design view of the Player Pop-up form, resize the First and Last labels and text boxes to about half of their current width.

   d. Move the Last and PlayerNo labels and text boxes close to the First label and text box so that the entire form can be narrowed to no larger than 3" wide. Resize the form to 3" wide.

   e. Open the Forms property sheet, change the Pop Up property on the form's Other tab to Yes. Close the property sheet.

   f. Save and close the Player Pop-up form.

   g. In the Design view of the Team Reports form, use the Toolbox and Command Button Wizard to create a command button on the right side of the form that opens the Player Pop-up form and shows all of the records.

   h. The Text for the new button should be "Open Player Pop-up" and the name of the button should be "Player Pop-up".

   i. Save and view the Team Reports form in Form view, then click the Open Player Pop-up command button to test it. Test the other buttons as well. The Player Pop-up form should stay on top of all other forms and reports unless you close it.

   j. Save and close all open forms and reports.

7. **Creating a Switchboard.**

   a. Click Tools, point to Database Utilities, click Switchboard Manager, then click Yes to create a new switchboard.

   b. Click Edit to edit the Main Switchboard, then click New to add the first item to it.

   c. The Text for the first item should be "Choose a Team Report", the Command should be Open Form in Add Mode, and the Form should be Team Reports.

   d. Click New to add a second item to the switchboard. The Text for the second item should be "Open Player Entry Form", the Command should be Open Form in Add Mode, and the form should be Player Entry Form.

   e. Close the Edit Switchboard manager dialog box, close the Switchboard Manager dialog box. Open the Switchboard form and click both command buttons to make sure they work. Notice that when you open a form in "Add Mode" (rather than using the Open Form in Edit Mode action within the Switchboard Manager), the navigation buttons indicate that you can only add a new record, and not edit an existing one.

   f. Close all open forms including the Switchboard form.

8. **Modifying a Switchboard.**

   a. Click Tools, point to Database Utilities, click Switchboard Manager, then click Edit to edit the Main Switchboard.

   b. Click Open Player Entry Form, then click Edit.

   c. Change the Command to Open Form in Edit Mode, choose the Player Entry Form in the Form list, then click OK.

   d. Move the Open Player Entry Form item above the Choose a Team Report item, then close the Switchboard Manager.

   e. In Design view of the Switchboard Manager, delete both the white and gray Basketball-M labels, add a label with your team's name, then add a label with your own name. Place the two new labels at the top of the Switchboard form, and be sure to format them with a color that is visible in Form view.

   f. Save, print, and close the Switchboard form.

   g. Close the Basketball-M database.

   h. Exit Access.

▶ Independent Challenges

1. As the manager of a doctor's clinic, you have created an Access database called Patients-M to track insurance claim reimbursements that are fixed (paid at a predetermined fixed rate), or denied (not paid by the insurance company). You wish to create two groups to organize database objects.

To complete this independent challenge:

a. Start Access and open the database Patients-M from your Project Disk.

b. Create two new groups: Fixed and Denied.

c. Add shortcuts for the Monthly Query – Fixed query, the Date of Service Report – Fixed report, and the Monthly Claims Report – Fixed report to the Fixed group.

d. Add shortcuts for the Monthly Query – Denied query, the Date of Service Report – Denied report, and the Monthly Claims Report – Denied report to the Denied group.

e. Click Queries on the Objects bar, click the Details button in the database window, then sort the queries by date they were modified.

f. For the two queries that were last modified in May, add the Description "For Board Meeting" by accessing their properties.

g. Click the Tools menu, point to Analyze, then click Documenter. On the Current Database tab, click Relationships, then click OK.

h. Print the Documenter's report, then close it.

i. Close the Patients-M database.

j. Exit Access.

2. As the manager of a doctor's clinic, you have created an Access database called Patients-M to track insurance claim reimbursements that are fixed (paid at a predetermined fixed rate) or denied (not paid by the insurance company). You wish to create a new dialog box for your database.

To complete this independent challenge:

a. Start Access and open the database Patients-M from your Project Disk.

b. Start a new form in Design view.

c. Using the Toolbox and the Command Button Wizard, add a command button to the form to preview the Date of Service Report – Denied.

d. The Text for the button should be "Preview Date of Service – Denied" and the name of the button should be "PDOSD".

e. Using the Toolbox and the Command Button Wizard, create a second button below the first to preview the Date of Service Report – Fixed.

f. The Text for the button should be "Preview Date of Service – Fixed" and the name of the button should be "PDOSF".

g. Create a third command button below the second to preview the Monthly Claims Report – Denied.

h. The Text for the button should be "Preview Monthly Claims – Denied" and the name of the button should be "PMCD".

i. Create a fourth and final command button below the third to preview the Monthly Claims Report – Fixed.

j. The text for the button should be "Preview Monthly Claims – Fixed" and the name of the button should be "PMCF".

k. Below the buttons, add a label to the form with your name in it.

l. Change the form's Border Style property to Dialog.

m. Change the form's Record Selectors property to No.

n. Change the form's Navigation Buttons property to No.

o. Close the property sheet, restore the form (if it is maximized), resize it to approximately 3" wide by 3" tall, save the form as "Report Dialog Box", click the Form View button, test the buttons, then print the form.

p. Close the Patients-M database.

q. Exit Access

3. As the manager of a doctor's clinic, you have created an Access database called Patients-M to track insurance claim reimbursements that are fixed (paid at a predetermined fixed rate), or denied (not paid by the insurance company). You wish to create a pop-up form to provide physician information. You'll access the pop-up form from the Claim Entry Form via a command button.

To complete this independent challenge:

a. Start Access and open the database Patients-M database from your Project Disk.

b. Use the Form Wizard to create a form with all three fields in the Doctors table.

c. Use a Tabular layout, a Standard style, and title the form "Doctor Pop-up".

d. In Design view of the Doctor Pop-up form, resize all three labels and text boxes to about half their current width.

e. Move the PodLastName and PodCode labels and text boxes close to the PodFirstName label and text box so that the entire form can be narrowed to no larger than 3" wide.

f. Change the Pop-Up property on the form's Other tab to Yes.

g. Save and close the Doctor Pop-up form.

h. In Design view of the Claim Entry Form, use the Toolbox and Command Button Wizard to create a command button to the right of the Form Header section that opens the Doctor Pop-up form and shows all of the records.

i. The Text for the new button should be "Open Doctor Pop-up" and the name of the button should be "Doctor Pop-up".

j. Save and view the Claim Entry Form in Form view, then click the Open Doctor Pop-up command button.

k. Move through the records of the Claim Entry form. The Doctor Pop-up form should stay on top of all other forms unless you close it.

l. Save and close all open forms.

m. Close the Patients-M database.

n. Exit Access.

4. MediaLoft has developed a Web site that provides internal information to their employees. In this independent challenge, you'll surf the Internet to find Web pages that present information organized similarly to how a switchboard is used to organize an Access database.

a. Connect to the Internet, go to the MediaLoft intranet site at http://www.course.com/illustrated/MediaLoft

b. Print the home page. Identify which hyperlinks on the home page are analogous to command buttons on a switchboard.

c. Click the center link Research, click the link for Competition: Other Bookstores, and browse for a Web page that organizes information like switchboards.

d. If you are not familiar with Web browsing techniques, click the Back button until you return to the MediaLoft Research page, where you can start a new search.

e. When you find a Web page that contains "switchboard-like" hyperlinks to organize information, print the Web page and identify the hyperlinks. Print at least two other non-MediaLoft Web pages that act like switchboards, providing an organized method to access the rest of the information on that Web site.

h. Close your browser window.

i. Disconnect from the Internet.

▶ Visual Workshop

As the manager of a doctor's clinic, you have created an Access database called Patients-M to track insurance claim reimbursements that are fixed (paid at a predetermined fixed rate), or denied (not paid by the insurance company). Create a switchboard form to give the users an easy interface, as shown in Figure M-24. Both command buttons on the switchboard open forms in edit mode. Add and modify the two labels in the switchboard's Design view, and be sure to add your own name as the manager.

FIGURE M-24

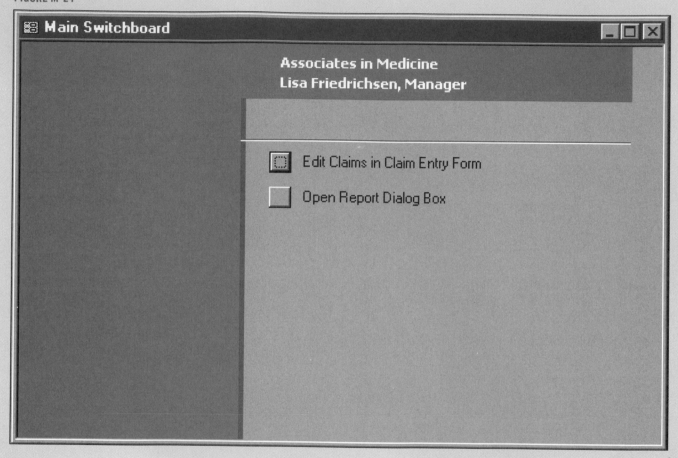

Creating
Macros

A **macro** is a database object that stores Access actions. When you run a macro, you execute the stored set of actions. Almost any repetitive Access task such as printing a report, opening a form, or exporting data is a good candidate for a macro. Automating routine and complex tasks as stored actions in a macro builds efficiency, accuracy, and flexibility into your database. ◄— Kristen noticed that several tasks are repeated on a regular basis and could be automated with macros. Although she hasn't worked with macros before, Kristen recognizes the benefits and is excited to get started.

Understanding Macros

A macro may contain one or more **actions**, the tasks that you want Access to perform. When you **run** a macro, the actions execute in the order in which they are listed in the **Macro window**. Each action has a specified set of **arguments** that provide additional information on how to carry out the action. For example, if the action were OpenForm, the arguments would include specifying the Form Name, the view (Form or Design) that the form should open to, and whether you want to apply any filters when you open the form. ◄━━ Kristen studies the major benefits of using macros, the key terminology she needs to know when developing macros, and the components of the Access Macro window before she builds her first macro.

Details

The major benefits of using macros:

- Save time by automating routine tasks.

- Increase accuracy by ensuring that tasks are executed consistently.

- Make forms and reports work together by providing command buttons bound to macros that enable users to quickly and easily move between the objects.

- Make the database easier to use by providing command buttons bound to macros to filter and find records automatically.

- Ensure data accuracy in forms by responding to errors in data entry with different messages developed in macros.

- Automate data transfers such as exporting data to an Excel workbook.

- Create your own customized environment by customizing toolbars and the menu system.

Key macro terminology:

- **macro**: An Access object that stores a series of actions to perform one or more tasks.

- **action**: Each task that you want the macro to perform. Each macro action occupies a single row in the macro window.

- **macro window**: The window in which you create a macro, as shown in Figure N-1. See Table N-1 for a description of the macro window components.

- **arguments**: Properties of an action that provide additional information on how the action should execute.

- **macro group**: An Access macro object that stores more than one macro. The macros in a macro group run independently of one another, but are grouped together to organize multiple macros that have similar characteristics. For example, you may wish to put all of the macros that print reports in one macro group.

- **expression**: A combination of values, identifiers (such as the value in a field), and operators that result in a value.

- **conditional expression**: An expression that results in either a "true" or "false" answer that determines if a macro action will execute or not. For example, if the field Country contained a null value, you may wish for the macro to execute an action that sends the user a message.

- **event**: Something that happens on a form, window, toolbar, or datasheet—such as the click of a command button or an entry in a field—that can be used to initiate the execution of a macro.

FIGURE N-1: Macro window of a macro group

Macro Names button

Macro names

Close macro is selected

Conditions evaluate to "true" or "false"

Suppliers macro group

Conditions button

Optional comments

Arguments for selected action

Macro actions

Descriptive information for selected argument

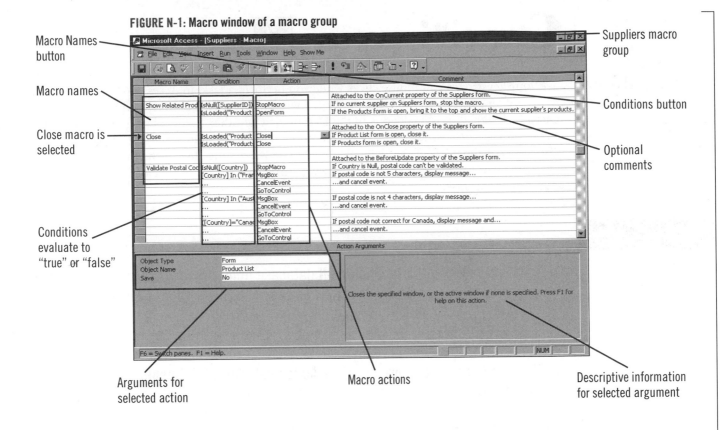

TABLE N-1: Macro window components

component	description
Macro Name column	Contains the names of individual macros within a macro group. If the macro object contains only one macro, it isn't necessary to use this column because you can run the macro by referring to the macro object's name. View this column by clicking the Macro Names button.
Condition column	Contains conditional expressions that are evaluated either "true" or "false." If "true," the macro action on that row is executed. If "false," the macro action on that row is skipped. View this column by clicking the Conditions button.
Action column	Contains the actions (steps, instructions, or commands) that the macro executes when it runs.
Comment column	Contains optional explanatory text for each macro action.
Close macro	Is only two actions long. Both actions are "close" actions and will be executed only if the conditional expression in the corresponding row is "true."
Action arguments	Displays action characteristics and values that further define the selected macro action. In Figure N-1, the Close action has three arguments. Action Arguments change based on the action.

Creating a Macro

In some software programs, you can create a macro by having a "macro recorder" monitor and save your keystrokes and mouse clicks while you perform a task. In Access, you create a macro by specifying a series of actions in the Macro window. Because the Macro window is where a macro is designed, it is analogous to the Design view of other Access objects. There are more than 50 macro actions, and many of the common ones are listed in Table N-2. ➤ Kristen observed that the users of the Technology database waste time closing the Employees form to open and print the All Equipment report several times a week, so she decides to create a macro to automate this task.

Steps

1. **Start Access, open the Technology-N database from your Project Disk, click Macros on the Objects bar, then click the New button 🔲 in the database window**
   The Macro1 Macro window opens, ready to accept your first action statement. The Macro Name and Condition columns are not visible by default, but could be toggled on by clicking their respective buttons on the Macro Design toolbar.

2. **Click the Action list arrow, scroll the Action list, then click OpenReport**
   The OpenReport action is added as the first line of the Macro window, and the arguments that further define the action appear in the Action Arguments panel. The Open Report action has two required arguments: the name of the report that you want to open and the view in which you want to open the report. The Filter Name and Where Condition arguments are optional.

3. **Click the Report Name text box in the Action Arguments panel, click the Report Name List arrow, then click All Equipment**
   All of the report objects in the Technology-N database display in the Report Name list when you choose the OpenReport action.

4. **Click the View text box in the Action Arguments panel, click the View list arrow, then click Print**
   Your screen should look like Figure N-2. Macro actions can contain conditional expressions that execute only if the result of the conditional expression is true. Macros can be one or many actions long. In this case, the macro is only one action long and there are no conditional expressions.

5. **Click the Save button 🔲 on the Macro Design toolbar, type Print All Equipment Report in the Macro Name text box, click OK, then close the Macro window**
   The Technology-N database window shows the Print All Equipment Report object as a Macro object.

QuickTip
Add a label with your name to the All Equipment report if you need to uniquely identify your printout.

6. **Click the Run button ⚠ in the Technology-N Database window**
   The All Equipment report prints.

FIGURE N-2: Macro window with OpenReport action

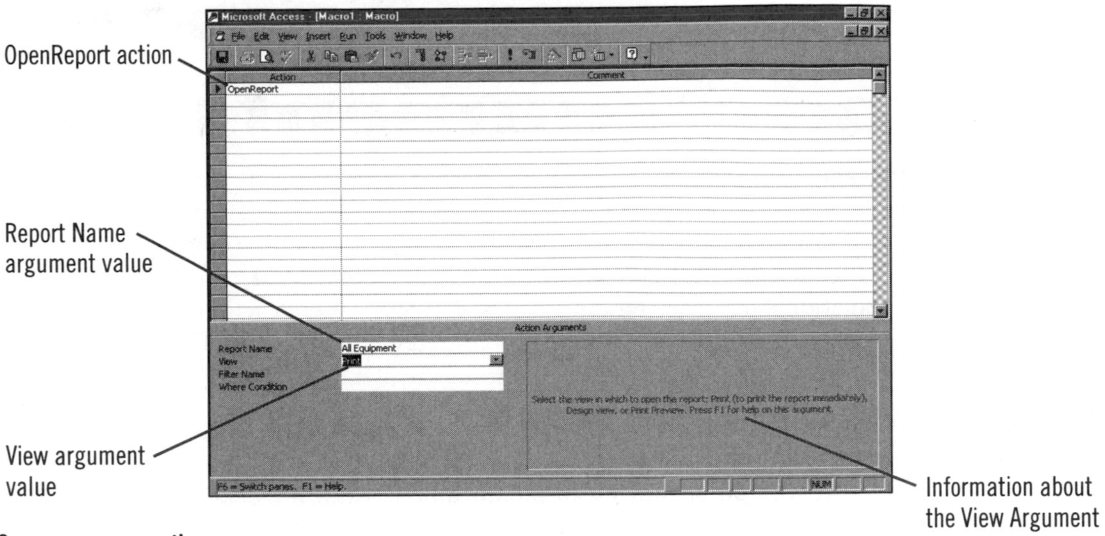

OpenReport action

Report Name
argument value

View argument
value

Information about
the View Argument

TABLE N-2: Common macro actions

subject area	macro action	description
Handling data in forms	ApplyFilter	Restricts the number of records that appear in the resulting form or report by applying limiting criteria
	FindRecord	Finds the first record that meets the criteria
	GoToControl	Moves the focus (where you are currently typing or clicking) to a specific field or control
	GoToRecord	Makes a specified record the current record
Executing menu options	RunCode	Calls a Visual Basic function (a series of programming statements that do a calculation or comparison and return a value)
	RunCommand	Carries out a specified menu command
	RunMacro	Runs a macro or attaches a macro to a custom menu command
	StopMacro	Stops the currently running macro
Importing/Exporting data	TransferDatabase TransferSpreadsheet TransferText	Imports, links, or exports data between the current Microsoft Access database and another database, spreadsheet, or text file
Manipulating objects	Close	Closes a window
	Maximize	Enlarges the active window to fill the Access window
	OpenForm	Opens a form in Form view, Design view, Print Preview, or Datasheet view
	OpenQuery	Opens a select or crosstab query in Datasheet view, Design view, or Print Preview; runs an action query
	OpenReport	Opens a report in Design view or Print Preview, or prints the report
	OpenTable	Opens a table in Datasheet view, Design view, or Print Preview
	PrintOut	Prints the active object, such as a datasheet, report, form, or module, in the open database
	SetValue	Sets the value of a field, control, or property
Miscellaneous	Beep	Sounds a beep tone through the computer's speaker
	MsgBox	Displays a message box containing a warning or an informational message
	SendKeys	Sends keystrokes directly to Microsoft Access or to an active Windows-based application

Modifying Actions and Arguments

Macros can contain as many actions as necessary to complete the process that you want to automate. Each action is evaluated in the order in which it appears in the Macro window, starting at the top. While some macro actions manipulate data or objects, others are used only to make the database easier to use. **MsgBox** is a particularly useful macro action because it displays an informational message. ▰▰▰▰ Kristen decides to add an action to the Print All Equipment Report macro to clarify what is happening when the macro runs. She adds a MsgBox action to the macro to display a descriptive message for the user.

Steps

QuickTip

Press [F1] to display Help text for the action and argument currently selected.

1. Click the **Design button** ▨ in the database window
   The Print All Equipment Report macro opens in Design view.

2. Click the **Action cell** just below the OpenReport action, click the **Action list arrow**, scroll the **Action list**, then click **MsgBox**
   Each action has its own arguments that further clarify what the action will accomplish.

3. Click the **Message text box** in the Action Arguments panel, then type **The All Equipment Report has just been sent to the printer**
   The Message argument determines what text appears in the message box. By default, the Beep argument is set to "Yes" and the Type argument is set to "None."

4. Click the **Type text box** in the Action Arguments panel, read the description in the lower-right corner of the Macro window, click the **Type list arrow**, then click **Information**
   The Type argument determines which icon will appear in the dialog box that is created by the MsgBox action.

5. Click the **Title text box** in the Action Arguments panel, then type **Important Information!**
   Your screen should look like Figure N-3. The Title argument specifies what text will display in the title bar of the resulting dialog box. If you leave the Title argument empty, the title bar of the resulting dialog box will display "Microsoft Access."

6. Click the **Save button** ▣ on the Macro Design toolbar, then click the **Run button** ▣ on the Macro Design toolbar
   If your speakers are turned on, you should hear a beep, then the message box should appear, as shown in Figure N-4. The report prints a second time.

7. Click **OK** in the dialog box, then close the Print All Equipment Report Macro window
   The modified Print All Equipment Report macro is saved.

FIGURE N-3: Print All Equipment Report macro with additional MsgBox action

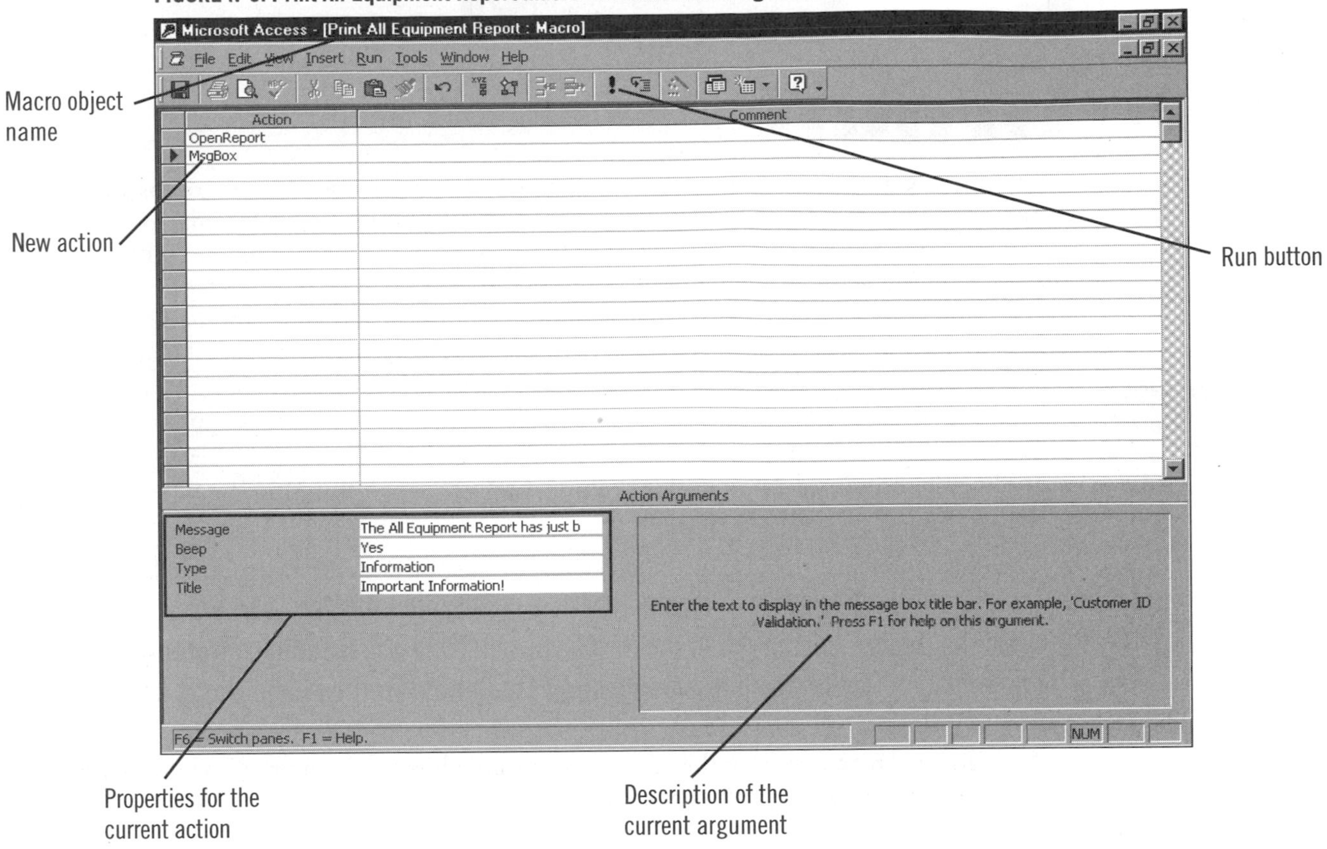

Macro object name

New action

Run button

Properties for the current action

Description of the current argument

FIGURE N-4: Dialog box created by MsgBox action

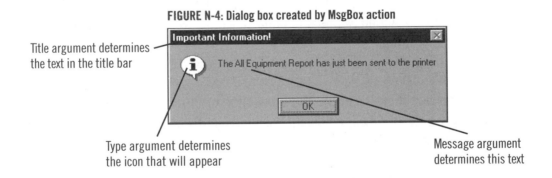

Title argument determines the text in the title bar

Type argument determines the icon that will appear

Message argument determines this text

Creating a Macro Group

A **macro group** is a macro object that stores several macros together. Macro groups are used to organize multiple macros that have similar characteristics, such as all the macros that print reports or all the macros that are attached to the same form through command buttons. When you put several macros in the same macro object to create a macro group, you must enter a unique name for each macro in the Macro Name column (in the same row as the first macro action) to identify where each macro starts. ✐ Kristen adds a macro that prints the Accounting Report to the Print All Equipment Report macro object. By adding this new macro and any additional macros that print reports in one object, she creates a macro object.

Steps 1234

1. Right-click the **Print All Equipment Report macro**, click **Rename**, type **Print Reports Macro Group**, then press **[Enter]**

   The object name should explain the contents of the object as clearly as possible. The name should reflect the fact that the macro object contains more than one macro.

2. Click the **Design button** 🔣 in the database window, click the **Macro Names button** 🔣 on the Macro Design toolbar, type **Print All Equipment** in the Macro Name column, then press **[Enter]**

   An individual macro is given the name of the macro object *unless* a macro name is entered in the Macro Name column. If several macros are stored as a macro group in one object, it is imperative that each be given a unique name so that each can be clearly referenced later.

3. Click in the **Macro Name cell** in the third row, type **Print Accounting Report**, then press **[Enter]**

   A new macro starts when a new name is entered in the Macro Name column.

> **QuickTip**
>
> Some macro developers leave a blank row between macros to further clarify where a new macro starts.

4. Click the **Action list arrow**, scroll and click **OpenReport**, click in the **Report Name text box** in the Action Arguments panel, click the **Report Name list arrow**, then click **Accounting Report**

   Your screen should look like Figure N-5. The other two arguments associated with the OpenReport action are already correctly specified.

5. Click the **row selector of the MsgBox action of the Print All Equipment macro**, click the **Copy button** 🔣 on the Macro Design toolbar, click the **fourth row selector**, then click the **Paste button** 🔣 on the Macro Design toolbar

   Being able to copy and paste actions in a Macro window is another benefit of using macro groups. Action argument values are copied and pasted along with the action, so they don't need to be reentered. Sometimes, however, the arguments need to be edited.

> **QuickTip**
>
> Add a label with your name to the Accounting Report if you need to uniquely identify your printout.

6. Delete **All Equipment** in the Message text box in the Action Arguments panel, type **Accounting**, then click the **Save button** 🔣 on the Macro Design toolbar

   To run a specific macro from within a macro group's window, you must use the menu.

7. Click **Tools** on the menu bar, point to **Macro**, click **Run Macro**, click the **Macro Name list arrow** in the Run Macro dialog box, click **Print Reports Macro Group.Print Accounting Report**, then click **OK**

   Your screen should look like Figure N-6. Referring to a specific macro within a macro group by separating them with a period is called **dot notation**. Dot notation syntax is also used when developing modules with Visual Basic programming code.

8. Click **OK**, then close the Macro window

   The Print Reports Macro Group object containing two macros is shown in the database window.

FIGURE N-5: Creating a macro group

Paste button

Macro name

Row selector

Macro Names button

Copy button

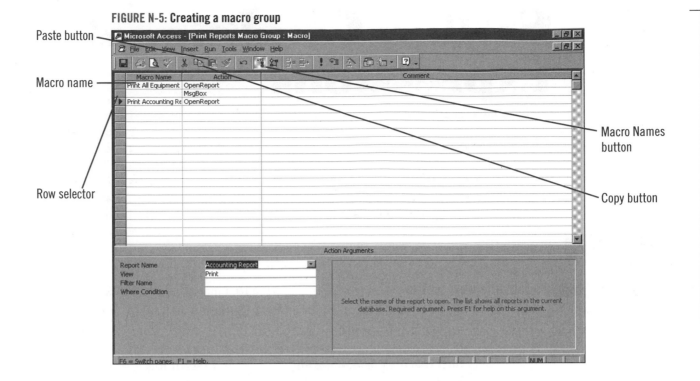

FIGURE N-6: Running the Print Accounting Report macro

MsgBox action was pasted

Message argument was edited

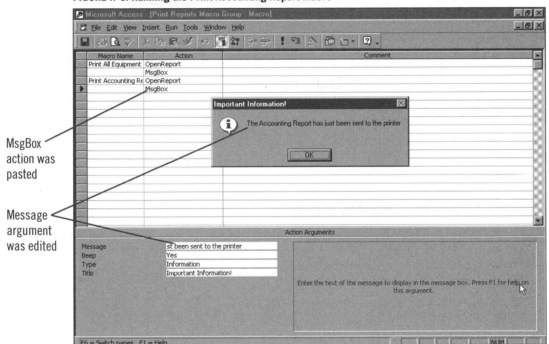

CLUES TO USE

Assigning a macro to a key combination

You can assign macros to a key combination (such as Ctrl+L) by creating a macro group object called **AutoKeys**. In the Macro Names column of the AutoKeys Macro window, enter the key combination to press when you want to run the macro. Any key combination assignments you make in the AutoKeys macro override those that Access has already specified (for example, Ctrl+C is the key combination for copy).

Setting Conditional Expressions

Conditional expressions are entered in the Condition column of the Macro window. They result in a true or false value. If the condition evaluates true, the action is executed: if false, the macro skips that row. When building a conditional expression, to refer to a value of a control on a form in a macro, use the following syntax: [Forms]![*formname*]![*controlname*]. To refer to a value of a control on a report, the syntax is [Reports]![*reportname*]![*controlname*]. Separating object types from object names from control names by using square brackets [] and exclamation points is called **bang notation**.  At MediaLoft, everyone who has been with the company longer than five years is eligible to take their old PC equipment home as soon as it has been replaced. Kristen uses a conditional macro to highlight this information in a form.

Steps

1. Click the **New button** 🖉 in the database window, click the **Conditions button** 🖅 on the Macro Design toolbar, right-click the **first Condition cell**, click **Zoom**, then type **[Forms]![Employees]![DateHired]<Date()-(5*365)** in the Zoom dialog box

   The Zoom dialog box should look like Figure N-7. This conditional expression says "Check the value in the DateHired field of the Employees form to see if it is earlier than five years before today's date."

2. Click **OK** to close the Zoom dialog box, click the **Action cell** for the first row, click the **Action list arrow**, scroll, then click **SetValue**

   The SetValue macro action has two arguments.

3. Click the **Item text box** in the Action Arguments panel, type **[Forms]![Employees]![PCProgram]**, click the **Expression text box** in the Action Arguments panel, then type **yes**

   Your screen should look like Figure N-8.

4. Click the **Save button** 🖫 on the Macro Design toolbar, type **5PC** in the Macro Name text box, click **OK**, then close the 5PC macro

   Test the macro using the Employees form.

5. Click **Forms on the Objects bar**, double-click the **Employees form**, maximize the Employees form, click the **Date Hired text box**, then click the **Sort Ascending button** 🔼 on the Form View toolbar

   The record for Evelyn Storey, hired 1/1/92, appears. Because she has five years of service with MediaLoft, she is eligible for the PC program.

6. Click **Tools** on the menu bar, point to **Macro**, click **Run Macro**, click the **Macro Name list arrow**, click **5PC**, then click **OK**

   After evaluating the date of this record and determining that this employee has been working at MediaLoft longer than five years, the PC Program check box was automatically checked (set to "Yes"), as shown in Figure N-9.

7. Click the **Last Record button** ▶❙ on the Main Form Navigation buttons, click **Tools** on the menu bar, point to **Macro**, click **Run Macro**, verify that **5PC** is in the **Macro Name text box**, then click **OK**

   Because Kristen Fontanelle was hired recently, the PC Program check box was not checked (set to "yes") by running the macro.

8. Close the Employees form

FIGURE N-7: Zoom dialog box

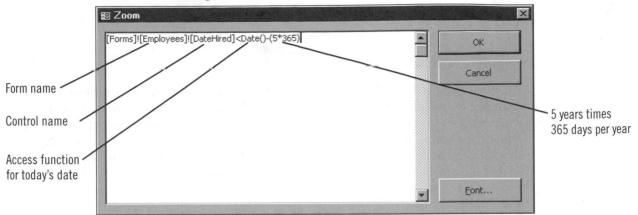

Form name

Control name

Access function
for today's date

5 years times
365 days per year

FIGURE N-08: Creating a conditional expression

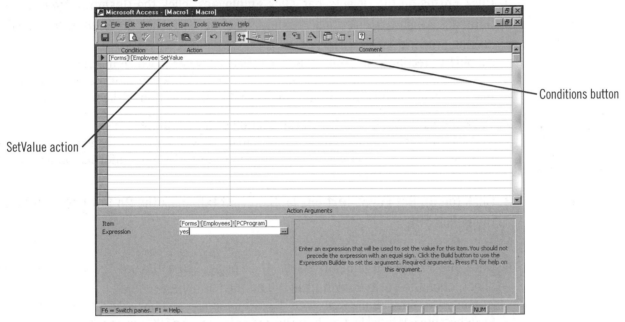

SetValue action

Conditions button

FIGURE N-9: Running the 5PC macro

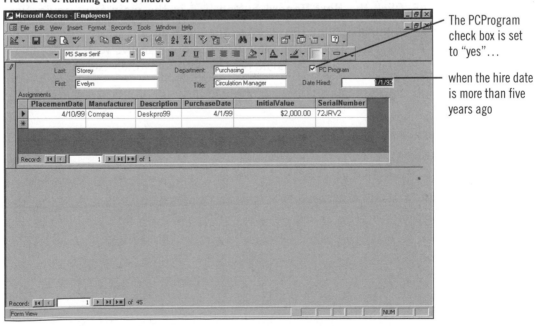

The PCProgram
check box is set
to "yes"...

when the hire date
is more than five
years ago

Assigning a Macro to an Event

An **event** is a specific action that occurs within the database such as clicking a command button, changing the data, or opening or closing a form. Events are usually the result of user action. By assigning a macro to an event, you can customize the response to an event that occurs on a form, report, or control, and therefore further automate and enhance your database.  Now that Kristen has developed the 5PC macro, she will attach it to an event on the Employees form so that she doesn't have to run the macro for each record.

Steps

QuickTip

Click any event property text box, then press [F1] for more help on that property.

1. Click **Forms** on the Objects bar, click **Employees**, click the **Design button** in the database window, double-click the **Detail section**, then click the **Event tab** in the Detail section property sheet

   All objects, sections, and controls have a variety of events to which macros can be attached. Most event names are self-explanatory, such as the On Click event for the Detail section. Any macro attached to this event would run when the Detail section of the form is clicked.

Trouble?

Close the Toolbox and Field list and move the property sheet to better view the form.

2. Click the **Last text box** in the Detail section of the Employees form

   There are 15 different events for a text box, many of which are very similar. Knowing which to use is a matter of experience. The Help manual provides more information on the subtle differences between the events.

3. Click the **On Got Focus text box** on the Event tab, click the **On Got Focus list arrow**, then click **5PC**

   Your screen should look like Figure N-10.

4. Click the **Properties button** on the Form Design toolbar to close the property sheet, click the **Form View button** on the Form View toolbar

   As you move through the records of the form, the Last text box will automatically have the focus because it is listed first in the form's tab order, and the 5PC macro will automatically run.

5. Click the **Next Record button** in the main form navigation buttons ten times while observing the PC Program check box

   For every Date Hired value that is more than five years earlier than today's date, the PC Program check box should be checked automatically (set to "yes").

6. Save and close the Employees form

FIGURE N-10: Assigning a macro to a text box event

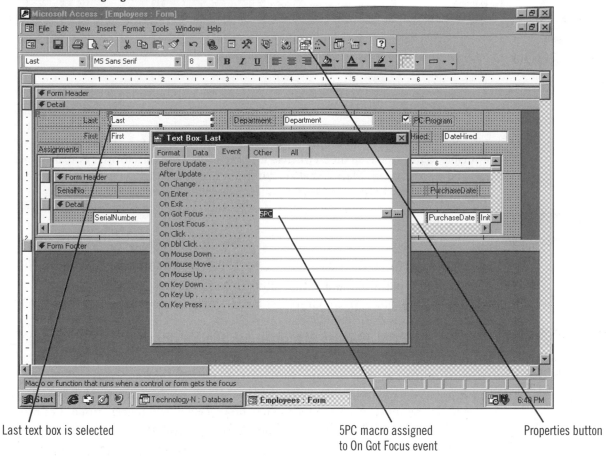

Last text box is selected

5PC macro assigned
to On Got Focus event

Properties button

Assigning a macro to a command button

You can add a command button on a form to run a macro. One way to accomplish this is to build the command button using the Command Button Wizard. Use the wizard to specify the Run Macro action found in the Miscellaneous category. Another way to assign a macro to a command button is to open the command button's property sheet and enter the macro name in the appropriate event property. The most common event property for a command button is the **On Click** event, which triggers as soon as you click the command button in Form view.

Access 2000

Customizing Toolbars with Macros

There are many ways to run a macro: by clicking the Run button in the Macro window, by going through the Tools menu, by assigning the macro to an event on a control, or by assigning it to a button on a toolbar, menu, or shortcut menu. The benefit of assigning a macro to a toolbar button over assigning it to a command button on a specific form is that the toolbar can be made available to the user at all times, whereas a command button on a form is available only when that specific form is open. Macros that are run from multiple forms are great candidates for custom toolbars. Kristen decides to create a new toolbar for the print macros.

Steps

1. **Click Macros on the Objects bar, click the Print Reports Macro Group, click Tools on the menu, point to Macro, then click Create Toolbar from Macro**
   The Print Reports Macro Group toolbar appears on your screen. All of the macros in that group are automatically added to the toolbar.

2. **Drag the Print Reports Macro Group toolbar title bar to dock it just below the Database toolbar, as shown in Figure N-11**
   Because this toolbar contains buttons for only two macros (the two found in the Print Reports Macro Group), the entire name of the macro fits comfortably on the toolbar. If you add several more macros to the toolbar, however, you will quickly run out of room.

3. **Right-click the Print Reports Macro Group toolbar, click Customize to open the Customize dialog box, right-click the Print All Equipment macro button on the Print Reports Macro Group toolbar, then point to Change Button Image**
   Your screen should look like Figure N-12. The shortcut menu that allows you to modify toolbar button images and text is available only when the Customize dialog box is open.

4. **Click the Shoes icon 🥾 on the icon palette, right-click the Print All Equipment macro button again, then click Default Style**
   The Default Style for a button displays only the button image, not the text.

5. **Right-click the Print Accounting Report macro button on the Print Reports Macro Group toolbar, point to Change Button Image, click the Scales icon ⚖ on the icon palette, right-click the Print Accounting Report macro button, then click Default Style**
   The image on a toolbar button can be edited.

6. **Right-click ⚖, then click Edit Button Image**
   The Button Editor dialog box opens, which allows you change the appearance of the picture pixel by pixel.

7. **Click the bright green color box on the Colors palette, then click all 11 squares in the left scale, as shown in Figure N-13**
   With enough time and patience, you could create any number of unique button images. Once created, the images can be copied and pasted from one button to another.

8. **Click OK, then click Close to close the Customize dialog box**
   The Print Reports Macro Group toolbar can be turned on or off from anywhere within the database. As with buttons on other toolbars, these buttons can be deleted and modified, and new ones can be added later.

9. **Point to the ⚖, then point to the 🥾 on the Print Reports Macro Group toolbar**
   Each button on the new Print Reports Macro Group toolbar has a ScreenTip and functions like the buttons on other toolbars.

Trouble?

If the new toolbar docks in an undesirable location, point to the left edge of the toolbar so that your mouse pointer changes to ✥, then drag it to the desired location.

FIGURE N-11: Print Reports Macro Group toolbar

New toolbar
with two macro
buttons

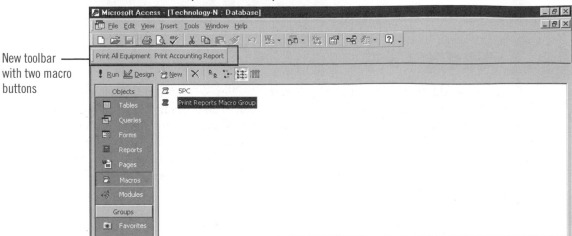

FIGURE N-12: Customizing a button image

Shoes

Scale

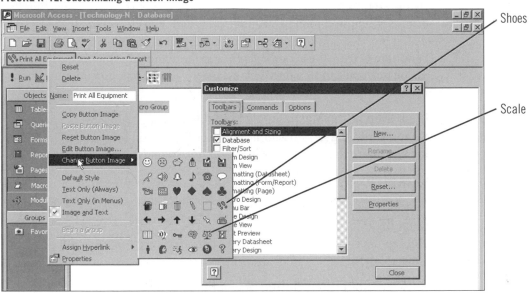

FIGURE N-13: Button Editor dialog box

Bright green

Left scale

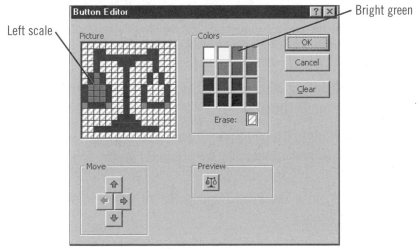

Troubleshooting Macros

When macros don't execute properly, Access supplies several techniques to debug them. **Debugging** means to determine why the macro doesn't run properly. **Single stepping** runs the macro one line at a time, so you can observe the effect of each macro action in the Macro Single Step dialog box while it executes. Another option is to disable a macro action by entering "False" in the Condition cell in the row of the action that you wish to temporarily skip. Before building more sophisticated macros, Kristen uses the Print Reports Macro Group to learn debugging techniques.

Steps 123 4

1. **Click Print Reports Macro Group, click the Design button**, **click the Single Step button** on the Macro Design toolbar, then click the **Run button** on the Macro Design toolbar
   The screen should look like Figure N-14, with the Macro Single Step dialog box open. This dialog box displays information including the macro's name, whether the current action's condition is true, the action's name, and the action arguments. From the Macro Single Step dialog box you can step into the next macro action, halt execution of the macro, or continue running the macro without single stepping.

2. **Click Step in the Macro Single Step dialog box**
   Stepping into the second action allows the first action to execute. The Macro Single Step dialog box now displays information about the second action.

3. **Click Step**
   The second action, the MsgBox action, executes, displaying the message box.

4. **Click OK**
   You can use the Condition column to temporarily ignore an action while you are debugging a macro.

5. **Click the Conditions button** on the Macro Design toolbar, click the **Condition cell** for the first row, then type **False**
   Your screen should look like Figure N-15.

6. **Click the Save button** on the Macro Design toolbar, then click
   The Macro Single Step dialog box still displays description information about the action, but because the Condition value is False, the OpenReport action will not execute, so the All Equipment report will not be sent to the printer.

7. **Click Halt in the Macro Single Step dialog box, double-click False in the Condition cell, then press [Delete]**

8. **Click the Single Step button** on the Macro Design toolbar to turn it off
   You could leave the Single Step feature on for future work, but you should turn it off now so that the next time you open a database and run a macro it will not be on.

9. **Save and close the Print Reports Macro Group, close the Technology–N database, then exit Access**

FIGURE N-14: Single stepping through a macro

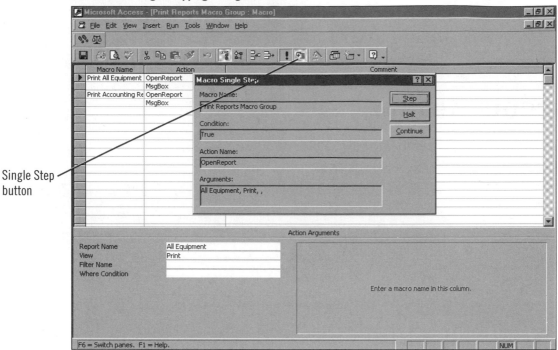

Single Step button

FIGURE N-15: Using a False condition

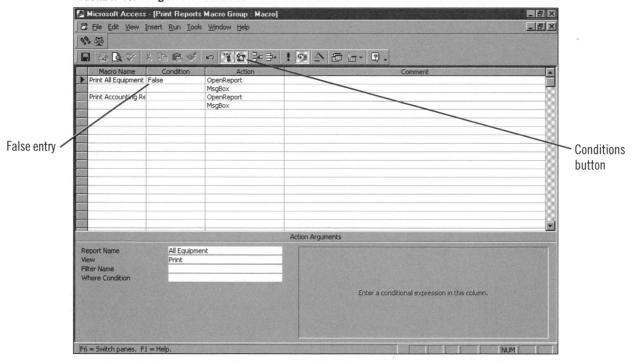

False entry

Conditions button

Practice

▶ Concepts Review

Identify each element of the macro window shown in Figure N-16.

FIGURE N-16

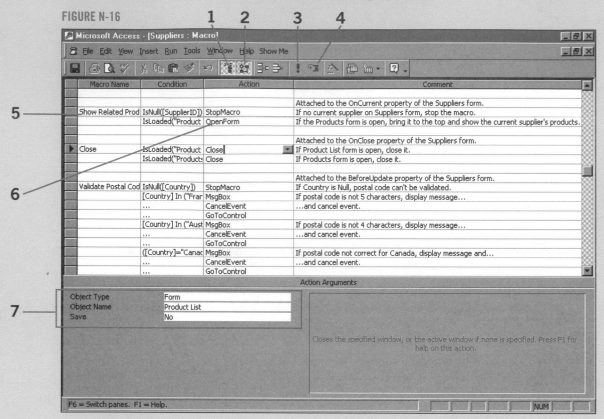

Match each term with the statement that describes its function.

8. Macro
9. Conditional expression
10. Arguments
11. Debugging
12. Actions
13. Event

a. Specific action that occurs within the database such as a mouse click, a change in data, or a form opening or closing
b. Individual tasks that you want the Access macro to perform
c. Access object that stores a series of actions that perform a series of tasks
d. Determining why a macro doesn't run properly
e. Provide additional information to define how an Access action will perform
f. Evaluates as either true or false, which determines whether Access will execute a macro action or not

Select the best answer from the list of choices.

14. Which of the following is *not* a major benefit of using a macro?
    a. To save time by automating routine tasks
    b. To ensure consistency in executing routine or complex tasks
    c. To make the database more flexible by adding macro command buttons to forms
    d. To redesign the relationships among the tables of the database

15. Which of the following *best* describes the process of creating an Access macro?
    a. Use the macro recorder to record clicks and keystrokes as you complete a task
    b. Use the single-step recorder feature to record clicks and keystrokes as you complete a task
    c. Use the Macro Wizard to determine which tasks are done most frequently
    d. Open the Macro window and add actions, arguments, and conditions to accomplish the desired task

16. Which of the following does *not* run a macro?
    a. Click the macro name in the Database window, then click Run
    b. Assign the macro to an event of a control on a form
    c. Add the macro to a toolbar
    d. Add the macro as an entry on the title bar

17. Which is *not* a reason to run a macro in single-step mode?
    a. You want to change the arguments of a macro while it runs
    b. You want to observe the effect of each macro action individually
    c. You want to debug a macro that isn't working properly
    d. You want to run only a few of the actions of a macro

18. Which is *not* a reason to use conditional expressions in a macro?
    a. More macro actions are available when you are also using conditional expressions
    b. Conditional expressions allow you to skip over actions when the expression evaluates to false
    c. You can enter "False" in the Conditions column of the Macro window to skip that action
    d. Conditional expressions give the macro more power and flexibility

19. Which example illustrates the proper syntax to refer to a specific control on a form?
    a. {Forms}!{*formname*}!{*controlname*}
    b. (Forms)!(*formname*)!(*controlname*)
    c. Forms!*formname.controlname*
    d. [Forms]![*formname*]![*controlname*]

▶ Skills Review

1. **Understanding Macros.**
    a. Start Access and open the Basketball-N database from your Project Disk.
    b. Open the Macro Design window of the Print Macro Group and record your answers to the following questions on a sheet of paper:
       • How many macros are in this macro group?
       • What are the names of the macros in this macro group?

- What actions does the first macro in this macro group contain?
- What arguments does the first action contain? What values were chosen for those arguments?

c. Close the Macro window for the Print Macro Group object.

2. Creating a Macro.

a. Open a new Macro window.

b. Add the OpenQuery action to the first row of the Macro window.

c. Select Score Delta as the value for the Query Name argument of the OpenQuery action.

d. Select Datasheet for the View argument of the OpenQuery action.

e. Select Edit for the Data Mode argument for the OpenQuery action.

f. Save the macro object with the name "Score Delta".

g. Run the macro to make sure it works, then close Score Delta query and the Score Delta Macro window.

3. Modifying Actions and Arguments.

f. Open the Score Delta macro in Macro Design view.

b. Add a MsgBox action in the second row of the Macro window.

c. Type "We had a great season!" for the Message argument in the Action Arguments panes of the MsgBox action.

d. Select Yes for the Beep argument of the MsgBox action.

e. Select Warning! for the Type argument of the MsgBox action.

f. Type "Iowa State Cyclones" for the Title argument of the MsgBox action.

g. Save the macro, then run it to make sure the MsgBox action works as intended.

h. Click OK in the dialog box created by the MsgBox action, then close the Score Delta query and close the Macro window.

4. Creating a Macro Group.

a. Rename the Score Delta macro with the name "Query Macro Group".

b. Open the Query Macro Group's Macro Design window.

c. Open the Macro Name column and type the name "Score Delta Macro" on the first line for the first macro.

d. Create another macro and name it "Forward FG Macro".

e. Add an OpenQuery action for the first action of the Forward FG Macro.

f. Select Forward Field Goals for the Query Name argument of the OpenQuery action and use the default entries for the other two arguments.

g. Add a MsgBox action for the second action of the Forward FG Macro.

h. Type "Forward Field Goals" as the Message argument for the MsgBox action.

i. Select Yes for the Beep argument of the MsgBox action.

j. Select Critical for the Type argument of the MsgBox action.

k. Type "2000-2001 Season" for the Title argument of the MsgBox action.

l. Save the macro.

m. Click Tools on the menu bar, point to Macro, click Run macro, then run the Forward FG Macro.

n. Click OK in the 2000-2001 Season dialog box created by the MsgBox action, then close the query datasheet and close the Macro window.

5. **Setting Conditional Expressions.**
   a. Open a new Macro window.
   b. Click the Conditions button to open the Condition column.
   c. Type the following condition in the condition cell of the first row: [Forms]![Game Summary Form]![Home Score]>[Opponent Score] (*Hint*: Use the Zoom dialog box or widen the column to more clearly view the entry.)
   d. Add the SetValue action to the first row.
   e. Type the following entry in the Item argument value for the SetValue action: [Forms]![Game Summary Form]![Victory]
   f. Type "Yes" for the Expression argument for the SetValue action.
   g. Save the macro as "Victory Calculator" and close the Macro window.

6. **Assigning a Macro to an Event.**
   a. Open the Game Summary Form in Design view.
   b. Open the Property sheet for the Detail section.
   c. Assign the Victory Calculator macro to the On Click event of the Detail section.
   d. Close the property sheet, save the form, then open it in Form view.
   e. Navigate through the first four records, while single clicking each record in the Detail section (click to the right of the text box controls). The Victory checkbox should be marked for the first three records, but not the fourth.
   f. Close the Game Summary form.

7. **Customizing Toolbars with Macros.**
   a. Click Macros on the Objects bar, click the Print Macro Group, click Tools on the menu bar, point to Macro, then click Create Toolbar from Macro.
   b. Dock the toolbar with the three text buttons just below the Database toolbar in the database window.
   c. Right-click the new toolbar, then click Customize to open the Customize dialog box.
   d. Change the button image for each of the three macros to the question mark icon and a default style (image only).
   e. Edit the button images so that the second macro question mark button is bright red (instead of yellow) and the third is bright blue (instead of yellow).
   f. Close the Customize dialog box and point to each icon to make sure that the ScreenTip relates to the three macro names in the Print Macro Group.

8. **Troubleshooting Macros.**
   a. Open the Print Macro Group's Macro window.
   b. Click the Single Step button on the Macro Design toolbar, then click the Run button.
   c. Click Step twice to step through the two actions of this macro, then click OK on the resulting message box.
   d. Open the Condition column by clicking the Conditions button on the Macro Design toolbar (if it's not already opened).
   e. Add the value "False" as a condition to the first row, the OpenReport action of the Games Summary macro.
   f. Save the macro, then click the Run button.
   g. Click the Step button twice to move through the actions of the macro. This time the Games Summary report should *not* be printed. Click OK when prompted.
   h. Delete the False condition in the first row, save the macro, then close the Macro window.
   i. Turn off the Single Step button.
   j. Close the Basketball-N database.
   k. Exit Access.

► Independent Challenges

1. As the manager of a doctor's clinic, you have created an Access database called Patients-N to track insurance claim reimbursements. You wish to use macros to help automate the database.

To complete this independent challenge:

a. Start Access and open the database Patients-N from your Project Disk.

b. Open the Macro window of the CPT Form Open macro (CPT stands for Current Procedural Terminology, which is a code that describes a medical procedure.)

c. On a separate sheet of paper, identify the macro actions, arguments for each action, and values for each argument.

d. In two or three sentences, explain in your own words what tasks this macro automates.

e. Close the CPT Form Open Macro window.

f. Open the Claim Entry Form in Design view. Maximize the window.

g. In the footer of the Claim Entry Form are several command buttons. (*Hint*: Scroll the main form to see these buttons.) Open the property sheet of the Add CPT Code button and click the Event tab.

h. On your paper, write the event to which the CPT Form Open macro is assigned.

i. Open the Claim Entry Form in Form view and click the Add CPT Code button in the form footer.

j. On your paper, write the current record number that is displayed for you.

k. Scroll up the CPT form and find the record for CPT Code 99243. Write the RBRVS value for this record, then close the CPT form and Claim Entry form. (RBRVS stands for Resource Based Relative Value System, a measurement of relative value between medical procedures.)

l. Close the Patients-N database.

m. Exit Access.

2. As the manager of a doctor's clinic, you have created an Access database called Patients-N to track insurance claim reimbursements. You wish to use macros to help automate the database.

To complete this independent challenge:

a. Start Access and open the database Patients-N from your Project Disk.

b. Open a new Macro Window and click the Macro Names button to open the Macro Name column.

c. Enter "Preview DOS-Denied" as the first macro name, and use the OpenReport macro action in the first row.

d. Select Date of Service Report – Denied for the ReportName argument, and Print Preview for the View argument of the OpenReport action. Leave the other two arguments blank.

e. Enter "Preview DOS-Fixed" as the second macro name, and use the OpenReport macro action in the second row.

f. Select Date of Service Report – Fixed for the ReportName argument, and Print Preview for the View argument of the OpenReport action. Leave the other two arguments blank.

g. Save the object with the name "Preview Group", then close the Macro window.

h. Run the Preview DOS-Fixed macro.

i. Close the Patients-N database.

j. Exit Access.

3. As the manager of a doctor's clinic, you have created an Access database called Patients-N to track insurance claim reimbursements. You wish to use macros to help automate the database.

To complete this independent challenge:

a. Start Access and open the Patients-N database from your Project Disk.

b. Open a blank Macro window and click the Conditions button to open the Condition column.

c. Enter the following in the Condition cell of the first row:
[Forms]![CPT Form]![RBRVS]=0

d. Select the SetValue action for the first row.

e. Type the following as the Item argument value for the SetValue action:
[Forms]![CPT Form]![Research]

f. Enter "Yes" as the Expression argument value for the SetValue action.

g. Save the macro with the name "Value Research" and close the Macro window.

h. Open the CPT Form in Design view, and open the property sheet for the CPTCode text box.

i. Assign the Value Research macro to the On Got Focus event of the CPTCode text box.

j. Close the property sheet, save the form, and open it in Form view.

k. Use the Next Record button to move quickly through all 64 records in the form. Notice that the macro automatically places a check mark in the Research check box when the RBRVS value is equal to zero.

l. Save and close the CPT form, and close the Patients-N database.

4. MediaLoft has developed a Web site that provides internal information to their employees. In this independent challenge, you will complete research on macros for upcoming MediaLoft projects.

a. Connect to the Internet, go to the MediaLoft intranet site at http://www.course.com/illustrated/MediaLoft

b. Click the link for the Research center, then click the link for Microsoft Access Information.

c. Find the Search This Site text box and enter "Access macro" to request information on this subject. (*Hint*: Web sites change often, and you may need to find and click a "Search" button before you are able to enter your search criteria.)

d. Refine your search as necessary, then find and print two articles with both the words "Access" and "macro" in the summary line.

e. Close your browser window.

► Visual Workshop

As the manager of a doctor's clinic, you have created an Access database called Patients-N to track insurance claim reimbursements. Develop the macro group called Query Group with the actions and argument values shown in Figure N-17 and Table N-3. Run both macros to test them. Debug them if necessary.

TABLE N-3: Macro actions and arguments for the Query Group

macro name	action	argument	argument value
Denied	OpenQuery	Query Name	Monthly Query – Denied
		View	Datasheet
		Data Mode	Edit
	Maximize		
	MsgBox	Message	These claims were denied
		Beep	Yes
		Type	Information
		Title	Denied
Fixed	OpenQuery	Query Name	Monthly Query – Fixed
		View	Datasheet
		Data Mode	Edit
	Maximize		
	MsgBox	Message	These claims were fixed
		Beep	Yes
		Type	Information
		Title	Fixed

FIGURE N-17

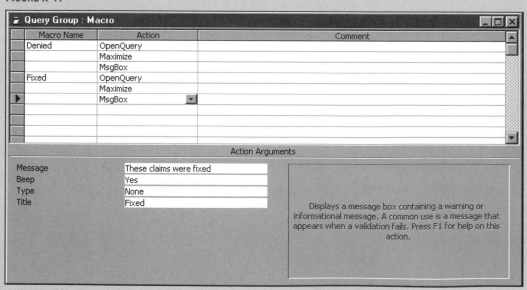

Creating
Modules

Objectives

► **Understand Modules**
► **Compare Macros and Modules**
► **Create a Function Procedure**
► **Use If Statements**
► **Document a Procedure**
► **Examine Class Modules**
► **Create a Sub Procedure**
► **Troubleshoot Modules**

Access is an extremely robust and easy-to-use relational database program. Reports and screens that took hours to create using complex programming code are now created using wizards, graphical tools, and property sheets. Macros that formerly took hours to debug can now be written, tested, and attached to a command button or control event in minutes. Because Access provides so many user-friendly tools to accomplish tasks, many Access database administrators don't need to work with the Access programming language, **Visual Basic for Applications (VBA)**, to meet the needs of the users. When programming is required, however, the Visual Basic code is stored in a database object called a **module**. ◄━━ Kristen learns about and creates some small Access modules to enhance the capabilities of the Technology database.

Access 2000

Understanding Modules

A **module** is an Access object that contains Visual Basic for Applications programming code, and it is written in the **Visual Basic Editor Code window** (**Code window**), shown in Figure O-1. The components and text colors of the Code window are described in Table O-1. Programming code contained within the module can be executed by clicking a command button or in response to an event. A database has two kinds of modules: **class modules**, which are used only with a particular form or report and are, therefore, stored as a part of the form or report object; and **standard modules**, which can be executed from anywhere in the database and are displayed as module objects in the database window. ✎ Kristen wants to learn more about VBA modules, so she studies several key questions that explain the purpose and terminology of modules.

Details

What does a module contain?

A module contains VBA programming code organized in units called **procedures**. A procedure may be a few or several lines (**statements**) long. Modules also contain **comment lines** to help document and explain the code. Comment lines in Visual Basic are preceded by an apostrophe.

What is a procedure?

A **procedure** is a series of VBA programming statements that perform an operation or calculate an answer. There are two types of procedures: Functions and Subs. **Declaration statements** precede procedure statements and help set rules for how the statements in the module are processed.

What is a function?

A **function** is a procedure that returns a value. Access supplies many built-in statistical, financial, and date functions, such as Sum, Pmt, and Now, that can be used in an expression in a query, form, or report to calculate a value. Using VBA, you could create a new function called StockOptions, for example, which calculates the date an employee is eligible for the corporate stock options, and use the unique method of calculating that date specified by your company.

What is a sub?

A **sub** (or **sub procedure**) performs a series of VBA statements, but does not return a value and cannot be used in an expression. You use subs to manipulate controls and objects. For example, you might create a sub called SetSchoolNameFocus that moves the focus on a form to a text box bound to a SchoolName field when the user marks a check box that indicates he or she is a college graduate.

What are arguments?

Arguments are constants, variables, or expressions passed to a procedure (function or sub) that are required for it to execute. For example, the full syntax for the Sum function is Sum(*expr*), where *expr* represents the argument for the Sum function. Arguments are specified immediately after a procedure's name and are enclosed in parentheses. When there are multiple arguments, they are separated by commas.

What is a method?

A **method** is an action that an object can perform. For example, the GoToPage method moves the focus to the first control on a specified page in the active form. Procedures are often written to invoke methods (database actions) in response to user actions. For example, you may wish to invoke the GoToPage method when the user clicks a command button.

FIGURE O-1: Visual Basic Editor Code window for a standard module

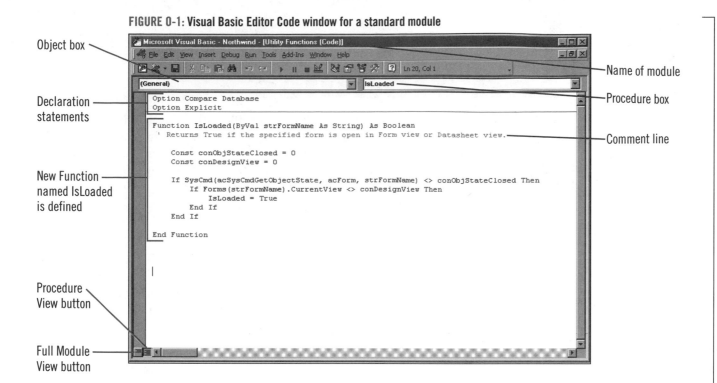

Object box — Microsoft Visual Basic - Northwind - [Utility Functions (Code)]

Name of module

Declaration statements — (General) — IsLoaded — Procedure box

```
Option Compare Database
Option Explicit

Function IsLoaded(ByVal strFormName As String) As Boolean
' Returns True if the specified form is open in Form view or Datasheet view.

    Const conObjStateClosed = 0
    Const conDesignView = 0

    If SysCmd(acSysCmdGetObjectState, acForm, strFormName) <> conObjStateClosed Then
        If Forms(strFormName).CurrentView <> conDesignView Then
            IsLoaded = True
        End If
    End If

End Function
```

Comment line

New Function named IsLoaded is defined

Procedure View button

Full Module View button

TABLE O-1: Components and Text Colors of the Code window

component or color	description
Procedure View button	Shows the statements that belong only to the current procedure
Full Module View button	Shows all the lines of VBA (all of the procedures) in the module
Declaration statements	Contains statements that apply to every procedure in the module such as declarations for variables, constants, user-defined data types, and external procedures in a dynamic link library
Object box	In a class module, lists the objects associated with the form or report (in VBA, "**objects**" are the form or report's controls, sections, the form or report itself, and subs already defined)
Procedure box	In a standard module, lists the procedures in that module. In a class module, lists the events (such as Click or Dblclick) that the item selected in the Object box can use
Comment line	Descriptive text that serves as explanatory documentation; comment lines start with an apostrophe
Blue	Keyword text—blue words are reserved by VBA and are already assigned specific meanings
Black	Normal text—black words are the unique VBA code developed by the user
Red	Syntax error text—a line of code in red indicates that it will not execute correctly because there is a syntax error (perhaps a missing parenthesis or a spelling error)
Green	Comment text—any text after an apostrophe is considered documentation, and is therefore ignored in the execution of the procedure

Comparing Macros and Modules

Both macros and modules help run your database more efficiently (faster) and effectively (with fewer errors). To create either requires some understanding of programming concepts, an ability to follow a process through its steps, and patience. Some tasks can be accomplished using either an Access macro or a module, but there are some guidelines and rules that will help guide your choice of which object is best for the task. Kristen learns how macros and modules compare by studying several key questions.

Details

For what types of tasks are macros best suited?

Macros are an easy way to handle repetitive, simple details such as opening and closing forms, showing and hiding toolbars, and printing reports.

Which is easier to create, a macro or a module, and why?

To create a module, you must know the correct syntax for each line of code, and write the statement yourself. Modules consist of VBA programming code, a robust programming language with endless possibilities. Macros are generally easier to create because you don't have to know about programming syntax. With a macro, you choose actions (a limited list of about 50) from a list. Once the action is chosen, the arguments associated with that action are displayed automatically in the Action Arguments panel.

Is there ever a situation when I must use a macro?

You must use macros to make global shortcut key assignments. You can also use an automatic macro that carries out a series of actions that are beyond the capabilities of the startup options when the database first opens.

When should I use a module?

There are at least five reasons to use a module rather than a macro:

- Class modules, like the one shown in Figure O-2, are stored as part of the form or report object in which they are created. Therefore, if you develop forms and reports in one database and copy them to another, class modules are copied with the object.

- You must use modules to create unique function procedures. For instance, you might want to create a function called COMMISSION that calculates the appropriate commission on a sale using your company's unique commission formula.

- Modules can contain procedures used to mask error messages. Access error messages can be confusing to the user. But using VBA procedures, you can detect the error when it occurs and display your own message or take some action.

- You can't use a macro to accomplish many tasks outside Access, but VBA code stored in modules works with other products in the Microsoft Office suite to pass information back and forth between the programs.

- VBA code can contain nested If statements, Case statements, and other programming code, which makes it more powerful and flexible than macros. Some of the most common VBA keywords are shown in Table O-2. Because each is a reserved VBA keyword, each appears in blue in the Code window.

FIGURE O-2: Code window for a class module

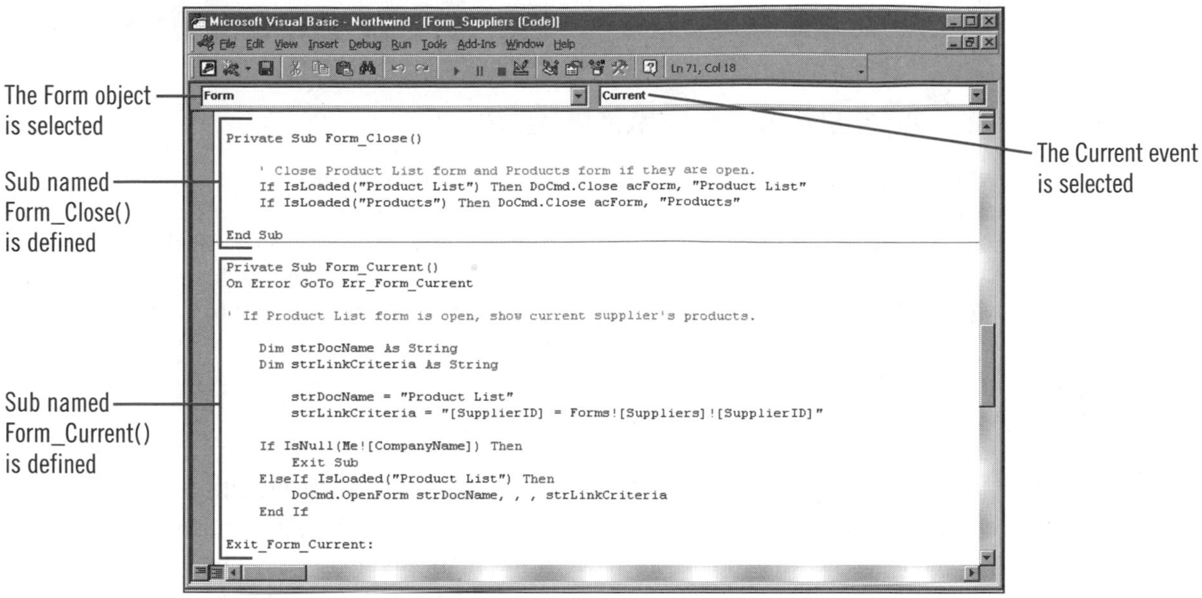

The Form object is selected →

Sub named Form_Close() is defined →

Sub named Form_Current() is defined →

→ The Current event is selected

```
Microsoft Visual Basic - Northwind - [Form_Suppliers (Code)]
File  Edit  View  Insert  Debug  Run  Tools  Add-Ins  Window  Help
                                                          Ln 71, Col 18

Form                                    Current

Private Sub Form_Close()

    ' Close Product List form and Products form if they are open.
    If IsLoaded("Product List") Then DoCmd.Close acForm, "Product List"
    If IsLoaded("Products") Then DoCmd.Close acForm, "Products"

End Sub

Private Sub Form_Current()
On Error GoTo Err_Form_Current

' If Product List form is open, show current supplier's products.

    Dim strDocName As String
    Dim strLinkCriteria As String

        strDocName = "Product List"
        strLinkCriteria = "[SupplierID] = Forms![Suppliers]![SupplierID]"

    If IsNull(Me![CompanyName]) Then
        Exit Sub
    ElseIf IsLoaded("Product List") Then
        DoCmd.OpenForm strDocName, , , strLinkCriteria
    End If

Exit_Form_Current:
```

TABLE O-2: Common VBA keywords

statement	explanation
Function	Declares the name and arguments that create a new function procedure
End Function	When defining a new function, the End Function statement is required as the last statement to mark the end of the VBA code that defines the function.
Sub	Declares the name, arguments, and code that create a new sub procedure. **Private Sub** indicates that the sub procedure is accessible only to other procedures in the module where it is declared
End Sub	When defining a new sub, the End Sub statement is required as the last statement to mark the end of the VBA code that defines the sub.
If **Then**	Used to execute code (code that follows the Then statement) if the value of the expression is true (the expression follows the If statement). The If...Then statement has additional optional parts including Then, and ElseIf statements.
End If	When creating an If...Then statement, the End If statement is required as the last statement.
Const	Declares the name and value of a **constant**, an item that retains a constant value throughout the execution of the code
Option Compare Database	A declaration statement that determines the way string values (text) will be sorted
Option Explicit	A declaration statement that specifies that you must explicitly declare all variables used in all procedures. If you attempt to use an undeclared variable name, an error occurs at **compile time**, the period during which source code is translated to executable code.
Dim	Declares a **variable**, a named storage location that contains data that can be modified during program execution
On Error GoTo	Upon error in the execution of a procedure, the On Error GoTo statement specifies the location (the statement) where the procedure should continue. If you don't use an On Error statement, any run-time error that occurs is fatal; that is, an error message is displayed and execution stops.
Select Case	Executes one of several groups of statements, depending on the value of an expression. Each group of statements is a new **Case**. Use the Select Case statement as an alternative to using **ElseIf** in **If...Then...Else** statements when comparing one expression to several different values.
End Select	When defining a new Select Case group of statements, the End Select statement is required as the last statement to mark the end of the VBA code.

Access 2000

Creating a Function Procedure

While there are hundreds of Access-supplied functions, there may be times when you want to create a unique function to accomplish a specific task. You can create a Function procedure in a standard module so that it can be used in any query, form, or report in the database. MediaLoft has implemented a program that allows employees to purchase corporate equipment when it is replaced. Equipment that is less than a year old will be sold to employees at 75% of its initial value, and equipment that is more than a year old will be sold at 50% of its initial value. Kristen defines a new function called StreetValue that will determine the employee purchase price of equipment that MediaLoft replaces.

Steps

Trouble?

If the Projects or Properties windows are open as small windows on the left side of the screen, click their Close buttons to close them.

1. **Start Access, open the Technology-O database, click Modules on the Objects bar, click the New button ⊠ in the database window, then maximize the Code window**
   The Code window opens, and Access automatically inserts the Option Compare Database declaration statement. The Technology-O database window minimizes on the taskbar.

2. **Type Function StreetValue(corpvalue), then press [Enter]**
   This statement declares a new function name, StreetValue, which contains one argument, corpvalue. VBA automatically adds the End Function statement because it is required to mark the end of the code that defines the new function. Because both Function and End Function are VBA keywords, they are colored blue. The insertion point is positioned between the statements so that you can further define how the new StreetValue function will calculate.

3. **Press [Tab], type StreetValue = corpvalue * 0.5, then press [Enter]**
   Your screen should look like Figure O-3. This statement explains how StreetValue will calculate. StreetValue will be equal to the corpvalue argument times 0.5. It is not necessary to indent statements, but many programmers indent code between matching Function/End Function, Sub/End Sub, or If/End If statements to enhance the program's readability.

4. **Click the Save button 🖫 on the Standard toolbar, type Functions in the Save As dialog box, then click OK**
   Now that the function is created, it can be used in a query, form, or report. You need to close the Visual Basic window and return to Access.

5. **Click File on the menu bar, then click Close and Return to Microsoft Access**
   The Visual Basic window closes, and the Microsoft Access window and the Technology-O database window are open on your screen.

6. **Click Queries on the Objects bar, click Employee Pricing, then click the Design button 🖾 in the database window**
   The Employee Pricing query opens in Design view. You can create calculated expressions in a query using either Access functions or the ones you define in modules.

QuickTip

Right-click the blank Field cell, then click Zoom to enter the calculated expression in a Zoom dialog box.

7. **Maximize the Query Design window, click the blank Field cell to the right of the InitialValue field, type EmployeePrice:StreetValue([InitialValue]), then click the Datasheet View button 🖩 on the Query Design toolbar**
   Your screen should look like Figure O-4. In this query you created a new field called EmployeePrice that used the StreetValue function that contains one argument (called corpvalue in the module). The value in the InitialValue field (stored in the Equipment table) was entered as the corpvalue argument. The StreetValue function multiplied the InitialValue field by 0.5 to determine the EmployeePrice field. By creating the StreetValue function in a module, you can add powerful logic to it that calculates different StreetValues depending on the age of the equipment and use it over and over again.

8. **Save the Employee Pricing query, then close the datasheet**

FIGURE O-3: Creating the StreetValue function

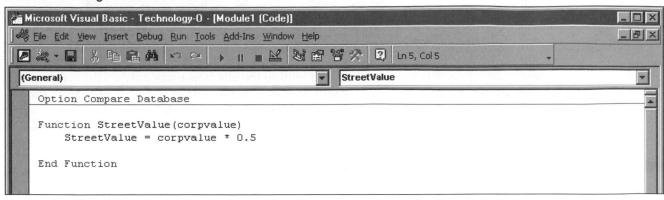

```
Microsoft Visual Basic - Technology-0 - [Module1 (Code)]
File  Edit  View  Insert  Debug  Run  Tools  Add-Ins  Window  Help
                                                                Ln 5, Col 5

(General)                                      StreetValue

   Option Compare Database

   Function StreetValue(corpvalue)
       StreetValue = corpvalue * 0.5

   End Function
```

FIGURE O-4: Creating the EmployeePrice field using the StreetValue function

Microsoft Access - [Employee Pricing : Select Query]

File Edit View Insert Format Records Tools Window Help

SerialNo	Manufacturer	Description	PurchaseDate	InitialValue	EmployeePrice
242XG1	Micron	Transtrek3000	7/1/99	$2,000.00	1000
242XG2	Micron	Transtrek3000	7/1/99	$2,000.00	1000
295XT4	Micron	Prosignet303	7/15/99	$1,800.00	900
295XT5	Micron	Prosignet303	7/15/99	$1,800.00	900
295XT6	Micron	Prosignet303	7/15/99	$1,800.00	900
295XT7	Micron	Prosignet303	7/15/99	$1,800.00	900
300RZ1	Micron	Prosignet303	8/1/99	$1,700.00	850
300RZ2	Micron	Prosignet303	8/1/99	$1,700.00	850
300RZ3	Micron	Prosignet303	8/1/99	$1,700.00	850
330RZ4	Micron	Prosignet303	8/1/99	$1,700.00	850
388MQS1	Compaq	Centuria8088	6/1/99	$1,500.00	750
388MQS2	Compaq	Centuria8088	6/1/99	$1,500.00	750
388MQS3	Compaq	Centuria8088	6/1/99	$1,500.00	750
388MQS4	Compaq	Centuria8088	6/1/99	$1,500.00	750
4848XH1	Micron	Transtrek3000	7/15/99	$1,900.00	950
4848XH2	Micron	Transtrek3000	7/15/99	$1,900.00	950
4848XJ3	Micron	Transtrek3000	8/1/99	$1,800.00	900
4848XJ4	Micron	Transtrek3000	8/1/99	$1,800.00	900
4848XK5	Micron	Transtrek3000	8/15/99	$1,750.00	875
511984CDE1	Lexmark	Optra2000	1/5/99	$2,000.00	1000
511984CDE2	Lexmark	Optra2000	1/5/99	$2,000.00	1000
72JRV1	Compaq	Deskpro99	4/1/99	$2,000.00	1000
72JRV2	Compaq	Deskpro99	4/1/99	$2,000.00	1000
72JRV3	Compaq	Deskpro99	4/1/99	$2,000.00	1000
72JRV4	Compaq	Deskpro99	4/1/99	$2,000.00	1000

Record: |◄| ◄ | 1 | ► | ►I | ►* | of 53

Datasheet View   NUM

Calculated
EmployeePrice field

Using If Statements

The **If...Then...Else** statement allows you to test a logical condition and execute commands only if the condition is true. The If...Then...Else statement can be one or several lines of code, depending on how many conditions you want to test and how many answers the result can be. Kristen needs to add logic to the StreetValue function. As originally designed, the calculation is *always* at 50%. If the equipment is less than one year old, the function should calculate the answer at 75% of the original value. She uses an If statement in the StreetValue function to determine the correct value based on age.

Steps

1. Click **Modules** on the Objects bar, click **Functions**, then click the **Design button**
   The Functions Code window with the StreetValue function opens. To determine the age of the equipment, which in turn determines whether 50% or 75% should be used in the calculation, the StreetValue function needs to evaluate another argument, which represents the purchase date.

Trouble?

Be sure to type the arguments exactly as specified to avoid getting errors later.

2. Click between the **e** in **corpvalue** and the **right parenthesis** in the Function statement, type **,** (a comma), press **[Spacebar]**, then type **corppurchasedate**
   Now that another argument has been established, the argument can be used in the function.

3. Click to the right of the **right parenthesis** in the Function statement, press **[Enter]**, then type **If (Now( ) – corppurchasedate) >365 Then**
   This expression evaluates whether today's date (represented by the Access function Now) minus the value represented by the corppurchasedate argument is greater than 365 days. If true, this would indicate that the equipment is older than one year old and the StreetValue should be recalculated at 50%.

4. Type the Else and End If statements precisely as shown in Figure O-5
   The Else statement will be executed only if the expression is false (if the equipment is less than 365 days old). The End If statement is needed to mark the end of the If block of code.

5. Click the **Save button** on the Visual Basic Standard toolbar, click **File** on the menu bar, click **Close and Return to Microsoft Access**, click **Queries** on the Objects bar, click **Employee Pricing**, then click in the database window
   Because you modified the StreetValue function to include two arguments, you have to change the expression in the query to include two arguments for the StreetValue function as well.

6. Right-click the **EmployeePrice field** in the query design grid, click **Zoom**, click to the right of the **right square bracket**, then type **,[PurchaseDate]**
   Your Zoom dialog box should look like Figure O-6. Both of the arguments used to calculate the StreetValue function are field names, so they must be typed exactly as shown and surrounded by square brackets. Commas separate multiple arguments in the function.

Trouble?

If you get a compile or syntax error, open the query design grid, check your function against Figure O-6, and correct any errors.

7. Click **OK** in the Zoom dialog box, then click the **Datasheet View button** on the Query Design toolbar

8. Click any entry in the **PurchaseDate field**, then click the **Sort Ascending button**
   The StreetValue function now calculates two ways, depending on the age of the equipment determined by the date in the PurchaseDate field, as shown in Figure O-7. The EmployeePrice will calculate based on the current date on your computer, so your results may vary. Check to make sure that all records with PurchaseDate values more recently than one year ago calculate the EmployeePrice field at 75% of the InitialValue field.

9. Save and close the Employee Pricing query

FIGURE O-5: If...Then...Else statements

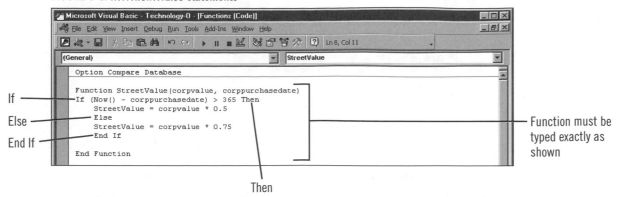

If ───
Else ───
End If ───

Function must be typed exactly as shown

Then

FIGURE O-6: Modifying the expression

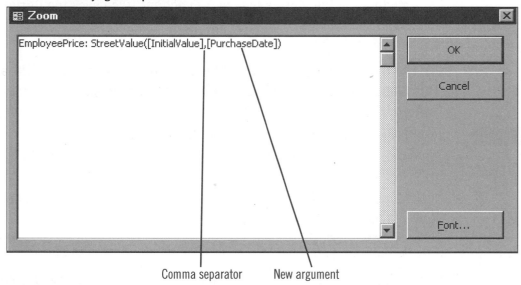

Comma separator   New argument

FIGURE O-7: Final EmployeePrice field is calculated using the StreetValue function

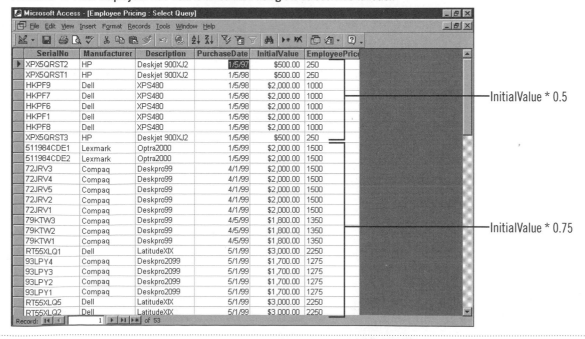

InitialValue * 0.5

InitialValue * 0.75

Documenting a Procedure

A good programmer documents code with frequent explanatory statements or comment lines. **Comment lines** are text in the code that do not affect the running of the program and are used simply to document the code. At any future time, when you want to modify the code, you'll be able to write the modifications much more quickly if the existing statements are properly documented. If you expect someone else to be able to maintain or modify the code, comment lines are a must. ➤ Kristen documents the StreetValue function in the Functions module with descriptive comments so she can easily follow the purpose and logic of the function.

Steps

1. Click **Modules** on the Objects bar, click **Functions**, then click the **Design button** 📧 in the database window
   The Code window for the Functions module opens.

2. Click to the left of the **Function statement**, press [**Enter**], press [**Up arrow**], type **'This function is called StreetValue and has two arguments**, then press [**Enter**]
   Comments always start with an apostrophe and are green in the Code window.

Trouble?

Be sure to use an ' (apostrophe) and not a " (quotation mark) to begin the comment line.

3. Type **'Created by Your Name on Today's Date**, then press [**Enter**]
   Your screen should look like Figure O-8. Comments also can be placed at the end of an existing line. Either way, however, they always start with an apostrophe.

4. Click to the right of **Then** at the end of the If statement, press [**Spacebar**], then type **'Now( ) is today's date**
   This comment explains that the Now() function is today's date. All comments are green, regardless of whether they are on their own line or at the end of an existing line.

5. Click to the right of **0.5**, press [**Spacebar**], then type **'If > 365 days, value is 50%**

6. Click to the right of **0.75**, press [**Spacebar**], then type **'If < 365 days, value is 75%**
   Your screen should look like Figure O-9. Table O-3 provides more information about the Standard toolbar buttons in the Code window.

7. Click the **Save button** 🖫 on the Standard toolbar, click **File** on the menu bar, click **Print**, then click **OK**

8. Click **File** on the menu bar, then click **Close and Return to Microsoft Access**

FIGURE O-8: Adding comments to the Code window

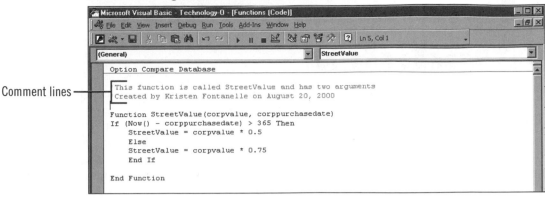

Comment lines ─────

FIGURE O-9: Adding comments at the end of a statement

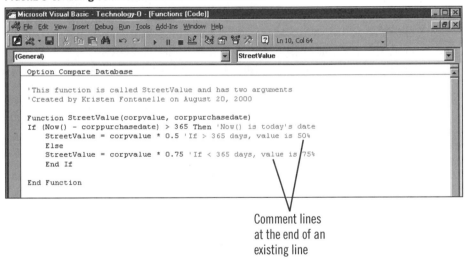

Comment lines
at the end of an
existing line

TABLE O-3: Standard toolbar buttons in the Code window

button name	button	description
View Microsoft Access		Toggles between the host application and the active Visual Basic document
Insert		Opens a new module or class module code window, or inserts a new procedure in the current code window
Run Sub/UserForm		Runs the current procedure if the insertion point is in a procedure or runs the UserForm if it is active
Break		Stops execution of a program while it's running and switches to **break mode**, the temporary suspension of program execution in which you can examine, debug, reset, step through, or continue program execution
Reset		Resets the procedure
Project Explorer		Displays the **Project Explorer**, which displays a hierarchical list of the currently open **projects**, (set of modules) and their contents
Object Browser		Displays the **Object Browser**, which lists the defined modules and procedures as well as available methods, properties, events, constants, and other items that you can use in the code

Examining Class Modules

Class modules are contained and executed within specific forms and reports. Class modules most commonly contain sub procedures and execute in response to an event such as the click of a command button. You do not always have to know VBA code to create class modules. The Command Button Wizard, for example, creates sub procedures. You can examine them to see how sub procedures work and how they are associated to specific events. ◤— Kristen used the Command Button Wizard to create four command buttons on the Equipment Entry Form. She examines the sub procedures in this form in order to understand class modules.

Steps 1 2 3 4

1. Click **Forms** on the Objects bar, click the **Equipment Entry Form**, then click the **Design button** 🔲 in the database window

    The Equipment Entry Form opens in Design view. The form has four command buttons: three to manipulate records and one to close the form.

QuickTip

The Command Button Wizard prompts you for the command button's name as its last question.

2. Maximize the form, click the **Add New Record command button**, view the **Object list** on the Formatting (Form/Report) toolbar, then click each command button while viewing the Object list

    Your screen should look like Figure O-10. The Object list identifies the name of the selected control as determined by the control's Name property. In this case, the word "object" is used as a VBA programmer would use it, and does not refer to the seven basic object types (tables, queries, forms, pages, reports, macros, and modules) of an Access database.

Trouble?

If the Immediate Window is open below the code window, close it.

3. Click the **Code button** 🔲 on the Form Design toolbar, then maximize the Form_Equipment Entry Form (Code) window

    The Code window for the VBA code stored in the Equipment Entry Form class module appears, as shown in Figure O-11. This code was created by using the Command Button Wizard. The names of the two subs displayed at the top of the code window correspond with the first two command buttons on the form, the AddNewRecordButton and the DeleteThisRecordButton. The _Click() suffix on the sub names identifies the event that will cause this sub to execute.

4. Click **File** on the menu bar, click **Close and Return to Microsoft Access**, double-click the **AddNewRecord command button** to open its property sheet, click the **Event tab**, click the **On Click text box**, then click the **Build button** 🔲

    The class module is opened in the specific location where the AddNewRecordButton_Click() sub is stored. If you wanted to create another sub that was executed from another event associated with that command button (for example, to display a message box when the command button gets the focus) you could use the property sheet to help you with the syntax of correctly defining the sub's name.

5. Click **File** on the menu bar, click **Close and Return to Microsoft Access**, click the **On Got Focus text box** on the Command Button AddNewRecordButton property sheet, click 🔲, click **Code Builder** in the Choose Builder dialog box, then click **OK**

    The class module Code window opens, as shown in Figure O-12. Because you entered the Code window through a specific event (On Got Focus) of a specific control (AddNewRecordButton), VBA knew what to name the sub and to automatically supply the last line of the procedure, the End Sub statement. The rest of the sub's statements, however, require individual programming, because you are not using a wizard to create the code.

6. Select all of the statements from **Private Sub AddNewRecordButton_GotFocus()** through the **End Sub** statement, press **[Delete]**, click the **Save button** 🔲 on the Microsoft Visual Basic Standard toolbar, click **File** on the menu bar, click **Close and Return to Microsoft Access**, close the property sheet, then close the Equipment Entry Form

FIGURE O-10: Four command buttons in Form Design view

Object list

Code button

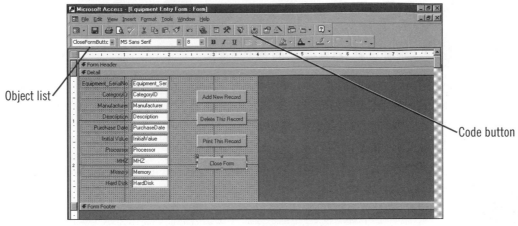

FIGURE O-11: Class module containing four subs that correspond with the four command buttons

DeleteThisRecordButton_
Click() sub

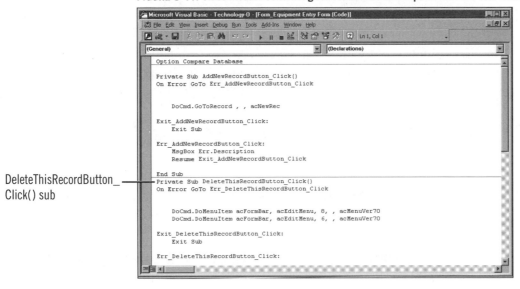

FIGURE O-12: Examining a new sub for a command button

New sub attached to the
On Got Focus event of the
AddNewRecordButton

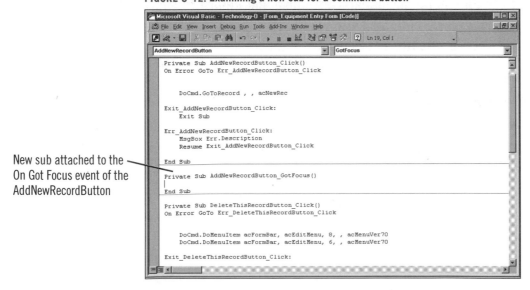

Creating a Sub Procedure

While it is easiest to create class module sub procedures using wizards, not all subs can be created this way. The Command Button Wizard, for example, always attaches its code to the Click event of a command button. You might want to create a sub that executes based on another action, such as double-click, or one that is assigned to a control (called objects in VBA) other than a command button. ◀ Kristen would like to create all of the Technology forms with built-in documentation that the user can access by clicking the form. To accomplish this, she writes a sub procedure in the form's class module.

Steps

1. Click the **Equipment Entry Form**, click the **Design button** 🗒 in the database window, then click the **Properties button** 🗐 to open the form's property sheet

2. Click the **Event tab**, click the **On Click text box**, click the **Build button** ▦, click **Code Builder** in the Choose Builder dialog box, then click **OK**
   The class module opens with two new statements to identify the new sub, which is called Form_Click( ). The name of the new sub references both the specific object and event you were examining through the property sheet. You can use the Object and Procedure lists within the Code window to find specific statements.

3. Click the **Object list arrow** below the Standard toolbar, click **FormFooter**, then scroll up so that your screen is similar to Figure O-13
   A new sub, named FormFooter_Click( ), was created.

4. Click the **Procedure list arrow** below the Standard toolbar, then click **DblClick**
   A new sub, named FormFooter_DblClick( ), was created. You do not wish to keep the FormFooter subs.

5. Click the **Undo button** 🔄 twice, type **MsgBox ("Created by Your Name on Today's Date")** as the single statement of the Form_Click() sub, then click the **Save button** 💾 on the Standard toolbar
   Your screen should look like Figure O-14.

6. Click **File** on the menu bar, click **Close and Return to Microsoft Access**, close the property sheet, click the **Form View button** 🗐 on the Form Design toolbar, then click the **record selector box** to the left of the record
   The MsgBox statement in the Form_Click() sub created the dialog box, as shown in Figure O-15.

7. Click **OK** in the message box, then close the form
   Visual Basic for Applications programming code is as robust and powerful as the Access application itself. It takes years of experience to appreciate the vast number of objects, events, methods, and properties that are available. With only modest programming skills, however, you can create basic modules as well as edit those that do not work as intended.

FIGURE O-13: Using the Object and Procedure lists

Undo button

Form_Click() sub

FormFooter_Click() sub

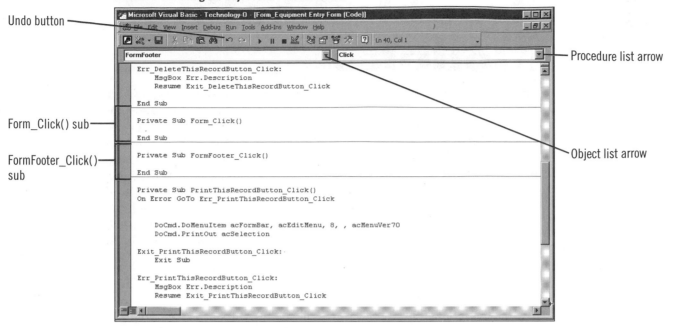

Procedure list arrow

Object list arrow

FIGURE O-14: Creating a sub procedure

MsgBox statement

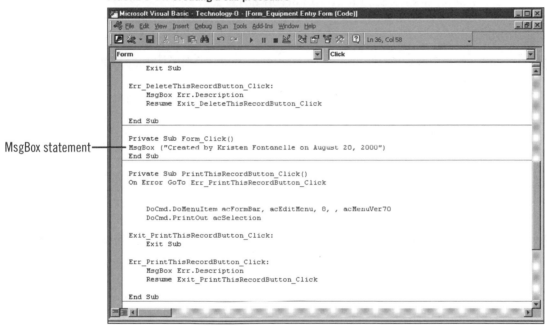

FIGURE O-15: The MsgBox action

Record selector box

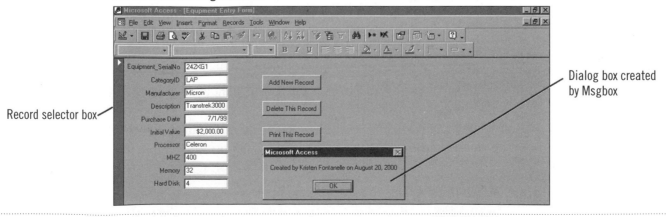

Dialog box created by Msgbox

Access 2000

Troubleshooting Modules

There are three types of errors you may encounter as your code runs, and Access provides several techniques to help you **debug** (find and resolve errors) them. **Compile-time errors** occur as a result of incorrectly constructed code. For example, you may have forgotten to write an End If statement following an If clause, or you may have a **syntax error**, such as a missing parenthesis. These are easiest to find because your code will turn red as soon as it detects a syntax error. **Run-time errors** occur after the code starts to run and include attempting an illegal operation such as dividing by zero or moving focus to a control that doesn't exist. When you encounter a run-time error, VBA will stop the execution of your procedure at the line in which the error occurred so you can examine it. **Logic errors** are more difficult to troubleshoot because they occur when the code runs without problems, but the procedure still doesn't produce the expected results. ✎ Kristen studies debugging techniques using the Functions module.

Steps

1. Click **Modules** on the Objects bar, click **Functions**, click the **Design button** 🔲 in the database window, click to the left of the **Option Compare Database** statement, type **Your Name**, then press the **[Down arrow key]**
   The Functions module opens in the Code window, and when you attempt to move out of that line of code, VBA notices the syntax error and displays the statement in bright red.

2. Click **OK** in the Compile error message box, delete **Your Name**, then click in another statement
   The Option Compare Database statement changes to blue (because it uses reserved VBA keywords) as soon as you successfully delete your name and click elsewhere in the code window. One debugging technique is to set a **breakpoint**, a bookmark that suspends execution of the procedure at that point in time to allow the user to examine what is happening.

   > **QuickTip**
   > Click the gray bar to the left of the VBA statement to toggle breakpoints on and off.

3. Click anywhere in the **If** statement, click **Debug** on the menu bar, then click **Toggle Breakpoint**
   Your screen should look like Figure O-16.

4. Click the **View Microsoft Access button** 🔲 on the Standard toolbar, click **Queries** on the Objects bar, then double-click **Employee Pricing**
   When the Employee Pricing query opens, it immediately runs the StreetValue function. Because you set a breakpoint at the If statement, that statement is highlighted, as shown in Figure O-17, indicating that the code has been suspended at that point.

   > **QuickTip**
   > If you suspend the execution of a procedure by using a breakpoint, pointing to an argument in the Code window will display a pop-up with the argument's current value.

5. Click **View** on the menu bar, click **Immediate Window**, type **? corppurchasedate**, then press **[Enter]**
   Your screen should look like Figure O-18. The **Immediate Window** is a scratch pad window in which statements are evaluated immediately, so you can determine the value of any argument at any point in the procedure. There are many other debugging tools available in the Code window when you are working with more complex code.

6. Click **Debug** on the menu bar, click **Clear All Breakpoints**, click the **Continue button** ▶ on the Standard toolbar to execute the rest of the function, close the **Immediate Window**, click **File** on the menu bar, then click **Close and return to Microsoft Access**
   The Employee Pricing query's datasheet should be visible.

7. Close the Employee Pricing datasheet, close the Technology-O database, save the changes to Functions, then exit Access

FIGURE O-16: Setting a breakpoint

Debug menu

Toggle breakpoint

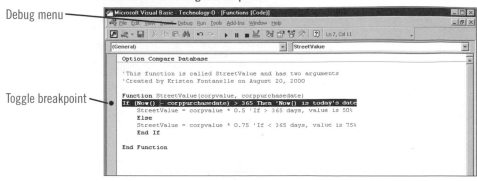

FIGURE O-17: Stopping execution at a breakpoint

Breakpoint highlighted

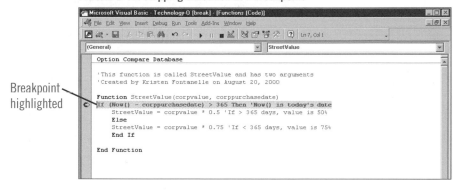

FIGURE O-18: Using the Immediate window

Continue button

Immediate window

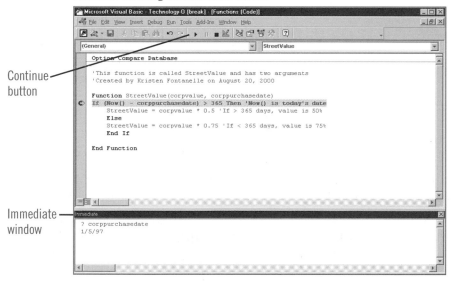

CLUES TO USE

Interpreting Visual Basic syntax

When you enter a Visual Basic keyword such as MsgBox, shown in Figure O-19, Visual Basic prompts appear to help you complete the statement. In the MsgBox function syntax, the bold italic words are **named arguments** of the function. **Arguments** enclosed in brackets are optional. (Do not type the brackets in your Visual Basic code.) For the MsgBox function, the only argument you must provide is the text for the prompt.

FIGURE O-19: MsgBox function

```
MsgBox |
MsgBox(Prompt, [Buttons As VbMsgBoxStyle = vbOKOnly], [Title], [HelpFile], [Context])
As VbMsgBoxResult
```

Practice

▶ Concepts Review

Identify each element of the code window shown in Figure O-20.

FIGURE O-20

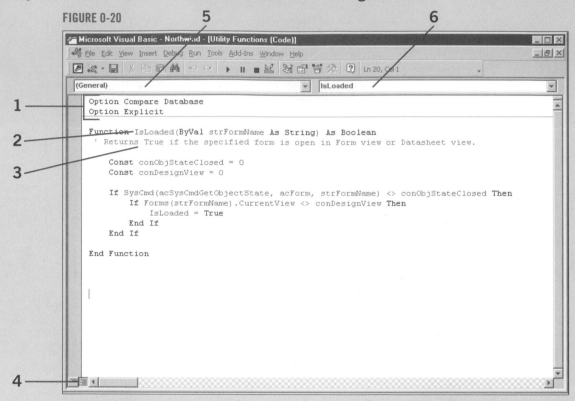

Match each term with the statement that describes its function.

7. Procedure
8. If...Then...Else statement
9. Debugging
10. Class modules
11. Visual Basic for Applications
12. Function
13. Arguments
14. Breakpoint
15. Module

a. Allows you to test a logical condition and execute commands only if the condition is true
b. The programming language used in Access modules
c. A line of code that automatically suspends execution of the procedure
d. A procedure that returns a value
e. Constants, variables, or expressions passed to a procedure to further define how it should execute
f. Stored as part of the form or report object in which they are created
g. The Access object where VBA code is stored
h. A series of VBA statements that perform an operation or calculate a value
i. A process to find and resolve programming errors

Select the best answer from the list of choices.

16. A module contains VBA programming code organized in units called:
   a. Macros.
   b. Arguments.
   c. Breakpoints.
   d. Procedures.

17. Which type of procedure does NOT return a value?
   a. Sub
   b. Function
   c. Module
   d. Macro

18. Which of the following is NOT a reason to use modules rather than macros?
   a. Modules are used to create unique functions.
   b. Modules contain code that can work with other Microsoft Office software programs.
   c. Modules can contain procedures that mask error messages.
   d. Modules are usually easier to write than macros.

19. Which of the following is NOT a type of VBA error?
   a. Compile time
   b. Run time
   c. Logic
   d. Class action

Skills Review

1. Understanding Modules.
   a. Start Access and open the Basketball-O database.
   b. Click Modules on the Objects bar, click the Shot Statistics module, then click the Design button.
   c. Record your answers to the following questions on a sheet of paper.

   - What is the name of the function defined in this module?
   - What are the names of the arguments defined in this module?
   - In your own words, what is the purpose of the If statement?
   - What is the purpose of the End Function statement?
   - Why is the End Function statement in blue?
   - Why are some of the lines indented?

2. Comparing Macros and Modules.
   a. If not already opened, open the Code window for the Shot Statistics module.
   b. Record your answers to the following questions on a sheet of paper.

   - Why was a module rather than a macro used to create this function?
   - Why is code written in the Shot Statistics code window generally more difficult to create than a macro?
   - Identify each of the keywords or keyword phrases, and explain the purpose for each.

3. Creating a Function Procedure.
   a. If not already opened, open the Code window for the Shot Statistics module.
   b. Create a function called "Contribution" below the End Function statement of the TotalShotPercentage function by typing the following VBA statements: (*Hint*: Type the function exactly as written below.)
   Function Contribution(fg, threept, ft, offreb, defreb, assists)
        Contribution = (fg * 2 + threept * 3 + ft + offreb * 2 + defreb + assists * 2)
   End Function

   c. Click the Save button to save the Shot Statistics code

   d. Close the Visual Basic Code window and return to Access.

   e. Use Query Design view to create a new query using the First and Last fields from the Players table and all of the fields from the Stats table.

   f. Create a calculated field called Rank in the first available column by carefully typing the Contribution function as follows:

   Rank: Contribution([FG],[3P], [FT], [Reb-O], [Reb-D], [Assists])

   g. View the query datasheet

   h. Change PlayerNo 21 to your first and last name, then print the first page of the datasheet in landscape orientation.

   i. Save the query as "Rankings" and close the datasheet.

4. Using If Statements.

   a. Click Modules on the Objects bar, open the Shot Statistics Code Design window, click to the right of the Function Contribution statement, press [Enter], then type the following If statements:

   (*Hint:* You can use copy and paste to copy repeating statements, then edit for the differences.)

```
        If fg+threept+ft = 0 Then
        Contribution = (fg * 2 + threept * 3 + ft + offreb * 2 + defreb + assists * 2)/2
        ElseIf offreb+defreb = 0 Then
        Contribution = (fg * 2 + threept * 3 + ft + offreb * 2 + defreb + assists * 2)/3
        Else
        Contribution = (fg * 2 + threept * 3 + ft + offreb * 2 + defreb + assists * 2)
        End If
End Function
```

   b. Save and close the Shot Statistics Code window and return to Access.

   c. Open the Rankings query, then print the first pages of the datasheet in landscape orientation. You should see the calculated Ranking field change for PlayerNo 21 for Games 1, 2, and 3 in which the player had either zero offense or zero rebounds.

   d. Close the datasheet.

5. Documenting a Procedure.

   a. Click Modules on the Objects bar, open the Shot Statistics Code design window, and edit the Contribution function to include the following five comment statements:

```
Function Contribution(fg, threept, ft, offreb, defreb, assists)
'If no field goals, 3 pointers, or free throws were made
        If fg + threept + ft = 0 Then
'Then the Contribution statistic should be divided by 2
        Contribution = (fg * 2 + threept * 3 + ft + offreb * 2 + defreb + assists * 2) / 2
'If no offensive or defensive rebounds were grabbed
        ElseIf offreb + defreb = 0 Then
'Then the Contribution statistic should be divided by 3
        Contribution = (fg * 2 + threept * 3 + ft + offreb * 2 + defreb + assists * 2) / 3
        Else
        Contribution = (fg * 2 + threept * 3 + ft + offreb * 2 + defreb + assists * 2)
        End If
End Function
'This function was created by Your Name on Today's Date
```

b. Save the changes to the Contribution function and Shot Statistics module, print and close the Code window, then return to Access.

6. Examining a Class Module.

a. Open the Player Entry Form in Design view.

b. Select the Command Button on the right side of the form that does the Print Record Action. It has the picture of a printer on the button and is named PrintCurrentRecord.

c. Open the property sheet for the button, click the Event tab, click the On Click property, then click the Build button to open the class module.

d. Edit the comment on the last line to document your name and the current date; save, print, then close the Code window.

7. Creating a Sub Procedure.

a. Open the Player Entry Form in Design view, if not already opened.

b. Open the property sheet for the form, click the Event tab, click the On Mouse Move text box, click the Build button, click Code Builder, then click OK.

c. Enter the following statement between the Private Sub and End Sub statements:
[First].ForeColor = 255

d. Enter a comment below this statement as follows:
'When the mouse moves, the First control will become bright red

e. Save and close the Code window. Return to Access.

f. Close the property sheet, then open the Player Entry Form in Form view.

g. Move the mouse beyond the edge of the Detail section of the form. The color of the First text box should turn bright red.

h. Save and close the Player Entry Form.

8. Troubleshooting a Module.

a. Open the Code window for the Shot Statistics module.

b. Click anywhere in the If fg + threept + ft = 0 statement in the Contribution function.

c. Click Debug on the menu bar, then click the Toggle Breakpoint option to set a breakpoint at the If fg + threept + ft = 0 statement in the Contribution function.

d. Save and close the Code window and return to Microsoft Access.

e. Click Queries on the Objects bar, then double-click the Rankings query. This action should call the Contribution function, which will stop and highlight the statement where you set a breakpoint.

f. Click View on the menu bar, click Immediate Window, type "?fg", then press [Enter].

g. Type ?offreb, then press [Enter].

h. View the results in the Immediate window, close the Immediate window, click Debug on the menu bar, click Clear All Breakpoints, click the Continue button on the Standard toolbar, then close the Code window and return to Access.

i. Close the Rankings query, close the Basketball-O database, then exit Access.

Independent Challenges

1. As the manager of a doctor's clinic, you have created an Access database called Patients-O to track insurance claim reimbursements and general patient health. You wish to modify an existing function within this database.
    To complete this independent challenge:

a. Start Access and open the database Patients-O from your Project Disk.

b. Open the Code window for the BMI Function, then record your answers to the following questions on another sheet of paper:

   • What is the name of the function?
   • What are the function arguments?
   • How many comments are in the function?

c. Edit the BMI Function by adding a comment at the end of the code with your name and today's date.

d. Edit the BMI Function by adding a comment above the Function statement with the following information: 'A healthy BMI is in the range of 21-24.

e. Edit the BMI Function by adding the following If statement between the Function and BMI statements: If height = 0 Then BMI = 0 Else

f. Edit the BMI Function by adding an End If statement between the BMI and End Function statements.

g. The final BMI function code should look as follows:

```
Function BMI(weight, height)
    If height = 0 Then
        BMI = 0
    Else
        BMI = (weight * 0.4536) / (height * 0.0254)^ 2
    End If
End Function
```

h. Save, print, and close the Code window.

i. Double-click the BMI Query to open its datasheet, and test the If statement by entering 0 in the Height field for the first record for Sara Johnson.

j. Edit the first record to contain your first and last names, then print, save, and close the BMI query datasheet.

k. Close the Patients-O database then exit Access.

2. As the manager of a doctor's clinic, you have created an Access database called Patients-O to track insurance claim reimbursements. You wish to study the existing sub procedures stored as class modules in the Claim Entry Form.
    To complete this independent challenge:

a. Start Access and open the database Patients-O from your Project Disk.

b. Click the Forms button on the Objects bar, click the Claim Entry Form, then click the Design button in the database window.

c. Click the Code button on the Form Design toolbar, then record your answers to the following questions on another sheet of paper:

   • What are the names of the Sub procedures that exist in this class module?
   • What event triggers each Sub procedure?
   • What Access function is used in the PtFirstName_AfterUpdate() sub, how many arguments does it have, and what does it do? (*Hint*: You may have to use the Help documentation if you are not familiar with this function. In the Code window, click Help on the menu bar, then click Microsoft Visual Basic Help.)

- What is the purpose of the On Error command? (*Hint*: Use the Visual Basic Help documentation to find information on this command.)

d. Close the Code window, close the Claim Entry Form, and close the Patients-O database.

e. Exit Access.

3. As the manager of a doctor's clinic, you have created an Access database called Patients-O to track insurance claim reimbursements that are fixed (paid at a predetermined fixed rate) or denied (not paid by the insurance company). You wish to enhance the database with a class module.

To complete this independent challenge:

a. Start Access and open the database Patients-O database from your Project Disk.

b. Open the CPT Form in Design view.

c. Expand the width of the CPT Form to about the 5" mark on the horizontal ruler.

d. Use the Command Button Wizard to add a command button in the Form Header section. Choose the Add New Record action from the Record Operations category.

e. Choose the text Add Record for the button and name it "AddRecordButton".

f. Use the Command Button Wizard to add a command button in the Form Header section to the right of the existing Add New Record button. (*Hint*: Move and resize controls as necessary to put two command buttons in the Form Header section.)

g. Choose the Delete Record action from the Record Operations category.

h. Choose the text Delete Record for the button and name it "DeleteRecordButton".

i. Save and view the CPT Form in Form view and click the Add Record command button.

j. Add a new record (it will be record number 65) with a CPTCode value of 999 and an RBRVS value of 1.5.

k. Click the new record you just entered, and then click the Delete Record command button to make sure it works.

l. Click the Design View button, click the Delete Record command button, then press [Delete] on the keyboard.

m. Click the Code button on the Standard toolbar to examine the class module associated with this form, then record your answers to the following questions on another sheet of paper:

- How many subs exist in this class module and what are their names?
- What was the effect of deleting the command button in Form Design view on the associated Visual Basic code?

n. Add a comment as the last line of code in the Code window with your name and the current date, then save, print, and close the Code window.

o. Save and close the CPT Form, close the Patients-O database; then exit Access.

4. MediaLoft has developed a Web site that provides internal information to their employees. In this independent challenge, you'll surf the Internet to find Web pages that present information about how Modules are used in Access databases.

a. Connect to the Internet, go to the MediaLoft intranet site at http://www.course.com/illustrated/MediaLoft

b. Click the link for the Research center, then click the link for Microsoft Access Information.

c. Find the Search This Site text box and enter "Visual Basic" to request information on this subject. (*Hint*: Web sites change often, and you may need to find and click a Search button before you are able to enter your search criteria).

d. Refine your search as necessary, then find and print two support articles with the words "Visual Basic" in the summary line.

e. Close your browser window.

▶ Visual Workshop

As the manager of a college basketball team, you are helping the coach build meaningful statistics to compare the relative value of the players in each game. The coach has stated that one offensive rebound is worth as much to the team as two defensive rebounds, and would like you to use this rule to develop a "rebounding impact statistic" for each game. Open the Basketball-O database and use Figure O-21 to develop a function called ReboundImpact in a module called Rebound Statistic to calculate this statistic. Be sure to put your own name and date as a comment in the last row. Print the function.

FIGURE O-21

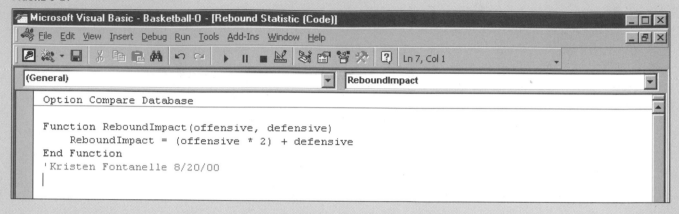

Managing
the Database

Objectives

- ⌐MOUS⌐ ► **Convert databases**
- ⌐MOUS⌐ ► **Set Passwords**
- ⌐MOUS⌐ ► **Change Startup Options**
- ⌐MOUS⌐ ► **Encrypt and Decrypt a database**
- ⌐MOUS⌐ ► **Analyze Performance**
- ⌐MOUS⌐ ► **Split a Database**
- ⌐MOUS⌐ ► **Replicate Using the Briefcase**
- ► **Synchronize Using the Briefcase**

After you have invested months of effort into developing an Access database, spending a few hours protecting the database, analyzing its use, and improving its performance is a practical and wise investment. As more and more users become dependent on the database, any effort you take to make the database faster, easier, and more secure will provide tremendous benefits. Proper administration of a database is an important responsibility. ◄━━ Kristen examines several administrative issues such as setting passwords, changing startup options, and analyzing database performance to protect, improve, and enhance the Technology database.

Converting databases

When you **convert** a database you change the file into one that can be opened in another version of Access. For example, it would be necessary to convert an Access 97 database to an Access 2000 database if your company upgraded from the Office 97 suite to the Office 2000 suite of Microsoft software. In Access 2000, you can convert an Access 2000 database to an Access 97 database with only a few conversion exceptions (links to data access pages are lost, for example). Access 2000 is the first Access database version that has supported this downward conversion capability. ▟▄▄ Kristen has been asked by the Training Department to convert the Technology-P database to a version that can be opened and used in Access 97 for use in their training classes. She uses the conversion capability of Access 2000 to accomplish this.

Steps 1234

1. Start Access, then open the **Technology-P database** on your Project Disk

   To convert a database, you must make sure that no other users have it open. Because you are the sole user of this database, you can start the conversion process.

2. Click **Tools** on the menu bar, point to **Database Utilities**, point to **Convert Database**, then click **To Prior Access Database Version**

   The Convert Database Into dialog box opens, prompting you for the name of the database.

3. Make sure the Save In list references your Project Disk, then type **Technology97** in the File name text box

   Your screen should look like Figure P-1. Because both Access 2000 and Access 97 databases have the same **.mdb** file extension, it is helpful to identify the version of Access in the filename if you are going to be working with both file types on the same computer.

4. Click **Save** in the Convert Database Into dialog box

   Access starts the conversion process; you can follow the progress on the status bar. Access creates a database file Technology97 in an Access 97 format on your Project Disk. There are no prompts indicating that the process is finished. Rather, you are returned to your original Access 2000 file, Technology-P.

Trouble?

You may need to click expand buttons (they appear as plus signs) in the Folders list to view all of the folders on the Project Disk.

5. Right-click the **Start button** on the taskbar, click **Explore**, locate your Project Disk, then view the contents on your Project Disk

6. Click the **Views button list arrow** 🔽 on the Explorer Standard Buttons toolbar, then click **Details**

   Your screen should look similar to Figure P-2. You can see a column of information for file types. Notice that the list includes Technology97, the database that was just created by converting the Technology-P Access 2000 database to an Access 97 version database. The filename Technology-P appears twice, as an .mdb and .ldb file. The **.ldb** file is a temporary file that keeps track of record-locking information when the database is open. It helps coordinate the multiuser capabilities of an Access database so that several people can read and update the same database at the same time. If you had Access 97 on your computer, you could open the Technology97 database into that application window without any conversion or error messages.

7. Click **File** on the menu bar, then click **Close**

   The Technology-P database window appears on your screen.

FIGURE P-1: Convert Database Into dialog box

Save the file to your Project Disk

New filename

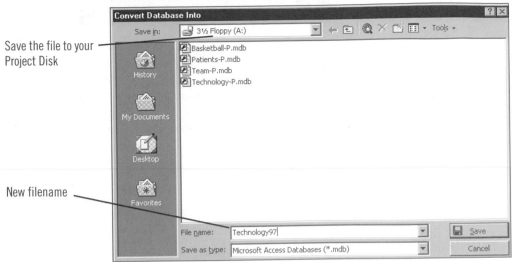

FIGURE P-2: Exploring the Project Disk

Views button

Technology97.mdb is an Access 97 database

Project Disk in drive A

Expand buttons

Files on Project Disk

Technology-P .mdb and .ldb files

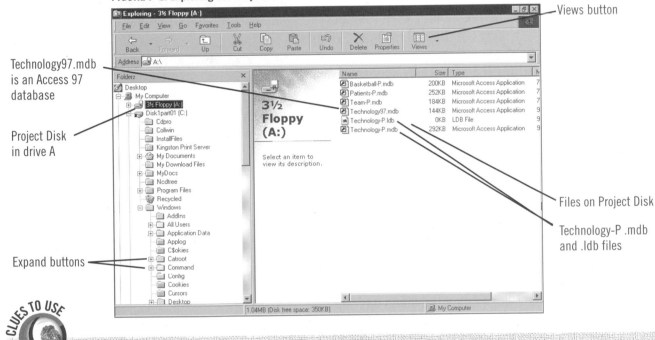

Converting from Access 97 to Access 2000

If you open an Access 97 database file in Access 2000, the dialog box shown in Figure P-3 will appear, enabling you to convert the database to an Access 2000 version as you open it or to just open it without converting it. If you open it without converting it, you will be able to view all objects and change data, but you will not be able to modify any of the objects in Access 2000. In this way, both Access 97 and Access 2000 users can share the same database.

FIGURE P-3: Convert/Open Database dialog box

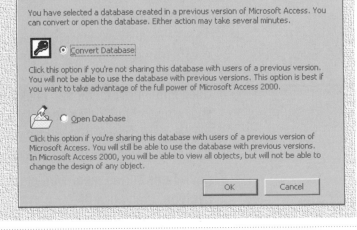

Setting Passwords

There are three types of passwords that can be set on an Access database: database, security account, and Visual Basic for Applications (VBA) passwords. If you set a **database password**, all users must enter that password before they are allowed to open the database, but they then have full access to the database. **Security account passwords** are applied to **workgroups**, files that determine the users, objects, and permissions to which the users are granted (such as read, delete, or edit) for specific objects in the database. **VBA passwords** prevent unauthorized users from modifying VBA code. The Technology database contains sensitive information about MediaLoft assets that Kristen wants to protect. She uses a database password to further secure the information.

Steps 1 2 3 4

QuickTip

It's always a good idea to back up a database on another disk before creating a database password.

1. **Click File on the menu bar, then click Close**
   The Technology-P database closes, and the Access window remains open.

2. **Click the Open button 📂 on the Database toolbar, navigate to your Project Disk, click Technology-P in the database window, click the Open list arrow in the Open dialog box, then click Open Exclusive**
   To set a database password, you must open it in exclusive mode. **Exclusive mode** means that you are the only person who has the database open, and others will not be able to open the file during this time.

3. **Click Tools on the menu bar, point to Security, then click Set Database Password**
   The Set Database Password dialog box opens, as shown in Figure P-4. Passwords are case sensitive, and if you lose or forget your password, it can't be recovered. For security reasons, your password will not appear as you type; for each keystroke, an asterisk will appear. Therefore, you must enter the exact same password in both the Password and Verify text boxes to make sure that you didn't make a typing error.

QuickTip

Check to make sure the Caps Lock light is not on if your password is lowercase letters.

4. **Type cyclone in the Password text box, press [Tab], type cyclone in the Verify text box, then click OK**
   Passwords should be easy enough to remember, but not obvious—such as your name, the word "password," the name of the database, or the name of the company.

5. **Click File on the menu bar, then click Close**
   You closed the Technology-P database, but left the Access window open. An important part of database administration is testing a new database password.

6. **Click 📂 on the Database toolbar, navigate to your Project Disk, then double-click Technology-P in the database window**
   The Password Required dialog box opens, as shown in Figure P-5.

7. **Type cyclone, then click OK**
   The Technology-P database opens, giving you full access to all of the objects. You must exclusively open a database to remove a database password, as was required to set a database password.

8. **Click File on the menu bar, click Close, click 📂 on the Database toolbar, navigate to your Project Disk, click Technology-P in the database window, click the Open list arrow in the Open dialog box, click Open Exclusive, type cyclone in the Password Required dialog box, then click OK**

9. **Click Tools on the menu bar, point to Security, click Unset Database Password, type cyclone, then click OK**

FIGURE P-4: Set Database Password dialog box

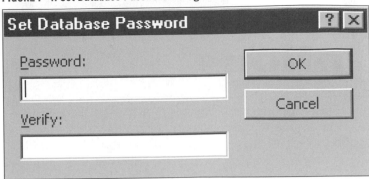

FIGURE P-5: Password Required dialog box

CLUES TO USE

Creating workgroups

To create workgroups that define the specific users and object permissions to which the users have access, use a program called **Workgroup Administrator**. Workgroup Administrator is started by double-clicking the Wrkgadm.exe file found in the C:\Program Files\Microsoft Office\Office folder of a typical installation. If you lose or forget any of the entries you make to workgroup information files, however, there is no way to recover them. Also, all entries in the workgroup information files are case sensitive, just like the database password.

Changing Startup Options

Startup options are a series of commands that execute when the database is opened. Many common startup options can be defined through the Startup dialog box, such as which form and menu bar to display when the database opens. Other startup options require that a **command-line option**, a special series of characters that starts with a forward slash added to the end of the path to the file (for example, C:\My Documents\MediaLoft.mdb /excl), execute a command when the file is opened. See Table P-1 for more information on several startup command-line options. ➤ Because she knows that most users immediately open the Employees form as soon as they open the Technology-P database, Kristen uses the Startup dialog box to specify that the Employees form opens as soon as the Technology-P database opens.

Steps

1. Click **Tools** on the menu bar, then click **Startup**
   The Startup dialog box opens, as shown in Figure P-6.

2. Click the **Display Form/Page list arrow**, then click **Employees**
   In addition to specifying which form will open when the Technology-P database opens, the Startup dialog box provides several other options as well.

3. Click in the **Application Title text box**, type **MediaLoft Computer Assets**, click the **Allow Toolbar/Menu Changes check box** to clear the check box, then click **OK**
   Clearing the Allow Toolbar/Menu Changes check box will not allow users to customize or change the view of toolbars or menus in any way. Provided the correct toolbars appear on each screen, not allowing the users to change them can simplify and improve the usability of the database. The text entered in the Application Title text box appears in the Access window title bar.

4. Close the Technology-P database, click the **Open button** 🖼 on the Database toolbar, navigate to your Project Disk, then double-click **Technology-P** in the database window
   The Technology-P database, followed by the Employees form, opens, as shown in Figure P-7. You can press and hold [Shift] while opening a database to bypass the startup options. If the database is also password protected, you would have to remove the password before you could bypass the startup options.

5. Close the Employees form, then click **View** on the menu bar
   The Toolbars option is no longer available because you disabled toolbar changes in the Startup dialog box.

6. Right-click the **database toolbar**
   There are no shortcut menus available from any toolbars because you disabled toolbar changes in the Startup dialog box.

FIGURE P-6: Startup dialog box

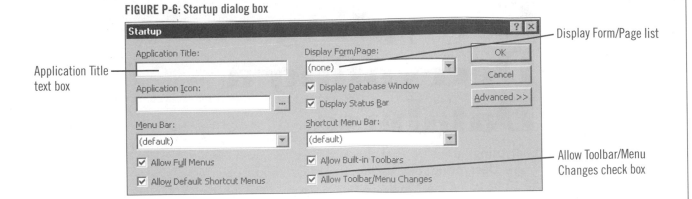

Application Title text box

Application Title:

Application Icon:

Menu Bar:
(default)

☑ Allow Full Menus

☑ Allow Default Shortcut Menus

Display Form/Page:
(none) — Display Form/Page list

☑ Display Database Window

☑ Display Status Bar

Shortcut Menu Bar:
(default)

☑ Allow Built-in Toolbars

☑ Allow Toolbar/Menu Changes — Allow Toolbar/Menu Changes check box

OK

Cancel

Advanced >>

FIGURE P-7: Employees form automatically opens

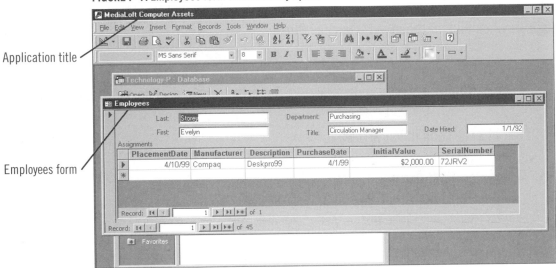

Application title

Employees form

TABLE P-1: Startup command-line options

option	effect
/excl	Opens the database for exclusive access
/ro	Opens the database for read-only access
/pwd *password*	Opens the database using the specified *password*
/repair	Repairs the database (In Access 2000, compacting the database also repairs it. So if the Compact on Close feature is chosen, the /repair option is not needed.)
/convert *target database*	Converts a previous version of a database to an Access 2000 database with the *target database* name
/x *macro*	Starts Access and runs specified *macro*
/nostartup	Starts Access without displaying the startup dialog box
/wrkgrp *workgroup information file*	Starts Access using the specified *workgroup information file*

Encrypting and Decrypting a Database

Encrypting means to make the database objects and data itself indecipherable to other programs. **Decrypting** reverses the encryption. If you are concerned that your Access database file might be stolen and the data stripped from it by another program (such as another database program, a word processor, or a utility program), encryption may be warranted. Other potential threats to the security of your database are described in Table P-2. ◄─── MediaLoft has recently connected their corporate file servers to the Internet, so Kristen is more concerned about securing corporate data than ever before. She uses Access encryption and decryption to learn how to secure the data within the Technology-P database.

Steps 123 4

1. Click **File** on the menu bar, click **Close**
   The Technology-P database window closes, but the Access window is still open. You cannot encrypt an open database.

2. Click **Tools** on the menu bar, point to **Security**, then click **Encrypt/Decrypt Database**
   The Encrypt/Decrypt Database dialog box opens, as shown in Figure P-8.

3. Click the **Look in list arrow**, navigate to your Project Disk, double-click **Technology-P**
   The Encrypt Database As dialog box appears, as shown in Figure P-9.

4. Type **Technology-P** in the File name text box, click **Save** in the Encrypt Database As dialog box, then click **Yes** to replace the existing file
   You can encrypt a database file to the same filename or to a new filename. In either case, a back-up copy of the database on a separate disk protects your file should the encryption be unsuccessful (unlikely but possible) or the equipment malfunctions during the encryption process. An encrypted database works in exactly the same way as the original file to users authorized to open the file. Encryption helps protect the data as it is being sent over network connections. You decrypt a database using the same steps.

5. Click **Tools** on the menu bar, point to **Security**, then click **Encrypt/Decrypt Database**

6. Click the **Look in: list arrow**, navigate to your Project Disk, then double-click **Technology-P**
   The Decrypt Database As dialog box opens, because Technology-P is currently encrypted. For now, decrypt the database back to its original state.

7. Double-click **Technology-P** in the Decrypt Database As dialog box, then click **Yes** when prompted to replace the existing file

FIGURE P-8: Encrypt/Decrypt Database dialog box

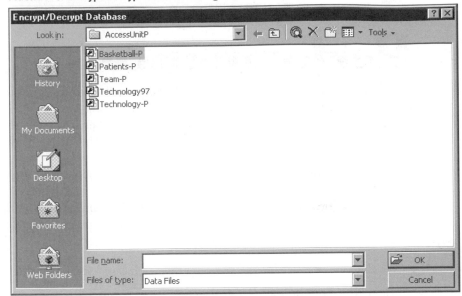

FIGURE P-9: Encrypt Database As dialog box

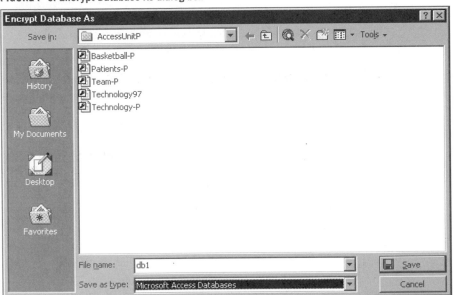

TABLE P-2: Database threats

incident	what can happen	appropriate action
Virus	Viruses can cause a vast number of damaging actions, ranging from profane messages to destruction of files.	Purchase the leading virus-checking software for each machine, and regularly update it.
Power outage	Power problems such as **brown-outs** (dips in power often causing lights to dim) and **spikes** (surges in power) can cause damage to the hardware, which may render the computer useless.	Purchase a **UPS** (Uninterruptible Power Supply) to maintain constant power to the file server (if networked); purchase a **surge protector** (power strip with surge protection) for each end user.
Theft or intentional damage	Computer thieves or other scoundrels steal or vandalize computer equipment.	Place the file server in a room that can be locked after hours; use network drives for end user data files that are backed up on a daily basis; use off-site storage for backups; set database passwords and encryption so that files that are stolen cannot be used; use computer locks for equipment that is at risk, especially laptops.

Unit **P**

Access 2000

Analyzing Performance

Access provides a powerful tool called the **Performance Analyzer** that studies the structure and size of your database and makes a variety of recommendations on how you could improve its performance. Usually, the decision whether to fix a database that runs too slowly boils down to two choices: time and money. With adequate time and knowledge of Access, you can alleviate many performance bottlenecks by using software tools and additional programming techniques. With extra money, however, you can purchase faster processors and more memory to accomplish the same thing. See Table P-3 for more tips on optimizing the performance of your computer. ➤ Kristen uses the Performance Analyzer to see whether Access has any easy recommendations on how to maintain peak performance of the Technology-P database.

Steps 1 2 3 4

1. Open the **Technology-P database** on your Project Disk, then close the **Employees form** that automatically opens

2. Click **Tools** on the menu bar, point to **Analyze**, then click **Performance**

   The Performance Analyzer dialog box opens, as shown in Figure P-10. You can choose to analyze selected objects or the entire database.

3. Click the **All Object Types tab**, click **Select All**, then click **OK**

   The Performance Analyzer examines each object and presents the results in a dialog box as shown in Figure P-11. The key shows that the analyzer gives four levels of advice regarding performance: recommendations, suggestions, ideas, and items that were fixed.

4. Click the **Table 'Assignments': Change data type of field 'SSN' from 'Text' to 'Long Integer'** in the Analysis Results list

   The icon tells you that this is an idea. The Analysis Notes section of the Performance Analyzer dialog box gives you additional information regarding that specific item. In this case, the idea is to change the data type of the field SSN from Text to Number (with a Long Integer field size). While this might not be an appropriate action for an SSN field, the three fields in the PCSpecs table—Memory, HardDisk, and MHz—all represent numeric values that could be changed from Text to Number with the suggested field size. All of the Performance Analyzer's ideas should be considered, but they are not as important as recommendations and suggestions.

5. Click **Close** to close the Performance Analyzer dialog box

FIGURE P-10: Performance Analyzer dialog box

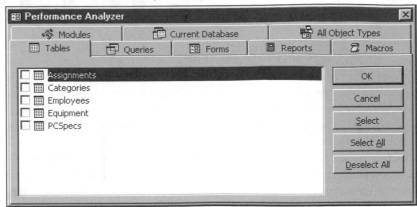

FIGURE P-11: Performance Analyzer results

Selected idea ——

Explains icons ——

Additional
explanation for the
selected item ——

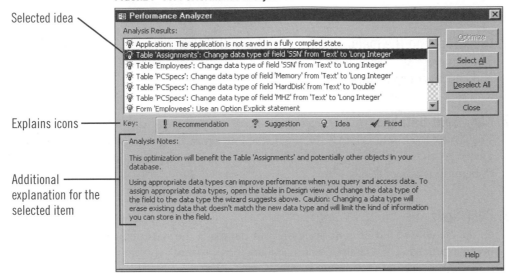

TABLE P-3: Tips for optimizing performance

degree of difficulty	tip
Easy	Close all applications that you don't currently need to free up memory and other computer resources.
Easy	Eliminate memory-resident programs such as complex screen savers, e-mail alert programs, and virus checkers if they can be run safely on an "as-needed" basis.
Easy	If you are the only person using a database, open it in exclusive mode.
Easy	Use the Compact on Close feature to regularly compact and repair your database.
Moderate	Add more memory to your computer; once the database is open, memory is the single most important determinant of overall performance.
Moderate	If others don't need to share the database, load it on your local hard drive instead of the network's file server (but be sure to back up local drives regularly, too).
Moderate	**Split** the database so that the data is stored on the file server, but other database objects are stored on your local, faster hard drive.
moderate to difficult	If using disk compression software, stop doing so or move the database to an uncompressed drive.
moderate to difficult	Run Performance Analyzer on a regular basis, examining and appropriately acting on each recommendation, suggestion, and idea.
moderate to difficult	Make sure that all PCs are running the latest versions of Windows and Access; this may involve purchasing more software or upgrading hardware to properly support these robust software products.

Splitting a Database

A successful database grows in many new ways and creates the need for higher levels of database connectivity. **Local area networks** (**LANs**) are installed to link multiple PCs together so they can share hardware and software resources. Once a LAN is installed, a shared database will often be moved to a **file server**, a centrally located computer in which every user can access the database through the network. The more users that share the same database, however, the slower it will respond. The **Database Splitter** feature improves the performance of a database shared among several users by allowing you to split the database into two files: the **back-end database**, which contains the actual table objects, and the **front-end database**, which contains the other database objects as well as links to the back-end database tables. The back-end database is stored on the file server. The front-end database is stored on user PCs. ⬤▬ Kristen uses the Database Splitter to split the Technology-P database into two databases in preparation for the new LAN being installed in the Information Systems Department.

Steps

QuickTip

It's always a good idea to back up a database on another disk before splitting it.

1. Click **Tools** on the menu, point to **Database Utilities**, then click **Database Splitter**

The Database Splitter dialog box opens, and provides additional information on the process and benefits of splitting a database, as shown in Figure P-12.

Trouble?

Verify that the file's path is to your Project Disk.

2. Click **Split Database**

The Create Back-end Database dialog box opens, prompting you for a name of the back-end database, the one that will hold the table objects. The suggested name Technology-P_be.mdb is acceptable.

3. Click **Split**

As the Database Splitter is working on your database, the status bar indicates that tables are being exported. The Database Splitter dialog box prompts you that the database is successfully split.

4. Click **OK**

The Technology-P database has become the front-end database, with all database objects intact except for the table objects. Technology-P no longer contains any table objects, but rather links to the Technology-P_be database that stores the actual data. See Figure P-13.

5. Click **File** on the menu bar, then click **Exit**

You closed the Technology-P database and exited Access. In a LAN environment, splitting a database then storing the back-end on the file server and the front-end on the **client** (the user's PC) dramatically improves performance when compared to using a database that is completely stored on the file server. On a split database, the only traffic that travels through the network is the actual data. All of the other objects that users need are stored on their local hard drives. (As many copies of the front-end database can be made as are needed so that each user has a copy of the front-end database on his or her own machine). Storing the actual tables in the back-end database on the file server maintains data integrity because all users update the same database file.

FIGURE P-12: Database Splitter dialog box

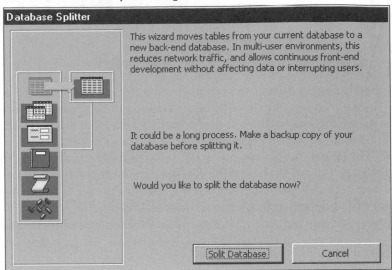

FIGURE P-13: Tables are linked in the front-end database

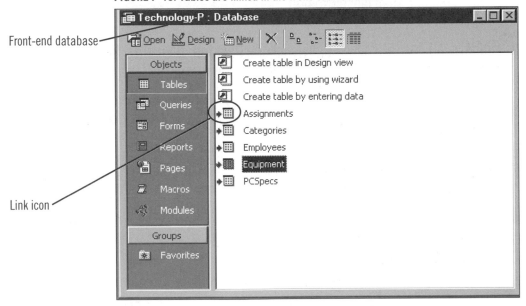

Front-end database

Link icon

Defining Client/Server computing

Splitting a database into a front-end and back-end database that work together is an excellent example of client/server computing. **Client/server computing** can be defined as two or more information systems cooperatively processing to solve a problem. In most implementations, the **client** is defined as the user's PC and the server is defined as the shared file server, mini-, or mainframe computer. The **server** usually handles corporate-wide computing activities such as

data storage and management, security, and connectivity to other networks. Within Access, client computers generally handle those tasks specific to each user such as storing all of the objects (other than table objects) used by that particular user. Effectively managing a vast client/server network in which many front-end databases link to a single back-end database is a tremendous task, but the performance and security benefits are worth the effort.

Replicating Using the Briefcase

If you want to copy a database to another computer, such as a home or laptop computer that you use on the road, the Windows Briefcase feature can help you. The **Briefcase** makes a special copy of the original database (called a **replica**) and keeps track of changes made in either the original database (called the **master**) or the replica so that they can be resynchronized at a later date. The master database and all replica database files created from the master are called the **replica set**. The process of making the copy is called **replication**, and the process of reconciling and updating changes between the replica and the master is called **synchronization**. Kristen is heading to a conference and wants to take the Technology-P_be database with her so that she can enter and update information in the Employee table. She uses the Briefcase program to keep the original database and the copy she will put on her laptop synchronized.

Steps

QuickTip

It's always a good idea to back up a database on another disk before replicating it.

1. Right-click the **Start button**, click **Explore**, locate your Project Disk in the Folders list, click **Technology-P_be** in the list of files, click the **Copy button** 🗐 on the Standard Buttons toolbar, then close Explorer
   You placed the Technology-P_be.mdb file on the Windows Clipboard.

2. Minimize all open windows, right-click the **Desktop**, then click **Paste**
   You copy the master database to the desktop because you can't create a replica set with a master and replica both stored on floppy disks.

Trouble?

To install Briefcase: open Control Panel, double-click Add/Remove Programs, click Windows Setup tab, double-click Accessories, click Briefcase check box, click OK.

3. Right-click the **Technology-P_be** file on the desktop, click **Copy**, double-click **My Briefcase** 💼, click **Edit** on the menu bar, click **Paste**, click **Yes** to continue, click **No** to not backup your database, click **OK** to accept the Original copy as the database that will allow design changes, click **View** on the menu bar, then click **Details**
   Your screen should look like Figure P-14.

Trouble?

The My Briefcase window may look different due to the Windows 98 settings on your computer.

4. Close the My Briefcase window, remove any existing disks from **drive A**, insert a blank formatted disk into **drive A**, right-click 💼 on the Desktop, point to **Send To**, then click **3½ Floppy (A)**
   For this lesson, you will update the replica on the floppy disk using your existing machine.

Trouble?

If the My Briefcase wizard is open on the desk top, click Finish to continue.

5. Double-click the **My Computer icon** 💻, double-click **3½ Floppy (A)** 🖫, double-click 💼 in the 3½ Floppy (A:) window, double-click **Technology-P_be** in the My Briefcase window, then double-click the **Employees table**
   The Replicated Employees table opens. You can add a new record to the table.

6. Click the **New Record button** ⏭️, then add yourself as a new record using the following information:

last	first	Department	title	location	e-mail	DateHired	SSN
Your Last Name	Your First Name	Information Systems	CIO	Corporate	yourname@ medialoft.com	1/1/00	444-33-2222

7. Close the Employees table datasheet
   Your screen should look like Figure P-15. Both the title bar of the database and the table icons indicate that you are working with a replica. The replica contains the record you just added, but the master does not.

8. Click **File** on the menu bar, then click **Exit**

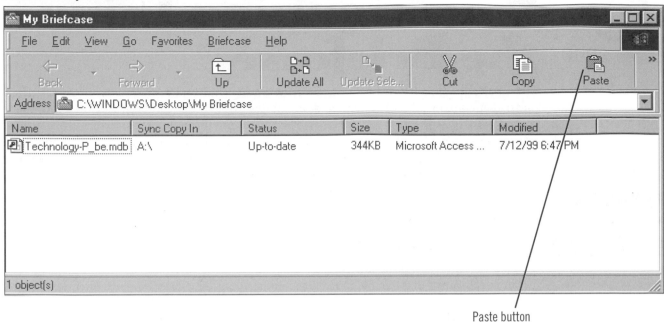

Paste button

Replica

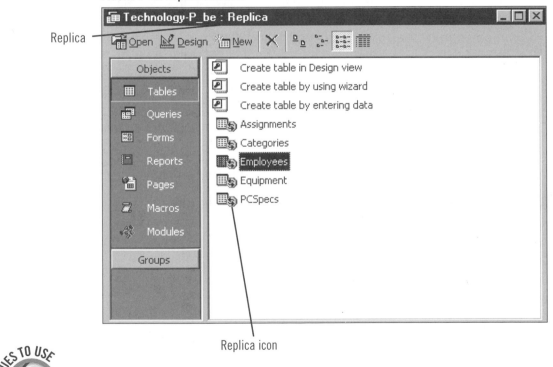

Replica icon

Access 2000

Creating a Briefcase folder

By default, the desktop displays a single Briefcase icon called "My Briefcase." Briefcase icons are actually a special type of folder designed to help users with two computers keep the files that are used on both computers updated. If you open the My Briefcase folder and find other files in it, or if there is no Briefcase on the desktop, you can easily create as many new Briefcase folders as you need. You create, delete, copy, and move a Briefcase folder in exactly the same manner as with a regular folder in Windows Explorer. For example, if you want to create a new Briefcase folder on the Desktop, you can right-click the Desktop, point to New, then click Briefcase.

Synchronizing Using the Briefcase

The Briefcase controls synchronization of the master and replica databases. If the Briefcase folder that contains the replica is stored on a floppy disk (which has been used in a secondary computer), the floppy disk would have to be inserted into the computer on which the master is stored before synchronization could occur. Synchronization updates all records and objects in each member of the replica set. The Briefcase reports on any synchronization discrepancies that it cannot resolve. Now that Kristen has created a replica of the Technology-P_be database and added a record to it, she is anxious to synchronize it with the master to see how the Briefcase keeps the replica set up-to-date.

Steps

Trouble?

If the A:/My Briefcase window is not open on the desktop, double-click the My Computer icon, double-click 3½ Floppy (A:) 💻, then double-click My Briefcase 💼 in the 3½ Floppy (A:) window

1. Click the **Update All button** 🔳 on the My Briefcase Standard Buttons toolbar

Your screen should look like Figure P-16. The Briefcase program read both database files and determined that the replica had been updated but the master had not. Therefore, it recommended the replace action. If there had been many files in the Briefcase, each one would be listed with a suggested action (replace, skip, merge).

2. Click **Update**

The Briefcase replaces the master file on your desktop with the replica file on your floppy and displays the My Briefcase window with an "Up-to-date" Status message for the Technology-P_be.mdb file, as shown in Figure P-17. Had you made changes to both the master and the replica, the Briefcase window would have recommended a more complex action (merge), as shown in Figure P-18. The **merge** action evaluates the changes in each object and applies them to the other. For example, the merge action will resynchronize the two databases if you edit or add records in both the master and replica. You also can add new objects to both. You can make design changes only to existing objects, however, in the master database.

3. Close the My Briefcase window

4. Close the 3½ Floppy (A:) window, then close the My Computer window

Trouble?

If you created a new Briefcase folder for this unit, delete it.

5. Delete the Technology-P_be Design Master from the desktop

CLUES TO USE

Using the Briefcase with a laptop computer

A common scenario in which Briefcase folders have tremendous value is when a master database is stored on a file server and the replica is stored on the hard drive of a laptop computer. When you are in the office, your laptop computer is connected to the network through a docking station so you can use the master database just like all of the other users. When you are in the field, however, your laptop computer is disconnected from the corporate database and you work on the replica stored in a Briefcase folder on the laptop's hard drive. When you return to the office, you use the Briefcase update features to resynchronize the two copies.

FIGURE P-16: Update My Briefcase window—Replace action

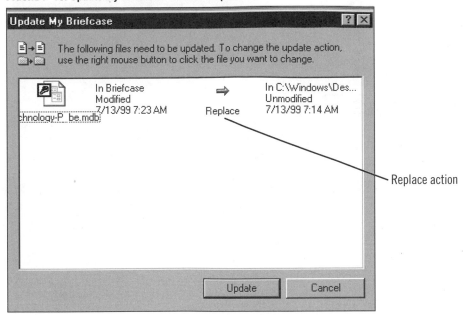

Replace action

FIGURE P-17: My Briefcase window showing an up-to-date file

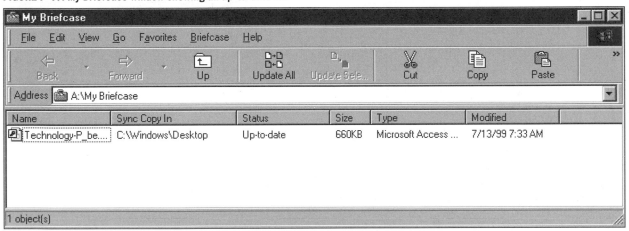

FIGURE P-18: Update My Briefcase window—Merge action

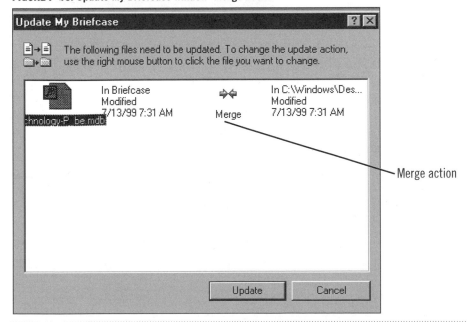

Merge action

Practice

▶ Concepts Review

Identify each element of the Explorer window shown in Figure P-19.

FIGURE P-19

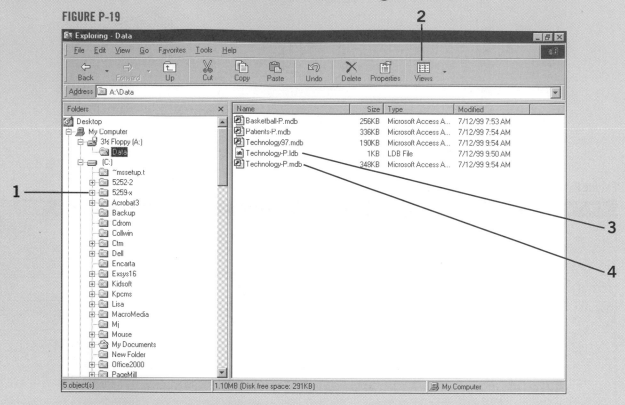

Match each term with the statement that describes its function.

5. Exclusive mode
6. Database Splitter
7. Encrypting
8. Performance Analyzer
9. Synchronization

a. Studies the structure and size of your database and makes a variety of recommendations on how you can improve its speed.

b. Breaks the database into two files to improve performance. One database contains the table objects and the other contains the rest of the objects with links to the table objects.

c. Updates the files in a replica set so that they all have the same information.

d. Scrambles a database so that it is indecipherable when opened by another program.

e. Means that no other users will have access to the database file while it's open.

Select the best answer from the list of choices.

10. Changing a database file into one that can be opened in another version of Access is called
    a. Splitting.
    b. Analyzing.
    c. Converting.
    d. Encrypting.

11. Which is NOT a type of password that can be set on an Access database?
    a. Database
    b. Security account
    c. Object
    d. Visual Basic for Applications

12. Which of the following determines the users, objects, and permissions to which the users are granted?
    a. Passwords
    b. Workgroups
    c. Permission logs
    d. Briefcase names

13. Which character precedes a command-line option?
    a. !
    b. @
    c. /
    d. ^

14. Which of the following is NOT an advantage of splitting the database using the Database Splitter?
    a. It keeps the data centralized in the back-end database for all users to access.
    b. It gives the users local control over form and report objects.
    c. It helps increase the overall performance of a LAN.
    d. It creates replica sets that can be used to synchronize files on laptops.

15. Startup command line options are:
    a. A special series of characters added to the end of the path to the file that start with a forward slash.
    b. Entered in the Startup dialog box.
    c. Used to automate the synchronization of a replica set.
    d. Special objects that execute first when the database is opened.

16. Client/server computing can be defined as:
    a. Two or more information systems cooperatively processing to solve a problem.
    b. A process to resynchronize a replica set.
    c. A LAN, WAN, or the Internet.
    d. A way to study the structure and size of your database to make a variety of recommendations on how you could improve its performance.

17. If you want to copy a database to another computer, such as a home or laptop computer you'll use on the road, which of the following features would keep the databases up-to-date?
    a. Database Splitter
    b. Performance Analyzer
    c. Startup Options
    d. Briefcase

▶ Skills Review

1. Converting databases.

   a. Start Access and open the Basketball-P database.

   b. Click Tools on the menu bar, point to Database Utilities, point to Convert Database, then click To Prior Access Version.

   c. Navigate to your Project Disk in the Convert Database Into dialog box, type "Basketball97" as the filename, then click Save.

   d. Open Windows Explorer, open your Project Disk, and check to make sure that both the Basketball-P and Basketball97 databases are stored on the Project Disk. You also will see a Basketball-P.ldb file, because Basketball-P.mdb is currently open.

   e. Close Explorer.

2. Setting Passwords.

   a. Close Basketball-P, but leave Access open.

   b. Click the Open button on the Database toolbar, navigate to your Project Disk, then click Basketball-P.

   c. Click the Open list arrow, then click Open Exclusive.

   d. Click Tools on the menu bar, point to Security, then click Set Database Password.

   e. Check to make sure the Caps Lock light is not on, type the word "colonial" in the Password text box, tab, type "colonial" in the Verify text box, then click OK. (Remember that passwords are case sensitive.)

   f. Close the Basketball-P database, but leave Access open.

   g. Open the Basketball-P database, type "colonial" in the Password Required dialog box, then click OK.

   h. Close the database, then open the Basketball-P database in Exclusive mode.

   i. Click Tools on the menu bar, point to Security, click Unset Database Password, type "colonial", then click OK.

3. Changing Startup Options.

   a. Click Tools on the menu bar, then click Startup to open the Startup dialog box.

   b. Type "SUNY Binghamton Women" in the Application Title text box, click the Display Form/Page list arrow, click the Player Entry Form, clear the Allow Toolbar/Menu Changes check box, then click OK. Notice the change in the title bar.

   c. Close the Basketball-P database, but leave Access open.

   d. Open the Basketball-P database.

   e. Close the Player Entry Form that automatically opened when the database was opened.

   f. Check the Access title bar to make sure it displays "SUNY Binghamton Women."

   g. Right-click the Database toolbar to make sure that you are unable to change or modify any of the toolbars.

   h. On a piece of paper, identify one reason for changing each of the three startup options modified in steps b, c, and d.

   i. Close the Basketball-P database, but leave Access open.

4. Encrypting and Decrypting a Database.

   a. To encrypt the database, click Tools on the menu bar, point to Security, then click Encrypt/Decrypt Database.

   b. Navigate to your Project Disk, click Basketball-P, then click OK.

   c. In the Encrypt Database As dialog box, click Basketball-P, then click Save.

   d. Click Yes when asked to replace the existing Basketball-P file.

   e. To decrypt the database, click Tools on the menu bar, point to Security, then click Encrypt/Decrypt Database.

   f. In the Decrypt Database dialog box, click Basketball-P, then click OK.

g. In the Decrypt Database As dialog box, click Basketball-P, click Save, then click Yes.

h. On a piece of paper, identify two database threats for which encryption could be used to protect the database.

5. Analyzing Performance.

a. Open Basketball-P, then close the Player Entry Form.

b. Click Tools on the menu bar, point to Analyze, then click Performance.

c. Click the All Object Types tab, click Select All, then click OK.

d. Click each of the Analysis Results and read the Analysis notes.

e. On a piece of paper, record the analysis results (there should be three entries), and identify whether they are recommendations, suggestions, ideas, or items that were fixed.

f. Close the Performance Analyzer dialog box.

6. Splitting a Database.

a. Click Tools on the menu, point to Database Utilities, then click Database Splitter.

b. Click Split Database, make sure that the Save in: list points to your Project Disk, then click Split to accept the default name of Basketball-P_be as the filename.

c. Click OK when prompted that the database was successfully split.

d. On a sheet of paper, identify two reasons for splitting a database.

e. On the paper, identify the back-end and front-end database filenames, and explain what these databases contain.

f. On the paper, explain what the table icons in the front-end database look like and what they represent.

g. Close the Basketball-P database.

7. Replicating Using the Briefcase.

a. Copy the Team-P database from your Project Disk, then paste it to the Desktop of your computer.

b. Copy the Team-P database from your Desktop, then paste it to an empty Briefcase folder. Click Yes when asked to continue, click No when asked to make a back-up copy, then click OK to choose the Original File.

c. Double-click the Team-P database in the New Briefcase window, double-click the Players table, then modify the record for PlayerNo 21 with your own First and Last names, HomeTown, and HomeState. (*Hint*: If no empty Briefcase window exists on your Desktop, create one by right-clicking the Desktop, pointing to New, then clicking Briefcase.)

d. Close the Players table, then close the Team-P Replica database and exit Access. Close the Briefcase window.

e. Open the Team-P Design Master database from your Desktop, then open the Players table. PlayerNo 21 will not be modified.

f. Change PlayerNo 22 so that a friend's First and Last names, HomeTown, and HomeState are entered.

g. Close the Players table, then close the Team-P Design Master database and Access window.

8. Synchronizing Using the Briefcase.

a. Open the Briefcase on the Desktop where the replicated Team-P database exists, click the Update All button, then click the Update button to merge the databases.

b. Double-click the Team-P entry in the Briefcase window to open the replica database, double-click the Players table, then print the Players datasheet. Both PlayerNo 21 and 22 should show the changes you made.

c. Close the Players datasheet, close the Team-P Replica, and close the Briefcase window.

d. Delete any files you created in the desktop.

▶ Independent Challenges

1. As the manager of a doctor's clinic, you have created an Access database called Patients-P to track insurance claims. You wish to set a database password on this file and also encrypt the database.

To complete this independent challenge:

a. Start Access.

b. Click the Open button on the Database toolbar, navigate to your Project Disk, click Patients-P, click the Open list arrow, then click Open Exclusive.

c. Click Tools, point to Security, then click Set Database Password.

d. Enter "health" in the Password text box as well as the Verify text box, then click OK.

e. Close the Patients-P database.

f. Open the Patients-P database, enter "health" in the Password Required dialog box.

g. Close the Patients-P database.

h. To encrypt the database, click Tools, point to Security, then click Encrypt/Decrypt Database.

i. In the Encrypt/Decrypt dialog box, click Patients-P, then click OK.

j. Enter "health" as the password, then click OK.

k. In the Encrypt Database As dialog box, click Patients-P, click Save, then click Yes to replace the existing file.

l. Exit Access.

2. As the manager of a doctor's clinic, you have created an Access database called Patients-P to track insurance claims. You wish to change the startup options.

To complete this independent challenge:

a. Start Access and open the database Patients-P from your Project Disk.

b. If prompted for a password (if you completed Independent Challenge 1, the file will be password protected), enter "health" and click OK.

c. To set startup options, click Tools on the menu, then click Startup.

d. In the Startup dialog box, enter "Dr. Biheller and Dr. Langguth" in the Application Title text box, choose the Claim Entry Form as the choice for the Display Form/Page option, clear the Allow Toolbar/Menu Changes check box, then click OK.

e. Close the Patients-P database.

f. Open the Patients-P database to test the Startup options. Enter the "health" password if prompted.

g. Close the Claim Entry Form, then right-click the Database toolbar to make sure that toolbars cannot be modified. Check to make sure that "Dr. Biheller and Dr. Langguth" appears in the title bar of the Access window.

h. Close the Patients-P database, then exit Access.

3. As the manager of a doctor's clinic, you have created an Access database called Patients-P to track insurance claims. You wish to use the Briefcase to synchronize a replica set.

To complete this independent challenge:

a. Open Windows Explorer, locate then copy the Patients-P database from your Project Disk, close Explorer, then paste the Patients-P database to your Desktop. (*Hint*: You can also use My Computer to find and copy the Patients-P database.)

b. If a password is set on the Patients-P database, you must remove it before you can use the database to create a replica set. If a password is not set on the Patients-P database, skip to step d. Open Access, then open the Patients-P database stored on your Desktop by using the Open Exclusive option.

c. Enter "health" as the password, close the Claim Entry Form if it automatically opened, click Tools, point to Security, click Unset Database Password, enter "health", click OK, then close the Patients-P database and Access window.

d. Copy the Patients-P database on your Desktop, then paste it into an empty Briefcase window. (*Hint*: If there is no empty Briefcase window on the Desktop, create one by right-clicking the Desktop, pointing to New, then clicking Briefcase.)

e. Click Yes to continue, click No about making a backup copy, and OK to choose the Original Copy as the one that will allow changes to the design of the database.

f. Double-click the Patients-P database in the Briefcase window, close the Claims Entry Form if it is opened, double-click the Doctors table, then enter your own information as a new record in the PodFirstName (your first name initial), PodLastName (your last name), and PodCode (your first and last name initials, which must be unique from the other records because it is the key field) fields.

g. Close the Doctors datasheet, then close the Patients-P Replica database.

h. Open the Patients-P database Design Master, which is stored on the Desktop.

i. Close the Claim Entry Form if it is opened, then double-click the Doctors table to open its datasheet.

j. Add a friend's name as a new record in the table, making sure that you enter unique initials in the PodCode field.

k. Close the Doctors datasheet, then close the Patients-P Design Master.

l. Open the Briefcase folder that contains the Patients-P replica, click the Update All button, then click Update to merge the changes in the Replica and Design Master.

m. Double-click either the Patients-P Replica or Design Master file to open it, close the Claim Entry Form as necessary, double-click the Doctors table, then print the datasheet. You should see both your name and your friend's name entered as records in the datasheet.

n. Close the Doctors datasheet, close the Patients-P database, and close Access.

o. Delete any files you created on the desktop.

4. MediaLoft has developed a Web site that provides internal information to their employees. In this independent challenge, you'll surf the Internet to find Web pages that present information on how to create a secure Access database and how to work with the Briefcase.

a. Connect to the Internet, and go to the MediaLoft intranet site at
http://www.course.com/ illustrated/MediaLoft

b. Click the link for Research center, then click the link for Microsoft Windows Information.

c. Find the Search This Site text box and enter "Briefcase" to request information on this subject. (*Hint*: Web sites change often, and you may need to find and click a Search button before you are able to enter your search criteria.)

d. Refine your search as necessary, then find and print two articles with the word "Briefcase" in the summary line.

e. Find the Search This Site text box and enter "Security" to request information on this subject. (*Hint*: Web sites change often, and you may need to find and click a Search button before you are able to enter your search criteria.)

f. Refine your search as necessary, then find and print two articles that discuss security options available in Access.

g. Close your browser window.

Access 2000

► Visual Workshop

As the manager of a doctor's clinic, you have created an Access database called Patients-P to track insurance claims. Use the Performance Analyzer to generate the results shown in Figure P-20 by analyzing all object types.

FIGURE P-20

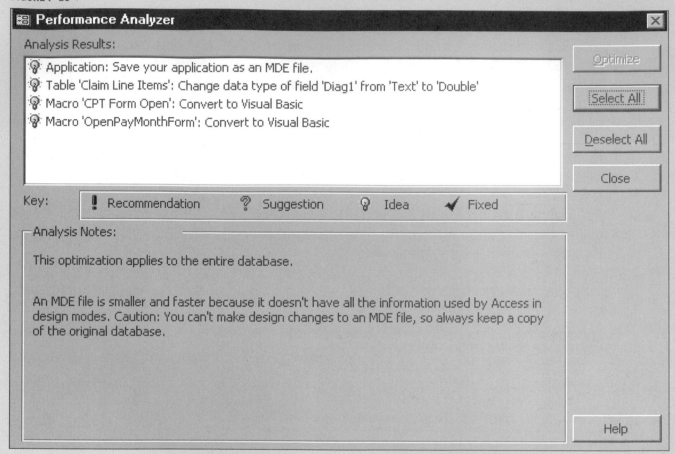

Access 2000 MOUS Certification Objectives

Below is a list of the Microsoft Office User Specialist program objectives for Core and Expert Access 2000 skills showing where each MOUS objective is covered in the Lessons and Practice. This table lists the Core and Expert MOUS certification skills covered in the units throughout this book. For more information on which Illustrated titles meet MOUS certification, please see the inside cover of this book.

MOUS standardized coding number	Activity	Lesson page where skill is covered	Location in lesson where skill is covered	Practice
AC2000.1	**Planning and designing databases**			
AC2000.1.1	Determine appropriate data inputs for your database	Access B-2 Access E-2	Details, Table B-1 Details	Skills Review, Independent Challenges 1–4, Visual Workshop
AC2000.1.2	Determine appropriate data outputs for your database	Access A-4 Access E-4	Table A-2 Details	Skills Review, Independent Challenges 1–4
AC2000.1.3	Create table structure	Access B-4 Access E-6	Steps 2–7 Steps 2–5	Skills Review, Independent Challenges 1–4
AC2000.1.4	Establish table relationships	Access E-16	Steps 1–5	Skills Review, Independent Challenges 1–4
AC2000.2	**Working with Access**			
AC2000.2.1	Use the Office Assistant	Access A-18	Steps 3–6	Skills Review
AC2000.2.2	Select an object using the Objects Bar	Access A-8 Access B-8	Steps 5–6 Steps 1–2	Skills Review, Independent Challenges 1–4
AC2000.2.3	Print database objects (tables, forms, reports, queries)	Access A-16 Access C-14 Access C-16	Steps 1–7 Step 7 Step 8	Skills Review, Independent Challenges 1–4
AC2000.2.4	Navigate through records in a table, query, or form	Access A-10 Access C-14	Steps 2–6 Steps 3–5	Skills Review, Independent Challenges 1–4
AC2000.2.5	Create a database (using a Wizard or in Design View)	Access H-2	Steps 1–6	Skills Review
AC2000.3	**Building and modifying tables**			
AC2000.3.1	Create tables by using the Table Wizard	Access B-4	Step 1	Skills Review, Independent Challenges 1–2
AC2000.3.2	Set primary keys	Access B-4 Access E-6	Steps 6–7 Step 6	Skills Review, Independent Challenges 1–4
AC2000.3.3	Modify field properties	Access B-6 Access E-6	Steps 5–6 Step 5	Skills Review, Independent Challenges 1–4
AC2000.3.4	Use multiple data types	Access B-6 Access E-6	Step 2 Steps 3–5	Skills Review, Independent Challenges 1–4
AC2000.3.5	Modify tables using Design View	Access B-6 Access E-6	Steps 1–8 Steps 3–6	Skills Review, Independent Challenges 1–4
AC2000.3.6	Use the Lookup Wizard	Access H-2	Steps 7–9	Skills Review
AC2000.3.7	Use the Input Mask wizard	Access E-8	Steps 4–8	Skills Review
AC2000.4	**Building and modifying forms**			
AC2000.4.1	Create a form with the Form Wizard	Access C-4	Steps 1–3	Skills Review, Independent Challenges 1–3

MOUS standardized coding number	Activity	Lesson page where skill is covered	Location in lesson where skill is covered	Practice
AC2000.4.2	Use the Control Toolbox to add controls	Access C-10 Access C-16	Steps 1–7 Steps 2–5	Skills Review, Independent Challenges 2–3
AC2000.4.3	Modify Format Properties (font, style, font size, color, caption, etc.) of controls	Access C-8 Access C-10	Steps 2–5 Steps 5–6	Skills Review, Independent Challenges 2–3
AC2000.4.4	Use form sections (headers, footers, detail)	Access C-6 Access C-12 Access C-16	Steps 1–6 Steps 2–5 Steps 2–5	Skills Review, Independent Challenges 2–3
AC2000.4.5	Use a Calculated Control on a form	Access C-10	Steps 2–7	Skills Review, Independent Challenge 2
AC2000.5	**Viewing and organizing information**			
AC2000.5.1	Use the Office Clipboard	Access D-10	Clues to Use	Skills Review, Independent Challenges 2–3
AC2000.5.2	Switch between object Views	Access B-6 Access B-18	Step 7 Step 6	Skills Review, Independent Challenges 1–4, Visual Workshop
AC2000.5.3	Enter records using a datasheet	Access A-12 Access E-12	Steps 2–4 Step 7	Skills Review Independent Challenges 3–4, Visual Workhop
AC2000.5.4	Enter records using a form	Access C-14 Access G-16	Step 2 Steps 2–4	Skills Review, Independent Challenge 1, Visual Workshop
AC2000.5.5	Delete records from a table	Access A-14	Step 9	Skills Review
AC2000.5.6	Find a record	Access B-10 Access B-12 Access B-14	Details Steps 4–7 Steps 4–8	Skills Review, Independent Challenge 1, Visual Workshop
AC2000.5.7	Sort records	Access B-10 Access B-12	Steps 1–3 Details	Skills Review, Independent Challenges 1–4
AC2000.5.8	Apply and remove filters (filter by form and filter by selection)	Access B-10 Access B-14	Details Steps 1–6	Skills Review
AC2000.5.9	Specify criteria in a query	Access B-16 Access B-18	Step 6 Step 4	Skills Review, Independent Challenges 1–4, Visual Workshop
AC2000.5.10	Display related records in a subdatasheet	Access E-16 Access H-22	Step 8	Independent Challenge 2
AC2000.5.11	Create a calculated field	Access C-10 Access F-10	Steps 1–6 Steps 2–3	Skills Review, Independent Challenge 3
AC2000.5.12	Create and modify a multi-table select query	Access F-2 Access F-6	Steps 2–6 Steps 2–4	Skills Review, Independent Challenges 1–4, Visual Workshop
AC2000.6	**Defining relationships**			
AC2000.6.1	Establish relationships	Access E-16	Steps 1–8	Skills Review, Independent Challenges 1–4, Visual Workshop
AC2000.6.2	Enforce referential integrity	Access E-16	Step 4	Skills Review, Independent Challenges 1–4
AC2000.7	**Producing reports**			
AC2000.7.1	Create a report with the Report Wizard	Access D-4 Access H-6 Access H-14	Steps 2–5 Steps 5–6 Step 1	Skills Review, Independent Challenges 1–4, Visual Workshop

MOUS standardized coding number	Activity	Lesson page where skill is covered	Location in lesson where skill is covered	Practice
AC2000.7.2	Preview and print a report	Access D-6 Access H-14	Step 7 Step 8	Skills Review, Independent Challenges 1–4, Visual Workshop
AC2000.7.3	Move and resize a control	Access D-12 Access H-14	Steps 2–5 Steps 4–6	Skills Review, Independent Challenges 1–4, Visual Workshop
AC2000.7.4	Modify format properties (font, style, font size, color, caption, etc.)	Access D-14 Access H-10	Steps 2–7 Steps 3–6	Skills Review, Independent Challenges 1–4, Visual Workshop
AC2000.7.5	Use the Control Toolbox to add controls	Access D-6 Access H-10 Access H-14	Steps 3–6 Step 6 Step 5	Skills Review, Independent Challenges 1–4, Visual Workshop
AC2000.7.6	Use report sections (headers, footers, detail)	Access D-3 Access D-6 Access H-14	Table D-1 Steps 1–7 Steps 3–6	Skills Review, Independent Challenges 1–4, Visual Workshop
AC2000.7.7	Use a Calculated Control in a report	Access D-12	Step 4	Skills Review, Independent Challenge 1
AC2000.8	**Integrating with other applications**			
AC2000.8.1	Import data to a new table	Access H-4	Steps 6–7	Skills Review
AC2000.8.2	Save a table, query, form as a Web page	Access G-17	Clues to Use	Skills Review, Independent Challenge 4
AC2000.8.3	Add Hyperlinks	Access C-17	Clues to Use	
AC2000.9	**Using Access Tools**			
AC2000.9.1	Print Database Relationships	Access E-16	Step 6	Skills Review, Independent Challenge 1
AC2000.9.2	Backup and Restore a database	Access H-16	Steps 4–6	Skills Review
AC2000.9.3	Compact and Repair a database	Access H-16	Steps 1–2	Skills Review
AC2000E.1.	**Building and modifying tables**			
AC2000E.1.1	Set validation text	Access E-14	Step 2	Skills Review, Independent Challenge 1
AC2000E.1.2	Define data validation criteria	Access E-14	Step 1	Skills Review, Independent Challenge 1
AC2000E.1.3	Modify an input mask	Access E-8 Access E-9	Steps 4–7 Clues to Use	Skills Review
AC2000E.1.4	Create and modify Lookup Fields	Access H-2	Steps 7–9	Skills Review
AC2000E.1.5	Optimize data type usage (double, long, int, byte, etc.)	Access E-10 Access E-11	Steps 2–6 Table E-4	Skills Review, Independent Challenges 2–3
AC2000E.2	**Building and modifying forms**			
AC2000E.2.1	Create a form in Design View	Access G-6	Steps 1–8	Skills Review
AC2000E.2.2	Insert a graphic on a form	Access C-16	Steps 2–4	Skills Review, Independent Challenge 3, Visual Workshop
AC2000E.2.3	Modify control properties	Access C-8 Access G-10 Access G-14 Access L-2 Access L-4	Steps 2–3 Steps 4–7 Steps 2–3 Step 5 Steps 2–4	Skills Review, Independent Challenges 1–4

MOUS standardized coding number	Activity	Lesson page where skill is covered	Location in lesson where skill is covered	Practice
AC2000E.2.4	Customize form sections (headers, footers, detail)	Access G-8 Access G-14	Step 3 Step 6	Skills Review, Independent Challenges 1–4, Visual Workshop
AC2000E.2.5	Modify form properties	Access G-6 Access G-14 Access L-2 Access L-8	Step 6 Steps 1–6 Step 3 Steps 1–6	Skills Review, Independent Challenges 1–4, Visual Workshop
AC2000E.2.6	Use the Subform Control and synchronize forms	Access G-6 Access G-7 Access G-8	Steps 7–8 Clues to Use Steps 1–5	Skills Review, Independent Challenges 1–4, Visual Workshop
AC2000E.2.7	Create a Switchboard	Access M-14	Steps 1-8	Skills Review, Independent Challenge 4, Visual Workshop
AC2000E.3	**Refining queries**			
AC2000E.3.1	Apply filters (filter by form and filter by selection) in a query's recordset	Access B-14 Access K-2 Access K-16	Steps 1–5 Step 6 Steps 6–7	Skills Review, Independent Challenge 2, Skills Review, Independent Challenges 3–4
AC2000E.3.2	Create a totals query	Access K-2	Steps 4–7	Skills Review, Independent Challenge 2
AC2000E.3.3	Create a parameter query	Access K-4 Access K-5	Steps 1–3 Clues to Use	Skills Review, Independent Challenges 1–4
AC2000E.3.4	Specify criteria in multiple fields (AND vs. OR)	Access F-6 Access F-8	Steps 2–4 Steps 2–4	Skills Review, Independent Challenges 1–3
AC2000E.3.5	Modify query properties (field formats, caption, input masks, etc.)	Access F-10 Access K-6	Steps 5–6 Steps 1–7	Skills Review, Independent Challenges 1–4, Visual Workshop
AC2000E.3.6	Create an action query (update, delete, insert)	Access K-8 Access K-10 Access K-12 Access K-14	Steps 1–6 Steps 1–6 Steps 1–6 Steps 1–6	Skills Review, Independent Challenges 1–4, Visual Workshop
AC2000E.3.7	Optimize queries using indexes	Access K-7	Clues to Use	
AC2000E.3.8	Specify join properties for relationships	Access K-16	Steps 2–4	Skills Review, Independent Challenges 3–4
AC2000E.4	**Producing reports**			
AC2000E.4.1	Insert a graphic on a report	Access H-10 Access H-14	Step 5 Steps 4–7	Skills Review, Independent Challenges 1–4
AC2000E.4.2	Modify report properties	Access D-8 Access H-8 Access L-2	Step 2 Step 2 Step 3	Skills Review, Independent Challenges 1–4, Visual Workshop
AC2000E.4.3	Create and modify a report in Design View	Access D-6 Access H-6	Steps 1–6 Steps 1–3	Skills Review, Independent Challenges 1–4, Visual Workshop
AC2000E.4.4	Modify control properties	Access H-8 Access H-10 Access L-16	Steps 1–7 Step 5 Step 5	Skills Review, Independent Challenges 1–4, Visual Workshop
AC2000E.4.5	Set section properties	Access H-8 Access L-16	Step 2 Steps 1–5	Skills Review, Independent Challenges 1–4
AC2000E.4.6	Use the Subreport Control and synchronize reports	Access L-14	Steps 1–4	Skills Review, Independent Challenges 1–4, Visual Workshop

MOUS standardized coding number	Activity	Lesson page where skill is covered	Location in lesson where skill is covered	Practice
AC2000E.5	**Defining relationships**			
AC2000E.5.1	Establish one-to-one relationships	Access I-4 Access I-5	Steps 2–6 Table I-2	Skills Review, Independent Challenges 1–3
AC2000E.5.2	Establish many-to-many relationships	Access I-5	Table I-2	
AC2000E.5.3	Set Cascade Update and Cascade Delete options	Access I-4	Steps 6	
AC2000E.6	**Utilizing web capabilities**			
AC2000E.6.1	Create hyperlinks	Access I-10 Access J-4	Steps 2-8 Steps 2–6	Skills Review, Skills Review, Independent Challenge 1
AC2000E.6.2	Use the group and sort features of data access pages	Access J-6 Access J-12	Steps 3–6 Steps 1–4	Skills Review, Independent Challenge 2
AC2000E.6.3	Create a data access page	Access J-6	Steps 1–3	Skills Review, Independent Challenges 1–3, Visual Workshop
AC2000E.7	**Using Access tools**			
AC2000E.7.1	Set and modify a database password	Access P-4	Steps 1–9	Skills Review, Independent Challenges 1–3
AC2000E.7.2	Set startup options	Access P-6	Steps 1–6	Skills Review, Independent Challenge 2
AC2000E.7.3	Use Add-ins (Database Splitter, Analyzer, Link Table Manager)	Access M-4 Access P-10 Access P-12	Steps 2–5 Steps 2–5 Steps 1–5	Skills Review, Independent Challenge 1, Skills Review, Independent Challenge 3, Visual Workshop
AC2000E.7.4	Encrypt and Decrypt a database	Access P-8	Steps 2–7	Skills Review, Independent Challenge 1
AC2000E.7.5	Use simple replication (copy for a mobile user)	Access P-14 Access P-15 Access P-16	Steps 1–8 Clues to Use Steps 1–4	Skills Review, Independent Challenges 3–4
AC2000E.7.6	Run macros using controls	Access N-12 Access N-13	Steps 1–5 Clues to Use	Skills Review, Independent Challenges 1–3, Visual Workshop
AC2000E.7.7	Create a macro using the Macro Builder	Access N-4	Steps 1–5	Skills Review, Independent Challenges 1–3, Visual Workshop
AC2000E.7.8	Convert database to a previous version	Access P-2	Steps 1–7	Skills Review
AC2000E.8	**Data Integration (New Skill Set)**			
AC2000E.8.1	Export database records to Excel	Access I-16	Steps 1–6	Skills Review, Visual Workshop
AC2000E.8.2	Drag and drop tables and queries to Excel	Access I-16	Step 5	Skills Review, Visual Workshop
AC2000E.8.3	Present information as a chart (MS Graph)	Access L-10 Access L-12	Steps 1–5 Steps 2–6	Skills Review, Independent Challenge 3
AC2000E.8.4	Link to existing data	Access I-8	Steps 1–6	Skills Review, Independent Challenges 1–3

Project Files List

To complete many of the lessons and practice exercises in this book, students need to use a Project File that is supplied by Course Technology and stored on a Project Disk. Below is a list of the files that are supplied, and the unit or practice exercise to which the files correspond. For information on how to obtain Project Files, please see the inside cover of this book. The following list only includes Project Files that are supplied; it does not include the files students create from scratch or the files students create by revising the supplied files.

Unit	File supplied on Project Disk	Location file is used in unit
Windows 98 Unit A	No files supplied	
Windows 98 Unit B	WIN B-1.bmp	Lessons
	WIN B-2.bmp	Skills Review
Access Unit A	MediaLoft-A.mdb	Lessons
	Recycle-A.mdb	Skills Review
	Recycle-A.mdb	Independent Challenge 2
	Recycle-A.mdb	Independent Challenge 3
	MediaLoft-A.mdb	Independent Challenge 4
	Recycle-A.mdb	Visual Workshop
Access Unit B	MediaLoft-B.mdb	Lessons
	Doctors-B.mdb	Skills Review
	Doctors-B.mdb	Independent Challenge 2
	MediaLoft-B.mdb	Independent Challenge 4
	MediaLoft-B.mdb	Visual Workshop
Access Unit C	MediaLoft-C.mdb Smallmedia.bmp	Lessons
	Membership-C.mdb Handin1.bmp	Skills Review
	Clinic-C.mdb	Independent Challenge 1
	Clinic-C.mdb	Independent Challenge 2
	Clinic-C.mdb Medical.bmp	Independent Challenge 3
	Clinic-C.mdb Medstaff.bmp	Visual Workshop
Access Unit D	MediaLoft-D.mdb	Lessons
	Club-D.mdb	Skills Review
	Therapy-D.mdb	Independent Challenge 1
	Therapy-D.mdb	Independent Challenge 2
	Club-D.mdb	Visual Workshop
Access Unit E	Training-E.mdb	Lessons
	Training-E.mdb	Independent Challenge 4
	Training-E.mdb	Visual Workshop
Access Unit F	Training-F.mdb	Lessons
	Training-F.mdb	Independent Challenge 4
	Training-F.mdb	Visual Workshop
	Music Store-F.mdb	Independent Challenges 1–3
	Membership-F.mdb	Skills Review

Unit	File supplied on Project Disk	Location file is used in unit
Access Unit G	Training-G.mdb	Lessons
	Training-G.mdb	Independent Challenge 4
	Training-G.mdb	Visual Workshop
	Membership-G.mdb	Skills Review
	Music Store-G.mdb	Independent Challenges 1–3
Access Unit H	Training.mdb *(Disk 1)*	Lessons
	Training-H.mdb *(Disk 2)*	
	Deptcodes.xls *(Disk 1)*	
	Training-H.mdb *(Disk 2)*	Independent Challenge 4
	Training-H.mdb *(Disk 2)*	Visual Workshop
	Prospects.xls *(Disk 3)*	Skills Review
	Membership-H.mdb *(Disk 3)*	
	Music Store-H.mdb *(Disk 3)*	Independent Challenges 1–3
Access Unit I	Training-I.mdb	Lessons
	New Courses.xls	
	Course Materials.xls	
	Directions to MediaLoft.doc	
	Final Attendance Log Report.xls	
	Machinery-I.mdb	Skills Review
	Machinery Employees.xls	
	Machinery Vendors.xls	
	Product Contacts.doc	
	Basketball-I.mdb	Independent Challenges 1–3
	BB Stats.xls	
	Course Load.xls	
	BB Player Information.doc	
	Training-I.mdb	Independent Challenge 4
	Basketball-I.mdb	Visual Workshop
Access Unit J	Training-J.mdb	Lessons Independent Challenge 4
	Machinery-J.mdb	Skills Review
	Basketball-J.mdb	Independent Challenges 1–3 Visual Workshop
Access Unit K	Training-K.mdb	Lessons Independent Challenge 4
	Seminar-K.mdb	Skills Review
	Basketball-K.mdb	Independent Challenges 1–3 Visual Workshop
Access Unit L	Training-L.mdb	Lessons
	Seminar-L.mdb	Skills Review
	Basketball-L.mdb	Independent Challenges 1–3 Visual Workshop
Access Unit M	Technology-M.mdb *(Disk 1)*	Lessons
	Basketball-M.mdb *(Disk 2)*	Skills Review
	Patients-M.mdb *(Disk 2)*	Independent Challenges 1–3 Visual Workshop

Unit	File supplied on Project Disk	Location file is used in unit
Access Unit N	Technology-N.mdb	Lessons
	Basketball-N.mdb	Skills Review
	Patients-N.mdb	Independent Challenges 1–3 Visual Workshop
Access Unit O	Technology-O.mdb *(Disk 1)*	Lessons 1-8
	Basketball-O.mdb *(Disk 2)*	Skills Review Visual Workshop
	Patients-O.mdb *(Disk 2)*	Independent Challenges 1–3 Visual Workshop
Access Unit P	Technology-P.mdb *(Disk 1)*	Lessons 1-8
	Basketball-P.mdb *(Disk 2)*	Skills Review
	Team-P.mdb *(Disk 2)*	
	Patients-P.mdb *(Disk 3)*	Independent Challenges 1–3 Visual Workshop

Windows 98

Glossary

Accessories Built-in progams that come with Windows 98.

Active Desktop The screen that appears when you first start Windows 98, providing access to your computer's programs and files and to the Internet. *See also* Desktop.

Active program The program that you are using, differentiated from other open programs by a highlighted program button on the taskbar and a differently colored title bar.

Active window The window that you are currently using, differentiated from other open windows by a differently colored title bar.

Address Bar The area below the toolbar in My Computer and Windows Explorer that you use to open and display a drive, folder, or Web page.

Back up To save files to another location in case you have computer trouble and lose files.

Browser A program, such as Microsoft Internet Explorer, designed to access the Internet.

Bullet mark A solid circle that indicates that an option is enabled.

Capacity The amount of information a disk can hold, usually measured in megabytes (Mb).

Cascading menu A list of commands from a menu item with an arrow next to it; pointing at the arrow displays a submenu from which you can choose additional commands.

Channel Bar The bar on the right side of the Active Desktop that shows buttons to access the Internet and view Web pages known as active channels (like those on television).

Check box A square box in a dialog box that you click to turn an option on or off.

Check mark A mark that indicates that a feature is enabled.

Classic style A Windows 98 setting in which you single-click to select items and double-click to open them.

Click To press and release the left mouse button once.

Clipboard Temporary storage space on your computer's hard disk containing information that has been cut or copied.

Close To quit a program or remove a window from the desktop. The Close button is usually located in the upper-right corner of a window.

Command A directive that provides access to a program's features.

Command button In a dialog box, a button that carries out an action. A command button usually has a label that describes its action, such as Cancel or Help. If the label is followed by an ellipses (…), clicking the button displays another dialog box.

Context-sensitive help Help that is specifically related to what you are doing.

Control Panel Used to change computer settings such as desktop colors or mouse settings.

Copy To place information onto the Clipboard in order to paste it in another location, but also leaving it in the original location.

Cut To remove information from a file and place it on the Clipboard, usually to be pasted into another location.

Default Settings preset by the operating system or program.

Delete To place a file or folder in the Recycle Bin, where you can either remove it from the disk permanently or restore it to its original location.

Desktop The screen that appears when you first start Windows 98, providing access to your computer's programs and files and to the Internet. *See also* Active Desktop.

Dialog box A window that opens when more information is needed to carry out a command.

Document A file that you create using a program such as WordPad.

Double-click To press and release the left mouse button twice quickly.

Drag To move an item to a new location using the mouse.

Drive A device that reads and saves files on a disk and is also used to store files; floppy drives read and save files on floppy disks, whereas hard drives read and save files on your computer's built-in hard disk.

Edit To change the content or format of an existing file.

Explorer Bar The pane on the left side of the screen in Windows Explorer that lists all drives and folders on the computer.

File An electronic collection of information that has a unique name, distinguishing it from other files.

File hierarchy A logical structure for folders and files that mimics how you would organize files and folders in a filing cabinet.

File management The process of organizing and keeping track of files and folders.

Floppy disk A disk that you insert into a disk drive of your computer (usually drive A or B) to store files.

Folder A collection of files and/or other folders that helps you organize your disks.

Font The design of a set of characters (for example, Times New Roman).

Format To enhance the appearance of a document by, for example, changing the font or font size, adding borders and shading to a document.

Graphical user interface (GUI) An environment made up of meaningful symbols, words, and windows in which you can control the basic operation of a computer and the programs that run on it.

Hard disk A disk that is built into the computer (usually drive C) on which you store files and programs.

Highlighting When an icon is shaded differently indicating it is selected. *See also* Select.

Icon Graphical representation of computer elements such as files and programs.

Inactive Refers to a window or program that is open but not currently in use.

Input device An item, such as a mouse or keyboard, that you use to interact with your computer.

Insertion point A blinking vertical line that indicates where text will appear when you type.

Internet A worldwide collection of over 40 million computers linked together to share information.

Internet style A Windows 98 setting in which you point to select items and single-click to open them. *See also* Web style.

Keyboard shortcut A keyboard alternative for executing a menu command (for example, [Ctrl][X] for Cut).

List box A box in a dialog box containing a list of items; to choose an item, click the list arrow, then click the desired item.

Maximize To enlarge a window so it fills the entire screen. The Maximize button is usually located in the upper-right corner of a window.

Menu A list of related commands in a program (for example, the File menu).

Menu bar A bar near the top of the program window that provides access to most of a program's features through categories of related commands.

Minimize To reduce the size of a window. The Minimize button is usually located in the upper-right corner of a window.

Mouse A hand-held input device that you roll on your desk to position the mouse pointer on the Windows desktop. *See also* Mouse pointer.

Mouse buttons The two buttons on the mouse (right and left) that you use to make selections and issue commands.

Mouse pointer The arrow-shaped cursor on the screen that follows the movement of the mouse. The shape of the mouse pointer changes depending on the program and the task being executed. *See also* Mouse.

Multi-tasking Working with more than one window or program at a time.

My Computer A program that you use to manage the drives, folders, and files on your computer.

Open To start a program or open a window; also used to describe a program that is running but not active.

Operating system A computer program that controls the basic operation of your computer and the programs you run on it. Windows 98 is an example of an operating system.

Option button A small circle in a dialog box that you click to select an option.

Paint A drawing program that comes with Windows 98.

Pane A section of a divided window.

Point To position the mouse pointer over an item on your computer screen; also a unit of measurement (1/72nd inch) used to specify the size of text.

Pointer trail A shadow of the mouse pointer that appears when you move the mouse; helps you locate the pointer on your screen.

Pop-up menu A menu that appears when you right-click an item on the desktop.

Program Task-oriented software that you use for a particular kind of work, such as word processing or database management. Microsoft Access, Microsoft Excel, and Microsoft Word are all programs.

Program button A button on the taskbar that represents an open program or window.

Properties Characteristics of a specific computer element (such as the mouse, keyboard, or desktop display) that you can customize.

Quick Launch toolbar A toolbar located next to the Start button on the taskbar that contains buttons to start Internet-related programs and show the desktop.

Random access memory (RAM) The memory that programs use to perform necessary tasks while the computer is on. When you turn the computer off, all information in RAM is lost.

Recycle Bin An icon that appears on the desktop that represents a temporary storage area on your computer's hard disk for deleted files, which remain in the Recycle Bin until you empty it.

Restore To reduce the window to its previous size before it was maximized. The Restore button is usually located in the upper-right corner of a window.

Right-click To press and release the right mouse button once.

ScreenTip A description of a toolbar button that appears when you position the mouse pointer over the button.

Scroll bar A bar that appears at the bottom and/or right edge of a window whose contents are not entirely visible; you click the arrows or drag the box in the direction you want to move. *See also* Scroll box.

Scroll box A rectangle located in the vertical and horizontal scroll bars that indicates your relative position in a window. *See also* Scroll bar.

Select To click and highlight an item in order to perform some action on it. *See also* Highlighting.

Shortcut A link that you can place in any location that gives you instant access to a particular file, folder, or program on your hard disk or on a network.

Shut down The action you perform when you have finished working with Windows 98; after you shut down it is safe to turn off your computer.

Slider An item in a dialog box that you drag to set the degree to which an option is in effect.

Spin box A box with two arrows and a text box; allows you to scroll in numerical increments or type a number.

Start button A button on the taskbar that you use to start programs, find and open files, access Windows Help and more.

Tab A place in a dialog box where related commands and options are organized.

Taskbar A strip at the bottom of the screen that contains the Start button, Quick Launch toolbar, and shows which programs are running.

Text box A rectangle in a dialog box in which you type text.

Title bar The area along the top of the window that indicates the filename and program used to create it.

Toolbar A strip with buttons that allow you to activate a command quickly.

Web page A document that contains highlighted words, phrases, and graphics that link to other documents on the Internet.

Web site A computer on the Internet that contains Web pages.

Web style A Windows 98 setting in which you point to select items and single-click to open them. *See also* Internet style.

Window A rectangular frame on a screen that can contain icons, the contents of a file, or other usable data.

Windows Explorer A program that you use to manage files, folders, and shortcuts; allows you to work with more than one computer, folder, or file at once.

Windows Help A "book" stored on your computer, complete with an index and a table of contents, that contains information about Windows 98.

WordPad A word processing program that comes with Windows 98.

World Wide Web Part of the Internet that consists of Web sites located on different computers around the world.

Zip disk A portable disk that can contain 100 Mb, far more than a regular floppy disk.

Zip drive A drive that can handle Zip disks.

Glossary

.ldb The file extension for a temporary file that exists when an Access database is open that keeps track of record locking information when the database is opened.

.mdb The file extension for Access databases.

Action A task that you want a macro to perform. Each macro action occupies a single row in the macro window.

Action query A query that makes changes to underlying data. There are four types of action queries: delete, update, append, and make-table.

Add-In An extra Access feature that extends the functionality of Access but is not part of the core program. Some add-ins are available through Microsoft and some by third parties. They are "added in" when the user chooses to install them.

Aggregate functions Special functions used in a summary query that calculate information about a group of records rather than a new field of information about each record.

Ampersand (&) The character used to concatenate items in an expression.

Analyze It with MS Excel An Access feature that quickly copies Access data to a blank Excel workbook.

And criteria Criteria placed in the same row of the query design grid. All criteria on the same row must be true in order for a record to appear on the resulting datasheet.

AND query A query which contains AND criteria (two or more criteria present on the same row of the query design grid. Both criteria must be true for the record to appear on the resulting datasheet).

Append query An action query that appends records to another table.

Argument For a macro, arguments are additional information for each action of a macro that further clarifies how the action is to execute. For a module, arguments are constants, variables, or expressions that are passed to a procedure and are required for it to execute.

Arguments The pieces of information a function needs to create the final answer. In an expression, multiple arguments are separated by commas. All of the arguments are surrounded by a single set of parentheses.

Arithmetic operators Plus (+), minus (-), multiply (*), divide (/), and exponentiation (^) characters used in a mathematical calculation.

Ascending order A sequence in which information is placed in alphabetical order or from smallest to largest. For a text field, numbers sort first, then letters.

Text ascending order: 123, 3H, 455, 98, 98B, animal, Iowa, New Jersey
Date ascending order: 1/1/57, 1/1/61, 12/25/61, 5/5/98, 8/20/98, 8/20/99
Number ascending order: 1, 10, 15, 120, 140, 500, 1200, 1500

AutoFormats Predefined formats provided by Access that contain background pictures and font, color, and alignment choices that can quickly be applied to an existing form or report.

AutoKeys A special name reserved for the macro group object that contains key combinations (such as Ctrl+L) that are used to run associated macros.

AutoNumber A data type in which Access enters a sequential integer for each record added into the datasheet. Numbers cannot be reused even if the record is deleted.

Back-end database When a database has been split using the Database Splitter, a back-end database is created which contains all of the data and is stored on a computer that is accessible by all users (which is usually the file server in a LAN).

Bang notation Syntax used to separate parts of an object (the parts are separated by an exclamation point, hence "bang") in the Visual Basic programming language.

Between . . . And operator Used when specifying limiting criteria between two values in a query; it is equivalent to >= (greater than or equal to) and <= (less than or equal to).

Body The basic design surface of the data access page that displays text, controls, and sections.

Bookmark A specific location within a Word document marked by an invisible code. Hyperlinks within Access can be created to open a Word document and display the text at a particular bookmark.

Bound control A control used in either a form or report to display data from the underlying record source; also used to edit and enter new data in a form.

Bound image control A bound control used to show OLE data such as a picture on a form or report.

Break mode Temporary suspension of program execution in which you can examine, debug, reset, step-through, or continue program execution.

Breakpoint A bookmark set in VBA code that temporarily suspends execution of the procedure at that point in time so that the user can examine what is happening.

Briefcase A Windows program used to help synchronize two computers that regularly use the same files.

Brown-out Dip in the level of electrical current causing the lights to dim or "brown-out."

Browser Software loaded on a microcomputer such as Microsoft's Internet Explorer (IE) or Netscape Navigator used to find and display Web pages.

Calculated control A control that uses information from existing controls to calculate new data such as subtotals, dates, or page numbers; used in either a form or report.

Calculated field A field created in Query Design view that results from an expression of existing fields, Access functions, and arithmetic operators. For example the entry Profit: [RetailPrice]-[WholesalePrice] in the field cell of the query design grid creates a calculated field called Profit that is the difference between the RetailPrice and WholesalePrice fields.

Caption property A field property used to override the technical field name with an easy-to-read caption entry when the field name appears on datasheets, forms, and reports.

Caption section A section available in the Design view of a page object used to display text.

Cascade Delete Related Records An option available when enforce referential integrity is applied that automatically deletes all records in the "many" table if the record with the matching key field in the "one" table is deleted.

Cascade Update Related Fields An option available when enforce referential integrity is applied that automatically updates the data in the foreign key field if the matching key field is changed.

Chart Graph: Visual representation of numeric data that helps a user see comparisons, patterns, and trends in data.

Chart placeholder A picture of a chart that represents the chart control within Report Design view. You must double-click the chart placeholder to edit the chart.

Chart Wizard Access Wizard that steps you through the process of creating charts within forms and reports.

Check box Bound control used to display "yes" or "no" answers for a field. If the box is "checked" it indicates "yes" information in a form or report.

Class modules Modules used only within a particular form or report object and therefore stored within the form or report object.

Client In client-server computer architectures, the client computer is generally the user's computer.

Client/server computing Two or more information systems cooperatively processing to solve a problem. In Access, a back-end and front-end database participate in client/server computing, each assigned to the tasks to which it is best suited.

Clipboard The temporary location that can store up to 12 items that are copied. When you paste, you paste information that is stored on the Clipboard.

Clipboard toolbar A toolbar that shows the contents of the Office Clipboard; contains buttons for copying and pasting items to and from the Office Clipboard.

Code window See *Visual Basic Code window.*

Collapse button A "minus sign" to the left of a record displayed in a datasheet that when clicked on, collapses the subdatasheet that is displayed. When you click a Collapse button on a page, less detail about the item being collapsed will appear.

Combo box A bound control used to display a list of possible entries for a field in which you can also type an entry from the keyboard. It is a "combination" of the list box and text box controls.

Command button An unbound control used to provide an easy way to initiate an action or run a macro.

Command Button Wizard A Wizard that steps you through the process of creating a command button.

Command-line option A special series of characters added to the end of the path to the database file that start with a forward slash and modify the way that the database is opened.

Comment line A VBA statement that does not execute any actions but is used to clarify or document other statements. Comment lines appear in green in the Code window and start with a single apostrophe.

Compacting Rearranging the data and objects on the storage medium so that space formerly occupied by deleted objects is eliminated. Compacting a database doesn't change the data, but it generally reduces the overall size of the database.

Compile time The period during which source code is translated to executable code.

Compile time error A VBA error that occurs because of incorrectly constructed VBA code.

Conditional expression An expression that results in either a "true" or "false" answer that determines whether a macro action will execute or not.

Conditional formatting Formatting applied to a control on a form or report that changes depending upon a value in a field, an expression, or on which field has the focus. For example, a text box may be conditionally formatted to display its value in red if the value is a negative number.

Constant In VBA, a constant is an item that retains a constant value throughout the execution of the code.

Control Source property The most important property of a bound control on a form or report because it etermines which field the bound control will display.

Control Any element on a form or report such as a label, text box, line, or combo box. Controls can be bound, unbound, or calculated.

ControlTip Text property Property of a control that determines what text displays in tip that pops up when you point to that control with the mouse.

Converting Changing a database file into one that can be opened by an earlier version of Access.

Criteria The entry that determines which records are displayed when finding or filtering records in a datasheet or form, or when building a query.

Crosstab query A query that presents data in a cross-tabular layout (fields are used for both column and row headings), similar to pivot tables in other database and spreadsheet products.

Crosstab Query Wizard A wizard used to create crosstab queries that helps identify which fields will be used for row and column headings, and which fields will be summarized within the datasheet.

Currency A data type used for monetary values.

Current record symbol A black triangle symbol that appears in the record select box to the left of the record that has the focus in either a datasheet or a form.

Data The unique entries of information that you enter into the fields of the records.

Data Access Page See *Page.*

Database A collection of data associated with a topic (for example, sales of products to customers).

Database password A password that is required to open a database.

Database software Software used to manage data that can be organized into lists of things such as customers, products, vendors, employees, projects, or sales.

Database Splitter An Access feature that improves the performance of a shared database by allowing you to split it into multiple files.

Database window The window that includes common elements such as the Access title bar, menu bar, and toolbar. It also contains an Objects bar to quickly work with the seven different types of objects within the database by clicking the appropriate object button.

Database Wizard A powerful Access wizard that creates a sample database file for a general purpose such as inventory control, event tracking, or expenses. The objects created by the Database Wizard can be used and modified.

Datasheet A spreadsheet-like grid that shows fields as columns and records as rows.

Datasheet view A view that lists the records of the object in a datasheet. Table, query, and most form objects have a Datasheet view.

Data type A required property for each field that defines the type of data that can be entered in each field. Valid data types include AutoNumber, Text, Number, Currency, Date/Time, OLE Object, Memo, Yes/No, and Hyperlink.

Date/Time A data type used for date and time fields.

Debug To determine why a macro doesn't run properly.

Declaration statements VBA statements that precede procedure statements and help set rules for how the statements in the module are processed.

Decrypt To reverse the encryption process.

Delete query An action query that deletes records based on an expression.

Delimited text file A file that contains one record on each line with the fields separated by a common character such as a comma, tab, or dash.

Descending order A sequence in which information is placed in reverse alphabetical order or from largest to smallest. For a text field, letters sort first, then numbers.

Text descending order: Zebra, Victory, Langguth, Bunin, 99A, 9854, 77, 740, 29, 270, 23500, 1

Date descending order: 1/1/99, 1/1/98, 12/25/97, 5/5/97, 8/20/61, 8/20/57

Number descending order: 1500, 1400, 1200, 140, 120, 15, 10, 1

Design view A view in which the structure of the object can be manipulated. Every Access object has a Design view.

Detail section The section of the form or report that contains the controls that are printed for each record in the underlying query or table.

Dialer Software that helps you dial-up to connect you to your ISP.

Dialog box A special form that is used to display information or to prompt a user for a choice.

Documenter An Access feature that creates reports on the properties and relationships between the objects in your database.

Domain Name The middle part of a URL such as www.course.com where "course" is the domain name.

Dot notation Syntax used to separate parts of an object (the parts are separated by a period, hence "dot") in the Visual Basic programming language.

Drag and drop A process which involves dragging an Access icon from the database window to another application window (the target window) in order to quickly copy and paste information. The target window is usually a Word document or Excel workbook window.

Dynamic HTML file An HTML file (Web page) that is tied to an underlying database and therefore displays current information and data.

Dynaset A type of recordset displayed within a query's datasheet that allows you to update all fields except for those on the "one" side of a one-to-many relationship.

Dynaset (inconsistent updates) A type of recordset displayed within a query's datasheet that allows you to update all fields.

E-mail Electronic mail sent and received without printed paper by using computers.

Edit mode The mode in which Access assumes you are trying to edit that particular field, so keystrokes such as [Ctrl][End], [Ctrl][Home], [←]and [→] move the insertion point within the field.

Edit record symbol A pencil-like symbol that appears in the record selector box to the left of the record that is currently being edited in either a datasheet or a form.

Embedded Refers to the relationship between a chart created within Access and the database itself. Although the chart is created through the MS Chart program, it is embedded and stored within the Access database. Sometimes embedded is compared to linked data. Linked data is physically stored outside the Access database file. Embedded data is stored within the file.

Encrypt To make the database objects and data within the database indecipherable to other programs.

Enforce referential integrity An option applied to a one-to-many relationship between two tables that does not allow a value to be entered into the foreign key field that is not first entered into the primary key field. It also does not allow records to be deleted in the "one" table if related records exist in the "many" table.

Event Something that happens within a database (such as the click of a command button or the entry of a field) that can be used to initiate the execution of a macro. Events are associated with toolbars, objects, and controls, and can be viewed by examining that item's property sheet.

Excel The spreadsheet software application within the Microsoft Office Suite.

Exclusive mode If you open an Access database in exclusive mode, others cannot open the file. You must open a database in exclusive mode before you can set a database password.

Expand button A "plus sign" to the left of a record that is displayed in datasheet view that when clicked, will show related records in a sub-datasheet. When you click an Expand button, more detail about the item being expanded will appear.

Explorer A Windows program used to manage files, folders, and disk drives.

Exporting A process that copies data from Access into a different Access database or file format.

Expression A combination of values, functions, and operators that calculates to a single value. Access expressions start with an equal sign and are placed in a text box in either Form or Report Design view.

Field The smallest piece or category of information in a database such as the customer's name, city, state, or phone number.

Field list A list of the available fields in the table or query that it represents.

Field names The names given each field in Table Design or Table Datasheet view. Field names can be up to 64 characters long.

Field Property See *Properties*.

File server A centrally-located computer to which every user has access on the network. The function of the file server is to store and serve application and data files to the individual client computers on the LAN.

File transfer Uploading and downloading of files through computing networks.

Filter A temporary view of a subset of records. A filter can be saved as a query object if you wish to apply the same filter later without recreating it.

Filter window A window that appears when you click the Filter by Form button when viewing data in a datasheet or in a form window. The Filter window allows you to define the filter criteria.

Find Duplicates Query Wizard A wizard used to create a query that determines whether a table contains duplicate values in one or more fields.

Find Unmatched Query Wizard A wizard used to create a query that finds records in one table that doesn't have related records in another table.

Focus The property that refers to which field would be edited if you started typing.

Footer Information that prints at the bottom of every printed page (or section when using forms and reports).

Foreign key field The field added to the "many" table involved in a one-to-many relationship.

Form An Access object that provides an easy-to-use data entry screen that generally shows only one record at a time.

Form Design toolbar The toolbar that appears when working in Form Design View with buttons that help you modify a form's controls.

Form Footer A section that appears at the bottom of screen in Form View for each record, but prints only once at the end of all records when the form is printed.

Form Header A section that appears at the top of the screen in Form View for each record, but prints only once at the top of all records when the form is printed.

Form View toolbar The toolbar that appears when working in Form View with buttons that help you print, edit, find, filter, and edit records.

Format Painter A tool used within Form and Report Design view to copy formatting characteristic from one control, and paint them on another.

Formatting Enhancing the appearance of the information in a form, report or datasheet.

Front-end database When a database has been split using the Database Splitter, a front-end database is created which contains links back to the data stored in the back-end database as well as any objects needed by the user. The front-end database is stored on the user's computer, which is also called the client computer.

Function Special, predefined formula such as Sum, Count, Date, Left, and Avg that are part of an expression and perform a specific calculation that returns a value. Access supplies many built-in functions. VBA allows you to create your own unique functions as well.

Functions A special, predefined formula that provides a shortcut for a commonly used calculation, for example, SUM

Graphic See *Image*.

Group Footer section The section of the report that contains controls that print once at the end of each group of records.

Group Header section The section of the report that contains controls that print once at the beginning of each group of records.

Grouping controls Specifying that several controls in the Design view of a form or report are in a "group" so that you can more productively format, move, and change them.

Grouping records In a report, grouping records means to sort them based on the contents of a field, plus provide a group header section that precedes the group of records as well as a group footer section that follows the group of records.

Groups bar Located just below the Objects bar in the database window, the Groups bar displays the Favorites and any user-created groups, which in turn contain shortcuts to objects. Groups are used to organize the database objects into logical sets.

GUI (Graphical User Interface) A characteristic of the design of the screens of a computer program. If GUI, the user interacts with the computer program using point-and-click, click-and-drag, and double-click techniques as well as graphical symbols such as icons, command buttons, and list arrows. Non-GUI screens use text-based menu options or command lines to prompt for user input.

Handles See *Sizing handles*.

Header Information that prints at the top of every printed page (or section when using forms and reports).

Help system Pages of documentation and examples that are available through the Help menu option, the Microsoft Access Help button on the Database toolbar, or the Office Assistant.

Home page The first page displayed on a Web server.

HTML (Hypertext Markup Language) A programming language used to create Web pages.

Hyperlink A data type that stores World Wide Web addresses.

If . . . Then . . . Else A series of VBA statements that allow you to test for a logical condition and execute one set of commands if the condition is true and another if the condition is false.

Image A nontextual piece of information such as a picture, piece of clip art, drawn object, or graph. Because images are graphical (not numbers or letters), they are sometimes referred to as graphical images.

Imported table A table created in another database product or application such as Excel, that is copied and pasted within the Access database through the import process.

Importing A process to quickly convert data from an external source, such as Excel or another database application, into an Access database

Index A field property used to speed up queries that are often sorted or grouped by that field.

Input mask A field property that controls both the values that the users can enter into a text box, as well as provides a visual guide for users as they enter data.

Input mask wizard A wizard that helps you determine the three parts of the input mask property.

Internet A worldwide network of computer networks that send and receive information through a common protocol called TCP/IP.

Intranet A WAN that is built with the same technologies as those used to support the Internet, yet is secured for the internal purposes of a business.

ISP (Internet Service Provider) A company that provides Internet access. To access the Internet from a home computer, your computer must first dial an ISP that in turn connects your computer with the Internet.

Junction table A table that links two other tables with a many-to-many relationship. The junction table holds two foreign key fields that create separate links to the original tables in separate one-to-many relationships.

Key field A field that contains unique information for each record. Also known as *Primary key field*. A key field cannot contain a null entry.

Key field combination Two or more fields that as a group, contain unique information for each record.

Key field symbol In a table's Design view, the symbol that appears as a miniature key in the field indicator box to the left of the field name. It identifies the field that contains unique information for each record.

Label An unbound control that displays static text on forms and reports.

LAN (Local Area Network) A computer network of local resources connected by a direct cable. LANs do not cross public thoroughfares such as streets or rivers.

Layout The general arrangement in which a form will display the fields in the underlying recordset. Layout types include Columnar, Tabular, Datasheet, Chart, and PivotTable. Columnar is most popular for a form, and Datasheet is most popular for a subform.

Leszynski Naming Convention A naming convention in which each object or field is preceded by a three-character tag to help identify it. For example, tables are named starting with the tag "tbl" as in "tblEmployees."

Line control An unbound control used to draw lines on a form or report that divide it into logical groupings.

Link Childs field A subform property that determines which field will serve as the "many" link between the subform and main form.

Link Masters fields A subform property that determines which field will serve as the "one" link between the main form and the subform.

Linked table A table created in another database product or application such as Excel, that is stored outside of the open database, but which can still be used within Access to modify and use its data.

Linking A way to connect data in an external source to an Access database in a way that does not copy or move the original data yet allows it to be manipulated within the Access database.

List box A bound control that displays a list of possible choices from which the user can choose. Used mainly on forms.

Logic error A VBA error that occurs because the code runs without problems, but the procedure still doesn't produce the desired results.

Lookup Wizard A wizard used in Table Design view that allows one field to "lookup" values from another table or query. For example, you might use the Lookup Wizard to specify that the CustomerNumber field in the Sales table display the CustomerName field entry from the Customers table.

Macro An Access object that stores a collection of keystrokes or commands such as printing several reports in a row or providing a toolbar when a form opens.

Macro group An Access macro object that contains more than one macro.

Macro window The Design View of a macro in which you specify which actions and the order in which they will run.

Main form A form that contains a subform control.

Main report A report that contains a subreport control is called the main report.

Make-table query An action query that creates a new table.

Many-to-many relationship The relationship between two tables in an Access database in which one field value in each table can have more than one matching record in the other. You cannot directly create a many-to-many relationship between two tables in an Access database. A junction table is used to connect two tables with this relationship.

Master The original Access database file that is copied to the Briefcase.

Memo A data type used for lengthy text such as comments or notes. It can hold up to 64,000 characters of information.

Merge An action that may occur during the synchronization of a replica and master database in which changes in each database are analyzed and applied to the other.

Merge It with MS Word An Access feature that begins the process of connecting Access data to a Word document for the purpose of creating merged letters, envelopes, or labels.

Method An action that an object can perform.

Microsoft Office Premium Edition The Microsoft software products of Word, Excel, Access, PowerPoint, and Outlook that are sold as an integrated set.

Modem Short for modulate-demodulate; hardware that converts digital computer signals to analog telephone signals to allow a computer to send and receive information across ordinary telephone lines.

Module An Access object that stores Visual Basic programming code that extends the functions and automated processes of Access.

MsgBox A macro action that displays an informational message.

Multimedia controls Non-textual controls such as those that display picture, sound, or motion information.

Multi-user The characteristic that allows multiple people to use the same file or resource at the same time.

My Computer A icon on the Windows desktop that gives the user access to the drives, folders, and files within the computer.

Name AutoCorrect An Access feature that fixes discrepancies between references to field names, controls, and objects when you rename them.

Navigation buttons Buttons in the lower-left corner of a datasheet or form that allow you to quickly navigate between the records in the underlying object as well as add a new record.

Navigation mode A mode in which Access assumes that you are trying to move between the fields and records of the datasheet (rather than edit a specific field's contents), so keystrokes such as [Ctrl][Home] and [Ctrl][End] move you to the first and last field of the datasheet, respectively.

Network administrator A person who builds or manages a networking infrastructure.

New Record button A button that, when clicked, presents a new record for data entry. It is found on both the Form View and Datasheet toolbars as well as part of the Navigation buttons.

Newsgroups Groups with a common interest that provide public mailboxes (accessible only by computers) in which members can send and read messages. Messages posted to a newsgroup are intended for anyone who cares to read the messages in that newsgroup.

Normalization The process of designing a relational database, which involves determining the appropriate fields, tables, and table relationships.

Null The term that refers to a state of "nothingness" in a field. Any entry such as 0 in a numeric field or an invisible space in a text field is *not* null. It is common to search for empty fields by using the criteria "Is Null" in a filter or query. "Is Not Null" criteria finds all records where there is an entry of any kind.

Number A data type used for numeric information used in calculations, such as quantities.

Object A table, query, form, report, page, macro, or module.

Objects bar In the opening database window, the toolbar that presents the seven Access objects. When you click an object button on the Objects bar, options and wizards to create an object of that type as well as existing objects of that type appear in the main portion of the database window.

Object Browser A window that lists the defined modules and procedures as well as available methods, properties, events, constants, and other items that you can use in the code.

ODBC (Open Database Connectivity) A protocol for accessing data in SQL database servers.

Office Assistant An animated character that appears to offer tips, answer questions, and provide access to the program's Help system.

Office Clipboard A temporary storage area shared by all Office programs that can be used to cut, copy and paste multiple items within and between Office programs. The Office Clipboard can hold up to 12 items collected from any Office program. See also *Clipboard* and *Clipboard toolbar.*

OfficeLinks buttons The set of three buttons on the Database toolbar that are used to quickly copy Access data to the Word or Excel programs.

OLE Object A data type that stores pointers that tie files created in other programs to a record such as pictures, sound clips, word-processing documents, or spreadsheets.

One-to-many line The line that appears in the Relationships window that shows which field is duplicated between two tables to serve as the linking field. The one-to-many line displays a "1" next to the field that serves as the "one" side of the relationship and an infinity symbol next to the field that serves as the "many" side of the relationship when referential integrity is specified for the relationship. Also called one-to-many join line.

One-to-many relationship The relationship between two tables in an Access database in which a common field links the tables together The field is a key field in the "one" table of the relationship, but can be listed "many" times in the "many" table of the relationship.

One-to-one relationship The relationship between two tables in an Access database in which a common field links the tables together. The same field value can be entered only one time in each of the tables. One-to-one relationships are rare, and tables linked in this way can be combined into one table.

Option Button A bound control used to display a limited list of mutually exclusive choices for a field such as "female" or "male" for a gender field in a form or report. Also called a radio button.

Option Group A bound control placed on a form that is used to group together several option buttons that provide a limited number of values for a field.

Or criteria Criteria placed on different rows of the query design grid. A record will appear in the resulting datasheet if it is true for any single row.

OR query A query that contains OR criteria (two or more criteria present on different rows in the query design grid. A record will appear on the resulting datasheet if it is true for either criteria.)

Orphan record A record in the "many" table of a one-to-many relationship between two tables that has no matching record in the "one" table. If referential integrity is enforced, it is not possible to create orphan records.

Page An Access object that creates Web pages from Access objects as well as provides Web page connectivity features to an Access database. Also called Data Access Page.

Page Design view The window in which you develop page objects by adding, moving, and manipulating controls.

Page Footer section The section of the form or report that contains controls that print once at the bottom of each page.

Page Header section The section of the form or report that contains controls that print once at the top of each page. On the first page of the report, the Page Header section prints below the Report Header section.

Parameter query A query that displays a dialog box prompting you for criteria each time you run it.

Parent/Child relationship The relationship between the main form and subform. The main form acts as the parent, displaying the information about the "one" side of a one-to-many relationship between the forms. The subform acts as the "child" displaying as many records as exist in the "many" side of the one-to-many relationship.

Password A combination of characters required to gain access to the user's computer or files. See also *Database password, Security account password,* and *VBA password.*

Performance Analyzer An Access feature that studies the size and structure of your database and makes a variety of recommendations on how you could improve its performance.

PivotTable list A bound control used with the page object that helps you reorganize data into summarized columns and rows similar to a crosstabular datasheet.

Pop-up form A special type of form that stays on top of other open forms, even when another form is active.

Positioning The relative space between the text, sections, and other elements on the body of a data access page.

Primary key field See *Key field.*

Primary sort field In a query grid, the left-most field that includes sort criteria. It determines the order in which the records will appear and can be specified "ascending" or "descending."

Print Preview A window that displays how the physical printout will appear if the current object is printed.

Procedure A series of VBA programming statements that perform an operation or calculate an answer. There are two types of procedures: functions and subs.

Properties Characteristics that further define the field (if field properties), control (if control properties), section (if section properties), or object (if object properties).

Property sheet A window that displays an exhaustive list of properties for the chosen control, section, or object within the form or report Design view.

Protocol A set of rules.

Publish It with MS Word An Access feature that quickly copies Access data to a blank Word document.

Publishing Sending (uploading) Web page files to a Web server.

Query An Access object which provides a spreadsheet-like view of the data similar to tables. It may provide the user with a subset of fields and/or records from one or more tables. Queries are created when the user has a "question" about the data in the database.

Query design grid The bottom pane of the Query Design view window in which you specify the fields, sort order, and limiting criteria for the query.

Query Design view The window in which you develop queries by specifying the fields, sort order, and limiting criteria that determine which fields and records are displayed in the resulting datasheet.

Raw data The individual pieces of information stored in the database in individual fields.

Record A group of related fields, such as all demographic information for one customer.

Record locking An Access feature that prevents two people from changing the same record at the same time.

Record Navigation section A section available in the Design view of a page object used to display the navigation toolbar.

Record selector box The small square to left of a record in a datasheet that marks the current record or edit record symbol when the record has focus or is being edited. Clicking the record selector box selects the entire record. In Form view, the record selector box expands to the entire height of the form because only one record is viewed at a time.

Record source In a form or report, either a table or query object that contains the fields and records that the form will display. It is the most important property of the form or report object. A bound control on a form or report also has a record source property. In this case, the record source property identifies the field to which the control is bound.

Record source property The most important property of a form or report because it determines the recordset that the form or report will display.

Recordset The fields and records that are displayed by the object.

Rectangle control An unbound control used to draw rectangles on the form that divide the other form controls into logical groupings.

Referential integrity Ensures that no orphaned records are entered or created in the database by making sure that the "one" side of a linking relationship (CustomerNumber in a Customer table) is entered before that same value can be entered in the "many" side of the relationship (CustomerNumber in a Sales table).

Relational database A database in which more than one table, such as the customer, sales, and inventory tables, can share information. The term "relational database" comes from the fact that the tables are linked or "related" with a common field of information. An Access database is relational.

Replica The copy of the Access database file that is stored in the Briefcase.

Replica set Both the original (master) and replicated (replica) database file. There may be more than one replica in a replica set, but there is only one master.

Replication The process of making replicas of a master database file using the Briefcase.

Report An Access object that creates a professional printout of data that may contain such enhancements as headers, footers, and calculations on groups of records

Report Footer section On a report, a section that contains controls that print once at the end of the last page of the report.

Report Header section On a report, a section that contains controls that print once at the top of the first page of the report.

Row selector The small square to the left of a field in Table Design view.

RTF (Rich Text Format) A document file format that retains many basic formatting embellishments such as fonts and colors but does not support advanced features such as bookmarks and clip art. The RTF format is commonly used when more than one word processing program needs to share a file, because an RTF file can be opened in most of the leading word processing software packages.

Run Executing actions. For example, you run an action query to change data and you run a macro to execute the actions contained therein.

Run-time error A VBA error which occurs because you are attempting an illegal or impossible operation; such as dividing by zero or moving focus to a control that doesn't exist.

ScreenTip A pop-up label that appears when you point to a button. It provides descriptive information about the button.

Secondary sort field In a query grid, the second field from the left that includes sort criteria. It determines the order in which the records will appear if there is a "tie" on the primary sort field. (For example, the primary sort field might be the State field. If two records both contained the data "IA" in that field, the secondary sort field, which might be the City field, would determine the order of the IA records in the resulting datasheet.)

Section A location of a form or report that contains controls. The section in which a control is placed determines where and how often the control prints.

Section properties Properties associated with form, report, or page sections that control how the sections will display and print.

Security account password A password applied to workgroups used to determine which objects each workgroup has access to and at what level.

Select query The most common type of query that retrieves data from one or more linked tables and displays the results in a datasheet.

Server In client-server computer architectures, the server computer is generally the one that serves files.

Server-generated HTML files Web pages created by the Web server. They are dynamic, and therefore show current data, but are read-only.

Shared network folder A folder on a computer network to which multiple people have access.

Shortcuts Pointers to objects placed in the Favorites or user-created groups in the Groups bar.

Show Check Box A check box in Query Design View that determines whether the chosen field will be displayed on the datasheet or not.

Simple Query Wizard A wizard used to create a select query.

Single stepping Running a macro one line at a time, and observing the effect of each line as it is executed.

Sizing handles Small squares at each corner of a selected control. Dragging a handle resizes the control. Also known as *handles*.

Snapshot A type of recordset displayed within a query's datasheet that does not allow you to update any field.

Sort To place records in an order (ascending or descending) based on the values of a particular field.

Source document The original paper document that records raw data such as an employment application. In some databases, there is no source document because raw data is entered directly into the computer.

Specific record box Part of the Navigation buttons that indicates the current record number. You can also click in the specific record box and type a record number to quickly move to that record.

Spike A surge in electricity that can cause damage to a computer.

SQL (structured query language) statement, A standard programming language for selecting and manipulating data stored in a relational database.

Standard modules Modules stored as objects within the database window. Standard modules can be executed from anywhere within the database.

Startup options A series of commands that execute when a database is opened.

Statement A line of VBA code.

Static HTML file An HTML file (Web page) that is current only as of the moment that the Web page was created. It is not linked to an underlying Access database.

Status bar The bar at the bottom of the Access window that provides informational messages and other status information (such as whether the Num Lock is active or not).

Status Bar Text property Property of a control that determines what text displays in the status bar when that control has the focus.

Sub A procedure that performs a series of VBA statements but does not return a value nor can it be used in an expression. You create subs to manipulate controls and objects.

Sub procedure See *Sub*.

Subdatasheet A datasheet that shows related records. It appears when the user clicks a record's expand button.

Subform A form placed within a form that shows related records from another table or query. A subform generally displays many records at a time in a datasheet arrangement.

Subreport A report placed as a control within another report.

Summary query A query used to calculate and display information about records grouped together.

Surge protector Equipment that protects computers in the event of surges or spikes in electricity.

Switchboard A special type of form that uses command buttons to simplify and secure access to database objects.

Switchboard Manager An Access feature that simplifies the creation and maintenance of switchboard forms.

Synchronization The process of reconciling and updating changes between the master and replicas of a replica set.

Syntax error A VBA error which occurs because of a typing error or misspelling. Syntax errors are highlighted in the Code window in red.

Tab control An unbound control used to create a three-dimensional aspect to a form so that other controls can be organized and shown in Form view by clicking the "tabs."

Tab order The sequence in which the controls on the form receive the focus when pressing [Tab] or [Enter] in Form view.

Table An Access object which is a collection of records for a single subject, such as all of the customer records. Tables can be linked with a common field to share information and therefore minimize data redundancy.

Table Datasheet toolbar The toolbar that appears when you are viewing a table's datasheet.

TCP/IP (Transmission Control Protocol/Internet Protocol) The communications protocol by which the Internet routes messages and Web pages through the Internet network.

Text A data type that allows text information or combinations of text and numbers such as a street address. By default, it is 50 characters but can be changed to 50 characters. The maximum length of a text field is 255 characters.

Text box A common control used on forms and reports to display data bound to an underlying field. A text box can also show calculated controls such as subtotals and dates.

Toggle button A bound control used to indicate "yes" or "no" answers for a field. If the button is "pressed" it displays "yes" information.

Toolbox toolbar The toolbar that has common controls that you can add to a report or form when working in the report or form's Design view.

Top Values feature A feature within Query Design view that allows you to limit the number of records in the resulting datasheet to a value or percentage of the total.

Unbound controls Controls that do not change from record to record and exist only to clarify or enhance the appearance of the form, such as labels, lines, and clip art.

Unbound image control An unbound control used to display clip art that doesn't change as you navigate from record to record on a form or report.

UNC (Universal Naming Convention) A convention used to locate a file on a network. The structure of a UNC is \\server\sharedfolder-name\filename and it is commonly used to locate files stored on a local area network.

Update query An action query that updates data based on an expression.

UPS (Uninterruptible Power Supply) Equipment that maintains constant electricity to a computer over a period of time in the event of brownouts, power surges, or power outages.

URL (Uniform Resource Locator) Each resource on the Internet (including Web pages) has an address so that other computers can accurately and consistently locate and view them.

Validation rule A field property that establishes criteria for an entry to be accepted into the database.

Validation text A field property that determines what message will appear if a user attempts to make a field entry that does not pass the validation rule for that field.

Variable A named storage location that can contain data that can be modified during program execution.

VBA (Visual Basic for Applications) The Access programming language that is very similar to Visual Basic and which is stored within module objects.

VBA password A password that prevents unauthorized users from modifying VBA code.

View buttons Four buttons in the database window that determines how the object icons are displayed (as Large Icons, Small Icons, List, and Details).

Visual Basic Code window The Design View of a module in which you write Visual Basic for Applications programming code.

Visual Basic for Applications See *VBA*.

WAN (Wide Area Network) A computer network that connects computers and LANs across public thoroughfares. WANs must use existing telecommunications networks (usually telephone lines) to accomplish this.

Web folder Special folders dedicated to storing and organizing Web pages on a Web server.

Web page A special type of file created with HTML code that contains hyperlinks to other files.

Web server A file server (large microcomputer) that stores, downloads, and routes Web pages.

Webmaster A person who works with Web servers, Web folders, and supporting Internet technologies.

What if analysis A process in which a user interactively applies assumptions to a set of numbers in an Excel spreadsheet to watch the resulting formulas recalculate automatically.

Wildcard characters Special characters used in criteria to find, filter, and query data. The asterisk (*) stands for any group of characters. For example, the criteria I* in a State field criteria cell would find all records where the state entry was IA, ID, IL, IN, or Iowa. The question mark (?) wildcard stands for only one character. The pound sign (#) can only be used as a wildcard in a numeric field and stands for a single number.

Wizard An interactive set of dialog boxes that guides you through an Access process such as creating a query, form, or report.

Word The word processing application within the Microsoft Office Suite.

Workgroup A description of users, objects, and permissions to which those users have access to the objects stored as a file.

Workgroup administrator A program used to create workgroups.

World Wide Web page A hyperlinked document that makes the Internet easy to navigate.

WorldWide Web See *WWW*.

WWW (World Wide Web) A vast number of linked documents stored on thousands of different Web servers.

Yes/No A data type that stores only one of two values (Yes/No, On/Off, True/False).

Zoom dialog box A dialog box that allows you to enter and view a large expression in a query or property text box.

Index

Index

Index

Index